Legal Interviewing

Analytics and Exercises

Version 1—Guardianship Client

Contents

Contributors

ZUBAIR W. BALOCH, MD, PHD • *Professor of Pathology, Director, Cytopathology Fellowship Program, Department of Pathology and Laboratory Medicine, University of Pennsylvania Medical Center, Philadelphia, PA 19104, USA, baloch@mail.med.upenn.edu*

REBECCA A. BRANNAN • *FRCPath MSc MBChB, Department of Histopathology, St James's University Hospital, Beckett Street, Leeds, LS9 7TF, United Kingdom, becky0000@hotmail.co.uk*

FAN CHEN, MD, MD, PHD • *Clinical Assistant Professor, NYU School of Medicine and Hospitals, Department of Surgical and Ob-Gyn pathology, Bellevue Hospital - Building H, Room 4west, NY 10016, USA, chenf04@nyumc.org*

RUNJAN CHETTY, MD, FRCPATH • *Professor of Pathology, Director of Surgical Pathology, Health Network/Toronto Medical Laboratories, Department of Laboratory Medicine and Pathobiology, University of Toronto, Toronto, Canada, runjan.chetty@uhn.on.ca*

RONALD R. DE KRIJGER, MD • *Department of Pathology, Erasmus MC, 3000 DR Rotterdam, The Netherlands, r.dekrijger@erasmusmc.nl*

RONALD A. DELELLIS, M.D. • *Pathologist-in-Chief, Lifespan AMC Pathology Laboratories, Professor and Associate Chair of Pathology and Laboratory Medicine, The Warren Alpert Medical School of Brown University, Department of Pathology, Rhode Island Hospital, Providence, RI 02903, USA, rdelellis@lifespan.org*

ANDREW M. HANBY, MD, FRCPATH • *Leeds Institute of Molecular Medicine, Yorkshire Cancer Research and Liz Dawn Pathology and Translational Sciences Centre Section of Pathology and Tumour Biology Wellcome Trust Brenner Building, Level 4, Room 4.13 St James's University Hospital, Beckett Street Leeds, LS9 7TF, United Kingdom, a.m.hanby@leeds.ac.uk*

EVA HORVATH, PHD • *Department of Pathology, St Michael's Hospital, Tronto, Ontario, CA, USA, horvathe@smh.toronto.on.ca*

ARMANDO E. FRAIRE, MD • *Professor of Pathology, Director, Pulmonary and Autopsy Pathology, University of Massachusetts Medical School, UMass Memorial Medical Center, Three Biotech, One Innovation Drive, Worcester, MA, USA, frairea@ummhc.org*

JENNIFER L. HUNT, M.D • *Associate Chief of Pathology, Director of Quality and Safety, James Homer Wright Pathology Laboratories, WRN225, Massachusetts General Hospital, 55 Fruit Street, Boston, MA 02114, huntj2@ccf.org*

ZHONG JIANG, MD • *Professor of Pathology, Director, Genitourinary Pathology, University of Massachusetts Medical School, Three Biotech, One Innovation Drive Worcester, MA, USA, jianz@ummhc.org*

ASHRAF KHAN, MD, FRCPATH • *Professor of Pathology, Director, Surgical Pathology, Department of Pathology, University of Massachusetts Medical School, UMass Memorial Medical Center, Three Biotech, One Innovation Drive, Worcester, MA 01605, USA e-mail: Khana@ummhc.org*

KALMAN KOVACS, MD, PHD • *Department of Pathology, St Michael's Hospital, Toronto, Ontario, CA, USA, kovacsk@smh.toronto.on.ca*

RICARDO V. LLOYD, M.D., PH.D • *Professor of Pathology and Laboratory Medicine, Division of Anatomic Pathology, Mayo Clinic, Rochester, MN 55905, USA, lloyd.ricardo@mayo.edu*

SANJAY LOGANI, MD • *Associate Professor of Pathology, Emory University School of Medicine, Department of Pathology, Suite H187, 1364 Clifton Rd, NE, Atlanta, GA 30322, USA, slogani@emory.edu*

KALPANA MANI, MD • *Department of Radiology, Beth Israel Deaconess Medical Center, Harvard Medical School, Boston, MA, USA, kmani1@bidmc.haravard.edu*

ANNE MARIE MCNICOL, MD, FRCPATH • *Professor Molecular and Cellular Pathology, School of Medicine, University of Queensland, Brisbane, Australia, a.mcnicol@uq.edu.au*

KHUSH MITTAL, MD • *Associate Professor of Pathology, NYU School of Medicine and Hospitals, Director, Surgical and Ob-Gyn pathology, Bellevue Hospital – Building H, Room 4west, NY 10016, USA, khush.mittal@med.nyu.edu*

Gul Moonis, MD • *Assistant professor of Radiology, Division of Neuroradiology, Beth Israel Deaconess Medical Center, Harvard Medical School, Boston, MA, USA, gmoonis@bidmc.harvard.edu*

Vânia Nosé, MD, Ph. D • *Associate Director of Surgical Pathology, Chief, Endocrine Pathology Service, Associate Professor of Pathology, Department of Pathology, Harvard Medical School, Brigham and Women's Hospital, Boston, MA 02115, USA, vnose@partners.org*

Ulrike M. Gruber-Moesenbacher, MD • *Institute of Pathology, Teaching Hospital Feldkirch Carinagasse 47, A-6800 Feldkirch, Austria, ulrike.gruber@lkhf.at*

Helmut H. Popper, MD, Prof.Path • *Institute of Pathology, Research Unit Molecular Lung and Pleura Pathology, Lab. Molecular Genetics, Environmental und Respiratory Pathology, Medical University of Graz, Auenbruggerplatz 25,A-8036, Graz, Austria, helmut.popper@meduni-graz.at*

Manju L. Prasad, MD • *Associate Professor, Director, Endocrine, Head & Neck Pathology, Director, Immunohistochemistry Laboratory, Department of Pathology, Yale University School of Medicine, 20 York Street, EP2-608B, New Haven, CT 06510, USA, manju.prasad@yale.edu*

Bernd W. Scheithauer, MD • *Department of Laboratory Medicine and Pathology, Mayo Clinic, 200 First St SW, Rochester MN 55905, USA, scheithauer.bernd@mayo.edu*

Arthur S. Tischler, MD • *Professor of Pathology, Department of Pathology, Tufts University Tufts Medical Center, Boston, MA, atishler@tuftsmedicalcenter.org*

Francoise Truong, MD FRCPC • *Consultant Pathologist, William Osler Health Center, 101 Humber College Blvd, Etobicoke, ON, Canada, M9V IR8, francoise_truong@oslerhc.org*

Imaging of Endocrine and Neuroendocrine Tumors

Gul Moonis and Kalpana Mani

Abstract Endocrine and neuroendocrine tumors, which secrete hormones or vasoactive substances, comprise a broad and divergent group of diseases. In the following section we have chosen some of the more common functional tumors to illustrate the spectrum of imaging findings, cross sectionally as well as scintigraphically.

Keywords Pituitary adenoma • Thyroid carcinoma • Parathyroid adenoma • Carcinoid • Pheochromocytoma • Pancreatic endocrine tumors • Imaging • CT • MRI • Nuclear medicine

Pituitary Tumors

The pituitary gland occupies the sella turcica. Pituitary adenomas are the most common pathology encountered in the sella. Pituitary adenomas can be classified into two categories: microadenomas (less than 10 mm in diameter) and macroadenomas (greater than 10 mm in diameter). Magnetic resonance imaging (MRI) is essential for radiologic evaluation of patients who present with symptoms related to overproduction of pituitary hormones. The most common microadenoma is a prolactinoma. On T1-weighted images, a pituitary microadenoma is seen as a round or oval intrasellar lesion, which is somewhat hypointense compared to normal anterior lobe. On T2-weighted images, these lesions tend to be slightly hyperintense compared to the normal anterior lobe. On post-gadolinium images, these lesions demonstrate focal hypoenhancement compared to normal, intense enhancement of the surrounding normal pituitary gland [1] (Fig. 1). Other variations of the characteristic imaging appearance can be seen.

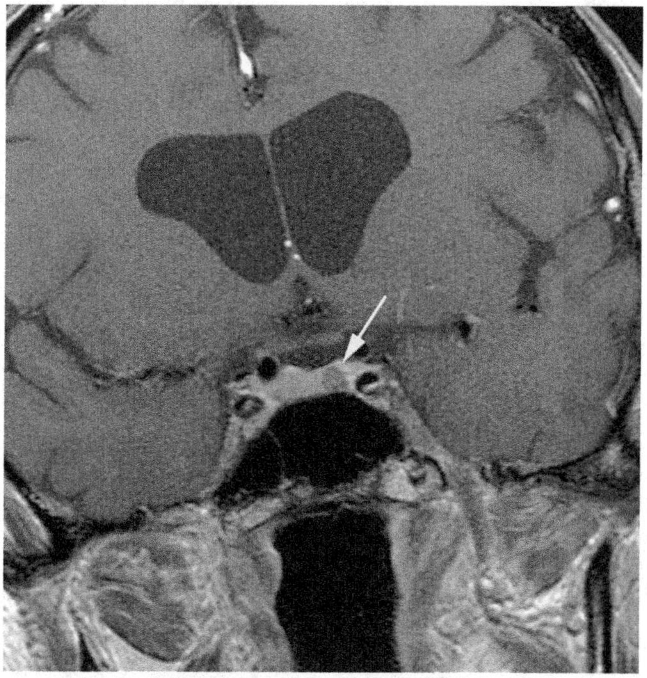

Fig. 1 Pituitary microadenoma. Coronal post-gadolinium MR image in a patient with hyperprolactinemia demonstrates a focus of decreased enhancement in the left aspect of the gland compatible with a microadenoma (*arrow*)

The lesion can be hyperintense on T1-weighted image due to hemorrhagic or proteinaceous transformation. Hypointensity on T2-weighted images may be seen in growth-hormone-secreting microadenomas compared to hyperintense T2 signal demonstrated by the majority of prolactinomas. Prolactinomas and growth-hormone-secreting adenomas tend to be located laterally within the gland whereas ACTH-producing microadenomas in Cushing's disease are more often located in the midline. Other techniques can be used to emphasize the contrast enhancement characteristics of microadenomas. Delayed imaging after administration of contrast may show late enhancement of the microadenoma. Dynamic imaging after

G. Moonis (✉)
Assistant professor of Radiology, Division of Neuroradiology, Beth Israel Deaconess Medical Center, Harvard Medical School, Boston, MA 02215, USA
e-mail: gmoonis@bidmc.harvard.edu

A. Khan (ed.), *Surgical Pathology of Endocrine and Neuroendocrine Tumors*, Current Clinical Pathology,
DOI 10.1007/978-1-60327-396-1_1,

contrast administration has also been employed, revealing a characteristic curve of enhancement over time, starting from hypoenhancement to gradual fill-in of the microadenoma over time [2].

Pituitary macroadenomas are lesions greater than 10 mm. On imaging, these present as intrasellar masses, often with suprasellar and parasellar extension. There is remodeling of the floor of the sella, and the sella turcica is enlarged. There may be destruction of the dorsum sella. Pituitary macroadenomas have a so-called "snowman appearance" or "figure of 8" appearance (Fig. 2). This represents an enlarged pituitary gland in the sella and a smaller suprasellar component with a "waist," which represents the level of the diaphragma sellae. On T1-weighted images, pituitary macroadenomas tend to be relatively hypointense to isointense to gray matter. On T2-weighted images, these lesions are heterogeneously hyperintense with portions of the lesion demonstrating hyperintense signal relating to cystic or necrotic transformation. On T1-weighted images, foci of hyperintense signal can be seen, which reflect hemorrhage or proteinaceous debris. Following gadolinium administration, macroadenomas are enhanced slightly compared to the pre-gadolinium images. The normal pituitary tissue forms a strongly enhancing pseudocapsule surrounding the adenoma. Coronal post-gadolinium images are crucial to determine extension into the cavernous sinus and to assess the degree of compression of the optic chiasm [1, 3].

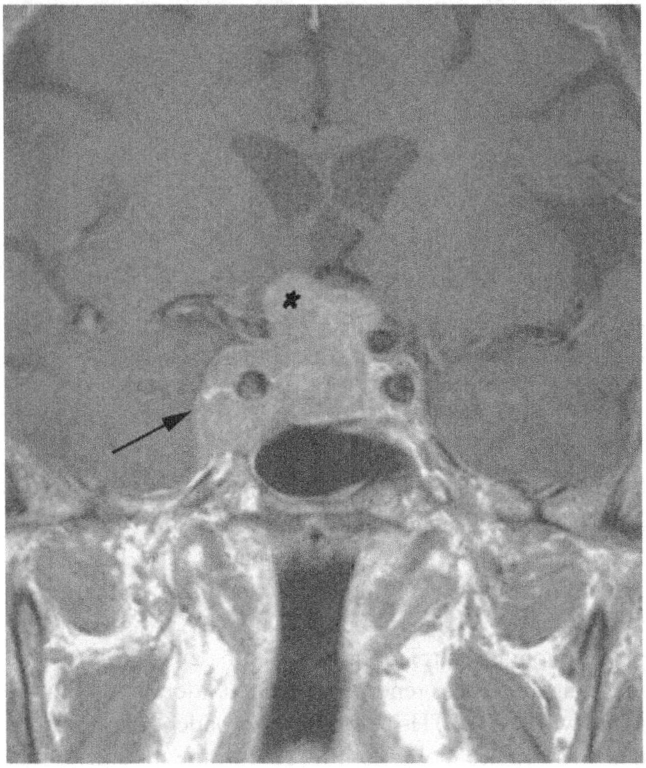

Fig. 2 Pituitary macroadenoma. Coronal post-gadolinium MR image demonstrates a large mass in the sella with suprasellar extension (*black asterisk*) as well as extension into the right cavernous sinus (*arrow*)

Pituitary apoplexy is a clinical syndrome of severe headaches, non-focal neurological deficits, and cranial neuropathies, relating to either hemorrhage or infarction of a pre-existing adenoma. Hemorrhage in seen as a fluid level within an enlarged adenomatous gland (Fig. 3).

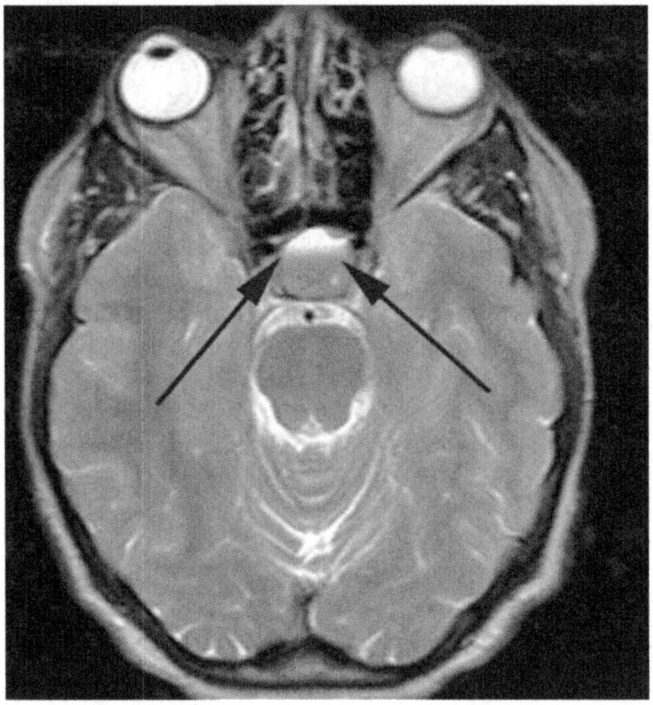

Fig. 3 Pituitary apoplexy. An axial T2-weighted MR image in a patient with acute headache demonstrates a hemorrhagic fluid level within an existing macroadenoma compatible with pituitary apoplexy

Thyroid Tumors

Ultrasound is often the first imaging modality employed to assess a thyroid nodule due to its ready accessibility, noninvasive nature, and no risk for radiation exposure. Microcalcifications (related to psammoma bodies) are considered to be relatively specific for thyroid malignancy [4]. Other ultrasound imaging features suggesting malignancy include marked hypoechogenicity, irregular margins, and lack of hypoechoic halo around the nodule [5](Fig. 4). In two recent reports a non-Doppler technology for blood flow imaging referred to as B-flow imaging (BFI) has been found to be very useful in the diagnosis of papillary thyroid carcinoma (PTC) [6, 7]. Brunese et al. [6,7] reported a BFI pattern 3 ($\geq$4 signs and distance >2 mm) to be almost 100% specific and 65% sensitive for diagnosis of PTC, with 43 of 45 nodules showing this

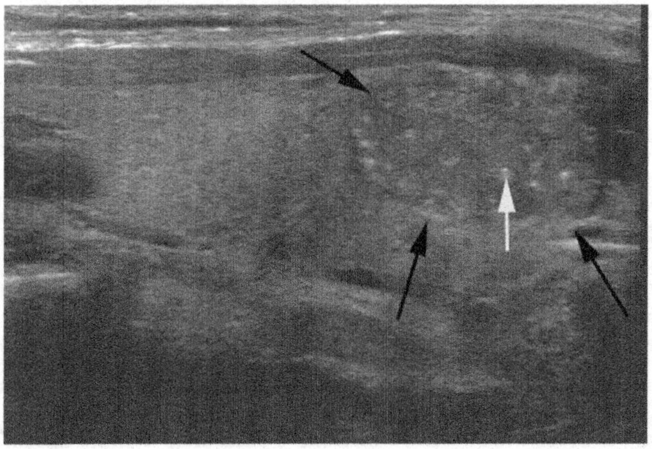

Fig. 4 Thyroid carcinoma on ultrasound. Sagittal ultrasound image of the right thyroid lobe demonstrates a hypoechoic mass in the lower pole (*black arrows*). There are multiple hyperechogenic foci which represent psammomatous calcifications (*white arrow*)

pattern resulted in PTC on final histologic diagnosis and remaining 2 (4.4%) were benign; this imaging finding has been referred to as "B-flow twinkling sign" [6]. Cross sectional imaging utilizing computed tomography (CT) and MRI is useful to depict the extent of neoplasm and assess the involvement of adjacent structures by invasive neoplasms as well as to delineate the full extent of cervical lymphadenopathy [8]. MRI or CT optimally achieves evaluation of a large T3 or T4 thyroid cancer. CT and MRI are also important to identify sites of recurrence of thyroid carcinoma. Psammomatous calcifications can also be seen on CT, most commonly in PTC. Papillary carcinomas may undergo necrosis and simulate a benign-appearing cyst. PTCs are well-differentiated tumors and often retain their ability to concentrate iodine and secrete thyroglobulin and colloid. A cyst with high thyroglobulin or colloid content can appear isodense or hyperdense compared to the surrounding thyroid gland on CT. On MRI, such cysts would be hyperintense on both T1- and T2-weighted images.

Regional lymph node metastases are commonly encountered with PTC and typically present early in the disease process. The first echelon of nodal metastasis consists of paralaryngeal, paratracheal, and prelaryngeal (delphian) nodes in the central compartment of the neck (Level VI). The lateral neck compartment (Level III/IV), the supraclavicular and the superior mediastinal nodes (Level VII) follow suit. Bilateral tumor spread is common. There is a high incidence of occult nodal disease, both in the central compartment and in the lateral neck in the absence of clinically palpable adenopathy [9, 10]. Metastatic nodes from papillary thyroid cancer can have psammomatous calcifications, appear as cysts with imperceptible walls (Fig. 5a), may be hypervascular and hemorrhagic, and may contain high concentrations of thyroglobulin or colloid [11] (Fig. 5b). Cystic change in lymph nodes (representing liquefaction necrosis) is characteristic of metastatic PTC with a PPV value of 100% and an NPV of 88% [12].

Medullary carcinoma of the thyroid (MTC) is a distinct thyroid carcinoma that originates in the parafollicular C cells of the thyroid gland, which produce calcitonin. MTC cells express somatostatin, which is the basis for using somatostatin analogues such as In-111 DTPA-octreotide [13, 14]. Iodine-123 meta-iodobenzlyguanidine (MIBG) has also been used for diagnosis since it is taken up and stored in the catecholamine vesicles of MTC, although its sensitivity for diagnosis is lower than that of In-111 DTPA-octreotide [15].

Parathyroid Tumors

About 80–85% of primary hyperparathyroidism is caused by a solitary adenoma. Scintigraphy with Tc-99m sestamibi provides high image contrast for detection of these

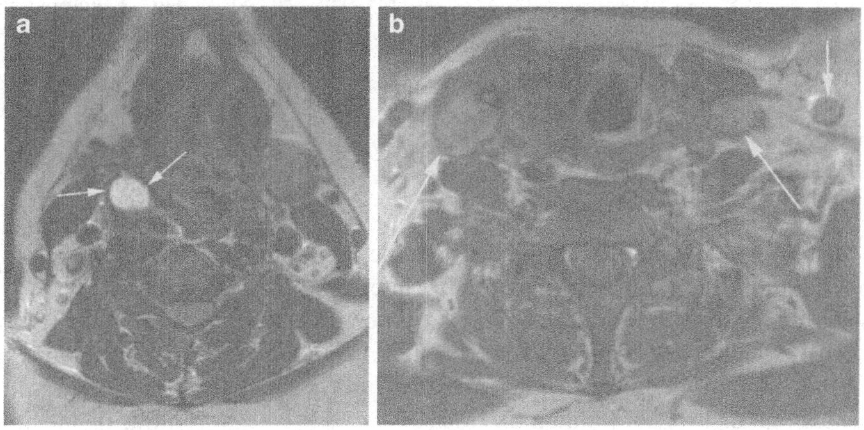

Fig. 5 Thyroid carcinoma metastasis. Axial T2-weighted MR image (**a**) in a 30-year-old woman with thyroid cancer demonstrates a cystic metastasis in the right neck (*arrows*). Axial T1-weighted MR image (**b**) demonstrates T1 hyperintensity of metastatic nodes in both sides of the neck related to colloid/thyroglobulin content of the metastasis (*arrows*)

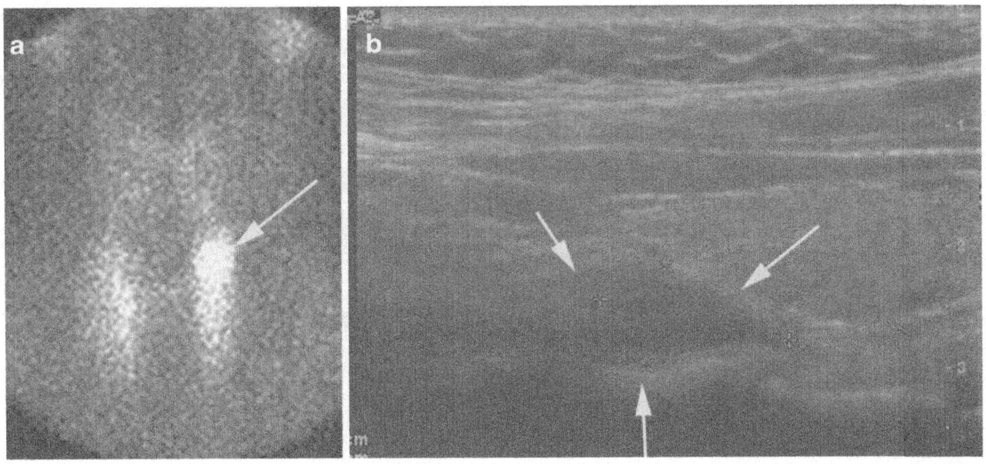

Fig. 6 Parathyroid adenoma imaging. Technetium-99m sestamibi scan (**a**) on a 32-year-old woman with hyperparathyroidism demonstrates a focus of increased uptake overlying the upper pole of the thyroid (*arrows*), which corresponded to a hypoechoic lesion in this locale (*arrows*) on the corresponding ultrasound examination (**b**). This was a surgically proven parathyroid adenoma

lesions (Fig. 6a). Initially the agent distribution is proportional to blood flow. Once intracellular the agent is sequestered within the mitochondria, especially in overactive parathyroid gland. The agent reaches maximum activity inside the thyroid gland within 5 min whereas parathyroid activity is sustained and washout is delayed allowing for a double phase study based on the differential washout rate from the thyroid versus the parathyroid [16–19]. Sensitivity of 68–95% and specificity of 75–100% have been attributed to the dual phase technique, particularly in conjunction with single photon emission tomography (SPECT)[20–24]. On ultrasound (US) the typical parathyroid adenoma is seen as an oval mass of low echogenicity, which is attributable to its uniform hypercellularity [25] (Fig. 6b). Preoperative imaging facilitates minimally invasive surgery as an alternative to bilateral neck dissection. A combined interpretation of Tc-99m sestamibi and US results is helpful in planning targeted exploration [26–28]. Cross sectional imaging (CT/MRI) is helpful for localizing ectopic adenomas, particularly in the mediastinum [29, 30] (Fig. 7). This is especially useful following failed surgery. On CT, these lesions are well defined and enhance intensely (Fig. 8). On MRI, these lesions are increased in signal on T2-weighted images, intermediate on T1-weighed images and demonstrate intense enhancement [8] (Fig. 7). No imaging modality can differentiate a parathyroid adenoma from a parathyroid carcinoma.

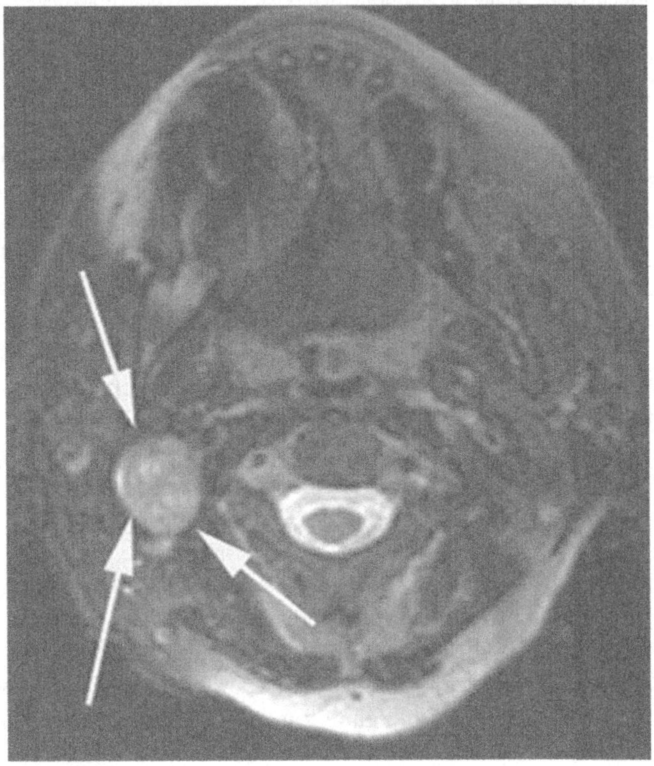

Fig. 7 Ectopic parathyroid adenoma. Axial T2-weighted MR image of the neck in a 60-year-old female with hyperparathyroidism not responsive to bilateral parathyroidectomy reveals a round hyperintense lesion in the right neck parapharyngeal space, which was surgically proven to be an ectopic PT adenoma (*arrows*)

Carcinoid Tumor

One of the most familiar of the neuroendocrine tumors is carcinoid tumor (also referred to in later chapters as neuroendocrine tumor), arising from enterochromaffin cells, which can occur widely throughout the body. Most commonly, however, they are found in the gastrointestinal or bronchopulmonary tracts.

Gastrointestinal Carcinoid Tumor (Neuroendocrine Tumor)

Carcinoid tumors as described in Chapter 12 can affect the gastrointestinal tract from the esophagus to the rectum, but are most common in midgut, including the jejunum, ileum, appendix, and ascending colon [31]. These

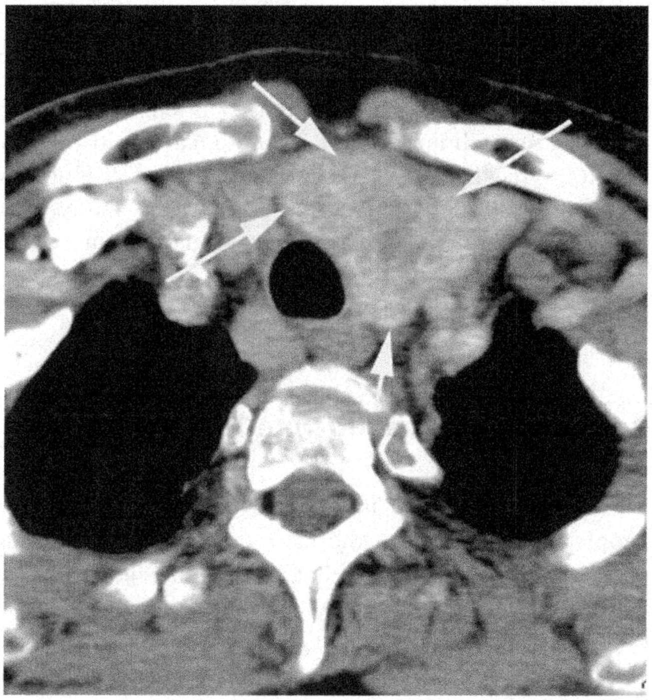

Fig. 8 Parathyroid adenoma CT. Enhanced axial CT image through the neck demonstrates a large enhancing mass in the left midline neck in a patient with hyperparathyroidism, which was surgically proven to be a parathyroid adenoma

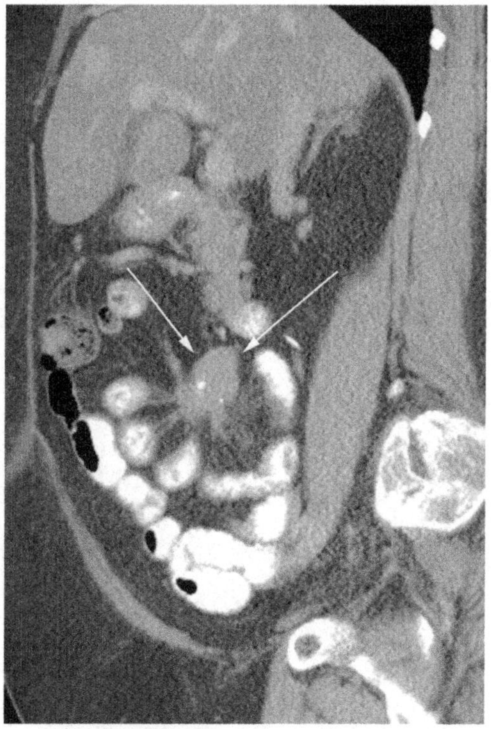

Fig. 9 Imaging of mesenteric carcinoid tumor. A 59-year-old woman with intermittent abdominal pain. Contrast-enhanced sagittal CT image demonstrates a typical spiculated mesenteric mass with tethering of adjacent small bowel loops (*arrows*); note the punctate calcifications within it

tumors typically secrete serotonin, serotonin precursors, or other hormones; however, 40–60% of patients are asymptomatic at presentation [31].

Historically, conventional fluoroscopic small bowel follow-through and enteroclysis studies have been used to assess luminal components and to indirectly visualize the bowel retraction and deformation from mesenteric abnormalities. However, cross sectional imaging is now one of the major diagnostic tools in initial workup and staging. Carcinoid tumors are submucosal and can be quite small, therefore, the findings on imaging may relate to adjacent mesenteric fibrosis and desmoplastic reaction (thought to be related to nearby release of hormones from the primary tumor). On CT, classically, the mesenteric mass is spiculated (stellate or spoke wheel in appearance) and demonstrates enhancement (Fig. 9). There is tethering of small bowel as well as small bowel wall thickening or edema, which is thought to be due to ischemia of the mesenteric vessels enveloped by fibrosis. Calcification within the mesenteric mass has been noted frequently and has been described as coarse, stippled, or diffuse [32].

On MR, primary small bowel carcinoid tumors are generally best seen on post-contrast fat-suppressed T1 images, which also nicely demonstrate associated bowel wall thickening. Liver metastatic disease is typically low signal on T1-weighted images, high signal on T2-weighted images, and avidly enhancing in the hepatic arterial phase after contrast administration [33].

Indium-111 pentetreotide can be a useful functional imaging agent, taking advantage of the presence of somatostatin receptors on many carcinoid tumors (Fig. 10). This functional imaging can frequently be done in conjunction with CT (SPECT-CT), giving an additional cross sectional perspective [31]. Newer techniques such as 18F-DOPA PET appear promising for functional imaging of carcinoid tumors [34].

Carcinoid syndrome is a clinical entity consisting of flushing, diarrhea, abdominal discomfort, bronchial constriction, and occasionally right heart failure which is seen with diffuse metastatic disease to the liver, preventing the liver from effectively performing its usual task of deactivating the neuropeptides and hormones released [35].

Pulmonary Carcinoid Tumor

Pulmonary carcinoid tumors arise from the enterochromaffin cells of the bronchial mucosa. They are classified as typical or atypical (see Chapter 10), with atypical being

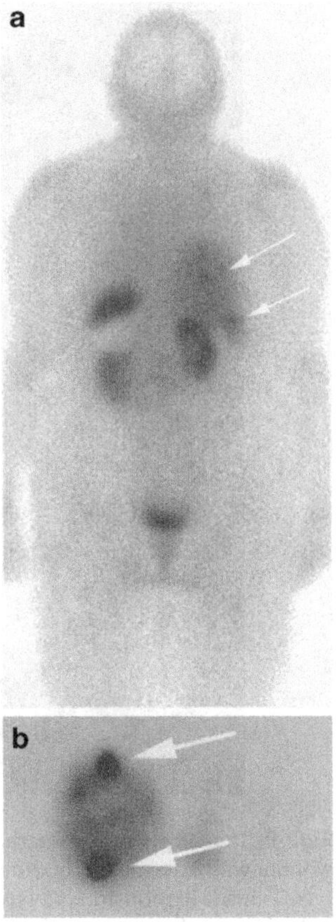

Fig. 10 Imaging of metastatic carcinoid tumor. A 78-year-old woman with prior resection of small bowel carcinoid. Whole body, posterior image from an In-111 pentetreotide study (**a**) reveals foci of tracer uptake corresponding to two lesions in the liver (*arrows*). The coned-down axial image from the SPECT study (**b**) demonstrates the same findings (*arrows*)

more aggressive histologically [31, 36]. Most lung carcinoids are incidentally discovered [35].

Carcinoids generally occur in the central bronchi and may present with symptoms of central airway obstruction. On chest radiographs, one might see a well-defined perihilar mass, possibly with distal obstructive findings such as collapse or mucous plugging.

On CT, pulmonary carcinoids appear as well-defined, rounded, or oval lesions, occasionally with lobulated borders, and can demonstrate punctuate or diffuse calcification (30%) (Fig. 11). They may be quite small upon discovery. The bronchi themselves are often narrowed or obstructed. These tumors intensely enhance post-contrast administration. Of note, carcinoid tumors are not typically very FDG-avid on PET-CT [36]. As with midgut carcinoid, due to the fact that many pulmonary carcinoid tumors contain somatostatin receptors, scintigraphy with somatostatin analogs such as In-111 pentetreotide is useful [35].

Pancreatic Neuroendocrine Tumors

This group of tumors is made up of islet cell tumors, neoplasms arising from the neuroendocrine cells of the pancreas, and includes insulinoma and gastrinoma, among others. If functioning (i.e., secreting hormones) they are often small (less than 2–3 cm) at initial diagnosis. MRI has proved quite valuable in the diagnosis and follow-up of these tumors.

On MR, these lesions are classically bright on T2-weighted images and demonstrate marked enhancement on post-contrast arterial-phase images. Fat suppression can be used to help distinguish these lesions from adjacent normal pancreatic parenchyma [37].

On CT, functioning tumors are also best seen separate from the pancreatic parenchyma on post-contrast arterial-phase studies. Non-functioning islet cell tumors can become much larger and can contain areas of cystic change or necrosis [38].

Finally, endoscopic ultrasound (EUS) has also been described as a valuable imaging tool in the workup of patients with pancreatic islet cell tumors, particularly in the facilitation of biopsy via EUS-assisted fine needle aspiration [39].

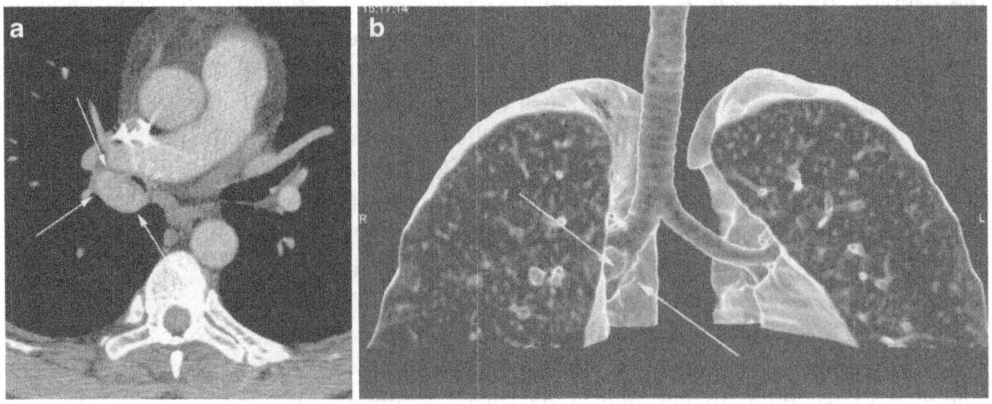

Fig. 11 Imaging of pulmonary carcinoid. A 55-year-old man with hemoptysis. Soft-tissue window (**a**) from a contrast-enhanced chest CT demonstrates an oval-shaped mass both within and adjacent to the right bronchus intermedius (*arrows*), causing severe bronchial narrowing (*arrowheads*). A 3D reformation (**b**) demonstrates the marked bronchial narrowing (*arrows*)

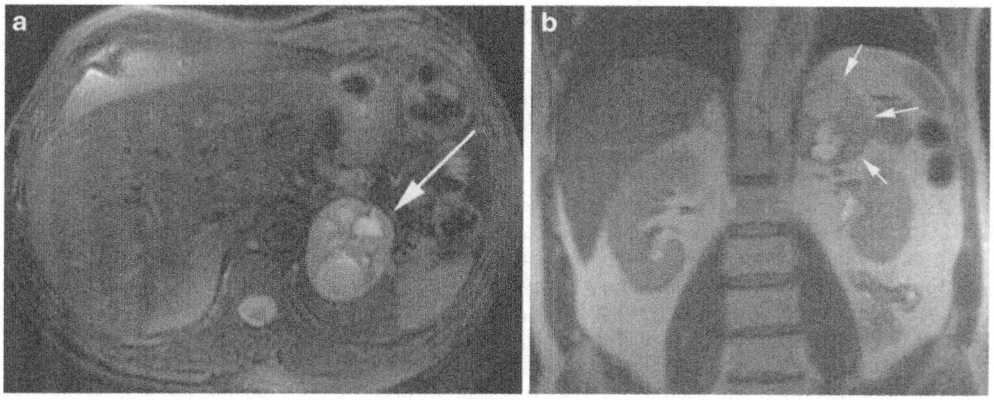

Fig. 12 Imaging of pheochromocytoma. A 68-year-old man with incidentally found left suprarenal mass. Axial T2-weighted image from an MRI (**a**) demonstrates a complex cystic and solid rounded supra-adrenal mass. The foci of T2 hyperintensity indicate the cystic areas. Coronal HASTE image (**b**) shows the same findings. This lesion demonstrated persistent, patchy areas of enhancement after contrast administration (not shown)

Pheochromocytoma

Pheochromocytoma is a tumor of the chromaffin cells derived from the adrenal medulla and typically secretes catecholamines, resulting in systemic effects such as hypertension. The vast majority of these are located within the adrenal gland (without metastatic extension) and more than 90% are unilateral [35]. Their imaging appearance can be varied, mainly due to degeneration within the lesion.

On CT, pheochromocytomas usually are soft-tissue attenuation suprarenal masses. Iodinated contrast has been avoided in the past for fear of precipitating a hypertensive crisis, but recent studies with non-ionic contrast have found no adverse reactions [40]; when contrast is given, these tumors enhance avidly. They can contain calcification, cystic or necrotic regions, areas of hemorrhage, and even lipid degeneration, making them occasionally difficult to differentiate from other adrenal lesions, such as adenoma, myelolipoma, or even adrenal carcinoma [41, 42].

On MR, typically they are low signal on T1-weighted images and high signal on T2-weighted images (Fig. 12). They demonstrate marked enhancement post gadolinium and typically less washout on delayed images than adenomas, and even in some cases foci of delayed enhancement [41]. As on CT, however, they can be quite variable in appearance [42].

Functional (scintigraphic) imaging often plays a role in the initial diagnosis of pheochromocytoma or in post-surgical follow-up to assess for recurrence or metastatic disease. The preferred radiopharmaceutical is MIBG, a derivative of guanethidine, which is taken up into membranes of cells in the sympathomedullary system. Indium-111 pentetreotide is less sensitive, primarily due to adjacent physiologic renal uptake, which can obscure uptake within a pheochromocytoma [35].

References

1. Bonneville JF, Bonneville F, Cattin F. Magnetic resonance imaging of pituitary adenomas. European Radiology 2005;15(3):543–8.
2. Miki Y, Matsuo M, Nishizawa S, et al. Pituitary adenomas and normal pituitary tissue: enhancement patterns on gadopentetate-enhanced MR imaging. Radiology 1990;177(1):35–8.
3. Cottier JP, Destrieux C, Brunereau L, et al. Cavernous sinus invasion by pituitary adenoma: MR imaging. Radiology 2000;215(2):463–9.
4. Frates MC, Benson CB, Charboneau JW, et al. Management of thyroid nodules detected at US: society of radiologists in ultrasound consensus conference statement. Radiology 2005;237(3):794–800.
5. Hoang JK, Lee WK, Lee M, Johnson D, Farrell S. US Features of thyroid malignancy: pearls and pitfalls. Radiographics 2007;27(3):847–60; discussion 61–5.
6. Brunese L, Romeo A, Iorio S, et al. A new marker for diagnosis of thyroid papillary cancer: B-flow twingling sign. Journal of Ultrasound in Medicine 2008;27:1187–94.
7. Brunese L, Romeo A, Iorio S, et al. Thyroid B-flow twingling sign: a new feature of papillary carcinoma. European Journal of Endocrinology 2008;159(4):447–51.
8. Kabala JE. Computed tomography and magnetic resonance imaging in diseases of the thyroid and parathyroid. European Journal of Radiology 2008;66(3):480–92.
9. Hay ID. Papillary thyroid carcinoma. Endocrinology and metabolism clinics of North America 1990;19(3):545–76.
10. Noguchi S, Noguchi A, Murakami N. Papillary carcinoma of the thyroid. I. Developing pattern of metastasis. Cancer 1970;26(5):1053–60.
11. Som PM, Brandwein M, Lidov M, Lawson W, Biller HF. The varied presentations of papillary thyroid carcinoma cervical nodal disease: CT and MR findings. American Journal of Neuroradiology 1994;15(6):1123–8.
12. Kessler A, Rappaport Y, Blank A, Marmor S, Weiss J, Graif M. Cystic appearance of cervical lymph nodes is characteristic of metastatic papillary thyroid carcinoma. Journal of Clinical Ultrasound 2003;31(1):21–5.
13. Arslan N, Ilgan S, Yuksel D, et al. Comparison of In-111 octreotide and Tc-99m (V) DMSA scintigraphy in the detection of medullary thyroid tumor foci in patients with elevated levels of tumor markers after surgery. Clinical Nuclear Medicine 2001;26(8):683–8.
14. Rufini V, Salvatori M, Garganese MC, Di Giuda D, Lodovica Maussier M, Troncone L. Role of nuclear medicine in the

diagnosis and therapy of medullary thyroid carcinoma. Rays 2000;25(2):273–82.
15. Kaltsas G, Korbonits M, Heintz E, et al. Comparison of somatostatin analog and meta-iodobenzylguanidine radionuclides in the diagnosis and localization of advanced neuroendocrine tumors. The Journal of Clinical Endocrinology and Metabolism 2001;86(2):895–902.
16. Lee VS, Spritzer CE, Coleman RE, Wilkinson RH, Jr., Coogan AC, Leight GS, Jr. The complementary roles of fast spin-echo MR imaging and double-phase 99m Tc-sestamibi scintigraphy for localization of hyperfunctioning parathyroid glands. American Journal of Roentgenology 1996;167(6):1555–62.
17. McHenry CR, Lee K, Saadey J, Neumann DR, Esselstyn CB, Jr. Parathyroid localization with technetium-99m-sestamibi: A prospective evaluation. Journal of the American College of Surgeons 1996;183(1):25–30.
18. Neumann DR, Esselstyn CB, Jr., Go RT, Wong CO, Rice TW, Obuchowski NA. Comparison of double-phase 99mTc-sestamibi with 123I-99mTc-sestamibi subtraction SPECT in hyperparathyroidism. American Journal of Roentgenology 1997;169(6):1671–4.
19. Taillefer R, Boucher Y, Potvin C, Lambert R. Detection and localization of parathyroid adenomas in patients with hyperparathyroidism using a single radionuclide imaging procedure with technetium-99m-sestamibi (double-phase study). Journal of Nuclear Medicine 1992;33(10):1801–7.
20. Ishibashi M, Nishida H, Hiromatsu Y, Kojima K, Tabuchi E, Hayabuchi N. Comparison of technetium-99m-MIBI, technetium-99m-tetrofosmin, ultrasound and MRI for localization of abnormal parathyroid glands. Journal of Nuclear Medicine 1998;39(2):320–4.
21. Ishibashi M, Nishida H, Hiromatsu Y, Kojima K, Uchida M, Hayabuchi N. Localization of ectopic parathyroid glands using technetium-99m sestamibi imaging: comparison with magnetic resonance and computed tomographic imaging. European Journal of Nuclear Medicine 1997;24(2):197–201.
22. Ishibashi M, Uchida M, Nishida H, et al. Pre-surgical localization of ectopic parathyroid glands using three-dimensional CT imaging, 99Tcm sestamibi, and 99Tcm tetrofosmin imaging. The British Journal of Radiology 1999;72(855):296–300.
23. Moka D, Voth E, Dietlein M, Larena-Avellaneda A, Schicha H. Preoperative localization of parathyroid adenomas using 99mTc-MIBI scintigraphy. The American Journal of Medicine 2000;108(9):733–6.
24. Nichols KJ, Tomas MB, Tronco GG, et al. Preoperative parathyroid scintigraphic lesion localization: accuracy of various types of readings. Radiology 2008;248(1):221–32.
25. Reading CC, Charboneau JW, James EM, et al. High-resolution parathyroid sonography. American Journal of Roentgenology 1982;139(3):539–46.
26. Prager G, Czerny C, Kurtaran A, et al. Minimally invasive open parathyroidectomy in an endemic goiter area: a prospective study. Archives of Surgery 2001;136(7):810–6.
27. Prager G, Czerny C, Ofluoglu S, et al. Impact of localization studies on feasibility of minimally invasive parathyroidectomy in an endemic goiter region. Journal of the American College of Surgeons 2003;196(4):541–8.
28. Sukan A, Reyhan M, Aydin M, et al. Preoperative evaluation of hyperparathyroidism: the role of dual-phase parathyroid scintigraphy and ultrasound imaging. Annals of Nuclear Medicine 2008;22(2):123–31.
29. Kang YS, Rosen K, Clark OH, Higgins CB. Localization of abnormal parathyroid glands of the mediastinum with MR imaging. Radiology 1993;189(1):137–41.
30. Stevens SK, Chang JM, Clark OH, Chang PJ, Higgins CB. Detection of abnormal parathyroid glands in postoperative patients with recurrent hyperparathyroidism: sensitivity of MR imaging. American Journal of Roentgenology 1993;160(3):607–12.
31. Scarsbrook AF, Ganeshan A, Statham J, et al. Anatomic and functional imaging of metastatic carcinoid tumors. Radiographics 2007;27(2):455–77.
32. Pantongrag-Brown L, Buetow PC, Carr NJ, Lichtenstein JE, Buck JL. Calcification and fibrosis in mesenteric carcinoid tumor: CT findings and pathologic correlation. Americal Journal of Roentgenology 1995;164(2):387–91.
33. Bader TR, Semelka RC, Chiu VC, Armao DM, Woosley JT. MRI of carcinoid tumors: spectrum of appearances in the gastrointestinal tract and liver. Journal of Magnetic Resonance Imaging 2001;14(3):261–9.
34. Jager PL, Chirakal R, Marriott CJ, Brouwers AH, Koopmans KP, Gulenchyn KY. 6-L-18F-fluorodihydroxyphenylalanine PET in neuroendocrine tumors: basic aspects and emerging clinical applications. Journal Nuclear Medicine 2008;49(4): 573–86.
35. Intenzo CM, Jabbour S, Lin HC, et al. Scintigraphic imaging of body neuroendocrine tumors. Radiographics 2007;27(5): 1355–69.
36. Chong S, Lee KS, Chung MJ, Han J, Kwon OJ, Kim TS. Neuroendocrine tumors of the lung: clinical, pathologic, and imaging findings. Radiographics 2006;26(1):41–57; discussion -8.
37. Herwick S, Miller FH, Keppke AL. MRI of islet cell tumors of the pancreas. American Journal of Roentgenology 2006;187(5): W472–80.
38. Horton KM, Hruban RH, Yeo C, Fishman EK. Multi-detector row CT of pancreatic islet cell tumors. Radiographics 2006; 26(2):453–64.
39. McLean A. Endoscopic ultrasound in the detection of pancreatic islet cell tumours. Cancer Imaging 2004;4(2):84–91.
40. Bessell-Browne R, O'Malley ME. CT of pheochromocytoma and paraganglioma: risk of adverse events with i.v. administration of nonionic contrast material. American Journal of Roentgenology 2007;188(4): 970–4.
41. Park BK, Kim CK, Kwon GY, Kim JH. Re-evaluation of pheochromocytomas on delayed contrast-enhanced CT: washout enhancement and other imaging features. European Radiology 2007;17(11):2804–9.
42. Blake MA, Kalra MK, Maher MM, et al. Pheochromocytoma: an imaging chameleon. Radiographics 2004;24(Suppl 1):S87–99.

Fine Needle Aspiration Cytology of Endocrine Tumors

Sanjay Logani and Zubair W. Baloch

Abstract Fine-needle aspiration biopsy (FNAB) has proved to be an excellent diagnostic tool in the initial management of various lesions affecting endocrine organs. Many studies have attested to its high sensitivity and specificity in diagnosing endocrine tumors, especially that of thyroid gland. However, as with other diagnostic tests its effectiveness is highly dependent upon the expertise of the operator performing the procedure, adequacy of the specimen, and interpretation of the cytomorphologic features. This chapter will address both old and new of the endocrine cytology: including brief description of cytologic features and differential diagnosis of various endocrine lesions and new techniques that have shown promise in their diagnosis

Keywords Endocrine • Cytology • FNA • Immunohistochemistry • Molecular markers

Introduction

During the past decade fine-needle aspiration (FNA) has become an essential tool in the management of common endocrine lesions. This chapter describes and illustrates the cytomorphologic features of the lesions affecting thyroid, parathyroid, pancreas, and adrenal. For the common lesions such as thyroid the cytological features are described and the differential diagnoses are discussed in detail. The discussion also includes an assessment of modern techniques such as immunohistochemistry and molecular analyses with emphasis on their validity for FNA samples as well as the pitfalls that are encountered in their use.

Z.W. Baloch (✉)
Professor of Pathology, Director, Cytopathology Fellowship Program, Department of Pathology and Laboratory Medicine, University of Pennsylvania Medical Center, Philadelphia, PA 19104, USA
e-mail: baloch@mail.med.upenn.edu

Cytopathology of Thyroid Gland

Thyroid nodules are common; they are often seen in women and a great majority are benign. Fine-needle aspiration (FNA) is considered an essential tool in providing a rational approach to the clinical management of these nodules. The results of FNA can determine whether a thyroid nodule should be followed clinically or undergo surgical removal [1, 2].

FNA Indications, Procedure, Specimen, and Classification

A palpable thyroid nodule is a candidate for FNA and further evaluation should be performed to determine if an FNA is needed. Thyroid nodules measuring 1.0–1.5 cm in dimension can be detected by palpation and are therefore clinically significant. However, thyroid nodules even though measuring >1.0 cm may not be readily palpated due to their location in the thyroid gland [2]. These and nodules measuring >1.0 cm are usually found during radiologic evaluation of the head and neck for non-thyroidal lesions. Thyroid nodules can be biopsied by palpation and/or under ultrasound guidance; the latter is becoming the method of choice since it provides precise information regarding the location, size, and structure (solid vs. cystic) of the nodule and is highly effective in getting an adequate sample for cytologic interpretation [3].

Thyroid FNA specimens can be prepared by making air-dried and alcohol fixed smears for staining with Romanowsky (Diff-Quik®, Wright-Giemsa) and Papanicolaou stains, respectively. The smears can be processed alone or with a liquid-based preparation or cell block [1]. Liquid-based preparations can be utilized either alone or as an adjunct to the smears [1].

The main purpose of the fine-needle aspiration (FNA) is to provide a rational approach for the management of

A. Khan (ed.), *Surgical Pathology of Endocrine and Neuroendocrine Tumors*, Current Clinical Pathology,
DOI 10.1007/978-1-60327-396-1_2, © Humana Press, a part of Springer Science+Business Media, LLC 2009

thyroid nodules and determine the correct surgical procedure when surgery is needed. Similar to other clinical tests in medicine, it is often expected that thyroid FNA results should demonstrate high degree of sensitivity and specificity. Therefore, it is prudent that thyroid FNA reporting should be close to uniform among pathologists to pave the path for rational management strategies and avoid confusion among clinicians, thus leading to optimal care of thyroid nodules [4].

At present several classification schemes have been proposed by various authors based on anecdotal/institutional experiences and clinical organizations including Papanicolaou Society, American Thyroid Association, and American Association of Clinical Endocrinologist [2, 4–6] (Table 1). Each of these reporting strategies claims to increase the diagnostic accuracy resulting in highest possible predictive value for a positive result.

Table 1 Thyroid FNA classification schemes

Papanicolaou Society of Cytopathology Task Force on Standards of Practice – 1997	1. Inadequate/unsatisfactory 2. Benign 3. Atypical cells present 4. Suspicious for malignancy 5. Malignant
American Thyroid Association (2006)	1. Inadequate 2. Malignant 3. Indeterminate ■ Suspect for neoplasia ■ Suspect for carcinoma 4. Benign
American Association of Clinical Endocrinologists & Associazione Medici Endocrinologi – 2006	1. Benign 2. Malignant or suspicious 3. Follicular neoplasia 4. Non-diagnostic or ultrasound Suspicious
NCI Thyroid FNA Consensus Conference – 2007	1. Benign 2. Follicular lesion of undermined significance. 3. Neoplasm (follicular or Hurthle) 4. Suspicious for malignancy 5. Malignant 6. Non-diagnostic

It has been shown that the predictive value of a positive result is highest with a reporting scheme using 4–5 categories. Thus, most studies favor a tiered system for classifying thyroid FNA, based upon risk of malignancy for each diagnostic category [7].

Thyroid FNA Diagnostic Categories Including Cytomorphology of Various Thyroid Lesions

Benign

This category implies low risk of neoplasm/malignancy, i.e., >1%. It includes the diagnostic terms such as *nodular goiter, hyperplastic/adenomatoid nodule in goiter, and chronic lymphocytic thyroiditis*. Patients with a benign nodule are usually followed by clinical and periodic ultrasound examination; some patients may undergo repeat FNA due to enlargement of the nodule [2].

The FNA specimen from a goitrous nodule shows (depending upon the preparation method) copious watery colloid in the background, small round to oval shaped follicular cells with dark nuclei with even chromatin pattern arranged in monolayer sheets, follicular groups, or as single cells [8, 9]. Macrophages are usually present and their number depends upon the presence or absence of degenerative changes or a cystic component in the nodule [9, 10].

The aspirates from a hyperplastic/adenomatoid nodule tend to be more cellular and contain an admixture of follicular cells and oncocytic cells arranged in monolayer sheets in a background of watery colloid and macrophages [9–11]. Hyperplastic nodules can also show a dominant papillary growth pattern and give rise to well-formed papillae in FNA specimens; however, most specimens contain oncocytic follicular cells with round nuclei, prominent nucleoli, and even chromatin pattern (Fig. 1).

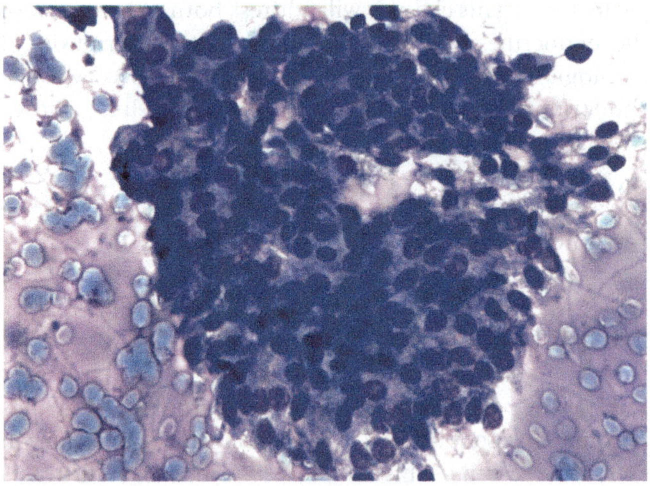

Fig. 1 Fine-needle aspiration smear of a hyperplastic nodule showing follicular cells arranged in loosely cohesive group in the background of watery colloid with a typical "chicken wire artifact" (Diff-Quik® stain, 60×)

The FNA specimens from a nodule arising in Graves' disease (usually hypofunctioning nodules undergo FNA) are usually cellular, show features similar to hyperplastic goiter with minimal colloid and may contain few lymphocytes and oncocytic cells. Rarely the follicular cells may display focal nuclear chromatin clearing and intranuclear grooves; however, other major diagnostic nuclear features of papillary carcinoma are not seen [12–15].

The FNA specimens from nodules arising in chronic lymphocytic thyroiditis contain oncocytes (Hürthle cells), follicular cells, lymphocytes, and few plasma cells in a background of scant colloid. The lymphocytes are usually seen in the background, percolating between cell groups and rarely as intact lymphoid follicle. The lymphocytes seen within the cell groups can be crushed due to mechanical force of smearing or centrifugation and lead to formation of "lymphocytic tangles." The oncocytes may display nuclear atypia and similarly follicular cells may show some chromatin clearing and intranuclear grooves. An extensive lymphocytic infiltrate can appear monotonous and mistaken for malignant lymphoma arising in lymphocytic thyroiditis [16–19]. Similarly, there may be a preponderance of oncocytic cells, which can lead to a diagnosis of oncocytic follicular neoplasm.

Follicular-Patterned Neoplasms

Thyroid (FNA) cannot distinguish between benign and malignant non-papillary follicular and oncocytic follicular (Hürthle cell) lesions, since both benign and malignant neoplasms demonstrate similar cytomorphology [20]. Often these lesions are diagnosed as either follicular lesion of undetermined significance, suspicious for follicular neoplasm, or follicular neoplasm.

The diagnostic term follicular lesion of undetermined significance represents a heterogeneous category, which reflects the difficulty in the cytologic diagnosis of the follicular lesions of thyroid. It includes cases in which the cytomorphologic findings are not representative of a benign lesion such as hyperplastic/adenomatoid nodule; yet the degree of cellular or architectural atypia is not sufficient to render the diagnosis of "follicular neoplasm" or "suspicious for follicular neoplasm/malignancy" that cannot be classified as either benign or follicular neoplasm. Risk of malignancy for this diagnosis has been reported as 10–15%, and it has been shown that these patients can benefit from repeat FNA and correlation with clinical and radiologic findings [1, 21].

The diagnostic terms follicular neoplasm/follicular neoplasm with oncocytic features (AKA Hürthle cell neoplasm)/suspicious for follicular neoplasm encompasses both benign and malignant tumors; i.e., follicular adenoma and carcinoma, and oncocytic follicular adenoma and carcinoma. The cytologic diagnosis of "neoplasm" reflects the limitations and is the "gray zone" of thyroid cytology [22, 23]. The diagnosis of follicular carcinoma is only possible by demonstration of capsular and/or vascular invasion in histologic preparations, since the FNA samples the center of the nodule and not the capsule, a definitive diagnosis of the invasive nature of the lesion is not possible. Several authors have shown that, at most, only 20–30% of cases diagnosed as "follicular neoplasm" are diagnosed as malignant on histological examination and the rest are either follicular adenomas or cellular adenomatoid nodules, i.e., benign [21, 24].

The FNA of a follicular neoplasm is usually hypercellular and show a monotonous population of either follicular or oncocytic follicular cells with minimal or absent background colloid. The cells can be seen as three dimensional groups or microfollicles with prominent nuclear overlapping and crowding [25] (Fig. 2). Random nuclear atypia is also commonly observed in oncocytic follicular (Hürthle cell) lesions; this can be seen in the form of nuclear enlargement, multinucleation, cellular pleomorphism, and prominent nucleoli. Some authors have reported the presence of intracytoplasmic lumens and transgressing vessels in FNA specimens of neoplastic oncocytic follicular (Hürthle cell) lesions [26].

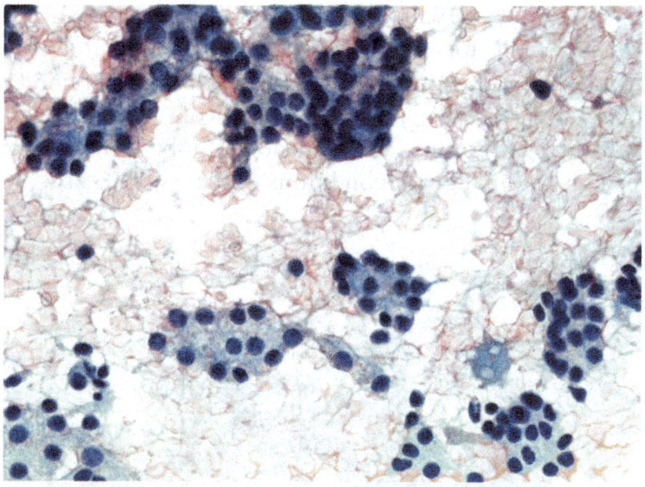

Fig. 2 Fine-needle aspiration smear showing a monotonous population of follicular cells arranged in microfollicles. This case was diagnosed as follicular neoplasm and the subsequent surgical excision was diagnosed as follicular adenoma (Papanicolaou stain, 40×)

Malignant

The well-differentiated thyroid carcinomas are the most common form of malignant thyroid tumors that behave in an indolent manner and have an excellent prognosis. They commonly occur in young adults, whereas, the less differentiated and anaplastic tumors of the thyroid are prevalent in older age [27].

Papillary Thyroid Carcinoma (PTC) and Its Variants

Papillary carcinoma is the most common (up to 80% of all thyroid malignancies) form of thyroid malignancy in non-endemic goiter regions [27].

The cytologic diagnosis of PTC is based on characteristic nuclear morphology regardless of cytoplasmic features, growth pattern, special stains, and immunohistochemical markers. This holds true for a majority of cases of PTC; however, some variants of PTC may be difficult to diagnose [28, 29]. The FNA specimen of PTC is usually cellular and shows tumor cells arranged in papillary groups, three-dimensional clusters, or as single cells in a background of watery or thick "ropy" colloid, nuclear or calcified debris, macrophages, and stromal fragments.

The individual tumor cells are enlarged, elongated, i.e., oval in shape with eosinophilic cytoplasm (cytoplasmic eosinophilia is common in Romanowsky stained preparations but is usually indistinct in alcohol fixed Papanicolaou stained preparations and liquid-based preparations) [8]. The nuclei show elongation, membrane thickening, chromatin clearing, grooves, and inclusions. The intranuclear inclusions may be scarce in monolayer preparations (Fig. 3). The nucleoli are usually small and eccentric; however, rare oncocytic variants of papillary thyroid carcinoma can demonstrate prominent nucleoli/macronucleoli. Intranuclear grooves and inclusions can be seen in other benign and malignant conditions of thyroid [30, 31].

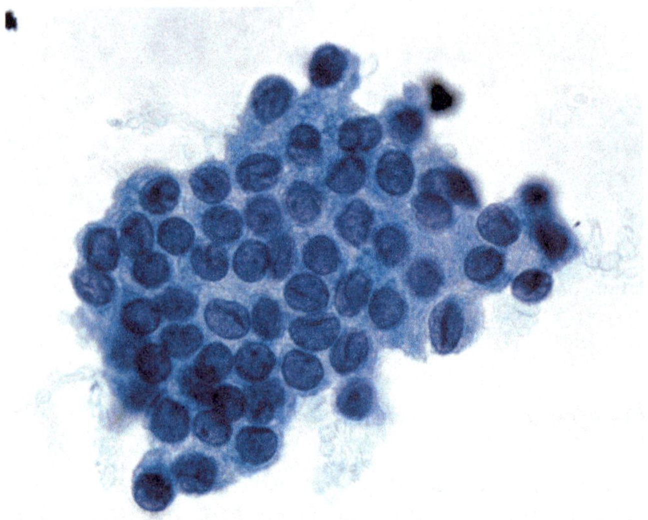

Fig. 3 A case of papillary thyroid carcinoma demonstrating typical nuclear features – nuclear elongation, chromatin clearing, intranuclear grooves and inclusions (Papanicolaou stained Thin-Prep preparation, 60×)

The FNA specimens from a ***follicular variant of papillary carcinoma (FVPTC)*** show enlarged follicular cells arranged in monolayer sheets and follicular groups in a background of thin and thick colloid. The individual tumor cells show nuclear elongation, chromatin clearing, and thick nuclear membranes; however, nuclear grooves and inclusions are rare. Thus, a majority of cytologic samples of FVPTC are diagnosed as suspicious for PTC [32].

The cytologic samples from ***tall cell variant of papillary carcinoma*** contain elongated cells with sharp cytoplasmic borders, granular eosinophilic cytoplasm, and variably sized nuclei with nuclear features of papillary carcinoma [33]. It has been shown that intranuclear grooves are readily found in specimens from this tumor; characteristic "soap bubble" like inclusions has been reported in this variant of papillary carcinoma [33].

Medullary Thyroid Carcinoma

Medullary thyroid carcinoma (MTC) originates from C cells of the thyroid and constitutes about 10% of all malignant thyroid tumors. This tumor also shows multiple growth patterns and variable cytomorphology [34].

Thus FNA specimens from MTC display a spectrum of morphologic patterns. They tend to be cellular and comprised of round-to-oval cells arranged mostly as single cells or loosely cohesive groups. The cytoplasm of the tumor cells shows distinct granules (calcitonin granules highlighted by immunostains) with eccentric nuclei, i.e., "plasma cell like/plasmacytoid" appearance to the tumor cells (Fig. 4). The nuclear chromatin is similar to that seen in other neuroendocrine tumors, i.e., "salt and pepper type." Intranuclear inclusions and multinucleated cells have been reported, thus this tumor being a great mimicker of other tumors of thyroid. The tumor cells can also assume a "spindle shape" and appear mesenchymal in origin. Amyloid may be observed as acellular material alone or in close association with tumor cells and can be distinguished from the thick colloid of papillary carcinoma by performing a Congo red stain. The diagnosis of MTC can

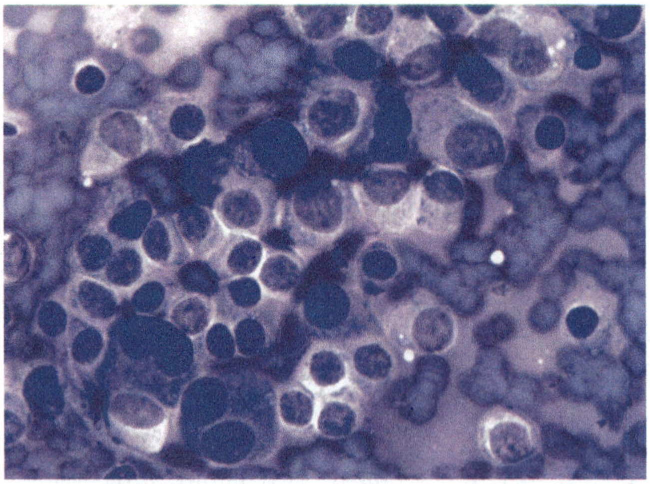

Fig. 4 A case of medullary carcinoma showing plasmacytoid cells with granular cytoplasm (Diff-Quik® stain, 60×)

be confirmed by performing immunostains for calcitonin and thyroglobulin [35, 36]. In a limited cellularity specimen it is advisable to recommend serum calcitonin levels to confirm the diagnosis of medullary carcinoma determination rather than performing immunostains [2, 6].

Anaplastic Carcinoma

Anaplastic carcinoma of the thyroid is one of the most clinically aggressive and fatal human tumors. The aspirates from anaplastic carcinoma usually do not pose any diagnostic difficulties; they can be readily classified as malignant due to extreme cellular pleomorphism, necrosis, and obvious malignant features [37].

Role of Special Studies in the Diagnosis of Thyroid Tumors in Cytologic Specimens

Immunohistochemistry

All follicular derived thyroid lesions, i.e., benign and malignant, express transcription factor (TTF-1) and thyroglobulin. This immunopanel is helpful in differentiating primary vs. secondary tumors of the thyroid [38]. The diagnosis of medullary carcinoma can be established in FNA specimens by performing immunostains for calcitonin and calcitonin gene related peptide (CGRP). Medullary carcinoma also stains positive for monoclonal carcinoembryonic antigen (CEA), chromogranin, synaptophysin, and TTF-1 [35, 39].

The use of various immunohistochemical markers in cytologic samples to differentiate papillary carcinoma from other follicular derived lesions of the thyroid have been explored by many authors. The immunopanel comprising of cytokeratin-19, HBME-1, and Galectin-3 have shown acceptable sensitivity and specificity, however, one must be aware of the fact that benign thyroid epithelium in chronic lymphocytic thyroiditis and post-FNA reactive foci can stain positive for both CK-19 and Galectin-3. This can lead to false positive diagnosis of malignancy [40–42]. Therefore, results of these stains must always be interpreted with care and correlated with the basic cytomorphology.

Molecular Genetics/Diagnosis

In the past decade much has been published on the role of various biologic events and genetic determinants in the pathogenesis of various thyroid tumors.

RET/PTC: Rearrangements of RET gene, known as RET/PTC have been identified in papillary carcinoma of thyroid [43]. RET/PTC 1 and 3 are the most common forms that occur in sporadic papillary carcinoma [44]. The prevalence of RET/PTC in papillary carcinoma varies significantly among various geographic regions [43, 45, 46]. Several authors have investigated the expression of RET/PTC rearrangements in thyroid aspirates to establish the diagnosis of papillary thyroid carcinoma [47, 48]; however, RET/PTC expression can also occur in some benign lesions, including hyalinizing trabecular neoplasm [49], chronic lymphocytic thyroiditis [50], hyperplastic nodules, and follicular adenoma [51, 52]. Thus, employing only RET/PTC analysis of FNA specimen to establish the diagnosis of PTC does not appear to be reliable.

BRAF: BRAF activating mutations in thyroid cancer are almost exclusively the BRAF V600E mutation, and have been found in 29–69% of papillary thyroid cancers, 13% of poorly differentiated cancers, and 10% of anaplastic cancers [53, 54, 55]. These mutations are independent of RET/PTC translocations or RAS mutations. BRAF mutational analysis of FNA samples has been shown to be of value in the diagnosis of papillary thyroid carcinoma. Some authors have suggested that since BRAF mutations, RET/PTC rearrangements, and RAS mutations are independent of each other, it may be helpful to analyze multiple markers in a given thyroid FNA specimen to establish the diagnosis of PTC [48].

DNA Microarray Analysis: Recently DNA microarray analysis of the thyroid FNA samples has been shown to successfully distinguish between the majority of benign and malignant thyroid lesions. It has been shown that based on these analyses FNA cohort could be separated into three clusters: malignant, benign, and indeterminate by unsupervised hierarchical cluster analysis [56].

Cytopathology of Parathyroid Gland

Most parathyroid lesions are not palpable; it is unusual to directly biopsy by FNA a parathyroid tumor. However, on occasion, parathyroid lesions present clinically as thyroid nodules or are large enough to be clinically evident. In such cases, an FNA may sample a proliferative parathyroid lesion [57]. With the advent of the image-guided fine-needle aspiration technique the number of FNA of neck masses is increasing, and so is the number of aspirated normal and/or neoplastic parathyroid tissue [57, 58]. Various studies have emphasized upon the difficulties in differentiating the parathyroid lesions from the neoplastic and non-neoplastic diseases of the thyroid in cytology specimens [59, 60]. The possibility of the ectopic location of parathyroid gland, including intrathyroidal location, clinical similarity between the parathyroid and thyroid lesions, overlap in their cytomorphology, and coexistence of pathology in both glands undoubtedly contribute to the misinterpretation of the fine needle aspirates [61]. Parathyroid lesions in the fine needle aspirates are most commonly confused with the thyroid neoplasms, papillary, follicular or Hürthle cell, adenomatoid thyroid nodules, or with lymphocytic thyroiditis. This is due to the presence of tissue fragments with papillary architecture, epithelial cells arranged in microfollicular pattern, colloid like material in the background, and due to the presence of oxyphil cells and naked nuclei of chief cells resembling Hürthle cells and lymphocytes, respectively [61, 62].

Although the literature dealing with the parathyroid FNA is sparse, most authors emphasize that there is no single diagnostic criterion that helps to reliably differentiate parathyroid lesions from those of thyroid, but rather a combination of cytomorphologic features should be used. Most helpful might be the presence in the parathyroid aspirates of three-dimensional fragments, naked nuclei admixed with cohesive cell clusters, (Fig. 5) nuclear overlapping, nuclear molding, and presence of mast cells [62]. In addition to cytomorphology, immunoperoxidase staining for the parathyroid hormone and thyroglobulin, chromogranin, and assays of PTH level of the aspirated fluid have shown to be of value in the cytologic diagnosis of parathyroid lesions [60, 62].

Cytopathology of Adrenal Gland

Fine-needle aspiration (FNA) is considered by many as the procedure of choice in the diagnosis of adrenal gland lesions [63, 64]. The possible causes for performing adrenal gland FNA include adrenal mass incidentally found on abdominal imaging, adrenal mass responsible for patients symptoms and altered adrenal function and adrenal mass encountered during the staging workup in a patient with known history of malignancy. However, the most important reason for performing adrenal FNA is to distinguish between primary and metastatic adrenal tumors [63, 64].

Benign adrenal cortical nodules are common and account for approximately 33% of adrenal lesions undergoing FNA. Though size is an important criterion for distinguishing between benign and malignant adrenal cortical nodules, one must be aware of the fact that metastatic nodules can also measure 1 cm or less [63, 65]. The most important criterion in making a diagnosis of neoplasm of adrenocortical origin is to be 100% sure that the FNA needle is within the nodule, since by morphology normal adrenocortical tissue is indistinguishable from the adrenocortical adenoma or adrenocortical tumors of undermined malignant potential [64]. The FNA specimens from adrenal tumors are usually cellular and show tumor cells in a lipid rich background (best seen in Diff-Quik stained slides). The individual cells display central or eccentrically placed nuclei with evenly dispersed chromatin and small nucleoli (Fig. 6). The cytoplasm is usually foamy and ill defined and a majority of cells can appear as stripped nuclei. The cells can occur as large cohesive fragments or singly scattered cells; some specimen can

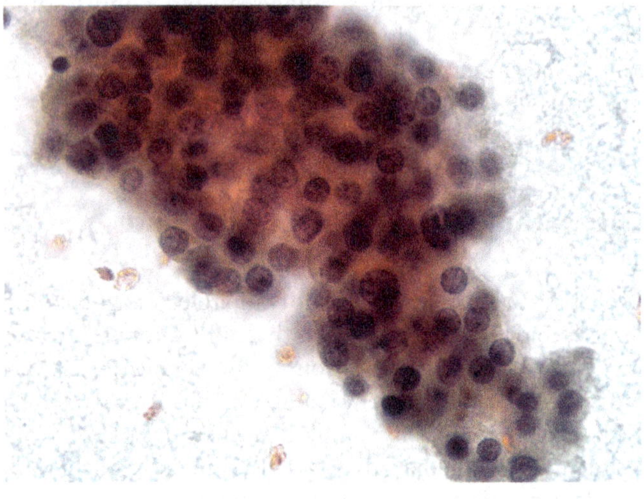

Fig. 5 Fine-needle aspiration of a parathyroid lesion demonstrating a monotonous population of cells arranged in cohesive group; notice the sharp cytoplasmic borders and clear cytoplasm. The PTH analysis of the aspirate confirmed the parathyroid origin. (Papanicolaou stained ThinPrep preparation, 60×)

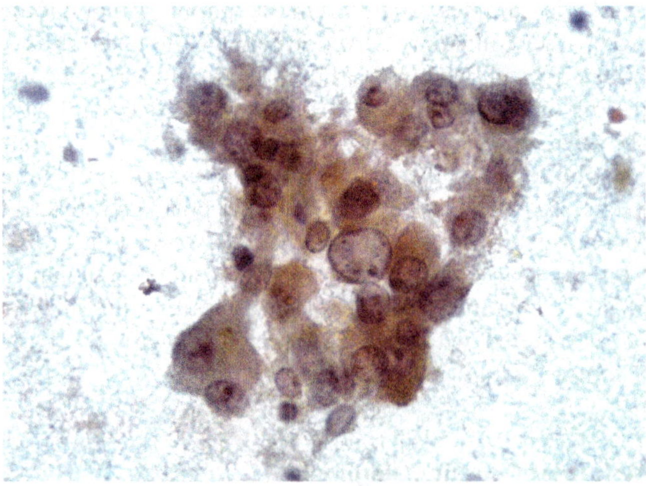

Fig. 6 Fine-needle aspiration of an adrenal cortical adenoma showing adrenal cortical cells with granular cytoplasm, round nuclei with prominent nucleoli (Papanicolaou stained Millipore® filter preparation, 60×)

show mostly singly scattered cells which can occur as a function of smearing technique or in large adrenal tumors with necrosis [63, 65, 66].

The differential diagnosis of FNA specimens from adrenocortical tumors includes renal cell carcinoma and metastatic mucinous adenocarcinoma. It is a challenge in cytology practice to differentiate between aspirates from renal cell carcinoma and adrenocortical tumors. Specimens from renal cell carcinoma usually lack lipid-rich background; however, in our practice, it is important to obtain enough material for immunostains to differentiate between these two entities. The aspirates from metastatic adenocarcinoma are mainly comprised of large cohesive fragments of tumor cells with marked nuclear pleomorphism with background necrosis [67, 68]. Mucicarmine stain can be helpful in the diagnosis of adenocarcinoma. Immunostains for CK-20, CK-7, CEA, EMA, Inhibin, and Calretinin, can be helpful in differentiating between primary adrenocortical tumors and metastatic adenocarcinoma [69, 70].

Rarely one may also encounter normal hepatocytes in FNA samples of right adrenal gland. Before making the diagnosis of accidental aspiration of normal liver, it is important to know that some adrenal tumors can show prominent oncocytic features. Normal hepatocytes are usually polygonal in shape with distinct cell borders, granular cytoplasm, and prominent nucleoli [70, 71].

There have been few reports describing the FNA cytology of pheochromocytoma. The cytology specimens are usually cellular and show many single cells and few tissue fragments. The latter may consist of a capillary rich stroma. The tumor cell cytoplasm is usually fragile leading to abundant bare nuclei; if present, the cytoplasm can show metachromatic granules, especially in Diff-Quik stained smears. Nuclear pleomorphism is readily evident (Fig. 7); usually the nuclei show salt and pepper chromatin with occasional intranuclear inclusions. In some cases one may also observe a variable number of ganglion-like cells [72, 73].

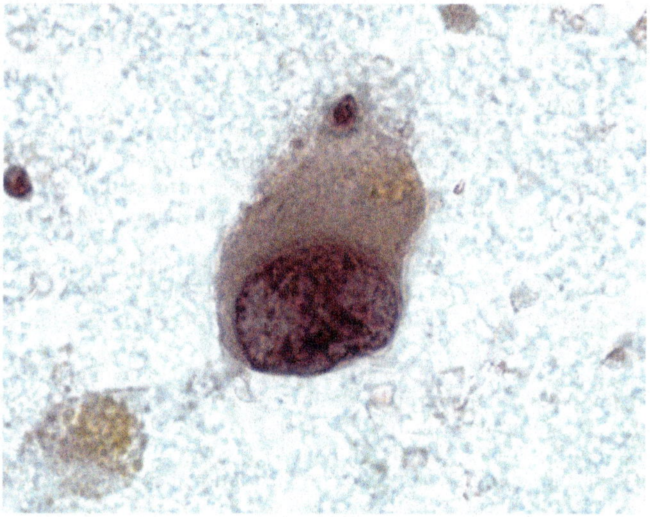

Fig. 7 Fine-needle aspiration specimen of a pheochromocytoma containing tumor cell displaying marked nuclear pleomorphism (Papanicolaou stained Millipore® filter preparation, 100×)

Cytopathology of Pancreatic Neuroendocrine Tumors

Pancreatic endocrine tumors (PET) account for approximately 1–2% of all neoplasms in the pancreas [74]. They may manifest clinically as functional tumors elaborating a variety of hormones or be nonfunctional. The nonfunctional tumors are detected as incidental findings on abdominal imaging or the patient may present with liver metastasis. The pancreas and the liver are amenable to percutaneous CT-guided fine-needle aspiration and fine-needle is often the first diagnostic test in an attempt to ascertain the nature of a pancreatic mass. More recently, endoscopic ultrasound-guided fine-needle aspiration (EUS FNA) has largely replaced percutaneous FNA due to the added advantage of visualizing peripancreatic lymph nodes and the liver and obtaining aspiration biopsies in a single procedure, thus staging the patient with a suspected pancreatic neoplasm [74–76].

Cytomorphologic Characteristics of PET

The cytomorphologic characteristics of PET are not dissimilar to the carcinoid tumors found elsewhere in the body [75–78]. Aspirates are generally cellular, with the tumor cells dispersed singly as well as forming cohesive groups or rosette-like structures (Fig. 8). The nuclear features are typical of a neuroendocrine tumor, with eccentrically placed nuclei imparting a plasmacytoid appearance to the tumor cells with salt and pepper chromatin (Fig. 9). Cystic degeneration has been reported in less than 2% of all PET [79]. Oncocytic metaplasia [80], clear cell change in the cytoplasm of the tumor cells mimicking a metastatic clear cell carcinoma, has also been reported [81, 82].

Ancillary Studies in the Diagnosis of PET

Immunohistochemical markers of neuroendocrine differentiation (synaptophysin, chromogranin-A, and CD56)

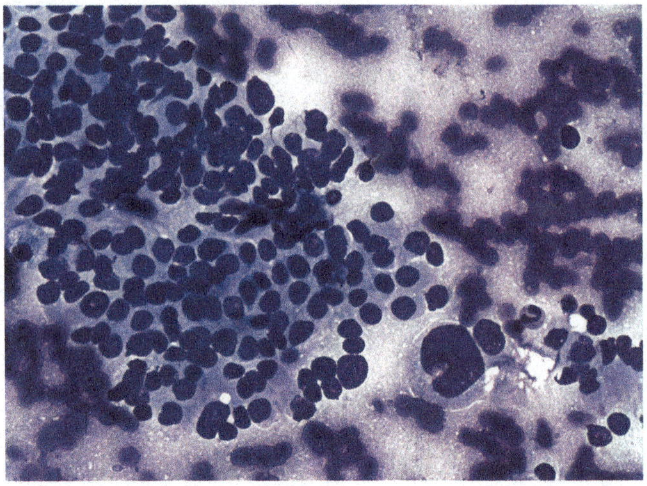

Fig. 8 Endoscopic-guided fine-needle aspiration specimen of a pancreatic endocrine tumor. The direct smear shows a group of uniform cells with round-to-oval nuclei arranged in an organoid pattern. Note the markedly enlarged cell in the *lower right* hand corner representing random nuclear atypia characteristic of endocrine tumors (Air-dried, Diff-Quik stained direct smear, 40×)

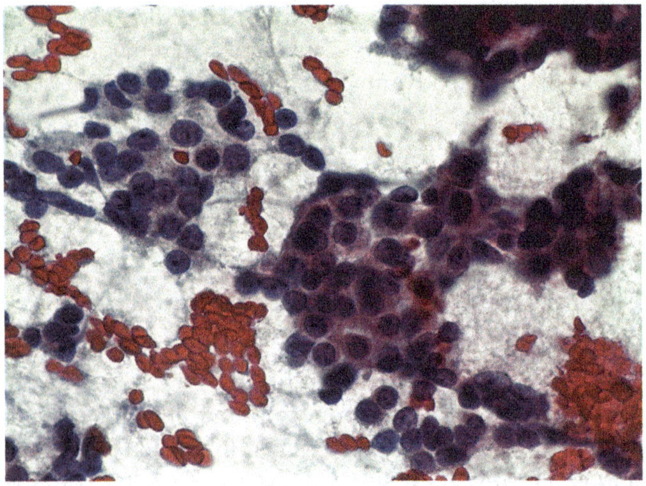

Fig. 9 Corresponding Papanicolaou stained smear from the above tumor exhibiting the characteristic nuclear characteristics of endocrine tumors. The tumor cells are arranged in a nested pattern with individual cells having moderate amount of cytoplasm. The chromatin pattern is finely granular and some of the nuclei do exhibit nucleoli (Alcohol fixed, Papanicolaou stained direct smear, 40×)

may be utilized on cell block material to confirm the diagnosis [75, 77, 83]. Two tumors that can be confused with PET on cytologic material include solid pseudopapillary tumor and acinar cell carcinoma of the pancreas. The former is characterized by the presence of tumor cells arranged in papillary fragments with fibrovascular cores. These tumors lack cytokeratin expression and stain strongly for ß-catenin, whereas PET shows diffuse and strong cytokeratin expression and stain negative for ß-catenin. Synaptophysin can be focally expressed in solid pseudopapillary tumor of the pancreas. Various authors have reported considerable overlap between immunohistochemical profile of PET and acinar cell carcinoma. Moreover, mixed acinar endocrine tumors of the pancreas make the differential diagnosis even more complicated. Skacel et al. [84] utilized a panel of immunohistochemical stains including synaptophysin, chromogranin-A, chymotrypsin, and α-1 antitrypsin to distinguish acinar cell from PET and concluded that the specificity of the neuroendocrine markers for PET and that of enzymatic markers for acinar cell carcinoma was too low to permit accurate classification using immunohistochemistry. One notable exception was the absence of chromogranin expression in acinar cell carcinoma and the expression of the same in about 60% of PET. Thus, caution should be exercised in distinguishing acinar cell carcinoma from PET in a limited cytology specimen [84, 85].

References

1. Baloch ZW, Cibas ES, Clark DP et al. The national cancer institute thyroid fine needle aspiration state of the science conference: a summation. *Cytojournal*. 2008;5:6.
2. Cooper DS, Doherty GM, Haugen BR et al. Management guidelines for patients with thyroid nodules and differentiated thyroid cancer. *Thyroid*. 2006;16:109–42.
3. Baskin HJ, Duick DS. The endocrinologists' view of ultrasound guidelines for fine needle aspiration. *Thyroid*. 2006;16:207–8.
4. American Association of Clinical Endocrinologists and Associazione Medici Endocrinologi medical guidelines for clinical practice for the diagnosis and management of thyroid nodules. *Endocr Pract*. 2006;12:63–102.
5. Guidelines of the Papanicolaou Society of Cytopathology for the Examination of Fine-Needle Aspiration Specimens from Thyroid Nodules. The Papanicolaou Society of Cytopathology Task Force on Standards of Practice. *Diagn Cytopathol*. 1996;15:84–9.
6. Baloch ZW, Livolsi VA, Asa SL et al. Diagnostic terminology and morphologic criteria for cytologic diagnosis of thyroid lesions: a synopsis of the national cancer institute thyroid fine-needle aspiration state of the science conference. *Diagn Cytopathol*. 2008;36:425–37.
7. Wang HH. Reporting thyroid fine-needle aspiration: literature review and a proposal. *Diagn Cytopathol*. 2006;34:67–76.
8. Kini SR. *Guides to Clinical Aspiration Biopsy Thyroid*. 2nd ed ed. New York, NY: Igaku-Shoin; 1996.
9. Layfield LJ, Wax T, Jones C. Cytologic distinction of goiterous nodules from morphologically normal thyroid: analyses of cytomorphologic features. *Cancer*. 2003;99:217–22.
10. Baloch ZW, Sack MJ, Yu GH, Livolsi VA, Gupta PK. Fine-needle aspiration of thyroid: an institutional experience. *Thyroid*. 1998;8:565–9.
11. Oertel YC, Oertel JE. Thyroid cytology and histology. *Baillieres Best Pract Res Clin Endocrinol Metab*. 2000;14:541–57.
12. Centeno BA, Szyfelbein WM, Daniels GH, Vickery AL, Jr. Fine needle aspiration biopsy of the thyroid gland in patients

with prior Graves' disease treated with radioactive iodine. Morphologic findings and potential pitfalls. *Acta Cytol.* 1996; 40:1189–97.

13. Anderson SR, Mandel S, LiVolsi VA, Gupta PK, Baloch ZW. Can cytomorphology differentiate between benign nodules and tumors arising in Graves' disease? *Diagn Cytopathol.* 2004;31: 64–7.
14. Kim WB, Han SM, Kim TY et al. Ultrasonographic screening for detection of thyroid cancer in patients with Graves' disease. *Clin Endocrinol (Oxf).* 2004;60:719–25.
15. Cantalamessa L, Baldini M, Orsatti A, Meroni L, Amodei V, Castagnone D. Thyroid nodules in Graves disease and the risk of thyroid carcinoma. *Arch Intern Med.* 1999;159:1705–8.
16. MacDonald L, Yazdi HM. Fine needle aspiration biopsy of Hashimoto's thyroiditis. Sources of diagnostic error. *Acta Cytol.* 1999;43:400–6.
17. Mechler C, Bounacer A, Suarez H et al. Papillary thyroid carcinoma: 6 cases from 2 families with associated lymphocytic thyroiditis harbouring RET/PTC rearrangements. *Br J Cancer.* 2001;85:1831–7.
18. Kumar N, Ray C, Jain S. Aspiration cytology of Hashimoto's thyroiditis in an endemic area. *Cytopathology.* 2002;13:31–9.
19. Kumarasinghe MP, De Silva S. Pitfalls in cytological diagnosis of autoimmune thyroiditis. *Pathology.* 1999;31:1–8.
20. Baloch ZW, Fleisher S, LiVolsi VA, Gupta PK. Diagnosis of "follicular neoplasm": A gray zone in thyroid fine-needle aspiration cytology. *Diagn Cytopathol.* 2002;26:41–4.
21. Yang J, Schnadig V, Logrono R, Wasserman PG. Fine-needle aspiration of thyroid nodules: a study of 4703 patients with histologic and clinical correlations. *Cancer.* 2007;111:306–15.
22. Renshaw AA. Follicular lesions of the thyroid. *Am J Clin Pathol.* 2001;115:782–5.
23. Sidawy MK, Del Vecchio DM, Knoll SM. Fine-needle aspiration of thyroid nodules: correlation between cytology and histology and evaluation of discrepant cases. *Cancer.* 1997;81:253–9.
24. Tuttle RM, Lemar H, Burch HB. Clinical features associated with an increased risk of thyroid malignancy in patients with follicular neoplasia by fine-needle aspiration. *Thyroid.* 1998; 8:377–83.
25. Kini SR, Miller JM, Hamburger JI, Smith-Purslow MJ. Cytopathology of follicular lesions of the thyroid gland. *Diagnostic Cytopathology.* 1985;1:123–32.
26. Elliott DD, Pitman MB, Bloom L, Faquin WC. Fine-needle aspiration biopsy of Hurthle cell lesions of the thyroid gland: A cytomorphologic study of 139 cases with statistical analysis. *Cancer.* 2006;108:102–9.
27. Carcangui ML ZG, Pupi A, Castagnoli A, Rosai J. Papillary carcinoma of the thyroid: a clinico-pathologic study of 241 cases treated at the University of Florence, Italy. *Cancer.* 1985;55:805–828.
28. Oertel YC. Fine-Needle Aspiration in the Evaluation of Thyroid Neoplasms. *Endocr Pathol.* 1997;8:215–224.
29. Das DK, Mallik MK, Sharma P et al. Papillary thyroid carcinoma and its variants in fine needle aspiration smears. A cytomorphologic study with special reference to tall cell variant. *Acta Cytol.* 2004;48:325–36.
30. Baloch ZW, LiVolsi VA. Cytologic and architectural mimics of papillary thyroid carcinoma. Diagnostic challenges in fine-needle aspiration and surgical pathology specimens. *Am J Clin Pathol.* 2006;125 Suppl:S135–44.
31. Albores-Saavedra J, Wu J. The many faces and mimics of papillary thyroid carcinoma. *Endocr Pathol.* 2006;17:1–18.
32. Zacks JF, de las Morenas A, Beazley RM, O'Brien MJ. Fine-needle aspiration cytology diagnosis of colloid nodule versus follicular variant of papillary carcinoma of the thyroid. *Diagn Cytopathol.* 1998;18:87–90.
33. Solomon A, Gupta PK, LiVolsi VA, Baloch ZW. Distinguishing tall cell variant of papillary thyroid carcinoma from usual variant of papillary thyroid carcinoma in cytologic specimens. *Diagn Cytopathol.* 2002;27:143–8.
34. Murray D. *The Thyroid Gland.* Malden, MA: Blackwell Science; 1998:295–380.
35. Collins BT, Cramer HM, Tabatowski K, Hearn S, Raminhos A, Lampe H. Fine needle aspiration of medullary carcinoma of the thyroid. Cytomorphology, immunocytochemistry and electron microscopy. *Acta Cytol.* 1995;39:920–30.
36. Papaparaskeva K, Nagel H, Droese M. Cytologic diagnosis of medullary carcinoma of the thyroid gland. *Diagn Cytopathol.* 2000;22:351–8.
37. Saunders CA, Nayar R. Anaplastic spindle-cell squamous carcinoma arising in association with tall-cell papillary cancer of the thyroid: A potential pitfall. *Diagn Cytopathol.* 1999;21:413–8.
38. Bejarano PA, Nikiforov YE, Swenson ES, Biddinger PW. Thyroid transcription factor-1, thyroglobulin, cytokeratin 7, and cytokeratin 20 in thyroid neoplasms. *Appl Immunohistochem Mol Morphol.* 2000;8:189–94.
39. Davila RM, Bedrossian CW, Silverberg AB. Immunocytochemistry of the thyroid in surgical and cytologic specimens. *Arch Pathol Lab Med.* 1988;112:51–6.
40. Cheung CC, Ezzat S, Freeman JL, Rosen IB, Asa SL. Immunohistochemical diagnosis of papillary thyroid carcinoma. *Mod Pathol.* 2001;14:338–42.
41. Sapio MR, Guerra A, Posca D et al. Combined analysis of galectin-3 and BRAFV600E improves the accuracy of fine-needle aspiration biopsy with cytological findings suspicious for papillary thyroid carcinoma. *Endocr Relat Cancer.* 2007;14:1089–97.
42. Barroeta JE, Baloch ZW, Lal P, Pasha TL, Zhang PJ, LiVolsi VA. Diagnostic value of differential expression of CK19, Galectin-3, HBME-1, ERK, RET, and p16 in benign and malignant follicular-derived lesions of the thyroid: an immunohistochemical tissue microarray analysis. *Endocr Pathol.* 2006;17:225–34.
43. Nikiforov YE. RET/PTC Rearrangement in Thyroid Tumors. *Endocr Pathol.* 2002;13:3–16.
44. Fischer AH, Bond JA, Taysavang P, O.Eugene B, Wynford-Thomas D. Papillary thyroid carcinoma oncogene (RET/PTC) alters the nuclear envelope and chromatin structure. *Am J Pathol.* 1998;153:1443–1450.
45. Zou M, Shi Y, Farid NR. Low rate of ret proto-oncogene activation (PTC/retTPC) in papillary thyroid carcinomas from Saudi Arabia. *Cancer.* 1994;73:176–80.
46. Motomura T, Nikiforov YE, Namba H et al. ret rearrangements in Japanese pediatric and adult papillary thyroid cancers. *Thyroid.* 1998;8:485–9.
47. Sapio MR, Posca D, Raggioli A et al. Detection of RET/PTC, TRK and BRAF mutations in preoperative diagnosis of thyroid nodules with indeterminate cytological findings. *Clin Endocrinol (Oxf).* 2007;66:678–83.
48. Pizzolanti G, Russo L, Richiusa P et al. Fine-needle aspiration molecular analysis for the diagnosis of papillary thyroid carcinoma through BRAF V600E mutation and RET/PTC rearrangement. *Thyroid.* 2007;17:1109–15.
49. Papotti M, Volante M, Giuliano A et al. RET/PTC activation in hyalinizing trabecular tumors of the thyroid. *Am J Surg Pathol.* 2000;24:1615–21.
50. Wirtschafter A, Schmidt R, Rosen D et al. Expression of the RET/PTC fusion gene as a marker for papillary carcinoma in Hashimoto's thyroiditis. [see comments]. *Laryngoscope.* 1997;107:95–100.
51. Elisei R, Romei C, Vorontsova T et al. RET/PTC rearrangements in thyroid nodules: studies in irradiated and not irradiated, malignant and benign thyroid lesions in children and adults. *J Clin Endocrinol Metab.* 2001;86:3211–6.

52. Inaba M, Umemura S, Satoh H et al. Expression of RET in follicular cell-derived tumors of the thyroid gland: Prevalence and implication of morphological type. *Pathol Int*. 2003;53:146–53.
53. Cohen Y, Xing M, Mambo E et al. BRAF mutation in papillary thyroid carcinoma. *J Natl Cancer Inst*. 2003;95:625–7.
54. Kimura ET, Nikiforova MN, Zhu Z, Knauf JA, Nikiforov YE, Fagin JA. High prevalence of BRAF mutations in thyroid cancer: genetic evidence for constitutive activation of the RET/PTC-RAS-BRAF signaling pathway in papillary thyroid carcinoma. *Cancer Res*. 2003;63:1454–7.
55. Fagin JA. How thyroid tumors start and why it matters: kinase mutants as targets for solid cancer pharmacotherapy. *J Endocrinol*. 2004;183:249–56.
56. Lubitz CC, Ugras SK, Kazam JJ et al. Microarray analysis of thyroid nodule fine-needle aspirates accurately classifies benign and malignant lesions. *J Mol Diagn*. 2006;8:490–8; quiz 528.
57. Liu F, Gnepp DR, Pisharodi LR. Fine needle aspiration of parathyroid lesions. *Acta Cytol*. 2004;48:133–6.
58. Maser C, Donovan P, Santos F et al. Sonographically guided fine needle aspiration with rapid parathyroid hormone assay. *Ann Surg Oncol*. 2006;13:1690–5.
59. Tseleni-Balafouta S, Gakiopoulou H, Kavantzas N, Agrogiannis G, Givalos N, Patsouris E. Parathyroid proliferations: a source of diagnostic pitfalls in FNA of thyroid. *Cancer*. 2007;111:130–6.
60. Owens CL, Rekhtman N, Sokoll L, Ali SZ. Parathyroid hormone assay in fine-needle aspirate is useful in differentiating inadvertently sampled parathyroid tissue from thyroid lesions. *Diagn Cytopathol*. 2008;36:227–31.
61. Giorgadze T, Stratton B, Baloch ZW, Livolsi VA. Oncocytic parathyroid adenoma: problem in cytological diagnosis. *Diagn Cytopathol*. 2004;31:276–80.
62. Abati A, Skarulis MC, Shawker T, Solomon D. Ultrasound-guided fine-needle aspiration of parathyroid lesions: a morphological and immunocytochemical approach. *Hum Pathol*. 1995;26:338–43.
63. Lumachi F, Borsato S, Brandes AA et al. Fine-needle aspiration cytology of adrenal masses in noncancer patients: clinicoradiologic and histologic correlations in functioning and nonfunctioning tumors. *Cancer*. 2001;93:323–9.
64. Lumachi F, Basso SM, Borsato S et al. Role and cost-effectiveness of adrenal imaging and image-guided FNA cytology in the management of incidentally discovered adrenal tumours. *Anticancer Res*. 2005;25:4559–62.
65. Fassina AS, Borsato S, Fedeli U. Fine needle aspiration cytology (FNAC) of adrenal masses. *Cytopathology*. 2000; 11:302–11.
66. Wu HH, Cramer HM, Kho J, Elsheikh TM. Fine needle aspiration cytology of benign adrenal cortical nodules. A comparison of cytologic findings with those of primary and metastatic adrenal malignancies. *Acta Cytol*. 1998;42:1352–8.
67. Sharma S, Singh R, Verma K. Cytomorphology of adrenocortical carcinoma and comparison with renal cell carcinoma. *Acta Cytol*. 1997;41:385–92.
68. Cochand-Priollet B. [Cytology of renal and adrenal gland masses in adults]. *Arch Anat Cytol Pathol*. 1997;45:299–304.
69. DeWitt J, Alsatie M, LeBlanc J, McHenry L, Sherman S. Endoscopic ultrasound-guided fine-needle aspiration of left adrenal gland masses. *Endoscopy*. 2007;39:65–71.
70. Jhala NC, Jhala D, Eloubeidi MA et al. Endoscopic ultrasound-guided fine-needle aspiration biopsy of the adrenal glands: analysis of 24 patients. *Cancer*. 2004;102:308–14.
71. Eloubeidi MA, Tamhane A, Jhala N et al. Agreement between rapid onsite and final cytologic interpretations of EUS-guided FNA specimens: implications for the endosonographer and patient management. *Am J Gastroenterol*. 2006;101:2841–7.
72. Jimenez-Heffernan JA, Vicandi B, Lopez-Ferrer P, Gonzalez-Peramato P, Perez-Campos A, Viguer JM. Cytologic features of pheochromocytoma and retroperitoneal paraganglioma: a morphologic and immunohistochemical study of 13 cases. *Acta Cytol*. 2006;50:372–8.
73. Saboorian MH, Katz RL, Charnsangavej C. Fine needle aspiration cytology of primary and metastatic lesions of the adrenal gland. A series of 188 biopsies with radiologic correlation. *Acta Cytol*. 1995;39:843–51.
74. Chatzipantelis P, Salla C, Konstantinou P, Karoumpalis I, Sakellariou S, Doumani I. Endoscopic ultrasound-guided fine-needle aspiration cytology of pancreatic neuroendocrine tumors: a study of 48 cases. *Cancer*. 2008.
75. Chang F, Vu C, Chandra A, Meenan J, Herbert A. Endoscopic ultrasound-guided fine needle aspiration cytology of pancreatic neuroendocrine tumours: cytomorphological and immunocytochemical evaluation. *Cytopathology*. 2006;17:10–7.
76. Gu M, Ghafari S, Lin F, Ramzy I. Cytological diagnosis of endocrine tumors of the pancreas by endoscopic ultrasound-guided fine-needle aspiration biopsy. *Diagn Cytopathol*. 2005; 32:204–10.
77. Jimenez-Heffernan JA, Vicandi B, Lopez-Ferrer P, Gonzalez-Peramato P, Perez-Campos A, Viguer JM. Fine needle aspiration cytology of endocrine neoplasms of the pancreas. Morphologic and immunocytochemical findings in 20 cases. *Acta Cytol*. 2004;48:295–301.
78. Saez A, Catala I, Brossa R, Funes A, Jaurrieta E, Ferrer JE. Intraoperative fine needle aspiration cytology of pancreatic lesions. A study of 90 cases. *Acta Cytol*. 1995;39:485–8.
79. Deshpande V, Lauwers GY. Cystic pancreatic endocrine tumor: a variant commonly confused with cystic adenocarcinoma. *Cancer*. 2007;111:47–53.
80. Pacchioni D, Papotti M, Macri L, Forte G, Bussolati G. Pancreatic oncocytic endocrine tumors. Cytologic features of two cases. *Acta Cytol*. 1996;40:742–6.
81. Guarda LA, Silva EG, Ordonez NG, Mackay B, Ibanez ML. Clear cell islet cell tumor. *Am J Clin Pathol*. 1983;79:512–7.
82. Hoang MP, Hruban RH, Albores-Saavedra J. Clear cell endocrine pancreatic tumor mimicking renal cell carcinoma: a distinctive neoplasm of von Hippel-Lindau disease. *Am J Surg Pathol*. 2001;25:602–9.
83. Shaw JA, Vance RP, Geisinger KR, Marshall RB. Islet cell neoplasms. A fine-needle aspiration cytology study with immunocytochemical correlations. *Am J Clin Pathol*. 1990;94:142–9.
84. Skacel M, Ormsby AH, Petras RE, McMahon JT, Henricks WH. Immunohistochemistry in the differential diagnosis of acinar and endocrine pancreatic neoplasms. *Appl Immunohistochem Mol Morphol*. 2000;8:203–9.
85. Labate AM, Klimstra DL, Zakowski MF. Comparative cytologic features of pancreatic acinar cell carcinoma and islet cell tumor. *Diagn Cytopathol*. 1997;16:112–6.

Fine Needle Aspiration Cytology of Neuroendocrine Tumors Arising in Non-endocrine Organs

Sanjay Logani and Zubair W. Baloch

Abstract The cytopathologic characteristics of endocrine tumors occurring in non-endocrine organs are not dissimilar to their counterparts commonly found in endocrine organs and detailed in the first half of this chapter. The terminology may be organ specific such as 'Merkel cell carcinoma' for neuroendocrine carcinoma native to the skin, but distinguishing Merkel cell from a metastatic small cell carcinoma of the lung or a small cell neuroendocrine carcinoma of paranasal sinuses may be difficult without knowledge of the clinical history and a selective immunohistochemical panel in appropriate cases. This chapter outlines the cytologic characteristics of the spectrum of neuroendocrine tumors occurring in non-neuroendocrine organs that are likely to be encountered in clinical practice by the cytopathologist.

Keywords Neuroendocrine tumor • Fine-needle aspiration • Immunohistochemistry • Non-endocrine organ

Introduction

The cytologic features of neuroendocrine tumors arising in non-endocrine organs are not markedly different from their counterparts in the endocrine system. In majority of the cases, it is the knowledge of the occurrence of endocrine variants of tumors native to the organ from which the needle aspirate is obtained, which leads to a correct interpretation in a fine-needle aspiration biopsy (FNAB) specimen. There are certain endocrine tumors that are encountered with some regularity on FNAB of non-endocrine organs and are the subject of discussion in the following paragraphs. For the sake of simplicity, they are discussed by organ system rather than tumor type.

Z.W. Baloch (✉)
Professor of Pathology, Director, Cytopathology Fellowship Program, Department of Pathology and Laboratory Medicine, University of Pennsylvania Medical Center, Philadelphia, PA 19104, USA
e-mail: baloch@mail.med.upenn.edu

Cytopathology of Neuroendocrine Tumors of the Lung

This group of tumors is thought to arise from the endocrine bronchial cells, also known as Kulchitsky's cells in recognition of the Russian histopathologist credited with the first description of the neuroendocrine cells in the gastrointestinal system in 1897 [1]. In the World Health Organization classification, endocrine tumors of the lung are classified into the following categories.

a) Carcinoid tumor and its variants (atypical carcinoid tumor)
b) Small cell carcinoma
c) Large cell neuroendocrine carcinoma.

Cytomorphologic Characteristics of Carcinoid Tumors and Its Variants

Carcinoid tumors are predominantly located centrally in the main stem and lobar bronchi and often present as submucosal polypoid tumors. Examples of carcinoid tumors located peripherally in the lung are described but these are rare. The central tumors are amenable to endobronchial brush cytology or may be encountered in bronchioalveolar lavage specimens and amenable to diagnosis by cytologic techniques. The peripheral tumors are more likely to be obtained on FNAB. The cytologic characteristics of carcinoid tumors are similar to carcinoid tumors elsewhere in the body, with the specimen showing a monotonous population of uniform oval to spindle-shaped cells containing moderate

A. Khan (ed.), *Surgical Pathology of Endocrine and Neuroendocrine Tumors*, Current Clinical Pathology,
DOI 10.1007/978-1-60327-396-1_3, © Humana Press, a part of Springer Science+Business Media, LLC 2009

amount of cytoplasm and fine granular chromatin described as 'salt and pepper' chromatin. The nuclei are often in eccentric location, imparting plasmacytoid appearance to the tumor cells. Nucleoli are generally not prominent but in occasional case may exhibit conspicuous nucleoli and should not detract the observer from the correct diagnosis. Focally, the tumor cells form rosettes and gland-like clusters and do not exhibit any nuclear molding or necrosis, features that are helpful in distinguishing small cell neuroendocrine carcinoma from carcinoid tumor in a limited sample. The mitotic activity of a typical carcinoid tumor should be less than 2 per 10 HPF. The presence of punctuate foci of necrosis and a mitotic activity of 2–10/10 HPF helps distinguish carcinoid from an atypical carcinoid tumor. Although some studies have described the presence of greater nuclear atypia and pleomorphism in atypical carcinoid, these features are unreliable to separate the two entities. For practical purposes, it is important to remember that carcinoid tumors are significantly more common than atypical carcinoid tumors and in the absence of punctuate necrosis, it may be impossible to distinguish the two entities on cytologic evaluation alone. In evaluating necrosis in carcinoid tumors, it is also important to remember that due to their endobronchial location, carcinoid tumors may show surface ulceration and granulation tissue that on endobronchial brush cytology may be mistaken for tumor type necrosis. Spindle cell variants of carcinoid tumors have the potential to be misinterpreted as small cell carcinoma [2]. In clinical practice, well-prepared cytologic specimen that includes a Diff-Quik smear, Pap smear, and cell block are optimal for obtaining a high rate of accuracy in diagnosing neuroendocrine tumors of the lung and helpful in distinguishing the four entities listed above from one another. Cell blocks are invaluable in immunohistochemical confirmation of neuroendocrine differentiation.

Small Cell Neuroendocrine Carcinoma (SCNC)

This tumor accounts for about 20% of lung carcinomas and has a significant association with smoking history in the patient. They are almost always located centrally and clinically present at an advanced stage. SCNC is comprised of cells that are smaller than the size of three small resting lymphocytes with scant cytoplasm, fine nuclear chromatin, and inconspicuous nucleoli. The tumor cells show oval to spindle-shaped nuclei with characteristic nuclear molding. Significant crush artifact is usually noted on the air-dried smears and the cell block preparation due to fragile tumor cells. Necrosis and high mitotic index are the hallmarks of this tumor (Fig. 1). The direct smears may show marked discohesion and mimic a lymphoma. Immunohistochemical demonstration of neuroendocrine differentiation can be obtained by staining the cell block with synaptophysin, chromogranin-A, or CD56. In

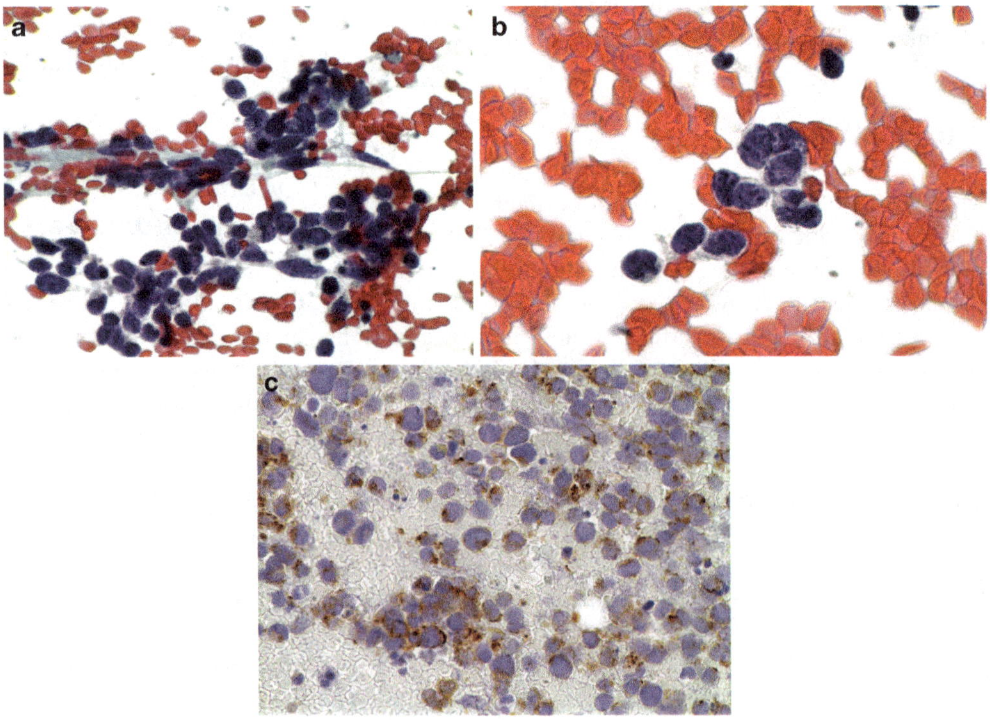

Fig. 1 Alcohol fixed direct smear of small cell carcinoma shows tumor cells with scant cytoplasm and oval to spindled-shaped nuclei (**A**). Characteristic nuclear molding (**B**) and dot-like staining pattern with cytokeratin AE1/3 (**C**, Papanicolaou stained smear, 60×)

approximately 10% of cases of SCNC, the neuroendocrine markers are negative and the diagnosis is based only on the morphologic characteristics [8]. The management of SCNC is often nonsurgical and due to the differences in the chemotherapeutic regimen between SCNC and non-small cell carcinoma, accuracy in diagnosis of this subtype of lung carcinoma is highly desirable.

Ancillary Techniques in the Diagnosis of Neuroendocrine Tumors of the Lung

Markers of neuroendocrine differentiation (chromogranin-A, synaptophysin, and CD56) are invaluable in confirming the diagnosis of a neuroendocrine tumor in challenging cases. The use of neuron-specific enolase is not recommended due to the nonspecific staining [8]. As aforementioned, the diagnosis of large cell neuroendocrine carcinoma of the lung (LCNEC) is highly dependent on the immunohistochemical demonstration of neuroendocrine differentiation in cytologic specimens. It has been shown that CDX2 and TTF 1 staining can be helpful in distinguishing primary carcinoid tumors in the lung from metastatic tumors originating in the gastrointestinal tract [9]. Markers of proliferative activity such as MIB-1 (Ki-67) have been utilized in difficult cases to distinguish carcinoid tumor from SCNC [10]. It is quite useful in cases where the tissue shows marked crush artifact. The proliferative index of carcinoid tumors is usually less than 10% and typically greater than 25% in SCNC.

Cytomorphology of Large Cell Neuroendocrine Carcinoma of the Lung (LCNEC)

The LCNEC shows considerable overlap with non-small cell carcinoma in cytology specimens. A few series that have dealt with the preoperative diagnosis of this tumor in cytologic specimens seem to rely more on immunohistochemical profile rather than on the cytologic characteristics alone. However, most authors agree that there are subtle cytomorphology clues that can prompt the pathologist to perform confirmatory immunohistochemical stains [3–7]. The specimens usually show large tumor cells with moderate cytoplasm. The presence of prominent nucleoli helps distinguish this tumor from small cell carcinoma; rosette formation and peripheral palisading of the nuclei in three-dimensional fragments offer clues to the neuroendocrine differentiation (Fig. 2). In some cases, the chromatin pattern may be fine and nucleoli may not be prominent, making its distinction from a small cell

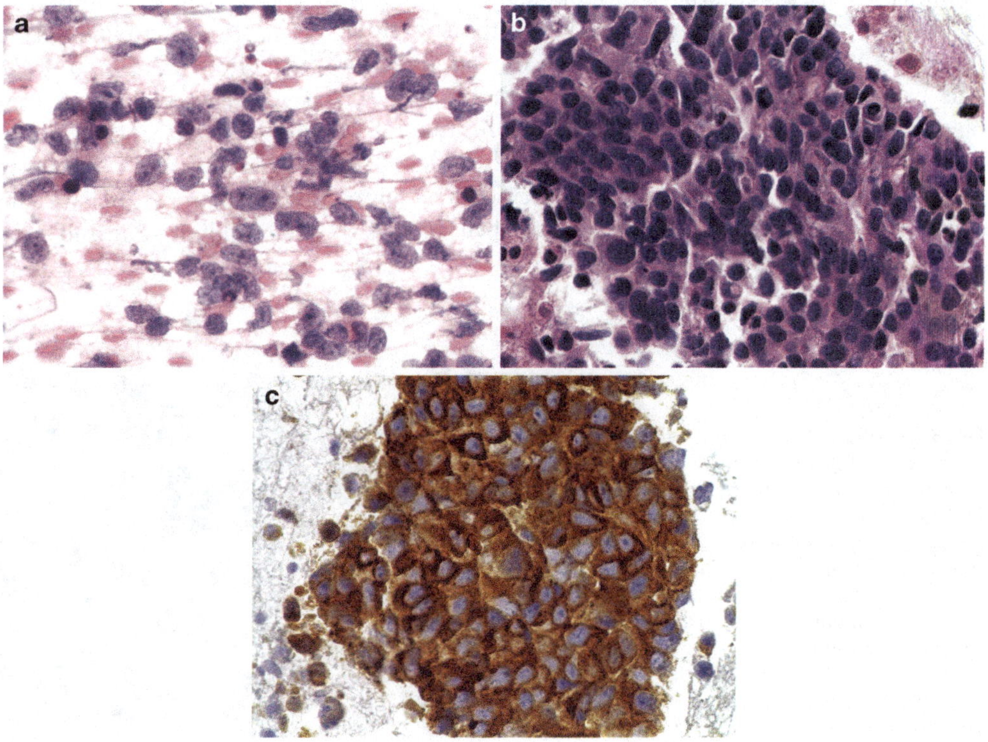

Fig. 2 Direct smear of a large cell neuroendocrine carcinoma shows cells with moderately pleomorphic nuclei and moderate amount of cytoplasm (**A**, hematoxylin and eosin, 60×). Corresponding cell block shows a neuroendocrine appearing tumor in sheet like arrangement (**B**, hematoxylin and eosin, 60×). The diagnosis can be confirmed by strong and diffuse expression for neuroendocrine markers (**C**, synaptophysin, 60×)

carcinoma quite challenging. The large nuclear size is the key distinguishing feature in these difficult cases, as nuclei of small cell carcinoma should be less than the diameter of three small resting lymphocytes.

Endocrine Tumors of the Nose and Paranasal Sinuses

Neuroendocrine tumors of the nose and paranasal sinuses include

a) Olfactory neuroblastoma
b) Small cell undifferentiated carcinoma

These tumors are rarely encountered on fine-needle aspiration cytology, especially as metastatic deposits in cervical lymph nodes. The cytologic characteristics of olfactory neuroblastoma have been described in isolated case reports [11–17]. More recently, Mahooti et al. studied a series of these tumors on cytology and compared them to the cytologic findings of metastatic small cell neuroendocrine carcinoma and Merkel cell carcinoma [18]. In their experience, the differential diagnosis of the above-mentioned tumors was quite challenging. Fibrillar neuropil previously reported as an important feature in the diagnosis of this tumor on cytologic material was not observed by Mahooti et al. in their series [18] (Fig. 3). Sinonasal undifferentiated carcinoma, malignant melanoma, and lymphoma can all have overlapping cytologic features in this region. These tumors produce a somewhat overlapping morphology in cytology specimens and separating them into the various categories often requires knowledge of the location and prior pertinent history [18–20]. Olfactory neuroblastoma typically arises from the olfactory mucosa in the nasal cavity and is often confined to the nasal cavity. Small cell undifferentiated carcinoma is more common in the paranasal sinuses and behaves as a locally aggressive tumor.

Ancillary Studies in the Diagnosis of Neuroendocrine Tumors of the Nose and Paranasal Sinuses

The major differential diagnostic considerations in an aspirate of a head and neck mass comprising of small blue cells includes olfactory neuroblastoma, Merkel cell carcinoma, small cell carcinoma, sinonasal undifferentiated carcinoma, lymphoma, and small cell variant of malignant melanoma. A panel of immunohistochemical stains including cytokeratin AE1/3, EMA, S100, LCA, synaptophysin, chromogranin, and CD-56 is helpful in arriving at correct diagnosis. Olfactory neuroblastoma shows synaptophysin expression in the majority of cases. A third of cases express cytokeratin focally but EMA is usually negative; this immunoprofile is helpful in distinguishing this tumor from a nasopharyngeal carcinoma [20]. The pattern of immunohistochemical staining for small cell undifferentiated carcinoma is similar to small cell carcinoma that occurs in other organs (positive expression for cytokeratin, synaptophysin, and chromogranin-A). Merkel cell carcinoma can be differentiated from the above by co-expression for cytokeratin 20 in the tumor cells.

Endocrine Tumors of the Skin

Merkel cell carcinoma is a primary cutaneous endocrine tumor, first described by the German anatomist Friedrich Merkel in 1872. Clinically, this tumor presents as a violaceous subcutaneous nodule, generally in the head and neck region. The tumor derives its name from the cell of origin; these cells are large sized with clear cytoplasm found in the stratum basale of mammalian skin and are associated with touch sensation [21].

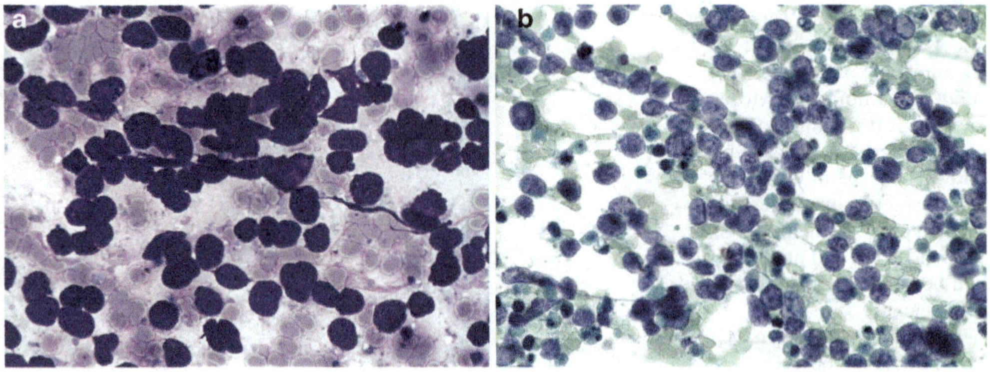

Fig. 3 Air-dried direct smear from a case of metastatic olfactory neuroblastoma (**A**, Diff-Quik, 60×) and the corresponding alcohol fixed smear (**B**, Papanicolaou stain, 60×). The morphologic features can be indistinguishable from a small cell carcinoma or lymphoma. The presence of neuropil in the background can be helpful, if present

Cytomorphologic Features of Merkel Cell Carcinoma

Fine-needle aspiration specimens are quite cellular with tumor cells dispersed singly or forming loosely cohesive groups; rosette formation can also occur. The individual tumor cells have scant cytoplasm that disintegrates easily upon smearing leaving a number of naked nuclei. The nuclear chromatin is generally fine and nucleoli are not prominent. Mitotic activity is generally brisk [22–24] (Fig. 4).

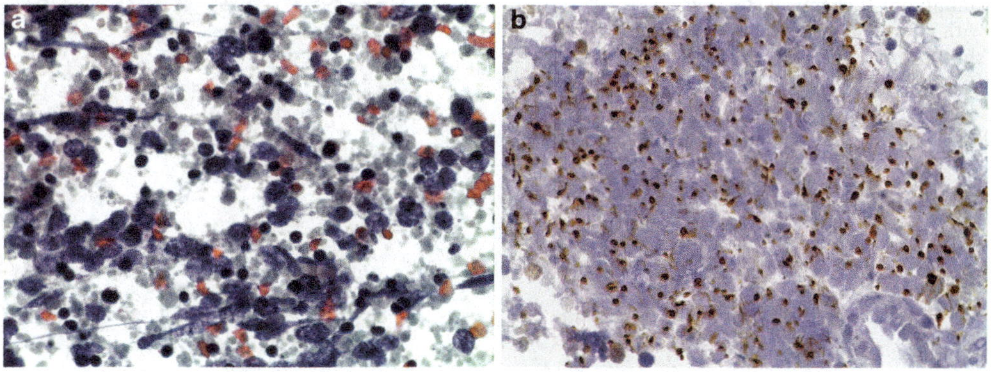

Fig. 4 Alcohol fixed direct smear from a case of metastatic Merkel cell carcinoma (**A**, Papanicolaou stain, 60×). The morphologic features of this tumor can be indistinguishable from other small round blue cell tumors on fine-needle aspiration biopsy. Staining with cytokeratin 20 in a 'dot-like' pattern is characteristic and helpful in distinguishing it from a small cell carcinoma (**B**, cytokeratin 20, 60×)

Ancillary Tests in Evaluation of Merkel Cell Carcinoma

Immunohistochemical staining for cytokeratin shows a characteristic perinuclear dot-like staining pattern in the tumor cells. In addition, the tumor cells express cytokeratin 20 but not cytokeratin 7. A panel of immunohistochemical stains including cytokeratin 20, TTF-1, chromogranin-A, and synaptophysin can be very helpful in confirming the diagnosis of Merkel cell carcinoma. Metastatic small cell carcinoma from lung may produce a subcutaneous mass but would express TTF-1 and show negative expression for cytokeratin 20 [25]. If lymphoma is a diagnostic consideration, a panel of stains comprising cytokeratin and leukocyte common antigen (LCA) is sufficient to distinguish the two. Interpretation of the keratin staining in these tumors sometimes requires careful scrutiny of the slide due to the small dot-like pattern of staining that can be easily overlooked if the slide is scanned on low to medium power magnification.

Endocrine Tumors of the Female Genital Tract

Neuroendocrine tumors encountered in the female genital tract include the following [26]:

a) Small cell carcinoma of the uterine cavity
b) Carcinoid tumor of the ovary
c) Small cell and large cell neuroendocrine carcinoma of the ovary
d) Small cell and large cell neuroendocrine carcinoma of the cervix

The tumor most likely to be encountered by cytopathologist in clinical practice is the small cell or large cell neuroendocrine carcinoma involving the cervix and therefore is discussed in detail.

Small cell and large cell neuroendocrine carcinomas of the cervix (Fig. 5) account for approximately 2% of all cervical carcinomas [27]. These tumors are likely to be encountered on a Pap smear and their recognition is important due to the rapidly progressive nature of the disease and poor prognosis if the diagnosis is delayed [28]. On a conventional smear, the diagnosis of small cell or large cell neuroendocrine carcinoma can be difficult and these are often misinterpreted as high-grade squamous intraepithelial lesion or worse; the small cells can potentially be ignored as small lymphocytes and can lead to a false-negative Pap test with dire consequences for the patient [29–31]. The correct identification of this tumor subtype is also challenging on liquid-based tests because the tumor cells tend to ball-up, shrink, and lack the smearing artifact seen on conventional smears with this group of tumors. A high index of suspicion and immunohistochemical confirmation of the diagnosis on a cell block prepared from the residual material can be invaluable in making the correct diagnosis.

Ancillary Tests in Evaluation of Neuroendocrine Carcinoma of the Cervix

If the diagnosis of neuroendocrine carcinoma is suspected on a Pap test, a cell block can be prepared from the residual material and stained for the usual markers of

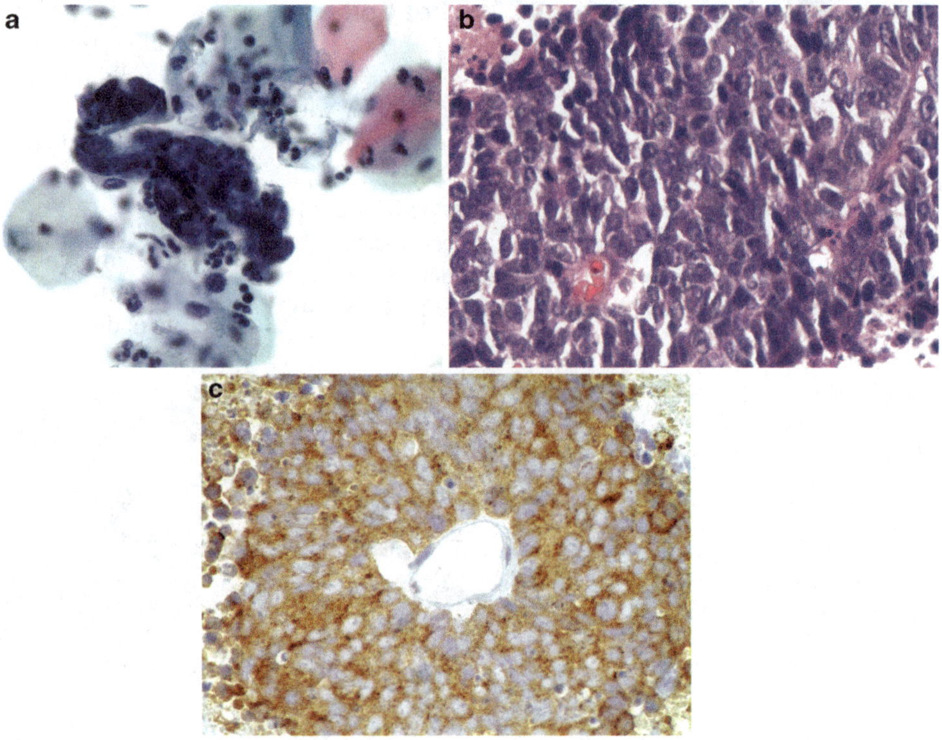

Fig. 5 Large cell neuroendocrine carcinoma of the cervix. The tumor cells show high-grade nuclei, nuclear molding, and can be mistaken for high-grade squamous intraepithelial lesion (**A**, Liquid-based preparation, Papanicolaou stain, 60×). The corresponding histologic section shows the neuroendocrine features of the tumor (**B**, hematoxylin and eosin staining, 60×). Immunohistochemical staining with neuroendocrine markers shows strong, diffuse expression (**C**, synaptophysin, 60×)

neuroendocrine differentiation. Small cell and large cell neuroendocrine carcinomas can express TTF-1 and thus this stain is not helpful in excluding the possibility of a lung primary metastatic to cervix. In all cases therefore, it is imperative that a clinicopathologic correlation to exclude the possibility of a metastatic tumor be performed before ascribing a diagnosis of primary neuroendocrine carcinoma of the cervix. HPV DNA can be detected in the vast majority of neuroendocrine carcinoma of the cervix and thus helpful in supporting a primary origin in the cervix [32, 33].

Endocrine Tumors of the Male Genitourinary Tract

The following neuroendocrine tumors occur in the male genitourinary tract [26, 34]

a) Small cell and large cell neuroendocrine carcinomas of the urinary bladder
b) Small cell carcinoma of the prostate
c) Carcinoid tumor of the testes

Neuroendocrine tumors of the prostate [35] and testes are unlikely to be encountered in cytology practice, and therefore, in the uncommon situation that an FNA is performed of a testicular mass, knowledge of the cytomorphologic features of endocrine tumors should permit a correct diagnosis. Due to the rarity of primary neuroendocrine tumors in these organs, the possibility of a metastasis should be considered and clinically excluded. Neuroendocrine tumors of the urinary bladder may potentially present in voided urine samples or bladder washings [36, 37]. The diagnosis may be challenging and in the absence of a

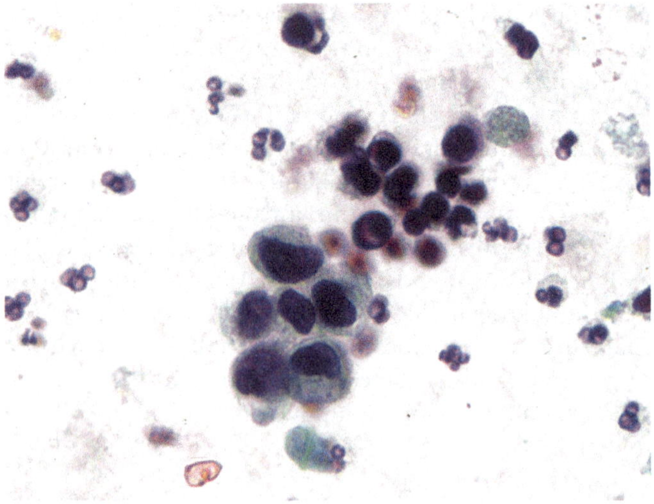

Fig. 6 Small cell neuroendocrine carcinoma of the urinary bladder. The tumor cells in a bladder washing specimen can be difficult to distinguish from conventional urothelial carcinoma. The presence of nuclear molding and lack of prominent nuclei can be helpful in suspecting this diagnosis on a urine sample (Millipore Filter, Papanicolaou staining, 40×)

high index of suspicion, the tumor cells may be considered to represent high-grade urothelial carcinoma or cells representing carcinoma in situ (CIS). Moreover, unlike the lung, the majority of small cell carcinoma of the bladder show conventional high-grade urothelial carcinoma component as well, making the pre-operative recognition of small cell carcinoma on cytology challenging [38, 39]. The observation of nuclear molding and tumor cells with very scant cytoplasm and lack of nucleoli are important cytologic features that can lead to the correct diagnosis of a neuroendocrine carcinoma on a urine sample (Fig. 6).

Ancillary Tests in the Diagnosis of Neuroendocrine Tumors of the Male Genital Tract

Immunohistochemical demonstration of neuroendocrine differentiation with synaptophysin, chromogranin-A, or CD56 on a cell block specimen is helpful in confirming the morphologic suspicion of neuroendocrine carcinoma on a urine or bladder washing specimen [36].

References

1. Drozdov I, Modlin IM, Kidd M, Goloubinov VV. From Leningrad to London: The Saga of Kulchitsky and the Legacy of the Enterochromaffin Cell. *Neuroendocrinology*. 2009;89(1):1–12.
2. Renshaw AA, Haja J, Lozano RL, Wilbur DC. Distinguishing carcinoid tumor from small cell carcinoma of the lung: correlating cytologic features and performance in the College of American Pathologists Non-Gynecologic Cytology Program. *Arch Pathol Lab Med*. May 2005;129(5):614–618.
3. Hiroshima K, Abe S, Ebihara Y, et al. Cytological characteristics of pulmonary large cell neuroendocrine carcinoma. *Lung Cancer*. Jun 2005;48(3):331–337.
4. Jimenez-Heffernan JA, Lopez-Ferrer P, Vicandi B, et al. Fine-needle aspiration cytology of large cell neuroendocrine carcinoma of the lung: a cytohistologic correlation study of 11 cases. *Cancer*. Jun 25 2008;114(3):180–186.
5. Kakinuma H, Mikami T, Iwabuchi K, et al. Diagnostic findings of bronchial brush cytology for pulmonary large cell neuroendocrine carcinomas: comparison with poorly differentiated adenocarcinomas, squamous cell carcinomas, and small cell carcinomas. *Cancer*. Aug 25 2003;99(4):247–254.
6. Peng WX, Sano T, Oyama T, Kawashima O, Nakajima T. Large cell neuroendocrine carcinoma of the lung: a comparison with large cell carcinoma with neuroendocrine morphology and small cell carcinoma. *Lung Cancer*. Feb 2005;47(2):225–233.
7. Wiatrowska BA, Krol J, akowski MF. Large-cell neuroendocrine carcinoma of the lung: proposed criteria for cytologic diagnosis. *Diagn Cytopathol*. Jan 2001;24(1):58–64.
8. Franks TJ, Galvin JR. Lung tumors with neuroendocrine morphology: essential radiologic and pathologic features. *Arch Pathol Lab Med*. Jul 2008;132(7):1055–1061.
9. Lin X, Saad RS, Luckasevic TM, Silverman JF, Liu Y. Diagnostic value of CDX-2 and TTF-1 expressions in separating metastatic neuroendocrine neoplasms of unknown origin. *Appl Immunohistochem Mol Morphol*. Dec 2007;15(4):407–414.
10. Aslan DL, Gulbahce HE, Pambuccian SE, Manivel JC, Jessurun J. Ki-67 immunoreactivity in the differential diagnosis of pulmonary neuroendocrine neoplasms in specimens with extensive crush artifact. *Am J Clin Pathol*. Jun 2005;123(6):874–878.
11. Chung J, Park ST, Jang J. Fine needle aspiration cytology of metastatic olfactory neuroblastoma: a case report. *Acta Cytol*. Jan–Feb 2002;46(1):40–45.
12. Fagan MF, Rone R. Esthesioneuroblastoma: cytologic features with differential diagnostic considerations. *Diagn Cytopathol*. Oct–Dec 1985;1(4):322–326.
13. Ferris CA, Schnadig VJ, Quinn FB, Des Jardins L. Olfactory neuroblastoma. Cytodiagnostic features in a case with ultrastructural and immunohistochemical correlation. *Acta Cytol*. May–Jun 1988;32(3):381–385.
14. Jelen M, Wozniak Z, Rak J. Cytologic appearance of esthesioneuroblastoma in a fine needle aspirate. *Acta Cytol*. May–Jun 1988;32(3):377–380.
15. Jobst SB, Ljung BM, Gilkey FN, Rosenthal DL. Cytologic diagnosis of olfactory neuroblastoma. Report of a case with multiple diagnostic parameters. *Acta Cytol*. May–Jun 1983;27(3):299–305.
16. Logrono R, Futoran RM, Hartig G, Inhorn SL. Olfactory neuroblastoma (esthesioneuroblastoma): appearance on fine-needle aspiration: report of a case. *Diagn Cytopathol*. Sep 1997;17(3):205–208.
17. Prasad N, Prasad P, Kishnani K. Diagnosis of olfactory neuroblastoma by cytology. *J Indian Med Assoc*. Mar 1990;88(3):86–88.
18. Mahooti S, Wakely PE, Jr. Cytopathologic features of olfactory neuroblastoma. *Cancer*. Apr 25 2006;108(2):86–92.
19. Bellizzi AM, Bourne TD, Mills SE, Stelow EB. The cytologic features of sinonasal undifferentiated carcinoma and olfactory neuroblastoma. *Am J Clin Pathol*. Mar 2008;129(3):367–376.
20. Iezzoni JC, Mills SE. "Undifferentiated" small round cell tumors of the sinonasal tract: differential diagnosis update. *Am J Clin Pathol*. Dec 2005;124(Suppl):S110–121.
21. Moll I, Moll R. Early development of human Merkel cells. *Exp Dermatol*. Nov 1992;1(4):180–184.
22. Collins BT, Elmberger PG, Tani EM, Bjornhagen V, Ramos RR. Fine-needle aspiration of Merkel cell carcinoma of the skin with cytomorphology and immunocytochemical correlation. *Diagn Cytopathol*. Apr 1998;18(4):251–257.
23. Dey P, Jogai S, Amir T, Temim L. Fine-needle aspiration cytology of Merkel cell carcinoma. *Diagn Cytopathol*. Nov 2004;31(5):364–365.
24. Kabukcuoglu F, Sungun A, Polat N, Evren I, Kabukcuoglu Y. Fine needle aspiration cytology of Merkel cell carcinoma. *Acta Cytol*. Mar–Apr 2003;47(2):311–313.
25. Cheuk W, Kwan MY, Suster S, Chan JK. Immunostaining for thyroid transcription factor 1 and cytokeratin 20 aids the distinction of small cell carcinoma from Merkel cell carcinoma, but not pulmonary from extrapulmonary small cell carcinomas. *Arch Pathol Lab Med*. Feb 2001;125(2):228–231.
26. Eichhorn JH, Young RH. Neuroendocrine tumors of the genital tract. *Am J Clin Pathol*. Jun 2001;115 Suppl:S94–112.
27. Gilks CB, Young RH, Gersell DJ, Clement PB. Large cell neuroendocrine [corrected] carcinoma of the uterine cervix: a clinicopathologic study of 12 cases. *Am J Surg Pathol*. Aug 1997;21(8):905–914.
28. Ciesla MC, Guidos BJ, Selvaggi SM. Cytomorphology of small-cell (neuroendocrine) carcinoma on ThinPrep cytology as compared to conventional smears. *Diagn Cytopathol*. Jan 2001;24(1):46–52.

29. Hoerl HD, Schink J, Hartenbach E, Wagner JL, Kurtycz DF. Exfoliative cytology of primary poorly differentiated (small-cell) neuroendocrine carcinoma of the uterine cervix in ThinPrep material: a case report. *Diagn Cytopathol.* Jul 2000;23(1):14–18.
30. Reich O, Pickel H, Purstner P. Exfoliative cytology of invasive neuroendocrine small cell carcinoma in a cervical cytologic smear. A case report. *Acta Cytol.* Sep–Oct 1996;40(5):980–984.
31. Zhou C, Hayes MM, Clement PB, Thomson TA. Small cell carcinoma of the uterine cervix: cytologic findings in 13 cases. *Cancer.* Oct 25 1998;84(5):281–288.
32. Grayson W, Rhemtula HA, Taylor LF, Allard U, Tiltman AJ. Detection of human papillomavirus in large cell neuroendocrine carcinoma of the uterine cervix: a study of 12 cases. *J Clin Pathol.* Feb 2002;55(2):108–114.
33. Ishida GM, Kato N, Hayasaka T, et al. Small cell neuroendocrine carcinomas of the uterine cervix: a histological, immunohistochemical, and molecular genetic study. *Int J Gynecol Pathol.* Oct 2004;23(4):366–372.
34. Fine SW. Neuroendocrine lesions of the genitourinary tract. *Adv Anat Pathol.* Jul 2007;14(4):286–296.
35. Evans AJ, Humphrey PA, Belani J, van der Kwast TH, Srigley JR. Large cell neuroendocrine carcinoma of prostate: a clinicopathologic summary of 7 cases of a rare manifestation of advanced prostate cancer. *Am J Surg Pathol.* Jun 2006;30(6):684–693.
36. Acs G, Gupta PK, Baloch ZW. Cytomorphology of high-grade neuroendocrine carcinoma of the urinary tract. *Diagn Cytopathol.* Aug 2000;23(2):92–96.
37. van Hoeven KH, Artymyshyn RL. Cytology of small cell carcinoma of the urinary bladder. *Diagn Cytopathol.* Jun 1996;14(4):292–297.
38. Ali SZ, Reuter VE, Zakowski MF. Small cell neuroendocrine carcinoma of the urinary bladder. A clinicopathologic study with emphasis on cytologic features. *Cancer.* Jan 15 1997;79(2):356–361.
39. Abbas F, Civantos F, Benedetto P, Soloway MS. Small cell carcinoma of the bladder and prostate. *Urology.* Nov 1995;46(5):617–630.

Tumors of the Pituitary Gland

Ricardo V. Lloyd, Bernd W. Scheithauer, Eva Horvath, and Kalman Kovacs

Abstract Anterior pituitary tumors are clonal proliferation of pituitary cells. They usually consist of one cell type, although some adenomas consist of more than one cell type.

Pituitary tumors can be characterized by broad spectrum markers such as synaptophysin and chromogranin. Reticulin histochemical staining is useful in separating normal hyperplastic and neoplastic pituitary tissues. Electron microscopy is a powerful tool to help separate various subtypes of adenomas including sparsely and densely granulated growth hormone adenomas and different subtypes of silent ACTH adenomas.

The major types of pituitary adenomas include GH, PRL, ACTH, TSH, gonadotroph (FSH/LH), and null cell adenomas. A combination of hematoxylin and eosin staining, immunohistochemistry, and electron microscopic studies are the most comprehensive ways of classifying pituitary tumors.

Keywords Pituitary • Pituitary adenomas • Immunohistochemistry • Electron microscopy • Growth hormone adenoma Prolactin adenoma • ACTH adenoma • and Gonadotroph adenoma

Tumors of the Pituitary Gland

Pituitary tumors are clonal proliferation and may consist of only one cell type or multiple hormone-expressing cells in the tumor. Most pituitary tumors are benign.

Hematoxylin and eosin staining remain the most commonly used method to examine and classify pituitary tumors. In addition, histochemical stains such as the reticulin stain and periodic acid Schiff (PAS) have been helpful in classifying pituitary tumors. Ultrastructural and immunohistochemical studies have contributed extensively to the classification of pituitary tumors.

Histochemical Studies

Silver stains for the demonstration of reticulin fibers are useful in distinguishing between normal anterior pituitary and pituitary tumors. In adenomas, the reticulin network that is present around acinar structures in the normal anterior pituitary is disrupted and irregular (Fig. 1A,B). PAS stain is useful for the diagnosis of ACTH adenomas because of the carbohydrate moiety present in pro-opiomelanocortin (POMC), which is the precursor for ACTH [1]. Calcification may be present in PRL adenomas, so the use of histochemical stains for calcium may help to confirm these findings. Endocrine amyloid deposits may be present in some pituitary tumors such as PRL, GH, or mixed PRL-GH tumors. Amyloid stains such as Congo red may be useful in these cases [2, 3].

Immunohistochemical Studies

Broad Spectrum Endocrine Markers

The use of broad-spectrum endocrine markers including chromogranin A [4, 5] and synaptophysin [6] can help to establish sellar-based tumor lesions as an endocrine tumor. This is especially useful with small biopsy specimens when there may be some questions as to whether the biopsy is a pituitary lesion. Other broad-spectrum endocrine markers such as CD56, 7B2, and proconvertase

R.V. Lloyd (✉)
Professor of Pathology and Laboratory Medicine, Division of Anatomic Pathology, Mayo Clinic, Rochester, MN 55905, USA
e-mail: lloyd.ricardo@mayo.edu

A. Khan (ed.), *Surgical Pathology of Endocrine and Neuroendocrine Tumors*, Current Clinical Pathology,
DOI 10.1007/978-1-60327-396-1_4, © Humana Press, a part of Springer Science+Business Media, LLC 2009

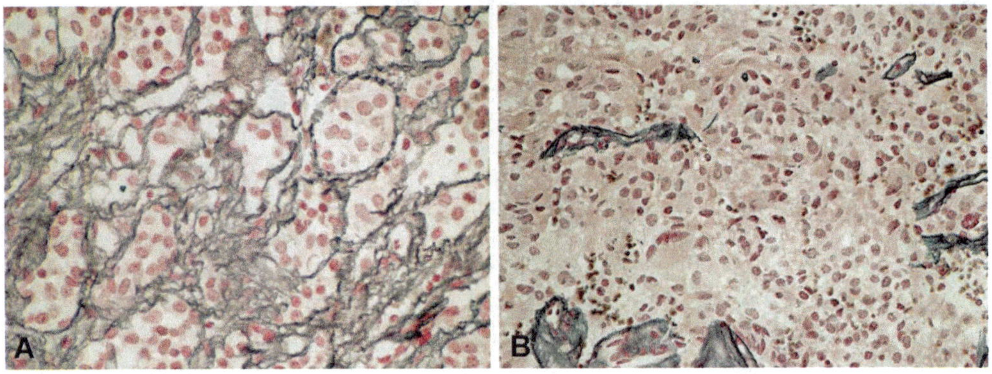

Fig. 1 Reticulin staining in pituitary.
A – Reticulin staining in normal pituitary with preservation of normal reticulin pattern.
B – Reticulin staining in pituitary adenoma showing disruption of the reticulin pattern

(PC)3 and PC2, are also expressed by pituitary cells but are not used as commonly as chromogranin A and synaptophysin.

Hormonal Markers

GH-Immunoreactivity

GH immunoreactive tumors may represent functioning tumors, which comprise the majority of GH-immunoreactive adenomas [7] as well as rare silent GH adenomas [8]. The various types of GH-producing pituitary adenomas will be discussed in a later section of the chapter.

PRL-Immunoreactivity

Most PRL-immunoreactive adenomas are functioning tumors [7]. There are reports of silent PRL adenomas, but they are extremely uncommon [7]. Treatment with bromocriptine and other dopamine agonists may lead to decreased immunoreactivity for PRL in the tumor cells in addition to perivascular and interstitial fibrosis which are related to suppression of hormone synthesis.

ACTH-Immunoreactivity

Although most ACTH immunoreactive tumors are functioning adenomas, this subtype of adenomas has the largest number of nonfunctioning tumors as well [7]. Between 5 and 10% of ACTH immunoreactive tumors may belong to this silent ACTH adenoma category [9–11]. The subtype of silent ACTH tumors will be discussed in another section of the chapter.

TSH-Immunoreactivity

TSH immunoreactive tumors may be associated with primary hypothyroidism, secondary hypothyroidism, or the patients may be euthyroid [12–15]. Hyperthyroidism secondary to a TSH-producing tumor is uncommon. There is usually no relationship between the degree of immunoreactive TSH and serum levels of TSH. In addition to the expression of TSH in these adenomas, other tumor types such as densely granulated GH adenomas, null cell adenomas, oncocytomas, and plurihormonal adenomas may also be positive for TSH.

FSH and LH-Immunoreactivity

The beta subunit of FSH and/or LH may be present with or without the alpha subunit of glycoprotein hormones in gonadotroph, null cell, and oncocytic adenomas [16]. Some gonadotroph adenomas may not have immunoreactive FSH and/or LH. This may be due to the sensitivity of the assay used, since highly sensitive assays usually reveal some immunoreactive FSH/LH or alpha subunit positive cells [16].

Alpha Subunit-Immunoreactivity

The alpha subunit (SU) of glycoprotein hormones may be present in gonadotroph, TSH, null cell, and oncocytic tumors. Alpha subunit-immunoreactivity may be associated with GH but also in rare cases PRL and ACTH immunoreactive adenomas. Adenomas immunoreactive for alpha SU only are rare. These are usually clinically inactive tumors. The tumors may be small or very large (macroadenomas) and many correspond to null cell adenomas or oncocytomas by electron microscopy [17].

Other Markers Present in Pituitary Adenomas

Chromogranins

Chromogranins are acidic proteins, which are associated with secretory granules of neuroendocrine cells. Chromogranin A is the most commonly studied member, but secretogranin I or chromogranin B, secretogranin II and protein 7B2 which are other members of the family may also be present [5, 18]. Chromogranin A may be decreased or absent in some PRL adenomas, but is present in all of the other tumor types, with the highest levels in glycoprotein hormone producing and null cell adenomas. Chromogranin B is present in all adenoma types.

Synaptophysin

Synaptophysin, a membrane protein of neuronal synaptic vesicle, is also present in most neuroendocrine cells and tumors. In the anterior pituitary, all hormone producing cell types are immunoreactive for synaptophysin [19].

S100 Acidic Protein

S100 protein is an acid binding protein that is present in the folliculostellate cells of the anterior pituitary [20, 21]. Tumors such as spindle cell oncocytomas, which are probably derived from folliculostellate cells in the anterior pituitary, are also positive for S100 protein.

Galectin-3

Galectin-3 is a beta galactosidase binding lectin that is selectively expressed in the anterior pituitary [22–24]. Galectin-3 is expressed by folliculostellate cells, PRL, and ACTH cells in the normal anterior pituitary but not in other cell types. Anterior pituitary tumors including PRL adenomas, ACTH adenomas, and spindle cell oncocytomas express galectin-3; but gonadotroph, GH, and null cell adenomas are usually negative for galectin-3 [24].

Cytokeratins

Cytokeratins are intermediate filaments ranging in size from 40K to 70K. Low and intermediate molecular weight cytokeratins such as CAM 5.2 are present in most pituitary adenomas [25–27]. ACTH cells with Crooke's hyaline change are usually positive for low molecular weight cytokeratin [27]. In GH adenomas, cytokeratin immunoreactivity is localized to the fibrous bodies in sparsely granulated adenomas [7].

Ki-67 and Other Proliferative Markers

Ki67 is a nuclear protein that is expressed in proliferating cells in all phases of the cell cycle except cells in the Go phase [28–30]. Antibodies such as MIB-1, which reacts with Ki-67, are used as proliferative markers. Other markers of proliferation including proliferating cell nuclear antigen (PCNA) and Topoisomerase 2α are other useful markers of proliferation; however, Ki-67 is the most frequently used marker.

p53

The p53 family of proteins includes p53, p63, p73, and MDM2 [31–34]. Mutations of p53 are associated with increased nuclear expression of this protein. However, other mechanisms may also lead to overexpression of p53 in pituitary and other tumors. A recent study has shown that some pituitary carcinomas with mutations of the p53 gene show high levels of p53 protein overexpression in most of the tumor cells [34].

Ultrastructural Features of Pituitary Adenomas

Electron microscopy provides a great deal of information that helps to classify pituitary adenomas. Ultrastructural classification has been used to subclassify adenomas into highly refined subtypes that have diagnostic and prognostic significance [9, 16]. There are some disadvantages to the ultrastructural study of pituitary tumors including the expense, need for special expertise, and the size of many small sample sizes, which can lead to errors in tissue sampling. However, the use of ultrastructural studies combined with H&E and immunohistochemical studies of adenomas have led to many new insights about the cytogenesis and pathogenesis of pituitary adenomas [9, 36, 37].

Anterior Pituitary Cell Hyperplasia

Anterior pituitary cell hyperplasia is very uncommon [38, 39]. Causes of anterior pituitary hyperplasia may be primary or idiopathic and secondary due to production of hypothalamic releasing hormones from tumors such as pulmonary or other neuroendocrine tumors producing GHRH, CRH, or other hypothalamic hormones. Other causes of secondary hyperplasia include end-organ failure such as thyroid or adrenal cortical atrophy leading to stimulation of TSH and ACTH cell proliferation, respectively, as part of the negative feedback mechanism. Secondary hyperplasia may also be related to hypothalamic hamartoma with production of hypothalamic hormones [9, 35]. Hyperplasia may be nodular or diffuse. Special stains such as reticulin and immunohistochemical stains for collagen 4 and/or pituitary hormones may help to establish the diagnosis of hyperplasia. Reticulin and collagen 4 stains show expansion of acinar unit. Immunohistochemical stains for specific hormones may show enlarged clusters of cells of a specific lineage in the expanded acini. The predominant cell type is often admixed with other types of cells in the acinar unit. It is important to appreciate the unique anatomical localization of specific cell types in the anterior pituitary in order to determine if the cells are increased. For example, ACTH cells are located predominately in the mucoid wedge, so the presence of abundant ACTH-positive cells in this region may not indicate hyperplasia. In addition, basophil invasion or the presence of abundant ACTH cells is the intermediate zone equivalent in a normal physiological change and does indicate ACTH cell hyperplasia.

PRL cell hyperplasia is present during pregnancy, where the pituitary weight and number of PRL cells can be increased up to two fold. Primary cell hyperplasia is rare in human pituitaries. PRL cell hyperplasia has been reported in the non-neoplastic pituitary cells adjacent to PRL adenomas [38].

ACTH cell hyperplasia may be nodular or diffuse. Nodular ACTH cell hyperplasia is characterized by an increase in the acinar size, hyperthyroidal ACTH cells, and expansion of the reticulin pattern. In contrast, diffuse ACTH cell hyperplasia is characterized by an increase in the number of ACTH cells, which may be more prominent in the mucoid wedge without significant distortion of the reticulin pattern. Patients with Addison's disease and adrenal cortical atrophy may develop diffuse and/or nodular ACTH cell hyperplasia.

GH cell hyperplasia may be striking under certain circumstances such as with GHRH producing tumors in the lungs or pancreas. Histologically, there is an expansion of the reticulin pattern with hypertrophic GH producing cells. Bi-hormonal cells producing GH and PRL may be present. Ultrastructural studies usually show cells with large dense core secretory glands, well-developed rough endoplasmic reticulin and prominent Golgi-complexes.

Hyperplasia of TSH cells may be nodular and/or diffuse. Patients with chronic hypothyroidism with atrophy of the thyroid can develop TSH cell hyperplasia with expanded acinar units and weakly staining TSH-positive cells.

Hyperplasia of gonadotrophic cells is uncommon. It may be associated with primary gonadal atrophy in a patient with Klinefelter and/or Turner syndrome [9, 35].

Pituitary Adenomas

GH-Producing Adenomas

Most GH-producing adenomas are manifested clinically as gigantism, if the tumor develops before the epiphyseal plates have closed. This is usually characterized by excessive linear growth. Acromegaly results when the GH-producing tumor develops after puberty. Patients usually develop increased stature, with enlarged extremities manifested by increases in hat and (glove) sizes, prognathism, and visceromegaly. The serum levels of IGF1 is increased and may be more sensitive than increased serum GH in establishing the diagnosis [9, 35].

Microscopic examination shows variable patterns depending on the cellular composition. Acidophilic cells are common (Fig. 2A), but chromophobic and amphophilic cells may also be present. Immunohistochemical staining is positive for GH, usually in a diffuse pattern (Fig. 2B). Other cell types such as PRL and/or immunoreactive alpha subunit cells may also be present in the tumors. Various subtypes of GH adenomas have been recognized, based largely on ultrastructural studies, which usually correlate with immunohistochemical findings.

Densely Granulated GH Cell Adenomas

These tumors correspond to the classical type of GH adenomas associated with acromegaly. These tumors are characterized by slow growth and limited invasion into tissues adjacent to the sella turcica. The tumors are strongly positive for GH, but may also be reactive for PRL, alpha subunit, and/or TSH. Ultrastructural examination shows dense, core granules measuring 150–600 nm in diameter, with most secretory granules between 400 and 500 nm in diameter (Fig. 2C) [7, 9, 35].

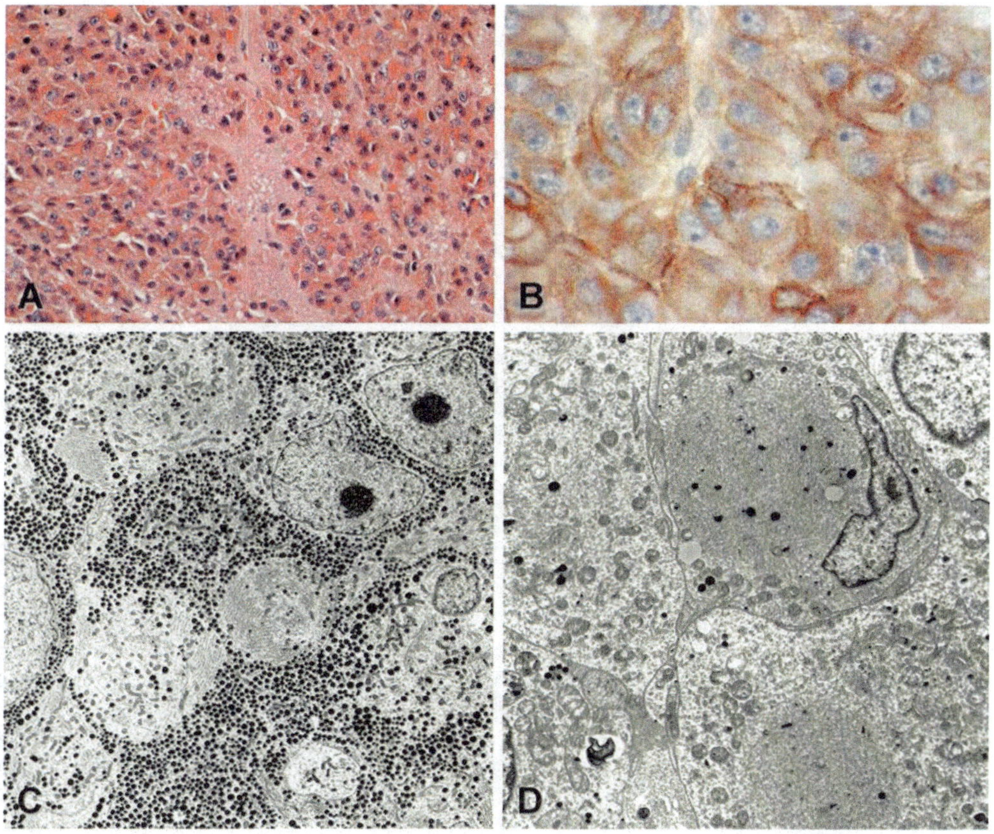

Fig. 2 GH adenoma
A) H&E section of a GH adenoma
B) Immunohistochemical staining for GH is positive.
C) Ultrastructure of a densely granulose GH adenoma showing ovoid cells with prominent rough endoplasmic reticulum and Golgi. X4000.
D) Ultrastructure of a sparsely granulose GH adenoma with prominent fibrous bodies and small secretory granules. X7500

Sparsely Granulated GH Adenomas

This subtype of GH adenoma is usually chromophobic on H&E sections. It is slightly more common in women and is more rapidly growing and more aggressive. GH immunoreactivity is usually prominent in the Golgi region. Cytokeratin immunoreactivity is also perinuclear.

Ultrastructural features include sparse secretory granules ranging from 100 to 200 nm in diameter. The fibrous body seen with cytokeratin staining is composed of intermediate filaments and smooth endoplasmic reticulin in the Golgi region in a perinuclear location (Fig. 2D) [7, 9, 35].

PRL-Producing Adenomas

PRL-producing adenomas used to be the most frequently encountered tumors in surgically resected series. With the frequent use of chronic medical therapy with dopamine agonist, the frequency with which these tumors are seen by the pathologist has declined. Hyperprolactinemia is commonly associated with amenorrhea, galactorrhea, and infertility in women and with decreased libido and impotence in men [73, 74]. Prolactinomas are frequently asymptomatic in men and often becomes symptomatic as space occupying lesions of macroadenomas.

Histologic examination usually shows chromophobic or amphophilic tumor cells (Fig. 3A). PRL immunostaining may be diffuse or juxtanuclear (Fig. 3B) [9, 35].

Sparsely Granulated PRL Cell Adenomas

This is the most common tumor type. The cells have abundant rough endoplasmic reticulin with prominent Golgi regions. Secretory granules range from 120 to 300 nm in diameter. A unique ultrastructural feature of this tumor subtype is the presence of misplaced exocytosis in which there is granule exocytosis between adjacent cells from the vascular pole of the cells (Fig. 3C) [9, 35].

Densely Granulated PRL Cell Adenomas

These are extremely rare tumors. They are acidophilic on H&E with diffuse PRL immunoreactivity. The cells have

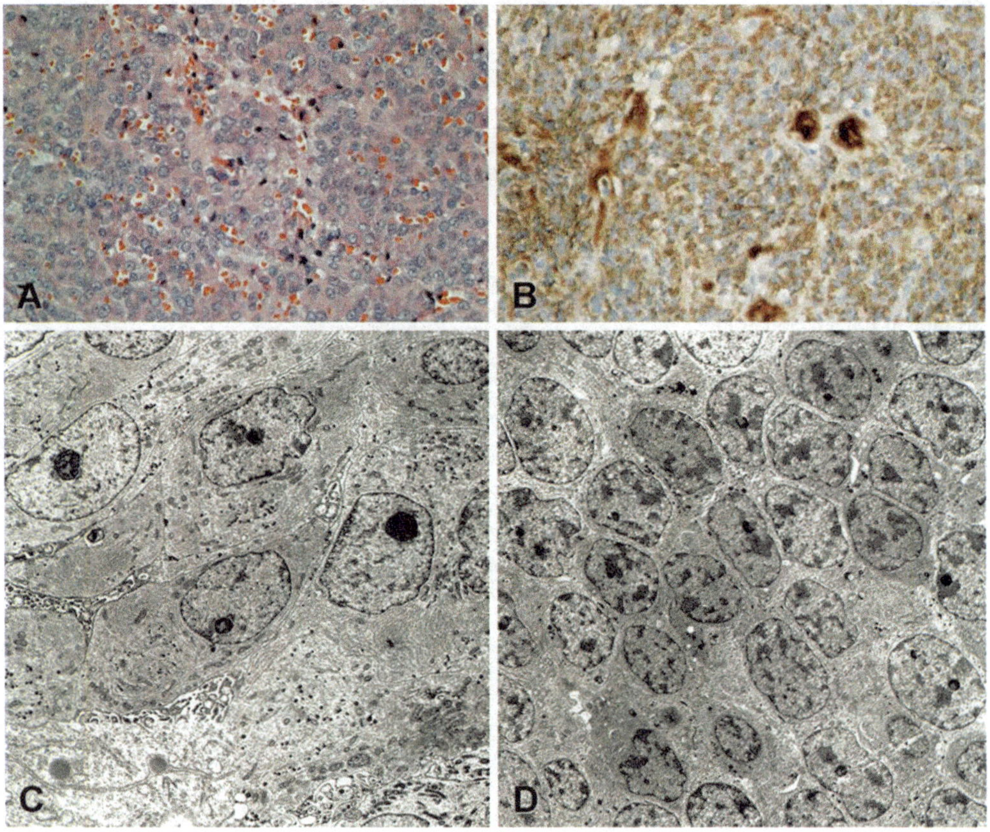

Fig. 3 PRL adenoma
A) H&E section of a PRL adenoma
B) Immunohistochemical staining for PRL is positive with a prominent juxtanuclear pattern.
C) Ultrastructure of a sparsely granulated PRL adenoma with well-organized rough endoplasmic reticulum and few secretory granules. X4000. Inset shows extrusion of secretory granules (exocytosis). X12000.
D) Ultrastructure of a PRL adenoma from a patient treated with dopamine agonist. There is massive shrinkage of the cytoplasm, with few cytoplasmic organelles. X4000

abundant secretory granules up to 600 nm in diameter. Patients with prolactinomas who have been treated with dopamine agonists usually showed dramatic cell shrinkage with decreased PRL immunoreactivity (Fig. 3D). With long-term treatment, the cells are extremely small and there is prominent perivascular and interstitial fibrosis. Ultrastructural studies show small cells with a narrow rim of cytoplasm and reduced number of membranous organelles and only a few scattered secretory granules. After cessation of treatment, there is a reversal of the ultrastructural changes.

ACTH Cell Adenomas

Patients with ACTH-producing tumors usually present with Cushing's disease and occasionally with Nelson's syndrome after adrenalectomy. There are also silent ACTH adenomas, which will be discussed below. Cushing's syndrome with moon facies, acne, truncal obesity, hirsutism, easy bruise ability, and diabetes mellitus, may be present. ACTH adenomas are usually basophilic or chromophobic on H&E staining (Fig. 4A). Crooke's hyaline changes are usually seen in the adjacent non-neoplastic ACTH-positive cells [40–42]. Crooke's changes are characterized by accumulation of 9 nm intermediate filaments, which are keratin positive in the cell cytoplasms. The secretory granules are pushed from the periphery of the cells next to the cell membrane. The adenoma cells may also be positive for other pro-opiomelanocortin processed peptides such as ACTH (Fig. 4B) endorphins and melanocyte stimulating hormones (MSH). On occasion, some of the tumor cells may be positive for LH, PRL, or alpha subunit.

Most ACTH-producing adenomas associated with Cushing's disease are microadenomas, which are less than 10 mm. Some tumors may be only 2–3 mm in diameter and not readily detected by imaging.

Patients with Nelson's syndrome usually have macroadenomas, which are frequently invasive tumors associated with hyperpigmentation due to increased secretion of MSH. Patients with Nelson's syndrome usually have visual field defects and headaches. A significant number of ACTH carcinomas arise in patients with Nelson's syndrome [7, 35].

In ACTH adenomas associated with Cushing's disease, the tumor cells are elongated or angular with ovoid nuclei. The cytoplasm contains abundant rough endoplasmic reticulin, polysomes, and conspicuous Golgi complexes. The secretory granules range from 150 to 450 nm in diameter and are characteristically spherical,

Fig. 4 ACTH adenoma
A) H&E section of an ACTH adenoma.
B) Immunohistochemical staining for ACTH is positive.
C) Ultrastructure of an ACTH adenoma with secretory granules and bundles of cytokeratin filaments. X11000

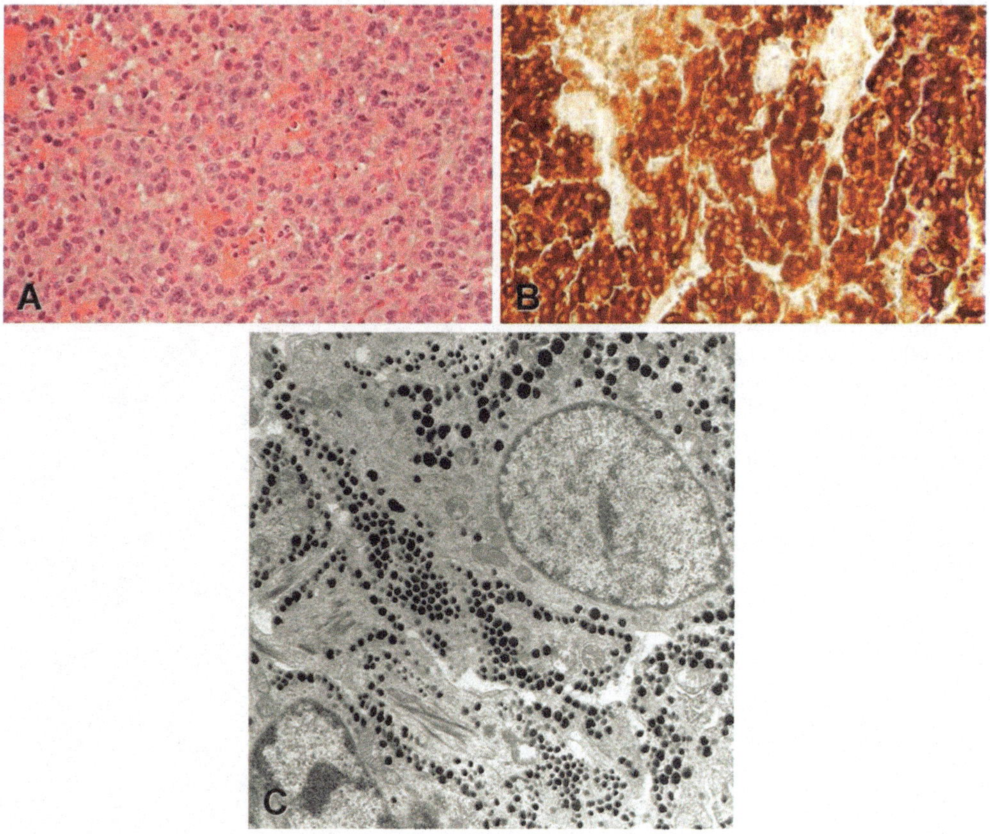

teardrop, or pear-shaped. (Fig. 4C). Keratin intermediate filaments are perinuclear in location and they constitute the filaments of Crooke's hyalinization secondary to excessive glucocorticoids, as previously described. Crooke's hyaline changes are usually present in the non-neoplastic ACTH cells, but a subtype of ACTH tumor, the Crooke cell adenoma, usually contains abundant intermediate filaments. Crooke cell adenomas are characteristically aggressive tumors, which are invasive, with a high recurrence rate (some).

The ultrastructural features of ACTH-producing tumors in Nelson's syndrome is similar to those of Cushing's disease except that keratin intermediate filaments are absent due to the lower levels of glucocorticoids associated with Nelson's syndrome, which is usually in a post-adrenalectomy setting.

TSH-Producing Adenomas

These are rare tumors. Patients usually present with signs and symptoms of hyperthyroidism. Patients usually have inappropriately high TSH levels in the presence of elevated perineural thyroid hormone levels. A few tumors may develop in a setting of hypothyroidism.

The histopathologic features of TSH adenomas are variable [43–45]. The tumor cells are generally chromophobic with an angular shape and can show a diffuse or sinusoidal pattern. Some tumors may show interstitial and/or perivascular fibrosis which is not related to prior treatment.

Immunohistochemical staining shows positive staining for TSH and usually for alpha subunit of glycoprotein hormones [43]. These may also be variable staining for GH and/or PRL in a few TSH adenomas.

Ultrastructural studies show spindle-shaped cells with long cytoplasmic processes, spherical to ovoid nuclei with prominent nucleoli. The secretory granules range from 50 to 200 nm in diameter and are usually located beneath the cell membrane [9, 35].

Gonadotroph Adenomas

Gonadotroph tumors producing FSH and/or LH occur most commonly in middle age or older patients. They are more common in men. Tumors that are hormonally active do not usually lead to clinical evidence of hyperfunction. Patients usually present with hypogonadism and symptoms related to mass effects such as visual disturbance.

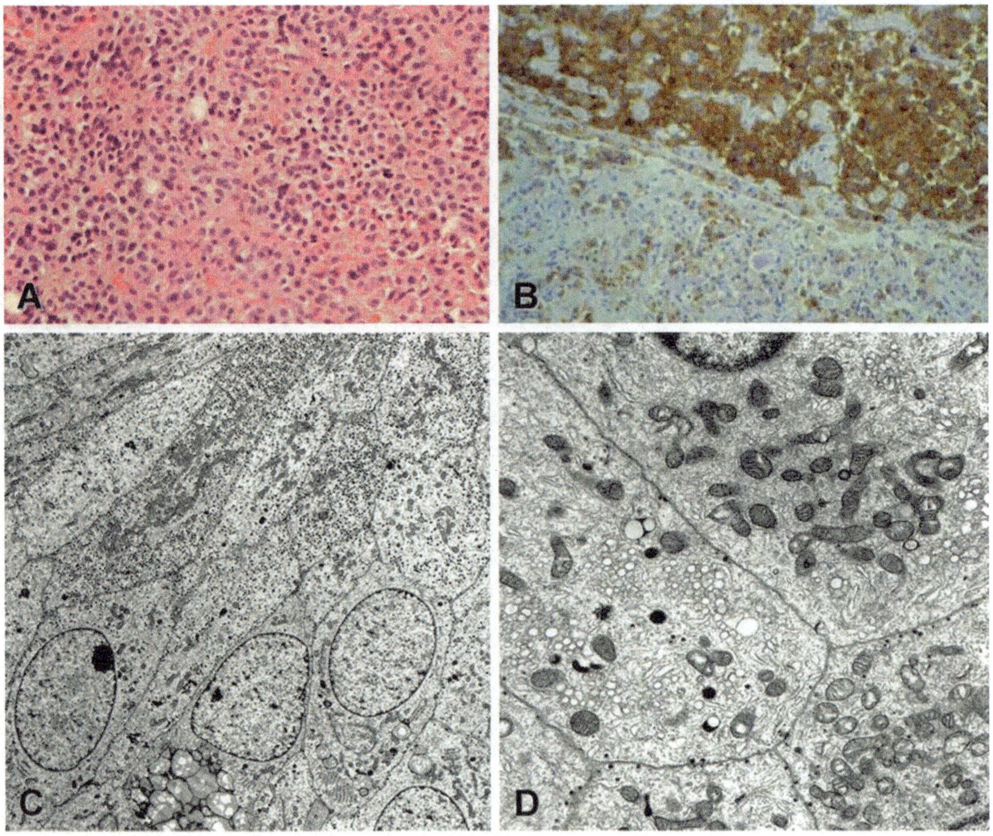

Fig. 5 Gonadotroph adenoma A) H&E section of a gonadotroph adenoma. B) Immunohistochemical staining for FSH in a gonadotroph adenoma. The tumor cells in the upper portion of the field are diffusely positive for FSH. Scattered positive cells are present in the non-neoplastic pituitary. C) Ultrastructure of a gonadotroph adenoma with polar cells containing long cytoplasmic processes and secretory granules. X4000. D) Ultrastructure of a gonadotroph adenoma in a female patient showing vacuolar transformation of the Golgi apparatus ("honeycomb Golgi"). X11000

Histopathologic examination shows chromophobic tumors with papillae or a diffuse growth pattern (Fig. 5A). Gonadotroph adenomas in men usually show variable immunoreactivity for FSH and/or LH (Fig. 5B). In women, the tumors show weak and sparse immunoreactivity for FSH and/or LH.

Ultrastructural studies also show sexual dimorphism [46] (Fig. 5C,D). The male-type gonadotroph adenomas show dilated rough endoplasmic reticulum, prominent Golgi complexes, and small but sparse secretory granules, about 200 nm in diameter (Fig. 5C). Oncocytic changes with increased numbers of mitochondria may be present. Gonadotroph adenomas in women ("female-type") contain a unique honeycomb Golgi complex, with the sacculi present as clusters of spheres containing a low density proteinaceous material (Fig. 5D). The secretory granules are small, around 200 nm in diameter [7, 9, 35].

Plurihormonal Adenomas

Plurihormonal adenomas are tumors producing hormone from more than one lineage [47, 48]. ACTH cells arise from a distinct lineage, which is influenced by specific transcription factors that are important for their development [49, 50]. These include Ptx1 and NeuroD1 [35].

The GH, PRL, and TSH adenomas have a common lineage, which is influenced by specific transcription factors such as Pit-1, Prop 1, and Lim 3 [35]. Gonadotroph cells (FSH/LH) developments are influenced by another group of transcription factors including: Ptx1, Lim 3, and SF-1 [35].

Mixed GH-PRL Adenomas

These tumors are composed of densely granulated GH cells and sparsely granulated PRL cells. The H&E sections show mostly acidophilic cells with chromophobic cells. Immunohistochemistry shows GH and PRL immunoreactivity in different cell types.

Acidophil Stem Cell Adenomas

These adenomas are associated with hyperprolactinemia, usually in younger patients. Histopathologic features include chromophobic or slightly acidophilic tumors. Immunohistochemical staining shows positive staining for PRL with less intense staining for GH. Ultrastructural features include one cell type with lactotroph and somatotroph features, such as unusual granule extension (reverse exocytosis) and fibrous bodies. The cells contain unique giant mitochondria and sparse small secretory granules 50–200 nm in diameter.

Mammosomatotroph Adenomas

These adenomas are composed of cells with GH and PRL. Histopathologic features show acidophilic cells, and immunohistochemical staining is positive for GH and PRL in the same cells. PRL staining is more variable and the tumors may also express alpha subunit. Ultrastructural studies show densely granulated GH cells in monomorphous tumor cells.

Silent Subtype 3 Adenoma

These tumors were placed into the plurihormonal category in the latest WHO Classification [7]. They have also been classified as silent adenomas. The tumors are immunoreactive for ACTH and other pro-opiomelanocortin-related peptides. Most tumors are immuno-negative for ACTH, but scattered tumor cells are positive for GH, PRL, and alpha subunit.

Ultrastructural features include: large polar cells with abundant smooth endoplasmic reticulum as well as rough endoplasmic reticulum and well-developed Golgi complexes. Secretory granules are variable and average about 200 nm in diameter. Based on the ultrastructural features, the tumors appear to be actively secreting some product(s). The diagnosis usually requires ultrastructural confirmation.

Silent Adenomas

These are clinically silent tumors that are not associated with excessive hormonal secretion. This group of tumors consists of two types of ACTH immunoreactive tumors. Null cell adenomas and rare cases of GH and PRL adenomas have been included in this group [7, 9, 35].

Silent Corticotroph Adenomas

Subtype 1

These are PAS-positive tumors that look similar to the adenomas associated with Cushing's disease. Immunohistochemistry is usually positive for ACTH. Ultrastructural

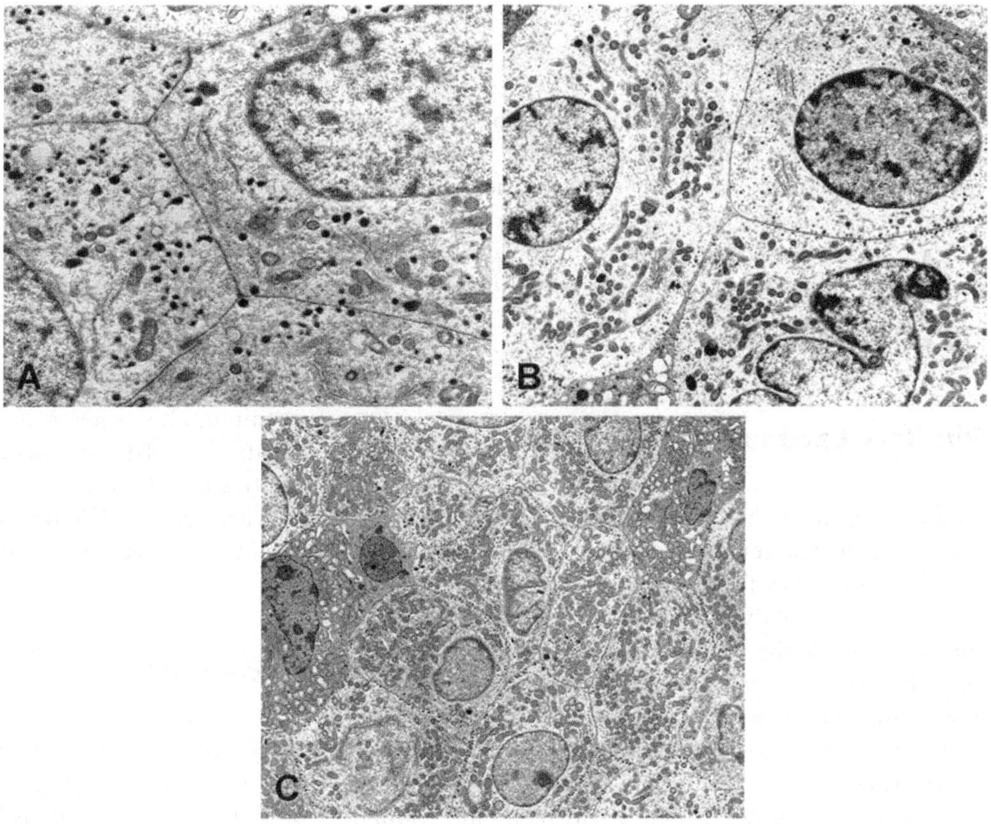

Fig. 6 Nonfunctioning adenomas
A) Ultrastructure of a silent ACTH adenoma, subtype 2. The secretory granules are small, but variable in size and shape. X11000.
B) Ultrastructure of a null cell adenoma showing no functional differentiation. X7500.
C) Ultrastructure of an oncocytic variant of a null cell adenoma showing abundant cytoplasmic mitochondria and few secretory granules. X4000

features are similar to the functional ACTH-positive tumors [7, 9, 35].

Subtype 2

These are silent ACTH-positive tumors, that are more common in men. Staining for ACTH and for PAS is often focal. Ultrastructural features include polygonal cells with smaller secretory granules (200–350 nm) than the functional ACTH tumors (Fig. 6A). Intermediate filaments are absent [7, 9, 35].

Null Cell Adenomas

These tumors are chromophilic and eosinophilic, with diffuse patterns on H&E [9, 35]. Immunohistochemical staining is positive for chromogranin, but only rare cells may stain for FSH, LH, or alpha subunit. Scattered cells positive for GH, PRL, or ACTH may be present. Ultrastructural features show poorly developed rough endoplasmic reticulum and Golgi complex and small secretory granules (100–250 nm) (Fig. 6B). The oncocytic variant contains numerous mitochondria (Fig. 6C).

Atypical Adenomas

These are adenomas with atypical morphologic features suggestive of aggressive behavior [51, 52]. This includes invasive growth and potential for recurrence. These features include elevated mitotic index and a MIB-1 labeling index greater than 3%. Some invasive adenomas also express p53 immunoreactivity which is usually not seen in noninvasive adenomas.

Pituitary Carcinomas

These are tumors that spread to the cerebrospinal fluid and/or develop systemic metastases [7]. Pituitary carcinomas usually arise from a pre-existing adenoma. The tumors grow rapidly and spread to neighboring tissues and may invade the brain. Metastasis occurs in the cerebrospinal space or spread systemically to the liver, lung, bone, and lymph nodes. Tumors are commonly associated with clinical syndromes of Cushing's disease or hyperprolactinemia. Occasional patients may have acromegaly or TSH excess and some may be nonfunctional.

Histologic features include invasive growth, cellular pleomorphism, mitotic activity, and necrosis.

Immunohistochemical findings include positive staining for chromogranin and synaptophysin. Immunoreactive tumors are most often PRL and/or ACTH. TP53 may be present in carcinomas and some carcinomas show mutation of the p53 gene. Ki67 staining is variable but generally higher than in adenomas.

Ultrastructural findings depend on the immunophenotype. Carcinomas tend to be less well differentiated compared to the same type of hormone-producing adenomas [7].

Other Tumor and Tumor-Like Lesions in the Sella Region That May Be Confused with Pituitary Tumors

Lymphocytic Hypophysitis

This inflammatory condition in the anterior pituitary is associated with hyperprolactinemia and lymphoplasmacytic infiltrate in the pituitary. Radiologic studies usually show an enlarged pituitary, which may be misdiagnosedas an adenoma. Lymphocytic hypophysitis is most common in postpartum women or during pregnancy [53, 54].

Granular Cell Tumor

These tumors are also known as choristomas and granular cell myoblastomas. They are thought to be derived from pituicytes, which are modified glial cells of the posterior pituitary and infundibulum [7].

The tumors are tan to gray and very vascular. They are composed of large polygonal cells forming sheets and small lobules. They have eosinophilic cytoplasm with coarse granularity and round nuclei.

Immunohistochemical staining is positive for NSE, but negative for S100 protein. Occasional tumors may be positive for GFAP.

Ultrastructural features show many lysosomes and absent neurosecretory granules and intermediate filaments.

Sarcoidosis

Sarcoidosis, which is a granulomatous inflammatory process of unknown etiology, may be present in the posterior pituitary and occasionally involves the anterior pituitary.

Histological features include non-caseating granulomas with numerous histiocytes and multinucleated giant cells. Immunostaining for CD68 is positive in the histocytes and giant cells. Special stains for organisms are consistently negative [55–57]. Sarcoidosis may be associated with galactorrhea and hyperprolactinemia [56, 57].

Secondary Tumors

Metastatic tumors to the pituitary can be from many sources. Autopsy series show between 3 and 23% of cancer patients with pituitary metastases. They are twice as common in the posterior pituitary compared to the anterior pituitary due to the direct blood supply to the posterior pituitary [7].

The most common tumors metastasizing to the pituitary include breast, lung, and gastrointestinal tract.

Other Tumors of the Pituitary

Gangliocytoma

These tumors are also know as hamartomas, choristomas, neuronal choristomas, and pituitary adenomas with neuronal choristomas (PANCH) [7, 9, 35].

These tumors arise in the pituitary and hypothalamus adjacent to the pituitary. They may present as mass lesions and look like typical adenomas. Patients may present with acromegaly/gigantism and precocious puberty. Histologically, there are neuronal cells with abundant necrophils. The other cells are larger polygonal ganglion cells and are binucleated or multinucleated. Many neuronal choristomas are associated with pituitary adenomas and rarely with pituitary hyperplasia.

Immunohistochemical staining is positive for synaptophysin, chromogranin, and neurofilament. The ganglion cells may contain hypothalamic hormones. Pituitary hormones are most commonly GH or PRL and rarely ACTH.

Ultrastructural findings show large nerve cells and well-developed rough endoplasmic reticulum with elongated interdigitating cell processes with many secretory granules of variable sizes.

Spindle Cell Oncocytoma

This is a low-grade neoplasm which is thought to be derived from folliculostellate cells [58, 59]. The tumors are composed of fascicles of spindle cells with eosinophilic granular cytoplasm. Immunophenotyping is positive for S100 protein, annexin, and galectin-3. Chromogranin and synaptophysin are both negative.

Ultrastructural features include cells with numerous mitochondria with lamellar cristae. Secretory granules are not present. Most tumors behave like low-grade neoplasms.

Pituicytoma

This is a rare benign tumor of sellar and suprasellar regions [60]. The tumors are characterized by bundles of elongated cells. They are positive for S100 protein, vimentin, NCAM, and NSE. Pituitary hormones and chromogranin are negative.

Ultrastructural features include intermediate filaments but no desmosomes. Scattered secretory granules have been reported [60].

Langerhans Cell Histiocytosis

This disorder is characterized by a proliferation of Langerhans cells with varying number of mature eosinophils. It is sometimes referred to as Histiocytosis X, Hand-Schuller-Christian syndrome, Letterer-Siwe disease, or eosinophilic granuloma. The disease may be present only in the hypothalamus posterior or anterior pituitary or it may be multifocal in various sites including bone [61].

The Langerhans' histocyte usually has a vesicular nucleus, which is vesicular or grooved. An increased number of eosinophils concentrated around areas of necrosis are frequently present.

Craniopharyngioma

This is a common epithelial tumor arising in the region of the sellar turcica. Most craniopharyngiomas are suprasellar and a small number is present in the sella turcica. They are primarily tumors of children and young adults. Patients may present with headache and visual disturbances. Endocrinopathies such as elevated serum PRL occurs with intrasellar tumors [62, 63].

Craniopharyngiomas are 3–4 cm in average diameter and are usually cystic. The cysts may have yellow or brown fluid. Calcifications are frequent and are present in solid and cystic regions. Histological features include an adenomatous pattern of the epithelium with pseudostratified columnar cells resting on a thin membrane and palisades around loose aggregates of stellate cells. Solid nests of keratinizing squamous epithelium may be present. Foreign body giant cell reactions and chronic inflammation are often seen as a secondary reaction to the cyst content.

Papillary craniopharyngioma is another type of craniopharyngioma composed of papillary squamous epithelium. This variant lacks calcification, palisade cells, cholesterol clefts, and foreign body giant cells. These tumors are very difficult to resect totally, so recurrences are common.

References

1. Herbert E, Roberts J, Phillips M, Allen R, Hinman M, Budarf M, Policastro P, Rosa P. (1980) Biosynthesis, processing and release of corticotropin, β-endorphin, and melanocyte-stimulating hormone in pituitary cell culture systems. In: Martini L, Ganong WF (eds). Frontiers in Nueroendocrinology. Vol 6. New York, Raven pp. 67–101.
2. Landolt AM, Heitz PU. (1988) Differentiation of two types of amyloid occurring in pituitary adenomas. Pathol Res Pract 183:552–554.
3. Voight C, Saeger W, Gerigk C, Ludecke DK. (1988) Amyloid in pituitary adenomas. Pathol Res Pract 183:555–557.
4. Lloyd RV, Cano M, Rosa P, Hille A, Huttner WB. (1988) Distribution of chromogranin and secretogranin I (chromogranin B) in neuroendocrine cells and tumors. Am J Pathol 130:296–304.
5. Lloyd RV, Wilson BS, Kovacs K, Ryan N. (1985) Immunohistochemical localization of chromogranin in human hypophyses and pituitary adenomas. Arch Pathol Lab Med 109:515–547.
6. Gould VE, Wiedenmann B, Lee I, Schwechheimer K, Dockhorn-Dworniczak B, Radosevich JA, Moll R, Franke WW. (1987) Synaptophysin expression in neuroendocrine neoplasm as determined by immunocytochemistry. Am J Pathol 126:243–257.
7. DeLellis RA, Lloyd RV, Heitz PU, Eng C. (2004) Tumours of Pathology and Genetics of Tumors of Endocrine Organs: IARC Press Lyon pages 9–45.
8. Kovacs K, Lloyd R, Horvath E, Asa SL, Stefaneanu L, Killinger DW, Smyth S. (1989) Silent somatotroph adenomas of the human pituitary. A morphologic study of three cases including immunocytochemistry, electron microscopy, in vitro examination, and in situ hybridization. Am J Pathol 134:345–353.
9. Kovacs K, Horvath E, Hartmannal WH, Sobin LH. (1986) Tumors of the pituitary gland. In: Atlas of Tumor Pathology. Fascicle 21. 2nd Series. Washington, DC, Armed Forces Institute of Pathology.
10. Horvath E, Kovacs K, Killinger DW, Smyth HS, Platts ME, Singer W. (1980) Silent corticotropic adenomas of the human pituitary gland: A histologic immunocytologic and ultrastructural study. Am J Pathol 98:617–638.
11. Lloyd RV, Fields K, Jin L, Horvath E, Kovacs K, (1990) Analysis of endocrine active and clinically silent corticotroph adenomas by in situ hybridization. Am J Pathol 137:479–488.
12. Duello T, Halmi NS. (1977) Endocrine and morphologic studies of pituitary adenomas secondary to primary hypothyroidism. J Clin Endocrinol Metab 45:903–911.
13. Katz MS, Gregerman RI, Horvath E, Kovacs K, Ezrin E. (1980) Thyrotroph cell adenoma of the human pituitary gland associated with primary hypothyroidism: Clinical and morphological features. Acta Endocrinol (Copenh) 95:41–48.
14. Afrasiabi A, Valenta L, Gwinup GA. (1979) A TSH-secreting pituitary tumour causing hyperthyroidism: presentation of a case and review of the literature. Acta Endocrinol (Copenh) 92:448–454.
15. Grisoli F, Leclerq T, Winteler JP, Jaquet P, Guibout M, Diaz-Vasquez P, Hassoun J, Nayak R. (1986) Thyroid-stimulating hormone pituitary adenomas and hyperthyroidism. Surg Neurol 25:361–368.
16. Horvath E, Kovacs K. (1984) Gonadotroph adenomas of the human pituitary: sex-related fine-structural dichotomy. A histologic, immunocytochemical, and electron-microscopic study of 30 tumors. Am J Pathol 117:429–440.
17. Landolt AM, Heitz PU. (1986) Alpha-subunit-producing pituitary adenomas. Immunocytochemical and ultrastructural studies. Virchows Arch (A) 409:417–431.
18. Rindi G, Buffa R, Sessa F, Tortora O, Solcia E. (1986) Chromogranin A, B and C immunoreactivities of mammalian endocrine cells. Distribution, distinction from costored hormones/prohormones and relationship with the argyrophil component of secretory granules. Histochemistry 85:19–28.
19. Stefaneanu L, Ryan N, Kovacs K. (1988) Immunocytochemical localization of synaptophysin in human hypophyses and pituitary adenomas. Arch Pathol Lab Med 112:801–804.
20. Lauriola L, Cocchia D, Sentinelli S, Maggiario N, Maira G, Michetti F. (1984) Immunohistochemical detection of folliculostellate cells in human pituitary adenomas. Virchows Arch (B) 47:189–197.
21. Yamashita M, Qian ZR, Sano T, Horvath E, Kovacs K. (2005) Immunohistochemical study on so-called follicular cells and folliculostellate cells in the human adenohypophysis. Pathol Int. 55:244–247.
22. Barondes, SH, Cooper DN, Gitt MA, Leffler H. (1994) Galectins: structure and function of a large family of animal lectin. J Biol Chem 269:20807–20810.
23. Amado M, Almeida R, Schwientek T, Clausen H. (1999) Identification and characterization of large galactosyltransferase gene familes: galactosyltransferases for all functions. Biochim Biophys Acta 1473:35–53.
24. Riss D, Jin L, Qian X, Bayliss J, Scheithauer BW, Young WF JR, Vidal S, Kovacs K, Raz A, Lloyd RV. (2003) Differential expression of galactin-3 in pituitary tumors. Cancer Res 63:2251–2255.
25. Ironside IW, Royds JA, Jefferson AA, Timperley WR. (1987) Immunolocalization of cytokeratins in the normal and neoplastic human pituitary gland. J Neurol Neurosurg Psychiatry 50:57–65.
26. Hofler H, Denk H, Walter GF. (1984) Immunohistochemical demonstration of cytokeratins in endocrine cells of the human pituitary gland and in pituitary adenomas. Virchows Arch (A) 404:359–368.
27. Neumann PE, Horoupian DS, Goldman JE, Hess MA. (1984) Cytoplasmic filaments of Crooke's hyaline change belongs to the cytokeratin class. Am J Pathol 116:142–222.
28. Gerdes J, Li L, Schlueter C, et al. (1991) Immunobiochemical and molecular biologic characterization of the cell proliferation-associated nuclear antigen that is defined by monoclonal antibody Ki-67. Am J Pathol 138:867.
29. Thapar K, Kovacs K, Scheithauer BW, et al. (1996) Proliferative activity and invasiveness among pituitary adenomas and

carcinomas: an analysis using the MIB-1 antibody. Neurosurgery 38:99–106.
30. Yamada S, Ohyama K, Taguchi M, Takeshita A, Morita K, Takano K, Sano T. (2007) A study of the correlation between morphological findings and biological activities in clinically nonfunctioning pituitary adenomas. Neurosurgery 61:580–584.
31. Hollstein M, Sidransky D, Vogelstein B, et al. (1991) P53 mutations in human cancers. Science 253:49.
32. Hosoi G, Hara J, Okamura T, et al. (1994) Low frequency of the p53 gene mutations in neuroblastoma. Cancer 73:3087.
33. Scheithauer BW, Gaffey TA, Lloyd RV, Sebo TJ, Kovacs KT, Horvath E, Yapicier O, Young WF Jr, Meyer FB, Kuroki T, Fiehle DL, Laws ER Jr. (2006) Pathobiology of pituitary adenomas and carcinomas. Neurosurgery 59:341–253.
34. Tanizaki Y, Jin L, Scheithauer BW, Kovacs K, Roncaroli F, Lloyd RV. (2007) P53 gene mutations in pituitary carcinomas. Endocr Pathol 18:217–222.
35. Asa SL. (1997) Tumors of the Pituitary Gland. In Atlas of Tumor Pathology. Fascicle 22 3rd ed. Washington, DC: Armed Forces Institute of Pathology.
36. Horvath E, Kovacs K. (1992) Ultrastructural diagnosis of human pituitary adenomas. Microsc Res Techn 20:107–135.
37. Horvath E. (1994) Ultrastructural markers in the pathologic diagnosis of pituitary adenomas. Ultrastruct Pathol 18:171–179.
38. Horvath E, Kovacs K, Scheithauer BW. (1999) Pituitary hyperplasia. Pituitary. 1:169–170.
39. Horvath E, Kovacs K. (1993) Ultrastructural diagnosis of pituitary adenomas and hyperplasias. In: Lloyd RV (ed). Surgical Pathology of the Pituitary Gland. Major Problems in Pathology. Philadelphia, Saunders, pp. 52–84.
40. Crooke A. (1935) A change in the basophil cells of the pituitary gland common to conditions which exhibit the syndrome attributed to basophil adenoma. J Pathol Bacteriol 41:339–349.
41. Horvath E, Kovacs K, Jossse R. (1983) Pituitary corticotroph cell adenoma with marked abundance of microfilaments. Ultrastruct Pathol 5:249–255.
42. Neumann PE, Horoupian DS, Goldman JE, Hess MA. (1984) Cytopasmic filaments of Crooke's hyaline change belong to the cytokeratin class. An immunocytochemical and ultrastructural study. Am J Pathol 116:214–222.
43. Girod C, Trouillas J, Claustrat B. (1986) The human thyrotropic adenoma: pathologic diagnosis in five cases and critical review of the literature. Semin Diagn Pathol 3:58–68.
44. Beck-Peccoz P, Piscitelli G, Amr S, et al. (1986) Endocrine, biochemical, and morphological studies of a pituitary adenoma secreting growth hormone, thyrotropin (TSH), and alpha-subunit: evidence for secretion of TSH with increased bioactivity. J Clin Endocrinol Metab 62:704–711.
45. Beck-Peccoz P, Brucker-Davis F, Persani L, Smallridge RC, Weintraub BD. (1996) Thyrotropin-secreting pituitary tumors. Endocr Rev 17:610–638.
46. Kontogeorgos G, Horvath E, Kovacs K. (1990) Sex-linked ultrastructural dichotomy of gonadotroph adenomas of the human pituitary: an electron microscopic analysis of 145 tumors. Ultrasatruct Pathol 14:475–482.
47. Scheithauer BW, Horvath E, Kovacs K, Laws ER Jr, Randall RV., Ryan N. (1986) Plurihormonal pituitary adenomas. Semin Diagn Pathol 3:69–82.
48. Matsumo A, Sasaki T, Kirino T. (1999) Plurihormonal pituitary tumor. J Neurosurg 90:608–609.
49. Osamura RY, Egashira N, Miyai S, Yamazaki M, Takekoski S, Sammo N, Teramoto A. (2004) Molecular pathology of the pituitary. Development and functional differentiation of pituitary adenomas. Front Horm Res 32:20–33.
50. Asa SL, Ezsat S. (2004) Molecular basis of pituitary development and cytogenesis. Front Horm Res 32:1–19.
51. Saeger W, Ludecke DK, Buchfelder M, Fahlbusch R, Quabbe HJ, Petersenn S. (2007) Pathohistological classification of pituitary tumors: 10 years of experience with the German Pituitary Tumor Registry. Eur J Endocrinol 156:203–216.
52. Kontogeorgos G. (2005) Classification and pathology of pituitary tumors. Endocrine 28:27–35.
53. Molitch ME, Gillam MP. (2007) Lymphocytic hypophysitis. Horm Res 68(Suppl 5):145–150.
54. Caturegli P, Newschaffer C, Olivi A, Pomper MG, Burger PC, Rose NR. (2005) Autoimmune hypophysitis. Endocr Rev 26:599–614.
55. Glezer A, Paraiba DB, Bronstein MD. (2008) Rare sellar lesion. Endocrinol Metab Clin North Am 37:195–211.
56. Bihan H, Christozova V, Dumas JL, Jomaa R, Valeyre D, Tazi A, Reach G, Krivitzky A, Cohen R. (2007) Sarcoidosis: clinical, hormonal, and magnetic resonance imaging (MRI) manifestations of hypothalamic-pituitary disease in 9 patients and review of the literature. Medicine (Baltimore) 86:259–268.
57. Miyoshi T, Otsuka F, Takeda M, Inagaki K, Otani H, Ogura T, Ichiki K, Amano T, Makino H. (2007) An elderly patient with sarcoidosis manifesting panhypopituitarism with central diabetes insipidus. Endocr J 54:425–430.
58. Roncaroli F, Scheithauer BW, Cenachi G, Horvath E, Kovacs K, Lloyd RV, Abell-Aleff P, Santi M, Yates AJ. (2002) 'Spindle cell oncocytoma' of the adenohypophysis: a tumor of folliculostellate cells? Am J Surg Pathol 26:1048–1055.
59. Vaitai I, Sahli R, Kappeler A. (2006) Spindle cell oncocytoma of the adenohypophysis: report of a case with a 16-year follow-up. Pathol Res Pract 202:745–750.
60. Figarella-Branger D, Dufour H, Fernandez C, Bourier-Labit C, Grisoli F, Pellissier JF. (2002). Pituicytomas, a mis-diagnosed benign tumor of the neurohypophysis: report of three cases. Acta Neuropathol 104:313–319.
61. Mahnel R, Tan KH, Fahlbusch R, Volk B, Ludecke D, Nagel HG, Jaursch-Hancke C. (2002) Problems in differential diagnosis of non Langerhans cell histiocytosis with pituitary involvement: case report and review of literature. Endocr Pathol 13:361–368.
62. Karavitaki N, Wass JA. (2008) Craniopharyngiomas. Endocrinol Metab Clin North Am 37:173–193.
63. Garre ML, Cama A. (2007) Craniopharyngioma: modern concepts in pathogenesis and treatment. Curr Opin Pediatr 19:471–479.

Tumors of Thyroid Gland: Non-C cell Tumors

Ashraf Khan and Manju Prasad

Abstract Thyroid tumors are one of the most common tumors of the endocrine system encountered in surgical pathology practice. They can arise from the follicular lining epithelial cells that produce the thyroid hormone or the C cells that secrete calcitonin. In this chapter we discuss non-C cell tumors of the thyroid. In this group of tumors papillary carcinoma is the most common malignancy and the conventional type of tumor can be easily diagnosed based on classical cytomorphologic features. However, variants of papillary carcinoma exist, the understanding of which is crucial for accurate diagnoses. The follicular patterned tumors may sometimes pose diagnostic challenge and approach to these thyroid lesions is suggested in this section along with ancillary studies that may help in the diagnosis of these tumors. Finally, thyroid cancer progression from differentiated carcinoma to poorly differentiated and anaplastic carcinoma is well known and is also presented along with clinical and pathological correlations.

Keywords Thyroid carcinoma • Follicular adenoma • Follicular variant of papillary carcinoma • Follicular-patterned lesions • Follicular carcinoma • Papillary thyroid carcinoma • Insular carcinoma • Anaplastic carcinoma • Oncocytic carcinoma • Oncocytic adenoma • Hyalanizing trabecular tumor • Papillary thyroid carcinoma variants

Thyroid Gland: Development and Embryology

The thyroid gland develops from the larger median anlage and the two lateral anlagen. The medial anlage, which forms the major portion of the thyroid, is derived from the floor of the foregut and the two lateral anlagen are derived from the endoderm of fourth and fifth branchial pouches like the ultimobranchial bodies. The medial anlage appears by day 24 as median endodermal diverticulum from the base of the tongue in the region of foramen cecum. The diverticulum descends down from the foramen cecum into the neck along the midline attached to the thyroglossal duct. It reaches its final position anterior to the trachea by about 7 weeks; it then grows laterally and becomes bilobed [1]. Aberrations in the descent of thyroid may lead to persistence of thyroid tissue anywhere along the path of the thyroglossal duct including posterior tongue, midline of the neck and the anterior mediastinum. As mentioned below, thyroid lesions including tumors may arise in any of these aberrant locations, which should be considered when investigating for thyroid disorders. Early during the fifth week, the thyroglossal duct loses its lumen and shortly afterward breaks into fragments [2]. However, the caudal end of the thyroglossal duct may persist in some embryos and this constitutes the pyramidal process, which is present in about 75% of mature human thyroids [3]. The lateral thyroid anlage becomes attached to the posterior surface of the thyroid during the fifth week and contributes up to 30% to the thyroid weight [2]. The causes of the fusion of the lateral and medial anlage are unknown. It is speculated that migration of the ultimobranchial body controls the growth of the medial anlage or that the growth of the medial anlage laterally and caudally inhibits expansion of the ultimobranchial body [2]. The lateral thyroid anlage is thought to give rise to the calcitonin producing C cells and the solid cell nests. It is believed that the C cells are derived from the neural crest; they migrate to the ultimobranchial body and are subsequently incorporated into the thyroid [4]. However, the existence of mixed follicular and C cell tumors raises the possibility of the common stem cell origin for both follicular and C cells, as is seen in the gastrointestinal tract [1].

A. Khan (✉)
Professor of Patholog, Director, Surgical Pathology, Department of Pathology, University of Massachusetts Medical School, UMassMemorial Medical Center, Three Biotech, One Innovation Drive, Worcester, MA 01605, USA
e-mail: khana@ummhc.org

A. Khan (ed.), *Surgical Pathology of Endocrine and Neuroendocrine Tumors*, Current Clinical Pathology,
DOI 10.1007/978-1-60327-396-1_5, © Humana Press, a part of Springer Science+Business Media, LLC 2009

The thyroid gland initially consists of a solid mass of endodermal cells, but small groups of epithelial cells are soon identified. The first follicles form epithelial plates at the beginning of eighth week and by twelfth week the plates are entirely converted into follicles. The development of the human fetal thyroid has been divided into three stages by LiVolsi to include precolloid stage (7–13 weeks); colloid stage (13–14 weeks); and follicular stage (after 14 weeks) [5]. Evidence of thyroxin comes with the appearance of colloid and T4 and TSH are detectable in the circulation of human fetuses after 12 weeks [2, 3].

Developemental and Embryological Anamolies Related to Thyroid Tumors

Ectopic Thyroid Tissue

Ectopic thyroid tissue may be seen anywhere in the midline along the path of the thyroglossal duct. In such situations ectopic thyroid tissue may be present in addition to the normal thyroid or ectopic tissue may be the only thyroid gland present. It is therefore important to search for normal thyroid before contemplating removal of the ectopic tissue to prevent hypothyroidism. Locations of ectopic thyroid tissue include lingual, sublingual, suprahyoid, and mediastinum. Additional sites in which ectopic thyroid tissue has been found include pericardium [4], heart, porta hepatis [6–8], gallbladder [9], inguinal region [1], vagina [10], sella turcica [11], trachea, and larynx; the tracheal and laryngeal ectopic tissue if sufficiently large may produce respiratory symptoms [12, 13]. While cutaneous and subcutaneous thyroid follicular tissue outside the anterior midline neck raises the possibility of metastatic carcinoma, there are recent reports of ectopic thyroid tissue in axilla and posterior neck in which total thyroidectomy failed to reveal an occult tumor and there was no uptake of radioactive iodine on scan outside the region of the thyroid [14, 15]. Maino et al. suggested that a somatic mutation in a transcription factor important in thyroid migration may play a role in this thyroid heterotopia [15].

Lingual thyroid resulting from complete arrest of the decent of the medial thyroid anlage is rare with a reported incidence of 1 in 4500 to 1 in 100,000. In most of the cases this is the only thyroid gland. Lingual thyroid lacks a capsule and on histology thyroid follicles are seen mixed with the striated muscle fibers of the tongue. While tumors have also been reported to occur in the lingual thyroid, pathologists must be careful in misinterpreting thyroid follicles intermingled with muscle as carcinoma. Diagnosis of carcinoma must only be made if there is marked desmoplasia or there are characteristic morphological features of papillary carcinoma [1]. Lingual thyroid may also be affected by thyroid disorders such as goiter and thyroiditis.

Ectopic thyroid tissue may also be found within the striated muscles and fibroadipose tissues of the neck and may sometimes mimic submandibular gland swelling [1, 16]. This usually is a result of a developmental defect due to a close association of thyroid and neck tissues during development. Sometimes benign-appearing thyroid tissue may be found within the perithyroidal soft tissues of the neck later in life, which is a result of detachment of a portion of thyroid tissue from a large multinodular goiter [1, 4]. It is important in these instances to differentiate this benign ectopic tissue or a detached portion of multinodular goiter from thyroid carcinoma.

"Lateral Aberrant Thyroid"

One of the most controversial and debated topics in thyroid heterotopia has been the finding of benign-appearing thyroid follicles within the subcapsular sinuses of the cervical lymph nodes. In the past these had been referred to as lateral aberrant thyroid. It is believed that benign-appearing thyroid follicles in lymph nodes medial to the jugular vein represent ectopic thyroid tissue and similar structures in nodes lateral to the jugular vein should be regarded as metastatic carcinoma [1, 3, 4, 17–19]. However, the latter deposits may be seen in cases where multiple serial sections of the thyroid gland failed to reveal any tumor [17, 20, 21]. It is possible that small microscopic thyroid carcinoma in these cases may have involuted leaving a scar behind [17]. It has been suggested that normal thyroid tissue may be transported to the lymph nodes by way of lymphatics [19]. Cacceta et al. reported a case of lateral aberrant thyroid presenting as a mass in the left submandibular area with no evidence thyroid malignancy; they suggested an anomaly of thyroid embryogenesis in their case primarily involving the left ultimobranchial body [22]. Architecture of the thyroid deposits has been suggested by some to be helpful in differentiating benign thyroid tissue from metastatic deposits, but it has not been reproduced in some other studies [17]. In practice there is no definitive way at present to resolve this issue, but the finding of thyroid follicles within cervical lymph nodes should be investigated and a careful search for a primary tumor should be made in the thyroid by examining multiple sections. While morphology alone may not help to distinguish benign thyroid rests in lymph nodes from metastatic carcinoma, molecular diagnostic techniques to determine clonality has been suggested to establish the etiology of thyroid tissue within cervical lymph nodes [23].

Thyroglossal Duct Cyst

The thyroglossal duct cyst (TDC) arises from the cystic dilatation of a persistent thyroglossal duct. It is located in the anterior midline of the neck and while they are more common in children, they can present at any age and in either sex. On gross examination, the TDC range in size from 1 to 4 cm in diameter and fistula may develop secondary to infection, which may open into the pharynx or the skin. On microscopic examination, the cyst is lined by respiratory and/or squamous epithelium. Thyroid tissue is seen in the cyst wall in approximately 60% of cases. Recurrent infection may cause denudation of the lining epithelium and chronic inflammation and scarring in the cyst wall leading to loss of the cystic architecture. However, a diagnosis of inflamed and fibrotic TDC may be made in the appropriate clinical setting, even in the absence of the cyst lining. Primary papillary thyroid carcinoma arising from the thyroid tissue within the thyroglossal duct cyst is a well-recognized complication [24–32]. Other primary thyroid tumors that have been reported to arise in thyroglossal duct cyst include Hurthle cell adenoma [33] and anaplastic carcinoma [34]. While primary thyroid tumors can occur in the TDC, the possibility of metastases from a thyroid primary must be ruled out by careful evaluation of the thyroid gland. The criteria for the diagnosis of primary papillary carcinoma arising in TDC are (1) histologic identification of TDC with cyst lining and thyroid tissue in the wall; (2) presence of normal tissue adjacent to the tumor; and (3) careful histopathologic evaluation of the thyroid fails to reveal a primary carcinoma [2]. There has been some debate over the years on the management of thyroid carcinoma arising in TDC. However, a consensus seems to be building that if the tumor is a papillary carcinoma, less than 1.5 cm, confined to the TDC, clinically the thyroid is normal and there is no nodal disease or history of neck irradiation; local resection of the TDC with the hyoid bone (Sistrunk procedure) is adequate treatment with excellent prognosis [28, 30].

Other developmental anomalies of the thyroid gland, which may be encountered in surgical pathology practice, include the finding of a lymphoepithelial cyst similar in morphology to the branchial cleft cyst (Fig. 1). These are derived from the branchial pouches four and five that give rise to the ultimobranchial body that is involved in the development of the thyroid gland [35]. Evidence of thyroid development from the fourth branchial pouch is further supported by the finding of ectopic thyroid tissue in branchial cysts in the neck [36].

Thyroid Gland: Normal Anatomy and Histology

The thyroid is normally located in the mid portion of the neck anterior to the trachea and larynx, just below the cricoid cartilage attached by a loose connective tissue capsule. The recurrent laryngeal nerves lie in the groove between the lateral lobes and the trachea. The superior and inferior parathyroid glands are found close to the posterior surface of the gland or they may be located within the gland itself.

The thyroid gland consists of two lobes joined by an isthmus. In adults, the two lobes measure about 2–2.5 cm wide and 4–5 cm long. In some glands a pyramidal lobe, derived from the distal portion of the thyroglossal duct, extends upward from the isthmus. At birth the thyroid weighs 1–2 g and it increases to 10–15 g at puberty [37]. In the adult the normal weight ranges from 15 to 35 g. The weight varies with iodine intake, sex, age, and functional status of the gland. In addition there are geographic variations ranging from an upper limit of up to 42 g in a Portuguese study [38] to about 10–20 g in North

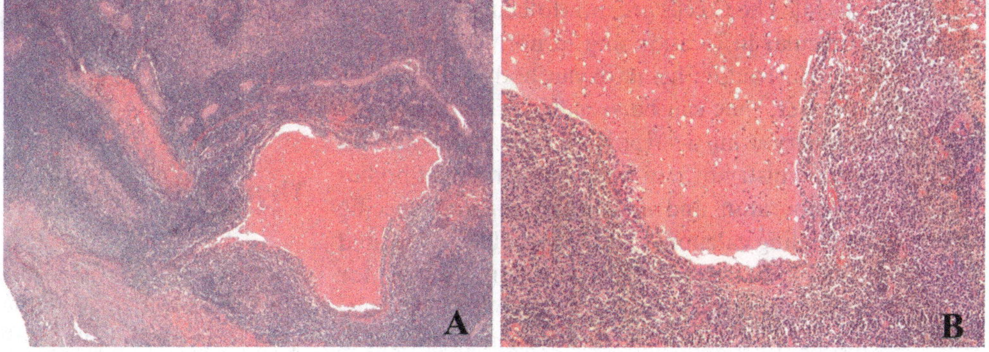

Fig. 1 Thyroid with branchial cleft remnant lined by pseudostratified columnar epithelium

American population [39, 40]. The mean weight is always higher in women and the weight varies in size with the menstrual cycle [41]. In the elderly the weight may sometimes reduce to as little as 10 g [1].

On section, the thyroid gland has a brown cut surface and it is composed of multiple lobules separated by thin fibrous septa. Each lobule is made up of 20–40 follicles and is supplied by a single intralobular artery. The thyroid contains three major types of epithelial cells. These include follicular cells, which line the follicles and secrete thyroxin and triiodothyronine; C cells, which secrete calcitonin; and the solid cell nests (SCN) that are remnants of the ultimobranchial body. The follicles are filled with colloid, range in size from 50 to 500 micron (average 200 micron) in diameter and are lined by cuboidal to low columnar epithelium. The cells lining the follicles have a basal nucleus and rest on a basement membrane composed of laminin and collagen IV [42]. The colloid includes thyroglobulin which is a glycoprotein giving it a PAS-positive diastase resistant staining characteristic. The amount of the colloid and the height of the follicular lining cells vary with the functional status of the gland. In a hyperactive state the follicles are lined by tall cells and have less amount of colloid. In addition to colloid the follicles contain birefringent calcium oxalate monohydrate crystals, the numbers of which may increase with age. This finding may be useful sometimes to differentiate between thyroid follicles and parathyroid tissue on frozen section evaluation [43]. Intracytoplasmic fat within thyroid follicular cells may be detected in 50% of glands on oil red O staining and this may increase with age [1]. Due to the intimate development of thyroid with the mesodermal structures of the neck, fat, cartilage, and/or muscle may be found within the thyroid capsule [5]. For the same reason normal thyroid tissue may be found intermingled with the neck soft tissues including muscle, which should not be mistaken for metastatic carcinoma.

On immunohistochemistry the follicular cells stain positively with low molecular weight cytokeratin, thyroglobulin, and thyroid transcription factor (TTF-1); vimentin co-expression may also be present. In situ hybridization studies have revealed thyroglobulin mRNA within the follicular cells [4]. The C cells are intrafollicular and sometimes parafollicular in location and in normal glands are not visualized on routine hematoxylin and eosin (H&E) staining. However, they can be visualized readily on special histochemistry using a sliver (Gremilius) stain and on immunohistochemistry by pan-neuroendocrine antibodies such as chromogranin and synaptophysin and specific antibodies including calcitonin and calcitonin gene related peptide (CGRP). In addition C cells stain positive for TTF-1 and may also express bombesin, somatostatin, gastrin-releasing peptide, low molecular weight cytokeratin, and CEA [4]. On electron microscopy, the C cells have the characteristic neurosecretory granules; these granules are of two types: the larger and moderately electron-dense type I granules measuring 280 nm and the smaller 130 nm more electron-dense type II granules. Both type I and II granules show calcitonin on immunoelectron microscopy [44]. On in situ hybridization, both calcitonin and CGRP mRNA can be localized in C cells [4].

The solid cell nests can be seen in up to 60% of thyroid glands in the mid portions of the lateral lobes [45]. They are solid irregular masses of epithelial cells measuring about 1 mm or less in maximum diameter and may be solitary or multiple, unilateral or bilateral. They are composed of polyhedral or oval cells with oval nuclei containing finely granular chromatin (Fig. 2); nuclear grooves may be seen [4]. SCN may sometimes show cystic change and show positive staining reaction with acid mucins [1]. On immunohistochemistry, the SCN are positive for low molecular weight cytokeratin and CEA and show variable staining with calcitonin [1, 4, 46, 47]. The latter finding gives support to the theory of the SCN being derivatives of the ultimobranchial body. On electron microscopy, SCN demonstrate desmosomes, intermediate filaments, and intracytoplasmic microvacuolar structures [48]. In addition there are dendritic antigen presenting cells present in the parafollicular thyroid stroma; mast cells, and T lymphocytes may also be seen around the follicles [49].

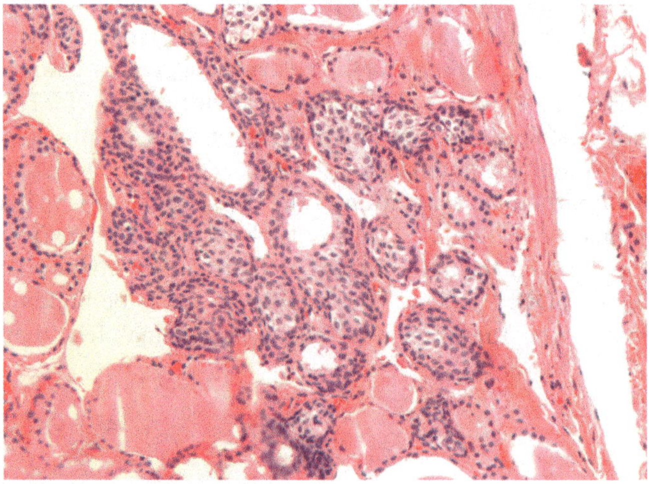

Fig. 2 Thyroid with solid cell nest

Thyroid Tumors

Majority of thyroid tumors are epithelial in origin and can be derived from either the follicular cells or the C (parafollicular) cells. Like in any other organ site, follicular tumors can be either benign or malignant. No benign counterpart of the C cell tumor is identified; however, various degrees of C cell hyperplasia may represent the precancerous stage of medullary carcinoma. A classification of thyroid tumors adapted from the 2004 WHO classification is outlined in Table 1. Tumors derived from the C cells will be covered in the next chapter. In this section tumors of thyroid follicular cells and all other non-C cell tumors will be discussed.

Table 1 Classification of thyroid tumors

Thyroid Adenoma and Related Tumors
- Follicular adenoma
  - Histologic types
- Hyalinizing trabecular tumor

Thyroid Carcinomas
- Papillary carcinoma
  - Conventional type
  - Variants
- Follicular carcinoma
  - Minimally Invasive
  - Encapsulated angioinvasive
  - Widely Invasive
- Poorly differentiated carcinoma
  - Insular carcinoma
  - NOS
- Undifferentiated (anaplastic) carcinoma
  - Squamoid type
  - Spindle cell (sarcomatoid) type
  - Small cell type
  - Giant cell type
- Squamous cell carcinoma
- Mucoepidermoid carcinoma
- Sclerosing mucoepidermoid carcinoma with eosinophilia
- Mucinous carcinoma
- Medullary carcinoma
- Mixed medullary and follicular cell carcinoma
- Spindle cell tumor with thymus-like differentiation
- Carcinoma showing thymus-like differentiation

Other Thyroid Tumors
- Mesenchymal tumors
- Lymphoma
- Metastatic carcinoma

Adapted From WHO Classification (2004)

Tumors of the Thyroid Follicular Cells Follicular Adenoma

Clinical Features and Etiology

Follicular adenoma is a benign tumor derived from the follicular cells. It is characterized by an encapsulated tumor showing a follicular architecture with varying degree of cellularity. The incidence of follicular adenoma in autopsy series has ranged from 3 to 4%, and no significant geographic variations exist [50, 51]. The dietary iodine has no significant role to play in the causation of conventional follicular adenoma. However, one of the rare variants, toxic adenoma appears to be more common in iodine deficient areas [52]. Follicular adenoma is more common in females than males and the patients are usually middle aged. While adenomas may occur in children and elderly patients, the chances of an alternative diagnosis of carcinoma are higher in this age group and should be ruled out by further sampling and careful histologic evaluation. The most common clinical presentation of follicular adenoma is a painless nodule in the thyroid, which may sometimes show gradual increase in size and become painful because of hemorrhage and necrosis. The patients are usually euthyroid except in rare cases of toxic adenoma that present with hyperthyroidism. On radionucleotide scan follicular adenoma in most cases presents as a "cold" (hypofunctioning) nodule, sometimes it may be "cool" or 'warm" (functioning) and very rarely "hot" (hyperfunctioning) in the case of toxic adenoma [51].

Pathology of Follicular Adenoma

On gross examination nearly all adenomas are present as a solitary nodule. However, in some instances two or more adenomas may be seen after applying strict criteria for excluding hyperplastic nodules. One other possibility that should be considered in the case of multiple nodules resembling follicular adenoma is that of an encapsulated follicular variant of papillary carcinoma (see below) and careful histological evaluation for nuclear features of papillary carcinoma should be performed. Follicular adenomas are well circumscribed, vary from 1 to 3 cm in size, have a firm and rubbery consistency, and on sectioning show a diffuse homogenous cut surface varying in color from grayish white to tan (Fig. 3) [51]. Secondary changes with areas of hemorrhage, degeneration necrosis, calcification, and ossification may be seen. On histologic examination, the architectural pattern of follicular adenoma may vary from solid/trabecular to that of large macrofollicles and accordingly they have been classified as solid/trabecular (Fig. 4), microfollicular, normofollicular, or macrofollicular type. The solid/trabecular type is also referred to as embryonal type because of its resemblance to thyroid tissue during the prefollicular embryonal stage of intrauterine life. Similarly microfollicular type is also called fetal type. The follicle size in the normofollicular type is same as that seen in the normal thyroid, therefore it is also called as simple type and macrofollicular type is

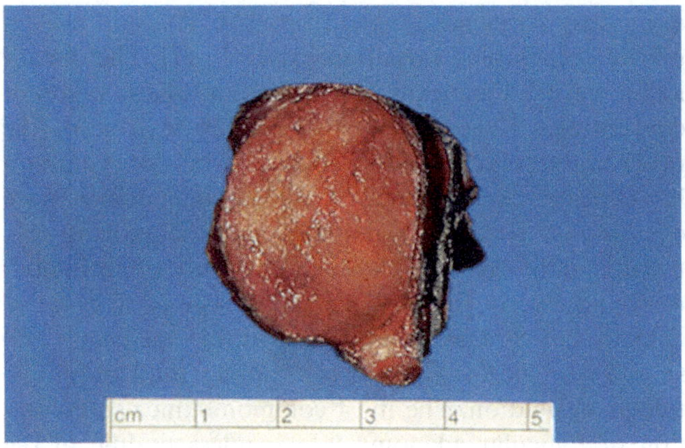

Fig. 3 Thyroid with follicular adenoma showing a well-circumscribed tumor with homogenous tan-brown cut surface

vascular network within the adenoma may be very prominent and sometimes may show a hemangiopericytoma-like pattern. This close intermingling of follicles with blood vessels may sometimes produce artefactual presence of intravascular epithelial cells, which should not be misdiagnosed as vascular invasion. Other histological changes that may be seen in follicular adenoma include foci of squamous metaplasia, which is exceptionally rare [51], areas of spindle cell metaplasia, which may in some cases involve up to 90% of the lesion [54–56], and papillary architecture mimicking papillary carcinoma [57]. The significance of spindle cell proliferation within a follicular adenoma lies in the importance of distinguishing this metaplastic change from an aggressive malignant process.

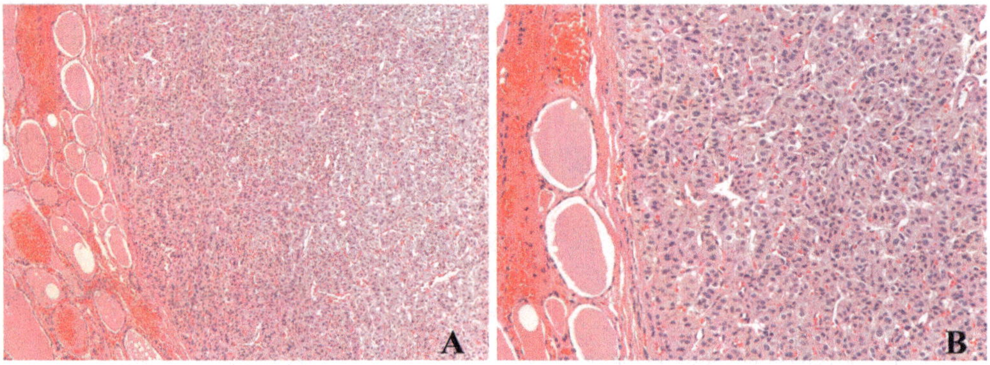

Fig. 4 Follicular adenoma, trabecular/embryonal type (**A**) (40×), (**B**) (100×)

called colloid type because of the large follicles mimicking hyperplastic colloid nodule. In most instances more than one architectural pattern is seen in follicular adenoma. No clinical significance is attributed to the various subtypes of follicular adenoma. The lining follicular cells are present as single layer of polygonal cells with distinct cell borders, round to oval uniform nuclei, and eosinophilic to amphophilic cytoplasm. No mitoses are usually seen. Almost all adenomas have a complete fibrous capsule, which may vary in thickness. A thick capsule should warrant a very careful evaluation of the entire capsule by examining multiple cuts of a section to rule out foci of capsular and vascular invasion. In addition studies utilizing picrosirius orange-red (PSR) staining techniques for the evaluation of capsular collagen have found qualitative differences in the staining characteristics of capsular collagen in follicular adenoma and follicular carcinoma, which may be helpful in the differential diagnosis [53]. Stromal changes in follicular adenoma include areas of edema, which are usually seen in the center of the lesion, and other changes that may be seen include hemorrhage, degeneration with cholesterol clefts, necrosis, dystrophic calcification, and ossification. In some cases the

Follicular Adenoma Variants

Atypical Follicular Adenoma

This term was proposed by Hazard and Kenyon in 1954 for follicular adenoma having some unusual features such as closely packed follicles lacking lumina, solid columns, with little intervening stroma and diffuse cellularity. Pathologists have come to include in this category adenoma showing necrosis and increased mitotic activity [51]. In such cases careful examination of the capsule should be performed to rule out capsular or vascular invasion. In a recent study atypical follicular adenoma on immunohistochemistry showed strong and diffuse expression of galectin-3 and HBME-1, similar to the pattern seen in papillary thyroid carcinoma in their series [58]. Furthermore another study reported that a subset of atypical follicular adenoma showed N2-RAS mutation and RET overexpression similar to the pattern seen in follicular carcinoma and follicular variant of papillary carcinoma [59]. These two studies have tried to make a case that atypical follicular adenoma may represent a precursor of differentiated thyroid carcinoma of both follicular and papillary phenotype. In our view these studies highlight the importance of morphologic correlation with immunohistochemistry and other ancillary molecular studies in reaching a diagnosis since relying on immunohistochemistry alone may lead to a false positive diagnosis of thyroid carcinoma. The diagnosis of carcinoma is based on well-established morphological features as described later.

Follicular Adenoma with Bizarre Nuclei

In this variant of follicular adenoma scattered large nuclei more than 10 times the size of adjacent cells is seen. These nuclei are hyperchromatic and irregular in shape and do not represent sign of malignancy on their own (Fig. 5) [51].

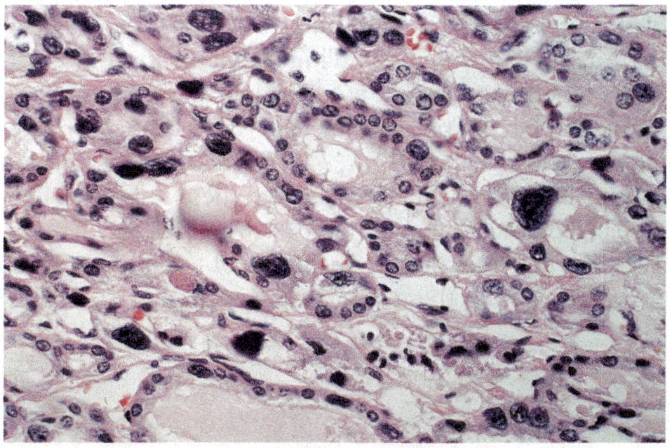

Fig. 5 Follicular adenoma with bizarre nuclei

Adenolipoma and Adenochondroma

Follicular adenoma with interspersed mature fat in between follicles are termed adenolipoma and accordingly tumors with islands of cartilage are called adenochondroma [51, 60].

Toxic Adenoma

Most conventional adenomas are hypofunctioning or "cold," on radionucleotide scan. Toxic adenoma is a rare variant comprising approximately 1% of all follicular adenoma, which is "hot" on radionucleotide scan, and the patients present with hyperthyroidism. It is also referred to as Plummer's disease. On microscopic examination toxic adenoma is either microfollicular or normofollicular and contains pseudopapillary projections. The cells lining the follicles are tall columnar and there is decrease in the amount of luminal colloid within the follicles. Ultrastructurally, the cells show similar features to that seen in Graves' disease, which include increase in rough endoplasmic reticulum, well-developed Golgi apparatus, numerous lysosomes, and numerous slender apical microvilli and pseudopods [51]. At the molecular level, there is mutation in the TSH receptor gene causing constitutive overexpression of the TSH receptor leading to hyperfunctioning of the thyrocytes [61–65]. In a recent study from NW Spain, an iodine-deficient region in addition to mutation in TSH receptor gene approximately 5% cases also showed adenylate cyclase-stimulating G alpha protein (GNAS) gene mutation [66].

Signet-Ring Cell Follicular Adenoma

This variant of follicular adenoma is characterized by the presence of large intracytoplasmic vacuole causing displacement of the nuclei to one side causing the signet ring-like appearance (Fig. 6) [67–69]. These foci with signet ring like areas may be focal or diffuse throughout the lesion. The cytoplasmic vacuoles contain thyroglobulin and on ultrastructural evaluation these vacuoles represent either intracellular lumina or dilated vesicles [17]. Mucin stain may sometimes be positive within the intracytoplasmic vacuoles and this is thought to be due to glycoprotein complexes produced as a result of thyroglobulin degradation [67].

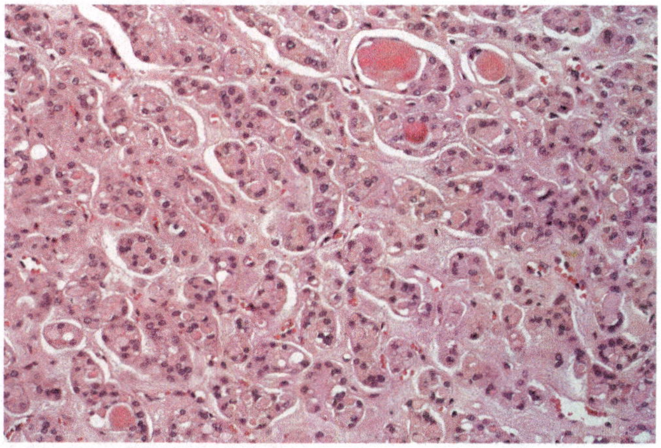

Fig. 6 Follicular adenoma signet-ring variant with intracytoplasmic vacuoles resembling signet-ring cells

Hyalanizing Trabecular Tumor

Hyalanizing trabecular tumor of the thyroid is known for the controversy around its terminology mainly due to an apparent uncertainty in the biological behavior of such tumors. Carney et al. in 1987 first coined the term hyalanizing trabecular adenoma (HTA) [70]. However, Carney in a more recent publication recognized that before their report in 1987, similar tumors were reported on three earlier occasions first by Rahel Zipkin in 1905, followed by Pierre Mason in 1922, and in 1982 by Ward and coworkers [71]. Carney et al. in their original paper described a series of 11 encapsulated tumors with a distinctive histology comprising polygonal and fusiform cells arranged in trabeculae separated by thin capillary network and hyalanized amyloid-like stroma which is often calcified (Fig. 7A,B). The cells on immunohistochemistry are negative for calcitonin. They considered these tumors as benign and called them adenoma. This pattern is reminiscent of a paraganglioma; hence the term paraganglioma-like adenoma of the thyroid (PLAT) has been suggested by some [72]. As shown in Fig. 7C,D, the cells within these trabecular islands may show longitudinal nuclear grooves, nuclear pseudo-inclusions, psammoma bodies, and paranuclear yellow cytoplasmic bodies [70, 73–75]. In view of these nuclear features, which resemble papillary carcinoma, HTA has been the subject of debate among thyroid pathologists and some have suggested that HTA is a variant of papillary carcinoma. These morphological observations were further supported in some studies by the finding of similarities in cytokeratin immunoprofile between papillary carcinoma and HTA, especially cytokeratin 19 that was positive in both [76, 77]. These findings have however not been reproduced in other studies. Hirokawa et al. reported a completely different cytokeratin profile in HTA and papillary carcinoma; in their study HTA were all CK-19 negative, while papillary carcinoma was positive [78]. A more recent study reported lack of CK 19 and HBME-1 immunoreactivity in all their HTA compared to diffuse positive staining noted in all papillary carcinoma [79]. In addition, another study used MIB staining to differentiate between HTA and papillary carcinoma, the peculiar pattern of cell membrane and cytoplasmic MIB-1 staining seen in HTA was not observed in papillary carcinoma [80]. RET/PTC rearrangement has been reported in HTA suggesting its similarity to papillary carcinoma at the molecular level [76]. Lloyd reviewed the status of HTA with respect to RET/PTC rearrangement and emphasized the limitations and practical usefulness of these analyses [81]. In view of the nuclear features resembling papillary thyroid carcinoma together with some studies reporting similar immunophenotype and presence of RET/PTC gene rearrangement in the so called HTA, World Health Organization consensus group in 2004 reclassified these tumors as hyalanizing trabecular tumor (HTT), which clearly emphasizes the uncertain biologic behavior of these tumors [82]. It is possible that these tumors may represent a group of

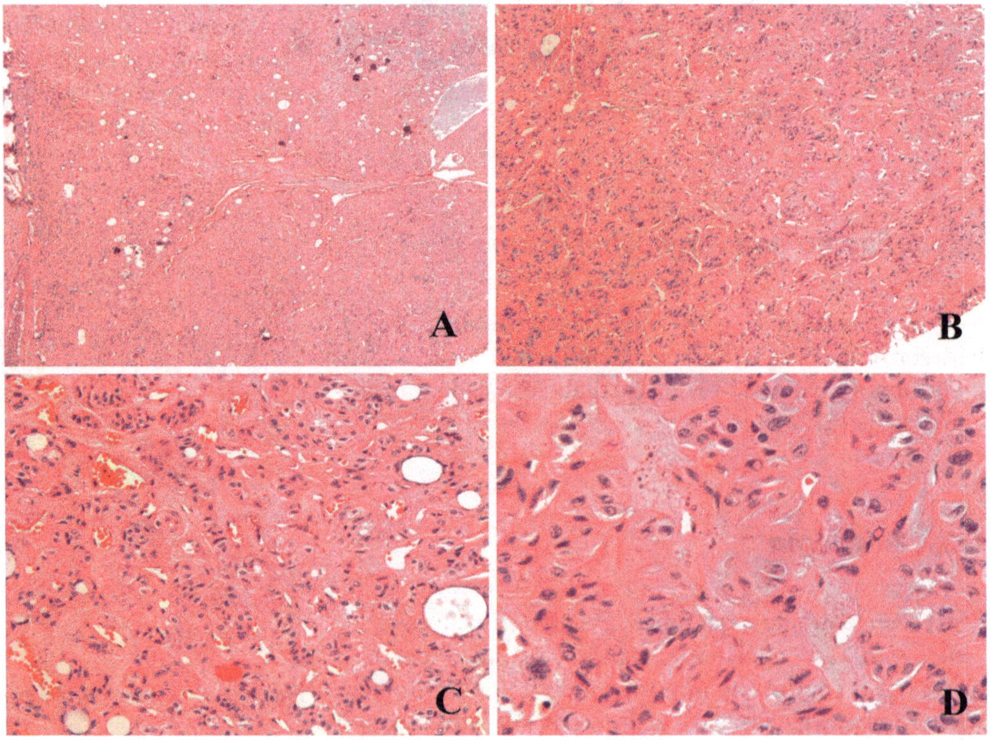

Fig. 7 Hyalanizing trabecular tumor, trabecular pattern with hyalanized stroma and focal calcification (**A**); ribbons of oval and elongated cells (**B, C**) with nuclear grooves and nuclear pseudoinclusions

thyroid tumors with very low malignant potential with an uncertain biology and further studies utilizing molecular diagnostic techniques with clinical correlation and long follow up may shed more light in the future [83]. There has been a recent report of hyalanizing trabecular carcinoma presenting as lung metastasis [84]. In this case, however, there was evidence of vascular invasion, with some nuclear groves and rare pseudoinclusions and the tumor was CK19 negative. We think that HTT must be differentiated from medullary carcinoma and poorly differentiated carcinoma and if the latter two are ruled out classified as HTT and most of these should have a relatively benign biology. In Carney's experience based on over 120 cases, "trabecular tumors of the thyroid that are circumscribed or encapsulated and exhibit intratrabecular hyalinization and PTC-type nuclei are benign neoplasms" [71].

Thyroid Carcinoma

Thyroid carcinoma, which constitutes more than 98% of thyroid malignancies accounts for 1% of all human cancers [85]. At a global level there is significant geographic variation in the incidence of thyroid carcinoma, which ranges from 0.5 to 10 cases per 100,000 [17]. In USA and Europe, the incidence is about 3 per 100,000-population [86]. Also incidence may change when people migrate from one area to another, for example, incidence of thyroid cancer in India is 1.0 but among the south Asians including Indians living in USA the incidence increased to 2.3 per 100,000 [87]. Females are three times more commonly affected than males. While thyroid carcinoma can be seen in all age groups, the most common age of onset is the fourth and the fifth decade. Most thyroid carcinomas are differentiated tumors and have an indolent course. Anaplastic carcinoma, which is one of the most aggressive forms of thyroid carcinoma, is seen in the elderly mainly in the seventh and the eighth decades of life [85]. Thyroid carcinoma can arise from either the thyroid hormone producing follicular cells or the calcitonin producing C cells. The later are referred to as medullary carcinoma and may be either sporadic or arise in a familial setting as part of multiple endocrine neoplasia (MEN) and are discussed in Chapter 6. The incidence of different types of thyroid carcinoma may vary worldwide depending on the iodine content of the diet. In a large multicenter prospective cohort study including more than 5,500 cases in USA, among the follicular cell derived thyroid carcinoma, the most common is papillary carcinoma (81%), followed by follicular carcinoma (10%), Hurthle cell carcinoma (3.6%), and anaplastic carcinoma (1.7%) [85]. Non-medullary thyroid carcinoma including papillary, follicular, and anaplastic carcinoma may also occur in a familial setting [88–91]. In iodine-deficient areas the incidence of follicular carcinoma is higher and may be as high as 45% [17]; however, in parts of the world with sufficient iodine supplementation the incidence of follicular carcinoma has declined over the past few decades; one of the reason in addition to iodine supplementation may be increase in the incidence of papillary carcinoma especially its follicular variant [92]. In a recent epidemiological review Maso et al. concluded that significant risk factors for thyroid carcinoma include exposure to ionizing radiation and iodine deficiency. Also there seems to be a strong association with history of benign thyroid nodules/adenoma or goiter. Diet rich in vegetables may help prevent thyroid cancer but a direct causal relationship with diet is yet to be established; worldwide mortality rates for thyroid cancer are 0.8/100,000 for women and 0.4/100,000 for men [93].

Papillary Thyroid Carcinoma

Clinical Features and Etiology

This is the most common form of thyroid carcinoma with no apparently known benign neoplastic counterpart [94]. It most often presents in the fourth and the fifth decades and three times being more common in females than males [85]. Most thyroid tumors in children are papillary carcinoma and rare reports of congenital tumors are also present. Papillary carcinoma may sometimes be seen in a familial setting, and family history of thyroid carcinoma was seen in 4.9% cases of papillary carcinoma in a large cohort of thyroid cancer [17, 85, 91]. In the same cohort, potential risk factors, which were seen associated with papillary carcinoma, include goiter (14.9% cases), thyroiditis (8.1% cases), history of prior exposure to radiation (4.8% cases), and Graves' disease (2.0% cases) [85]. Somatic rearrangements of the *ret* proto-oncogene which is located on the long arm of chromosome 10 and encodes a membrane-associated tyrosine kinase receptor have been seen in papillary thyroid carcinoma and the rearranged form of the *ret* oncogene is designated as ret/PTC gene; this RET/PTC rearrangement is believed to play a role in papillary thyroid carcinogenesis (for review see [95, 96]; also see Chapter 18). In experimental models ret/PTC rearrangements have been observed in mice exposed to ionizing radiation, suggesting the role of ionizing radiation in the causation of papillary thyroid carcinoma [97]. More recently BRAF mutations have also been reported in a subset of papillary thyroid carcinoma, this is discussed later in Chapter 18. The role of ionizing radiation in the causation of thyroid cancer is well recognized and has been reviewed by Moysich et al. [98]. Furthermore there is increased incidence of childhood PTC as a second malignancy following radiotherapy involving the head and neck and upper thorax for malignant neoplasm [99].

Pathology of Papillary Thyroid Carcinoma

The typical gross appearance of papillary carcinoma is an ill-defined tumor with irregular borders and firm consistency with granular pale white cut surface, sometimes associated with calcification (Fig. 8). Other presentation of conventional papillary carcinoma is a cystic tumor with attached papillary growth. Some variants may show a well-circumscribed nodule with a fleshy cut surface often encapsulated and may show partial cystic change [51]. The latter form of presentation on gross examination may resemble an adenoma and careful microscopic evaluation for nuclear changes of papillary carcinoma should be performed in these cases.

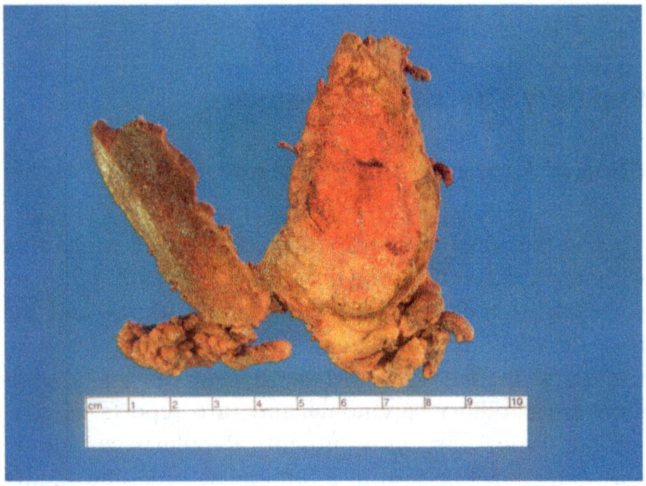

Fig. 8 Papillary thyroid carcinoma with ill-defined gray-white tumor and infiltrative edges involving almost the entire left lobe with smaller foci of tumor in the right lobe

On microscopic examination the architecture of papillary carcinoma may be papillary comprising of complex arborizing papillary process with well-defined fibrovascular cores (Fig. 9A); it may be follicular, solid/trabecular, or mixed. The hallmarks of the diagnosis of papillary thyroid carcinoma are the characteristic nuclear changes, which are seen in the conventional papillary carcinoma and all its variants. These changes include elongation of the nuclei with nuclear groove present along the long axis of the nuclei; optical clearing of the chromatin referred to as "Orphan Annie" nuclei, and the presence of nuclear pseudoinclusions, which are eosinophilic and represent extension of the cytoplasmic contents that appear to lie in the nucleus due to the highly irregular and undulated nuclear membrane (Fig. 9B,C). On immunohistochemical studies β-catenin localization has been reported in these nuclear pseudoinclusions (Fig. 10) suggesting its role in nuclear envelope changes [100, 101]. While nuclear grooves may be seen in other types of thyroid lesions, both neoplastic and non-neoplastic [102], the overall appearance of the lesion both at architectural and cytologic level is helpful in distinguishing these conditions from papillary thyroid carcinoma. These nuclei in papillary carcinoma often show overlapping features. Additional histologic changes include the presence of psammoma bodies which are concentric calcific bodies within in the stroma of the papillae; desmoplastic stroma with infiltrative growth of the tumor, and variable degree of lymphocytic infiltrate in the stroma. Foci of squamous

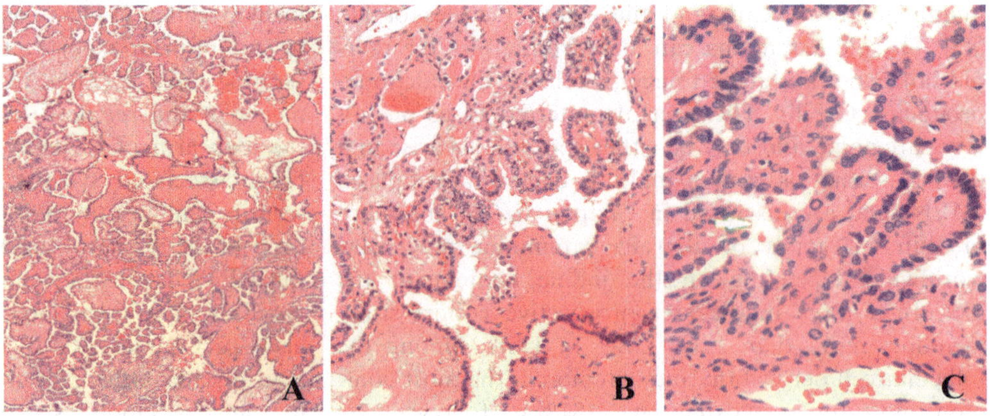

Fig. 9 Papillary thyroid carcinoma, with conventional papillary architecture (**A**), piling up of nuclei (**B**) and characteristic nuclear morphology including optically clear chromatin, nuclear grooves, and nuclear pseudoinclusions

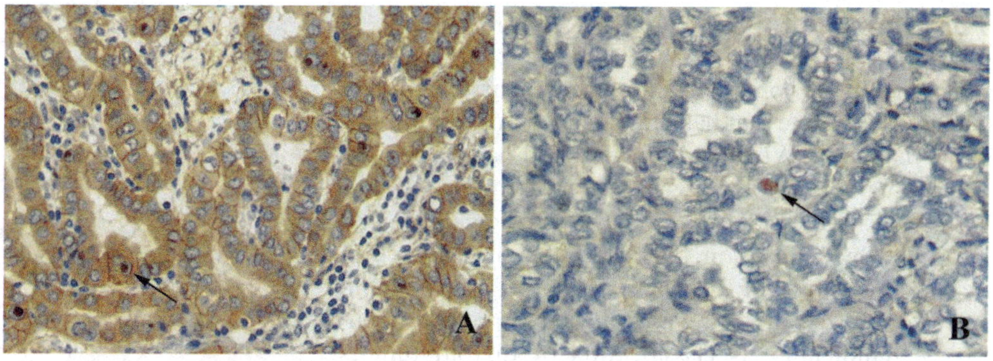

Fig. 10 Papillary thyroid carcinoma with β-catenin accumulation on immunostaining in nuclear pseudoinclusions (*arrow*); evidence of cytoplasmic and membrane immunostaining is also seen in (**A**)

differentiation may sometimes be seen [17, 51]. Papillary carcinoma may show multicentricity and may be present in bilateral lobes justifying the near total thyroidectomy that most surgeons prefer, especially for tumors larger than 1.0 cm in size. It is not completely clear whether the multicentricitry is due to intrathyroidal spread of the tumor via lymphatics, or it represents multiple synchronous primaries. While some studies have shown that these multiple foci of tumors are clonal, others have shown that they represent separate clones. In a recent study on multifocal PTC, molecular analysis was able to separate intrathyroidal metastasis (ITM) seen in 67% cases by having a similar profile of loss of heterozygosities (LOH) and presence of BRAF mutation from other cases which were labeled as multiple independent primaries; cases with ITM in their study had a higher incidence of lymph node metastasis [103]. Papillary carcinoma usually disseminates through lymphatics and it is not uncommon to find metastases in regional lymph nodes. Some authors have suggested sentinel lymph node biopsy as an accurate method for the diagnosis of metastatic papillary carcinoma avoiding significant morbidity associated with lymph node dissection [104–108].

On electron microscopy, the nuclear membrane of papillary carcinoma is highly irregular showing infolding, the chromatin is scant, and nuclear pseudoinclusions containing cytoplasmic contents are seen [17]. Numerous immunohistochemical markers such as cytokeratin 19, HBME-1, CD57, CD44, galectin 3, p27, cyclin D1, retinoblastoma protein, and CITED have been reported to help in the diagnosis of papillary thyroid carcinoma, especially in the follicular patterned lesions. While some have shown promising results, especially when used in a panel as discussed below, no single marker on its own is absolutely specific and nuclear cytomorphology still may be the gold standard for the diagnosis of papillary thyroid carcinoma. Some recent studies have shown deregulation of a subset of microRNA (miRNA) in PTC, which may potentially be used in FNA samples and aid in preoperative diagnosis [109–111].

Histologic Variants of Papillary Carcinoma

While the characteristic nuclear features described above are common to all histologic types of papillary carcinoma, a number of variants have been described based on either size or architectural patterns of the tumor. The diagnosis of some of these variants is important because they behave in a more aggressive fashion compared to the conventional papillary carcinoma and the knowledge of some other variants such as follicular and oncocytic variants is important to prevent misdiagnosis.

Papillary Microcarcinoma

Papillary microcarcinoma is defined as tumor less than 1.0 cm in size, it is also referred to as occult sclerosing carcinoma and is not an uncommon incidental finding at autopsy and in surgical resection of thyroid for benign conditions [17]. Because of its high prevalence up to 35% in autopsy series and in up to 24% in total thyroidectomies for unrelated benign condition this tumor is regarded as an indolent tumor with a relatively benign course [112–114]. For the same reason some have suggested that this may be an earlier stage in the papillary carcinogenesis [94]. However, up to 11% of microcarcinomas may show lymph node metastases and local recurrence, which is usually seen in multifocal and bilateral tumors [17]. In one study tumor size >/= 0.8 cm was significantly associated with more aggressive disease [115]. However, in a recent meta-analysis of the literature, significant risk factors for recurrence included younger age group, clinically overt tumor, multifocality, and lymph node involvement at diagnosis; tumor size was not associated with recurrence [116].

Follicular Variant of Papillary Carcinoma

This is the most common variant of papillary carcinoma and is also the one that has generated a lot of controversy in its diagnosis. While Crile and Hazard had recognized carcinoma with a follicular pattern as early as 1953, the term follicular variant of papillary carcinoma was first proposed by Lindsay in 1960 [117–119] but it was still regarded as a type of follicular carcinoma. The WHO in 1974 recognized the entity as follicular variant of papillary carcinoma in its classification of thyroid tumors [120]. Later in 1977 Chen and Rosai described six additional cases elaborating the morphologic features and proposed the use of the terminology follicular variant of papillary carcinoma (FVPC), proposed by Lindsay [121]. Since the description by Chen and Rosai this variant of papillary carcinoma is now more readily recognized and in some series 29% of papillary carcinoma have 70% or more of the tumor showing a follicular architecture [122]. The follicular pattern in this tumor may be microfollicular, normofollicular, macrofollicular, or a mixed pattern. These tumors may be infiltrative (noncapsulated) (Fig. 11) or be partially or completely encapsulated (Fig. 12). In a recent study from Memorial Sloan-Kettering Cancer Center, FVPC with an infiltrative and noncapsulated pattern showed significantly higher rate of regional lymph node metastasis (65% vs. 5%), intratumoral fibrosis (88% vs. 18%), exrathyroidal extension (65% vs. 5%), and positive margins (50% vs. 2%), compared to encapsulated tumors [123]. One of the most controversial and challenging diagnoses in thyroid surgical pathology may be the identification focal nuclear changes of papillary carcinoma in an encapsulated follicular pattern lesion which many pathologists may have faced [124]. It has been suggested that there may be a tendency to overdiagnose follicular variant of papillary carcinoma [125], and furthermore, if these encapsulated follicular lesions with apparently equivocal nuclear changes of papillary carcinoma are sent out for consultation, more often than not divergent opinions may be obtained, which reflects the lack of uniform diagnostic criteria and interobserver variability [126, 127]. Since the nuclear changes are not diffuse, they may sometimes be missed and the lesion may be misdiagnosed as follicular adenoma. These nuclear changes are most often seen in the subcapsular region of the tumor [17]. The importance of diagnosing these lesions as encapsulated follicular variant of papillary carcinoma cannot be overemphasized because these tumors may later present with bone metastases, some doing so 15–17 years after the initial diagnosis justifying their appropriate treatment at the time of presentation [128]. In view of this difficulty in their diagnosis some have suggested that encapsulated follicular lesions with questionable nuclear changes be diagnosed as well-differentiated tumor of uncertain malignant potential (WDT-UMP) [124]. The features that may help in the differential diagnosis of these follicular pattern lesions are outlined in Table 2.

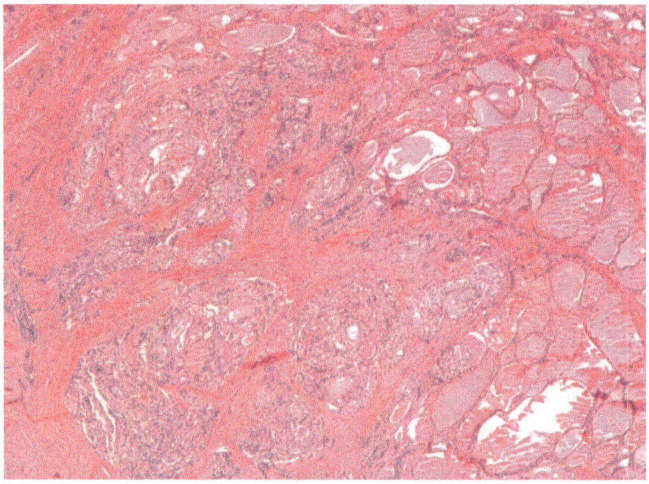

Fig. 11 Follicular variant of papillary carcinoma, infiltrative type with desmoplastic stroma

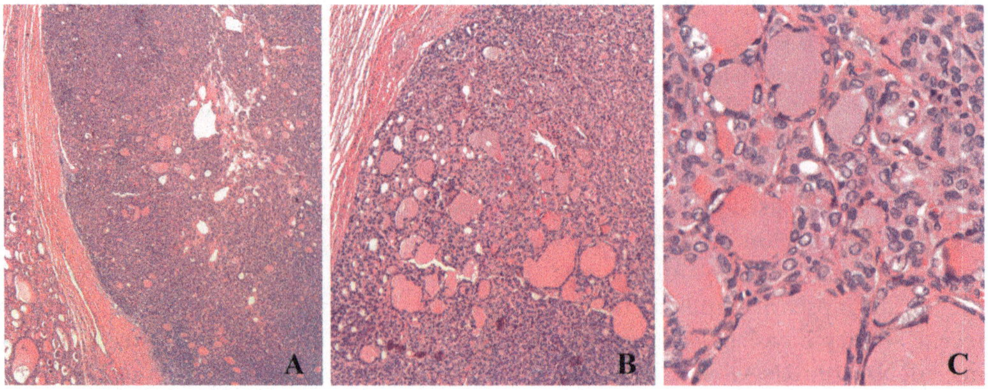

Fig. 12 Follicular variant of papillary carcinoma, encapsulated type, follicular architecture (**A** and **B**) and characteristic nuclear features of papillary carcinoma are seen (**C**)

Table 2 Differential diagnosis of thyroid follicular lesions

Pathological Features	Diagnosis			
	HCN	FA	FC	FVPC
Macroscopic Appearance	usually multiple nodules of varying size	usually solitary nodule	usually solitary nodule	may be solitary or multiple nodules
Microscopic Appearance				
capsule	usually absent, sometimes may be present	continuous fibrous capsule of varying thickness	thick capsule with evidence of invasion	may or may not be present
vascular invasion	not present	not present	may be present	may be present
architecture	usually normo or macrofollicular	usually micro or normofollicular	usually micro or normofollicular	usually micro or normofollicular
colloid	amphophilic or pale eosinophilic	amphophilic or pale eosinophilic	amphophilic or pale eosinophilic	diffusely eosinophilic
lining cells	single layer of flat to low cuboidal	single layer of uniform polygonal cells	polygonal cells with cellular areas	multilayered polygonal cells
nuclei	round uniform normochromatic	round uniform normochromatic	may show mitoses, pleomorphism and prominent nucleoli	nuclear grooves, clear chromatin, pseudoinclusions
Ancillary Studies Immunohistochem				
CK19	usually negative	usually negative,	usually negative	strongly positive
HBME-1	usually negative,	usually negative	strongly positive	strongly positive
Galectin 3	usually negative	usually negative	usually positive	usually positive
CD57	usually negative	usually negative	may be positive	usually positive
CITED 1	negative	negative	usually negative	positive in subset
P27	strongly positive	strongly positive	focally positive	focally positive
Rb protein	positive	positive	negative	negative
Cytogenetics				
RET/PTC rearrangement	absent	absent	absent	present in a subset
BRAF mutation	absent	absent	usually absent	may be present
PAX8/PPARγ rearrangement	absent	usually absent	present in a subset	may be present

HCN: Hyperplastic colloid nodule FA: Follicular adenoma
FC: Follicular carcinoma FVPC: Follicular variant of papillary carcinoma

In addition to the encapsulated pattern of FVPC, another distinct pattern that has been described in FVPC includes a diffuse variant which involves the entire thyroid, may be associated with stromal calcification and ossification, and shows a high incidence of lymph node and distant metastases [129, 130] (Fig. 13); and the macrofollicular variant described by Albores-Saavedra et al., which should be distinguished from colloid nodule [131, 132]. Some cases of macrofollicular variant in a later publication by the same authors showed focal transformation into a poorly differentiated (insular) phenotype with evidence of lung and bone metastases [133]. While some cases as described above have shown evidence of lung and bone metastases, in general the natural history of FVPC is the same as that of conventional papillary carcinoma, especially with respect to spread to the lymph nodes and prognosis. In a recent Japanese study, FVPC was associated with a higher incidence of distant metastases and more aggressive behavior compared to conventional PTC [134]. Other studies with long-term follow-up have reported similar 10- and 15-year disease-specific survival in both FVPC and conventional PTC [135, 136]. Furthermore, immunophenotypically the keratin expression profile of these tumors resembles that of the conventional papillary carcinoma as opposed to the follicular carcinoma [51]. One recent study has also showed overexpression of microRNA (miR-146b) similar to that seen in conventional PTC [109]. However, there is also evidence that FVPC shares some features with follicular carcinoma such as higher frequency of systemic spread, presence of PAX8-PPARγ rearrangement seen approximately in one-third patients and higher frequency of ras mutations compared to conventional PTC [137–140]. These morphologic and molecular features suggest that FVPC may be related to both conventional PTC and follicular carcinoma and larger series with clinicopathological correlations and molecular data may shed some more light in the classification of these tumors.

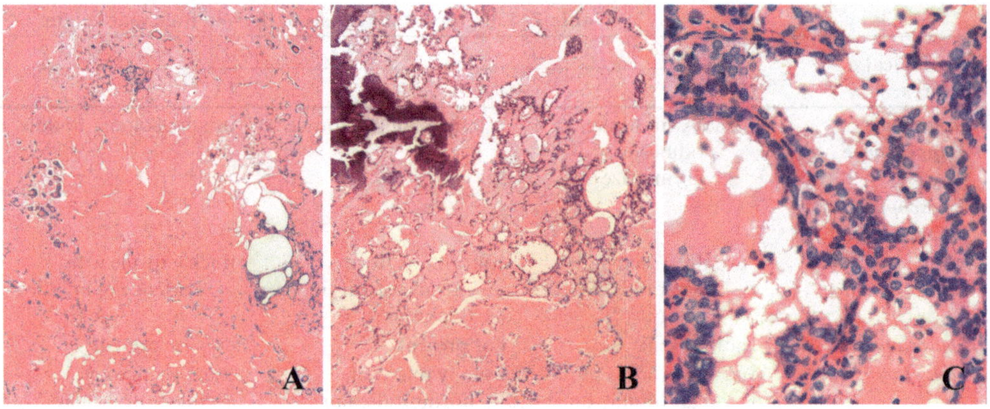

Fig. 13 Follicular variant of papillary carcinoma, diffuse type with stromal fibrosis and calcification (**A**), follicular architecture (**B**) and nuclear changes are seen (**C**)

Tall Cell Variant of Papillary Carcinoma

Tall cell variant (TCV) is one of the more aggressive variants of papillary carcinoma, first described in 1976 by Hawk and Hazard [141]. In one series of 650 PTC over a 30-year period, tall cell variant comprised 4% of all PTC [142]. These tumors usually present in the elderly and are more common in males. On gross examination, they are usually larger than 5.0 cm in size and on histologic examination show papillary structures lined by elongated tumor cells with height being at least twice that of the width having an eosinophilic cytoplasm and characteristic nuclear features of papillary carcinoma (Fig. 14). Ultrastructurally there are increased mitochondria in the cytoplasm, but it is less than that seen in Hurthle cells [17]. The tall cell variant of papillary carcinoma is associated with adverse prognostic features such as large tumor size, extrathyroidal extension, and vascular invasion and is associated with high incidence of locoregional recurrence, distant metastasis, and shorter disease-free survival [143–150]. Furthermore TCV even without extrathyroidal extension has more aggressive phenotype compared to conventional PTC, independent of age, gender, and tumor size [151]. In addition evaluation of cell cycle regulatory proteins such as p27, Ki67 cyclin D1, P53, and eukaryotic translation initiation factors 4E and 2 alpha expression, show a profile which is similar to that seen in thyroid tumors with an unfavorable prognosis [152–156]. The tall cell variant has been found to be associated with squamous cell and Hurthle cell carcinoma of thyroid, which are both more aggressive types of thyroid carcinoma [152, 157].

Columnar Cell Variant of Papillary Carcinoma

This is one of the rare and also a more aggressive variant of papillary carcinoma first described by Evans [17]. LiVolsi later highlighted an important morphologic alteration in these cells, which includes subnuclear vacuolation, mimicking early secretory endometrium (Fig. 15) [5]. This latter feature is important and helps in differentiating this from the tall cell variant. Encapsulated tumors tend to have a better prognosis compared to tumors without a capsule that are associated with extrathyroidal extension and higher local regional recurrence [158, 159]. In metastatic sites, however, because of the lack of colloid and presence cytoplasmic vacuolation these tumors may sometimes be confused with other primaries, and to complicate matters further this tumor may show variable thyroglobulin immunostaining but TTF-1 immunoexpression is more consistent (Fig. 16) [160].

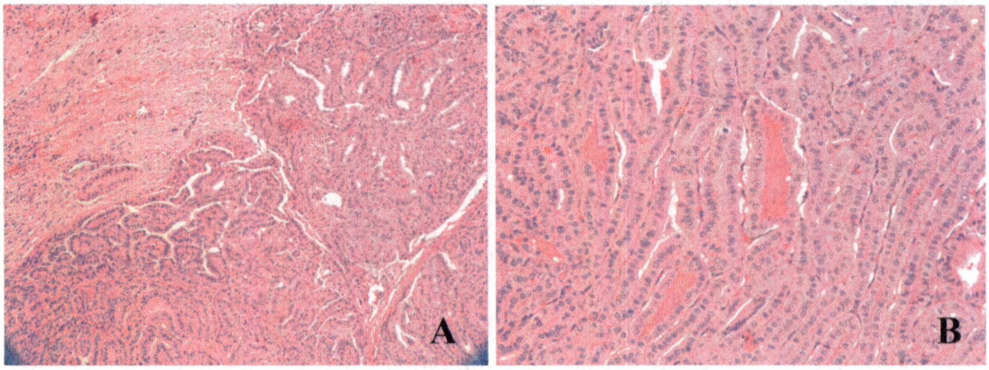

Fig. 14 Papillary thyroid carcinoma, tall cell variant, with invasive edges (**A**), tumor showed extrathyroidal extension; elongated nuclei with eosinophilic cytoplasm and nuclear features of papillary carcinoma are seen (**B**)

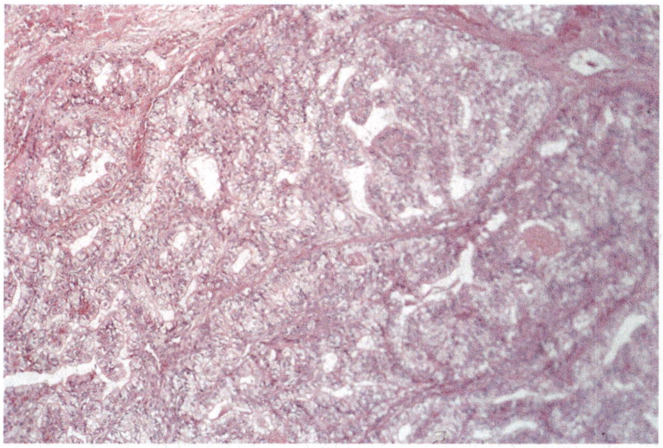

Fig. 15 Papillary thyroid carcinoma, columnar cell variant with elongated cells and vacuolated cytoplasm

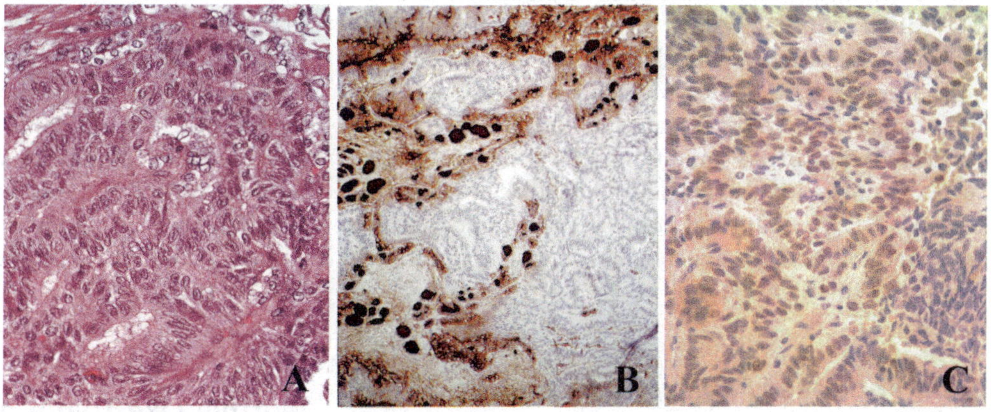

Fig. 16 Papillary thyroid carcinoma, columnar cell variant with elongated cells (**A**), focal thyroglobulin immunostaining (**B**), and diffuse TTF-1 nuclear staining (**C**) and vacuolated cytoplasm

Clinicopathologic correlation and positive TTF1 and thyroglobulin immunostaining is helpful in these cases to make the diagnosis of metastatic thyroid carcinoma.

Cribriform-morular Variant of Papillary Carcinoma

This is a rare but distinct variant of papillary carcinoma, which may be associated with familial adenomatous polyposis (FAP) and germline mutations in the APC gene [161–166]. Tumors in FAP patients that do not show APC gene mutation, there may be aberrant nuclear accumulation of mutant β-catenin that is thought to play a role in the histogenesis of these tumors [167]. Sporadic cribriform-morular variants of PC have also been reported without associated FAP, but the diagnosis of this tumor warrants a full workup to rule out associated colonic polyposis [168–171]. Cribriform variant of PC occurs almost exclusively in females and may be solitary or multifocal. They may be encapsulated and histologically are characterized by a cribriform, solid/trabecular, morular (squamoid) growth pattern with intermixed papillary and follicular areas (Fig. 17). The diagnosis of papillary carcinoma is based on the finding of characteristic nuclear features. Immunohistochemistry shows reactivity with thyroglobulin, epithelial membrane antigen, cytokeratin, vimentin, estrogen and progesterone receptors, and behavior of these tumors is similar to that of the conventional PC [168].

Oncocytic Variant of Papillary Carcinoma

This variant of papillary carcinoma usually displays papillary architecture in which cubo-columnar cells with eosinophilic cytoplasm and nuclear features of papillary carcinoma line the papillae. While majority have a papillary morphology, areas with follicular pattern or in some cases predominantly a follicular pattern tumor may be seen (Fig. 18) [172]. This tumor should be differentiated from papillary variant of Hurthle cell carcinoma and TCV of PTC because of different clinical course of the

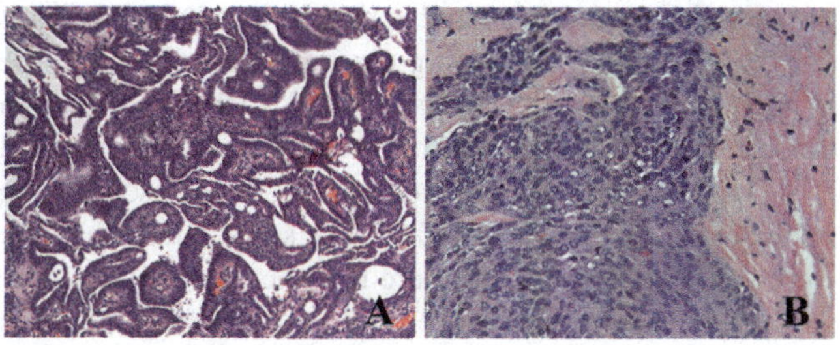

Fig. 17 Papillary thyroid carcinoma, cribriform-morular variant including cribriform and papillary areas (**A**) and solid morular/squamoid foci (**B**). *Photomicrograph courtesy Dr. Vania Nose, Brigham and Women's Hospital, Boston, MA*

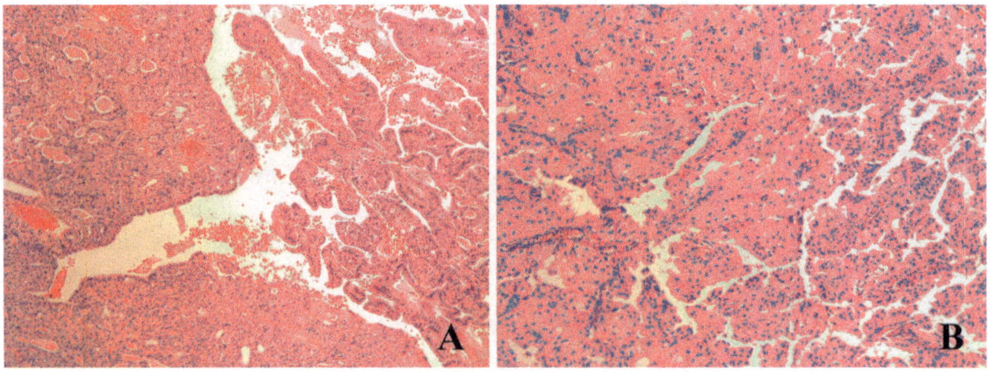

Fig. 18 Papillary thyroid carcinoma, Hurthle cell (oncocytic) variant, In (**A**), pseudopapillary foci (*right half*) and follicular architecture (*left half*) are seen; (**B**) shows solid trabecular pattern and nuclear features of papillary carcinoma

two tumors. In the former characteristic nuclear features of PTC are not seen, the papillary structures are not true papillae, and there is very little stroma. In TCV of PTC, the height of the cells is at least two times the width. Oncocytic variant may sometimes be associated with the TCV of PTC and may show higher propensity for extra-thyroidal invasion and vascular invasion compared to the conventional PTC [173]. Molecular analysis of these tumors has revealed the presence of both RET/PTC rearrangement and BRAF mutations [174, 175]. However, it seems tumors with a follicular architecture are less likely to have BRAF mutation compared to tumors with a papillary architecture, again making a case for a different biology of the FVPC [176].

Solid Variant of Papillary Carcinoma

This variant of papillary carcinoma is most often seen in the pediatric population and is the most common variant of PTC in children following the radiation exposure due to the Chernobyl nuclear disaster [177–179]. However, a more recent study found no difference between childhood PTC tumor types in patients who were exposed to the nuclear disaster and those from the same countries who were not, suggesting that there may be other geographic variations such as dietary iodine that may play a role in the genesis of these tumors [180]. The solid variant of PTC is associated with adverse prognostic factors such as lymph node metastases, extrathyroidal extension, and venous invasion. On histology, they are composed of solid islands of oval cells separated by thin fibrous septae. The cells show nuclear features of papillary carcinoma. Areas of follicular and papillary architecture may also be seen intermixed [181]. They are associated with slightly higher incidence of distant metastases and less favorable prognosis than conventional PTC [182], but they must be differentiated from insular carcinoma which may seen associated with differentiated thyroid carcinoma of both papillary and follicular types, and have a worse prognosis [17, 51, 183].

Warthin-Like Tumor of the Thyroid

This variant of papillary carcinoma resembles the Warthin tumor of the salivary gland and because of this feature Apel et al termed this variant as "Warthin-like thyroid tumor" [184]. It is associated with lymphocytic thyroiditis and is composed of papillae lined by tall eosinophilic cells with nuclear features of papillary carcinoma separated by abundant lymphocyte-rich stroma (Fig. 19). This tumor behaves like the conventional PTC

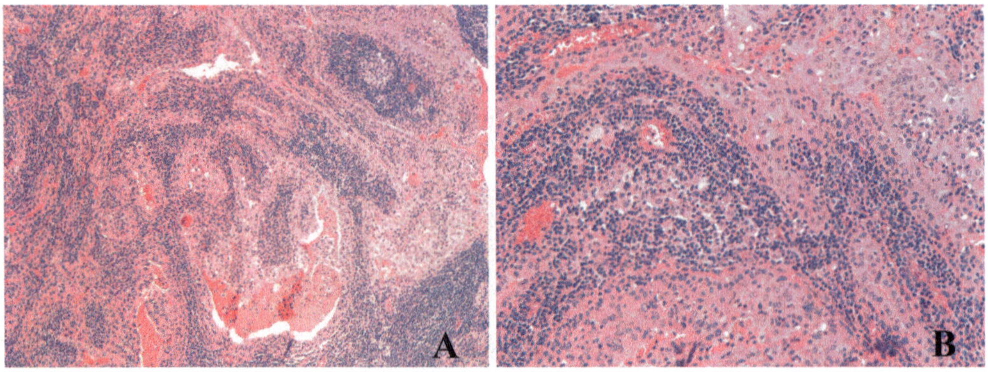

Fig. 19 Papillary thyroid carcinoma, Warthin tumor-like with papillary architecture and dense lymphoid stroma (**A**); cells are eosinophilic with nuclear features of papillary carcinoma (**B**)

[185–188]. Lam et al. reported a case with progression to anaplastic carcinoma leading to systemic spread and death 18 months after first surgery [142].

Papillary Carcinoma with Nodular Fasciitis-Like Stroma

This is a rare variant of PTC in which there is marked fibroblastic proliferation in the stroma mimicking granulation tissue, which may sometimes mask the tumor cells; the tumor cells show nuclear features of papillary carcinoma (Fig. 20) [189–194]. In surgical pathology practice it is important to recognize this variant so that in the presence of exuberant fibroblastic proliferation careful search may be made to look for tumor islands. Furthermore, this variant must be distinguished and not misdiagnosed as a more aggressive anaplastic thyroid carcinoma [190]. Other differential diagnosis includes solitary fibrous tumor of the thyroid [195]. The presence of fibroblastic stroma may pose problems in its diagnosis on fine-needle aspiration biopsy [196]. Few case studies available show the behavior of this variant similar to the conventional PTC [189].

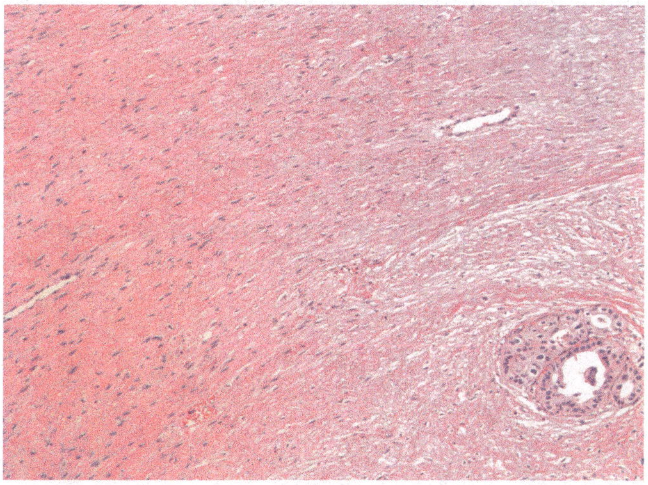

Fig. 20 Papillary thyroid carcinoma with fibromatosis like stroma showing abundant spindle cell stroma and scattered islands of tumor cells

Diffuse Sclerosing Variant of Papillary Carcinoma

This variant of PTC is more common in children and adolescents and shows diffuse involvement of the thyroid by a widely invasive tumor associated with dense fibrous stroma (Fig. 21). Focal squamous metaplasia, numerous

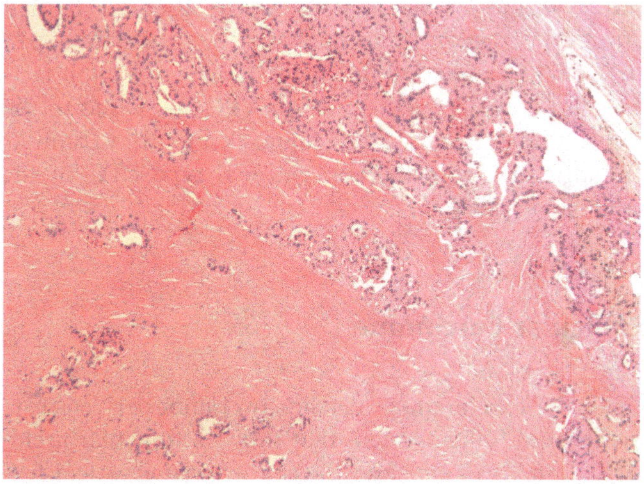

Fig. 21 Papillary thyroid carcinoma, diffuse sclerosing variant with a desmoplastic stroma and infiltrating islands of tumor cells

psammoma bodies, and lymphocytic infiltrate are additional histologic features. Due to the diffuse infiltrative pattern these tumors may not produce a clinically palpable mass, so these patients tend to present at later stage [51]. On ultrasound, they usually manifest diffuse calcification associated with a suspicious mass, which in children and young adults must alert to this diagnosis [197]. The overall survival in these patients is similar to the conventional PTC of same stage but since they tend to present at a higher stage with extrathyroidal extension and higher frequency of lymph node metastasis, a more aggressive surgical treatment is recommended in these patients [198–200]. In Thompson et al.'s series of 22 cases, 5-year disease free survival was seen in 95% and one patient died of disease following transformation of the tumor to squamous cell carcinoma [200].

Prognosis in Papillary Thyroid Carcinoma

With the exception of some more aggressive histologic variants mentioned above papillary carcinoma has an excellent prognosis. The overall 5-year survival rate is 90–95% and 10-year survival rate is 80–95%. Independent adverse prognostic factors include older age (above 45 years), extrathyroidal spread, aggressive histologic variants, and distant metastases [51, 86]. The significance of lymph node metastasis (LNM) as a prognostic factor and the extent of lymph node dissection needed at surgery has been subject of debate. Some studies have shown that while 10-year probability for recurrence is significantly higher in patients with macroscopic LNM the figures for microscopic LNM were similar to patients with no LNM and so in the absence of gross nodal disease a limited prophylactic node dissection may be sufficient [201–203]. While some studies have shown a higher incidence of distance metastasis in FVPC compared to the conventional PTC [134], prognosis in this variant is not different from the conventional type PTC of the same stage [204].

Follicular Carcinoma

Follicular carcinoma is a malignant tumor derived from the thyroid follicular cells that shows a follicular architecture and *does not* show the characteristic nuclear features associated with papillary carcinoma. The latter feature is very important and may be one of the reasons for the decline in the incidence of follicular carcinoma over the years, ever since the follicular variant of papillary carcinoma gained recognition after its description by Chem and Rosai in 1977 [92, 121, 205]. However, follicular carcinoma is still the second commonest malignant tumor after papillary carcinoma accounting for 10% of all thyroid cancers in the USA [85]. In other parts of the world especially in areas with iodine deficiency, the incidence of follicular carcinoma is higher and may be up to 45% of all thyroid cancers [17]. It has been shown that addition of iodine to the diet results in relative increase in papillary carcinoma and corresponding decrease in follicular carcinoma [51]. Follicular carcinoma may occur at any age but most commonly presents in the fifth decade, is rare in childhood unlike PTC, and has the same female predilection of 3:1 as PTC [85, 206–208]. It typically presents as a solitary thyroid nodule that is usually "cold" on radionucleotide scan, sometimes bone metastases may be the presenting feature and unlike PTC follicular carcinoma are not clinically occult [51].

According to the WHO classification of thyroid tumors, follicular carcinoma is subdivided into two groups namely *minimally invasive or encapsulated* and *widely invasive* follicular carcinoma [209]. The distinction into these two groups is important because of their significantly different clinical behavior and treatment [205, 210]. However, what constitutes minimally invasive follicular carcinoma has been the subject of debate and lacks uniform criteria among pathologists, endocrinologists, and surgeons [205, 211]. Some authors have suggested that since angioinvasion is associated with a worse outcome these tumors be separated from minimally invasive carcinoma and terms such as encapsulated angioinvasive carcinoma [212, 213] and moderately invasive [214] have been proposed.

Minimally Invasive (Encapsulated) Follicular Carcinoma

Minimally invasive follicular carcinoma (MIFC) is defined as an encapsulated follicular tumor showing foci of full thickness capsular invasion (Fig. 22) and/or vascular invasion within or outside the capsule (Fig. 23). The capsule in most of these tumors is thick, but cases with thin capsule or uneven poorly formed capsule may also be seen [211]. However, what constitutes *capsular invasion* lacks consensus and both partial and full thickness capsule invasion has been cited as criteria for capsular invasion in the past [17]. A survey of endocrine pathologists revealed lack of consensus on the definition of capsular invasion to diagnose MIFC [205]. In the recent WHO series on classification of tumors, capsular invasion is defined as penetration through the capsule unassociated with previous fine-needle aspiration biopsy (Fig. 22) [82]. There, however, remains a significant interobserver variability in diagnosis of MIFC [215]. For encapsulated follicular tumors with questionable capsular invasion showing no vascular invasion some authors have suggested that they should be classified as follicular tumor of uncertain malignant potential (FT-UMP) [124]. There are reports of follicular carcinoma with capsular invasion only showing distant metastases justifying their designation as carcinoma and appropriate management [216, 217]. The presence of *vascular invasion* is regarded as a definite sign of malignancy; the vascular invasion, however, should be in a blood vessel within or immediately outside the capsule [51, 82]. In minimally invasive carcinoma, the blood vessels outside the capsule are of small or medium size and lack a continuous muscular layer [210, 211]. The tumor cells

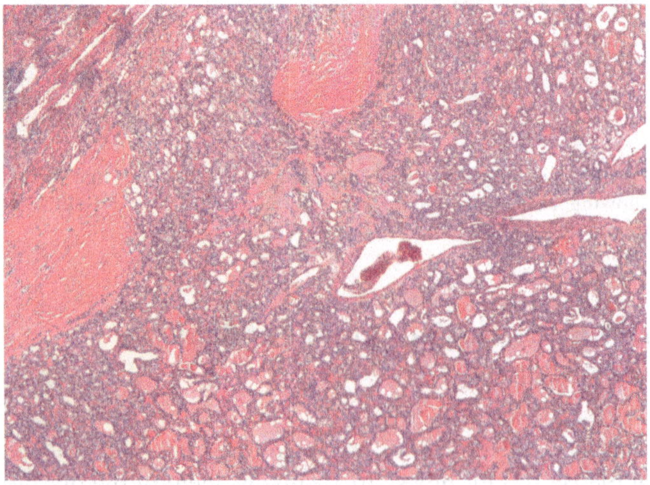

Fig. 22 Minimally invasive follicular carcinoma with full thickness capsular invasion

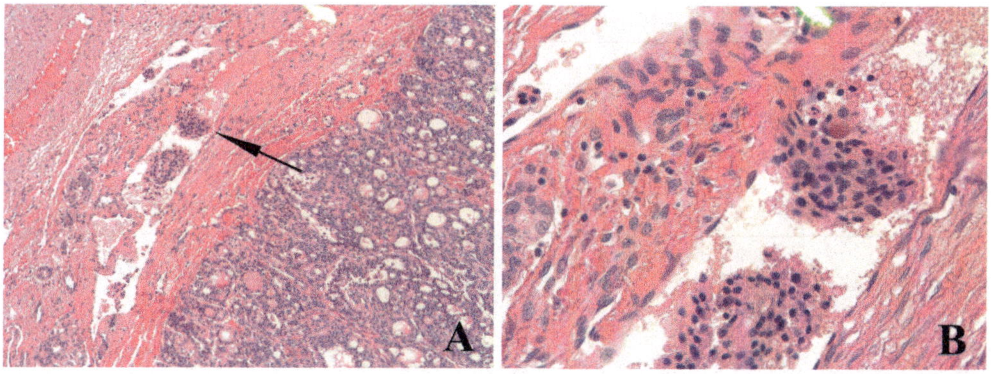

Fig. 23 Follicular carcinoma, encapsulated with angioinvasion. Extracapsular blood vessel with tumor emboli attached to the endothelial surface (*arrow*), with higher magnification of the same in (**B**)

should be present within the vascular lumen like a fibrin thrombus and show attachment to the endothelial surface at some point (Fig. 23) to avoid overdiagnosis by artefactual presence of tumor cells in the blood vessel as a result of dislodging of tumor cells during handling of the specimen at surgery or gross examination. At times tumor cells are seen pushing into the a thin blood vessel from outside causing protrusion of the tumor cells into the lumen with intact endothelial cells on the surface, this should also not be regarded as vascular invasion if strict criteria are adopted [51]. LiVolsi has suggested an approach, which seems practical in that tumors with capsular invasion only are regarded as minimally invasive carcinoma and tumors with vascular invasion designated as angioinvasive grossly encapsulated follicular carcinomas. The angioinvasive tumors have a capacity for hematogenous spread and 50% of these patients die of tumor at 10 years and patients with capsular invasion only have a better prognosis [17]. Further larger series with long-term outcome data applying this classification may be useful in validating its clinical significance. Prognosis in MIFC is excellent and some have suggested that patients may not need to undergo completion thyroidectomy following a diagnosis of MIFC in a lobectomy [218]. Thomson et al. in a series of 95 MIFC, which included cases both with capsular and/or vascular invasion, showed excellent survival. All but one patient were alive after a mean follow-up of 16.8 years. Four patients showed recurrent disease, one of whom died after 15 years; this latter patient was a female who was 49 years old at presentation and had a large 7.0 cm tumor [211]. Distant metastases in MIFC are seen more often in tumors showing vascular invasion so it may be best to regard this as a distinct group as suggested earlier when evaluating the prognosis [219]. In view of the focal nature of capsular and vascular invasion it is important that encapsulated follicular tumors should be evaluated by thorough sampling, which must include examination of the entire capsule. We have found doing multiple serial sections of the capsular region especially in cases with thick fibrous capsule to be helpful in identifying foci of capsular and vascular invasion. The differential diagnosis of MIFC as discussed later includes other follicular patterned lesions such as follicular adenoma, follicular variant of papillary carcinoma, and hyperplastic colloid nodule (see Table 2). Furthermore, many ancillary tests using immunohistochemistry and molecular diagnosis techniques as mentioned later have been found to be helpful in the diagnosis of equivocal follicular lesions (Table 2). However, thorough sampling and careful morphologic evaluation still may be the best diagnostic method at present, which can be supported by additional ancillary studies in difficult cases.

Widely Invasive Follicular Carcinoma

The diagnosis of this subtype of follicular carcinoma is fairly straightforward; on gross examination, the tumor has widely invasive edges with foci of necrosis; microscopy reveals a follicular tumor, often with solid or trabecular areas and invasion of the surrounding thyroid parenchyma. The tumor cells may show high mitotic rate and areas of necrosis may be seen. In some cases there may be transformation into a poorly differentiated (insular) or an anaplastic phenotype indicating the progression of differentiated carcinoma to poorly differentiated and anaplastic phenotype (Fig. 24). These tumors spread to distant organs through blood vessels and up to 80% may develop systemic metastases. The prognosis is much worse than MIFC, the 10-year survival in these patients is 25–45% as opposed to 70–100% in the MIFC group [17, 51]. Various prognostic scoring schemes have been suggested, most including variables such as patient's age, tumor size and extent of invasion, presence of vascular invasion,

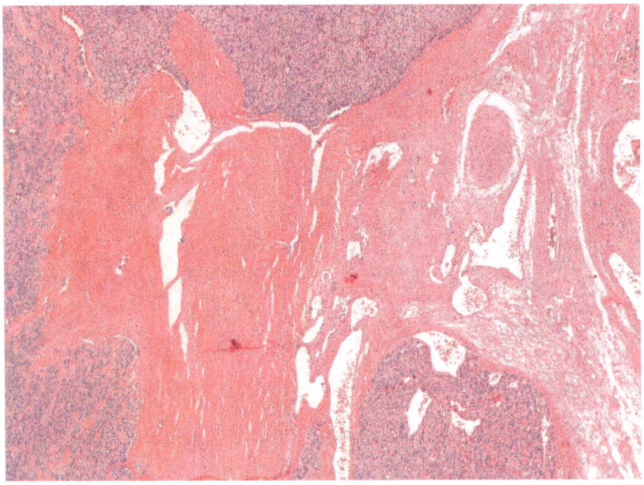

Fig. 24 Widely invasive follicular carcinoma with a broad front of capsular invasion

and metastasis, all of which seem to be important prognostic factors [220].

Oncocytic (Hurthle Cell) Tumors

Thyroid follicular cells with oncocytic feature including finely granular abundant eosinophilic cytoplasm were first described by Askanazy in 1898, the cells that were described by Hurthle in the thyroid of a dog are thought to represent the parafollicular C cells [51]. However, the term Hurthle cell for oncocytic thyroid cells that were actually described by Askanazy has been so engrained in our minds that people continue to use this terminology. The AFIP fascicle on thyroid tumors has proposed to designate these tumors as oncocytic tumors and in the recent WHO classification of thyroid tumors, these tumors are classified as variants of follicular adenoma and follicular carcinoma [51, 82]. Montone et al. recently reviewed oncocytic lesions of the thyroid that include both neoplastic and non-neolastic types [172]. Oncocytic tumors are a rare group of thyroid neoplasm, with oncocytic (Hurthle cell) carcinoma comprising 3.6% of all thyroid cancers in the USA [85]. While it is derived from the thyroid follicular cells, oncocytic carcinoma has a distinct oncogenic expression, which is different from the follicular and papillary carcinoma [221]. Oncocytic tumors are divided in to two categories, the benign tumor as adenoma and the malignant counterpart as oncocytic carcinoma [222]. Some earlier studies suggested that all oncocytic (Hurthle cell) neoplasms irrespective of their size have the propensity of distant metastases and should be regarded as carcinoma [223, 224]. This view, however, now is universally not accepted and oncocytic tumors are classified as adenoma or carcinoma based on the capsular and/or vascular invasion criteria identical to the follicular adenoma/carcinoma discussed above.

Oncocytic Adenoma

Oncocytic adenoma is a completely encapsulated tumor with a distinct brown smooth and homogenous cut surface; foci of hemorrhage and necrosis may be seen as secondary changes. On microscopic examination the tumor is composed of large polygonal cells with abundant finely granular eosinophilic cytoplasm arranged in a follicular pattern with areas of solid/trabecular growth. Predominance of solid or trabecular pattern should raise the suspicion for malignancy and warrants careful evaluation of the capsule [51]. The tumor cell nuclei have a vesicular chromatin and may show significant atypia, hyperchromasia, and pleomorphism, which should not be mistaken as malignancy. Foci of clear cell change may be seen, which is regarded as a degenerative phenomenon, and sometimes the predominant lesion may have clear cell morphology (Fig. 25). The tumor may show areas of ischemic necrosis, which may sometimes involve the entire lesion making histologic evaluation difficult, this is most commonly seen following needle aspiration biopsy [51].

The distinction between oncocytic adenoma and carcinoma is based on the finding of capsular and/or vascular invasion like in the case of follicular tumors. This can sometimes be difficult and require extensive sampling of the capsule. Some studies have suggested that size is helpful in differentiating oncocytic adenoma from carcinoma with tumors larger than 4.0 cm being more likely to be malignant compared to the smaller tumors, other immunohistochemical markers such as Ki67 and cyclin D1 expression have also been found to help in the differential diagnosis of oncocytic adenoma and carcinoma [224–227].

Oncocytic Carcinoma

Oncocytic carcinoma is a rare malignant thyroid tumor that is more common in females, with a female to male ratio approaching 2:1, which is less than papillary or follicular carcinoma (female to male ratio for oncocytic adenoma is 8:1). While it can occur at any age it is most commonly seen in the elderly, which is a decade later than the oncocytic adenoma [85]. Therefore, an oncocytic

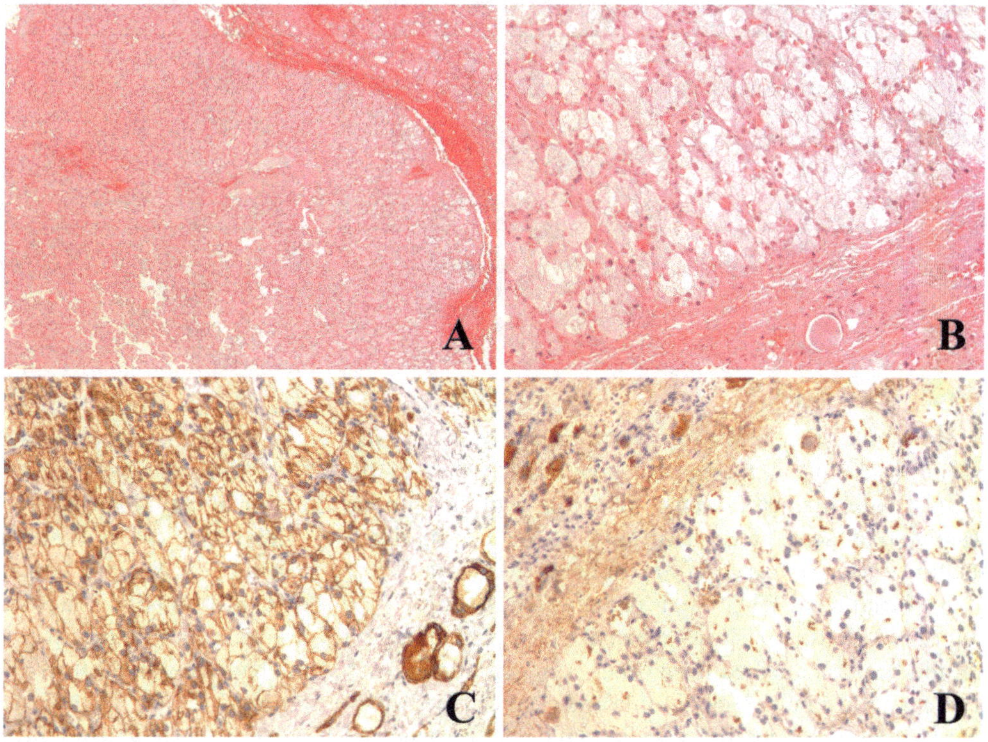

Fig. 25 Hurthle cell (oncocytic) adenoma with diffuse clear cell change (**A, B**). On immunohistochemistry the tumor cells are positive for pancytokeratin (**C**), and thyroglobulin (**D**)

tumor in an elderly male especially if it is larger than 5.0 cm should raise suspicion of malignancy.

On gross examination oncocytic carcinoma are larger than their benign counterpart, although with a wide size range, show a brown cut surface with more marked areas of hemorrhage and necrosis and at times may show cystic degeneration in the center (Fig. 26). Histological examination most often shows a solid/trabecular growth pattern (Fig. 27B) as opposed to predominantly follicular pattern seen in adenoma and while the hallmark of malignancy is the presence of capsular and vascular invasion as described earlier in follicular carcinoma, certain cytological feature may be helpful. In carcinoma there is increase in the nuclear size with greater percentage of cells being tall columnar as opposed to round or polygonal seen in adenoma [51]. In addition there is more hyperchromasia and mitoses in carcinoma compared to adenoma. In some cases areas of clear cell change may be seen and these may sometimes predominate. Oncocytic carcinoma is also designated as *minimally invasive* or *widely invasive* using the same criteria as described earlier in follicular carcinoma. This distinction is important because of significant difference in the biologic behavior of the two groups. In one study, no patient with minimally invasive carcinoma died of disease after median follow-up of 8 years, while of the widely invasive carcinoma group 73% relapsed and 55% died of disease. Adverse prognostic factors include extrathyroidal extension, nodal metastases, positive margin at surgery, and solid growth pattern. Of these, extrathyroidal extension and nodal metastases are independent predictors of prognosis on a multivariate analyses [222, 228]. Ghossein et al. reported high mitotic rate and solid/trabecular growth pattern is associated with four or more foci of vascular invasion that carried a high risk of local recurrence [229].

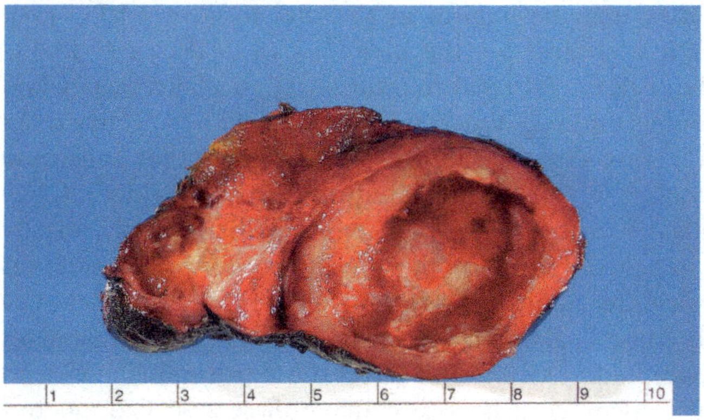

Fig. 26 Hurthle cell (oncocytic) carcinoma, minimally invasive with central area of cystic degeneration

Differential Diagnosis

The diagnosis of oncocytic neoplasm in most cases is made by the distinctive oncocytic nature of the cells.

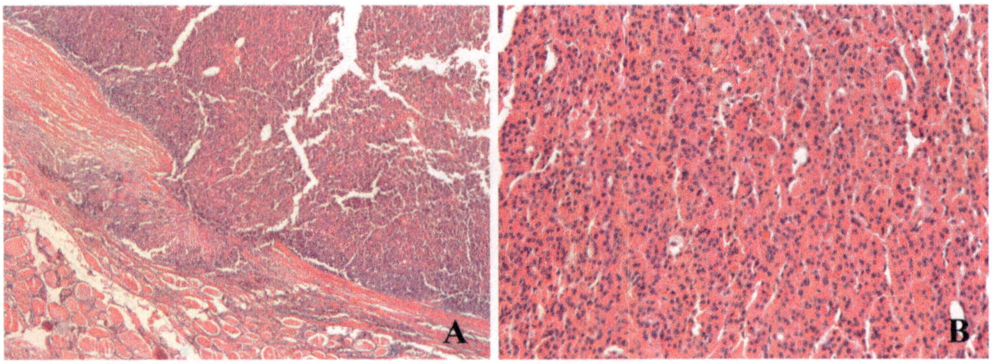

Fig. 27 Hurthle cell (oncocytic) carcinoma, minimally invasive with focal transcapsular invasion (**A**) and trabecular and solid architecture and characteristic oncocytic cytomorphology (**B**)

Evaluation of the tumor capsule is needed to distinguish adenoma from carcinoma, as mentioned earlier in the case of follicular carcinoma. In the case of carcinoma, lesions that sometimes may have to be distinguished include oncocytic variant of medullary carcinoma, oncocytic variant of PTC, and parathyroid oxyphil type tumor. If the tumor shows extensive clear cell change it should be distinguished from other clear cell tumors such as metastatic renal cell carcinoma and clear cell medullary carcinoma. For medullary carcinoma, the presence of amyloid and positive immunohistochemical staining with chromogranin, calcitonin, calcitonin gene-related peptide, and CEA are helpful. Nuclear changes of PTC can help in distinguishing oncocytic tumor from oncocytic variant of PTC. Oncocytic tumors may sometimes exhibit a predominantly papillary architecture comprising of papillae without a well developed fibrovascular core, these tumors are sometimes designated as oncocytic papillary neoplasms and should be distinguished from oncocytic variant of PTC [51].

Differential Diagnosis of Follicular-Patterned Lesions of the Thyroid

Morphology

Thyroid follicular lesions that can sometimes pose a challenge to the surgical pathologist include capsulated or unencapsulated lesions with a follicular architecture comprising varying sized follicles filled with variable amount of colloid. The four most important and common lesions that have to be differentiated in this category include *hyperplastic(adenomatous) colloid nodule (HPN)*, *follicular adenoma (FA)*, *follicular carcinoma (FC)*, and *follicular variant of papillary carcinoma (FVPC)*. The problems most often encountered are in the distinction of HPN from FA and differentiation of FA from minimally invasive follicular carcinoma (MIFC) and FVPC.

The features that help in the differential diagnosis of these follicular lesions are outlined in Table 2 and a practical diagnostic approach is outlined in Fig. 28

Hyperplastic nodules usually lack a well-developed capsule, occur in the background of multinodular goiter, and are mostly macrofollicular or normofollicular. Some lesions may have an incomplete capsule and be microfollicular [230]. While the demonstration of capsular and/or vascular invasion is the sole criteria of distinguishing follicular adenoma from follicular carcinoma, what constitutes capsular and vascular invasion as discussed earlier is controversial with significant inter and intraobserver variability and lacks consensus among pathologists, surgeons, and endocrinologists [205, 215, 231, 232]. A thick fibrous capsule should raise suspicion and warrants a careful and complete evaluation of the tumor capsule in search for vascular and/or capsular invasion. Multiple cuts of a section may have to be examined. The diagnosis of follicular variant of papillary carcinoma (FVPC) is based on the presence of characteristic nuclear features of papillary carcinoma as discussed earlier [51, 231–233]. These nuclear changes however may at times be focal and not be well appreciated making diagnosis of FVPC difficult in these cases. In addition to the nuclear changes the staining quality of the colloid and presence of stromal fibrous bands may sometimes be helpful in the diagnosis of FVPC [51]. While criteria for the diagnosis of MIFC and FVPC have been discussed in multiple studies and clearly laid out as outlined above, from a practical perspective there remains a minor subset of these tumors that constitute the 'gray zone lesions' and are difficult to definitively classify as benign or malignant. Williams et al. initially proposed a terminology for such 'borderline' lesions that was later adopted by the WHO working group and has become a part of their classification. However, this is not accepted by all and still leaves the treating clinicians with the dilemma of how to manage these so-called indeterminate lesions [231, 232]. Immunohistochemistry, which is now widely used in most laboratories and easy to

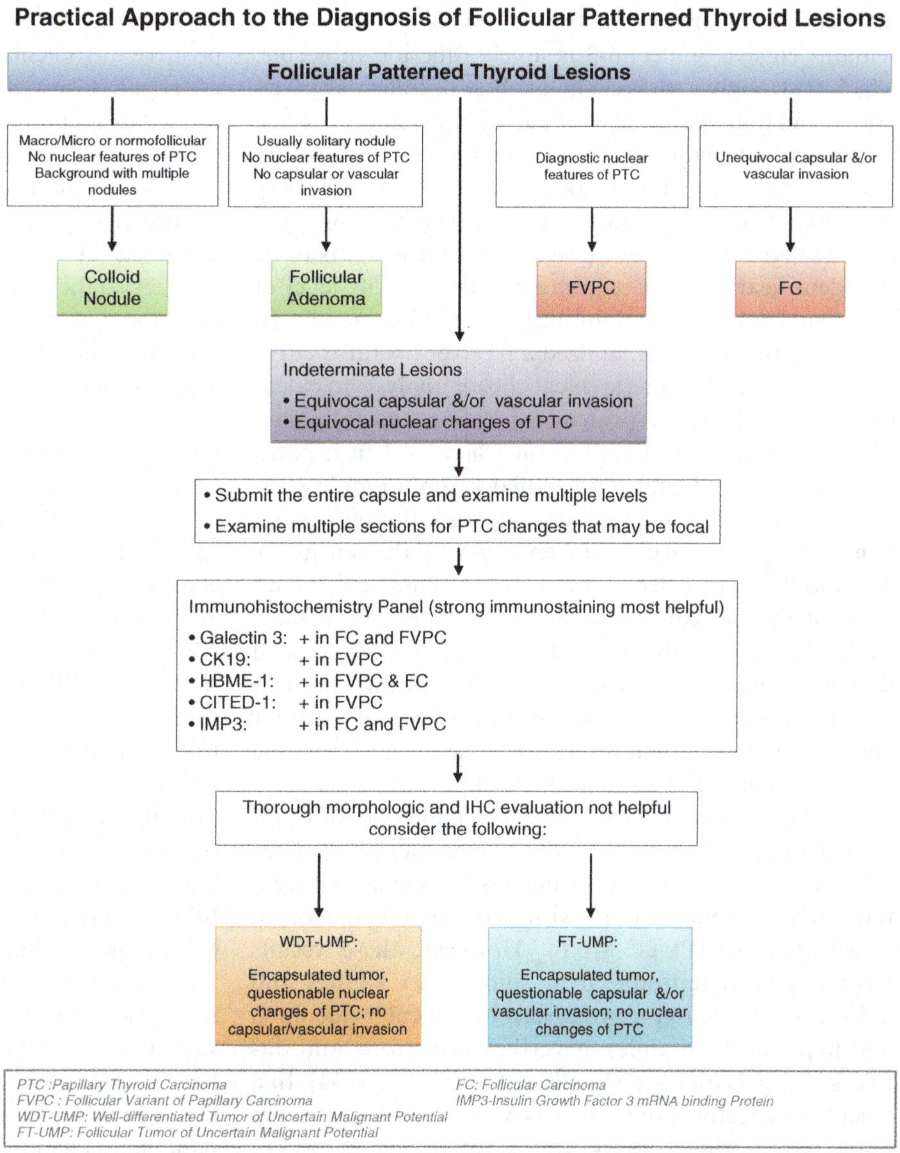

Fig. 28 Diagnostic approach to follicular patterned thyroid lesions

perform, may some times help in this differential diagnosis. As discussed later in Chapter 18 some studies have found molecular diagnostic tests also to be helpful. However, there seems to be some overlap in the immunophenotype and molecular diagnostic tests between morphologically benign, malignant, and so called indeterminate group of lesions suggesting that if additional larger studies with clinical correlations can reproduce these observations we may in the future be able reclassify thyroid follicular tumors based on their molecular signature.

Immunohistochemistry

There is a long list of immunohistochemical markers that have been studied to evaluate thyroid follicular lesions and to differentiate benign from malignant lesions; some that have been found to be helpful include galectin-3, HBME-1-1, high molecular weight cytokeratin (CK19), CITED-1, ret/PTC oncogene, peroxisome proliferator-activated receptor γ (PAX8-PPARγ), CD44v6, CD57, and intracellular sodium/iodide symporter (iNIS) (for review see [234–236]. While some have shown great promise especially when used as part of a panel, the 'magic marker' with high sensitivity and 100% specificity still remains elusive. Galectin-3 is a cell adhesion molecule, which is strongly expressed in a subset of follicular carcinoma, and follicular variant of papillary carcinoma, while the normal thyroid tissue and benign follicular lesions are either negative or show weak expression [234, 237–247]. Since expression of galectin-3 may be seen in benign and normal thyroid tissue one practical problem seems to be the identification of a semi-quantitative cut-off level of expression as a threshold for diagnosis of malignancy. To overcome this Liu et al. utilized a receiver operator curve (ROC) analysis and hierarchical cluster analysis to calculate the threshold for protein expression and they concluded that galectin-3 expression when used in a panel with fibronectin-1 and intracellular sodium/iodide symporter had a 98% accuracy in diagnosis thyroid malignancy [243]. In a large multicenter study, the sensitivity and specificity of galectin-3 immunostaining in the diagnosis of thyroid carcinoma was 99% and 98%, respectively. In view of this data, Bartolazzi et al. suggested that if a encapsulated follicular tumor (adenoma) was galectin-3 positive but did not show evidence of capsular and/or vascular invasion on morphology, it is possible that malignant transformation in these cases may have taken place at the molecular level preceding the morphological alteration associated with malignancy [237]. They referred these tumors to as suspicious adenomas or potential early thyroid cancers with molecular evidence of transformation (PETC-MET). However, these results have not been reproduced in some other studies and galectin-3 expression may be seen in follicular adenoma and hyperplastic nodules, nevertheless a strong and diffuse staining is highly suggestive of carcinoma [234]. In a recent prospective study on FNA samples for selecting patients requiring surgery, the sensitivity of galectin-3 was 78% with a 93% specificity, suggesting that while galectin-3 immunostaining cannot replace the morphologic evaluation it can serve as complimentary test [248]. HBME-1, which is strongly positive in more than 40% of thyroid carcinoma of both follicular and papillary types and is negative or focally positive in hyperplastic colloid nodule and follicular adenoma [234, 249–251]. When used in combination with galectin-3, Rossi et al. found that co-expression of HBME-1 and galectin-3 has a diagnostic accuracy rate of almost 98% for the diagnosis of papillary carcinoma including the follicular variant [252]. Furthermore, in follicular tumors of uncertain malignant potential, Papotti et al. found that strong and diffuse expression of galectin-3 and HBME-1 is helpful in classifying some of these lesions as malignant [253]. Cell cycle regulatory proteins such as p27 are downregulated in follicular carcinoma and follicular variant of papillary carcinoma and is diffusely positive in hyperplastic nodules and follicular adenoma [254, 255]. Cytokeratin19 and CD57 are also positive in follicular variant of papillary carcinoma and are negative or weakly positive in hyperplastic nodule and follicular adenoma [249, 256–260]. However, in another study a subset of follicular adenomas were also positive for CK 19 along with follicular carcinoma suggesting caution in relying on one single marker for the differential diagnosis of benign versus malignant follicular lesion [260]. Also the sensitivity of CK19 expression in papillary carcinoma is around 60% and therefore a negative staining is not helpful [234]. Some authors have suggested that a panel including CK-19, HBME-1 and ret/PTC [249], CK-19, HBME-1, and CD57 [257] improves sensitivity and specificity in differentiating benign and malignant follicular lesions of the thyroid. Kroll et al. first reported in 2000 that PAX8-PPARγ fusion oncogene is highly specific for follicular carcinoma [261]. Following Kroll et al.'s report there have been a number of studies looking at PAX8-PPARγ expression in thyroid follicular tumors, while some have supported their findings others did not find PAX8-PPARγ fusion to be specific for follicular carcinoma and it may be seen in a significant number of follicular adenoma and follicular variant of papillary carcinoma [138, 139, 231, 234, 262–265]. Retinoblastoma protein expression is decreased in follicular variant of papillary carcinoma compared to follicular adenoma [266]. Other biomarkers that have been found to be helpful in differentiating benign and malignant thyroid follicular tumors include CITED-1 [267], CD44v6, and CD57 [256, 268–270], ret/PTC rearrangement and immunohistochemical expression while commonly associated with a subset of conventional papillary thyroid carcinoma [271] has also been reported in FVPC [272]. Since no one marker is both highly sensitive and specific using some in a panel may be more helpful and some studies have found these panels very valuable. These panels include galectin-3 and HBME-1 [253], HBME-1 and galectin-3 [252], galectin-3, fibronectin-1, CITED-1, HBME-1, CK19, PAX-8-PPARγ [243], galectin-3, fibronectin-1, CITED-1, HBME-1, CK19 [273–275], galectin-3, CITED-1, HBME-1, CK19, cyclin D1, p27 [276], and galectin-3 and TPO [277]. We have recently reported another potential marker, insulin growth factor 3 mRNA binding protein (IMP3) that has 100% specificity for diagnosing thyroid malignancy with a follicular pattern but has a low sensitivity [278] (Fig. 29B, unpublished data). We think careful morphologic evaluation is still most important in the differential diagnosis of follicular thyroid lesions and immunohistochemistry when used by employing a panel of markers may be helpful in a small group of lesions where morphology alone is not diagnostic. In our practice we use a panel of CK19, HBME-1, CITED-1, galectin-3, and IMP3 and have found it to be helpful in

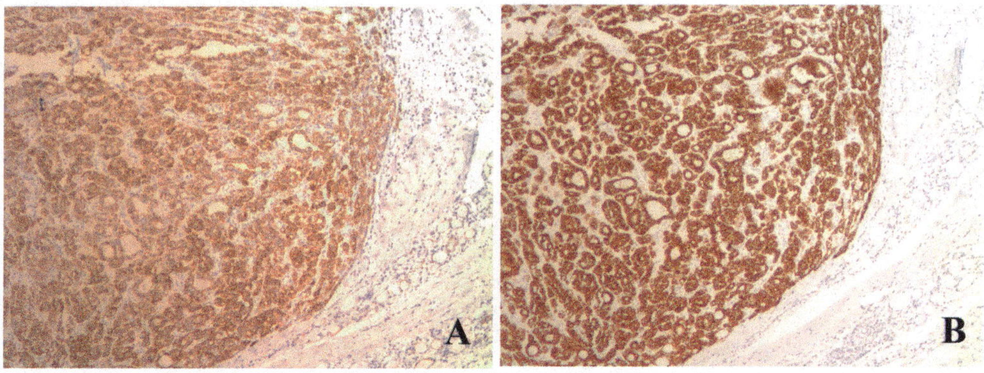

Fig. 29 Follicular variant of papillary carcinoma on immunohistochemistry strongly positive for CK19 (**A**) and IMP3 (**B**). Normal residual thyroid on the *right* in both A and B is negative

the diagnosis of morphologically challenging follicular lesions (Fig. 26A–D). However, the search for newer biomarkers is still on and with progress made in the field of molecular diagnostic methods and informatics, gene expression profiling using cDNA microarray is being employed to identify new candidate genes that can be studied at the protein level by immunohistochemistry. Some genes identified by gene expression profile that have been studied by immunohistochemistry and found useful include, PDGF, Bax, P-cadherin, and c-MET [244, 279, 280].

Poorly Differentiated Carcinoma

Differentiated thyroid carcinoma of both papillary and follicular type may progress to a more poorly differentiated phenotype. Poorly differentiated thyroid carcinoma (PDTC) is a heterogenous group that may present as more distinct morphologic entity referred to as insular carcinoma or a group of less well-defined morphologic phenotype. The latter group of PDTC, which has included entities such as columnar and tall variants of papillary carcinoma and tumors with solid and trabecular architecture, has been controversial with its inclusion as distinct category in question [281]. In the non-insular group after excluding the aggressive variants of PTC, this group of tumor presents as a distinct biological group similar to the insular group, so their classification as PDTC seems justified (see Volante et al. for review [282]). Hiltzik et al. from Memorial Sloan-Kettering Cancer Center defined PDTC on the basis of mitosis (5 or more per 10 HPF) and necrosis and found that these criteria identified a more aggressive subset of thyroid carcinoma independent of the growth pattern [283]. More recently a working group comprising of thyroid pathologists from USA, Europe, and Japan at a consensus meeting following review of 83 cases have come up with a uniform diagnostic criteria for the diagnosis of PDTC, that includes presence of solid/trabecular/insular growth pattern, absence of nuclear features of PTC, and presence of at least one of the following: convoluted nuclei; mitotic activity of 3 or more per 10 HPF; and tumor necrosis; This has come to be known as the "Turin proposal" [284].

Insular Carcinoma

Insular carcinoma is a morphologically distinct form of PDTC derived from the thyroid follicular cells having an aggressive biological course. The incidence of these tumors varies from being rare in the USA to about 4% of all thyroid cancers seen in an Italian study [51]. It is not uncommon to see foci of insular growth associated with differentiated thyroid carcinoma of both papillary and follicular types. Yamashita et al. in a series of 82 follicular carcinoma reported presence of an insular component in eight (10%) and furthermore, presence of insular component was an independent risk factor for distant metastasis [285]. Insular carcinoma tends to involve elderly patients with a slight female predilection.

On gross examination these tumors are large in size, exhibit an invasive growth with associated areas of necrosis (Fig. 30). On histology they are composed of

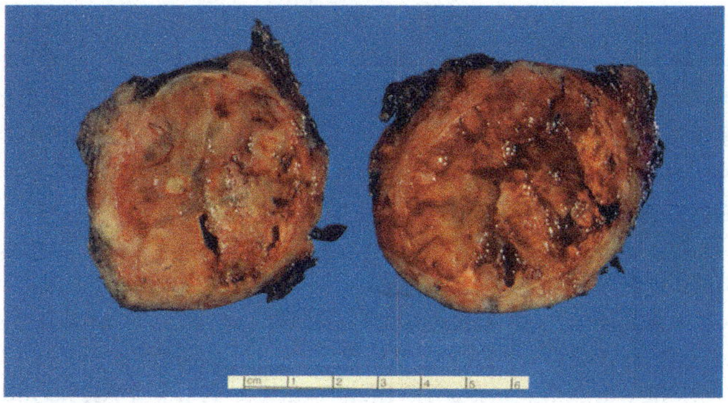

Fig. 30 Insular carcinoma, diffusely invasive involving the entire lobe with a variegated cut surface and areas of hemorrhage and necrosis

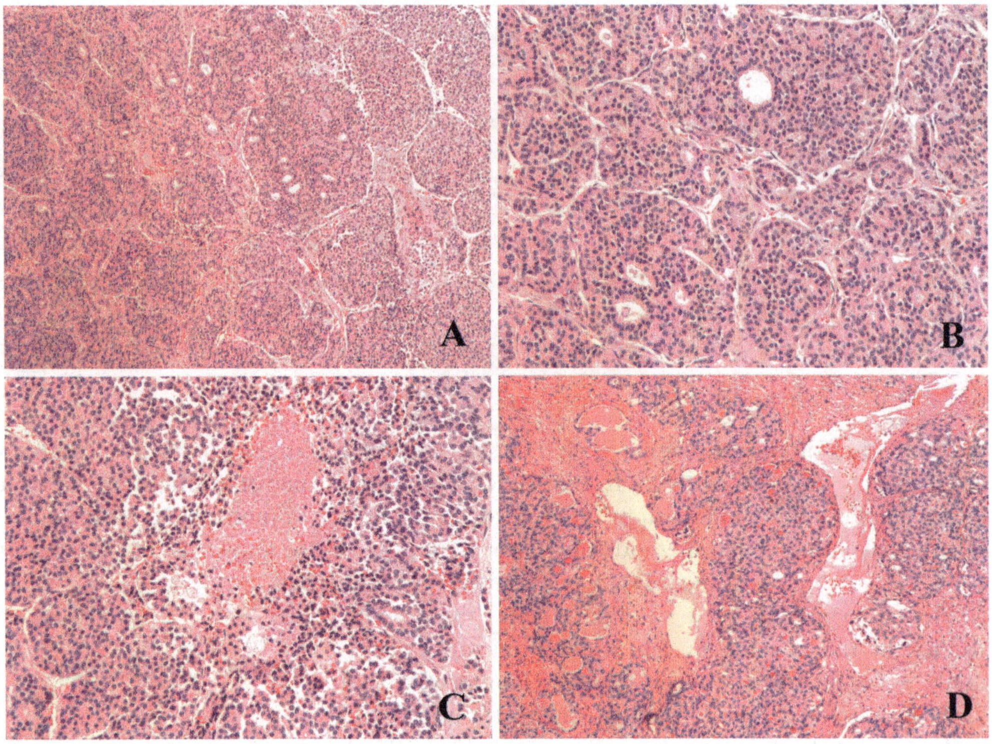

Fig. 31 Insular carcinoma, with typical islands of tumor cells including microfollicular areas (**A, B**), foci of central necrosis in these islands (**C**) and a peritheliomatous infiltration of tumor cells around vascular structures

well-defined islands of round or oval cells which lack significant pleomorphism. Small microfollicular structures may be seen within these islands, it is not uncommon to see necrosis in the center of these islands and a peritheliomatous pattern of infiltration by tumor cells (Fig. 31A–D). Foci of vascular invasion are not infrequent and rhabdoid type cells with eosinophilic intracytoplasmic inclusions have also been reported [286].

Differential Diagnosis

The tumor that insular carcinoma should be differentiated from and can pose problems on morphology is medullary carcinoma. Immunohistochemistry is very useful in these situations. Insular carcinoma cells are positive for thyroglobulin and TTF-1 and negative for calcitonin and other neuroendocrine markers. Other primary tumor that may have to be differentiated is the solid variant of papillary carcinoma in which the nuclear features of papillary carcinoma are helpful in the differential diagnosis [178, 179].

PDTC is associated with a prognosis worse than differentiated thyroid carcinoma but better than anaplastic carcinoma. In a series of 49 PDTC Jung et al. reported a 5-year survival rate of 68%, which was similar in both insular and non-insular type. In their study adverse prognostic factors on univariate analysis included age 45 years or more, tumor size larger than 4 cm, extra-thyroidal invasion, cervical node metastasis, distant metastasis, absence of high-dose radioactive iodine (RAI) therapy, and TNM stage II, III, and IV. However, distant metastasis was the only independent prognostic factor [287].

Anaplastic Carcinoma

Anaplastic thyroid carcinoma is a highly aggressive and rare thyroid tumor accounting for 1.7% of all thyroid cancers in the USA [85]. Its incidence is higher in regions endemic for goiter [288]. The patients are usually elderly in their seventh or eight decade of life, with a female preponderance of around 2.5:1. Personal history of goiter may be seen in approximately 25% of cases and prior exposure to radiation in 9.4% cases. Clinical presentation includes rapidly enlarging neck mass associated with compressing symptoms such as dysphagia, hoarseness, and stridor. Often signs and symptoms related to metastatic tumor may be the first presentation [51, 85]. On gross examination the tumor is usually large, majority being larger than 4.0 cm, often replacing the entire thyroid and spreading in to the perithyroidal soft tissues. On microscopic examination, the tumor may exhibit one of the several patterns or a mixture of more than one of these patterns including squamoid pattern resembling the nonkeratinizing squamous cell carcinoma, spindle cell pattern

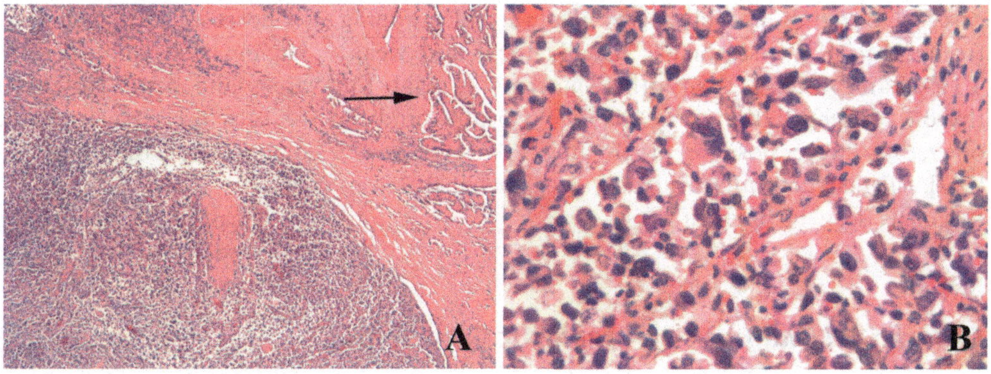

Fig. 32 Anaplastic carcinoma, giant cell type arising in the background of differentiated papillary carcinoma (*arrow*)

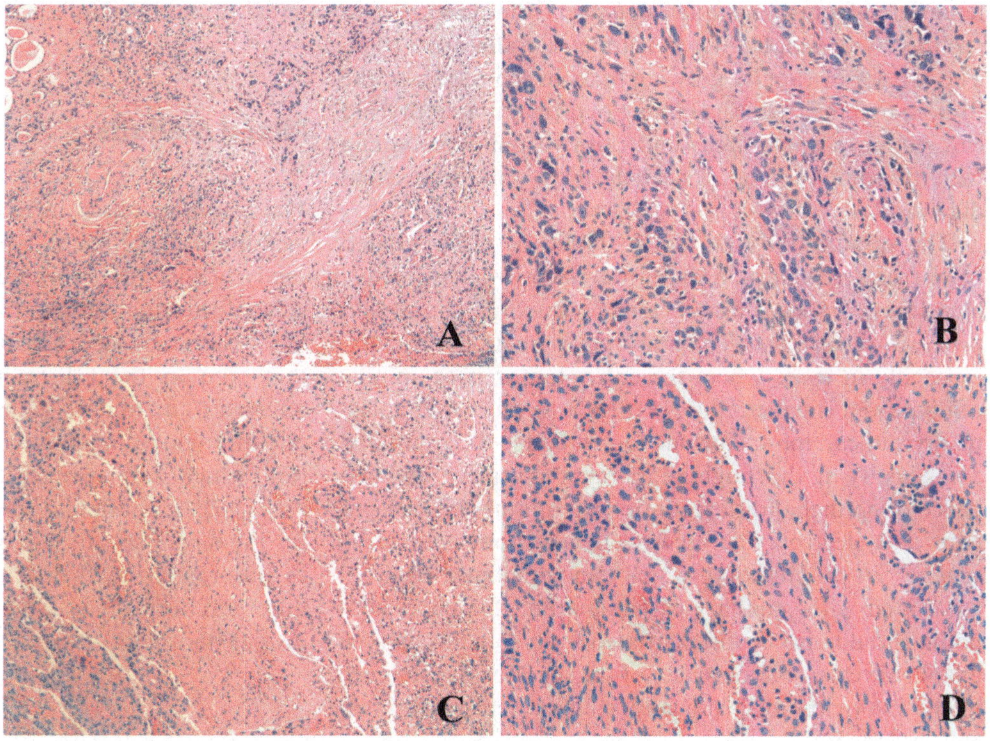

Fig. 33 Anaplastic carcinoma with spindle cell areas (**A, B**) and squamoid foci with focal keratinization (**C, D**)

resembling sarcoma, and giant cell type (Figs. 32 and 33) and small cell carcinoma-like pattern. All these types of patterns are associated with high mitotic rate and focal necrosis may be seen. The spindle cell sarcoma-like pattern may show paucicellular areas with dense fibrosis, which may alternate, with cellular areas that aid in the diagnosis of anaplastic thyroid carcinoma [17, 51]. The giant cell pattern is associated with marked degree of pleomorphism with large multinucleated cells including tumor giant cells. The tumors are highly invasive with infiltration of the perithyroidal soft tissues. In some cases heterologous stromal elements including cartilage, bone, and rhabdomyoblastic differentiation may be seen [51, 289, 290]. The key to the diagnosis of ATC in most cases is the identification of differentiated thyroid carcinoma that may have progressed to ATC. Albores-Saavedra et al. reported rhabdoid inclusions in PDTC and ATC but not in differentiated component of the tumor, which instead had intracytoplasmic thyroglobulin inclusions suggesting dedifferentiation of PTC and FC to ATC [291]. There is evidence of alteration of certain molecular pathways [51, 292] in the progression of thyroid cancer such as p53 and β-catenin mutations, the latter leading to derangement of E-cadherin/β-catenin complex [293–296]. These studies and others have also provided some insights into potential targets for treating ATC; these targets include EGFR, β-catenin, cyclin E, and cyclin D1 [297, 298].

On immunohistochemistry the squamoid type tumors are positive for high and low molecular weight keratin, EMA, and sometimes CEA. The spindle cell pattern shows variable positivity with low molecular weight keratin ranging in incidence from 47 to 100%

cases. Thyroglobulin staining is also variable ranging from 9 to 71% cases and is usually focal and weak, TTF-1 and TTF-2, two other markers crucial for thyroid differentiation may also be variable and in one study were positive in 18 and 7% respectively [292]. Ultrastructurally evidence of epithelial differentiation is seen in most tumors.

Differential Diagnosis of Anaplastic Carcinoma

The squamoid type anaplastic carcinoma should be differentiated from *metastatic carcinoma* from primary sites such as lung, esophagus, and upper aerodigestive tract. The history of rapidly growing mass in the region of the thyroid together with the finding of differentiated thyroid carcinoma in some areas and positive immunostaining with thyroglobulin may be helpful in this differential diagnosis.

The spindle cell type tumor should be differentiated from true *sarcoma* such as *fibrosarcoma, leimyosarcoma, malignant fibrous histiocytoma, angiosarcoma*, and *hemangiopericytoma.* This may pose greatest difficulty, especially in cases where the entire tumor is of spindle cell type and is paucicelluar. Features that favor anaplastic thyroid carcinoma include foci of better-differentiated areas justifying thorough sampling of the tumor and evidence of epithelial differentiation on immunohistochemistry and electron microscopy. In addition *metaplastic spindle cell proliferation,* which can sometimes be seen, associated with papillary carcinoma and follicular adenoma should also be differentiated from spindle cell type anaplastic carcinoma because of the significant difference in the biological behavior and management of the two entities [54–56].

Medullary thyroid carcinoma may show a variety of growth patterns and this may have to be differentiated from the spindle cell type and pleomorphic variants of anaplastic carcinoma. Immunohistochemistry plays a very important role in this differentiation and must be performed using antibodies to calcitonin, chromogranin, and CEA, which are all positive in medullary carcinoma [51].

Malignant lymphoma may also be considered in cases with small cells; however, the even distribution of smaller, uniform cells in lymphoma and lack of focal epithelial islands are helpful in this differential diagnosis [51].

Riedel's thyroiditis may be confused with the paucicellular spindle cell type anaplastic thyroid carcinoma, which may show marked sclerosis and lack significant pleomorphism and mitotic activity. In these cases, features that favor anaplastic carcinoma include presence of necrosis, more cellular areas, and evidence of vascular invasion and metastases [17]. The more cellular areas and better differentiated thyroid carcinoma may be seen on extensive sampling, which is crucial in the diagnosis of anaplastic carcinoma in these problematic cases.

The prognosis in anaplastic thyroid carcinoma is extremely poor with 5-year survival ranging from 0 to 14%, and mean survival being 7.2 +/−10 months [51, 82]. Prognosis is related to extent of disease at presentation and rare cases that do better are tumors localized to thyroid that are less than 5 cm in size and include microscopic foci of anaplastic carcinoma, in the background of differentiated thyroid carcinoma [82].

Mixed Medullary and Follicular Carcinoma

These tumors show mixed morphology including both medullary and follicular patterns and mixed immunoreactivity with thyroglobulin and calcitonin [299–305]. In view of this dual differentiation some have proposed the idea of common stem cell origin for thyroid cells similar to that seen in the GI tract [1]. Composite tumors are referred to as tumors with two distinct cell populations, one thyroglobulin positive and the other of C cell derivation, which stains with calcitonin on immunohistochemistry [17]. Immunohistochemistry should be performed for the diagnosis of these mixed tumors and will also aid in differentiating these tumors from progression of a differentiated tumor with follicular architecture to an insular poorly differentiated phenotype.

Role of Intraoperative Frozen Sections in the Management of Thyroid Nodules

Intraoperative evaluation of thyroid nodules by frozen section (FS) has been the subject of numerous studies over the years. It was used with a higher frequency in the past when preoperative diagnosis by fine-needle aspiration cytology (FNAC) was not widely available making intraoperative evaluation a valuable exercise [306]. The accuracy of FNAC for thyroid malignancy is 90–97% and approaches close to 100% in papillary thyroid carcinoma (PTC), [307–310] based on which definitive surgery can be planned without doing FS. The problem, however, seems to be the follicular pattern lesions in which the accuracy of both FNAC and FS is lower and almost similar [311, 312]. There are studies in the literature on both sides, some making a case for intraoperative frozen section being a valuable tool in the surgical management of thyroid nodules [313–317], while others arguing that FS adds little to the surgical planning in this era of improved preoperative diagnosis of thyroid nodules by FNAC [311, 312, 318, 319]. In two studies; one from Johns Hopkins and the other from Memorial Sloan Kettering, surgical management was altered in less than 5% of cases due to a FS diagnosis [312, 318]. We think that FS is not needed in cases diagnosed as malignant on FNAC because of a high specificity. Secondly, in cases diagnosed as follicular neoplasm or suspicious for follicular neoplasm FS may add little because of limited sampling during intraoperative evaluation. FS may fail to show capsular or vascular invasion needed for diagnosis of follicular carcinoma and nuclear changes required for the diagnosis of follicular variant of papillary carcinoma may be focal and at times better appreciated in formalin fixed tissue. Furthermore, it is well known that freezing may cause artefactual nuclear clearing leading to a false positive diagnosis of follicular variant of papillary carcinoma [320]. One situation where FS may be useful is in the cases where the FNAC is either nondiagnostic/unsatisfactory [314] or is suspicious for papillary thyroid carcinoma [310]. In the latter situation imprint cytology along with FS may be valuable since the nuclear changes of papillary carcinoma are better appreciated on a cytological preparation [306].

Other Rare Epithelial Tumors of the Thyroid

Mucoepidermoid Carcinoma

Primary mucoepidermoid carcinoma (MEC) of the thyroid is rare but has generated interest among pathologists with respect to its cell of origin, which has included solid cell nests, follicular cells, and even C cells. On histologic examination some thyroid MEC may show marked stromal sclerosis and tissue eosinophilia in addition to the characteristic squamoid and mucin producing areas, as seen in these tumors in other locations (Fig. 34) [17, 321–325]. The presence of marked tissue eosinophilia and sclerosis may mimic Hodgkin's disease in lymph node metastases of these tumors and should be considered in the differential diagnosis [326] and this may be even more important when evaluating cervical lymph nodes involved by the tumor [327]. Other diagnostic pitfall includes nodular tumor like squamous metaplasia that may be associated with fibrosing variant of Hashimoto's thyroiditis [328].

Squamous Cell Carcinoma

Primary squamous cell carcinoma of the thyroid is rare; spindle cell squamous cell carcinoma has been described in association with tall cell variant of papillary carcinoma and is regarded as an unusual type of anaplastic carcinoma with an aggressive behavior [329–331].

Spindle Epithelial Tumor with Thymus-Like Differentiation (SETTLE)

This is a rare thyroid tumor, which predominantly occurs in children and young adults. These tumors are slow growing and present as painless thyroid mass. Local recurrence and distant metastases involving lungs may be seen later in the course of the disease [332–338]. SETTLE is thought to be derived from ectopic thymus or branchial pouch remnant [335, 339]. On microscopic examination, the tumor shows lobules of tumor cells separated by fibrous bands, the tumor cells are spindle shaped mixed with tubulopapillary epithelial islands including foci of

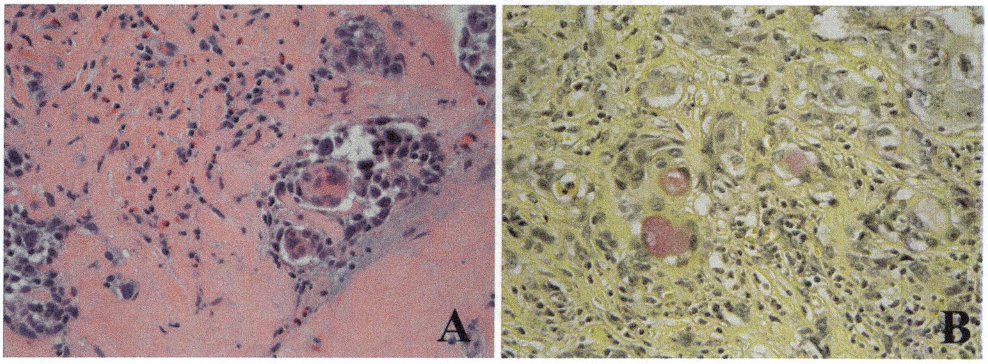

Fig. 34 Sclerosing mucoepidermoid carcinoma with eosinophilia showing islands of tumor cells in a collagenous desmoplastic stroma including eosinophils (**A**) and intracytoplasmic mucin on mucicarmine stain (**B**). *Photomicrograph courtesy Dr. Vania Nose, Brigham and Women's Hospital, Boston, MA*

squamoid areas and structures resembling Hassall's corpuscles. Cystic change may be seen in the epithelial islands [333–335]. While most tumors are biphasic, monophasic SETTLE has been reported, which must be distinguished from medullary carcinoma and monophasic synovial sarcoma [340]. On immunohistochemistry the tumor cells stain positive with cytokeratin and muscle-specific actin and they are negative for thyroglobulin and calcitonin [334].

Differential Diagnosis

Differential diagnosis of thyroid spindle cell lesions include anaplastic carcinoma, medullary carcinoma, intrathyroidal thymoma, metaplastic spindle cell proliferation associated with follicular cell derived tumors, teratoma of the thyroid, synovial sarcoma, and other mesenchymal tumors. The age of presentation in SETTLE (children) helps rule out anaplastic carcinoma and intrathyroidal thymoma. Positive immunoreactivity with cytokeratin rules out mesenchymal tumor except synovial sarcoma. Medullary carcinoma and synovial sarcoma both may be seen in childhood, medullary carcinoma will stain positive for neuroendocrine markers on immunohistochemistry and synovial sarcoma is usually highly mitotic and lacks cyst formation [17].

Carcinoma Showing Thymus-Like Differentiation (CASTLE)

This is a rare tumor first described by Miyauchi et al. in 1985 and has also been referred to as intrathyroidal thymoma (ITET) [341]. It occurs in the elderly, involves lower or middle third of the gland, and may invade surrounding soft tissues and regional lymph nodes. On histology it shows lobulated architecture composed of groups of tumor cells with large vesicular nuclei, prominent nucleoli and associated prominent lymphocytic infiltrate reminiscent of the so-called lymphoepithelioma (Fig. 35A) [338, 342]. On immunohistochemistry tumor cells are positive for CD5 suggesting a thymic origin, they are also positive for cytokeratin and CEA (Fig. 35B–D); both thyroglobulin and calcitonin are negative [343]. Differential diagnosis of CASTLE includes metastatic carcinoma, particularly from lung and upper aerodigestive tract. CD5 immunoreactivity is useful in this differential diagnosis since most metastatic carcinomas from the sites mentioned above are CD5 negative [341]. CASTLE without node metastasis has low risk of local recurrence and surgery alone may be sufficient treatment [344]. In a series of 25 cases of CASTLE, Ito et al. reported a 5- and 10-year cause-specific survival 90 and 82%, respectively; nodal metastasis and tumor extension predict a worse prognosis [345].

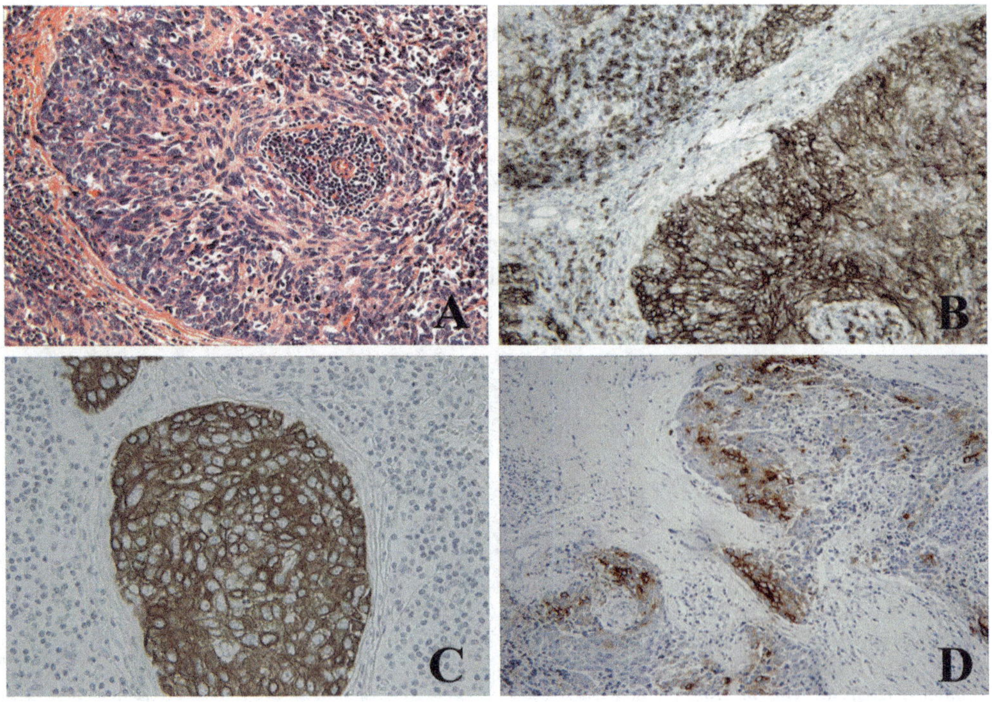

Fig. 35 Carcinoma showing thymus like differentiation (CASTLE). Tumor cells show a lobulated architecture with associate lymphocytic stroma (**A**) and CD5 (**B**), cytokeratin (**C**) and CEA (**D**) positive on immunohistochemistry. *Photomicrograph courtesy Dr. Vania Nose, Brigham and Women's Hospital, Boston, MA*

Rare Non-epithelial Thyroid Tumors

Lymphoma

Thyroid lymphoma is rare and accounts for 2.2–2.5% of all lymphomas [17]. It usually occurs in the background of Hashimoto's thyroiditis and is thought to arise from the mucosa associated lymphoid tissue (MALT). There have been rare case reports of primary thyroid lymphoma associated with Graves' disease [346]. Most common type of lymphoma is the diffuse large B cell lymphoma followed by low-grade MALT lymphoma. Diffuse large B cell lymphoma must be differentiated from anaplastic carcinoma and immunohistochemistry can be very helpful in this situation [347–349]. Bacon et al. recently described 22 cases of follicular lymphoma of the thyroid which included two distinct groups with different clinical stage at presentation and biological behavior: one group showed t(14;18) translocation and/or expressed Bcl2 and was CD10 positive and the other lacked Bcl2 expression and was negative for CD10. It may be important to distinguish the two for better management of these patients [350].

Other Non-epithelial Tumors

Mesenchymal tumors, which are more commonly seen in other parts of the body, are rare in thyroid. Primary mesenchymal tumors that have been described in the thyroid include vascular tumors such as cavernous hemangioma [351]; and epithelioid hemangioendothelioma [352]; granular cell tumor [353]; solitary fibrous tumor [195, 354]; fibrosarcoma [355]; smooth muscle tumors including leiomyoma and leiomyosarcoma [356, 357]; osteosarcoma [358]; malignant fibrous histiocytoma [359]. Other tumors and tumor-like lesions that have been described in thyroid include Langerhans cell histiocytosis [360], plasma cell granuloma [361], and extramedullary hematopoesis [362]. There are reports in the literature of metastatic uterine sarcoma to the thyroid which have to be differentiated from primary sarcoma [363, 364].

Metastatic Carcinoma

Metastases to thyroid from another primary source are infrequent, tumors that most commonly spread to the thyroid include kidney (Fig. 36), breast, and lung carcinoma, but metastasis from hepatocelluar carcinoma has also been reported [51, 365]. Metastatic carcinoma should be considered in the differential diagnosis of poorly differentiated carcinoma, especially with a non-insular growth pattern and clinicopathological correlation, and immunostaining with thyroglobulin may be helpful in these situations [366, 367]. When investigating metastatic carcinoma in the females it should be kept in mind that

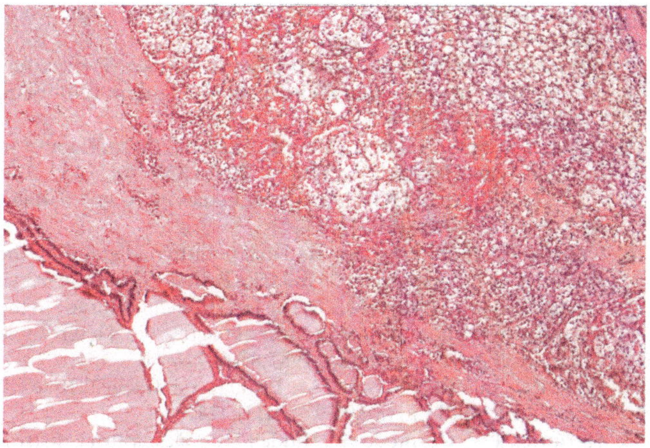

Fig. 36 Thyroid with metastatic renal cell carcinoma, clear cell type. Normal thyroid is seen on the left bottom corner. Patient had history of nephrectomy for renal cell carcinoma

thyroid carcinoma can strongly express estrogen and progesterone receptors (Fig. 37) [368] and may be negative for thyroglobulin on immunohistochemistry; TTF-1

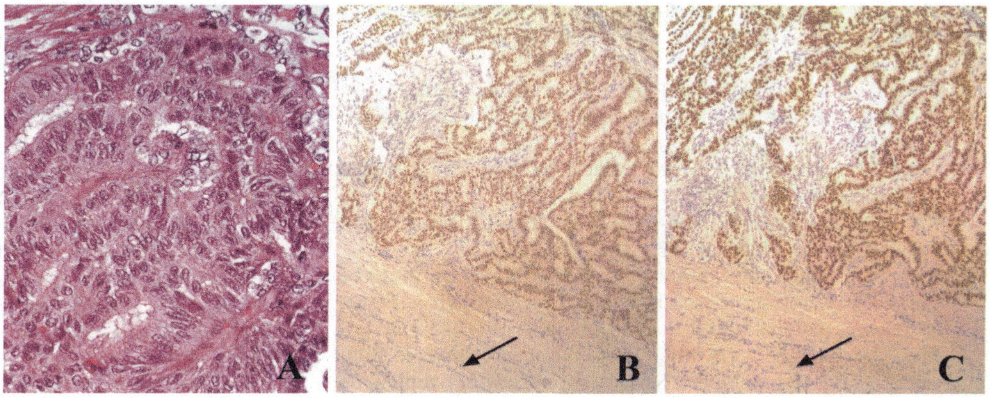

Fig. 37 Papillary thyroid carcinoma, columnar cell variant (similar to Fig. 16) with diffuse estrogen receptor (**B**) and progesterone receptor (**C**) immunostaining. Normal thyroid (*arrow*) is negative for both ER and PR

immunostaining (Fig. 16) along with other clinical and pathological features may be helpful in this situation.

References

1. McNicol AM, Lewis PD. The Endocrine System. In: Lewis PD, ed. Systemic Pathology. Edinburgh: Churchill Livingstone; 1996:131–85.
2. Organ GM, Organ CH, Jr. Thyroid gland and surgery of the thyroglossal duct: exercise in applied embryology. World J Surg 2000;24(8):886–90.
3. Murray D. The Thyroid Gland. In: Kalman K, Asa SL, eds. Functional Endocrine Pathology. 2nd ed. Oxford, UK: Blackwell; 1998:295–380.
4. Lloyd RV, Douglas BR, Young WF. Thyroid Gland. In: Lloyd RV, Douglas BR, and Young WF, eds. Atlas of Non-tumor Pathology: Endocrine Diseases (First Series Fascicle 1). Washington DC: Armed Forces Institute of Pathology; 2002:91–169.
5. Livolsi V. Surgical Pathology of the Thyroid. Philadelphia: Saunders; 1990.
6. Jamshidi M, Kasirye O, Smith DJ. Ectopic thyroid nodular goiter presenting as a porta hepatis mass. Am Surg 1998;64(4):305–6.
7. Pistono M, Occhetta E, Sarasso G, et al. Intracardiac ectopic thyroid: a report of a clinical case with a long-term follow-up. Cardiologia 1999;44(1):83–8.
8. Pollice L, Caruso G. Struma cordis. Ectopic thyroid goiter in the right ventricle. Arch Pathol Lab Med 1986;110(5):452–3.
9. Curtis LE, Sheahan DG. Heterotopic tissues in the gallbladder. Arch Pathol 1969;88(6):677–83.
10. Kurman RJ, Prabha AC. Thyroid and parathyroid glands in the vaginal wall: report of a case. Am J Clin Pathol 1973;59(4):503–7.
11. Ruchti C, Balli-Antunes M, Gerber HA. Follicular tumor in the sellar region without primary cancer of the thyroid. Heterotopic carcinoma? Am J Clin Pathol 1987;87(6):776–80.
12. Bone RC, Biller HF, Irwin TM. Intralaryngotracheal thyroid. Ann Otol Rhinol Laryngol 1972;81(3):424–8.
13. Hardwick DF, Cormode EJ, Riddell DG. Respiratory distress and neck mass in a neonate. J Pediatr 1976;89(3):501–5.
14. Kuffner HA, McCook BM, Swaminatha R, Myers EN, Hunt JL. Controversial ectopic thyroid: a case report of thyroid tissue in the axilla and benign total thyroidectomy. Thyroid 2005;15(9):1095–7.
15. Maino K, Skelton H, Yeager J, Smith KJ. Benign ectopic thyroid tissue in a cutaneous location: a case report and review. J Cutan Pathol 2004;31(2):195–8.
16. Kumar R, Sharma S, Marwah A, Moorthy D, Dhanwal D, Malhotra A. Ectopic goiter masquerading as submandibular gland swelling: a case report and review of the literature. Clin Nucl Med 2001;26(4):306–9.
17. Baloch ZW, Livolsi V. Pathology of Thyroid Gland. In: Livolsi V, Asa SL, eds. Endocrine pathology: Churchill Livingstone; 2002:61–88.
18. Gerard-Marchant R. Thyroid Follicle Inclusions in Cervical Lymph Nodes. Arch Pathol 1964;77:633–7.
19. Roth LM. Inclusions of Non-Neoplastic Thyroid Tissue within Cervical Lymph Nodes. Cancer 1965;18:105–11.
20. Escofet X, Khan AZ, Mazarani W, Woods WG. Lessons to be learned: a case study approach. Lateral aberrant thyroid tissue: is it always malignant? J R Soc Health 2007;127(1):45–6.
21. Meyer JS, Steinberg LS. Microscopically benign thyroid follicles in cervical lymph nodes. Serial section study of lymph node inclusions and entire thyroid gland in 5 cases. Cancer 1969;24(2):302–11.
22. Caccetta TP, Kumar A, Ishak H. Lateral aberrant thyroid tissue presenting as a lateral neck mass. ANZ J Surg 2005;75(12):1123–4.
23. Kakudo K, Shan L, Nakamura Y, Inoue D, Koshiyama H, Sato H. Clonal analysis helps to differentiate aberrant thyroid tissue from thyroid carcinoma. Hum Pathol 1998;29 (2):187–90.
24. Arabi A, Zayour D, Salti I. Papillary carcinoma arising in a thyroglossal duct cyst; two case reports and review of the literature. Int Surg 2007;92(6):327–30.
25. Hilger AW, Thompson SD, Smallman LA, Watkinson JC. Papillary carcinoma arising in a thyroglossal duct cyst: a case report and literature review. J Laryngol Otol 1995;109(11):1124–7.
26. Martin-Perez E, Larranaga E, Marron C, Monje F. Primary papillary carcinoma arising in a thyroglossal duct cyst. Eur J Surg 1997;163(2):143–5.
27. McNicoll MP, Hawkins DB, England K, Penny R, Maceri DR. Papillary carcinoma arising in a thyroglossal duct cyst. Otolaryngol Head Neck Surg 1988;99(1):50–4.
28. Patel SG, Escrig M, Shaha AR, Singh B, Shah JP. Management of well-differentiated thyroid carcinoma presenting within a thyroglossal duct cyst. J Surg Oncol 2002;79(3):134–9; discussion 40–1.
29. Patti G, Ragni G, Calisti A. Papillary thyroid carcinoma in a thyroglossal duct cyst in a child. Med Pediatr Oncol 2000;34(1):67–9.
30. Plaza CP, Lopez ME, Carrasco CE, Meseguer LM, Perucho Ade L. Management of well-differentiated thyroglossal remnant thyroid carcinoma: time to close the debate? Report of five new cases and proposal of a definitive algorithm for treatment. Ann Surg Oncol 2006;13(5):745–52.
31. Samara C, Bechrakis I, Kavadias S, Papadopoulos A, Maniatis V, Strigaris K. Thyroglossal duct cyst carcinoma: case report and review of the literature, with emphasis on CT findings. Neuroradiology 2001;43(8):647–9.
32. Berni Canani F, Dall'Olio D, Chiarini V, Casadei GP, Papini E. Papillary carcinoma of a thyroglossal duct cyst in a patient with thyroid hemiagenesis: effectiveness of conservative surgical treatment. Endocr Pract 2008;14(4):465–9.
33. Tovi F, Fliss DM, Inabar-Yanai I. Hurthle cell adenoma of the thyroglossal duct. Head Neck Surg 1988;10:346–9.
34. Nussbaum M, Buchwald RP, Ribner A, Mori K, Litwins J. Anaplastic carcinoma arising from median ectopic thyroid (thyroglossal duct remnant). Cancer 1981;48(12):2724–8.
35. Apel RL, Asa SL, Chalvardjian A, LiVolsi VA. Intrathyroidal lymphoepithelial cysts of probable branchial origin. Hum Pathol 1994;25(11):1238–42.
36. Ohri AK, Ohri SK, Singh MP. Evidence for thyroid development from the fourth branchial pouch. J Laryngol Otol 1994;108(1):71–3.
37. Kay C, Abrahams S, McClain P. The weight of normal thyroid glands in children. Arch Pathol 1966;82(4):349–52.
38. Sobrinho-Simoes MA, Sambade MC, Goncalves V. Latent thyroid carcinoma at autopsy: a study from Oporto, Portugal. Cancer 1979;43(5):1702–6.
39. Mochizuki Y, Mowafy R, Pasternack B. Weights of Human Thyroids in New York City. Health Phys 1963;9:1299–301.
40. Pankow BG, Michalak J, McGee MK. Adult human thyroid weight. Health Phys 1985;49(6):1097–103.
41. Hegedus L, Karstrup S, Rasmussen N. Evidence of cyclic alterations of thyroid size during the menstrual cycle in healthy women. Am J Obstet Gynecol 1986;155(1):142–5.
42. Kendall CH, Sanderson PR, Cope J, Talbot IC. Follicular thyroid tumours: a study of laminin and type IV collagen in basement membrane and endothelium. J Clin Pathol 1985;38(10):1100–5.

43. Isotalo PA, Lloyd RV. Presence of birefringent crystals is useful in distinguishing thyroid from parathyroid gland tissues. Am J Surg Pathol 2002;26(6):813–4.
44. DeLellis RA, May L, Tashjian AH, Jr., Wolfe HJ. C-cell granule heterogeneity in man. An ultrastructural immunocytochemical study. Lab Invest 1978;38(3):263–9.
45. Harach HR. Solid cell nests of the thyroid. J Pathol 1988;155(3):191–200.
46. Mizukami Y, Nonomura A, Michigishi T, et al. Solid cell nests of the thyroid. A histologic and immunohistochemical study. Am J Clin Pathol 1994;101(2):186–91.
47. Pianzola HM, Ottino A, Castelletto RH. Solid cell nests of the thyroid. Hum Pathol 1995;26(8):929–30.
48. Martin V, Martin L, Viennet G, Hergel M, Carbillet JP, Fellmann D. Ultrastructural features of "solid cell nest" of the human thyroid gland: a study of 8 cases. Ultrastruct Pathol 2000;24(1):1–8.
49. Kabel PJ, Voorbij HA, De Haan M, van der Gaag RD, Drexhage HA. Intrathyroidal dendritic cells. J Clin Endocrinol Metab 1988;66(1):199–207.
50. Bisi H, Fernandes VS, de Camargo RY, Koch L, Abdo AH, de Brito T. The prevalence of unsuspected thyroid pathology in 300 sequential autopsies, with special reference to the incidental carcinoma. Cancer 1989;64(9):1888–93.
51. Rosai J, Carangui ML, DeLellis RA. Atlas of Tumor Pathology: Tumors of the Thyroid Gland. Washington DC: Armed Forces Institute of Pathology; 1992.
52. Belfiore A, Sava L, Runello F, Tomaselli L, Vigneri R. Solitary autonomously functioning thyroid nodules and iodine deficiency. J Clin Endocrinol Metab 1983;56(2):283–7.
53. Koren R, Yaniv E, Kristt D, et al. Capsular collagen staining of follicular thyroid neoplasms by picrosirius red: role in differential diagnosis. Acta Histochem 2001;103(2):151–7.
54. Aker FV, Bas Y, Ozkara S, Peker O. Spindle cell metaplasia in follicular adenoma of the thyroid gland: case report and review of the literature. Endocr J 2004;51(5):457–61.
55. Shikama Y, Mizukami H, Sakai T, Yagihashi N, Okamoto K, Yagihashi S. Spindle cell metaplasia arising in thyroid adenoma: characterization of its pathology and differential diagnosis. J Endocrinol Invest 2006;29(2):168–71.
56. Vergilio J, Baloch ZW, LiVolsi VA. Spindle cell metaplasia of the thyroid arising in association with papillary carcinoma and follicular adenoma. Am J Clin Pathol 2002;117 (2):199–204.
57. Mai KT, Landry DC, Thomas J, et al. Follicular adenoma with papillary architecture: a lesion mimicking papillary thyroid carcinoma. Histopathology 2001;39(1):25–32.
58. Coli A, Bigotti G, Parente P, Federico F, Castri F, Massi G. Atypical thyroid nodules express both HBME-1 and Galectin-3, two phenotypic markers of papillary thyroid carcinoma. J Exp Clin Cancer Res 2007;26(2):221–7.
59. Vasko VV, Gaudart J, Allasia C, et al. Thyroid follicular adenomas may display features of follicular carcinoma and follicular variant of papillary carcinoma. Eur J Endocrinol 2004;151(6):779–86.
60. DeRienzo D, Truong L. Thyroid neoplasms containing mature fat: a report of two cases and review of the literature. Mod Pathol 1989;2(5):506–10.
61. Farfel Z, Bourne HR, Iiri T. The expanding spectrum of G protein diseases. N Engl J Med 1999;340(13):1012–20.
62. Parma J, Duprez L, Van Sande J, et al. Somatic mutations in the thyrotropin receptor gene cause hyperfunctioning thyroid adenomas. Nature 1993;365(6447):649–51.
63. Tonacchera M, Chiovato L, Pinchera A, et al. Hyperfunctioning thyroid nodules in toxic multinodular goiter share activating thyrotropin receptor mutations with solitary toxic adenoma. J Clin Endocrinol Metab 1998;83(2):492–8.
64. Trulzsch B, Krohn K, Wonerow P, et al. Detection of thyroid-stimulating hormone receptor and Gsalpha mutations: in 75 toxic thyroid nodules by denaturing gradient gel electrophoresis. J Mol Med 2001;78(12):684–91.
65. Van Sande J, Parma J, Tonacchera M, Swillens S, Dumont J, Vassart G. Somatic and germline mutations of the TSH receptor gene in thyroid diseases. J Clin Endocrinol Metab 1995;80(9):2577–85.
66. Lado-Abeal J, Palos-Paz F, Perez-Guerra O, Cameselle-Teijeiro J, Rueda-Chimeno JC, Barreiro-Morandeira F. Prevalence of mutations in TSHR, GNAS, PRKAR1A and RAS genes in a large series of toxic thyroid adenomas from Galicia, an iodine deficient area in NW Spain. Eur J Endocrinol 2008;159:623–31.
67. Brisigotti M, Lorenzini P, Alessi A, Fabbretti G, Baldoni C. Mucin-producing adenoma of the thyroid gland. Tumori 1986;72(2):211–4.
68. Carcangiu ML, Sibley RK, Rosai J. Clear cell change in primary thyroid tumors. A study of 38 cases. Am J Surg Pathol 1985;9(10):705–22.
69. Rigaud C, Peltier F, Bogomoletz WV. Mucin producing microfollicular adenoma of the thyroid. J Clin Pathol 1985;38(3):277–80.
70. Carney JA, Ryan J, Goellner JR. Hyalinizing trabecular adenoma of the thyroid gland. Am J Surg Pathol 1987;11(8):583–91.
71. Carney JA. Hyalinizing trabecular tumors of the thyroid gland: quadruply described but not by the discoverer. Am J Surg Pathol 2008;32(4):622–34.
72. Chetty R, Beydoun R, LiVolsi VA. Paraganglioma-like (hyalinizing trabecular) adenoma of the thyroid revisited. Pathology (Phila) 1994;26(4):429–31.
73. Evenson A, Mowschenson P, Wang H, et al. Hyalinizing trabecular adenoma–an uncommon thyroid tumor frequently misdiagnosed as papillary or medullary thyroid carcinoma. Am J Surg 2007;193(6):707–12.
74. Papotti M, Riella P, Montemurro F, Pietribiasi F, Bussolati G. Immunophenotypic heterogeneity of hyalinizing trabecular tumours of the thyroid. Histopathology 1997;31(6):525–33.
75. Rothenberg HJ, Goellner JR, Carney JA. Hyalinizing trabecular adenoma of the thyroid gland: recognition and characterization of its cytoplasmic yellow body. Am J Surg Pathol 1999;23(1):118–25.
76. Cheung CC, Boerner SL, MacMillan CM, Ramyar L, Asa SL. Hyalinizing trabecular tumor of the thyroid: a variant of papillary carcinoma proved by molecular genetics. Am J Surg Pathol 2000;24(12):1622–6.
77. Fonseca E, Nesland JM, Sobrinho-Simoes M. Expression of stratified epithelial-type cytokeratins in hyalinizing trabecular adenomas supports their relationship with papillary carcinomas of the thyroid. Histopathology 1997;31(4):330–5.
78. Hirokawa M, Carney JA, Ohtsuki Y. Hyalinizing trabecular adenoma and papillary carcinoma of the thyroid gland express different cytokeratin patterns. Am J Surg Pathol 2000;24(6):877–81.
79. Galgano MT, Mills SE, Stelow EB. Hyalinizing trabecular adenoma of the thyroid revisited: a histologic and immunohistochemical study of thyroid lesions with prominent trabecular architecture and sclerosis. Am J Surg Pathol 2006;30(10):1269–73.
80. Hirokawa M, Carney JA. Cell membrane and cytoplasmic staining for MIB-1 in hyalinizing trabecular adenoma of the thyroid gland. Am J Surg Pathol 2000;24(4):575–8.
81. Lloyd RV. Hyalinizing trabecular tumors of the thyroid: a variant of papillary carcinoma? Adv Anat Pathol 2002;9(1):7–11.
82. DeLellis RA, Williams ED, et al. Tumors of Thyroid and Parathyroid. In: DeLellis RA, Lloyd RV, Heitz PU, Eng C, eds.

Pathology and Genetics: Tumors of Endocrine Organs. Lyon: IARC; 2004:49–123.
83. LiVolsi VA. Hyalinizing trabecular tumor of the thyroid: adenoma, carcinoma, or neoplasm of uncertain malignant potential? Am J Surg Pathol 2000;24(12):1683–4.
84. Gowrishankar S, Pai SA, Carney JA. Hyalinizing trabecular carcinoma of the thyroid gland. Histopathology 2008;52(4):529–31.
85. Hundahl SA, Cady B, Cunningham MP, et al. Initial results from a prospective cohort study of 5583 cases of thyroid carcinoma treated in the united states during 1996. U.S. and German Thyroid Cancer Study Group. An American College of Surgeons Commission on Cancer Patient Care Evaluation study. Cancer 2000;89(1):202–17.
86. Gimm O. Thyroid cancer. Cancer Lett 2001;163(2):143–56.
87. Rastogi T, Devesa S, Mangtani P, et al. Cancer incidence rates among South Asians in four geographic regions: India, Singapore, UK and US. Int J Epidemiol 2008;37(1): 147–60.
88. Malchoff CD, Malchoff DM. Familial nonmedullary thyroid carcinoma. Semin Surg Oncol 1999;16(1):16–8.
89. Malchoff CD, Malchoff DM. The genetics of hereditary nonmedullary thyroid carcinoma. J Clin Endocrinol Metab 2002;87(6):2455–9.
90. Malchoff CD, Sarfarazi M, Tendler B, Forouhar F, Whalen G, Malchoff DM. Familial papillary thyroid carcinoma is genetically distinct from familial adenomatous polyposis coli. Thyroid 1999;9(3):247–52.
91. Ruben Harach H. Familial nonmedullary thyroid neoplasia. Endocrine pathology 2001;12(2):97–112.
92. LiVolsi VA, Asa SL. The demise of follicular carcinoma of the thyroid gland. Thyroid 1994;4(2):233–6.
93. Dal Maso L, Bosetti C, La Vecchia C, Franceschi S. Risk factors for thyroid cancer: an epidemiological review focused on nutritional factors. Cancer Causes Control 2008;20:75–86.
94. Stephenson TJ. Papillary carcinoma of the thyroid: a tumour still with no benign neoplastic counterpart. Histopathology 2001;39(5):536–8.
95. Nikiforov YE. RET/PTC rearrangement in thyroid tumors. Endocr Pathol 2002;13(1):3–16.
96. Tallini G, Asa SL. RET oncogene activation in papillary thyroid carcinoma. Adv Anat Pathol 2001;8(6):345–54.
97. Nikiforov YE, Koshoffer A, Nikiforova M, Stringer J, Fagin JA. Chromosomal breakpoint positions suggest a direct role for radiation in inducing illegitimate recombination between the ELE1 and RET genes in radiation-induced thyroid carcinomas. Oncogene 1999;18(46):6330–4.
98. Moysich KB, Menezes RJ, Michalek AM. Chernobyl-related ionising radiation exposure and cancer risk: an epidemiological review. Lancet oncol 2002;3(5):269–79.
99. Brignardello E, Corrias A, Isolato G, et al. Ultrasound screening for thyroid carcinoma in childhood cancer survivors: a case series. J Clin Endocrinol Metab 2008.
100. Lantsov D, Meirmanov S, Nakashima M, et al. Cyclin D1 overexpression in thyroid papillary microcarcinoma: its association with tumour size and aberrant beta-catenin expression. Histopathology 2005;47(3):248–56.
101. Rezk S, Brynes RK, Nelson V, et al. beta-Catenin expression in thyroid follicular lesions: potential role in nuclear envelope changes in papillary carcinomas. Endocr pathol 2004;15(4):329–37.
102. Scopa CD, Melachrinou M, Saradopoulou C, Merino MJ. The significance of the grooved nucleus in thyroid lesions. Mod Pathol 1993;6(6):691–4.
103. Lin X, Finkelstein SD, Zhu B, Silverman JF. Molecular analysis of multifocal papillary thyroid carcinoma. J Mol Endocrinol 2008;41(4):195–203.
104. Arch-Ferrer J, Velazquez D, Fajardo R, Gamboa-Dominguez A, Herrera MF. Accuracy of sentinel lymph node in papillary thyroid carcinoma. Surgery 2001;130(6):907–13.
105. Chow TL, Lim BH, Kwok SP. Sentinel lymph node dissection in papillary thyroid carcinoma. ANZ J Surg 2004;74(1–2):10–2.
106. Fukui Y, Yamakawa T, Taniki T, Numoto S, Miki H, Monden Y. Sentinel lymph node biopsy in patients with papillary thyroid carcinoma. Cancer 2001;92(11):2868–74.
107. Shindo M, Wu JC, Park EE, Tanzella F. The importance of central compartment elective lymph node excision in the staging and treatment of papillary thyroid cancer. Arch Otolaryngol Head Neck Surg 2006;132(6):650–4.
108. Roh JL, Park CI. Sentinel lymph node biopsy as guidance for central neck dissection in patients with papillary thyroid carcinoma. Cancer 2008;113(7):1527–31.
109. Chen YT, Kitabayashi N, Zhou XK, Fahey TJ, 3rd, Scognamiglio T. MicroRNA analysis as a potential diagnostic tool for papillary thyroid carcinoma. Mod Pathol 2008;21(9):1139–46.
110. Nikiforova MN, Tseng GC, Steward D, Diorio D, Nikiforov YE. MicroRNA expression profiling of thyroid tumors: biological significance and diagnostic utility. J Clin Endocrinol Metab 2008;93(5):1600–8.
111. Pallante P, Visone R, Ferracin M, et al. MicroRNA deregulation in human thyroid papillary carcinomas. Endocrine-related cancer 2006;13(2):497–508.
112. Fink A, Tomlinson G, Freeman JL, Rosen IB, Asa SL. Occult micropapillary carcinoma associated with benign follicular thyroid disease and unrelated thyroid neoplasms. Mod Pathol 1996;9(8):816–20.
113. Hubert JP, Jr., Kiernan PD, Beahrs OH, McConahey WM, Woolner LB. Occult papillary carcinoma of the thyroid. Arch Surg 1980;115(4):394–8.
114. Lang W, Borrusch H, Bauer L. Occult carcinomas of the thyroid. Evaluation of 1,020 sequential autopsies. Am J Clin Pathol 1988;90(1):72–6.
115. Roti E, Rossi R, Trasforini G, et al. Clinical and histological characteristics of papillary thyroid microcarcinoma: results of a retrospective study in 243 patients. J Clin Endocrinol Metab 2006;91(6):2171–8.
116. Roti E, Degli Uberti E, Braverman L, Bondanelli M. Thyroid papillary microcarcinoma. A descriptive and meta-analysis study. Eur J Endocrinol 2008;159:659–73.
117. Crile G, Jr., Hazard JB. Relationship of the age of the patient to the natural history and prognosis of carcinoma of the thyroid. Ann Surg 1953;138(1):33–8.
118. Hazard JB, Crile G, Jr., Dinsmore RS, Hawk WA, Kenyon R. Neoplasms of the thyroid: classification, morphology, and treatment. A M A 1955;59(4):502–13.
119. Lindsay S. Carcinoma of the Thyroid Gland. A Clinical and Pathological Study of 293 Patients at University of California Hospital. In: Thomas CC, ed. Springfield, IL; 1960.
120. Hedinger C, Sobin LH. Histologic Typing of Thyroid Tumors. International Histological Classfication of Tumors. 1st ed. Geneva: World Health Organization; 1974.
121. Chen KT, Rosai J. Follicular variant of thyroid papillary carcinoma: a clinicopathologic study of six cases. Am J Surg Pathol 1977;1(2):123–30.
122. Hay ID. Papillary thyroid carcinoma. Endocrinol Metab Clin North Am 1990;19(3):545–76.
123. Liu J, Singh B, Tallini G, et al. Follicular variant of papillary thyroid carcinoma: a clinicopathologic study of a problematic entity. Cancer 2006;107(6):1255–64.
124. Williams ED. Guest Editorial: Two Proposals Regarding the Terminology of Thyroid Tumors. International journal of surgical pathology 2000;8(3):181–3.

125. Renshaw AA, Gould EW. Why there is the tendency to "over-diagnose" the follicular variant of papillary thyroid carcinoma. Am J Clin Pathol 2002;117(1):19–21.
126. Chan JK. Strict criteria should be applied in the diagnosis of encapsulated follicular variant of papillary thyroid carcinoma. Am J Clin Pathol 2002;117(1):16–8.
127. Lloyd RV, Erickson LA, Casey MB, et al. Observer variation in the diagnosis of follicular variant of papillary thyroid carcinoma. Am J Surg Pathol 2004;28(10):1336–40.
128. Baloch ZW, LiVolsi VA. Encapsulated follicular variant of papillary thyroid carcinoma with bone metastases. Mod Pathol 2000;13(8):861–5.
129. Ivanova R, Soares P, Castro P, Sobrinho-Simoes M. Diffuse (or multinodular) follicular variant of papillary thyroid carcinoma: a clinicopathologic and immunohistochemical analysis of ten cases of an aggressive form of differentiated thyroid carcinoma. Virchows Arch 2002;440(4):418–24.
130. LiVolsi VA. Well differentiated thyroid carcinoma. Clin Oncol (R Coll Radiol) 1996;8(5):281–8.
131. Albores-Saavedra J, Gould E, Vardaman C, Vuitch F. The macrofollicular variant of papillary thyroid carcinoma: a study of 17 cases. Hum Pathol 1991;22(12):1195–205.
132. Lugli A, Terracciano LM, Oberholzer M, Bubendorf L, Tornillo L. Macrofollicular variant of papillary carcinoma of the thyroid: a histologic, cytologic, and immunohistochemical study of 3 cases and review of the literature. Arch Pathol Lab Med 2004;128(1):54–8.
133. Albores-Saavedra J, Housini I, Vuitch F, Snyder WH, 3rd. Macrofollicular variant of papillary thyroid carcinoma with minor insular component. Cancer 1997;80(6):1110–6.
134. Chang HY, Lin JD, Chou SC, Chao TC, Hsueh C. Clinical presentations and outcomes of surgical treatment of follicular variant of the papillary thyroid carcinomas. Jpn J Clin Oncol 2006;36(11):688–93.
135. Lang BH, Lo CY, Chan WF, Lam AK, Wan KY. Classical and follicular variant of papillary thyroid carcinoma: a comparative study on clinicopathologic features and long-term outcome. World J Surg 2006;30(5):752–8.
136. Passler C, Prager G, Scheuba C, et al. Follicular variant of papillary thyroid carcinoma: a long-term follow-up. Arch Surg 2003;138(12):1362–6.
137. Castro P, Eknaes M, Teixeira MR, et al. Adenomas and follicular carcinomas of the thyroid display two major patterns of chromosomal changes. J Pathol 2005;206(3): 305–11.
138. Castro P, Rebocho AP, Soares RJ, et al. PAX8-PPARgamma rearrangement is frequently detected in the follicular variant of papillary thyroid carcinoma. J Clin Endocrinol Metab 2006;91(1):213–20.
139. Castro P, Roque L, Magalhaes J, Sobrinho-Simoes M. A subset of the follicular variant of papillary thyroid carcinoma harbors the PAX8-PPARgamma translocation. International journal of surgical pathology 2005;13(3):235–8.
140. Zhu Z, Gandhi M, Nikiforova MN, Fischer AH, Nikiforov YE. Molecular profile and clinical-pathologic features of the follicular variant of papillary thyroid carcinoma. An unusually high prevalence of ras mutations. Am J Clin Pathol 2003;120(1):71–7.
141. Hawk WA, Hazard JB. The many appearances of papillary carcinoma of the thyroid. Cleve Clin Q 1976;43(4):207–15.
142. Lam AK, Lo CY, Lam KS. Papillary carcinoma of thyroid: A 30-yr clinicopathological review of the histological variants. Endocrine pathology 2005;16(4):323–30.
143. Flint A, Davenport RD, Lloyd RV. The tall cell variant of papillary carcinoma of the thyroid gland. Comparison with the common form of papillary carcinoma by DNA and morphometric analysis. Arch Pathol Lab Med 1991;115(2):169–71.
144. Ito Y, Hirokawa M, Fukushima M, et al. Prevalence and prognostic significance of poor differentiation and tall cell variant in papillary carcinoma in Japan. World J Surg 2008;32(7):1535–43; discussion 44–5.
145. Jobran R, Baloch ZW, Aviles V, Rosato EF, Schwartz S, LiVolsi VA. Tall cell papillary carcinoma of the thyroid: metastatic to the pancreas. Thyroid 2000;10(2):185–7.
146. Johnson TL, Lloyd RV, Thompson NW, Beierwaltes WH, Sisson JC. Prognostic implications of the tall cell variant of papillary thyroid carcinoma. Am J Surg Pathol 1988;12(1):22–7.
147. Lawrence E, Lord ST, Leon Y, et al. Tall cell papillary thyroid carcinoma metastatic to femur: evidence for thyroid hormone synthesis within the femur. Am J Med Sci 2001;322(2):103–8.
148. Leung AK, Chow SM, Law SC. Clinical features and outcome of the tall cell variant of papillary thyroid carcinoma. Laryngoscope 2008;118(1):32–8.
149. Michels JJ, Jacques M, Henry-Amar M, Bardet S. Prevalence and prognostic significance of tall cell variant of papillary thyroid carcinoma. Hum Pathol 2007;38(2):212–9.
150. Ostrowski ML, Merino MJ. Tall cell variant of papillary thyroid carcinoma: a reassessment and immunohistochemical study with comparison to the usual type of papillary carcinoma of the thyroid. Am J Surg Pathol 1996;20(8):964–74.
151. Ghossein RA, Leboeuf R, Patel KN, et al. Tall cell variant of papillary thyroid carcinoma without extrathyroid extension: biologic behavior and clinical implications. Thyroid 2007;17(7):655–61.
152. Kleer CG, Giordano TJ, Merino MJ. Squamous cell carcinoma of the thyroid: an aggressive tumor associated with tall cell variant of papillary thyroid carcinoma. Mod Pathol 2000;13(7):742–6.
153. Putti TC, Bhuiya TA. Mixed columnar cell and tall cell variant of papillary carcinoma of thyroid: a case report and review of the literature. Pathology (Phila) 2000;32(4):286–9.
154. Tallini G, Garcia-Rostan G, Herrero A, et al. Downregulation of p27KIP1 and Ki67/Mib1 labeling index support the classification of thyroid carcinoma into prognostically relevant categories. Am J Surg Pathol 1999;23(6):678–85.
155. Wang S, Lloyd RV, Hutzler MJ, et al. Expression of eukaryotic translation initiation factors 4E and 2alpha correlates with the progression of thyroid carcinoma. Thyroid 2001;11(12):1101–7.
156. Wang S, Lloyd RV, Hutzler MJ, Safran MS, Patwardhan NA, Khan A. The role of cell cycle regulatory protein, cyclin D1, in the progression of thyroid cancer. Mod Pathol 2000;13(8): 882–7.
157. Baloch ZW, Mandel S, LiVolsi VA. Combined tall cell carcinoma and Hurthle cell carcinoma (collision tumor) of the thyroid. Arch Pathol Lab Med 2001;125(4):541–3.
158. Sobrinho-Simoes M, Nesland JM, Johannessen JV. Columnar-cell carcinoma. Another variant of poorly differentiated carcinoma of the thyroid. Am J Clin Pathol 1988;89(2):264–7.
159. Wenig BM, Thompson LD, Adair CF, Shmookler B, Heffess CS. Thyroid papillary carcinoma of columnar cell type: a clinicopathologic study of 16 cases. Cancer 1998;82(4): 740–53.
160. Albores-Saavedra J, Wu J. The many faces and mimics of papillary thyroid carcinoma. Endocrine pathology 2006; 17(1):1–18.
161. Bulow C, Bulow S. Is screening for thyroid carcinoma indicated in familial adenomatous polyposis? The Leeds Castle Polyposis Group. Int J Colorectal Dis 1997;12(4):240–2.
162. Civitelli S, Tanzini G, Cetta F, Petracci M, Pacchiarotti MC, Civitelli B. Papillary thyroid carcinoma in three siblings with familial adenomatous polyposis. Int J Colorectal Dis 1996;11(1):34–7.

163. Fenton PA, Clarke SE, Owen W, Hibbert J, Hodgson SV. Cribriform variant papillary thyroid cancer: a characteristic of familial adenomatous polyposis. Thyroid 2001;11(2):193–7.
164. Hizawa K, Iida M, Yao T, et al. Association between thyroid cancer of cribriform variant and familial adenomatous polyposis. J Clin Pathol 1996;49(7):611–3.
165. Soravia C, Sugg SL, Berk T, et al. Familial adenomatous polyposis-associated thyroid cancer: a clinical, pathological, and molecular genetics study. Am J Pathol 1999;154(1):127–35.
166. Uchino S, Noguchi S, Yamashita H, et al. Mutational analysis of the APC gene in cribriform-morula variant of papillary thyroid carcinoma. World J Surg 2006;30(5):775–9.
167. Xu B, Yoshimoto K, Miyauchi A, et al. Cribriform-morular variant of papillary thyroid carcinoma: a pathological and molecular genetic study with evidence of frequent somatic mutations in exon 3 of the beta-catenin gene. J Pathol 2003;199(1):58–67.
168. Cameselle-Teijeiro J, Chan JK. Cribriform-morular variant of papillary carcinoma: a distinctive variant representing the sporadic counterpart of familial adenomatous polyposis-associated thyroid carcinoma? Mod Pathol 1999;12 (4):400–11.
169. Dalal KM, Moraitis D, Iwamoto C, Shaha AR, Patel SG, Ghossein RA. Clinical curiosity: cribriform-morular variant of papillary thyroid carcinoma. Head Neck 2006;28(5):471–6.
170. Ng SB, Sittampalam K, Goh YH, Eu KW. Cribriform-morular variant of papillary carcinoma: the sporadic counterpart of familial adenomatous polyposis-associated thyroid carcinoma. A case report with clinical and molecular genetic correlation. Pathology (Phila) 2003;35(1):42–6.
171. Tomoda C, Miyauchi A, Uruno T, et al. Cribriform-morular variant of papillary thyroid carcinoma: clue to early detection of familial adenomatous polyposis-associated colon cancer. World J Surg 2004;28(9):886–9.
172. Montone KT, Baloch ZW, LiVolsi VA. The thyroid Hurthle (oncocytic) cell and its associated pathologic conditions: a surgical pathology and cytopathology review. Arch Pathol Lab Med 2008;132(8):1241–50.
173. Mai KT, Thomas J, Yazdi HM, Commons AS, Lamba M, Stinson AW. Pathologic study and clinical significance of Hurthle cell papillary thyroid carcinoma. Appl Immunohistochem Mol Morphol 2004;12(4):329–37.
174. Cheung CC, Ezzat S, Ramyar L, Freeman JL, Asa SL. Molecular basis off hurthle cell papillary thyroid carcinoma. J Clin Endocrinol Metab 2000;85(2):878–82.
175. Trovisco V, Soares P, Preto A, et al. Type and prevalence of BRAF mutations are closely associated with papillary thyroid carcinoma histotype and patients' age but not with tumour aggressiveness. Virchows Arch 2005;446(6):589–95.
176. Trovisco V, Vieira de Castro I, Soares P, et al. BRAF mutations are associated with some histological types of papillary thyroid carcinoma. J Pathol 2004;202(2):247–51.
177. Collini P, Mattavelli F, Pellegrinelli A, Barisella M, Ferrari A, Massimino M. Papillary carcinoma of the thyroid gland of childhood and adolescence: Morphologic subtypes, biologic behavior and prognosis: a clinicopathologic study of 42 sporadic cases treated at a single institution during a 30-year period. Am J Surg Pathol 2006;30(11):1420–6.
178. Nikiforov Y, Gnepp DR. Pediatric thyroid cancer after the Chernobyl disaster. Pathomorphologic study of 84 cases (1991–1992) from the Republic of Belarus. Cancer 1994;74(2):748–66.
179. Tronko MD, Bogdanova TI, Komissarenko IV, et al. Thyroid carcinoma in children and adolescents in Ukraine after the Chernobyl nuclear accident: statistical data and clinicomorphologic characteristics. Cancer 1999;86(1):149–56.
180. Williams ED, Abrosimov A, Bogdanova T, et al. Morphologic characteristics of Chernobyl-related childhood papillary thyroid carcinomas are independent of radiation exposure but vary with iodine intake. Thyroid 2008;18(8):847–52.
181. Pilotti S, Collini P, Manzari A, Marubini E, Rilke F. Poorly differentiated forms of papillary thyroid carcinoma: distinctive entities or morphological patterns? Semin Diagn Pathol 1995;12(3):249–55.
182. Nikiforov YE, Erickson LA, Nikiforova MN, Caudill CM, Lloyd RV. Solid variant of papillary thyroid carcinoma: incidence, clinical-pathologic characteristics, molecular analysis, and biologic behavior. Am J Surg Pathol 2001;25(12):1478–84.
183. Volante M, Papotti M. A practical diagnostic approach to solid/trabecular nodules in the thyroid. Endocrine pathology 2008;19(2):75–81.
184. Apel RL, Asa SL, LiVolsi VA. Papillary Hurthle cell carcinoma with lymphocytic stroma. "Warthin-like tumor" of the thyroid. Am J Surg Pathol 1995;19(7):810–4.
185. Baloch ZW, LiVolsi VA. Warthin-like papillary carcinoma of the thyroid. Arch Pathol Lab Med 2000;124(8):1192–5.
186. Kim HH, Myssiorek D, Heller KS, Zahurullah F, Bhuiya T. Warthin-like tumor of the thyroid gland: an uncommon variant of papillary thyroid cancer. Ear Nose Throat J 2006;85(1):56–9.
187. Urano M, Abe M, Kuroda M, et al. Warthin-like tumor variant of papillary thyroid carcinoma: case report and literature review. Pathol Int 2001;51(9):707–12.
188. Vera-Sempere FJ, Prieto M, Camanas A. Warthin-like tumor of the thyroid: a papillary carcinoma with mitochondrion-rich cells and abundant lymphoid stroma. A case report. Pathol Res Pract 1998;194(5):341–7.
189. Basu S, Nair N, Shet T, Borges AM. Papillary thyroid carcinoma with exuberant nodular fasciitis-like stroma: treatment outcome and prognosis. J Laryngol Otol 2006; 120(4):338–42.
190. Chan JK, Carcangiu ML, Rosai J. Papillary carcinoma of thyroid with exuberant nodular fasciitis-like stroma. Report of three cases. Am J Clin Pathol 1991;95(3):309–14.
191. Lee YS, Nam KH, Hong SW, Yun JS, Chung WY, Park CS. Papillary thyroid carcinoma with nodular fasciitis-like stroma. Thyroid 2008;18(5):577–8.
192. Mizukami Y, Kurumaya H, Kitagawa T, et al. Papillary carcinoma of the thyroid gland with fibromatosis-like stroma: a case report and review of the literature. Mod Pathol 1995;8(4):366–70.
193. Mizukami Y, Nonomura A, Matsubara F, Michigishi T, Ohmura K, Hashimoto T. Papillary carcinoma of the thyroid gland with fibromatosis-like stroma. Histopathology 1992;20(4):355–7.
194. Terayama K, Toda S, Yonemitsu N, Koike N, Sugihara H. Papillary carcinoma of the thyroid with exuberant nodular fasciitis-like stroma. Virchows Arch 1997;431(4):291–5.
195. Rodriguez I, Ayala E, Caballero C, et al. Solitary fibrous tumor of the thyroid gland: report of seven cases. Am J Surg Pathol 2001;25(11):1424–8.
196. Yang YJ, LiVolsi VA, Khurana KK. Papillary thyroid carcinoma with nodular fasciitis-like stroma. Pitfalls in fine-needle aspiration cytology. Arch Pathol Lab Med 1999;123 (9):838–41.
197. Kwak JY, Kim EK, Hong SW, et al. Diffuse sclerosing variant of papillary carcinoma of the thyroid: ultrasound features with histopathological correlation. Clin Radiol 2007;62(4):382–6.
198. Lam AK, Lo CY. Diffuse sclerosing variant of papillary carcinoma of the thyroid: a 35-year comparative study at a single institution. Ann Surg Oncol 2006;13(2):176–81.

199. Lee JY, Shin JH, Han BK, et al. Diffuse sclerosing variant of papillary carcinoma of the thyroid: imaging and cytologic findings. Thyroid 2007;17(6):567–73.
200. Thompson LD, Wieneke JA, Heffess CS. Diffuse sclerosing variant of papillary thyroid carcinoma: a clinicopathologic and immunophenotypic analysis of 22 cases. Endocrine pathology 2005;16(4):331–48.
201. Alfalah H, Cranshaw I, Jany T, et al. Risk Factors for Lateral Cervical Lymph Node Involvement in Follicular Thyroid Carcinoma. World J Surg 2008;32:2623–26.
202. Bardet S, Malville E, Rame JP, et al. Macroscopic lymph-node involvement and neck dissection predict lymph-node recurrence in papillary thyroid carcinoma. Eur J Endocrinol 2008;158(4):551–60.
203. Pereira JA, Jimeno J, Miquel J, et al. Nodal yield, morbidity, and recurrence after central neck dissection for papillary thyroid carcinoma. Surgery 2005;138(6):1095–100, discussion 100–1.
204. Ito Y, Hirokawa M, Uruno T, et al. Prevalence and biological behaviour of variants of papillary thyroid carcinoma: experience at a single institute. Pathology (Phila) 2008;40(6):617–22.
205. Perrier ND, Ituarte PH, Treseler P, et al. Classification and treatment of follicular thyroid neoplasms are discordant between and within medical specialties. Surgery 1999;126(6):1063–8; discussion 9.
206. Cooper DS, Schneyer CR. Follicular and Hurthle cell carcinoma of the thyroid. Endocrinol Metab Clin North Am 1990;19(3):577–91.
207. Lang W, Choritz H, Hundeshagen H. Risk factors in follicular thyroid carcinomas. A retrospective follow-up study covering a 14-year period with emphasis on morphological findings. Am J Surg Pathol 1986;10(4):246–55.
208. Young RL, Mazzaferri EL, Rahe AJ, Dorfman SG. Pure follicular thyroid carcinoma: impact of therapy in 214 patients. J Nucl Med 1980;21(8):733–7.
209. Hedinger C, Williams ED, Sobin LH. Histologic Typing of Thyroid Tumors. 2nd edition ed. Hiedelberg: Springer-Verlag; 1988.
210. Heffess CS, Thompson LD. Minimally invasive follicular thyroid carcinoma. Endocr pathol 2001;12(4):417–22.
211. Thompson LD, Wieneke JA, Paal E, Frommelt RA, Adair CF, Heffess CS. A clinicopathologic study of minimally invasive follicular carcinoma of the thyroid gland with a review of the English literature. Cancer 2001;91(3):505–24.
212. Kesmodel SB, Terhune KP, Canter RJ, et al. The diagnostic dilemma of follicular variant of papillary thyroid carcinoma. Surgery 2003;134(6):1005–12; discussion 12.
213. LiVolsi VA. Pure versus follicular variant of papillary thyroid carcinoma: clinical features, prognostic factors, treatment, and survival. Cancer 2003;98(9):1997; author reply -8.
214. D'Avanzo A, Treseler P, Ituarte PH, et al. Follicular thyroid carcinoma: histology and prognosis. Cancer 2004;100(6):1123–9.
215. Franc B, de la Salmoniere P, Lange F, et al. Interobserver and intraobserver reproducibility in the histopathology of follicular thyroid carcinoma. Hum Pathol 2003;34(11):1092–100.
216. Evans HL. Follicular neoplasms of the thyroid. A study of 44 cases followed for a minimum of 10 years, with emphasis on differential diagnosis. Cancer 1984;54(3):535–40.
217. Kahn NF, Perzin KH. Follicular carcinoma of the thyroid: an evaluation of the histologic criteria used for diagnosis. Pathol Annu 1983;18 Pt 1:221–53.
218. Ito Y, Miyauchi A. Prognostic factors and therapeutic strategies for differentiated carcinomas of the thyroid. Endocr J 2008.
219. Goldstein NS, Czako P, Neill JS. Metastatic minimally invasive (encapsulated) follicular and Hurthle cell thyroid carcinoma: a study of 34 patients. Mod Pathol 2000;13(2):123–30.
220. Zeiger MA, Dackiw AP. Follicular thyroid lesions, elements that affect both diagnosis and prognosis. J Surg Oncol 2005;89(3):108–13.
221. Masood S, Auguste LJ, Westerband A, Belluco C, Valderama E, Attie J. Differential oncogenic expression in thyroid follicular and Hurthle cell carcinomas. Am J Surg 1993;166 (4):366–8.
222. Stojadinovic A, Ghossein RA, Hoos A, et al. Hurthle cell carcinoma: a critical histopathologic appraisal. J Clin Oncol 2001;19(10):2616–25.
223. Gundry SR, Burney RE, Thompson NW, Lloyd R. Total thyroidectomy for Hurthle cell neoplasm of the thyroid. Arch Surg 1983;118(5):529–32.
224. Thompson NW, Dunn EL, Batsakis JG, Nishiyama RH. Hurthle cell lesions of the thyroid gland. Surg Gynecol Obstet 1974;139(4):555–60.
225. Azadian A, Rosen IB, Walfish PG, Asa SL. Management considerations in Hurthle cell carcinoma. Surgery 1995;118(4):711–4; discussion 4–5.
226. Chen H, Nicol TL, Zeiger MA, et al. Hurthle cell neoplasms of the thyroid: are there factors predictive of malignancy? Ann Surg 1998;227(4):542–6.
227. Erickson LA, Jin L, Goellner JR, et al. Pathologic features, proliferative activity, and cyclin D1 expression in Hurthle cell neoplasms of the thyroid. Mod Pathol 2000;13(2):186–92.
228. Mills SC, Haq M, Smellie WJ, Harmer C. Hurthle cell carcinoma of the thyroid: Retrospective review of 62 patients treated at the Royal Marsden Hospital between 1946 and 2003. Eur J Surg Oncol 2008;35:230–34.
229. Ghossein RA, Hiltzik DH, Carlson DL, et al. Prognostic factors of recurrence in encapsulated Hurthle cell carcinoma of the thyroid gland: a clinicopathologic study of 50 cases. Cancer 2006;106(8):1669–76.
230. Baloch ZW, Livolsi VA. Follicular-patterned lesions of the thyroid: the bane of the pathologist. Am J Clin Pathol 2002;117(1):143–50.
231. Baloch ZW, LiVolsi VA. Our approach to follicular-patterned lesions of the thyroid. J Clin Pathol 2007;60(3):244–50.
232. Suster S. Thyroid tumors with a follicular growth pattern: problems in differential diagnosis. Arch Pathol Lab Med 2006;130(7):984–8.
233. Rosai J. Handling of thyroid follicular patterned lesions. Endocr Pathol 2005;16(4):279–83.
234. Asa SL. The role of immunohistochemical markers in the diagnosis of follicular-patterned lesions of the thyroid. Endocr Pathol 2005;16(4):295–309.
235. Fonseca E, Soares P, Cardoso-Oliveira M, Sobrinho-Simoes M. Diagnostic criteria in well-differentiated thyroid carcinomas. Endocr Pathol 2006;17(2):109–17.
236. Rezk S, Khan A. Role of immunohistochemistry in the diagnosis and progression of follicular epithelium-derived thyroid carcinoma. Appl Immunohistochem Mol Morphol 2005;13 (3):256–64.
237. Bartolazzi A, Gasbarri A, Papotti M, et al. Application of an immunodiagnostic method for improving preoperative diagnosis of nodular thyroid lesions. Lancet 2001;357(9269):1644–50.
238. Bryson PC, Shores CG, Hart C, et al. Immunohistochemical distinction of follicular thyroid adenomas and follicular carcinomas. Arch Otolaryngol Head Neck Surg 2008;134(6): 581–6.
239. Coli A, Bigotti G, Zucchetti F, Negro F, Massi G. Galectin-3, a marker of well-differentiated thyroid carcinoma, is expressed in thyroid nodules with cytological atypia. Histopathology 2002;40(1):80–7.
240. Cvejic D, Savin S, Paunovic I, Tatic S, Havelka M, Sinadinovic J. Immunohistochemical localization of galectin-3 in

malignant and benign human thyroid tissue. Anticancer Res 1998;18(4A):2637–41.

241. Gasbarri A, Martegani MP, Del Prete F, Lucante T, Natali PG, Bartolazzi A. Galectin-3 and CD44v6 isoforms in the preoperative evaluation of thyroid nodules. J Clin Oncol 1999;17(11):3494–502.
242. Inohara H, Honjo Y, Yoshii T, et al. Expression of galectin-3 in fine-needle aspirates as a diagnostic marker differentiating benign from malignant thyroid neoplasms. Cancer 1999;85(11):2475–84.
243. Liu YY, Morreau H, Kievit J, Romijn JA, Carrasco N, Smit JW. Combined immunostaining with galectin-3, fibronectin-1, CITED-1, Hector Battifora mesothelial-1, cytokeratin-19, peroxisome proliferator-activated receptor-{gamma}, and sodium/iodide symporter antibodies for the differential diagnosis of non-medullary thyroid carcinoma. Eur J Endocrinol 2008;158(3):375–84.
244. Murphy KM, Chen F, Clark DP. Identification of immunohistochemical biomarkers for papillary thyroid carcinoma using gene expression profiling. Hum Pathol 2008;39 (3):420–6.
245. Orlandi F, Saggiorato E, Pivano G, et al. Galectin-3 is a presurgical marker of human thyroid carcinoma. Cancer Res 1998;58(14):3015–20.
246. Saggiorato E, Cappia S, De Giuli P, et al. Galectin-3 as a presurgical immunocytodiagnostic marker of minimally invasive follicular thyroid carcinoma. J Clin Endocrinol Metab 2001;86(11):5152–8.
247. Xu XC, el-Naggar AK, Lotan R. Differential expression of galectin-1 and galectin-3 in thyroid tumors. Potential diagnostic implications. Am J Pathol 1995;147(3):815–22.
248. Bartolazzi A, Orlandi F, Saggiorato E, et al. Galectin-3-expression analysis in the surgical selection of follicular thyroid nodules with indeterminate fine-needle aspiration cytology: a prospective multicentre study. The lancet oncology 2008;9(6):543–9.
249. Cheung CC, Ezzat S, Freeman JL, Rosen IB, Asa SL. Immunohistochemical diagnosis of papillary thyroid carcinoma. Mod Pathol 2001;14(4):338–42.
250. Miettinen M, Karkkainen P. Differential reactivity of HBME-1 and CD15 antibodies in benign and malignant thyroid tumours. Preferential reactivity with malignant tumours. Virchows Arch 1996;429(4–5):213–9.
251. Sack MJ, Astengo-Osuna C, Lin BT, Battifora H, LiVolsi VA. HBME-1 immunostaining in thyroid fine-needle aspirations: a useful marker in the diagnosis of carcinoma. Mod Pathol 1997;10(7):668–74.
252. Rossi ED, Raffaelli M, Mule A, et al. Simultaneous immunohistochemical expression of HBME-1 and galectin-3 differentiates papillary carcinomas from hyperfunctioning lesions of the thyroid. Histopathology 2006;48(7):795–800.
253. Papotti M, Rodriguez J, De Pompa R, Bartolazzi A, Rosai J. Galectin-3 and HBME-1 expression in well-differentiated thyroid tumors with follicular architecture of uncertain malignant potential. Mod Pathol 2005;18(4):541–6.
254. Erickson LA, Jin L, Wollan PC, Thompson GB, van Heerden J, Lloyd RV. Expression of p27kip1 and Ki-67 in benign and malignant thyroid tumors. Mod Pathol 1998;11(2):169–74.
255. Wang S, Wuu J, Savas L, Patwardhan N, Khan A. The role of cell cycle regulatory proteins, cyclin D1, cyclin E, and p27 in thyroid carcinogenesis. Hum Pathol 1998;29 (11):1304–9.
256. Khan A, Baker SP, Patwardhan NA, Pullman JM. CD57 (Leu-7) expression is helpful in diagnosis of the follicular variant of papillary thyroid carcinoma. Virchows Arch 1998;432(5):427–32.
257. Mai KT, Ford JC, Yazdi HM, Perkins DG, Commons AS. Immunohistochemical study of papillary thyroid carcinoma and possible papillary thyroid carcinoma-related benign thyroid nodules. Pathol Res Pract 2000;196(8):533–40.
258. Raphael SJ, Apel RL, Asa SL. Brief report: detection of high-molecular-weight cytokeratins in neoplastic and non-neoplastic thyroid tumors using microwave antigen retrieval. Mod Pathol 1995;8(8):870–2.
259. Raphael SJ, McKeown-Eyssen G, Asa SL. High-molecular-weight cytokeratin and cytokeratin-19 in the diagnosis of thyroid tumors. Mod Pathol 1994;7(3):295–300.
260. Sahoo S, Hoda SA, Rosai J, DeLellis RA. Cytokeratin 19 immunoreactivity in the diagnosis of papillary thyroid carcinoma: a note of caution. Am J Clin Pathol 2001;116(5):696–702.
261. Kroll TG, Sarraf P, Pecciarini L, et al. PAX8-PPARgamma1 fusion oncogene in human thyroid carcinoma [corrected]. Science 2000;289(5483):1357–60.
262. French CA, Alexander EK, Cibas ES, et al. Genetic and biological subgroups of low-stage follicular thyroid cancer. Am J Pathol 2003;162(4):1053–60.
263. Marques AR, Espadinha C, Catarino AL, et al. Expression of PAX8-PPAR gamma 1 rearrangements in both follicular thyroid carcinomas and adenomas. J Clin Endocrinol Metab 2002;87(8):3947–52.
264. Nikiforov YE. Thyroid carcinoma: molecular pathways and therapeutic targets. Mod Pathol 2008;21 Suppl 2:S37–43.
265. Nikiforova MN, Biddinger PW, Caudill CM, Kroll TG, Nikiforov YE. PAX8-PPARgamma rearrangement in thyroid tumors: RT-PCR and immunohistochemical analyses. Am J Surg Pathol 2002;26(8):1016–23.
266. Anwar F, Emond MJ, Schmidt RA, Hwang HC, Bronner MP. Retinoblastoma expression in thyroid neoplasms. Mod Pathol 2000;13(5):562–9.
267. Prasad ML, Pellegata NS, Kloos RT, Barbacioru C, Huang Y, de la Chapelle A. CITED1 protein expression suggests Papillary Thyroid Carcinoma in high throughput tissue microarray-based study. Thyroid 2004;14(3):169–75.
268. Bohm J, Niskanen L, Tammi R, et al. Hyaluronan expression in differentiated thyroid carcinoma. J Pathol 2002;196 (2):180–5.
269. Chandan VS, Faquin WC, Wilbur DC, Khurana KK. The role of immunolocalization of CD57 and GLUT-1 in cell blocks in fine-needle aspiration diagnosis of papillary thyroid carcinoma. Cancer 2006;108(5):331–6.
270. Nasir A, Catalano E, Calafati S, Cantor A, Kaiser HE, Coppola D. Role of p53, CD44V6 and CD57 in differentiating between benign and malignant follicular neoplasms of the thyroid. In Vivo 2004;18(2):189–95.
271. Adeniran AJ, Zhu Z, Gandhi M, et al. Correlation between genetic alterations and microscopic features, clinical manifestations, and prognostic characteristics of thyroid papillary carcinomas. Am J Surg Pathol 2006;30(2):216–22.
272. Boutross-Tadross O, Saleh R, Asa SL. Follicular variant papillary thyroid carcinoma arising in struma ovarii. Endocr Pathol 2007;18(3):182–6.
273. de Matos PS, Ferreira AP, de Oliveira Facuri F, Assumpcao LV, Metze K, Ward LS. Usefulness of HBME-1, cytokeratin 19 and galectin-3 immunostaining in the diagnosis of thyroid malignancy. Histopathology 2005;47(4):391–401.
274. Prasad ML, Pellegata NS, Huang Y, Nagaraja HN, de la Chapelle A, Kloos RT. Galectin-3, fibronectin-1, CITED-1, HBME1 and cytokeratin-19 immunohistochemistry is useful for the differential diagnosis of thyroid tumors. Mod Pathol 2005;18(1):48–57.
275. Scognamiglio T, Hyjek E, Kao J, Chen YT. Diagnostic usefulness of HBME1, galectin-3, CK19, and CITED1 and

evaluation of their expression in encapsulated lesions with questionable features of papillary thyroid carcinoma. Am J Clin Pathol 2006;126(5):700–8.
276. Park YJ, Kwak SH, Kim DC, et al. Diagnostic value of galectin-3, HBME-1, cytokeratin 19, high molecular weight cytokeratin, cyclin D1 and p27(kip1) in the differential diagnosis of thyroid nodules. J Korean Med Sci 2007;22 (4):621–8.
277. Weber KB, Shroyer KR, Heinz DE, Nawaz S, Said MS, Haugen BR. The use of a combination of galectin-3 and thyroid peroxidase for the diagnosis and prognosis of thyroid cancer. Am J Clin Pathol 2004;122(4):524–31.
278. Khan A, Vohra P, Prasad ML, Fischer A, Quinlan RM, Rock KL. IMP3 (Insulin Growth Factor 3 mRNA Binding Protein) is Differentially Expressed in Benign and Malignant Follicular Patterned Lesions of the Thyroid. In: International Academy of Pathology. Athens, Greece; 2008.
279. Siraj AK, Bavi P, Abubaker J, et al. Genome-wide expression analysis of Middle Eastern papillary thyroid cancer reveals c-MET as a novel target for cancer therapy. J Pathol 2007;213(2):190–9.
280. Yano Y, Uematsu N, Yashiro T, et al. Gene expression profiling identifies platelet-derived growth factor as a diagnostic molecular marker for papillary thyroid carcinoma. Clin Cancer Res 2004;10(6):2035–43.
281. Akslen LA, LiVolsi VA. Poorly differentiated thyroid carcinoma–it is important. Am J Surg Pathol 2000;24(2):310–3.
282. Volante M, Rapa I, Papotti M. Poorly Differentiated Thyroid Carcinoma: Diagnostic Features and Controversial Issues. Endocr Pathol 2008;19:150–55.
283. Hiltzik D, Carlson DL, Tuttle RM, et al. Poorly differentiated thyroid carcinomas defined on the basis of mitosis and necrosis: a clinicopathologic study of 58 patients. Cancer 2006;106(6):1286–95.
284. Volante M, Collini P, Nikiforov YE, et al. Poorly differentiated thyroid carcinoma: the Turin proposal for the use of uniform diagnostic criteria and an algorithmic diagnostic approach. Am J Surg Pathol 2007;31(8):1256–64.
285. Yamashita H, Noguchi Y, Noguchi S, et al. Significance of an insular component in follicular thyroid carcinoma with distant metastasis at initial presentation. Endocr Pathol 2005; 16(1):41–8.
286. Agarwal S, Sharma MC, Aron M, Sarkar C, Agarwal N, Chumber S. Poorly differentiated thyroid carcinoma with rhabdoid phenotype: a diagnostic dilemma–report of a rare case. Endocr Pathol 2006;17(4):399–405.
287. Jung TS, Kim TY, Kim KW, et al. Clinical features and prognostic factors for survival in patients with poorly differentiated thyroid carcinoma and comparison to the patients with the aggressive variants of papillary thyroid carcinoma. Endocr J 2007;54(2):265–74.
288. Venkatesh YS, Ordonez NG, Schultz PN, Hickey RC, Goepfert H, Samaan NA. Anaplastic carcinoma of the thyroid. A clinicopathologic study of 121 cases. Cancer 1990;66(2):321–30.
289. Cerilli LA, Frable WJ, Spafford MF. Anaplastic carcinoma of the thyroid with chondroblastoma features mimicking papillary carcinoma: a case report. Acta Cytol 2007;51(5):825–8.
290. Olthof M, Persoon AC, Plukker JT, van der Wal JE, Links TP. Anaplastic Thyroid Carcinoma with Rhabdomyoblastic Differentiation: A Case Report with a Good Clinical Outcome. Endocr Pathol 2008;19:62–65.
291. Albores-Saavedra J, Hernandez M, Sanchez-Sosa S, Simpson K, Angeles A, Henson DE. Histologic variants of papillary and follicular carcinomas associated with anaplastic spindle and giant cell carcinomas of the thyroid: an analysis of rhabdoid and thyroglobulin inclusions. Am J Surg Pathol 2007;31(5):729–36.
292. Nonaka D, Tang Y, Chiriboga L, Rivera M, Ghossein R. Diagnostic utility of thyroid transcription factors Pax8 and TTF-2 (FoxE1) in thyroid epithelial neoplasms. Mod Pathol 2008;21(2):192–200.
293. DeLellis RA. Pathology and genetics of thyroid carcinoma. J Surg Oncol 2006;94(8):662–9.
294. Nikiforov YE. Genetic alterations involved in the transition from well-differentiated to poorly differentiated and anaplastic thyroid carcinomas. Endocr Pathol 2004;15(4):319–27.
295. Wiseman SM, Griffith OL, Deen S, et al. Identification of molecular markers altered during transformation of differentiated into anaplastic thyroid carcinoma. Arch Surg 2007;142(8):717–27; discussion 27–9.
296. Wiseman SM, Masoudi H, Niblock P, et al. Derangement of the E-cadherin/catenin complex is involved in transformation of differentiated to anaplastic thyroid carcinoma. Am J Surg 2006;191(5):581–7.
297. Elliott DD, Sherman SI, Busaidy NL, et al. Growth factor receptors expression in anaplastic thyroid carcinoma: potential markers for therapeutic stratification. Hum Pathol 2008;39(1):15–20.
298. Wiseman SM, Masoudi H, Niblock P, et al. Anaplastic thyroid carcinoma: expression profile of targets for therapy offers new insights for disease treatment. Ann Surg Oncol 2007;14(2):719–29.
299. Baloch ZW, LiVolsi VA. Unusual tumors of the thyroid gland. Endocrinol Metab Clin North Am 2008;37(2):297–310, vii.
300. Goyal R, Nada R, Rao KL, Radotra BD. Mixed medullary and follicular cell carcinoma of the thyroid with lymph node metastasis in a 7-year-old child. Pathol Int 2006;56(2):84–8.
301. Hsieh MH, Lin MC, Shun CT, Chang TC. Fine needle aspiration cytology of mixed medullary-follicular thyroid carcinoma: a case report. Acta Cytol 2008;52(3):361–5.
302. Kostoglou-Athanassiou I, Athanassiou P, Vecchini G, Gogou L, Kaldrymides P. Mixed medullary-follicular thyroid carcinoma. Report of a case and review of the literature. Horm Res 2004;61(6):300–4.
303. Mizukami Y, Nonomura A, Michigishi T, Noguchi M, Ishizaki T. Mixed medullary-follicular carcinoma of the thyroid gland: a clinicopathologic variant of medullary thyroid carcinoma. Mod Pathol 1996;9(6):631–5.
304. Papotti M, Volante M, Komminoth P, Sobrinho-Simoes M, Bussolati G. Thyroid carcinomas with mixed follicular and C-cell differentiation patterns. Semin Diagn Pathol 2000;17(2):109–19.
305. Sobrinho-Simoes M. Mixed medullary and follicular carcinoma of the thyroid. Histopathology 1993;23(3):287–9.
306. LiVolsi VA, Baloch ZW. Use and abuse of frozen section in the diagnosis of follicular thyroid lesions. Endocrine pathology 2005;16(4):285–93.
307. Bugis SP, Young JE, Archibald SD, Chen VS. Diagnostic accuracy of fine-needle aspiration biopsy versus frozen section in solitary thyroid nodules. Am J Surg 1986;152(4):411–6.
308. Gharib H. Fine-needle aspiration biopsy of thyroid nodules: advantages, limitations, and effect. Mayo Clin Proc 1994;69(1):44–9.
309. Gharib H, Goellner JR. Fine-needle aspiration biopsy of the thyroid: an appraisal. Ann Intern Med 1993;118(4):282–9.
310. Haymart MR, Greenblatt DY, Elson DF, Chen H. The role of intraoperative frozen section if suspicious for papillary thyroid cancer. Thyroid 2008;18(4):419–23.
311. Lin HS, Komisar A, Opher E, Blaugrund SM. Follicular variant of papillary carcinoma: the diagnostic limitations of preoperative fine-needle aspiration and intraoperative frozen section evaluation. Laryngoscope 2000;110(9):1431–6.

312. Udelsman R, Westra WH, Donovan PI, Sohn TA, Cameron JL. Randomized prospective evaluation of frozen-section analysis for follicular neoplasms of the thyroid. Ann Surg 2001;233(5):716–22.
313. Basolo F, Ugolini C, Proietti A, Iacconi P, Berti P, Miccoli P. Role of frozen section associated with intraoperative cytology in comparison to FNA and FS alone in the management of thyroid nodules. Eur J Surg Oncol 2007;33(6):769–75.
314. Chang HY, Lin JD, Chen JF, et al. Correlation of fine needle aspiration cytology and frozen section biopsies in the diagnosis of thyroid nodules. J Clin Pathol 1997;50 (12):1005–9.
315. Makay O, Icoz G, Gurcu B, et al. The ongoing debate in thyroid surgery: should frozen section analysis be omitted? Endocr J 2007;54(3):385–90.
316. Miller MC, Rubin CJ, Cunnane M, et al. Intraoperative pathologic examination: cost effectiveness and clinical value in patients with cytologic diagnosis of cellular follicular thyroid lesion. Thyroid 2007;17(6):557–65.
317. Paphavasit A, Thompson GB, Hay ID, et al. Follicular and Hurthle cell thyroid neoplasms. Is frozen-section evaluation worthwhile? Arch Surg 1997;132(6):674–8; discussion 8–80.
318. Brooks AD, Shaha AR, DuMornay W, et al. Role of fine-needle aspiration biopsy and frozen section analysis in the surgical management of thyroid tumors. Ann Surg Oncol 2001;8(2):92–100.
319. Boyd LA, Earnhardt RC, Dunn JT, Frierson HF, Hanks JB. Preoperative evaluation and predictive value of fine-needle aspiration and frozen section of thyroid nodules. J Am Coll Surg 1998;187(5):494–502.
320. Baloch ZW, LiVolsi VA. Cytologic and architectural mimics of papillary thyroid carcinoma. Diagnostic challenges in fine-needle aspiration and surgical pathology specimens. Am J Clin Pathol 2006;125 Suppl:S135–44.
321. Arezzo A, Patetta R, Ceppa P, Borgonovo G, Torre G, Mattioli FP. Mucoepidermoid carcinoma of the thyroid gland arising from a papillary epithelial neoplasm. Am Surg 1998;64(4):307–11.
322. Baloch ZW, Solomon AC, LiVolsi VA. Primary mucoepidermoid carcinoma and sclerosing mucoepidermoid carcinoma with eosinophilia of the thyroid gland: a report of nine cases. Mod Pathol 2000;13(7):802–7.
323. Franssila KO, Harach HR, Wasenius VM. Mucoepidermoid carcinoma of the thyroid. Histopathology 1984;8(5):847–60.
324. Rhatigan RM, Roque JL, Bucher RL. Mucoepidermoid carcinoma of the thyroid gland. Cancer 1977;39(1):210–4.
325. Viciana MJ, Galera-Davidson H, Martin-Lacave I, Segura DI, Loizaga JM. Papillary carcinoma of the thyroid with mucoepidermoid differentiation. Arch Pathol Lab Med 1996;120(4):397–8.
326. Solomon AC, Baloch ZW, Salhany KE, Mandel S, Weber RS, LiVolsi VA. Thyroid sclerosing mucoepidermoid carcinoma with eosinophilia: mimic of Hodgkin disease in nodal metastases. Arch Pathol Lab Med 2000;124(3):446–9.
327. Das S, Kalyani R. Sclerosing mucoepidermoid carcinoma with eosinophilia of the thyroid. Indian J Pathol Microbiol 2008;51(1):34–6.
328. Musso-Lassalle S, Butori C, Bailleux S, Santini J, Franc B, Hofman P. A diagnostic pitfall: nodular tumor-like squamous metaplasia with Hashimoto's thyroiditis mimicking a sclerosing mucoepidermoid carcinoma with eosinophilia. Pathol Res Pract 2006;202(5):379–83.
329. Bronner MP, LiVolsi VA. Spindle cell squamous carcinoma of the thyroid: an unusual anaplastic tumor associated with tall cell papillary cancer. Mod Pathol 1991;4(5):637–43.
330. Makay O, Kaya T, Ertan Y, et al. Primary squamous cell carcinoma of the thyroid: report of three cases. Endocr J 2008;55(2):359–64.
331. Zhou XH. Primary squamous cell carcinoma of the thyroid. Eur J Surg Oncol 2002;28(1):42–5.
332. Abrosimov AY, LiVolsi VA. Spindle epithelial tumor with thymus-like differentiation (SETTLE) of the thyroid with neck lymph node metastasis: a case report. Endocrine pathology 2005;16(2):139–43.
333. Cheuk W, Jacobson AA, Chan JK. Spindle epithelial tumor with thymus-like differentiation (SETTLE): a distinctive malignant thyroid neoplasm with significant metastatic potential. Mod Pathol 2000;13(10):1150–5.
334. Hofman P, Mainguene C, Michiels JF, Pages A, Thyss A. Thyroid spindle epithelial tumor with thymus-like differentiation (the "SETTLE" tumor). An immunohistochemical and electron microscopic study. Eur Arch Otorhinolaryngol 1995;252(5):316–20.
335. Kirby PA, Ellison WA, Thomas PA. Spindle epithelial tumor with thymus-like differentiation (SETTLE) of the thyroid with prominent mitotic activity and focal necrosis. Am J Surg Pathol 1999;23(6):712–6.
336. Kloboves-Prevodnik V, Jazbec J, Us-Krasovec M, Lamovec J. Thyroid spindle epithelial tumor with thymus-like differentiation (SETTLE): is cytopathological diagnosis possible? Diagn Cytopathol 2002;26(5):314–9.
337. Satoh S, Toda S, Narikawa K, et al. Spindle epithelial tumor with thymus-like differentiation (SETTLE): youngest reported patient. Pathol Int 2006;56(9):563–7.
338. Su L, Beals T, Bernacki EG, Giordano TJ. Spindle epithelial tumor with thymus-like differentiation: a case report with cytologic, histologic, immunohistologic, and ultrastructural findings. Mod Pathol 1997;10(5):510–4.
339. Haberal AN, Aydin H, Turan E, Demirhan B. Unusual spindle cell tumor of thyroid (SETTLE). Thyroid 2008;18(1):85–7.
340. Tong GX, Hamele-Bena D, Wei XJ, O'Toole K. Fine-needle aspiration biopsy of monophasic variant of spindle epithelial tumor with thymus-like differentiation of the thyroid: report of one case and review of the literature. Diagn Cytopathol 2007;35(2):113–9.
341. Dorfman DM, Shahsafaei A, Miyauchi A. Intrathyroidal epithelial thymoma (ITET)/carcinoma showing thymus-like differentiation (CASTLE) exhibits CD5 immunoreactivity: new evidence for thymic differentiation. Histopathology 1998;32(2):104–9.
342. Cappelli C, Tironi A, Marchetti GP, et al. Aggressive thyroid carcinoma showing thymic-like differentiation (CASTLE): case report and review of the literature. Endocr J 2008;55(4):685–90.
343. Reimann JD, Dorfman DM, Nose V. Carcinoma showing thymus-like differentiation of the thyroid (CASTLE): a comparative study: evidence of thymic differentiation and solid cell nest origin. Am J Surg Pathol 2006;30(8): 994–1001.
344. Roka S, Kornek G, Schuller J, Ortmann E, Feichtinger J, Armbruster C. Carcinoma showing thymic-like elements–a rare malignancy of the thyroid gland. Br J Surg 2004;91(2):142–5.
345. Ito Y, Miyauchi A, Nakamura Y, Miya A, Kobayashi K, Kakudo K. Clinicopathologic significance of intrathyroidal epithelial thymoma/carcinoma showing thymus-like differentiation: a collaborative study with Member Institutes of The Japanese Society of Thyroid Surgery. Am J Clin Pathol 2007;127(2):230–6.
346. Doi Y, Goto A, Murakami T, Yamashita H, Yamashita H, Noguchi S. Primary thyroid lymphoma associated with Graves' disease. Thyroid 2004;14(9):772–6.

347. Green LD, Mack L, Pasieka JL. Anaplastic thyroid cancer and primary thyroid lymphoma: a review of these rare thyroid malignancies. J Surg Oncol 2006;94(8):725–36.
348. Kossev P, Livolsi V. Lymphoid lesions of the thyroid: review in light of the revised European-American lymphoma classification and upcoming World Health Organization classification. Thyroid 1999;9(12):1273–80.
349. Skacel M, Ross CW, Hsi ED. A reassessment of primary thyroid lymphoma: high-grade MALT-type lymphoma as a distinct subtype of diffuse large B-cell lymphoma. Histopathology 2000;37(1):10–8.
350. Bacon CM, Diss TC, Ye H, et al. Follicular Lymphoma of the Thyroid Gland. Am J Surg Pathol 2008.
351. Rios A, Rodriguez JM, Martinez E, Parrilla P. Cavernous hemangioma of the thyroid. Thyroid 2001;11(3):279–80.
352. Rhomberg W, Bohler FK, Eiter H, Fritzsche H, Breitfellner G. [Malignant hemangioendothelioma of the thyroid gland: new results on pathogenesis, therapy and prognosis]. Wien Klin Wochenschr 1998;110(13–14):479–84.
353. Paproski SM, Owen DA. Granular cell tumor of the thyroid. Arch Pathol Lab Med 2001;125(4):544–6.
354. Deshmukh NS, Mangham DC, Warfield AT, Watkinson JC. Solitary fibrous tumour of the thyroid gland. J Laryngol Otol 2001;115(11):940–2.
355. Ally N, Kumar D, Wodajo FM. Synchronous fibrosarcoma and medullary thyroid cancer in a man with AIDS. Am J Clin Oncol 2006;29(5):532–3.
356. Mansouri H, Gaye M, Errihani H, Kettani F, Gueddari BE. Leiomyosarcoma of the thyroid gland. Acta Otolaryngol 2008;128(3):335–6.
357. Wang TS, Ocal IT, Oxley K, Sosa JA. Primary leiomyosarcoma of the thyroid gland. Thyroid 2008;18(4):425–8.
358. Tong GX, Hamele-Bena D, Liu JC, Horst B, Remotti F. Fine-needle aspiration biopsy of primary osteosarcoma of the thyroid: report of a case and review of the literature. Diagn Cytopathol 2008;36(8):589–94.
359. Hsu KF, Lin YS, Hsieh CB, et al. Primary malignant fibrous histiocytoma of the thyroid: review of the literature with two new cases. Thyroid 2008;18(1):51–5.
360. Yap WM, Chuah KL, Tan PH. Langerhans cell histiocytosis involving the thyroid and parathyroid glands. Mod Pathol 2001;14(2):111–5.
361. Martinez F, Filipowicz E, Hudnall SD. Plasma cell granuloma of the thyroid. Arch Pathol Lab Med 2002;126(5):595–8.
362. Lazzi S, Als C, Mazzucchelli L, Kraft R, Kappeler A, Laissue J. Extensive extramedullary hematopoiesis in a thyroid nodule. Mod Pathol 1996;9(11):1062–5.
363. Giannikaki E, Mantadakis E, Mamalaki E, Delides G, Samonis G. Metastatic uterine leiomyosarcoma coexisting with papillary carcinoma of the thyroid gland. Int J Gynecol Cancer 2006;16(1):442–5.
364. Leath CA, 3rd, Huh WK, Straughn JM, Jr., Conner MG. Uterine leiomyosarcoma metastatic to the thyroid. Obstet Gynecol 2002;100(5 Pt 2):1122–4.
365. Liang HH, Wu CH, Tam KW, Chai CY, Lin SE, Chen SC. Thyroid metastasis in a patient with hepatocellular carcinoma: case report and review of literature. World journal of surgical oncology 2007;5:144.
366. Lam KY, Lo CY. Metastatic tumors of the thyroid gland: a study of 79 cases in Chinese patients. Arch Pathol Lab Med 1998;122(1):37–41.
367. Nakhjavani MK, Gharib H, Goellner JR, van Heerden JA. Metastasis to the thyroid gland. A report of 43 cases. Cancer 1997;79(3):574–8.
368. Tavangar SM, Monajemzadeh M, Larijani B, Haghpanah V. Immunohistochemical study of oestrogen receptors in 351 human thyroid glands. Singapore Med J 2007;48(8): 744–7.

Tumors of the Thyroid Gland (C-Cells)

Ronald A. DeLellis

Abstract Medullary thyroid carcinoma (MTC) comprises 5–10% of all thyroid malignancies and occurs sporadically in 75% of cases, while the remainder develop in association with multiple endocrine neoplasia (MEN) 2A, MEN2B, or familial MTC (FMTC). The MEN2 syndromes, which have autosomal dominant patterns of inheritance, occur as the result of germline mutations in the RET proto-oncogene (10q 11.2). Guidelines for age-stratified prophylactic thyroidectomies in MEN2A, MEN2B, and FMTC are now based on the results of mutational analyses. The tumors exhibit a remarkably wide spectrum of histological appearances and may mimic every type of thyroid malignancy. A small proportion of the cases represent mixed follicular and C cell neoplasms. The heritable tumors are preceded in their development by phases of C cell hyperplasia although there is a growing body of data to support the view that the proliferating C cells represent preinvasive malignancies (carcinomas in situ). C cell hyperplasia (CCH) also occurs in patients with hypercalcemia, hypergastrinemia, Hashimoto's disease, and in the immediate vicinity of follicular cell neoplasms (peritumoral CCH). The latter types of hyperplasia have been classified as physiological or secondary CCH as compared to the C cell proliferative changes in the MEN2 syndromes. In contrast to physiological hyperplasia in which C cells most often appear normal cytologically, the C cells in MEN2 syndromes are frequently dysplastic. However, these distinctions may not always be apparent in individual cases, including some normal glands, which may demonstrate considerable variations in C cell distribution and morphology.

R.A. DeLellis (✉)
Pathologist-in-Chief, Lifespan AMC Pathology Laboratories, Professor and Associate Chair of Pathology and Laboratory Medicine, The Warren Alpert Medical School of Brown University, Department of Pathology, Rhode Island Hospital, Providence, RI 02903, USA
e-mail: rdelellis@lifespan.org

Introduction

Neuroendocrine tumors occur in virtually all organs, but with the notable exception of medullary carcinoma, they are exceedingly rare in the thyroid gland. Medullary thyroid carcinoma (MTC) is a malignant thyroid tumor with evidence of C cell differentiation as manifested by the presence of immunoreactive calcitonin and/or calcitonin messenger RNA [1, 2]. Although earlier reports had suggested the existence of this tumor type, Horn in 1951 reported a series of cases of a primary thyroid cancer characterized by sharply defined rounded or ovoid compact cell groups of moderate size in a background of hyalinized connective tissue [3]. Importantly, their prognosis was intermediate between undifferentiated (anaplastic) thyroid carcinomas and the differentiated carcinomas of papillary or follicular types. The major histopathologic features of this tumor type, including the presence of stromal amyloid deposits, were describe subsequently by Hazard and co-workers who suggested the term, medullary thyroid carcinoma (MTC) based on the solid appearance of many of the cases in their series. E.D. Williams proposed that MTCs were derived from the thyroid parafollicular cells based on comparative studies in dogs and other animals [5]. Subsequent immunofluorescence studies confirmed the parafollicular cell origin of calcitonin [6] and the presence of this hormone in tumor extracts and in the serum of affected patients [7, 8].

Medullary carcinomas comprise 5–10% of all thyroid malignancies in most series [1, 2, 9]. In patients with nodular thyroid disease subjected to serum basal and pentagastrin stimulated calcitonin studies, the prevalence of MTC ranges from 0.24 to 2.85% (mean 0.61%) based on nine reported series, primarily from Europe [10]. Pacini et al. have further underscored the relatively high prevalence of MTC in more than 1300 patients with nodular thyroid disease [10]. In their study, MTC represented approximately 15% of all incidentally discovered thyroid carcinomas.

A. Khan (ed.), *Surgical Pathology of Endocrine and Neuroendocrine Tumors*, Current Clinical Pathology,
DOI 10.1007/978-1-60327-396-1_6, © Humana Press, a part of Springer Science+Business Media, LLC 2009

Clinical Features of Sporadic and Heritable MTC

Medullary thyroid carcinomas (MTCs) occur sporadically or in association with the MEN2 syndromes, which are inherited as autosomal dominant traits [11–13]. Sporadic tumors represent approximately 75% of cases while MEN2 associated tumors account for the remainder [2]. Sporadic tumors occur with equal frequency in different parts of the world, but little is known about their etiology. In contrast to papillary and follicular carcinomas, there is no apparent relationship between exposure to radiation and the development of MTC.

Sporadic MTC occurs primarily in middle-aged adults, with a slightly increased female to male preponderance. Most patients present with a painless tumor mass with or without associated cervical lymphadenopathy. In Kebebew's series, approximately 75% of patients presented with a thyroid mass while 15% had symptoms of dysphagia, dyspnea, or hoarseness [14]. Cervical lymph node metastases may be present, and in some cases, distant metastases may also be evident at presentation. Affected patients can present with a variety of signs and symptoms associated with the production of calcitonin, other peptides, amines, or prostaglandins. Patients with metastatic disease, for example, may have severe diarrhea or flushing and these symptoms may be related to the high circulating levels of calcitonin. In Kebebew's series, approximately 10% of patients presented with systemic symptoms [14]. Cushing's syndrome, which occurs in less than 1% of patients with MTC, is a result of tumor production of adrenocorticotrophin (ACTH). Survival following the appearance of the syndrome is poor [15]. Although very high levels of calcitonin may be present in patients with these tumors, hypocalcemia is virtually nonexistent.

MEN2 has an incidence of approximately $1.25–7.5/10^7$ per year and an estimated prevalence of 1/35,000 [13]. More than 90% of patients with MEN2 will develop MTC [13]. MEN2A [MIM# (Mendelian Inheritance in Man Number) 1714007] accounts for more than 75% of all heritable MTC cases. Affected patients also have pheochromocytomas in approximately 40–60% of cases and hyperparathyroidism (10–30%). Some kindreds with MEN2A or FMTC may also have cutaneous lichen amyloidosis, which appears as pruritic plaques over the upper back [16]. It has been suggested that pruritus plays a pivotal role in the development of cutaneous lichen amyloidosis with the amyloidosis resulting from repeated scratching [17]. Hirschsprung's disease has been associated with MEN2A in a few families [18].

Patients with MEN2A generally present with thyroid tumors between the ages of 25 and 35. However, age at presentation became progressively younger with the development of calcitonin screening studies in the 1970s and molecular diagnostic testing for RET mutations in the past decade [13, 16]. In approximately 10% of cases, pheochromocytomas become evident before the appearance of the thyroid tumors. Pheochromocytomas in this syndrome are usually bilateral and multicentric and are preceded in their development by phases of adrenal medullary hyperplasia [19, 20]. The frequency of malignancy in MEN2A associated pheochromocytomas does not differ significantly from that observed in patients with non-syndromic tumors. Hyperparathyroidism occurs in up to 30% of affected patients and the resected parathyroid glands are typically hyperplastic.

MEN2B (MIM# 162300) is the most phenotypically distinctive type of the MEN2 syndromes [13, 21]. It accounts for approximately 5% of the heritable forms of MTC, with a significant proportion of cases representing de novo mutations. Patients with MEN2B have pheochromocytomas in 40–60% of cases, but parathyroid abnormalities are virtually nonexistent. Affected patients may also have neuromas of the tongue and/or ganglioneuromatosis of the gastrointestinal tract, a marfanoid habitus, and/or medullated corneal nerve fibers. The MTCs in this syndrome have an earlier onset and more aggressive clinical course than those occurring in patients with MEN2A or FMTC.

Some kindreds with familial MTC syndromes may manifest thyroid tumors exclusively and these patients are classified as having FMTC (MIM# 155240) [13, 22]. Affected patients typically present at the same age as those with nonfamilial MTCs. Importantly, a significant proportion of patients presenting with apparent sporadic MTCs will prove to have FMTC on the basis of molecular analyses [23].

Pathological Features and Differential Diagnosis

Medullary carcinomas vary in size from those that are barely visible to those that replace the entire lobe of the thyroid [1, 2, 24]. The tumors are generally sharply circumscribed but are nonencapsulated. Many of the tumors are tan to pink with a generally soft consistency while others are firm and fibrotic with areas of granular yellow discoloration that represent focal calcifications. The smaller tumors generally occur at the junction of the upper and middle thirds of the lobes, an area in which C cells normally predominate. When the tumors become very large, they replace the entire lobe with extension into the perithyroidal soft tissues and trachea. In contrast, heritable tumors are typically bilateral and multicentric.

Sporadic and familial medullary carcinomas have a wide spectrum of histological patterns that may mimic virtually all other primary thyroid tumors [1, 2]. The usual medullary carcinoma has a lobular, trabecular, insular, or sheet-like growth pattern, with evidence of focal extension of tumor into the adjacent normal thyroid (Figs. 1 and 2). Individual tumor cells may be round, polygonal, or spindle shaped, with frequent admixtures of these cell types. The nuclei have coarsely clumped or speckled (salt and pepper) chromatin and generally inconspicuous nucleoli (Fig. 2). A few nuclei may contain pseudo-inclusions similar to those seen in papillary carcinomas. Binucleate cells are common and occasional multinucleate giant cells may be evident. Most MTCs exhibit moderate degrees of pleomorphism but mitotic activity is generally low.

The cytoplasm varies from eosinophilic to basophilic and appears finely granular in well-fixed preparations. Prior to the advent of immunohistochemistry, argyrophil stains (e.g., Grimelius technique) were the methods of choice for the identification of MTCs. Occasional mucin

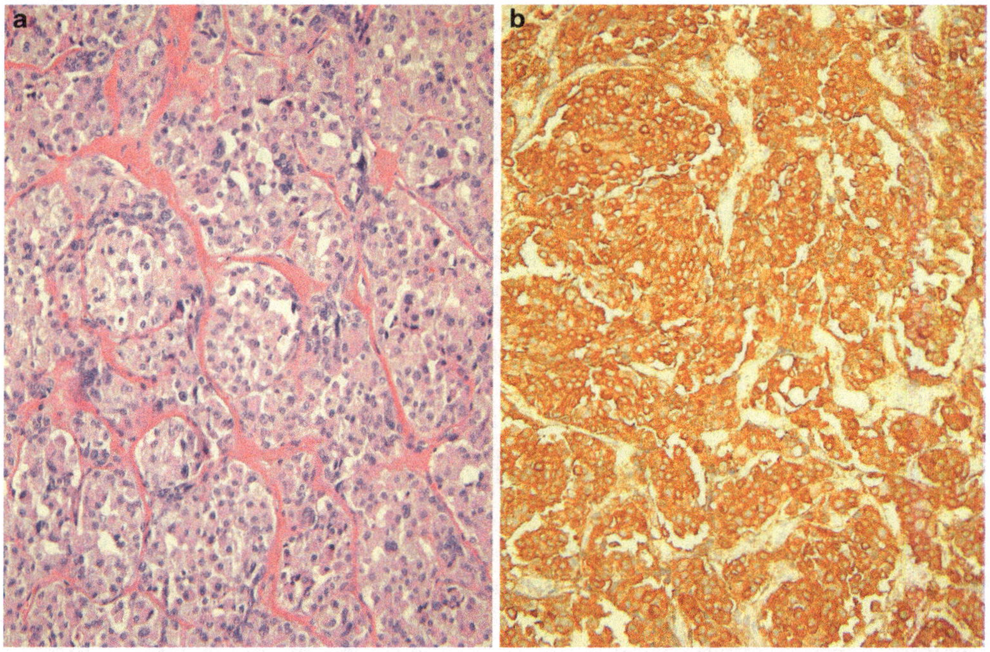

Fig. 1 (**A**) Medullary thyroid carcinoma. The tumor has a nesting growth pattern (H&E stain). (**B**) Immunoperoxidase stain for calcitonin. The tumor cells are strongly positive for calcitonin

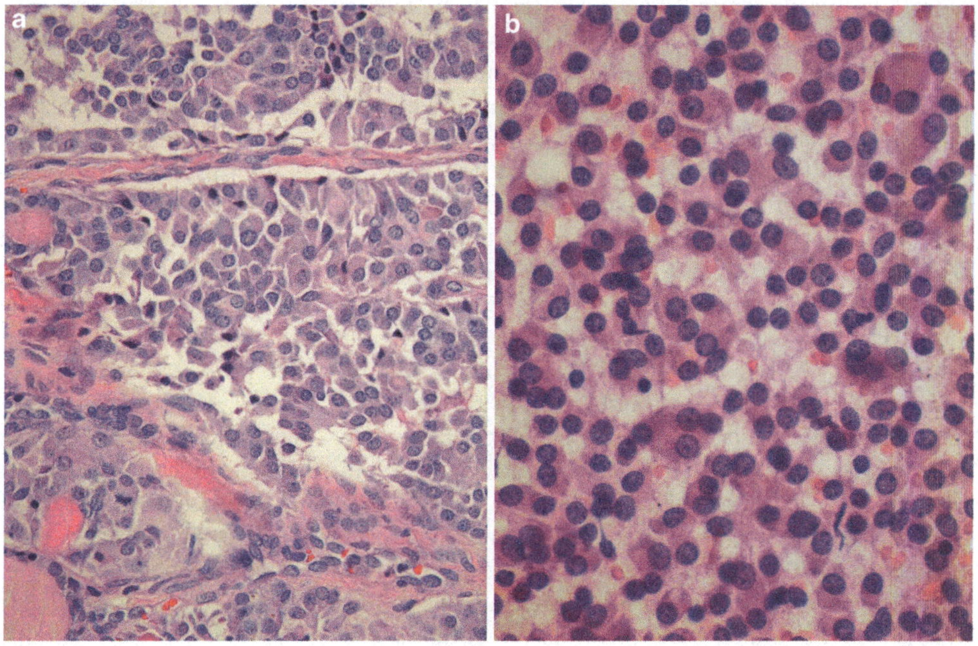

Fig. 2 (**A**) Medullary thyroid carcinoma. These tumor cells have a plasmacytoid appearance with eccentric nuclei (H&E stain). (**B**) Touch preparation of same case as A (H&E stain). The plasmacytoid appearance of the tumor cells is accentuated in this preparation. Occasional multinucleate tumor cells are present

positive cytoplasmic vacuoles may be present in some cases [25].

Foci of necrosis and hemorrhage are uncommon in small tumors; however, larger tumors exhibit these features more commonly. Lymphatic and vascular invasion may be seen at the advancing front of the tumor. In large tumors, foci of lymphatic invasion may be present in the contralateral lobe. Occasionally, nodal and distant metastases may be present in association with tumors measuring less than 1 cm. Some MTCs contain prominent areas of fibrosis, and stromal amyloid deposits are present in up to 80% of cases. Ultrastructurally, the amyloid deposits have a fibrillar ultrastructure that is identical to that seen in other forms of amyloidosis. Calcitonin immunostains frequently demonstrate positive staining within the amyloid deposits. Although earlier studies had suggested that the amyloid was derived from the calcitonin precursor [26], more recent studies indicate that full-length calcitonin is the sole constituent of the amyloid [27]. Calcification of the amyloid may occur and occasional tumors may contain psammoma bodies. A few medullary carcinomas may consist almost exclusively of amyloid and these cases may be difficult to distinguish from amyloid goiters.

Cytological Features and Ultrastructure

Medullary carcinomas are variably cellular in cytological preparations [2, 28]. Cells are usually present singly or in loosely cohesive groups with poorly defined cell margins. Aspirates typically appear pleomorphic and while some cells are small and round, others may be cuboidal, polyhedral, or spindle shaped. The nuclei tend to be located eccentrically within the cytoplasm, and this feature imparts a plasmacytoid appearance to the tumor cells (Fig. 2B). The chromatin is coarsely granular and nucleoli are usually small and inconspicuous. Occasional nuclear pseudo-inclusions may be present.

The cytoplasm is generally pale and fibrillary in Papanicolaou stained preparations with occasional areas of process formation [2, 28]. In Wright-Giemsa stained slides, cytoplasmic granularity may be evident, and in some instances, the granules appear metachromatic. Amyloid may be indistinguishable from colloid in Papanicolaou stains, but a Congo red stain can be performed to confirm the presence of amyloid. The diagnosis of medullary carcinoma should be confirmed with immunostains for calcitonin or chromogranin.

Ultrastructurally, MTCs contain membrane-bound dense core secretory granules which represent the sites of storage of calcitonin and other peptide and amine products [9, 29]. Type 1 granules, which have an average diameter of 280 mm contain moderately dense finely granular contents that are closely applied to their limiting membranes. The type 2 granules have an average diameter of 130 mm and are characterized by electron dense contents that are separated from their limiting membranes by a narrow electron lucent space. Both granule types contain calcitonin.

Immunohistochemistry

Medullary thyroid carcinomas are positive for thyroid transcription factor-1 (TTF-1), similar to tumors of follicular cell origin [30]. Stains for thyroglobulin are typically negative, although entrapped normal thyroid follicles may stain positively. The tumors are typically positive for low molecular weight cytokeratins and most commonly have a cytokeratin 7 positive/cytokeratin 20 negative phenotype [31]. Vimentin is variably present within the tumor cells and some tumors contain subpopulations of neurofilament positive cells [32].

The tumors are usually positive for calcitonin (Fig. 1) and a wide spectrum of generic neuroendocrine markers including chromogranin and synaptophysin [33–35]. Chromogranin is a sensitive marker for medullary carcinoma and in fact, may be more sensitive than calcitonin for the identification of this tumor type [36]. Other products found in these tumors include calbindin-D28K and polysialic acid of NCAM [37, 38].

Calcitonin is present in 80–90% of the tumors. Although many cases demonstrate extensive calcitonin immunoreactivity throughout the tumor, others may show only focal and weak reactivity [39, 40]. The calcitonin gene related peptide is also present in many cases [41]. Some tumors which are negative for calcitonin peptide and the calcitonin gene-related peptide give positive signals for calcitonin messenger RNA using in situ hybridization procedures [42].

A variety of other peptides have been localized within these tumors and their presence has been confirmed by radioimmunoassays of tumor extracts. Both somatostatin and gastrin releasing peptide are present in subpopulations of normal C cells and both of these peptides are commonly expressed in medullary carcinomas [43, 44]. Somatostatin receptors are also frequently expressed in these tumors. Other peptides that are commonly present include ACTH, leu-enkephalin, neurotensin, substance P, vasoactive intestinal peptide, and chorionic gonadotropin [45–47]. Rarely, the tumors may contain subpopulations of cells immunoreactive for glucagon, gastrin, and insulin, and both [50] catecholamines and serotonin may also be present [48].

Galectin-3 has been reported in 92% of heritable medullary thyroid carcinomas [49]. The staining is focal in 26% of the carcinomas and diffuse in the remainder. Interestingly, galectin-3 is reduced or absent in nodal metastases while foci of C cell hyperplasia are negative for galectin-3.

CEA levels are typically increased in the plasma of patients with MTC [50, 51], and correlative immunohistochemical studies have demonstrated that virtually all of the tumors are CEA positive. Several groups have demonstrated that a subset of MTCs may lose the ability to synthesize and secrete calcitonin while maintaining their capacity for CEA synthesis. In fact, calcitonin negative areas in medullary carcinoma are frequently positive for CEA. The finding of decreasing levels of calcitonin in the face of increasing levels of CEA generally predicts an aggressive clinical course [52].

Medullary Thyroid Carcinoma Variants

Numerous variants of medullary carcinoma have been described, as summarized in Table 1 and illustrated in Fig. 3 [53–64].

Table 1 Variants of medullary thyroid carcinoma

Variant	Features
Papillary [53]	Tumor cells aligned along fibrovascular stalks with frequent solid areas. A pseudopapillary pattern, resulting from necrosis of tumor cells at a distance from the vascular supply, is considerably more common.
Follicular/tubular [54]	Follicle formation within the tumor. Colloid like material is thyroglobulin negative and variably positive for calcitonin.
Small cell [55]*	Cells with hyperchromatic nuclei and scant cytoplasm. Mitotic activity and foci of necrosis may be prominent.
Giant cell [57]	Numerous multinucleate tumor cells.
Clear cell [58]	Optically clear cytoplasm
Melanotic [59, 60]	Melanin-positive tumor cells.
Oncocytic [61]	Abundant granular eosinophilic cytoplasm.
Squamous [61]	Foci of keratinization.
Amphicrine [62]	Mucin and calcitonin present in tumor cells.
Paraganglionoma-like [63]	Encapsulated with broad trabecular growth pattern resembling hyalinizing trabecular tumors.
Angiosarcoma-like [64]	Anastomosing pseudovascular channels lined by flattened cells and with groups of neoplastic cells admixed with red blood cells

*Eusebi et al. have also reported two cases of apparent primary small (oat) cell carcinomas of the thyroid that were positive for chromogranin and synaptophysin but were negative for thyroglobulin and calcitonin and calcitonin messenger RNA, by immunohistochemistry and in situ hybridization [56].

All C cell neoplasms have been considered to represent carcinomas although occasional examples of apparent C cell adenomas have been reported [65]. Kodama and coworkers [66] reported two cases of C cell adenoma, each of which measured 4 cm in diameter. Both tumors were composed of cells that were fusiform to cuboidal with small ovoid nuclei. Neither tumor contained amyloid or foci of calcification. In contrast to most medullary carcinomas, stains for CEA were negative and there was no evidence of increased CEA levels in the serum. Calcitonin levels were markedly elevated and the tumor cells stained strongly for this peptide. Although the term "C cell adenoma" has been suggested for completely encapsulated C cell tumors [70], it is best to regard the tumors as encapsulated medullary carcinomas until more is known about their natural history.

Medullary microcarcinomas, by definition, measure less than 1 cm in diameter and may occur sporadically or in association with MEN2 [24]. They may exhibit nesting, trabecular or diffuse growth patterns, and occasional microcarcinomas may have a microfollicular growth pattern resembling small follicular adenomas or adenomatous foci. Most of the reported cases have been incidental findings in thyroids removed for other reasons or in patients with nodular thyroid disease who have been screened for calcitonin abnormalities. Occasional microcarcinomas may give rise to metastases.

Differential Diagnosis

Medullary carcinomas can mimic the entire spectrum of benign and malignant thyroid tumors. Both papillary/pseudopapillary and other MTC variants may contain nuclear pseudo-inclusions and psammoma bodies; however, they lack the nuclear clearing that is typical of papillary thyroid carcinomas (PTCs). Moreover, medullary carcinomas are positive for chromogranin, calcitonin, and synaptophysin while PTCs are negative for these markers. Since medullary carcinomas may contain follicles, they also must be distinguished from follicular cell neoplasms which are typically positive for thyroglobulin and negative for calcitonin, chromogranin, and synaptophysin. Poorly differentiated carcinomas of insular type are composed of nests and islet like arrangements of follicular cells and may contain microfollicles. These tumors are also positive for thyroglobulin and are typically negative for calcitonin, chromogranin, and synaptophysin. However, a few poorly differentiated carcinomas may express generic neuroendocrine markers, as discussed in a subsequent section. Medullary carcinomas of spindle and giant cell types must be distinguished from undifferentiated carcinomas of follicular cell origin. The latter tumors are negative for neuroendocrine markers, calcitonin, thyroglobulin, and TTF-1.

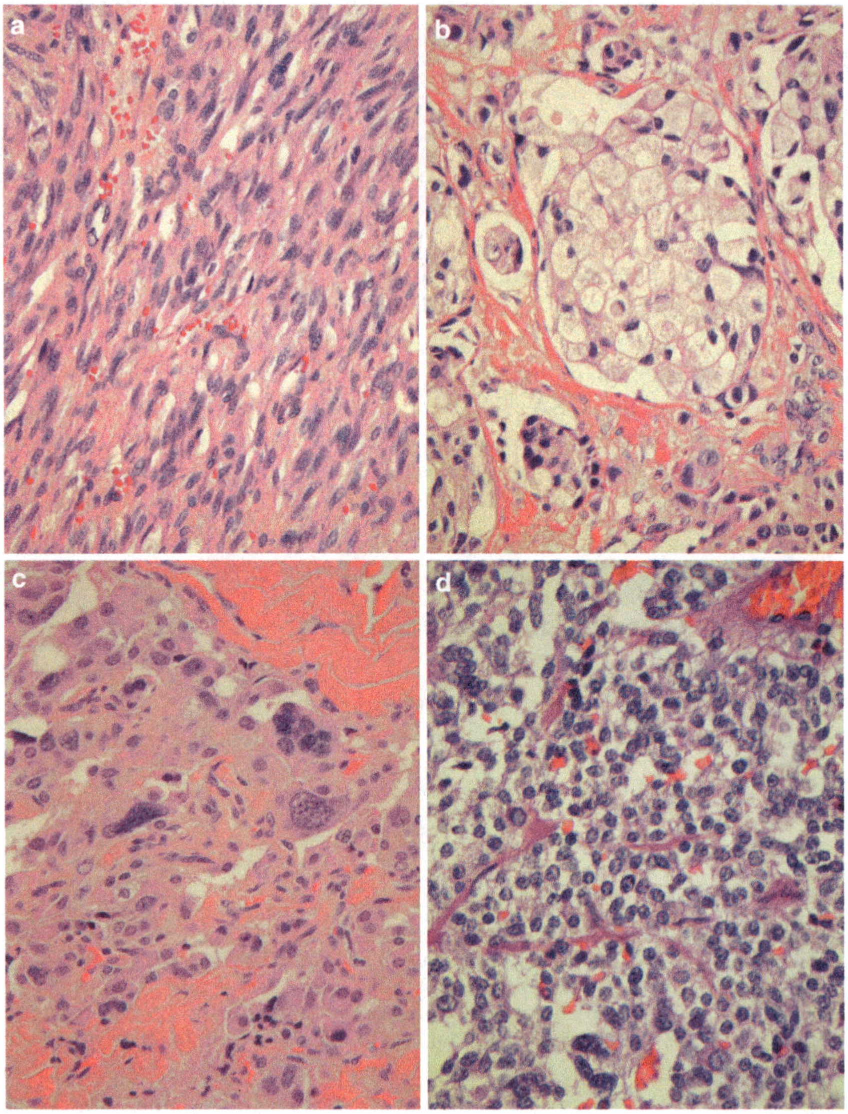

Fig. 3 Medullary thyroid carcinoma variants. (**A**) Spindle cell. (**B**) Clear cell. (**C**) Giant cell. (**D**) Small cell (H&E stains)

The distinction of small cell medullary carcinoma from malignant lymphomas may be difficult, particularly in small biopsy or cytological samples. The demonstration of CD45 and markers of T and B cell lineage establishes the diagnosis of lymphoma. Small cell carcinoma of the lungs and other sites may metastasize to the thyroid and may mimic medullary carcinoma of small cell type [68]. Since TTF-1 is expressed both in lung and in thyroid tumors in addition to small cell carcinomas of diverse sites of origin, the presence of this marker is not a useful discriminant. Moreover, calcitonin and generic neuroendocrine markers may be present in other small cell carcinomas. In these instances, careful clinical and radiological examination may be helpful in identifying a pulmonary or extra pulmonary primary tumor. Since mucin may be present in medullary carcinomas, these tumors must also be distinguished from mucinous carcinomas that have metastasized to the thyroid.

Oncocytic medullary carcinomas must be distinguished from oncocytic tumors of follicular cell origin and oncocytic parathyroid neoplasms. Oncocytic follicular cell tumors are positive for thyroglobulin while parathyroid tumors are positive for parathyroid hormone. The hyalinizing trabecular tumor is typically encapsulated, as are some variants of medullary carcinoma. A trabecular pattern is present in both tumor types and both may exhibit areas of hyalinization. However, the stroma of medullary carcinoma is positive for amyloid, whereas the stroma of hyalinizing trabecular tumors stains only for collagen. While medullary carcinomas stain positively for calcitonin and CEA, these markers are negative in hyalinizing trabecular tumors. It should be noted that occasional hyalinizing trabecular tumors may be positive for generic neuroendocrine markers [69].

Medullary carcinomas may be difficult to distinguish from paragangliomas. The latter tumors have a "Zellballen" architecture and are positive for chromogranin and synaptophysin but are negative for calcitonin. A population of S-100-positive sustentacular cells is typically present at the peripheries of the cell nests in paragangliomas but is absent from MTCs. Intrathyroidal parathyroid adenomas also may be difficult to distinguish from medullary carcinomas. Parathyroid tumors are positive for parathyroid hormone and chromogranin, but stains for calcitonin are negative and should serve to distinguish these tumor types.

Metastatic neuroendocrine carcinomas involving the thyroid gland may be particularly difficult to distinguish from MTCs [68]. Features that favor a diagnosis of metastatic neuroendocrine carcinoma include an interstitial pattern of spread, occurrence of multiple tumor foci, folliculotropism (tumor cells lining follicles), rosette formations with cuticular borders, and lack of reactivity for calcitonin and CEA [68]. The presence of folliculotropism may be particularly difficult to distinguish from C cell hyperplasia, as described below.

Heritable Forms of Medullary Thyroid Carcinoma and C Cell Hyperplasia

Medullary carcinomas occurring in patients with MEN2-associated tumors are identical to those occurring sporadically, except for the bilaterality and multifocality of the heritable cases. Studies based on enhanced calcitonin secretory responses to calcium and pentagastrin in patients at risk for the development of heritable forms of these tumors established that they were preceded in their development by C cell hyperplasia which is characterized by increased numbers of C-cells within follicular spaces [21, 29, 70, 71] (Fig. 4). With further progression, C cells expand the follicles to produce

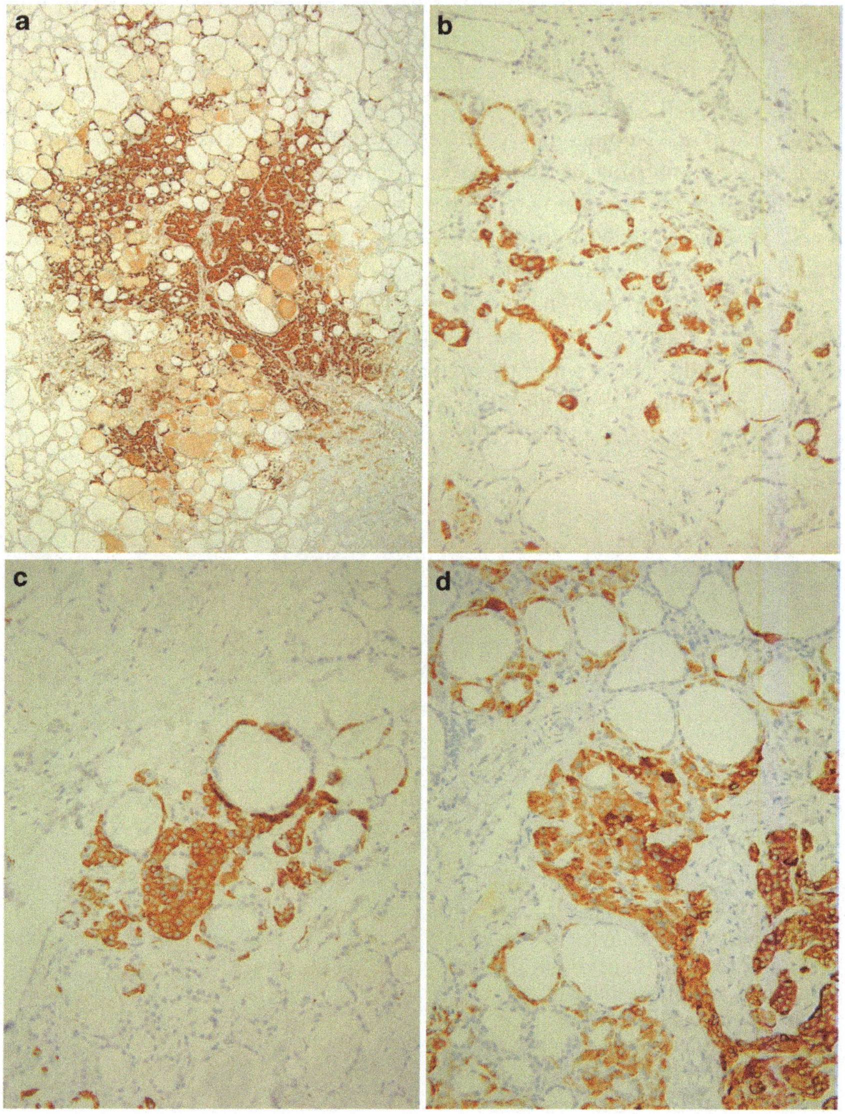

Fig. 4 MEN2A associated C cell hyperplasia and medullary thyroid carcinoma, immunoperoxidase stains for calcitonin. (**A**) Low-power view of early medullary thyroid cancer (center) with surrounding areas of C cell hyperplasia (periphery). (**B**) Area of diffuse C cell hyperplasia. (**C**) Area of early nodular C cell hyperplasia. (**D**) Area of early medullary carcinoma with surrounding fibrosis

foci of nodular hyperplasia. Transition of this phase of C cell growth to medullary carcinoma is characterized by areas of fibrosis between the proliferating C cells, as they begin to invade the interstitium (Fig. 4). With further progression, there are increasing degrees of fibrosis between the groups of neoplastic C cells. At the ultrastructural level, the earliest feature of malignancy is the extension of intrafollicular C cells through the follicular basement membranes into the interstitium of the gland [29]. McDermott and coworkers confirmed these observations using an immunoperoxidase technique for the demonstration of type IV collagen in the follicular basement membranes [72].

The distinction of normal C cell distribution from the earliest phases of C cell hyperplasia is both difficult and controversial. Early studies suggested that the presence of 10 C cells per low power field constituted sufficient evidence for C cell hyperplasia; however, more recent studies indicate that this diagnosis should be made only when there are at least 50 C cells per low power field [73] (Fig. 5). However it should be noted that in some regions of the lobes, particularly in the vicinity of solid cell nests, the numbers of C cells may exceed 50 per low power field in occasional normal individuals.

Guyetant and colleagues demonstrated that C cells were more numerous in male patients than in females, correlating with the known higher plasma calcitonin levels in men [74]. Moreover, this study demonstrated that 33% of the adult population, including 15% of women and 41% of men, had evidence of CCH as defined by having at least 3 microscopic fields (100×) with greater than 50 C cells. These findings suggest that either a substantial portion of the population has CCH or that the criteria for the definition of this entity are inaccurate. Interestingly, abnormal pentagastrin tests are found in only approximately 5% of the normal population as compared to the 30% frequency of CCH, as defined histologically. These observations suggest that there may be considerable variation in normal C cell distribution and that these variations may not be accompanied necessarily by hypercalcitoninemia.

C cell hyperplasia also occurs in patients with hypercalcemia (Fig. 5A), hypergastrinemia, Hashimoto's thyroiditis, and adjacent to a variety of follicular cell tumors, including follicular adenomas and carcinomas and papillary carcinomas (peritumoral C cell hyperplasia). The latter type of hyperplasia has been referred to as physiologic or secondary C cell hyperplasia, in contrast to MEN2-associated CCH, which has been referred to as primary or "neoplastic" hyperplasia [75]. Perry and coworkers reported that physiologic CCH is primarily a diffuse process characterized by increased numbers of normal C cells and can be diagnosed with only on the basis of calcitonin immunostains [75]. "Neoplastic" CCH, on the other hand, involves the proliferation of dysplastic C cells and can be diagnosed on the basis of H&E stains alone. While "neoplastic"/MEN2-associated CCH is generally regarded as a precursor of MTC, the neoplastic potential of physiologic CCH remains unknown, notwithstanding the rare cases of MTC reported in patients with chronic hypercalcemia or Hashimoto's thyroiditis (Fig. 5B).

Carney and coworkers in 1978 proposed that CCH associated with MEN2 syndromes is a preinvasive carcinoma or carcinoma in situ [76]. Further evidence for the neoplastic nature of CCH has come from molecular studies of microdissected foci of thyroid glands from patients with MEN2A [77]. The latter studies have

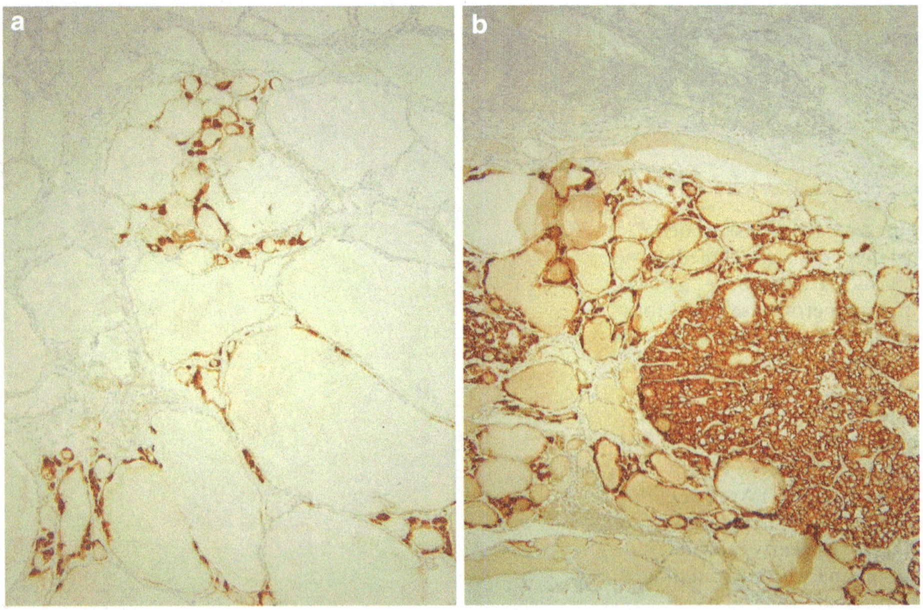

Fig. 5 (**A**) Mild diffuse C cell hyperplasia in a 70-year-old man with adenomatous (follicular cell) hyperplasia, immunoperoxidase stain for calcitonin. (**B**) C cell hyperplasia with a microscopic medullary carcinoma in a patient with Hashimoto's thyroiditis, immunoperoxidase stain for calcitonin

shown that foci of CCH are monoclonal with inactivation of the same allele in both thyroid lobes. Moreover, the foci have different secondary alterations involving the tumor suppressor genes p53, RB1, WT1, and NF1. These findings, together with the down regulation of apoptosis, are consistent with an intraepithelial neoplastic process and suggest that early clonal expansions precede migration of C cell precursors into each thyroid lobe.

C cell hyperplasia has been regarded as a precursor and marker of MEN2 associated medullary carcinoma; however, this view has been challenged by several recent reports. In a series of 30 patients with nodular thyroid disease and abnormal pentagastrin-stimulated calcitonin levels, Kaserer et al. reported 19 patients (F:M;14:5) with MTC and 11 males but no females with CCH only, as defined by greater than 50 C cells per low power field [78]. Six of 16 patients with sporadic MTC had concomitant CCH and three of these patients proved to be new MEN2 index cases, as demonstrated by genetic studies. On the basis of these studies, Kaserer et al. concluded that CCH was an unreliable marker for heritable MTC and that CCH had a preneoplastic potential in the absence of RET germline mutations.

In a second study of 16 familial and 34 sporadic MTCs, Kaserer et al. noted CCH in 16/16 (100%) of familial cases and in 24/34 (71%) of sporadic cases [79]. Among familial cases, CCH was of neoplastic type in 85% (14/16), nodular type in 6% (1/14), and focal type in 6% (1/14). In sporadic cases, on the other hand, neoplastic CCH was present in 18% (6/34), nodular hyperplasia in 21% (7/34), diffuse hyperplasia in 18% (6/34), and focal hyperplasia in 14% (5/34). There was no evidence of CCH in 29% (10/34) of the sporadic cases. On the basis of this study, Kaserer et al. concluded that many sporadic MTCs develop on a background of CCH [79].

Since there is such a wide variation in C cell counts in normal thyroid glands, two possible interpretations of these observations are (1) that the observed "CCH" in sporadic tumor cases represents the upper limit of normal C cell distribution or (2) that the CCH is analogous to the secondary CCH found adjacent to follicular and papillary tumors. Mears and Diaz-Cano have reanalyzed the data in the Kaserer study [80] and have concluded that multifocal and bilateral invasive MTCs associated with expansile intraepithelial neoplasia (nodular and neoplastic hyperplasia) represent familial disease in 98% of cases. The probability of sporadic disease associated with nodular and neoplastic C cell hyperplasia was calculated as 1.87% [80].

In summary, C cell distribution has a remarkably wide variation in normal individuals. The current criterion of 50 C cells per 100× microscopic field is, in all likelihood, an underestimate since up to 40% of normal males would have CCH according to this definition. MEN2-associated CCH has characteristic topographic, cytological, and molecular features, which permits its distinction from secondary C cell hyperplasia in most cases, and this can be confirmed by the presence of germline RET mutations. Whether physiologic/secondary CCH has a significant preneoplastic potential remains to be determined.

Molecular Features of Sporadic and Heritable MTC

A major advance in the study of the molecular origins of the familial MTC syndromes was the observation that the putative MEN2A gene mapped to the pericentromeric region of chromosome 10 [81, 82]. Subsequent studies led to the use of restriction length polymorphisms to identify carriers of the familial MTC syndromes [83, 84]. Ultimately the responsible gene was mapped to the region of chromosome 10 (10q11.2) that contained the RET proto-oncogene and germline missense RET mutations were demonstrated in affected individuals [85–96].

The RET proto-oncogene contains 21 exons and encodes a cell surface tyrosine kinase receptor with a cadherin ligand binding site and a cysteine rich extracellular domain, a transmembrane region, and two cytoplasmic tyrosine kinase domains [97, 98]. The cadherin binding site plays an important role in cell signaling while the cysteine rich extracellular domain is important for receptor dimerization. RET is expressed in a variety of neural crest derivatives (C cells, adrenal medulla, extraadrenal paraganglia, sympathetic and enteric ganglia), parathyroid gland, and urogenital tract [99]. Mice homozygous for a targeted RET mutation develop to term and develop both renal agenesis or dysgenesis and absence of enteric neurons; however, they do not have evidence of neoplastic disorders [100].

Germline mutations in RET resulting in aberrant activation of RET receptors have been characterized in MEN2A, MEN2B, and FMTC (Table 2) [13, 88–96]. The mutations are of the missense type and most commonly affect exons 10 and 11 and less commonly exons 13, 14, 15, and 16. Most of the mutations affect the cysteine rich extracellular domain (MEN2A, FMTC). Codon 634 mutations are present in approximately 80% of MEN2A patients while codon 609, 618, and 620 mutations account for more than 60% of FMTC cases and those patients with the Hirschsprung's phenotype. Codon 634 mutations have a strong genotype-phenotype correlation with the development of pheochromocytoma and hyperparathyroidism [94]. Substitution of cysteine with several other amino acids increases the formation of active RET dimers resulting in their transforming potential [101–103]. Mutations affecting codons 768 or 804 (tyrosine kinase domain) may also occur (Table 2).

Table 2 RET mutations in MEN2 syndromes

Site	Codon	Syndrome	Frequency (%)
Cysteine-rich domain	609	MEN2A, FMTC	0–1
	611	MEN2A, FMTC	2–3
	618	MEN2A, FMTC	3–5
	620	MEN2A, FMTC	6–8
	630	MEN2A, FMTC	0–1
	634	MEN2A, FMTC	80–90
Transmembrane domain	768	FTMC	Rare
	790	MEN2A	Rare
	791	FMTC	Rare
	804	MEN2A/FMTC	0–1
	844	FMTC	Rare
Tyrosine kinase domain	883	MEN2B	Rare
	891	FMTC	Rare
	918	MEN2B	3–5
	922	MEN2B	Rare

Mutations affecting the tyrosine kinase domain (codon 918) occur in patients with MEN2B and in some sporadic medullary carcinomas [91–93]. This mutation results in the replacement of methionine with threonine. Codon 883 mutations resulting in the substitution of phenylalanine for alanine also occur in a small subset of patients with MEN2B [104, 105]. The MEN2B mutations result in RET activation in its monomeric form [102, 103]. These mutations are present in the catalytic core region of the tyrosine kinase domain and it has been suggested that they induce a conformational change in this region leading to increased tyrosine kinase activity or alteration in its substrate specificity [102]. Mutations commonly detected in MEN2A and 2B have high transforming activities for NIH 3T3 cells, suggesting that the underlying tumorigenic mechanism of RET mutations results from dominant oncogenic conversion rather than from a loss of tumor suppressor function [102, 103]. Moreover, targeting of MEN2A mutant RET forms to C cells in transgenic mice results in the development of CCH or MTC in 100% of the animals in addition to mammary and parotid gland carcinomas in approximately 50% [106].

The frequency of RET germline mutations in cases of apparent sporadic MTC has been assessed in several studies [95]. In one study, 6 of 101 individuals harbored mutations involving codons 609, 611, 618, or 634 [107]. Four of the affected patients were the probands of previously unrecognized kindreds while the remaining two patients were examples of de novo mutations. Combining the results of several studies, it has been estimated that approximately 7% of patients with apparent sporadic tumors have germline mutations [95]. These findings support the view that analysis of RET should be performed in all patients presenting with apparent sporadic medullary carcinoma.

Somatic mutations in codon 918 have been observed in up to 70% of sporadic MTCs [92, 95]. This mutation, which is identical to the 918-germline mutation in MEN2B, results in the substitution of threonine for methionine. Although Zedenius et al. [108] and Eng et al. [109] have suggested that sporadic tumors with this mutation pursue a more aggressive course, this point has been controversial [110]. The studies of Eng et al. have suggested that the codon 918 mutation can arise as an event in tumor progression within a single tumor or in a metastatic clone [109]. Somatic mutations in codons 630, 634, 766, 768, 804, and 833 have been observed considerably less commonly than codon 918 mutations in sporadic medullary carcinomas [95].

The relationship of physiological/secondary CCH to the development of non-familial MTC is controversial. Recent studies based on laser capture microdissection studies of 24 cases of CCH either isolated or associated with nonfamilial MTC failed to show RET mutations in foci of CCH, despite the presence of codon 918 mutations in three concomitant MTCs [111].

RET mutations involving codons 620, 630, 634, and 918 occur in 10–20% of sporadic pheochromocytomas [112–114]. In contrast, RET mutations have not been detected in parathyroid hyperplasias or adenomas, pituitary adenomas, pancreatic endocrine tumors, carcinoids, or neuroblastomas [115, 116].

RET mutations are also responsible for up to 40% of the autosomal dominant forms of Hirschsprung's disease and a subset of patients with sporadic disease [95, 117]. Mutations are scattered throughout the gene and result in the loss of function of the RET protein. Rarely, FMTC or MEN2A may be present in association with Hirschsprung's disease, and in five kindreds with this association, mutations in codons 609, 618, and 620 were identified [92].

Treatment and Prognosis

Molecular genetic testing has had a profound impact on the management of patients with these syndromes [96, 118, 119]. The decision to perform a prophylactic thyroidectomy is now based exclusively on the use of this type of testing rather than the use of the calcium and pentagastrin provocative tests used in the past. Based on a negative test result, family members at risk for the development of the syndrome need not be subjected to additional testing.

A number of studies have assessed the value of genetic analyses as the basis for prophylactic thyroidectomies in patients with MEN2 [120–122]. In a survey of thyroidectomies in 75 children and adolescents with proven RET mutations, MTC was found in 61% and C cell hyperplasia alone was found in 39%. Testing for RET mutations is now the standard of care for patients with MEN2 [133]. For patients with MEN2A, a prophylactic thyroidectomy is recommended between the ages of 5 and 10 years. For patients with MEN2B, thyroidectomy between the ages of 6 months and 3 years is recommended. The optimal therapeutic strategy for those patients with mutations associated with FMTC remains to be determined.

Surgical treatment of patients with medullary thyroid carcinoma is guided by the known pattern of spread of these tumors, which includes central compartment lymph nodes followed by ipsilateral and then contralateral cervical lymph nodes [124, 125]. Approximately 50% of patients with palpable primary tumors, in fact, will have evidence of cervical nodal metastases. Both sporadic and heritable MTCs, therefore, are generally treated by total thyroidectomy with central lymph node dissection. In those patients with palpable primary tumors, some surgeons advocate the use of ipsilateral and even contralateral cervical lymph node dissections to optimize the chances for complete local control. Postoperative reduction of basal and stimulated calcitonin levels as well as other biomarkers is highly effective in providing information on biochemical cure.

The survival of patients with MTCs is strongly correlated with stage [126]. Surgery provides cure in nearly all patients whose tumors measure less than a few millimeters in diameter, in 90% when tumors are less than one centimeter and in 50% with tumors measuring more than one centimeter [127]. Overall 10-year survival rates average 75–85%. In a series of 104 patients with sporadic and heritable MTC, 49.4% of the patients were cured, 12.3% had recurrent tumor, and 38.3% had persistent tumor [14]. The mean follow-up time was 8.6 years with 10.7% and 13.5% cause specific mortalities at 5 and 10 years, respectively. In this series, 32% of the patients with heritable tumors were diagnosed by genetic or biochemical screening studies. As would be expected, these patients had a lower incidence of cervical node metastases than patients with sporadic tumors and 94.7% were cured at last follow-up. Patients with systemic symptoms of diarrhea, bone pain, and flushing had widespread metastatic disease, and one third of these patients died within 5 years.

Age greater than 50 years and stage are the most important prognostic factors in patients with MTC. In fact, in the study reported by Kebebew et al. age and stage were the only two independent prognostic factors [14]. Male gender approached statistical significance in univariate analyses and most likely represents a minor risk factor. While patients with cervical lymph node metastases were more likely to have recurrent or persistent disease, this parameter was not associated with a significantly higher mortality.

The type of MTC (sporadic MTC, FMTC, MEN2A, MEN2B) has been reported to be an important prognostic factor in some studies. However, when controlling for stage or in multivariate analyses, the subtype of MTC does not appear to be an important prognostic factor according to one study [128].

Numerous histological and immunohistochemical parameters, including cellular composition (spindle cell vs. round cell), pleomorphism, extent of amyloid deposition, and extent of calcitonin staining, have been examined as potential prognostic parameters but none has proven to be significant in multivariate analyses [129]. Koperek et al. have demonstrated that desmoplasia in the primary tumor is a reliable and reproducible parameter to predict nodal metastatic potential [130]; however, additional studies will be required to confirm this hypothesis. Both calcitonin and CEA serum doubling times have also been used as prognostic indices in patients with MTC [131]. Patients with rapid calcitonin doubling times have a poorer prognosis than those with longer doubling times.

The presence of a somatic RET mutation, particularly involving codon 918, has been linked to poor prognosis [108, 109]. RET mutations involving codon 918 are more frequent in large tumors and in those tumors with nodal and distant metastases [132]. Among all prognostic factors found to be correlated with a worse outcome, only advanced stage at diagnosis and the presence of RET mutations showed an independent correlation [132].

Mixed Medullary and Follicular Cell Carcinomas

Mixed tumors with neuroendocrine and follicular cell differentiation include mixed medullary and follicular/papillary carcinoma, medullary carcinoma with thyroglobulin immunoreactivity, and thyroglobulin positive tumors that co-express neuroendocrine markers [133–148]. Among the latter group are occasional poorly differentiated (insular) carcinomas, mucoepidermoid tumors, and hyalinizing trabecular tumors [149–151]. For example, poorly differentiated carcinomas of the insular type may co-express thyroglobulin and somatostatin while hyalinizing trabecular tumors may stain positively for neuroendocrine markers and may contain electron dense neuroendocrine type granules [149, 150].

According to the *WHO Classification of Endocrine Tumors*, mixed tumors are defined as those tumors "showing the morphological features of both medullary carcinoma together with immunoreactive calcitonin and the morphological features of follicular (or papillary) carcinomas with immunoreactive thyroglobulin" [152]. Although this definition may seem straightforward, the distinction of entrapped normal follicles from neoplastic follicles may be difficult, if not impossible. In general, entrapped follicles are present in the peripheral regions of the tumors, but on occasion, they may be present in more central areas (Fig. 6). Moreover, the distinction of true thyroglobulin immunoreactivity from passively absorbed or phagocytosed thyroglobulin is often difficult. Mixed medullary and follicular (or papillary) carcinomas are rare. Most cases have been sporadic; however, rare examples of familial mixed tumors also occur [148].

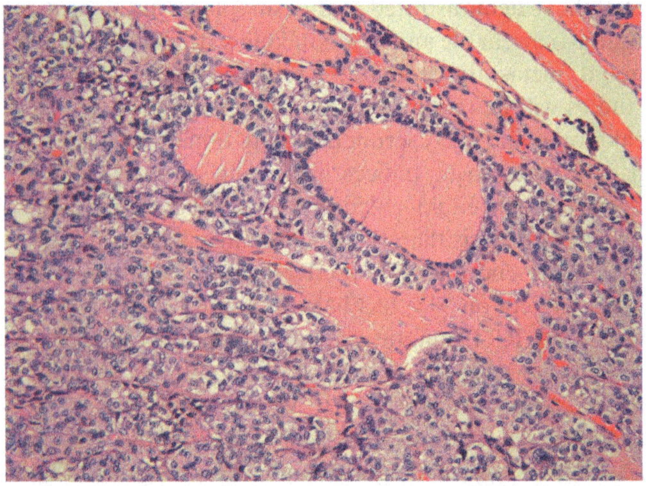

Fig. 6 Medullary thyroid carcinoma with an entrapped thyroid follicle at its periphery (H&E stain)

Mixed tumors with papillary and medullary components also occur [139]. The papillary components are thyroglobulin positive but are negative for calcitonin and CEA. The medullary components, on the other hand, are calcitonin and CEA positive but are negative for thyroglobulin. Both components have been recognized in the primary tumors and in metastatic sites. The existence of such tumors has raised the same histogenetic issues as those of the mixed follicular and medullary carcinomas.

Volante and coworkers utilized molecular approaches to study a series of 12 mixed medullary and follicular/papillary carcinomas [147]. These studies supported the view that the two components were derived from different cells since the components of seven cases consistently showed differences in patterns of RET mutations, allelic losses, and clonal composition. According to their "hostage" hypothesis, Volante et al. postulated that entrapped non-neoplastic follicles were stimulated by medullary carcinoma-derived trophic factors leading to hyperplastic follicular foci. The nature of the putative trophic factors, however, is unknown. Subsequently acquired genetic defects in the follicular cells lead to their neoplastic transformation and the development of papillary or follicular carcinoma components that have the capacity to metastasize. Interestingly, a subset of "mixed tumors" is composed of a medullary carcinoma containing hyperplastic follicles, based on the fact that such follicles are often polyclonal or oligoclonal.

Rarely, families with germline RET point mutations develop both MTC and papillary thyroid carcinoma (PTC), suggesting that RET point mutations rather than rearrangements can drive the development of PTC. The mutant RET found in such families scored constitutive kinase activity and mitogenic effects for cultured thyroid follicular cells (PCC13) although at a significantly lower level than RET/PTC1 [153]. These findings indicate that RET point mutants have the capacity to function as dominant oncogenes for thyroid follicular cells.

It is clear that medullary and follicular/papillary carcinomas represent a heterogeneous group [146]. In addition to those tumors explained by the "hostage" hypothesis, some mixed tumors may represent collision tumors or derivatives of a stem cell capable of differentiating into C cells or follicular cells [146, 148].

References

1. Rosai J, Carcangiu MI, DeLellis RA. (1992) Tumors of the Thyroid Gland Atlas of tumor Pathology. Washington DC: Armed Forces Institute of Pathology 207–258
2. Matias-Guiu X, DeLellis RA, Moley JF et al. (2004) Medullary thyroid carcinoma. In: R.A. DeLellis, R.V. Lloyd, P.U. Heitz and C. Eng (Ed.) Pathology and Genetics of Tumours of Endocrine Organs. WHO Classification of Tumours (pp. 86–91) IARC Press, Lyon
3. Horn RC, (1951) Carcinoma of the thyroid. Description of a distinctive morphological variant and report of seven cases. Cancer 4:697–707
4. Hazard JB, Hawke WA, Crile G (1959) Medullary (solid) carcinoma of the thyroid: A clinicopathological entity. J Clin Endocrinol Met 19:152–161
5. Williams ED (1966) Histogenesis of medullary carcinoma of the thyroid. J Clin Pathol 19:114–118
6. Bussolati G, Pearse AGE (1967) Immunofluorescent localization of calcitonin in the 'C'-cells of the dog and pig thyroid. J Endocrinol 37: 205–209
7. Tashjian AH, Melvin EW (1968) Medullary carcinoma of the thyroid gland. Studies of thyrocalcitonin in plasma and tumor extracts. N Engl J Med 279:279–283
8. Melvin KE, Miller HH, Tashjian AH Jr. (1971) Early diagnosis of medullary carcinoma of the thyroid means of calcitonin assay. N Engl J Med 285:1115–1120
9. DeLellis RA, Wolfe HJ (1981) The pathology of human calcitonin (C)-cell. A Rev Pathol Annu 16:25–52
10. Pacini F, Fontanelli M, Fugazzola L et al. (1994) Routine measurement of serum calcitonin in nodular thyroid disease allows the preoperative diagnosis of unsuspected sporadic

medullary thyroid carcinoma. J Clin Endocrinol Metab 78:826–829
11. DeLellis RA (1995) Multiple endocrine neoplasia syndromes revisited. Clinical, morphological and molecular features. Lab Invest 72:494–505
12. Lips CMJ, Vasen HFA, Lamers CBHW (1988) Multiple endocrine neoplasia syndromes. CRC Crit Rev. Oncol Hematol 2:117–184
13. Gimm O, Morrison CD, Suster S et al. (2004) Multiple endocrine neoplasia type 2. In: R.A. DeLellis, R.V. Lloyd, P.U. Heitz and C. Eng (Ed.) Pathology and Genetics of Tumours of Endocrine Organs. WHO Classification of Tumours (pp. 211–217) IARC Press, Lyon
14. Kebebew E, Ituarte PHG, Siperstein AE et al. (2000) Medullary thyroid carcinoma. Clinical characteristics; treatment, prognostic factors and a comparison of staging systems. Cancer 88:1139–1148
15. Barbosa SL-S, Rodien P, Leboulleux S et al. (2005) Ectopic adrenocorticotropic hormone-syndrome in medullary carcinoma of the thyroid: a retrospective analysis and review of the literature. Thyroid 15:618–623
16. Gagel RF, Tashjian AH, Jr., Cummings T et al. (1988) The clinical outcome of prospective screening for multiple endocrine neoplasia type 2a: An 18 year experience. N Engl J Med 318:478–484
17. Verga U, Fugazzola L, Cambiaghi S et al. (2005) Frequent association between MEN2A and cutaneous lichen amyloidosis. Clin Endocrinol (Oxf) 59:156–161
18. Verdy M, Weber AM, Roy CC et al. (1982) Hirschsprung's disease in a family with multiple endocrine neoplasia type 2. J Pediatr Gastroenterol Nutr 1:603–607
19. DeLellis RA, Wolfe HJ, Gagel RF et al. (1976) Adrenal medullary hyperplasia: A morphometric analysis in patients with familial medullary thyroid carcinoma. Am J Pathol 183: 177–196
20. Carney JA, Sizemore GW, Tyce, GM (1975) Bilateral adrenal medullary hyperplasia in multiple endocrine neoplasia type 2: the precursor of bilateral pheochromocytoma. Mayo Clin Proc 50:3–10
21. Carney JA, Sizemore GW, Hayles AB (1978) Multiple endocrine neoplasia type 2B. Pathobiol Ann 8:105–153
22. Farndon JR, Leight GS, Dilley WG et al. (1986) Familial medullary thyroid carcinoma without associated endocrinopathies: a distinct clinical entity. Br J Surg 73 (4):278–281
23. Elisei R, Romei C, Cosci B et al. (2007) RET genetic screening in patients with medullary thyroid cancer and their relatives: experience with 807 individuals at one center. J Clin Endocrinol Metab 92:4725–4729
24. Mizukami Y, Kurumaya H, Nonomura A et al. (1992) Sporadic medullary microcarcinoma of the thyroid. Histopathology 21:373–377
25. Zaatari GS, Saigo PC, Huvos AG (1983) Mucin production in medullary carcinoma of the thyroid. Arch Pathol Lab Med 107:70–74
26. Sletton K, Westermark P, Natwig JB (1976) Characterization of amyloid fibril proteins from medullary carcinoma of the thyroid. J Exp Med 143:993–998
27. Khurana R, Agarwal A, Bajpai VK et al. (2004) Unraveling the amyloid associated with human medullary carcinoma. Endocrinol 154:5465–5470
28. Kini S (2008) Thyroid Cytopathology: An Atlas and Text. Philadelphia: Lippencott Williams and Wilkins
29. DeLellis RA, Nummemacher G, Wolfe HJ. (1977) C-cell hyperplasia: An ultrastructural analysis. Lab Invest 36:237–248
30. Kaufmann O, Dietel M (2000) Expression of thyroid transcription factor-1 in pulmonary and extrapulmonary small cell carcinomas and other neuroendocrine carcinomas of various primary sites. Histopathol 36:415–420
31. Bejarano PA, Nikiforov YE, Swenson ES, Biddinger PW (2000) Thyroid transcription factor-1, thyroglobulin, cytokeratin 7 and cytokeratin 20 in thyroid neoplasms. Appl Immunohistochem Mol Morphol 8:189–194
32. Kimura N, Nakazato Y, Nagura H, Sasano N (1990) Expression of intermediate filaments in neuroendocrine tumors. Arch Pathol Lab Med 114:506–510
33. DeLellis RA (1993) The pathology of medullary thyroid carcinoma and its precursors. In: LiVolsi, VA, DeLellis, RA (ed) Pathology of the Parathyroid and Thyroid Glands, pp. 77–102. Baltimore Williams and Wilkins
34. Holm R, Sobrinho-Simoes M, Nesland JM Fould VE, Johannessen JV (1985) Medullary carcinoma of the thyroid gland: and immunocytochemical study. Ultrastruct Pathol 8:25–41
35. Portela-Gomes GM, Luckinius GM, Grimeluis L (2000) synaptic vesicle protein 2, a new neuroendocrine cell marker. Am J Pathol 157:1299–1309
36. Schmid KW, Fisher-Colbrie R, Hagn C, Jasani B, Williams, Ed, Winkler H (1987) Chromogranin A and B and secretogranin II in medullary carcinomas of the thyroid. Am J Surg Pathol 11:551–556
37. Katsetos CD, Jami MM, Krishna L, Jackson R, Patchefsky AS, Cooper HS (1994) Novel immunohistochemical localization of 28,000 molecular weight (Mr) calcium binding protein (Calbindin-$D_{28\ k}$) in enterochromaffin cells of the human appendix and neuroendocrine tumors (carcinoids and small cell carcinomas) of the midgut and foregut. Arch Pathol Lab Med 11:633–639
38. Komminoth P, Roth J, Saremaslani P, Matias-Guiu T, Wolfe HF, Heitz PU (1994) Polysialic acid of the neural cell adhesion molecule in the human thyroid: a marker for medullary thyroid carcinoma and primary C-cell hyperplasia. An immumohistochemical study of 70 thyroid lesions. Am J Surg Pathol 18:399–411
39. Saad MF, Ordonez NG, Guido JJ, Samaan Na (1984) the prognostic value of calcitonin immunostaining in medullary carcinoma of the thyroid. J Clin Endocrinol Metab 59:850–856
40. Sikri KL, Varndell IM, Hamid QA et al. (1985) Medullary carcinoma of the thyroid. An immunocytochemical and histochemical study of 25 cases using 8 separate markers. Cancer 56:2481–2491
41. Steenbergh PH, Heppner JW, Zandberg J et al. (1984) Calcitonin gene related peptide coding sequence is conserved in the human genome and is expressed in medullary thyroid carcinoma. J Clin Endocrinol Metab 5:358–360
42. Zajac JD, Penschow J, Mason T et al. (1986) Identification of calcitonin and calcitonin gene-related peptide messenger RNA in medullary thyroid carcinoma by hybridization histochemistry. J Clin Endocrinol Metab 62:1037–1043
43. Scopsi L Ferrari C, Pilotti S et al. (1990) Immunocytochemical localization and identification of prosomatostatin gene products in medullary carcinoma of human thyroid gland. Hm Pathol 21:820–830
44. Sunday ME, Wolfe HJ, Roos BA, Chin WW, Spindel ER (1988) Gastrin releasing peptide gene expression in developing, hyperplastic and neoplastic thyroid C-cell. Endocrinol 122:1551–1558
45. Williams ED, Morales AM, Horn RC (1968) Thyroid carcinoma and Cushing's syndrome. A report of two cases with review of the common features of the non-endocrine tumours associated with Cushing's syndrome. J Clin Pathol 21:129–135
46. Roth KA, Bensch KG, Hoffman AR (1987) Characterization of opioid peptides in human thyroid medullary carcinoma. Cancer 59:850–856

47. Birkenhäger JC, Upton GV, Seldenrath HJ, Krieger DT, Tashjian AH Jr. (1976) Medullary thyroid carcinoma: ectoic production of peptides with ACTH-like, corticotropin-releasing factor-like and prolactin production—stimulating activities. Acta Endocrinol (Copenh) 83:280–292
48. Uribe M, Fenoglio-Preiser CN, Grimes M, Feind C. (1985) Medullary carcinoma of the thyroid gland. Clinical, pathological, and immunohistochemical features with review of the literature. Am J Surg Pathol 9:577–594
49. Faggiano A, Talbot M, Lacroix L et al. (2002) Differential expression of galectin-3 in medullary thyroid carcinoma and C-cell hyperplasia. Clin Endocrinol 57:813–819
50. DeLellis RA, Rule AH, Spiler I, Nathanson L, Tashjian AH, Jr., Wolfe HJ (1978) Calcitonin and carcinoembryonic antigen as tumor markers in medullary thyroid carcinoma. Am J Clin Pathol 70:587–594
51. Schroder S, Klöppel G (1987) Carcinoembryonic antigen and non-specific cross-reacting antigen in thyroid cancer. An immunocytochemical study using polyclonal and monoclonal antibodies. Am J Surg Pathol 11:100–108
52. Mendelsohn G, Wells SA, Baylin SB (1984) Relationship of tissue carcinoembryonic antigen and calcitonin to tumor virulence in medullary thyroid carcinoma. An immunohistochemical study in early, localized and virulent disseminated stages of disease. Cancer 54:657–662
53. Kakudo K, Miyauchi A, Yakai SI et al. (1979) C-cell carcinoma of the thyroid, papillary type. Acta Pathol (Jpn) 29:663–659
54. Harach HR, Williams ED (1983) Glandular (tubular and follicular) variants of medullary carcinoma of the thyroid. Histopathology 7:83–97
55. Harach HR, Bergholm U (1992) Small cell variant of medullary carcinoma of the thyroid with neuroblastoma-like features. Histopathol 21:378–380
56. Eusebi V, Damiani S, Riva C, Lloyd RV, Capella C (1990) Calcitonin free oat cell carcinoma of the thyroid gland. Virchows Arch [A] 417:267–271
57. Mendelsohn G, Baylin SB, Bigner SH et al. (1980) Anaplastic variants of medullary thyroid carcinoma: a light microscopic and immunohistochemical study. Am J Surg Pathol 4:333–341
58. Landon G, Ordóñex NG (1985) Clear cell variant of medullary carcinoma of the thyroid. Hum Pathol 16:844–847
59. Marcus JN, Dise CA, LiVolsi VA (1982) Melanin production in a medullary thyroid carcinoma. Cancer 49:2518–2526
60. Beerman H, Rigaud C, Bogomeletz WV, Hollander H, Veldhuizen H (1990) Melanin production in black medullary thyroid cancer (MTC). Histopathology 16:227–234
61. Dominguez-Malagon H, Delgardo-Chavez R, Torres-Najera M, Gould E, Albores-Saavedra J (1989) Oxyphil and squamous variants of medullary thyroid carcinoma. Cancer 63:1183–1188
62. Golough R, Us-Krasovec M, Auersperg M, Jancar J, Bondi A, Eusebi V (1985) Amphicrine-composite calcitonin and mucin producing carcinoma of the thyroid. Ultrastruct Pathol 8:197–206
63. Huss LJ, Mendlesohn G (1990) Medullary carcinoma of the thyroid gland: an encapsulated variant resembling the hyalinizing trabecular (paraganglioma-like) adenoma of thyroid. Mod Pathol 3:581–585
64. Laforga JB, Aranda FI (2007) Pseudoangiosarcomatous features in medullary thyroid carcinoma spindle cell variant. Report of a case studied by FNA and immunohistochemistry. Diagn Cytopathol 34:424–428
65. Beskid M, Lorenc R, Rôsciszewska A (1971) C-cell thyroid adenoma in man. J Pathol 103:3343–346
66. Kodama T, Okamoto T, Fujjimoto Y et al. (1988) C-cell adenoma in the thyroid: a rare but distinct clinical entity. Surgery 104:997–1003
67. Mendelsohn G, Oertel JE (1981) Encapsulated medullary thyroid carcinoma [Abstract]. Lab Invest 44:43A
68. Matias-Guiu X, LaGuette J, Puras-Gil AM, Rosai, J (1997) Metastatic neuroendocrine tumors to the thyroid mimicking medullary carcinoma: a pathological and immunohistochemical study of six cases. Am J Surg Pathol 21:754–762
69. Shikama Y, Osawa T, Yagihashis N et al. (2003) Neuroendocrine differentiation in hyalinizing trabecular tumors of the thyroid. Virchows Arch 443:792–796
70. Wolfe HJ, Melvin KE, Cervi-Skinner SJ et al. (1973) C-cell hyperplasia preceding medullary thyroid carcinoma. N Engl J Med 289: 437–441
71. Wells SA, Ontjes DA, Cooper CW et al. (1975) The early diagnosis of medullary carcinoma of the thyroid gland in patients with multiple endocrine neoplasia type II. Ann Surg 182:362–370
72. McDermott MB, Swanson PE, Wick MR (1995) Immunostains for collagen type IV discriminate between C-cell hyperplasia and microscopic medullary carcinoma in multiple endocrine neoplasia, type 2A. Hum Pathol 26:1308–1312
73. Albores-Saavedra J, Monforte H, Nadji M, Morales AR (1988) C-cell hyperplasia in thyroid tissue adjacent to follicular cell tumors. Hum Pathol 19:795–799
74. Guyetant S, Rousselet MC, Durigon M et al. (1997) Sex related C-cell hyperplasia in the normal human thyroid: a quantitative autopsy study. J Clin Endocrinol Metab 82:42–47
75. Perry A, Molberg K, Albores-Saavedra J (1996) Physiologic versus neoplastic C-cell hyperplasia of the thyroid: separation of distinct histologic and biologic entities. Cancer 77:750–756
76. Carney JA, Sizemore GW, Hales AB (1978) Multiple endocrine neoplasia, type 2B. Pathobiol Annu 8:105–153
77. Diaz-Cano S, DeMiguel M, Blanes A et al. (2001) Germline RET634 mutation positive MEN2A related C-cell hyperplasias have genetic features consistent with intraepithelial neoplasias. J Clin Endocrinol Metab 86:3948–3951
78. Kaserer K, Scheuba C, Neuhold N et al. (1998) C-cell hyperplasia and medullary thyroid carcinoma in patients routinely screened for serum calcitonin. Am J Surg Pathol 22:722–728
79. Kaserer K, Scheuba C, Neuhold N et al. (2001) sporadic versus familial medullary thyroid microcarcinoma: a histopathologic study of 50 consecutive patients. Am J Surg Pathol 25:1245–1251
80. Mears L, Diaz-Cano S (2003) Difference between familial and sporadic medullary thyroid carcinomas (Letter). Am J Surg Pathol 27:266–267
81. Mathew CG, Chin KS, Easton DF et al. (1987) A linked genetic marker for multiple endocrine neoplasia type 2A on chromosome 10. Nature 328:527–528
82. Simpson NE, Kidd KK, Goodfellow PJ et al. (1987) Assignment of multiple endocrine neoplasia type 2A to chromosome 10 by linkage. Nature 328:528–530
83. Ponder BA, Coffe R, Gagel RF et al. (1988) Risk estimation and screening of families of patients with medullary thyroid carcinoma. Lancet 1:397–401
84. Sobol H, Narod SA, Nakamura Y et al. (1989) Screening for multiple endocrine neoplasia type 2A with DNA polymorphism analysis. N Engl J Med 321:996–1001
85. Gardner E, Papi L, Easton DF et al. (1993) Genetic linkage studies map the multiple endocrine neoplasia type 2 loci to a small interval of chromosome 10q 11.2 Hum Mol Gent 2:241–246
86. Lairmore TC, Dou S, Howe JR et al. (1993) A 1.5 megabase yeast artificial chromosome contig from human chromosome 10q 11.2 connecting 3 genetic loci (RET,D10S94, and D10S102) closely linked to the MEN2A locus. Proc Nat'l Acad Sci USA 90: 492–496
87. Mole SE, Mulligan LM, Healey CS et al. (1993) Localization of the gene for localization of the gene for multiple endocrine neoplasia type 2A to a 480 kb region in chromosome band 10q 11.2. Hum Mol Genet 2:247–252

88. Mulligan LM, Kwok JBJ, Healey CS et al. (1993) Germline mutations of the RET proto-oncogene in multiple endocrine neoplasia type 2A Nature 363:458–460
89. Donis-Keller H, Dou S, Chi D et al. (1993) Mutations in the RET proto-oncogene are associated with MEN2A and FMTC. Hum Mol Genet 2:851–856
90. Mulligan LM, Eng C, Healey CS et al. (1994) Specific mutations of the RET proto-oncogene are related to disease phenotype in MEN2A and FMTC. Nature Genet 6:70–74
91. Hofstra RM, Landsvater RM, Ceccherini I et al. (1994) A mutation in the RET proto-oncogene associated with multiple endocrine neoplasia type 2B and sporadic medullary thyroid carcinoma. Nature 367:375–376
92. Eng C, Smith DP, Mulligan LM et al. (1994) Point mutations within the tyrosine kinase domain of the RET proto-oncogene in multiple endocrine neoplasia type 2B and related sporadic tumors. Hum Mol Genet 3:237–241
93. Carlson KM, Dou S, Chi D et al. (1994) single missense mutation in the tyrosine kinase catalytic domain of the RET proto-oncogene is associated with multiple endocrine neoplasia type 2B. Proc Natl Acad Sci USA 91:1579–1583
94. Eng C, Clayton D, Schuffenecker I et al. (1996) The relationship between specific RET proto-oncogene mutations and disease phenotype in multiple endocrine neoplasia type 2. International RET mutation consortium analysis. JAMA 276:1575–1579
95. Eng C (1999) RET proto-oncogene in the development of human cancer. J Clin Oncol 17:380–393
96. Hoff AO, Cote GJ, Gagel RF (2000) Multiple endocrine neoplasias. Annu Rev Physiol 62:377–341
97. Takahashi M, Buma Y, Iwamoto T (1988) Cloning and expression of the ret proto-oncogene encoding a tyrosine kinase with two potential transmembrane domains. Oncogene 3:571–578
98. Pasini B, Hofstra RM, Yin L et al. (1995) The physical map of the RET proto-oncogene. Oncogene 11:1737–1743
99. Pachnis V, Mankoo B, Costantiri F (1993) Expression of the C-ret proto-oncogene during mouse embryogenesis. Development 119:1005–1017
100. Schuchardt A, D'Agati V, Larsson-Bloomberg L, Costantini F, Pachnis V (1994) Defects in the kidney and enteric nervous system of mice lacking the tyrosine kinase receptor ret. Nature 367:380–383
101. Lai AZ, Gujral TS, Mulligan LM (2007) RET signalling in endocrine tumors: delving deeper into molecular mechanisms. Endocrin Pathol 18:57–67
102. Santoro, M, Carlomagno F, Romano A et al. (1995) Activation of RET as a dominant transforming by germline mutations of MEN2A and MEN2B. Science 267:381–383
103. Iwashita T, Asai N, Murakami H et al. (1976) Identification of tyrosine residues that are essential for transforming activity of the ret proto-oncogene with MEN2A or MEN2B mutations. Oncogene 12:481–487
104. Gimm O, Marsh DJ Andrew SD et al. (1997) Germline dinucleotide mutation in codon 883 of the RET proto-oncogene in multiple endocrine neoplasia type 2B without codon 918 mutation. J Clin Endocrinol Metab 81:3902–3904
105. Smith DP, Houghton C, Ponder BA (1997) Germline mutation of RET codon 883 in two cases of de novo MEN2B. Oncogene 15:1213–1217
106. Kawai K, Iwashita T, Murakami H et al. (2000) Tissue specific carcinogenesis in neoplasia type 2A mutation. Cancer Res 60:5254–5260
107. Wohllk N, Cote GJ, Bugalho MM et al. (1996) Relevance of RET proto-oncogene mutations in sporadic medullary thyroid carcinoma. J Clin Endocrinol Metab 81:3740–3745
108. Zedenius J, Wallin G, Hamberger B et al. (1994) Somatic and MEN2A de novo mutations identified in the RET proto-oncogene by screening of sporadic MTCs. Hum Mol Genet 3:1259–1262
109. Eng C, Mulligan LM, Healey CS et al. (1996) Heterogeneous mutation of the RET proto-oncogene in subpopulations of medullary thyroid carcinoma. Cancer Res 56:2167–2170
110. Marsh DJ, Learoyd DL, Andrew SD et al. (1996) Somatic mutations in the RET proto-oncogene in sporadic medullary thyroid carcinoma. Clin Endocrinol 44:249–257
111. Saggiorato E, Rapa I, Garino F et al. (2007) Absence of RET gene point mutation in sporadic C-cell hyperplasia. J Mol Diagn 9:214–219
112. Eng C, Crossey PA, Mulligan LM et al. (1995) Mutations of the RET proto-oncogene and von Hippel Lindau disease tumour suppressor gene in sporadic and syndromic pheochromocytoma. J Med Genet 32:934–937
113. Lindor LM, Honchel R, Khosla S et al. (1995) Mutations in the RET proto-oncogene in sporadic pheochromocytomas. J Clin Endocrinol Met 80:627–629
114. Beldjord B, Desclaux-Arranond F, Raffin-Samson M et al. (1995) The RET proto-oncogene in sporadic pheochromocytomas. Frequent MEN2-like mutations and new molecular defects. J Clin Endocrinol Metab 80:2063–2068
115. Padberg BC,Schroder S, Jochum W et al. (1995) Absence of RET proto-oncogene point mutations in sporadic hyperplastic and neoplastic lesions of the parathyroid gland. Am J Pathol 147:1600–1607
116. Komminoth P, Roth J, Mulletta-Feurer S et al. (1996) RET proto-oncogene point mutations in sporadic neuroendocrine tumors. J Clin Endocrinol Metab 81:2041–2046
117. Eng C, Mulligan LM, Mutations of the RET proto-oncogene in the multiple endocrine neoplasia type 2 syndrome, related sporadic tumours and Hirschsprung disease. Hum Mut 9:97–109
118. Peacock ML, Borst MJ, Sweet JD, Decker RA (1996) Detection of RET mutations in multiple endocrine neoplasia type 2A and familial medullary thyroid carcinoma by denaturing gel electrophoresis. Hum Mut 7:100–104
119. Wohllk N, Cote GJ, Evans DB et al. (1996) Application of genetic screening information to the management of medullary thyroid carcinoma and multiple endocrine neoplasia type 2. Endocrinol Metab Clinics North Am 25:1–25
120. Wells SA, Chi DD, Toshima K et al. (1994) Predictive DNA testing and prophylactic thyroidectomy in patients at risk for multiple endocrine neoplasia type 2A. Ann Surg 220:237–250
121. Lips CJ, Landsvater RM, Hoppener JW et al. (1994) Clinical screening as compared with DNA analysis in families with multiple endocrine neoplasia type 2A. N Engl J Med 331:828–835
122. Dralle H, Gimm O, simon D et al. (1998) Prophylactic thyroidectomy in 75 children and adolescents with hereditary mudullary thyroid carcinoma: German and Austrian experience. World J Surg 22 (7):744–751
123. Offit K, Biesecker BB, Burt RW et al. (1996) Statement of the American Society of Oncology: Genetic Testing for Cancer Susceptibility. J Clin Oncol 14:1730–1736
124. Fialkowski EA, Moley JF (2006) Current approaches to medullary thyroid carcinoma, sporadic and familial. J Surg Oncol 94:737–747
125. Moley JF, Fialkowski EA (2007) Evidence based approach to the management of sporadic medullary thyroid carcinoma. World J Surg 31:946–956
126. Modigliani E, Cohen R, Campos JM et al. (1998)Prognostic factors for survival and for biochemical cure in medullary thyroid carcinoma: results in 819 patients. The GETC Study Group. Groupe d'etude des tumeurs a calcitonine. Clin Endocrinol (Oxf) 48:265–273

127. Vezzosi D, Bennet A, Caron P (2007) Recent advances in treatment of medullary thyroid carcinoma. Ann Endocrinol (Paris) 68:147–153
128. Leboulleux S, Travagli JP, Caillou B et al. (2002) Medullary thyroid carcinoma as part of a multiple endocrine neoplasia type 2B syndrome. Influence of the stage on the clinical course. Cancer 94:44–50
129. Schröder S, Böcker w, Baisch H et al. (1998) Prognostic factors in medullary thyroid carcinoma. Survival in relation to age, sex, stage, histology, immunohistochemistry and DNA content. Cancer 61:806–816
130. Koporek O, Scheuba C, Cherenko M, et al. (2008) Desmoplasia in medullary thyroid carcinoma: a reliable indicator of metastatic potential. Histopathol 52:623–630
131. Barbet J, Campion L, Kraeber-Bodere F, Chatal JF (2005) Prognostic impact of serum calcitonin and carcinoembryonic antigen doubling times in patients with medullary thyroid carcinoma. J Clin Endocrinol Metab 90:6077–6084
132. Elisei R, Cosci B, Romei C et al. (2008) Prognostic significance of somatic RET oncogene mutations in sporadic medullary thyroid carcinoma: a 10-year follow-up study. J Clin Endocrinol Metab 93:682–687
133. Hales, M, Rosenau, W, Okerlund, MD, Galante, M. (1982) Carcinoma of the thyroid with a mixed medullary and follicular pattern: morphological, immunohistochemical and clinical laboratory studies. Cancer 50:1352–1359
134. Pfaltz, M, Hedinger, Chr. E, Muhlethales, JP. (1983) Mixed medullary and follicular carcinoma of the thyroid. Virchows Arch [Pathol. Anat] 400:53–59
135. Ljungberg, O, Ericsson, U-B, Bondeson, L, Thorell, J. (1984) A compound follicular-parafollicular cell carcinoma of the thyroid: A new tumor entity? Cancer 52:1053–1061
136. Ljungberg O. Bondeson L. Bondeson AG (1984) A-G. Differentiated thyroid carcinoma, intermediate type: a new tumor entity with features of follicular and parafollicular cell carcinoma. Hum Pathol 15:218–228
137. Holm R, Sobrinho-Simoes M, Nesland JM, Sambade C, Johannessen JV (1987) Medullary thyroid carcinoma with thyroglobulin immunoreactivity. A special entity? Lab Invest 57:258–268
138. LiVolsi, VA. (1987) Mixed thyroid carcinoma: A real entity? Lab Invest 57:237–239
139. Albores-Saavedra J, de la Mora TG, de la Torra-Rendon F, Gould E. (1990) Mixed medullary-papillary carcinoma of the thyroid: A previously unrecognized variant of thyroid carcinoma. Hum Pathol 21:1151–1155
140. Mizukami Y, Michigishi T, Nonomura A, et al. (1993) Mixed medullary-follicular carcinoma of the thyroid occurring in familial form. Histopathol 22:284–287
141. Matias-Guiu X, Caixas A, Costa I, Cabezas R, Prat J. (1994) Compound medullary-papillary carcinoma of the thyroid: true mixed versus collision tumour. Histopathol 25:183–185
142. Lax SF, Beham A, Kronberger-Schönecker D, Langsteger W, Denk H. (1994) Coexistence of papillary and medullary carcinoma of the thyroid gland-mixed or collision tumors? Clinicopathological analysis of three cases. Virchows Archiv 424:441–447
143. Kobayashi K, Teramoto S, Maeta H, Ishiguro S, Mori T, Horie Y. (1995) Simultaneous occurrence of medullary carcinoma and papillary carcinoma of the thyroid. J Surg Onc 59:276–279
144. Mizukami Y, Nonomura A, Michigishi T, Noguchi M, Ishizaki T. (1996) Mixed medullary-follicular carcinoma of the thyroid gland: a clinicopathologic variant of medullary thyroid carcinoma. Mod Pathol 9:631–635
145. Papotti M, Negro F, Carney JA, Bussolati G, Lloyd RV. (1997) Mixed medullary-follicular carcinoma of the thyroid. A morphological, immunohistochemical and in situ hybridization analysis of 11 cases. Virchows Arch 430:397–405
146. Matias-Guiu X. (1999) Mixed medullary and follicular carcinoma of the thyroid. On the search for its histogenesis. Am J Pathol 155:1413–1418
147. Volante, M, Papotti, M, Roth, J. et al. (1999) Mixed medullary-follicular thyroid carcinoma. Molecular evidence for a dual origin of tumor components. Am J Pathol 155: 1499–1509
148. Pappoti M, Volante M, Komminoth P, Sobrinho-Simoes M, Bussolati G. (2000) Thyroid carcinomas with mixed follicular and C-cell differentiation patterns. Semin Diagn Pathol 17:109–119
149. Katoh R, Jasani B, Williams ED. (1989) Hyalinizing trabecular adenomas of the thyroid: A report of three cases with immunohistochemical and ultrastructural studies. Histopathol 15:211–224.
150. Carcangiu ML, Zampi G, Rosai J (1984) Poorly differentiated ("insular") thyroid carcinoma. A reinterpretation of Langhans "wuchernde struma". Am J Surg Pathol 8:655–668
151. Sobrinho-Simoes M. (1996) Poorly differentiated carcinomas of the thyroid. Endocrine Pathol 7:99–102
152. Papotti M, Bussolati G, Kommoth P, et al. (2004) Mixed medullary and follicular cell carcinoma. In R.A. DeLellis, R.V. Lloyd, P.U. Heitz, C Eng (ed). Pathology and Genetics of Tumours of Endocrine Organs. WHO Classification of Tumours, pp. 92–92. Lyon: IARC Press
153. Mellilo RM, Cirafici AM, DeFalco V et al. (2004) The oncogenic activity of RET point mutants for follicular thyroid cells may account for the occurrence of papillary thyroid carcinoma in patients affected by familial medullary thyroid carcinoma. Am J Pathol 165:511–521

Tumors of Parathyroid Gland

Manju L. Prasad and Ashraf Khan

Abstrac The most common parathyroid gland pathology in primary hyperparathyroidism is parathyroid adenoma, followed by hyperplasia and carcinoma. Adenoma, hyperplasia, and carcinoma have distinct molecular genetic profiles, however, their pathologic features are often overlapping leading to significant diagnostic dilemma, even on permanent sections. Final diagnosis must be arrived at after taking into consideration the abnormal gland, the status of the remaining glands, and the pre- and post-operative blood parathyroid hormone levels. The goal of treatment is achievement of normocalcemia, but recurrences occur in a significant number of patients. Differentiating between different pathologic entities is important in predicting recurrences and choosing the appropriate extent of surgical resection. Several genetic syndromes are associated with primary hyperparathyroidism and include multiple endocrine neoplasia (MEN1 and MEN2a), familial isolated hyperparathyroidism, and hyperparathyroidism-jaw tumor syndrome.

Keywords Parathyroid gland • Hyperparathyroidism • Adenoma • Carcinoma • Atypical adenoma • Parathyromatosis

Embryology

Parathyroid glands develop from the dorsal buds of pharyngeal pouches in the human embryo at about 5–6 weeks, hence their location on the dorsal surface of the thyroid. The inferior parathyroid glands develop in the third pharyngeal pouch along with the thymus and descend with it to their final position. The superior parathyroid glands develop from the fourth pharyngeal pouch [1]. An understanding of the path of descent of the parathyroid glands is critical to locating the parathyroid gland at surgery.

Histology

The normal parathyroid gland is about 6 mm long and weighs up to 40 mg in the adult. A thin fibrous capsule is seen around the gland but its presence is inconsistent [2]. The epithelial component of the gland comprises of, predominantly, the chief or principal cells and oxyphil cells. The chief cells develop from the endodermal pharyngeal pouch epithelium in the embryo while the oxyphil cells appear 5–7 years after birth and increase with age [1]. The chief cells are small, 8–10 μm in size with central, pyknotic nuclei and indistinct nucleoli (Fig. 1). The cytoplasm may be clear, vacuolated, or amphophilic, and contains glycogen and lipid. Glycogen may be demonstrated as PAS-positive diastase sensitive staining and fat stains may demonstrate intracytoplasmic lipid. The cells are arranged in lobules or solid sheets separated by fibrovascular stroma. Well-formed glands with PAS-positive colloid-like intraluminal contents may be seen. The oncocytic cells are larger than the chief cells and have abundant, densely eosinophilic granular cytoplasm. Transitional cells may be seen in abnormal parathyroid glands and have features that overlap with chief and oncocytic cells (Fig. 1). Stromal adipose cells are characteristically intermingled with the parathyroid cells in the adult, and its proportion depends on age and body fat content [3, 4]. The parathyroid cells show positive expression of chromogranin A, parathyroid hormone, parathyroid hormone-related protein (PTHrP), cytokeratin, and calcium sensing receptor [5–7].

M.L. Prasad (✉)
Associate Professor, Department of Pathology, Yale University School of Medicine, 20 York Street, New Haven, CT, USA
e-mail: manju.prasad@yale.edu

A. Khan (ed.), *Surgical Pathology of Endocrine and Neuroendocrine Tumors*, Current Clinical Pathology,
DOI 10.1007/978-1-60327-396-1_7, © Humana Press, a part of Springer Science+Business Media, LLC 2009

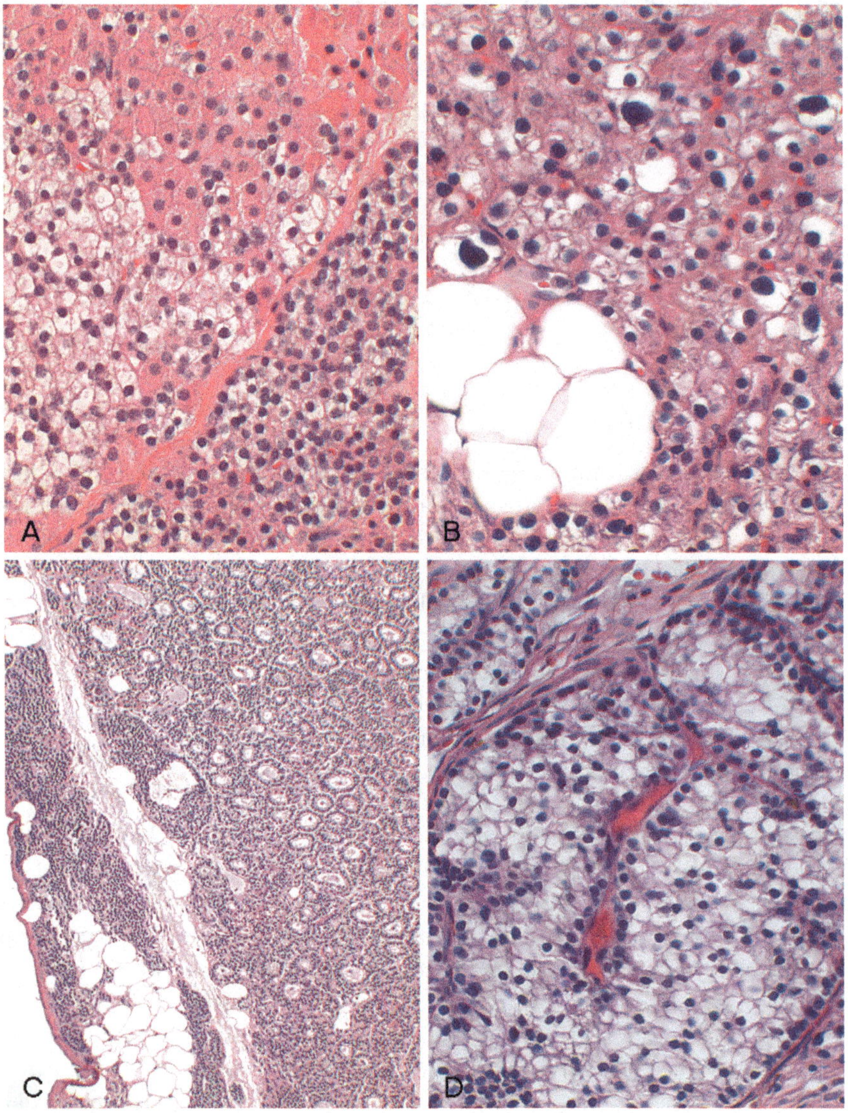

Fig. 1 Parathyroid adenoma, (**A**) comprising of chief cells (*lower right*), oncocytic cells (*upper third*), and transitional cells (*lower left*). The chief cells are small with central, pyknotic nuclei and indistinct nucleoli. The cytoplasm may be clear and amphophilic. The oncocytic cells are larger and have abundant, densely eosinophilic granular cytoplasm. Transitional cells (*lower left*) have features overlapping with chief and oncocytic cells, (**B**) comprising of predominantly chief cells showing nuclear atypia and a small amount of stromal fat. As in other benign endocrine tumors, atypia may be seen in parathyroid adenoma, and does not have any significance. (**C**) Adenoma with microfollicular architecture. The tumor is separated from the compressed normal residual parathyroid gland (*left*) by a thin fibrous capsule. The normal compressed gland shows stromal fat cells, which are significantly reduced in the adenoma. (**D**) Water clear cells in parathyroid adenoma. The cells have abundant vacuolated cytoplasm

Primary Hyperparathyroidism

Hyperparathyroidism is defined as high serum parathyroid hormone levels and may be *primary, secondary,* or *tertiary*. The most common cause for *primary* hyperparathyroidism is parathyroid adenoma (85–90%), followed by multiglandular hyperplasia (10–14%), and, infrequently, carcinomas (1–3.5%) [8, 9]. *Secondary* hyperparathyroidism is a compensatory reaction to low serum calcium levels as in chronic renal failure while *tertiary* hyperparathyroidism indicates the development of autonomously functioning abnormal parathyroid glands in the background of secondary hyperparathyroidism. Serum calcium levels are increased in primary and tertiary hyperparathyroidism and low in secondary hyperparathyroidism [10].

Predisposing factors for primary hyperparathyroidism include radiation. A fourfold increase in primary hyperparathyroidism was reported in atomic bomb survivors [11]. Even low doses of radiation have been reported to increase the risk for hyperparathyroidism [12, 13]. Various familial and inheritable disorders can also predispose to hyperparathyroidism, as discussed in the chapter on *Application of Molecular Diagnosis Techniques in the Diagnosis and Management of Endocrine Tumors* and later in this chapter.

The incidence of hyperparathyroidism has increased significantly with the introduction of the multichannel autoanalyzer in the clinical chemistry laboratories in the early seventies [14]. Mayo Clinic reported an increase from 15/100,000 person-years before 1974 to 112/100,000 person-years after 1974 [8]. However, recent studies show an incidence of about 21–29/100,000 person-years [15].

Patients tend to be asymptomatic as hypercalcemia is incidentally detected on routine serum chemistry. Symptoms of hyperparathyroidism are due to the complications of hypercalcemia and include gastric ulcers, band keratopathy, neuromuscular weakness, depression, renal stones, osteoporosis, fractures, brown tumors of bones, and osteitis fibrosa cystica [16, 17, 18]. The higher incidence of hyperparathyroidism in postmenopausal women may be due to age-associated decline in endogenous estrogens and withdrawal of its protective action on bones. As expected, the incidence of clinical presentation with complications of hyperparathyroidism has undergone a dramatic decrease from 22% in the pre-screening era before 1974 to <10% in the post-screening era [8, 14].

Parathyroid Adenoma

The predisposing factors and signs and symptoms are those of primary hyperparathyroidism, as discussed above. Patients are usually in their fifth and sixth decade with a female to male predilection of nearly 2–3:1 [8, 14, 15]. A small proportion of parathyroid adenomas may be nonfunctional and discovered incidentally on imaging of the neck [19]. Adenomas may occur sporadically or as part of one of the genetic syndromes, discussed later in this chapter.

Macroscopic Pathology

The adenomatous glands are generally located in the neck (90%), however, adenomas in ectopic locations where normal parathyroid tissue may be found, can occur, e.g., in the mediastinum. The affected parathyroid gland is enlarged measuring <1 cm to several centimeters and weighing <1 g to several grams, well-circumscribed, and encapsulated [20]. In contrast, the other three

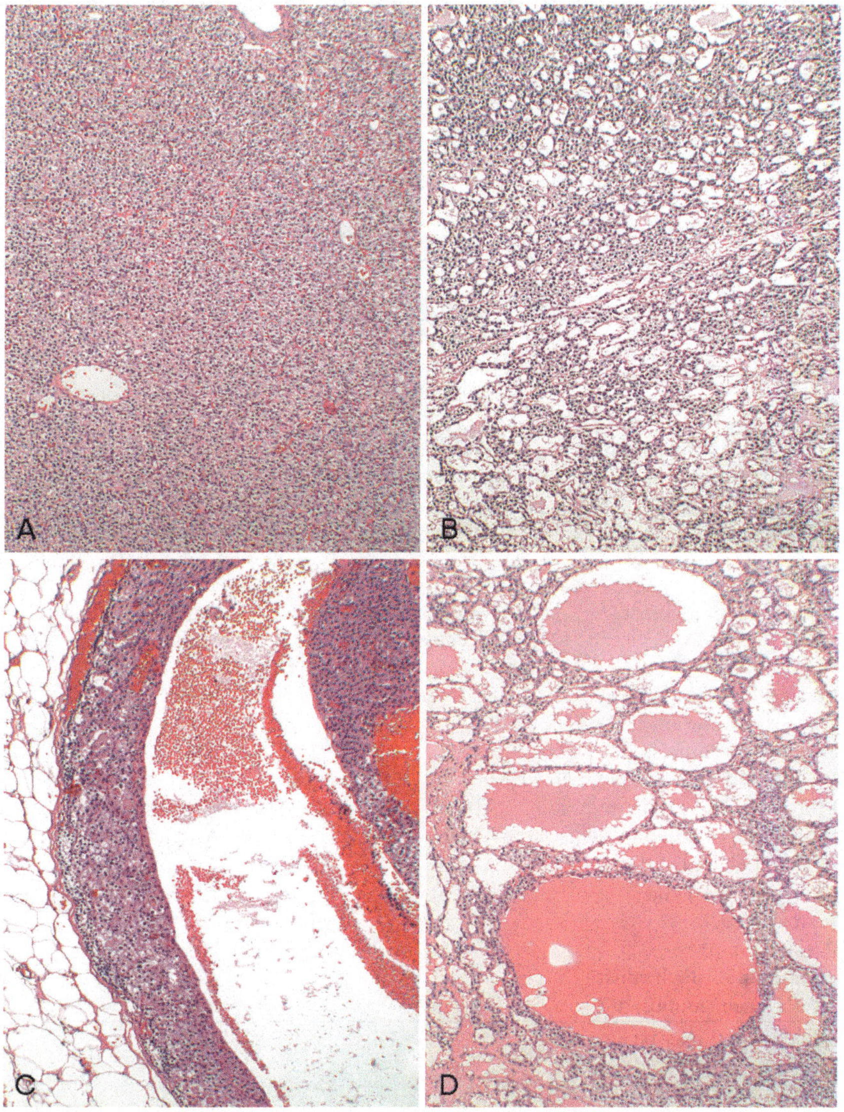

Fig. 2 Parathyroid adenoma with (**A**) solid, sheet like growth intersected by rich capillary network, (**B**) microfollicular architecture, (**C**) macrofollicular architecture with eosinophilic, colloid-like, luminal contents mimicking thyroid (**D**)

parathyroid glands are normal or small. In a study published from the Massachusetts General Hospital, 99% of adenomas were solitary involving a single gland and only about 1% was *double adenomas* involving two glands [9]. Multiple adenomas, when present, tend to be synchronous but may be metachronous. Triple adenomas are rare [21]. Roth and Faquin did not find any triple adenomas in a series of 2787 parathyroid adenomas diagnosed between 1930 and 2002 and concluded that convincing cases of triple adenoma were nonexistent [9]. The tumor may be nodular or multinodular, soft in consistency, and has a tan brown cut surface. Adenomas composed of predominantly oncocytic cells may have a mahogany brown cut surface. Large tumors may be cystic or hemorrhagic.

Microscopy

Most adenomas comprise of predominantly or exclusively chief cells. However, other cells e.g., oncocytic, transitional, or a mixture of cells, can also be seen (Fig. 1). The intracytoplasmic lipid in chief cells is significantly reduced, as is the stromal fat within the tumor. Mitoses, pleomorphism, and necrosis are typically absent, but some atypia may be seen infrequently (Fig. 1B). The tumor cells may be arranged in solid sheets with a rich capillary network or in nests separated by thin fibrous septa. A compressed residual normal parathyroid gland is frequently present at the periphery of the adenoma (Fig. 1C). Micro and macrofollicular patterns with colloid-like intraluminal contents mimicking thyroid may be seen, as may be cystic degeneration, hemorrhage, and fibrosis (Fig. 2).

Various morphologic subtypes of adenoma are described, e.g., *oxyphilic type, water clear cell type, and lipoadenoma*. These morphologic types have little functional significance. Tumor cells in *oxyphil (oncocytic) adenoma* contain abundant eosinophilic granular cytoplasm and small pyknotic nuclei. Electron microscopy shows abundant intracytoplasmic mitochondria. Water clear cells are not part of the normal parathyroid gland [22] but rarely abnormal glands may be composed of predominantly water clear cells. These cells have abundant vacuolated cytoplasm due to intracytoplasmic vesicles (Fig. 1D). *Lipoadenoma* is rare and contains abundant stromal fat [23, 24]. The latter may be very large (up to 40 g) [23]. Parathyroid *microadenomas* are defined as

Table 1 Pathology of primary hyperparathyroidism

	Adenoma (85–90%)*	Hyperplasia (10–14%)*	Atypical adenoma (rare)*	Carcinoma (1–3.5%)*
Number	Single gland	Multiglandular	Single gland	Single gland
Size	Increased size and weight of affected gland	Increased size and weight of >1 gland	Increased size and weight of affected gland	Increased size and weight of affected gland
Microscopy: Architecture	Solitary, well-circumscribed nodule	Diffuse or multinodular	Solitary, well-circumscribed nodule	Solitary, well-circumscribed nodule
Capsule	Present	Absent	May be Present, dense, or incomplete	Absent or very dense fibrous incomplete capsule
Stromal fat content	No or little fat within enlarged nodule	Variable fat, may be as much as in normal gland	No or little fat within enlarged nodule	No or little fat within enlarged nodule
Intracellular fat content in chief cells	Reduced	Reduced	Reduced	Reduced
Peripheral compressed uninvolved parathyroid gland	±	Absent	±	Absent
Fibrous septae within nodule	Absent	Absent	±	Usually present
Infiltration of adjacent tissue	Absent	Absent	Microscopic infiltration ±	Present, usually gross
Atypia, pleomorphism, mitoses	Absent	Absent	±	±
Enlarged nuclei and macronucleoli	Absent	Absent	±	±
Parafibromin** immunohistochemistry	Positive	Positive	±	Negative
HRPT2 gene mutation**	Absent	Absent	±	Present

± Present but may be absent
*References [8, 9, 54]
**References [53, 54]

functional solitary adenomas less than 6 mm in size with no enlargement of the affected parathyroid gland and biochemical improvement after surgical excision [25]. The pathologic diagnoses of *microadenoma* and *double adenomas* are difficult and need to be supported by biochemical evidence, i.e., normalization of serum parathyroid hormone levels after surgical removal with no recurrence on follow-up. Differential diagnoses of parathyroid tumors are discussed in Table 1 and later in this chapter.

Atypical Parathyroid Adenoma

Atypical parathyroid adenoma or parathyroid neoplasm of uncertain malignant potential is a histopathologic entity, diagnosed on the basis of aggressive histological features. Aggressive histological features include broad intratumoral fibrous bands, pleomorphism and atypia, mitoses, necrosis, and microscopic capsular infiltration (Fig. 3). These features do not fulfill the criteria for carcinoma but are too worrisome for a diagnosis of adenoma [2, 19, 20]. The clinical and biochemical features are similar to parathyroid adenoma.

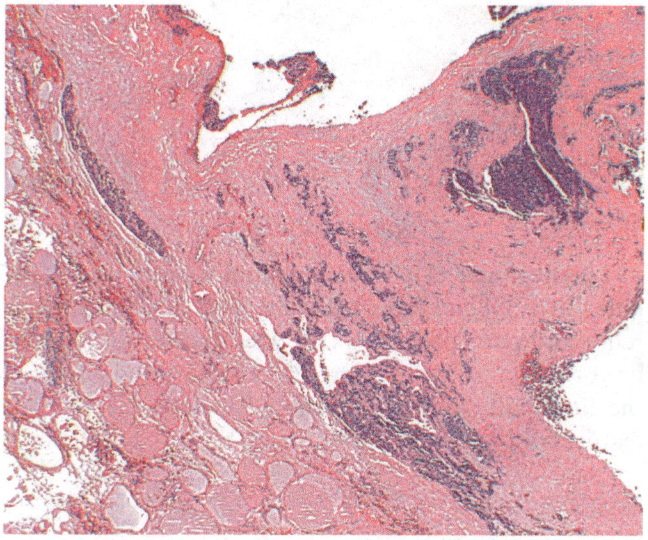

Fig. 3 Atypical adenoma. The tumor shows thick fibrosis and capsular invasion. Tumor cell nests are adjacent to thyroid follicles (*lower left*). These features are worrisome but do not qualify for carcinoma

Parathyroid Carcinoma

Carcinoma of the parathyroid gland is rare. The incidence in the United States is <1 per million population per year [26], accounting for 0.005% of all cancers in the National Cancer Data Base [27]. However, according to the national Surveillance, Epidemiology, and End Results (SEER) data, its incidence has increased significantly from 3.58 per 10,000,000 during 1988–1991 to 5.73 per 10,000,000 during 2000–2003 [26]. Among patients who undergo parathyroidectomy for primary hyperparathyroidism the incidence of parathyroid carcinoma is <1–3.5% [8, 9].

There are no predisposing factors [26], however, rare cases may be associated with MEN1 [28, 29]. In a case reported from Mayo Clinic, a MEN1 syndrome patient had a parathyroid carcinoma with mediastinal metastasis with a concurrent parathyroid adenoma and pancreatic gastrinoma [28]. Mutations in the tumor suppressor gene *HRPT2* (hyperparathyroidism 2 gene, *CDC73*) leading to familial isolated hyperparathyroidism (FIHPT) are associated with a relatively higher frequency of aggressive parathyroid disease, namely atypical adenoma and carcinoma [30].

Parathyroid carcinoma affects adults in the sixth decade (median age 55, range 14–90 years) and has no gender or race predilection [6, 26, 27, 31]. Most patients present with primary hyperparathyroidism and its complications [32]. Severe hypercalcemia with renal and bone disease and a neck mass is suggestive of parathyroid carcinoma over adenoma [10]. However, the diagnosis of carcinoma is rarely made preoperatively.

Macroscopically, the affected gland is enlarged and firm to hard with grey white cut surface. The mean tumor size is approximately 3 cm (range 1–7 cm) [27, 32] and the average weight is approximately 3 g although tumors as large as 67 g have been reported [31, 33]. The tumors may grossly infiltrate adjacent structures and may be difficult to resect at surgery, leading the surgeon to suspect its malignant nature intraoperatively.

Microscopically, the majority (80%) of parathyroid carcinomas are well differentiated and cytoarchitecturally resemble adenomas. The tumor cells are generally chief cells but may have a mixture of other cell types arranged in solid sheets, trabeculae, nests, and nodules, with pushing edges intersected by broad fibrous or hyalinized bands (Fig. 4). Poorly differentiated and undifferentiated variants account for <10% of carcinomas [27]. Increased nuclear cytoplasmic ratio, nuclear atypia with macronucleoli, and increased mitoses (>5/10 HPF) may be present (Fig. 5), but are inconstant features [10]. However, the *two absolute diagnostic criteria* are *extensive invasion* of adjacent tissues and *metastasis* (Fig. 4–5) [34]. In a review of 358 cases Koea et al. found that the most commonly invaded tissues were the ipsilateral thyroid (89%), skeletal muscles (71%), recurrent laryngeal nerve (26%), esophagus (18%), and trachea (17%) [35]. Due to the intrathyroidal location of some normal parathyroid glands, thyroid invasion alone should not be used as sufficient

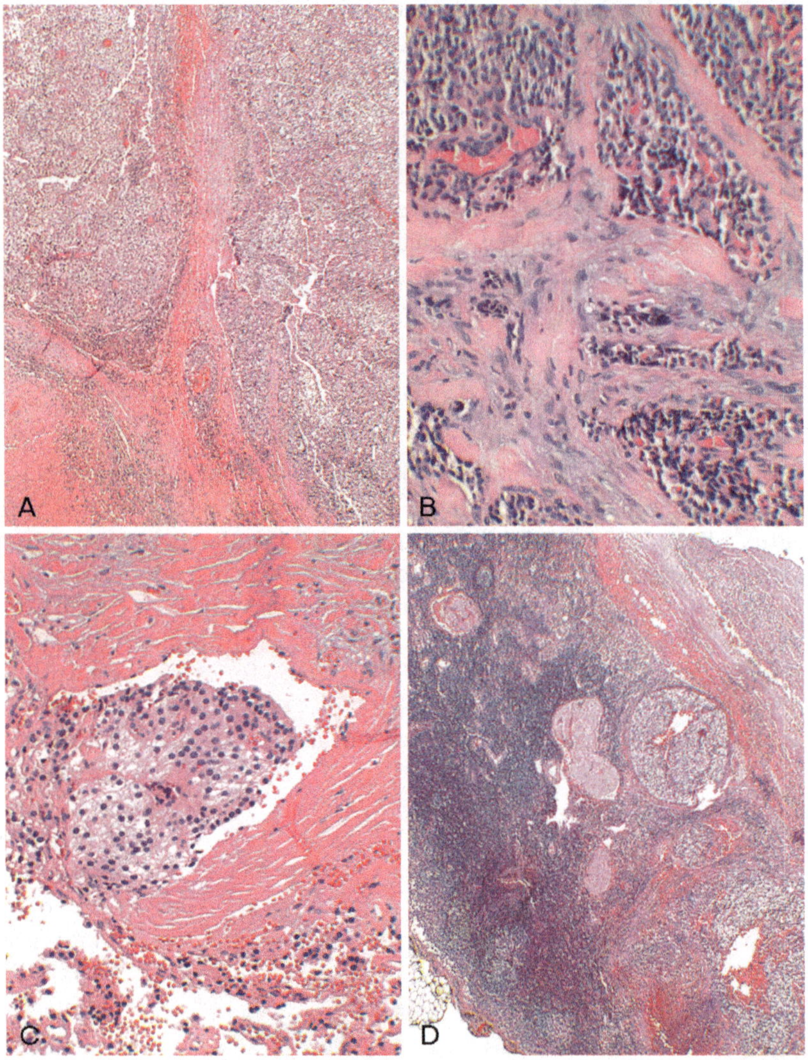

Fig. 4 Parathyroid carcinoma: (**A**) Multinodular tumor with fibrous bands and necrosis (*lower left*), (**B**) Thick hyalinizing fibrosis and desmoplasia associated with tumor cell nests, (**C**) Vascular invasion with tumor emboli, (**D**) Lymph node metastasis

for diagnosis. Other important criteria for malignancy are irregular thick fibrosis including hyaline bands intersecting the tumor, dense fibrous capsule, focal coagulative necrosis, capsular, vascular, and/ or neural invasion (Figs. 4–5, Table 1).

Approximately 10–15% of tumors develop nodal metastasis [27, 31, 35]. Older age, male gender, and distant metastases at diagnosis appear to be associated with a worse overall survival, whereas tumor size and lymph node status do not seem to affect the overall survival rate [26, 27]. Therefore, the TNM staging where size and nodal status are two of the three major components is not used for parathyroid carcinoma. Distant metastasis to lung and bone develops in a small number of cases [31, 36–39]. *En bloc* resection of the tumor with the adjacent neck structures results in reduced recurrence (10%) and long survival (67–90%) [31, 35]. Incomplete resection leads to neck recurrence in nearly 50% of patients and to 46% disease-related mortality [35].

Locoregional extension at initial surgery and Ki-67 index of $\geq$5% are reported to be associated with recurrence and poor prognosis [33]. Despite the absence of a uniform staging and grading system, the authors feel that the final pathology report should include the standard features of the tumor (Table 2).

Parathyromatosis

This is a condition where numerous parathyroid nodules develop in the soft tissues of the neck and mediastinum, generally after parathyroid surgery, but may occur de novo (primary parathyromatosis, e.g., in MEN1) [40]. It has also been reported after autotransplantation of the parathyroid tissue in the arm. The disease presents as recurrent or persistent hyperparathyroidism. There are three theories for its origin [41]: (1) seeding theory: it

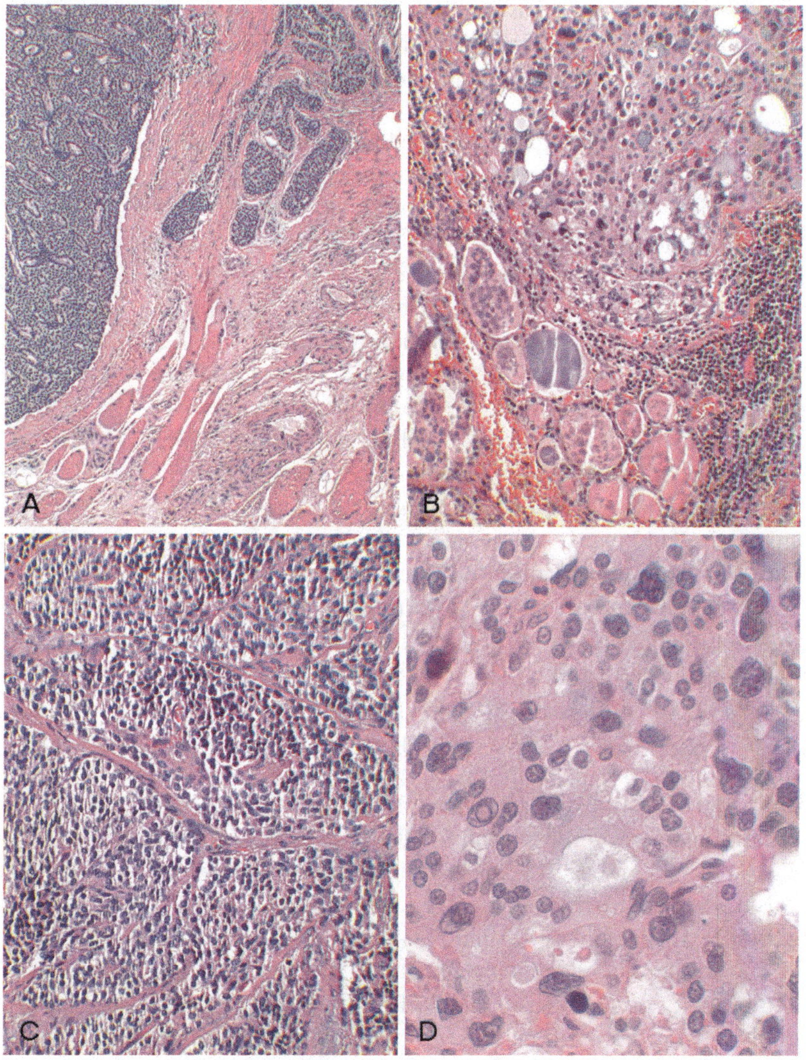

Fig. 5 Parathyroid carcinoma: (**A**) Thick tumor capsule with solid tumor nests invading skeletal muscle (*lower right*), (**B**) Tumor infiltrating thyroid (*lower left*), (**C**) Tumor nests intersected by thick fibrovascular septae, (**D**) A poorly differentiated parathyroid carcinoma with severe nuclear atypia, pleomorphism, macronucleoli, and a pseudonucleolus (*left of center*)

Table 2 Pathology report for parathyroid carcinoma

1. Diagnosis
2. Size, weight
3. Extent of resection: Complete/incomplete (margin status)
4. Extent of invasion: Capsular, vascular, lymphatic, neural, soft tissue (fat, skeletal muscle, etc.), and adjacent structures (thyroid, trachea, thymus); Focal vs. extensive invasion
5. Metastases: Regional lymph nodes or distant metastasis

occurs due to rupture of an abnormal parathyroid gland during surgery leading to seeding of the tissue [42]; (2) embryonic rest theory: it is an overgrowth of multiple embryonic rests [43, 44]; and the least popular, (3) malignant theory: it is a low-grade malignancy [45]. Parathyromatosis may involve the soft tissues of the neck, mediastinum including the thymus [46], or the arm, as in autotransplantation [47]. Microscopically, there are multiple miliary-type or larger nodules of bland looking parathyroid glandular tissue in the fat and skeletal muscle. The lesion is differentiated from parathyroid carcinoma by the absence of extensive fibrosis, mitosis, and other features of malignancy, as discussed above.

Management of Parathyroid Gland Abnormality and the Pathologist's Role

Identification of hyperfunctioning parathyroid gland is critical for their removal and the subsequent achievement of normocalcemic state by the patient. Pre-operative imaging techniques, such as sestamibi scans with technetium-99m label are highly accurate in localizing the abnormal parathyroid gland [48]. The traditional role of intraoperative pathology (frozen section) involves identification of (1) the parathyroid gland and (2) the abnormality. Frozen sections can help distinguish parathyroid gland from thyroid nodules, lymph node, thymus, or other tissues.

The use of intraoperative cytology such as touch or imprint smears to distinguish parathyroid from other tissues is not popular due to an unacceptably high rate of inaccuracies [9]. The parathyroid gland should be weighed after removing any attached fat or thymic tissue. Increased size and weight is consistent with abnormal gland. Intraoperative use of fat stain in assessing normal and abnormal gland is useful. Chief cells in normal glands have abundant intracellular lipid as against hyperplastic and neoplastic glands [9, 22]. However, fat stains like oil red O and Sudan IV require more labor and increase the time needed to arrive at the diagnosis. A rapid toluidine blue stain (30 sec) is used on frozen section to assess intracellular fat in the department of pathology at the University of Pennsylvania with good results [49]. Differential diagnosis of abnormal parathyroid gland is discussed in Table 1. It is critical to diagnose hyperplasia correctly, as missing this entity could lead to inadequate treatment and recurrence of hyperparathyroidism. The preoperative clinical and biochemical features are similar in neoplastic and hyperplastic glands. Morphologically there may be little or no intratumoral stromal fat in adenoma, which may show a compressed residual parathyroid gland at the periphery (Fig. 1). The hyperplastic parathyroid gland contains variable amount of stromal fat and may vary only in weight and size from the normal parathyroid gland. Multiglandular disease indicates hyperplasia whereas single gland involvement with the remaining glands being normal or atrophic would support neoplasia. Hyperplasia may be cystic or multinodular (Fig. 6) and is comprised of predominantly chief cells, similar to neoplastic glands. Indeed the single most important distinguishing feature between hyperplasia and neoplasia is the number of involved glands (single or multiglandular disease) and the status of the uninvolved glands (normal, enlarged, or atrophic), with a caveat, that a single dominant hyperplastic nodule may mimic adenoma, contain little fat, a compressed residual parathyroid gland at the periphery, and even suppress the other parathyroid glands. Thus, the histopathologic distinction of adenoma vs. hyperplasia is fraught with pitfalls even on permanent sections when only one gland is available for review [49]. In one study, prediction of normocalcemia after parathyroidectomy, based on intraoperative pathology, was incorrect in 62% of cases, in contrast to quantitative intraoperative parathyroid hormone monitoring which was incorrect in only 3% of patients [50]. These authors suggest that intraoperative frozen sections have little or no role in deciding multiglandular disease, and exploration of the neck for multiglandular disease should be replaced by functional evaluation of parathyroid using intraoperative hormone monitoring. A significant fall ($\geq$50% of pre-incision levels) in parathyroid hormone levels after removal of the hyperfunctioning gland or glands accurately predicts removal of all abnormal parathyroid tissue [51]. Complete surgical removal of the affected gland or subtotal parathyroidectomy with removal of three and a half glands in parathyroid hyperplasia provides the best chance of achieving normocalcemic state in the patient. Hypercalcemia may recur in approximately 5% of patients even after many years, especially in cases where the traditional surgical exploration of the neck was performed to identify abnormal parathyroid glands rather than intraoperative parathyroid hormone assessment [52]. Recurrence has been reported in both neoplasia and hyperplasia, and may be due to the metachronous development of a second adenoma, or single gland predominant hyperplasia that suppressed the other glands leading to an initial erroneous impression of adenoma, parathyroid carcinoma that was initially missed or accidental seeding of the cervical soft tissue by parathyroid tissue during surgery (parathyromatosis).

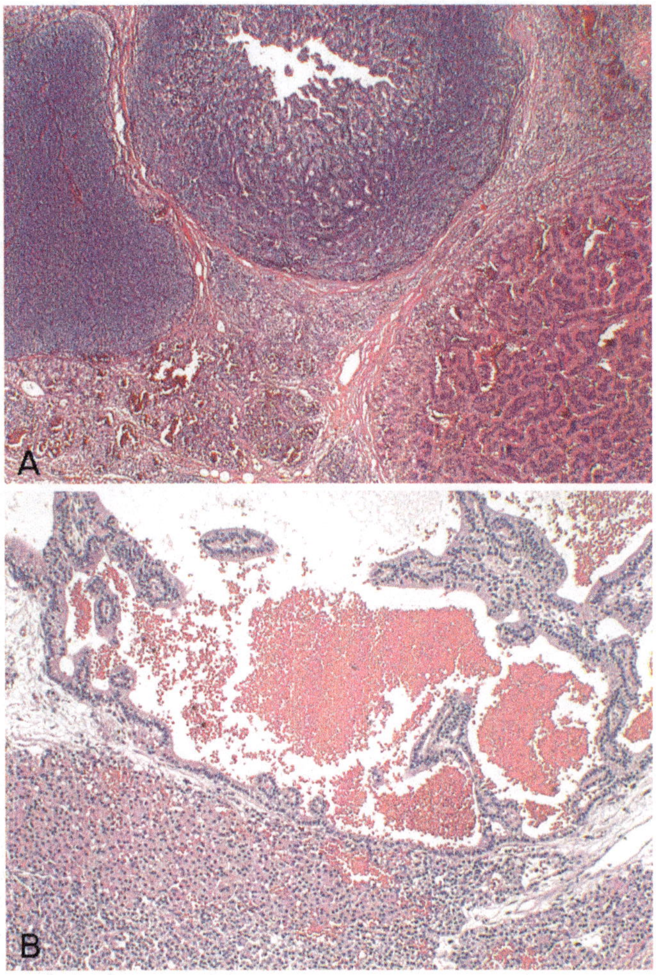

Fig. 6 Parathyroid hyperplasia: (**A**) Multinodular hyperplasia, (**B**) Hyperplastic gland with cystic change and papillary hyperplasia

Special Techniques in Parathyroid Gland Pathology

Immunohistochemistry for parafibromin shows its loss in almost all parathyroid carcinomas and correlates with inactivating *HRPT2* gene mutations, while parafibromin expression is retained in adenomas and sporadic primary hyperparathyroidism [53, 54]. Mitoses of >5/10 HPF, high proliferative index (>5%) with Ki-67, and Galectin-3 expression may suggest carcinoma over adenoma [10, 33, 55]. Cyclin D1 is believed to be expressed in abnormal parathyroid glands and absent in normal but does not appear to be useful in differentiating among the different types of parathyroid abnormalities (Table 3, Fig. 7).

Ectopic parathyroid tumors may be diagnostically challenging. Intrathyroidal parathyroid tumors may resemble follicular neoplasms of the thyroid. Ordonez and colleagues (1983) reported an intrathyroidal parathyroid carcinoma associated with amyloid production raising the suspicion of medullary thyroid carcinoma [56]. Immunohistochemistry for parathyroid hormone, neuroendocrine markers, e.g., chromogranin A is positive in parathyroid while positive expression of thyroglobulin and TTF1 would support thyroid origin (Table 3).

Inactivating mutation of the *HRPT2* gene are a hallmark of carcinoma, hyperparathyroidism-jaw tumor-syndrome, and some cases of familial isolated hyperparathyroidism, but is not seen in sporadic adenoma or primary hyperplasia [54]. Gene expression profiling has shown distinct profiles for adenoma and hyperplasia but these techniques are limited to research only [57, 58].

Familial Primary Hyperparathyroidism

Several genetic syndromes may include primary hyperparathyroidism either as a predominant feature or as part of the syndrome. These syndromes and their associated gene mutations are listed in Table 3 in the chapter on *Application of Molecular Diagnosis Techniques in the Diagnosis and Management of Endocrine Tumors.*

Multiple Endocrine Neoplasia (MEN)

This is a group of syndromes where multiple endocrine organs develop hyperplasia, adenoma, or carcinoma. The group is categorized as MEN1 and MEN2a and MEN2b. In MEN1 patients, the presenting symptoms are those primary hyperparathyroidism in 80–95% of patients with hyperplasia being the most common parathyroid gland pathology. These patients also develop pancreatic neuroendocrine tumors and pituitary tumors. MEN2 is characterized by medullary thyroid carcinoma and pheochromocytoma. In addition, in MEN2a 20–30% of patients may develop parathyroid hyperplasia, as part of the syndrome [59].

Familial Idiopathic Hyperparathyroidism (FIHPT)

Familial isolated primary hyperparathyroidism (FIHPT) is an autosomal dominant inheritable disorder characterized by isolated primary hyperparathyroidism. It may represent an early stage of either the multiple endocrine neoplasia type 1 (MEN1) or the hyperparathyroidism-jaw tumor (HPT-JT) syndrome. The condition may be caused by allelic variants of *MEN1*. *HRPT2* mutations in FIHPT is rare and are associated with a relatively higher frequency of aggressive parathyroid disease, namely atypical adenoma and carcinoma. Kelly et al. recommend that a personal or family history of parathyroid carcinoma in FIHPT should mandate an evaluation of

Table 3 Immunohistochemistry in parathyroid pathology

Protein/Antigen	Expression in Parathyroid Tissue	Comment/Utility
Chromogranin A	Positive	Helps identify parathyroid tissue from thyroid, lymph node, and other tissues
Parathormone	Positive	Helps identify parathyroid tissue from thyroid, lymph node, and other tissues
TTF-1	Negative	Helps distinguish from thyroid follicular cells, which are positive
Thyroglobulin	Negative	Helps distinguish from thyroid follicular cells, which are positive
Parafibromin	Negative in most parathyroid carcinomas	Helps distinguish malignant from benign parathyroid gland (positive), may be positive in secondary and tertiary hyperplasia
Ki-67	Increased in parathyroid carcinoma	>5/10HPF may suggest malignancy and poorer prognosis; may be negative or not increased in carcinoma
Galectin-3	Positive in parathyroid carcinoma	May be positive in benign tumors
Cyclin-D1	Positive in abnormal parathyroid	Helps identify abnormal from normal but does not distinguish between various types of pathology, i.e., Hyperplasia, adenoma, carcinoma

Abbreviations: HPF High power field, TTF-1 Thyroid transcription factor-1

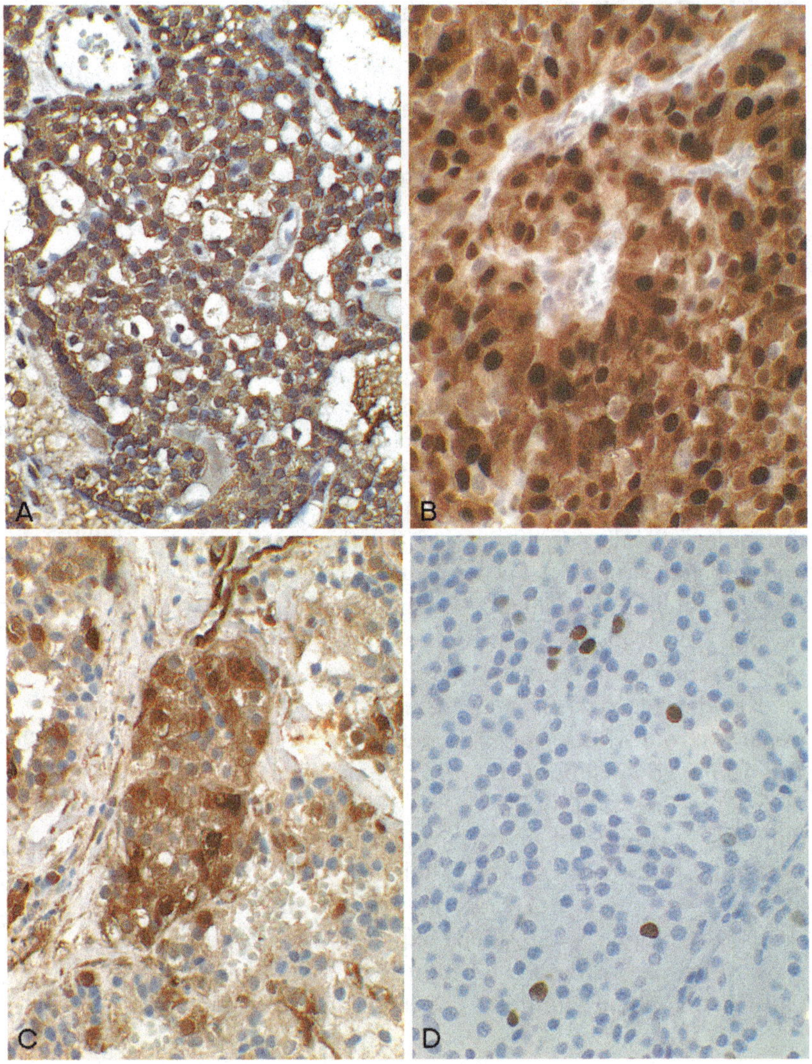

Fig. 7 Immunohistochemistry in parathyroid disease: (**A**) Chromogranin A is uniformly expressed in parathyroid cells. Parathyroid carcinoma with (**B**) nuclear expression of Cyclin-D1, (**C**) nuclear and cytoplasmic expression of Galectin-3, and (**D**) nuclear expression Ki-67 proliferation marker

germline *HRPT2* mutation status [30]. The genetic information can be used in diagnostic and management considerations leading to early detection and removal of potentially malignant parathyroid tumors.

Hyperparathyroidism-Jaw Tumor Syndrome

Hyperparathyroidism-jaw tumor (HPT-JT) is an autosomal dominant genetic disease where primary hyperparathyroidism is associated with recurrent parathyroid adenomas or carcinoma, fibro-osseous tumors of the jaw (mandible or maxilla), and various types of renal lesions, including benign cysts, renal tumors, and hamartomas. The affected individuals carry *HRPT2* gene mutations. *HRPT2* gene encodes the protein parafibromin, which is present in normal parathyroid glands but is uniformly lost in the parathyroid glands of HPT-JT patients and also parathyroid carcinomas due to an inactivating mutation in *HRPT2* [53, 54, 60]. The parathyroid adenomas in these patients tend to be cystic and there is a higher incidence of parathyroid carcinoma.

References

1. Moore, K. L., Persaud, T. V. N. (2003) The Pharyngeal Apparatus. In *The Developing Human: Clinically Oriented Embryology*. WB Saunders 7th ed, pp. 201–40.
2. Harach, H. R. (2004) The Parathyroid. In *Endocrine Pathology: Differential Diagnosis and Molecular Advances* (Ed. Lloyd RV). Humana, pp. 109–30.
3. Hamperle, H. (1936) Uber das Vorkommen von Onkocyten in verschiedenen Organen und ihren Geschwulsten (Mundspeicheldrusen, Bausch-peicheldruse, Epithelkorperchen, Hypophyse, Schilddruse, Eileiter). *Virchows Arch* [A] **298**, 327–75.

4. Roth, S. I., Abu-Jawdeh, G. (1997) Parathyroid Glands. In *Histology for Pathologists* (Ed. Sternberg SS) 2nd ed. Lippincott-Raven, pp. 1093–106.
5. Miettinen, M., Clark, R., Lehto, V. P., Virtanen, I. (1985) Intermediate-filament proteins in parathyroid glands and parathyroid adenomas. *Arch Pathol Lab Med* **109**, 986–9.
6. Kitazawa, R., Kitazawa, S., Fukase, M., et al. (1992) The expression of parathyroid hormone-related peptide (PTHrP) in normal parathyroid histochemistry and in situ hybridization. *Histochemistry* **98**, 211–5.
7. Kifor, O., Moore, F. D. Jr., Wang, P., et al. (1996) Reduced immunostaining for the extracellular Ca^{2+}-sensing receptor in primary and uremic secondary hyperparathyroidism. *J Clin Endocrinol Metab* **81**, 1598–606.
8. Wermers, R. A., Khosla, S., Atkinson, E. J., Hodgson, S. F., O'Fallon, W. M., Melton, L. J. 3rd. (1997) The rise and fall of primary hyperparathyroidism: a population-based study in Rochester, Minnesota, 1965–1992. *Ann Intern Med* **126**, 433–440.
9. Roth, S. I., Faquin, W. C. (2003) The Pathologist's intraoperative role during parathyroid surgery. *Arch Pathol Lab Med* **127**, 15.
10. Chan, J. K. C. (2007) The parathyroid gland. In *Diagnostic Histopathology of Tumors* (Ed. Fletcher CDM). Churchill Livingston Elsevier 3rd ed, pp. 1080–97.
11. Fujiwara, S., Sposto, R., Ezaki, H., Akiba, S., Neriishi, K., Kodama, K., et al. (1992) Hyperparathyroidism among atomic bomb survivors in Hiroshima. *Radiat Res* **130**, 372–8.
12. Beard, C. M., Heath, H. 3rd, O'Fallon, W.M., Anderson, J.A., Earle, J.D., Melton, L. J. 3rd. (1989) Therapeutic radiation and hyperparathyroidism. A case-control study in Rochester, Minn. *Arch Intern Med* **149**, 1887–90.
13. Schneider, A. B., Gierlowski, T. C., Shore-Freedman, E., Stovall, M., Ron, E., Lubin, J. (1995) Dose-response relationships for radiation-induced hyperparathyroidism. *J Clin Endocrinol Metab* **80**, 254–7.
14. Heath H., Hodgson, S. F., Kennedy, M. A. (1980) Primary hyperparathyroidism. Incidence, morbidity, and potential economic impact in a community. *N Engl J Med* **302**, 189–193.
15. Wermers R. A., Khosla S., Atkinson E. J., et al. (2006) Incidence of primary hyperparathyroidism in Rochester, Minnesota, 1993–2001: an update on the changing epidemiology of the disease. *J Bone Miner Res* **21**, 171–77.
16. Turken, S. A., Cafferty, M., Silverberg S. J., et al. (1989) Neuromuscular involvement in mild, asymptomatic primary hyperparathyroidism. *Am J Med* **87**, 553–7.
17. Solomon, B. L., Schaaf, M., Smallridge, R. C. (1994) Psychologic symptoms before and after parathyroid surgery. *Am J Med* **96**,101–6.
18. Bilezikian, J. P., Silverberg, S. J. (2004) Asymptomatic primary hyperparathyroidism. *N Engl J Med* **350**, 1746–51.
19. Grimelius, L., DeLellis, R. A., Bondeson, L., et al. (2004) Parathyroid Adenoma. In *World Health Organization Classification of Tumors: Pathology & Genetics: Tumors of Endocrine Organs* (Eds. DeLellis RA, Lloyd RV, Heitz PU, Eng C). IARC Press, pp. 128–132.
20. DeLellis R. A. (1993) Parathyroid Adenoma. In *Atlas of Tumor Pathology: Tumors of the Parathyroid Gland.* 3rd series. Armed Forces Institute of Pathology, pp. 25–51.
21. Attie, J. N., Bock, G., Auguste, L. J. (1990) Multiple parathyroid adenomas: report of thirty-three cases. *Surgery* **108**, 1014–9.
22. Faquin, W. C., Roth, S. I. (2006) Frozen section of thyroid and parathyroid specimens. *Arch Pathol Lab Med* **130**, 1260.
23. Turner, W. J. D., Bergen, R. N., Pelliteri, P. K., Orloff, L. A. (1996) Parathyroid lipoadenoma: Case report and review of the literature. *Otolaryngol Head Neck Surgery* **114**, 313–316.
24. Chow, L. S., Erickson, L. A., Abu-Lebdeh, H. S., Wermers, R. A. (2006) Parathyroid lipoadenomas: a rare cause of primary hyperparathyroidism. *Endocr Pract* **12**, 131–136.
25. Rasbach, D. A., Monchik, J. M., Geelhoed, G. W., Harrison, T. S. (1984) Solitary parathyroid microadenoma. *Surgery* **96**, 1092–8.
26. Lee, P. K., Jarosek, S. L., Vernig, B. A., Evasovich, M., Tuttle, T. M. (2007) Trends in the incidence and treatment of parathyroid carcinoma in the United States. *Cancer* **109**,1736–41.
27. Hundahl, S. A., Fleming, I. D., Fremgen, A. M., Menck, H. R. (1999) Two hundred eighty-six cases of parathyroid carcinoma treated in the U.S. between 1985–1995: a National Cancer Data Base Report. The American College of Surgeons Commission on Cancer and the American Cancer Society. *Cancer* **86**, 538–44.
28. Dionisi, S., Minisola, S., Pepe, J., De Geronimo, S., Paglia, F., Memeo, L., Fitzpatrick, L. A. (2002) Concurrent parathyroid adenomas and carcinoma in the setting of multiple endocrine neoplasia type 1: presentation as hypercalcemic crisis. *Mayo Clin Proc* **77**, 866–9.
29. Agha, A., Carpenter, R., Bhattacharya, S., Edmonson, S.J., Carlsen, E., Monson, J. P. (2007) Parathyroid carcinoma in multiple endocrine neoplasia type 1 (MEN1) syndrome: two case reports of an unrecognised entity. *J Endocrinol Invest* **30**, 145–9.
30. Kelly, T. G., Shattuck, T. M., Reyes-Mugica, M., et al. (2006) Surveillance for early detection of aggressive parathyroid disease: carcinoma and atypical adenoma in familial isolated hyperparathyroidism associated with a germline HRPT2 mutation. *J Bone Miner Res* **21**, 1666–71.
31. Kleinpeter, K. P., Lovato, J. F., Clark, P. B., et al. (2005) Is parathyroid carcinoma indeed a lethal disease? *Ann Surg Oncol* **12**, 260–6.
32. Pelizzo, M. R., Piotto, A., Bergamasco, A., Rubello, D. Casara, D. (2001) Parathyroid carcinoma. Therapeutic strategies derived from 20 years of experience. *Minerva Endocrinol* **26**, 23–9.
33. Iihara, M., Okamoto, T., Suzuki, R., Kawamata, A., Nishikawa, T., Kobayashi, M., Obara, T. (2007) Functional parathyroid carcinoma: Long-term treatment outcome and risk factor analysis. *Surgery* **142**, 936–43.
34. Bondeson, L., Grimelius, L., DeLellis, R. A., et al. (2004) Parathyroid Carcinoma. In *World Health Organization Classification of Tumors: Pathology & Genetics: Tumors of Endocrine Organs* (Eds. DeLellis RA, Lloyd RV, Heitz PU, Eng C). IARC Press, pp. 124–127.
35. Koea, J. B., Shaw, J. H. (1999) Parathyroid cancer: biology and management. *Surg Oncol* **8**, 155–65.
36. Sandelin, K., Auer, G., Bondeson, L., Grimelius, L., Farnebo, L. O. (1992) Prognostic factors in parathyroid cancer: a review of 95 cases. *World J Surg* **16**, 724–31.
37. Munson, N. D., Foote, R. L., Northcutt, R. C., et al. (2003) Parathyroid carcinoma: Is there a role for adjuvant radiation therapy? *Cancer* **98**, 2378–84.
38. Busaidy, N. L., Jimenez, C., Habra, M. A., et al. (2004) Parathyroid carcinoma: a 22-year experience. *Head Neck* **26**, 716–26.
39. Wiseman, S. M., Rigual, N. R., Hicks, W. L. Jr, et al. (2004) Parathyroid carcinoma: a multicenter review of clinicopathologic features and treatment outcomes. *Ear Nose Throat J* **83**, 491–4.
40. Carpenter J. M., Michaelson P. G., Lidner T. K., Hinni M. L. (2007) Parathyromatosis. *Ear Nose Throat J* **86**, 21.
41. Fernandez-Ranvier G. G., Khanafshar E., Jensen K., et al. (2007) Parathyroid carcinoma, atypical parathyroid adenoma, or parathyromatosis? *Cancer* **110**, 255–64.
42. Palmer J. A., Brown W. A., Kerr W. H., Rosen I. B., Watters N. A. (1975) The surgical aspects of hyperparathyroidism. *Arch Surg* **110**, 1004–7.

43. Reddick R. L., Costa J. C., Marx S. J. (1977) Parathyroid hyperplasia and parathyromatosis. *Lancet* **1**, 549.
44. Aly A, Douglas M. (2003) Embryonic parathyroid rests occur commonly and have implications in the management of secondary hyperparathyroidism. *ANZ J Surg* **73**, 284–8.
45. Barnes, B. A., Cope, O. (1961) Carcinoma of the parathyroid glands: Report of 10 cases with endocrine function. *JAMA* **178**, 556–559.
46. Kollmorgen C. F., Aust M. R., Ferreiro J. A., McCarthy J. T., van Heerden J.A. (1994) Parathyromatosis: a rare yet important cause of persistent or recurrent hyperparathyroidism. *Surgery* **116**, 111–5.
47. Falvo L., Catania A., Sorrenti S., D'Andrea V., Santulli M., De Antoni E. (2003) Relapsing secondary hyperparathyroidism due to multiple nodular formations after total parathyroidectomy with autograft. *Am Surg* **69**, 998–1002.
48. Calcutt, V. G. Franco-Saenz, R. Morrow, L. B. et al. (1998) Localization of abnormal parathyroid tissue with use of technetium-99m-seastamibi. *Endocr Pract* **4**, 184–9.
49. Baloch, Z. W., LiVolsi, V. A. (2002) Intraoperative assessment of thyroid and parathyroid lesions. *Semin Diagn Pathol* **19**, 219–26.
50. Carneiro-Pla, D. M., Romaguera, R., Nadji, M., Lew, J.I., Solorzano, C.C., Irvin, G. L. 3rd. (2007) Does histopathology predict parathyroid hypersecretion and influence correctly the extent of parathyroidectomy in patients with sporadic primary hyperparathyroidism? *Surgery* **142**, 930–5.
51. Irvin, G. L., Solorzano, C. C., Carneiro, D. M. (2004) Quick intraoperative parathyroid hormone assay: surgical adjunct to allow limited parathyroidectomy, improve success rate, and predict outcome. *World J Surg* **28**, 1287–92.
52. Hedbäck, G., Odén, A. (2003) Recurrence of hyperparathyroidism; a long-term follow-up after surgery for primary hyperparathyroidism. *Eur J Endocrinol* **148**, 413–21.
53. Tan M. H., Morrison C., Wang P., et al. (2004) Loss of parafibromin immunoreactivity is a distinguishing feature of parathyroid carcinoma. *Clin Cancer Res* **10**, 6629–37.
54. Cetani F., Ambrogini E., Viacava P., et al. (2007) Should parafibromin staining replace HRTP2 gene analysis as an additional tool for histologic diagnosis of parathyroid carcinoma? *Eur J Endocrinol* **156**, 547–54.
55. Bergero, N., De Pompa, R., Sacerdote, C., et al. (2005) Galectin-3 expression in parathyroid carcinoma: immunohistochemical study of 26 cases. *Hum Pathol* **36**, 908–14.
56. Ordoñez N. G., Ibañez M. L., Samaan N. A., Hickey R. C. (1983) Immunoperoxidase study of uncommon parathyroid tumors. Report of two cases of nonfunctioning parathyroid carcinoma and one intrathyroid parathyroid tumor-producing amyloid. *Am J Surg Pathol* **7**, 535–42.
57. Morrison C., Farrar W., Kneile J., et al. (2004) Molecular classification of parathyroid neoplasia by gene expression profiling. *Am J Pathol* **165**, 565–76.
58. Velázquez-Fernández D., Laurell C., Saqui-Salces M., et al. (2006) Differential RNA expression profile by cDNA microarray in sporadic primary hyperparathyroidism (pHPT): primary parathyroid hyperplasia versus adenoma. *World J Surg* **30**, 705–13.
59. Maitra, A., Abbas, A. K. (2005) The Endocrine System. In *Robbins and Cotran Pathologic Basis of Disease* (Eds. Kumar V, Abbas AK, Fausto N). Elsevier Saunders, pp. 1155–1226.
60. Carpten J. D., Robbins C. M., Villablanca A., et al. (2002) HRPT2, encoding parafibromin, is mutated in hyperparathyroidism-jaw tumor syndrome. *Nat Genet* **32**, 676–80.

Tumors of the Adrenal Cortex

Anne Marie McNicol

Abstract Adrenal cortical tumors may present clinically with evidence of excess hormone secretion, local mass effects, or symptoms and signs associated with malignancy. They are now also identified incidentally when the abdomen is scanned in the investigation of other disease. Although adrenal cortical carcinoma is rare, it is important to recognize it as an aggressive tumor.

This chapter discusses first the aspects of the normal adrenal gland and clinical and epidemiological features of adrenal cortical tumors. The pathologic features of benign and malignant tumors are described, also the application of immunohistochemistry in differential diagnosis and an outline of the molecular pathogenesis.

Keywords Adrenal cortex • Adenoma • Carcinoma • Immunohistochemistry • Molecular genetics

Introduction

Adrenal cortical tumors are now more commonly part of diagnostic surgical pathology practice because they are increasingly identified when the abdomen is scanned in the investigation of other diseases. Although adrenal carcinoma is rare it is important to recognize as it has a very poor prognosis and adequate surgical treatment is the mainstay of therapy. Diagnosis is still based on basic histological analysis and prognosis is linked mainly to tumor stage. However, immunohistochemistry and molecular investigations are beginning to provide information that may be useful for the future. This chapter will discuss clinical and pathologic aspects of adrenal adenoma and carcinoma, the use of immunohistochemistry in differential diagnosis, and relevant aspects of molecular pathogenesis.

The Normal Adrenal Cortex

The human adrenal glands sit at the upper poles of the kidneys, the right having a pyramidal shape and the left a more crescentic appearance. The normal weight in the adult at surgery [1] or in cases of sudden death [2] is 4.0 ± 0.8 g, while it is 6 g at hospital autopsy, presumably reflecting stimulation by adrenocorticotrophic hormone (ACTH) in the stress of terminal illness. It is divided along the long axis into head, body, and tail, and the alae are flattened extensions on the medial and lateral aspects. The medulla accounts for ~10% of the total weight and is present in the head and body and focally in the alae [2, 3]. The cortex comprises three zones with distinctive histologic features. The zona glomerulosa (ZG) comprises small angular cells dispersed in a discontinuous manner below the capsule. It is responsible for the synthesis of aldosterone, the main mineralocorticoid. The zona fasciculata (ZF) is the main component, with large lipid-laden cells arranged in columns from the ZG or capsule to the inner zona reticularis (ZR). It is thought to be the main source of glucocorticoids (cortisol in the human gland). The ZR comprises eosinophilic, or compact, cells with little lipid storage. These are arranged in cords around vascular sinusoids. This zone is also capable of producing cortisol and is the source of adrenal androgens. The control of aldosterone secretion is mainly by the renin–angiotensin system, while cortisol production is regulated by ACTH. The medulla lies centrally and the border between it and the cortex is often not clearly defined, with foci of cortical cells lying within the medulla. There is also a cuff of cortex that invaginates into the medulla around the central vein.

A.M. McNicol (✉)
Professor Molecular and Cellular Pathology, School of Medicine, University of Queensland, Brisbane, Australia
e-mail: a.mcnicol@uq.edu.au

A. Khan (ed.), *Surgical Pathology of Endocrine and Neuroendocrine Tumors*, Current Clinical Pathology,
DOI 10.1007/978-1-60327-396-1_8, © Humana Press, a part of Springer Science+Business Media, LLC 2009

Clinical Aspects of Adrenal Cortical Tumors

Both benign and malignant tumors may present with signs and symptoms of secretion of excess steroids. Production of aldosterone causes Conn syndrome, with hypertension, low renin levels, and, in many patients, hypokalemia [4]. Excessive secretion of cortisol gives rise to the well-recognized features of Cushing syndrome [5]. Production of sex steroids causes adrenogenital syndrome, with virilization, feminization, or precocious puberty, depending on the age and sex of the patient and the nature of the steroids produced. Androgen production is much more common than estrogen. Adrenal cortical carcinoma may present with metastases or with abdominal or loin pain, fullness, or other more general tumor-related effects, such as fever or weight loss.

Both adenomas and carcinomas also present as 'incidentalomas,' when the abdomen is scanned for the investigation of other disease [6]. High resolution computed tomography (CT) scans detect lesions in ~4% of people [7]. They are more common with increasing age and have a prevalence of about 7% over 70 years of age [8]. Some are found to be functional and a number are associated with subclinical Cushing syndrome [9]. These are usually removed, but there is still a debate as to what to do with nonfunctional cortical lesions [10]. Decisions may be made on the basis of size since larger adrenal cortical tumors are more likely to be malignant.

Adrenal Adenoma

The true incidence of adrenal cortical adenomas is unknown as, until recently, most were identified in life only if they secreted excess steroids. Cortical nodules are reported in up to 54% of unselected autopsy series [11]. These may be single nodules, but many are small, multiple, and bilateral [12]. They are more common with increasing age and in hypertension and diabetes mellitus. They are usually unencapsulated but circumscribed and larger lesions often show an expansile pattern of growth. Large nodules may cause disparity in weight between the two glands. Micronodules are usually seen in the outer ZF (Fig. 1) and larger nodules occupy more of the cortex. They may also be found in the cortical cuff surrounding the central vein. The cut surface is yellow, often with focal brown areas. Most comprise large lipid-laden cells but compact cells may predominate. Myelolipomatous change and osseous change are found occasionally. These nodules were thought to represent compensatory hyperplasia following ischemia and atrophy on the basis that they were found more commonly in glands showing

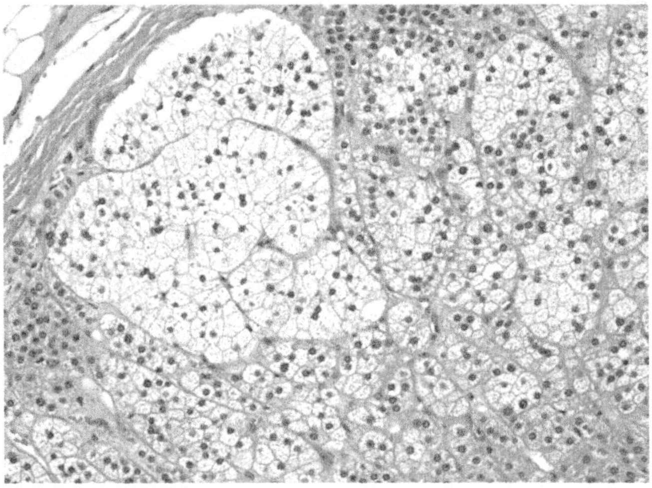

Fig. 1 Adrenal cortical micronodule in the outer zona fasciculata. The capsule lies at the upper left hand corner. Hematoxylin and eosin. Original magnification ×200

hyalinization and luminal occlusion of capsular vessels [12]. However, others have challenged this because they can be found in glands without evidence of vascular changes and abnormal vessels may actually be present within the nodules themselves [13].

Most would regard larger solitary nodules as adenomas and multiple bilateral nodules as hyperplastic. Clonal analysis supports this approach as it suggests that most nodules with the morphologic characteristics of adenoma are monoclonal, consistent with a neoplasm [14, 15]. However, a minority are polyclonal, raising the possibility that they are of hyperplastic origin or that some adenomas arise from neoplastic transformation of more than one cell. This requires further clarification.

Using the presence of a solitary nodule as one of the main diagnostic criteria, an autopsy study has reported adenomas in 5% of glands [16], more commonly in women. Occasional cases of bilateral adenomas have been reported [17, 18]. Adenomas often weigh less than 50 g but occasionally are large [11]. They are intra-adrenal, often unencapsulated (Fig. 2), but may have a pseudocapsule or a true capsule. The cut surface is usually yellow with focal brown areas. Although the reason is unclear, adenomas associated with Conn syndrome are often a brighter yellow than those of Cushing syndrome. Occasional tumors are very dark, so-called 'black adenoma' [19]. This is due to the accumulation of lipofuscin and/or neuromelanin. In patients with Cushing syndrome the adjacent normal gland is usually atrophic because of the suppression of ACTH release from the anterior pituitary caused by the excess levels of cortisol. Histologically, they are composed mainly of ZF-like cells with foci of compact cells and show an alveolar architectural pattern

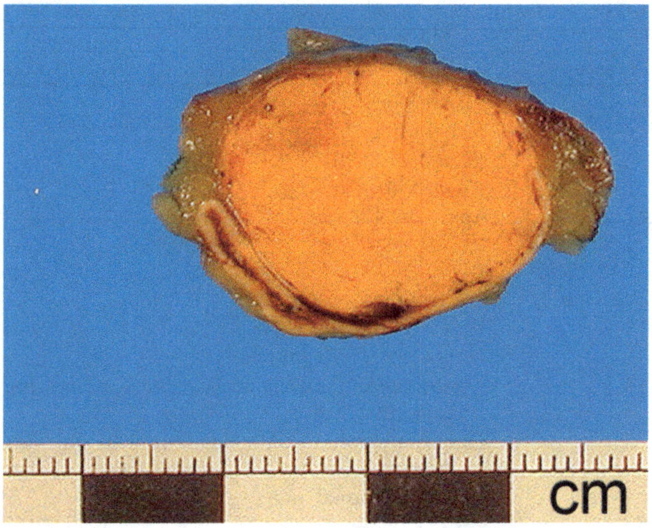

Fig. 2 Adrenal cortical adenoma from a patient with Conn syndrome. The normal gland is seen in the lower part of the picture and attenuated around the tumor

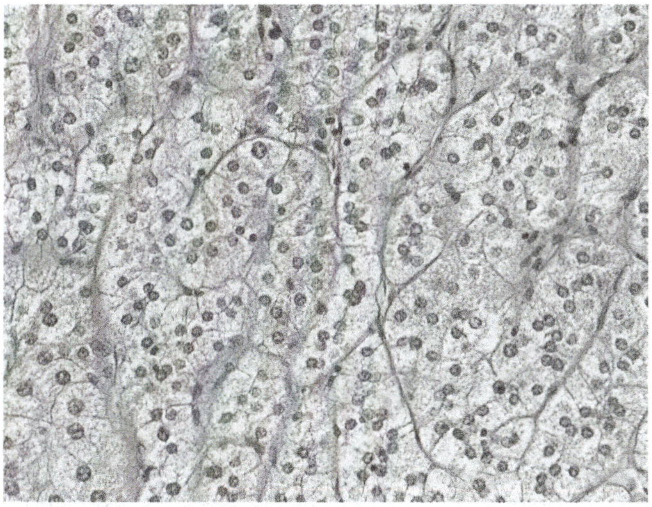

Fig. 3 Adrenal cortical adenoma. The tumor comprises lipid-laden cells arranged in a mixture of alveolar groups and short cords. Hematoxylin and eosin. Original magnification×400

mixed with short cords of cells (Fig. 3). In tumors associated with Conn syndrome there may be foci of ZG-like cells and cells showing mixed characteristics of ZG and ZF cells – 'hybrid' cells. In patients treated with spironolactone, small intracytoplasmic whorled inclusions (spironolactone bodies) may be found in the tumor cells and in the outer ZF and ZG [20]. These measure up to 20 μm in diameter and are often surrounded by a clear halo. They stain positively with periodic acid-Schiff. Compact cells may be the dominant subtype in tumors associated with virilization and this may cause problems in the diagnosis of malignancy as outlined later.

Adrenal Carcinoma

Adrenal cortical carcinoma is a rare tumor with an estimated prevalence of between 0.5 and 2 per million [6, 21–23] and it accounts for 0.05% to 2% of all malignancies [24–26]. It is more common in women. There is a bimodal age distribution, with a peak in early childhood and another in the fifth to seventh decades [27–29]. The outcome is still poor [30, 31] with reported mortality rates between 67% and 94% [32–34]. The median or mean survival lies between 4 and 46 months [24, 34, 35]. Over half of patients have invasion of adjacent organs or distant metastases at the time of first presentation [31, 36]. The common sites of metastases are liver, lung, retroperitoneum, lymph nodes, and bone [37, 38].

Functioning tumors account for between 24% and 74% of cases [11, 38, 39]. Cushing syndrome is the commonest, often accompanied by androgen excess (mixed Cushing syndrome). Virilization may be the only feature. Feminization is rare as is Conn syndrome. In recurrence or metastatic disease the clinical syndrome is usually the same, but changes from virilization to feminization [40] and Conn to Cushing syndrome [41] have been reported. Surgery is the main therapeutic approach and most tumors have a poor response to chemotherapy. This may be due to the expression of P-glycoprotein [42, 43] and glutathione-S-transferases [44] that play a role in various types of drug resistance. Mitotane is a compound with a nonspecific adrenolytic effect that has been shown to prolong disease-free survival [45].

Most adrenal cortical carcinomas weigh more than 100 g [46] although some would use 50 g as the cut-off for suspicion of malignancy [27]. In some series, the average weight has been >1 kg [47]. They may range from 3 cm to 40 cm in diameter. However, smaller lesions may behave in a malignant fashion [48]. Some are encapsulated, but others are adherent to, or invade, surrounding fat and adjacent organs. On slicing, the lesion is often lobulated with fibrous bands separating the tumor lobules. The cut surface is fleshy (Fig. 4), ranging in color from yellow to pink/brown. Necrosis and hemorrhage are common and there may be cystic change. Occasionally gross vascular invasion is seen.

Histologically, the architecture is less ordered than in adenomas. Trabecular and diffuse patterns are common (Fig. 5). The architecture may be uniform or mixed. Compact cells often predominate. Nuclear pleomorphism is seen sometimes with multinucleated cells. Mitoses are usually present and atypical forms may be seen. Confluent necrosis is common. Broad fibrous

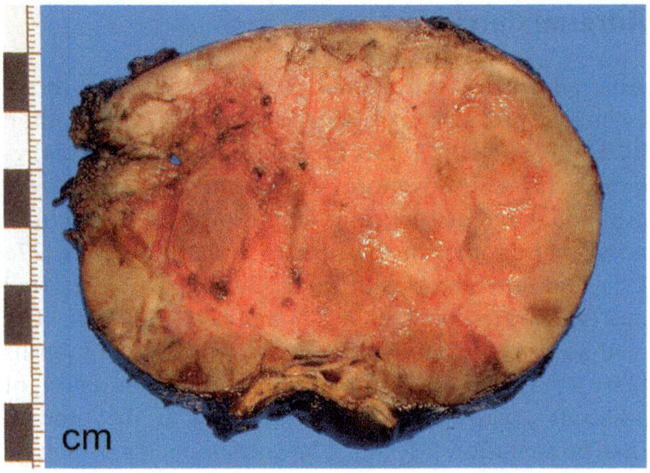

Fig. 4 Adrenal cortical carcinoma. The cut surface is fleshy and shows some lobulation. There is necrosis and hemorrhage, particularly in the upper left of the picture

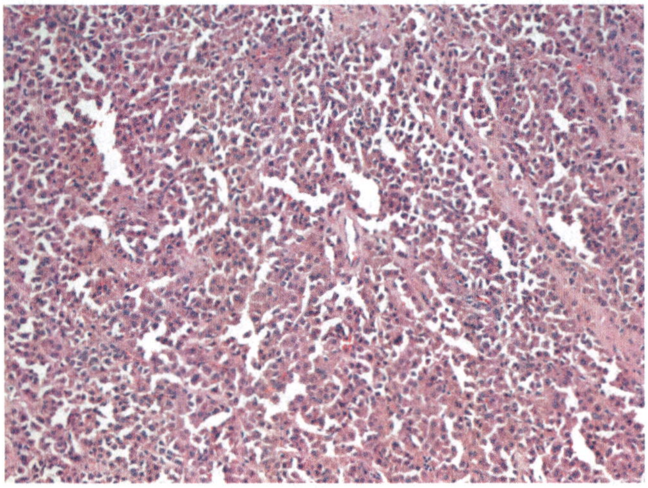

Fig. 5 Adrenal cortical carcinoma. The tumor comprises sheets of eosinophilic compact cells. Hematoxylin and eosin. Original magnification × 100

bands are present in many cases. Invasion of sinusoidal and venous channels can be identified. Capsular invasion may also be seen, and infiltration of surrounding fat or adjacent organs. In contrast to pheochromocytoma, both local invasion and distant metastases define malignancy.

There is no formal staging system from either the International Union against Cancer (UICC) or the American Joint Committee on Cancer (AJCC), but the most commonly used approach is that of Macfarlane [26] modified by Sullivan [49] (Table 1). Seventy per cent of patients present with stage 3 or 4 disease [50].

Table 1 Staging of adrenal cortical carcinoma using Sullivan's modification [49] of MacFarlane's method [26]

Stage	
1	T1 N0 M0
2	T2 N0 M0
3	T1 or T2 N1 M0
	T3 N0 M0
4	Any T or N M1
	T3 N1
	T4
Criterion	
T1	Tumor $\geq$ 5 cm, no invasion
T2	Tumor >5 cm, no invasion
T3	Tumor any size, locally invasive but not involving adjacent organs
T4	Tumor any size, invading adjacent organs or with distant metastases
N0	Negative regional nodes
N1	Positive regional nodes
M0	No distant metastases
M1	Distant metastases

Diagnosis of Malignancy

The diagnosis of malignancy is easy in most cases. However, all adrenal cortical tumors must be assessed for malignant potential. There is no one diagnostic feature, so a number of multifactorial systems have been proposed. These have been developed by comparing findings in tumors with known benign or malignant behavior. Hough et al. incorporated clinical and biochemical findings as well as histologic features [27]. Some systems give a numerical weighting to each feature and the total defines the tumor as benign, of uncertain malignant potential, or malignant [27, 47]. However, since pathologists may not have access to clinical information or to the numerical weightings when reporting a case, the most widely used system is that of Weiss [51, 52] in which nine histologic features are assessed (Table 2). The presence of three or more indicates malignant potential. This system has been validated in a recent study [53] with a specificity of 96% and a sensitivity of 100%, with good correlation between the observers ($r = 0.94$). However, the authors reported poorer correlation on features such as nuclear pleomorphism and vascular invasion and proposed a modification in which they were omitted and the others were incorporated into a weighted numerical score (Table 3). This modified system has been compared to those of Weiss and van Slooten in classifying cases as benign or malignant [54] and performed well ($p < 0.005$). However, although all of these systems have value, they may occasionally give different diagnoses on the same case. Therefore, in difficult cases all clinical, biochemical, and histologic information should be taken into account, and, in a

Table 2 Diagnosis of malignancy in adrenal cortical tumors using the Weiss system [51, 52]

Histological features to be assessed
Diffuse architecture greater than one third
Clear cells ≤ 25% of total
Significant nuclear pleomorphism
Confluent necrosis
Mitotic count ≥ 6 per 50 HPF
Atypical mitoses
Capsular invasion
Sinusoidal invasion
Venous invasion

Table 3 Diagnosis of malignancy in adrenal cortical tumors using the Aubert modification of the Weiss system [53]

Histological features to be assessed
Mitotic count ≤ 6 per 50 HPF
Atypical mitoses
Clear cells ≥ 25% of total (cytoplasmic)
Confluent necrosis
Capsular invasion

Each feature is scored 1 when present and 0 when absent. The final score is obtained by summing as follows, resulting in scores of 0–7: 2 × mitotic rate score + 2 × cytoplasmic score + atypical mitoses score + necrosis score + capsular invasion score.
A total score of ≥ 3 indicates malignant potential.

few cases, a diagnosis of indeterminate or borderline tumor may have to be made. It should also be noted that occasional tumors in which an initial benign diagnosis is made do metastasize [55]. When the reported case recurred, it had a high score and the authors queried whether tumor heterogeneity might have limited the application of Weiss, since the tumor was large and there may have been sampling problems. It is very important therefore to sample tumors widely and to take blocks from any unusual areas.

Some additional tests may be helpful in problem cases. The Ki-67 (MIB-1) index is higher in carcinomas with levels over 5% found only in malignant tumors [56–58]. However, a low Ki-67 index is not diagnostic of benign behavior, as many carcinomas lie below this threshold. Immunopositivity for p53 has been detected in around 50% of carcinomas and rarely in adenomas [56, 59]. Carcinomas also overexpress insulin-like growth factor 2 (IGF-2) [60, 61].

An area in which there is difficulty in applying the Weiss criteria is that of oncocytic tumors (Fig. 6). These resemble oncocytic tumors at other sites and are composed of large eosinophilic cells with accumulation of mitochondria. Originally reported as nonfunctioning and benign [62, 63], functional [64] and malignant [65], variants have now been described. The diagnostic problem arises because most have less than 25% clear cells,

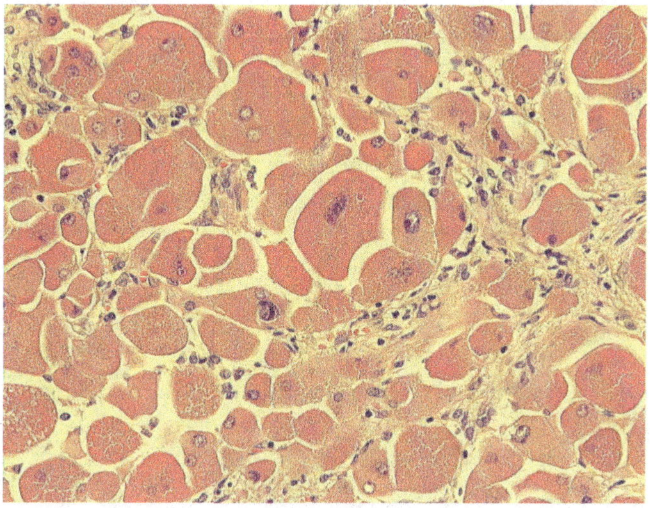

Fig. 6 Adrenal cortical oncocytoma. The tumor comprises large pleomorphic eosinophilic cells arranged in a diffuse pattern. Hematoxylin and eosin. Original magnification×400

pleomorphic nuclei, and diffuse architecture, a combination giving a Weiss score of 3, and thus a malignant diagnosis. A modification of the Weiss approach has been put forward [66]. Three *major criteria* have been proposed for diagnosis: a mitotic rate of > 5 per 50 high power fields, any atypical mitoses, and venous invasion. The presence of any one of these defines the tumor as malignant. Four *minor criteria* are: large size (>10 cm or >200 g), necrosis, capsular invasion, and sinusoidal invasion. Tumors with one or more of these are defined as of uncertain malignant potential. Where none of these criteria is present, the tumor is diagnosed as benign. Other groups have used a similar approach [63, 67] but have not been so specific in their recommendations. This is a useful way of dealing with this problem but it will obviously have to be validated prospectively.

Immunohistochemistry

The main area where immunohistochemistry is applied is in the differential diagnosis. Adrenal cortical tumors may need to be distinguished from hepatocellular carcinoma (HCC) and renal cell carcinoma (RCC) [68] and, occasionally, from pheochromocytoma. Specific identification of adrenal cortical tumors is difficult. Immunopositivity for inhibin-α [69, 70] and with melan A antibody (clone A103) [71] (Fig. 7) has high sensitivity and specificity when compared with other solid organ carcinomas. The combination of the two identified 82.5% of cases in a recent report [68]. Calretinin is also highly sensitive, but not specific [72]. Expression of steroidogenic enzymes can

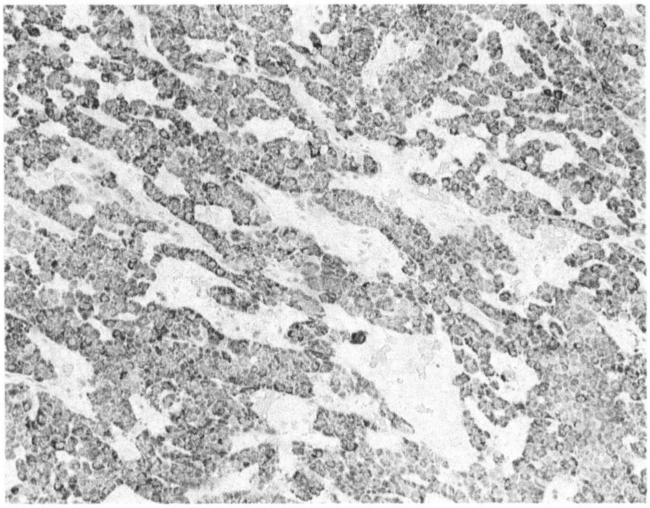

Fig. 7 Adrenal cortical carcinoma showing immunopositivity with Melan A antibody, clone A103. Immunoperoxidase technique. Original magnification ×200

be of use [73, 74] as can identification of nuclear proteins involved in steroidogenesis, such as the transcription factor SF1 (steroidogenic factor 1) and nuclear hormone receptor DAX-1 (dosage sensitive sex reversal, adrenal hypoplasia critical region on chromosome X gene 1) [75, 76]. These have not yet found their way into diagnostic practice, probably because of the lack of good commercial antibodies. Adrenal cortical tumors are usually negative or only weakly positive for cytokeratins [77, 78] and are negative for epithelial membrane antigen [77], while RCC is usually positive for both of these. In addition, RCC is positive for CD10 in 70–89% of cases [68, 79] and the antibody RCC that recognizes a brush border protein of the proximal kidney tubule has 99% specificity for RCC, with 55% sensitivity [68] while adrenal cortical carcinomas are negative. The antibody Hepar-1 (hepatocyte paraffin 1) has a specificity of 98% for HCC when compared to RCC and adrenal cortical carcinoma [68] and a canalicular pattern of staining with polyclonal antibody to carcinoembryonic antigen (pCEA) has reasonable sensitivity and 100% specificity. Adrenal cortical tumors can show positivity for general neuroendocrine markers, including synaptophysin [80, 81], and chromogranin A is the only marker that can be used to positively identify pheochromocytoma.

Prognostic Features in Carcinoma

The most important factor is still tumor stage. It has been reported that the van Slooten and modified Weiss scores correlate with metastatic behavior and with cancer-specific survival in tumors that had metastasized [54]. High proliferative activity is associated with poorer outcome. A mitotic rate of >20 per 50 high power fields was associated with lower median survival ($p<0.02$) [52]. A Weiss score of ≥ 6 correlated with poorer disease-free and overall survival [82]. Patients with a Ki-67 index of >3% [57] or >7% [82] had a lower disease-free survival and the Ki-67 index had an inverse correlation with survival [83]. Some of the molecular genetic studies discussed below are beginning to suggest that more aggressive carcinomas can be identified by gene profiling [84] or by overexpression of IGF-2 or loss of heterozygosity (LOH) at 17p13 [85]. Specific chromosomal gains and losses may also be linked to survival, with poorer outcome as the number of changes increases [86].

Genetic Aspects of Adrenal Cortical Tumors

Adrenal cortical tumors occur more frequently in a number of familial syndromes. These include Li-Fraumeni syndrome, associated with germline mutations in the *TP53* tumor suppressor gene on 17q13.1 [87]; Beckwith-Wiedemann syndrome, linked to the 11p15 locus with paternal disomy and involvement of a number of genes including *IGF2* and *H19*, and overexpression of IGF-2 [88]; Carney complex, with inactivating mutations in the protein kinase A regulatory subunit 1A (*PRKAR1A*) gene at 17q22-24 [89]; and Multiple Endocrine Neoplasia type 1 (MEN1) with mutations in the *MEN1* gene on 11q13 [90, 91].

A variety of approaches have been used to investigate the molecular pathogenesis of sporadic adrenal cortical tumors. Loss of heterozygosity (LOH) studies, comparative genomic hybridization (CGH), and interphase cytogenetics have examined changes in individual chromosomes. These studies have yielded inconsistent data, probably because of the small numbers of cases and differences in methodology. However, there is general agreement that changes are present in all carcinomas and in up to 61% of adenomas [85, 92]. In situ hybridization has demonstrated chromosomal gains and less frequent losses [93–95]. Losses on chromosomes 2, 11q, and 17p and gains on 4 and 5 were first described by CGH with increasing numbers of changes with tumor size and malignancy [96]. In carcinomas the most frequent gains were reported on chromosomes 5,12, 9, and 4 and losses were frequent at 1p, 17p, 22, 2q, and 11q, while the most frequent change in adenomas was gain of 4q [92]. High-level amplifications were found in another study [97]. Interestingly, in sporadic tumors, LOH has been reported at loci associated with the familial tumors discussed above, suggesting that the genes involved may have a role. LOH at 17p13 [85, 98, 99], 11q13 [100, 101], and 11p15 [85, 102] is more common in carcinoma than adenoma. However, LOH at 17q22-24 has been reported only in adenoma [103]. LOH has also been reported in a minority of cases at 18p11, the locus of the gene encoding the ACTH receptor [104].

A number of tumor suppressor genes and oncogenes have been investigated. Acquired mutations in *TP53* have been reported in only up to 27% of carcinomas and 6% of adenomas [105, 106]. However, a higher proportion shows immunopositivity for p53 protein [59, 106]. An unusual germline mutation has been shown to be involved in carcinomas in southern Brazil, where the incidence is ten times greater than in other geographic regions [107]. There is no evidence for significant involvement of *MEN1* in sporadic tumors [100, 108]. In view of the presence of LOH at this locus, this raises the possibility of another tumor suppressor gene.

Overexpression of IGF-2 is the most commonly reported abnormality in carcinoma, occurring in $\sim$90% of cases [61, 109, 110] and associated with paternal disomy. Other growth factors involved may include transforming growth factor α (TGFα); IGF-1, its receptors, and binding proteins [61, 111, 112]; and inhibins and activins [113, 114]. There is recent evidence for involvement of the Wnt signaling pathway with activating mutations of *β-catenin* gene in 27% of adenomas and 31% of carcinomas and accumulation of the protein in 13% and 77% [115].

ACTH acts through a G-protein linked receptor, cyclic adenosine monophosphate (cAMP), and protein kinase A (PKA), and components of this pathway have been studied. No activating mutations of the ACTH receptor have been identified [116, 117] and mutations in G proteins are rare [118, 119]. There is some evidence for a role for PKA, but only in adenomas [103, 120]. Indeed, it has been proposed that this pathway is important in the pathogenesis of adrenal cortical hyperplasia and adenoma, while other changes are associated with the development of carcinoma [121].

There have now been a number of publications on gene expression profiling in adrenal cortical tumors. A study on 11 carcinomas and 4 adenomas, starting with 10,000 genes and progressing to a selected 91 genes, demonstrated that distinction could be made between benign and malignant tumors [122]. It also confirmed the overexpression of IGF-2 in carcinoma and showed high expression of other proliferation related genes. Another investigation used a different approach selecting 230 genes in two groups: adrenal related genes, including steroidogenic enzymes and cAMP signaling components, and cancer related genes including components of the IGF-2 pathway [84]. In a series of 33 adenomas and 24 carcinomas, they identified a combination of 14 genes from the adrenal cluster and 8 genes from the IGF-2 cluster that permitted distinction between benign and malignant tumors with a similar predictive value to the Weiss score. The adrenal cluster predominated in adenoma and the IGF-2 in carcinoma. They were also able to select a panel of 14 genes that allowed distinction between recurring and non-recurring carcinomas. These findings are of interest, but need validation and refinement before they can be incorporated into clinical practice.

References

1. Studzinski, G.P., Hay, D.C.F. and Symington, T. (1963) Observations on the weight of the human adrenal gland and the effect of preparations of corticotropin of different purity on the weight and morphology of the human adrenal gland. *J Clin Endocrinol Metab* 23, 248–254.
2. Quinan, C. and Berger, A.A. (1933) Observations on human adrenals with especial reference to the relative weight of the normal medulla. *Ann Int Med* 6, 1180–1192.
3. Dobbie, J.W. and Symington, T. (1966) The human adrenal gland with special reference to the vasculature. *J Endocrinol* 34, 479–489.
4. Young, W.F. (2007) Primary aldosteronism: renaissance of a syndrome. *Clin Endocrinol (Oxf)* 66, 607–18.
5. Pivonello, R., De Martino, M.C., De Leo, M., Lombardi, G. and Colao, A. (2008) Cushing's Syndrome. *Endocrinol Metab Clin North Am* 37, 135–49, ix.
6. Grumbach, M.M., Biller, B.M., Braunstein, G.D., et al. (2003) Management of the clinically inapparent adrenal mass ("incidentaloma"). *Ann Intern Med* 138, 424–9.
7. Bovio, S., Cataldi, A., Reimondo, G., et al. (2006) Prevalence of adrenal incidentaloma in a contemporary computerized tomography series. *J Endocrinol Invest* 29, 298–302.
8. Kloos, R.T., Gross, M.D., Francis, I.R., Korobkin, M. and Shapiro, B. (1995) Incidentally discovered adrenal masses. *Endocr Rev* 16, 460–483.
9. Beuschlein, F. and Reincke, M. (2006) Adrenocortical tumorigenesis. *Ann N Y Acad Sci* 1088, 319–34.
10. Nawar, R. and Aron, D. (2005) Adrenal incidentalomas – a continuing management dilemma. *Endocr Relat Cancer* 12, 585–98.
11. Lack, E.E. (1997) Tumors of the adrenal gland and extra-adrenal paraganglia Atlas of Tumor Pathology. Armed Forces Institute of Pathology Washington DC
12. Dobbie, J.W. (1969) Adrenocortical nodular hyperplasia.The ageing adrenal. *J Pathol* 99, 1–18.
13. Hedeland, H., Östberg, G. and Hökfelt, B. (1968) On the prevalence of adrenocortical adenomas in autopsy material in relation to hypertension and diabetes. *Acta Med Scand* 184, 211–214.
14. Beuschlein, F., Reincke, M., Karl, M., et al. (1994) Clonal composition of human adrenocortical neoplasms. *Cancer Res* 54, 4927–32.

15. Gicquel, C., Leblond-Francillard, M., Bertagna, X., et al. (1994) Clonal analysis of human adrenocortical carcinomas and secreting adenomas. *Clin Endocrinol (Oxf)* 40, 465–77.
16. Reinhard, C., Saeger, W. and Schubert, B. (1996) Adrenocortical nodules in post-mortem series. Development, functional significance, and differentiation from adenomas. *Gen Diagn Pathol* 141, 203–8.
17. Favre, L., Jacot-des-Combes, E., Morel, P., et al. (1980) Primary aldosteronism with bilateral adrenal adenomas. *Virchows Arch A (Pathol Anat)* 388, 229–236.
18. Desai, N., Kapoor, A., Singh, B.K. and Liu, J. (2006) Bilateral adrenal adenomas and persistent leukocytosis: a unique case of Cushing's syndrome. *Am J Med* 119, e3–5.
19. Ueda, Y., Tanaka, H., Murakami, H., et al. (1997) A functioning black adenoma of the adrenal gland. *Intern Med* 36, 398–402.
20. Aiba, M., Suzuki, H., Kageyama, K., et al. (1981) Spironolactone bodies in aldosteronomas and in the attached adrenals. Enzyme histochemical study of 19 cases of primary aldosteronism and a case of aldosteronism due to bilateral diffuse hyperplasia of the zona glomerulosa. *Am J Pathol* 103, 404–10.
21. Brennan, M.F. (1987) Adrenocortical carcinoma. *CA-A Canc J Clin* 37, 348–353.
22. Correa, P. and Chen, V.W. (1995) Endocrine gland cancer. *Cancer* 75, 338–52.
23. Lubitz, J.A., Freeman, L. and Okun, R. (1973) Mitotane use in inoperable adrenal cortical carcinoma. *Jama* 223, 1109–1112.
24. Hutter, A.M.J. and Kayhoe, D.E. (1966) Adrenal cortical carcinoma. *Am J Med* 41, 572–580.
25. Ibanez ML. The Pathology of Adrenal Cortical Carcinomas. Study of 22 Cases. Endocrine and Nonendocrine Hormone-Producing Tumors. Chicago: Year Book Medical Publishers; 1971, p. 231–9.
26. MacFarlane, D.A. (1958) Cancer of the adrenal cortex. The natural history, prognosis and treatment in a study of fifty-five cases. *Ann Royal Coll Surg Engl* 23, 155–186.
27. Hough, A.J., Hollifield, J.W., Page, D.L. and Hartmann, W.H. (1979) Prognostic factors in adrenal cortical tumours. *Am J Clin Pathol* 72, 390–399.
28. Javadpour, N., Woltering, E.A. and Brennan, M.F. (1980) Adrenal neoplasms. *Cur Prob Surg* 17, 3–52.
29. Wooten, M.D. and King, D.K. (1993) Adrenal cortical carcinoma. Epidemiology and treatment with mitotane and a review of the literature. *Cancer* 72, 3145–55.
30. Crucitti, F., Bellantone, R., Ferrante, A., Boscherini, M. and Crucitti, P. (1996) The Italian Registry for Adrenal Cortical Carcinoma: analysis of a multiinstitutional series of 129 patients. The ACC Italian Registry Study Group. *Surgery* 119, 161–70.
31. Paton, B.L., Novitsky, Y.W., Zerey, M., et al. (2006) Outcomes of adrenal cortical carcinoma in the United States. *Surgery* 140, 914–20; discussion 919–20.
32. Huvos, A.G., Hajdu, S.I., Brasfield, R.D. and Foote, F. (1970) Adrenal cortical carcinoma. *Cancer* 25, 354–361.
33. Didolkar, M.S., Bescher, R.A., Elias, E.G. and Moore, R.H. (1981) Natural history of adrenal cortical carcinoma: A clinicopathologic study of 42 patients. *Cancer* 47, 2153–2161.
34. King, D.R. and Lack, E.E. (1979) Adrenal cortical carcinoma: a clinical and pathologic study of 49 cases. *Cancer* 44, 239–44.
35. Lee, J.E., Berger, D.H., el-Naggar, A.K., et al. (1995) Surgical management, DNA content, and patient survival in adrenal cortical carcinoma. *Surgery* 118, 1090–8.
36. Hogan, T.F., Gilchrist, K.W., Westring, D.W. and Citrin, D.L. (1980) A clinical and pathological study of adrenocortical carcinoma. *Therapeutic implications Cancer* 45, 2880–2883.
37. Lack EE, Travis WD, Oertel JE. Adrenal cortical neoplasms. In: Lack EE, ed. Pathology of the Adrenal Glands. New York: Churchlll Livingstone; 1990:115–171.
38. Zografos, G.C., Driscoll, D.L., Karakousis, C.P. and Huben, R.P. (1994) Adrenal adenocarcinoma: a review of 53 cases. *J Surg Oncol* 55, 160–4.
39. Ng, L. and Libertino, J.M. (2003) Adrenocortical carcinoma: diagnosis, evaluation and treatment. *J Urol* 169, 5–11.
40. Halmi, K.A. and Lascari, A.D. (1971) Conversion of virilization to feminization in a young girl with adrenal cortical carcinoma. *Cancer* 27, 931–935.
41. Barzon, L., Masi, G., Fincati, K., et al. (2005) Shift from Conn's syndrome to Cushing's syndrome in a recurrent adrenocortical carcinoma. *Eur J Endocrinol* 153, 629–36.
42. Flynn, S.D., Murren, J.R., Kirby, W.M., Honig, J., Kan, L. and Kinder, B.K. (1992) P-glycoprotein expression and multidrug resistance in adrenocortical carcinoma. *Surgery* 112, 981–6.
43. McNicol AM. The human adrenal gland: aspects of structure, function and pathology. In: James VHT, ed. The Adrenal Gland. Second ed. New York: Raven Prees Ltd; 1992:1–42.
44. Sundberg, A.G., Nilsson, R., Appelkvist, E.L. and Dallner, G. (1993) Immunohistochemical localization of alpha and pi class glutathione transferases in normal human tissues. *Pharmacol Toxicol* 72, 321–31.
45. Terzolo, M., Angeli, A., Fassnacht, M., et al. (2007) Adjuvant mitotane treatment for adrenocortical carcinoma. *N Engl J Med* 356, 2372–80.
46. Tang, C.K. and Gray, G.F. (1975) Adrenocortical neoplasms. Prognosis and morphology. *Urology* 5, 691–5.
47. Van Slooten, H., Schaberg, A., Smeenk, D. and Moolenaar, A. J. (1985) Morphologic characteristics of benign and malignant adrenocortical tumors. *Cancer* 55, 766–773.
48. Gandour, M.J. and Grizzle, W.E. (1986) A small adrenocortical carcinoma with aggressive behavior. An evaluation of criteria for malignancy. *Arch Pathol Lab Med* 110, 1076–9.
49. Sullivan, M., Boileau, M. and Hodges, C.V. (1978) Adrenal cortical carcinoma. *J Urol* 120, 660–5.
50. Sidhu, S., Gicquel, C., Bambach, C.P., et al. (2003) Clinical and molecular aspects of adrenocortical tumourigenesis. *ANZ J Surg* 73, 727–38.
51. Weiss, L.M. (1984) Comparable histologic study of 43 metastasizing and non metastasizing adrenocortical tumors. *Am J Surg Pathol* 8, 163–169.
52. Weiss, L.M., Medeiros, L.J. and Vickery, A.L., Jr. (1989) Pathologic features of prognostic significance in adrenocortical carcinoma. *Am J Surg Pathol* 13, 202–6.
53. Aubert, S., Wacrenier, A., Leroy, X., et al. (2002) Weiss system revisited: a clinicopathologic and immunohistochemical study of 49 adrenocortical tumors. *Am J Surg Pathol* 26, 1612–9.
54. van't Sant, H.P., Bouvy, N.D., Kazemier, G., et al. (2007) The prognostic value of two different histopathological scoring systems for adrenocortical carcinomas. *Histopathology* 51, 239–45.
55. Pohlink, C., Tannapfe, A., Eichfeld, U., et al. (2004) Does tumor heterogeneity limit the use of the Weiss criteria in the evaluation of adrenocortical tumors? *J Endocrinol Invest* 27, 565–9.
56. Arola, J., Salmenkivi, K., Liu, J., Kahri, A.I. and Heikkila, P. (2000) p53 and Ki67 in adrenocortical tumors. *Endocr Res* 26, 861–5.
57. McNicol, A.M., Struthers, A.J., Nolan, C.E., Hermans, J. and Haak, H.R. (1997) Proliferation in adrenocortical tumors: correlation with clinical outcome and p53 status. *Endocr Pathol* 8, 29–36.
58. Sasano, H., Suzuki, T. and Moriya, T. (2001) Discerning malignancy in resected adrenocortical neoplasms. *Endocr Pathol* 12, 397–406.

59. McNicol, A.M., Nolan, C.E., Struthers, A.J., Farquharson, M. A., Hermans, J. and Haak, H.R. (1997) Expression of p53 in adrenocortical tumours: clinicopathological correlations. *J Pathol* 181, 146–52.
60. Gicquel, C. and Le Bouc, Y. (1997) Molecular markers for malignancy in adrenocortical tumors. *Horm Res* 47, 269–72.
61. Ilvesmaki, V., Kahri, A.I., Miettinen, P.J. and Voutilainen, R. (1993) Insulin-like growth factors (IGFs) and their receptors in adrenal tumors: high IGF-II expression in functional adrenocortical carcinomas. *J Clin Endocrinol Metab* 77, 852–8.
62. Sasano, H., Suzuki, T., Sano, T., Kameya, T., Sasano, N. and Nagura, H. (1991) Adrenocortical oncocytoma. A true nonfunctioning adrenocortical tumor. *Am J Surg Pathol* 15, 949–56.
63. Lin, B.T., Bonsib, S.M., Mierau, G.W., Weiss, L.M. and Medeiros, L.J. (1998) Oncocytic adrenocortical neoplasms: a report of seven cases and review of the literature. *Am J Surg Pathol* 22, 603–14.
64. Xiao, G.Q., Pertsemlidis, D.S. and Unger, P.D. (2005) Functioning adrenocortical oncocytoma: a case report and review of the literature. *Ann Diagn Pathol* 9, 295–7.
65. Golkowski, F., Buziak-Bereza, M., Huszno, B., et al. (2007) The unique case of adrenocortical malignant and functioning oncocytic tumour. *Exp Clin Endocrinol Diabetes* 115, 401–4.
66. Bisceglia, M., Ludovico, O., Di Mattia, A., et al. (2004) Adrenocortical oncocytic tumors: report of 10 cases and review of the literature. *Int J Surg Pathol* 12, 231–43.
67. Hoang, M.P., Ayala, A.G. and Albores-Saavedra, J. (2002) Oncocytic adrenocortical carcinoma: a morphologic, immunohistochemical and ultrastructural study of four cases. *Mod Pathol* 15, 973–8.
68. Pan, C.C., Chen, P.C., Tsay, S.H. and Ho, D.M. (2005) Differential immunoprofiles of hepatocellular carcinoma, renal cell carcinoma, and adrenocortical carcinoma: a systemic immunohistochemical survey using tissue array technique. *Appl Immunohistochem Mol Morphol* 13, 347–52.
69. McCluggage, W.G., Burton, J., Maxwell, P. and Sloan, J.M. (1998) Immunohistochemical staining of normal, hyperplastic, and neoplastic adrenal cortex with a monoclonal antibody against alpha inhibin. *J Clin Pathol* 51, 114–6.
70. Munro, L.M., Kennedy, A. and McNicol, A.M. (1999) The expression of inhibin/activin subunits in the human adrenal cortex and its tumours. *J Endocrinol* 161, 341–347.
71. Ghorab, Z., Jorda, M., Ganjei, P. and Nadji, M. (2003) Melan A (A103) is expressed in adrenocortical neoplasms but not in renal cell and hepatocellular carcinomas. *Appl Immunohistochem Mol Morphol* 11, 330–3.
72. Zhang, H., Bu, H., Chen, H., et al. (2008) Comparison of immunohistochemical markers in the differential diagnosis of adrenocortical tumors: immunohistochemical analysis of adrenocortical tumors. *Appl Immunohistochem Mol Morphol* 16, 32–9.
73. Sasano, H., Sasano, N. and Okamoto, M. (1989) Immunohistochemical demonstration of cholesterol side-chain cleavage cytochrome P-450 in bovine and human adrenals. *Pathol Res Pract* 184, 337–42.
74. Sasano, H., White, P.C., New, M.I. and Sasano, N. (1988) Immunohistochemical localization of cytochrome P-450C21 in human adrenal cortex and its relation to endocrine function. *Hum Pathol* 19, 181–5.
75. Shibata, H., Ikeda, Y., Mukai, T., et al. (2001) Expression profiles of COUP-TF, DAX-1, and SF-1 in the human adrenal gland and adrenocortical tumors: possible implications in steroidogenesis. *Mol Genet Metab* 74, 206–16.
76. Sasano, H., Suzuki, T. and Moriya, T. (2006) Recent advances in histopathology and immunohistochemistry of adrenocortical carcinoma. *Endocr Pathol* 17, 345–54.
77. Schroder, S., Padberg, B.C., Achilles, E., Holl, K., Dralle, H. and Kloppel, G. (1992) Immunocytochemistry in adrenocortical tumours: a clinicomorphological study of 72 neoplasms. *Virchows Arch A Pathol Anat Histopathol* 420, 65–70.
78. Gaffey, M.J., Traweek, S.T., Mills, S.E., et al. (1992) Cytokeratin expression in adrenocortical neoplasia: an immunohistochemical and biochemical study with implications for the differential diagnosis of adrenocortical, hepatocellular, and renal cell carcinoma. *Hum Pathol* 23, 144–53.
79. Chu, P. and Arber, D.A. (2000) Paraffin-section detection of CD10 in 505 nonhematopoietic neoplasms. Frequent expression in renal cell carcinoma and endometrial stromal sarcoma. *Am J Clin Pathol* 113, 374–82.
80. Komminoth, P., Roth, J., Schroder, S., Saremaslani, P. and Heitz, P.U. (1995) Overlapping expression of immunohistochemical markers and synaptophysin mRNA in pheochromocytomas and adrenocortical carcinomas. Implications for the differential diagnosis of adrenal gland tumors. *Lab Invest* 72, 424–31.
81. Haak, H.R. and Fleuren, G.J. (1995) Neuroendocrine differentiation of adrenocortical tumors. *Cancer* 75, 860–4.
82. Morimoto, R., Satoh, F., Murakami, O., et al. (2008) Immunohistochemistry of a proliferation marker Ki67/MIB1 in adrenocortical carcinomas: Ki67/MIB1 labeling index is a predictor for recurrence of adrenocortical carcinomas. *Endocr J* 55, 49–55.
83. Terzolo, M., Boccuzzi, A., Bovio, S., et al. (2001) Immunohistochemical assessment of Ki-67 in the differential diagnosis of adrenocortical tumors. *Urology* 57, 176–82.
84. de Fraipont, F., El Atifi, M., Cherradi, N., et al. (2005) Gene expression profiling of human adrenocortical tumors using complementary deoxyribonucleic acid microarrays identifies several candidate genes as markers of malignancy. *J Clin Endocrinol Metab* 90, 1819–29.
85. Gicquel, C., Bertagna, X., Gaston, V., et al. (2001) Molecular markers and long-term recurrences in a large cohort of patients with sporadic adrenocortical tumors. *Cancer Res* 61, 6762–7.
86. Stephan, E.A., Chung, T.H., Grant, C.S., et al. (2008) Adrenocortical carcinoma survival rates correlated to genomic copy number variants. *Mol Cancer Ther* 7, 425–31.
87. Srivastava, S., Zou, Z., Pirollo, K., Blattner, W. and Chang, E. H. (1990) Germline transmission of a mutated p53 gene in a cancer-prone family with Li-Fraumeni syndrome. *Nature* 348, 747–749.
88. Cohen, M.M., Jr. (2005) Beckwith-Wiedemann Syndrome: Historical, Clinicopathological, and Etiopathogenetic Perspectives. *Pediatr Dev Pathol* 8, 287–304.
89. Bertherat, J. (2006) Carney complex (CNC). *Orphanet J Rare Dis* 1, 21.
90. Agarwal, S.K., Kester, M.B., Debelenko, L.V., et al. (1997) Germline mutations of the MEN1 gene in familial multiple endocrine neoplasia type 1 and related states. *Hum Mol Genet* 6, 1169–75.
91. Courseaux, A., Grosgeorge, J., Gaudray, P., et al. (1996) Definition of the minimal MEN1 candidate area based on a 5-Mb integrated map of proximal 11q13. The European Consortium on Men1, (GENEM 1; Groupe d'Etude des Neoplasies Endocriniennes Multiples de type 1). *Genomics* 37, 354–65.
92. Sidhu, S., Marsh, D.J., Theodosopoulos, G., et al. (2002) Comparative genomic hybridization analysis of adrenocortical tumors. *J Clin Endocrinol Metab* 87, 3467–74.
93. Shono, T., Sakai, H., Takehara, K., Honda, S. and Kanetake, H. (2002) Analysis of numerical chromosomal aberrations in adrenal cortical neoplasms by fluorescence in situ hybridization. *J Urol* 168, 1370–3.

94. Takehara, K., Sakai, H., Shono, T., Irie, J. and Kanetake, H. (2005) Proliferative activity and genetic changes in adrenal cortical tumors examined by flow cytometry, fluorescence in situ hybridization and immunohistochemistry. *Int J Urol* 12, 121–7.
95. Russell, A.J., Sibbald, J., Haak, H., Keith, W.N. and McNicol, A.M. (1999) Increasing genome instability in adrenocortical carcinoma progression with involvement of chromosomes 3, 9 and X at the adenoma stage. *Br J Cancer* 81, 684–9.
96. Kjellman, M., Kallioniemi, O.P., Karhu, R., et al. (1996) Genetic aberrations in adrenocortical tumors detected using comparative genomic hybridization correlate with tumor size and malignancy. *Cancer Res* 56, 4219–23.
97. Dohna, M., Reincke, M., Mincheva, A., Allolio, B., Solinas-Toldo, S. and Lichter, P. (2000) Adrenocortical carcinoma is characterized by a high frequency of chromosomal gains and high-level amplifications. *Genes Chromosomes Cancer* 28, 145–52.
98. Soon, P.S., McDonald, K.L., Robinson, B.G. and Sidhu, S.B. (2008) Molecular markers and the pathogenesis of adrenocortical cancer. *Oncologist* 13, 548–61.
99. Yano, T., Linehan, M., Anglard, P., et al. (1989) Genetic changes in human adrenocortical carcinomas. *J Natl Cancer Inst* 81, 518–23.
100. Heppner, C., Reincke, M., Agarwal, S.K., et al. (1999) MEN1 gene analysis in sporadic adrenocortical neoplasms. *J Clin Endocrinol Metab* 84, 216–9.
101. Kjellman, M., Roshani, L., Teh, B.T., et al. (1999) Genotyping of adrenocortical tumors: very frequent deletions of the MEN1 locus in 11q13 and of a 1-centimorgan region in 2p16. *J Clin Endocrinol Metab* 84, 730–5.
102. Gicquel, C., Raffin-Sanson, M.L., Gaston, V., et al. (1997) Structural and functional abnormalities at 11p15 are associated with the malignant phenotype in sporadic adrenocortical tumors: study on a series of 82 tumors. *J Clin Endocrinol Metab* 82, 2559–65.
103. Bertherat, J., Groussin, L., Sandrini, F., et al. (2003) Molecular and functional analysis of PRKAR1A and its locus (17q22-24) in sporadic adrenocortical tumors: 17q losses, somatic mutations, and protein kinase a expression and activity. *Cancer Res* 63, 5308–19.
104. Reincke, M., Mora, P., Beuschlein, F., Arlt, W., Chrousos, G. P. and Allolio, B. (1997) Deletion of the adrenocorticotropin receptor gene in human adrenocortical tumors: implications for tumorigenesis. *J Clin Endocrinol Metab* 82, 3054–8.
105. Ohgaki, H., Kleihues, P. and Heitz, P.U. (1993) p53 mutations in sporadic adrenocortical tumors. *Int J Cancer* 54, 408–10.
106. Reincke, M., Karl, M., Travis, W.H., et al. (1994) p53 mutations in human adrenocortical neoplasms: immunohistochemical and molecular studies. *J Clin Endocrinol Metab* 78, 790–4.
107. Ribeiro, R.C., Sandrini, F., Figueiredo, B., et al. (2001) An inherited p53 mutation that contributes in a tissue-specific manner to pediatric adrenal cortical carcinoma. *Proc Natl Acad Sci U S A* 98, 9330–5.
108. Schulte, K.M., Mengel, M., Heinze, M., et al. (2000) Complete sequencing and messenger ribonucleic acid expression analysis of the MEN I gene in adrenal cancer. *J Clin Endocrinol Metab* 85, 441–8.
109. Boulle, N., Logie, A., Gicquel, C., Perin, L. and Le Bouc, Y. (1998) Increased levels of insulin-like growth factor II (IGF-II) and IGF- binding protein-2 are associated with malignancy in sporadic adrenocortical tumors. *J Clin Endocrinol Metab* 83, 1713–20.
110. Gicquel, C., Bertagna, X., Schneid, H., et al. (1994) Rearrangements at the 11p15 locus and overexpression of insulin-like growth factor-II gene in sporadic adrenocortical tumors. *J Clin Endocrinol Metab* 78, 1444–53.
111. Ilvesmaki, V., Liu, J., Heikkila, P., Kahri, A.I. and Voutilainen, R. (1998) Expression of insulin-like growth factor binding protein 1–6 genes in adrenocortical tumors and pheochromocytomas. *Horm Metab Res* 30, 619–23.
112. Weber, M.M., Auernhammer, C.J., Kiess, W. and Engelhardt, D. (1997) Insulin-like growth factor receptors in normal and tumorous adult human adrenocortical glands. *Eur J Endocrinol* 136, 296–303.
113. Hofland, J., Timmerman, M.A., de Herder, W.W., van Schaik, R.H., de Krijger, R.R. and de Jong, F.H. (2006) Expression of activin and inhibin subunits, receptors and binding proteins in human adrenocortical neoplasms. *Clin Endocrinol (Oxf)* 65, 792–9.
114. Beuschlein, F., Looyenga, B.D., Reincke, M. and Hammer, G. D. (2004) Role of the inhibin/activin system and luteinizing hormone in adrenocortical tumorigenesis. *Horm Metab Res* 36, 392–6.
115. Tissier, F., Cavard, C., Groussin, L., et al. (2005) Mutations of beta-catenin in adrenocortical tumors: activation of the Wnt signaling pathway is a frequent event in both benign and malignant adrenocortical tumors. *Cancer Res* 65, 7622–7.
116. Latronico, A.C. (2000) Role of ACTH receptor in adrenocortical tumor formation. *Braz J Med Biol Res* 33, 1249–52.
117. Light, K., Jenkins, P.J., Weber, A., et al. (1995) Are activating mutations of the adrenocorticotropin receptor involved in adrenal cortical neoplasia? *Life Sci* 56, 1523–7.
118. Demeure, M.J., Doffek, K.M., Komorowski, R.A. and Gorski, J. (1996) Gip-2 codon 179 oncogene mutations: absent in adrenal cortical tumors. *World J Surg* 20, 928–31; discussion 931–2.
119. Gicquel, C., Dib, A., Bertagna, X., Amselem, S. and Le Bouc, Y. (1995) Oncogenic mutations of alpha-Gi2 protein are not determinant for human adrenocortical tumourigenesis. *Eur J Endocrinol* 133, 166–72.
120. Vincent-Dejean, C., Cazabat, L., Groussin, L., et al. (2008) Identification of a clinically homogenous subgroup of benign cortisol-secreting adrenocortical tumors characterized by alterations of the protein kinase A (PKA) subunits and high PKA activity. *Eur J Endocrinol* 158, 829–39.
121. Stratakis, C.A. (2008) Cushing syndrome caused by adrenocortical tumors and hyperplasias (corticotropin- independent cushing syndrome). *Endocr Dev* 13, 117–32.
122. Giordano, T.J., Thomas, D.G., Kuick, R., et al. (2003) Distinct transcriptional profiles of adrenocortical tumors uncovered by DNA microarray analysis. *Am J Pathol* 162, 521–31.

Tumors of the Adrenal Medulla and Extra-adrenal Paraganglia

Arthur S. Tischler and Ronald R. de Krijger

Abstract According to World Health Organization definitions updated in 2004, pheochromocytomas (PCC) are tumors derived from chromaffin cells in the adrenal medulla. Closely related tumors arising outside the adrenal medulla are called extra-adrenal sympathetic paragangliomas (PGL). The latter can occur anywhere in the vicinity of sympathetic ganglia or visceral branches of sympathetic nerves and, like PCC, are often associated with signs and symptoms of catecholamine overproduction. A pheochromocytoma is an intra-adrenal sympathetic PGL. The arbitrary separation between PCC and other sympathetic PGL emphasizes distinctive properties of adrenal tumors, including frequent production of epinephrine rather than norepinephrine, relatively low rate of malignancy, and tendency to occur in particular hereditary syndromes. A third group of related tumors consists of parasympathetic PGL in the head and neck. Those tumors are usually not clinically functional.

In recent studies the number of genes involved in the pathogenesis of hereditary PCC and PGL has expanded to six including *RET*, *VHL*, *SDHB*, *SDHC*, *SDHD*, and *NF1*. Together they account for almost 30% of PCC and PGL, with several geographic areas reaching even higher figures due to founder effects. This means that the familiar "10% rule" for PCC has to be abandoned. It has also become clear that location and genetic background have a profound effect on the frequency of malignancy, which, according to the WHO, is defined by presence of metastases, not local invasion, and ranges from less than 5% for VHL-related PCC to approximately 50% for SDHB-related sympathetic PGL.

The role for the pathologist has expanded from histopathological diagnosis, including the identification of malignancy, to guidance of clinicians in detection of hereditary disease. PCC and PGL show many morphological variations in addition to the classic "Zellballen" pattern and must be distinguished from various other neoplasms, both endocrine and non-endocrine. The tumor cells typically stain intensely for chromogranin A and synaptophysin, while associated sustentacular cells are positive for S100. Clues pointing to hereditary tumor syndromes include multiple tumors or a combination of neoplasia and hyperplasia. However, they can be subtle, often do not occur synchronously, and may not be present at all in some patients. There are currently no validated means to diagnose malignancy before metastases occur. Although histopathological scoring systems have been proposed, their use is optional and a high score should not be considered equivalent to a diagnosis of malignancy.

Keywords Chromaffin cell • Paraganglia • Paraganglioma • Pheochromocytoma

Nomenclature

Paraganglia are neural crest derived neuroendocrine organs that form part of the sympathetic and parasympathetic autonomic nervous system. Sympathetic paraganglia are located throughout the distribution of sympathetic ganglia and visceral branches of sympathetic nerves. Parasympathetic paraganglia are located along branches of the vagus and glossopharyngeal nerves above the diaphragm. Most paraganglia are microscopic and their distribution is variable. Exceptions are the adrenal medulla and organ of Zuckerkandl, which are the prototypical sympathetic paraganglia, and the carotid body, which is the prototypical parasympathetic paraganglion [1].

The nomenclature of paraganglia and their corresponding tumors has been a source of controversy and confusion for more than a century. Normal paraganglia

A.S. Tischler (✉)
Professor of Pathology, Department of Pathology, Tufts University Tufts Medical Center, Boston, MA, USA
e-mail: atishler@tuftsmedicalcenter.org

A. Khan (ed.), *Surgical Pathology of Endocrine and Neuroendocrine Tumors*, Current Clinical Pathology,
DOI 10.1007/978-1-60327-396-1_9,

were originally identified on the basis of brown coloration that they exhibited after immersion in chromate salts. Believing that the color change was due to affinity for chromium, Alfred Kohn, the first proponent of a unitary paraganglionic system, coined the term "chromaffin reaction" for the color change and "chromaffin cell" for the cells in which it was elicited ("Chromaffin" won out over "chromophile" in one of the first nomenclature controversies!) [2]. Kohn also coined the term "paraganglia" in order to denote embryological and functional analogies of these cells, which were not quite neuronal, to true neurons [3], thus perhaps becoming the first person to conceptualize a neuroendocrine phenotype.

Ultimately, it was recognized that the chromaffin reaction is caused mostly by oxidation of stored catecholamines, rather than affinity for chromium. The term "pheochromocyte" (from Greek *phaeos*, dusky) was therefore proposed as an alternative to chromaffin cell, in order to describe the color change without implying a mechanism. Although that term was never widely accepted for normal chromaffin cells, it did take hold for catecholamine-producing tumors, mostly associated with sympathetic paraganglia, which may have been described clinically as early as 1800 [4] but were not named until they were termed pheochromocytomas by Pick in 1912 [5]. Because parasympathetic paraganglia produce smaller quantities of catecholamines than their sympathetic counterparts, their tumors usually did not show a chromaffin reaction and therefore went by various names including "non-chromaffin paraganglioma," "glomus tumor" (a major source of confusion with myoarterial glomus tumor of soft tissue, which is a completely different entity), and "chemodectoma." All of those terms are now obsolete, as is the chromaffin reaction itself.

The current World Health Organization (WHO) classification, updated in 2004 [6], reserves the term pheochromocytoma for tumors that arise in the adrenal medulla, i.e., "A pheochromocytoma is an intra-adrenal sympathetic paraganglioma." Tumors associated with the sympathetic nervous system but outside the adrenal gland are called extra-adrenal sympathetic paragangliomas (often abbreviated in practice to "extra-adrenal paraganglioma," "sympathetic paraganglioma," or just "paraganglioma"). Parasympathetic paragangliomas are similarly classified, with optional incorporation of the specific anatomic site (e.g., "carotid body paraganglioma"). Restricting the term pheochromocytoma to the adrenal while excluding closely related tumors elsewhere in the sympathetic nervous system is an arbitrary convention that originated in the first series of the Armed Forces Institute of Pathology Atlas of Tumor Pathology fascicle, *Tumors of the Adrenal*, published in 1950. The intention at the time was to reduce confusion caused by inconsistent diagnosis of various tumors in extra-adrenal locations [7]. While its ultimate wisdom may in some respects be debated, the convention does serve to emphasize that intra- and extra-adrenal sympathetic paragangliomas do behave differently. The differences include a predominantly noradrenergic phenotype for extra-adrenal PGL, a lower rate of malignancy for PCC [8], and different genetic associations [9, 10]. It is, therefore, important for clinical practice and imperative for research purposes to adhere to the proposed nomenclature in order to avoid obscuring these differences and to be able to compare various studies. Similarly, although many clinicians still refer to head and neck PGL as "glomus tumors" or chemodectomas, that usage should be discouraged.

Epidemiology

The overall annual incidence of PCC has been reported to be 2–8 per million, with a wide range due to geographic variation and differences in diagnostic practice. Indeed, it has been shown in autopsy studies that a significant proportion of PCC go unnoticed during life [5]. The frequency of head and neck PGL, which are parasympathetic and are associated with catecholamine overproduction in less than 1% of cases, is about one third that of PCC.

Genetics and Heredity

In the last 5 years it has become clear that many patients with apparently sporadic PCC or PGL harbor occult germline mutations of genes associated with hereditary endocrine tumor syndromes. Almost one third of PCC and PGL are caused by germline mutations in one of six candidate genes: *RET*, *VHL*, *SDHB*, *SDHC*, *SDHD*, and *NF1* [9, 11, 12]. Hereditary disorders known for many years to be associated with development of PCC and PGL are multiple endocrine neoplasia (MEN) types 2A and 2B, von Hippel-Lindau disease (VHL), and neurofibromatosis type 1 (NF1), due respectively to mutations of the *RET* protooncogene and the *VHL* and *NF1* tumor-suppressor genes. VHL is now divided into types 1 and 2, defined by the absence or presence of susceptibility to PCC and PGL, and those tumors can occur in the absence of other VHL stigmata [6]. In addition, the list of hereditary susceptibility disorders is now expanded to include familial PGL syndromes caused by mutations of succinate dehydrogenase genes *SDHD*(PGL1), *SDHC*

(PGL3), and *SDHB*(PGL4), which also appear to function as tumor-suppressor genes [13, 14, 6]. In large series of apparently sporadic PCC, the germline mutation frequency of *SDHB* and *SDHD* varies from 2% to 11%, while it is between 5% and 10% in similar series of head and neck PGL. Differences in reported prevalence of hereditary PCC and PGL are due in part to certain geographical areas displaying a founder effect, as for germline mutations of *SDHD* in The Netherlands and *VHL* in Germany.Epidemiological data are further complicated by a novel mode of transmission of tumor susceptibility in patients with *SDHD* mutations that involves genomic imprinting, i.e., tumors occur only after paternal transmission of the mutated gene [13, 14]. As a consequence, the family history of patients often appears to be negative as a result of generation skipping. Finally, several kindreds susceptible to tumors harbor mutations that have still not been identified [15]. Somatic mutations of the genes responsible for hereditary PCC and PGL are uncommon but have been reported by some groups at low frequency or as individual cases [16–19].

Striking genotype–phenotype correlations exist for tumors in each of the familial syndromes with respect to malignancy, distribution, and function. Estimated rates of malignancy are quite low for most of the known mutations, ranging from 1% to 10%. However, at least 50% of tumors with *SDHB* mutations are malignant [20]. In addition, tumors with any of the *SDH* mutations are often extra-adrenal, while those with mutated *RET* are confined to the adrenal medulla or immediate vicinity. SDH mutations are also suggested by the combined occurrence of sympathetic and parasympathetic PGL. *VHL* mutations are associated with PCC that produce norepinephrine and little or no epinephrine [20].

Pathology

General Considerations

Pathology of the paraganglia should be approached with three objectives in mind. The first, which is the same as for any other organ, is diagnosis. For practical purposes, the only significant pathological changes encountered are neoplasia and hyperplasia. PCC and PGL show great morphological variation and must be distinguished from a variety of other tumors, both endocrine and non-endocrine. The second is identification of clues pointing to hereditary tumor syndromes. Those clues take the form of multiple tumors or a combination of neoplasia and hyperplasia. However, they can be subtle, often do not occur synchronously, and may not be present at all in some patients with hereditary disease.The third and most problematic function is assessment of malignancy. According to the current WHO classification, malignancy of PCC and PGL is defined by the presence of metastases [6], not local invasion which, though potentially lethal, is a poor predictor of metastases. Despite the WHO criteria, the literature shows tremendous inconsistency and controversy surrounding this point, suggesting a need for a new approach to classification that precisely specifies the type of aggressive behavior.

Macroscopic and Microscopic Pathology

Gross examination of PCC and PGL shows fleshy pink-gray-to-dark-brown tumors that range to more than 10 cm in diameter. In the adrenal, color can be particularly important in grossly distinguishing PCC from typically golden yellow cortical lesions (Fig. 1). PCC may be very hemorrhagic, but in PGL this is less apparent. Focal or extensive local invasion may be present. Presently, a size threshold of 1 cm for PCC is mentioned in many textbooks, below which lesions of the adrenal medulla are designated as hyperplastic. However, there is no scientific justification for classification of a lesion as a hyperplastic nodule purely on the basis of size, particularly if the lesion is solitary. Recently, identical genetic abnormalities were found in adrenal medullary hyperplasia and PCC from multiple endocrine neoplasia type 2 patients, supporting the above view. Diffuse hyperplasia is more clearcut conceptually but sometimes difficult to identify because of normal anatomic variation. It is most readily recognized when gray medullary tissue expands into the tail and alae of the gland.

PCC and PGL show enormous variability in cytology and histological patterns, often within the same tumor, and must be distinguished from a variety of endocrine and non-endocrine neoplasms. The classic pattern is that of so-called "Zellballen," formed by nests of large uniform polygonal cells with granular amphophilic or basophilic cytoplasm surrounded by S100-positive sustentacular cells that usually become evident only after immunohistochemical staining. However, the Zellballen pattern may not be evident and one may instead observe diffuse architecture, spindle cells, admixtures of large and small cells, and extreme cytological atypia (Fig. 2). Areas of ganglioneuroma or ganglioneuroblastoma are occasionally admixed with PCC or PGL in sympathoadrenal tumors (composite PCC or PGL) (Fig. 3). "Hyaline globules" (Fig. 2A) and intranuclear pseudoinclusions (actually invaginations of cytoplasm) are prominent in some PCC/PGL [21] but can also be seen in some adrenal

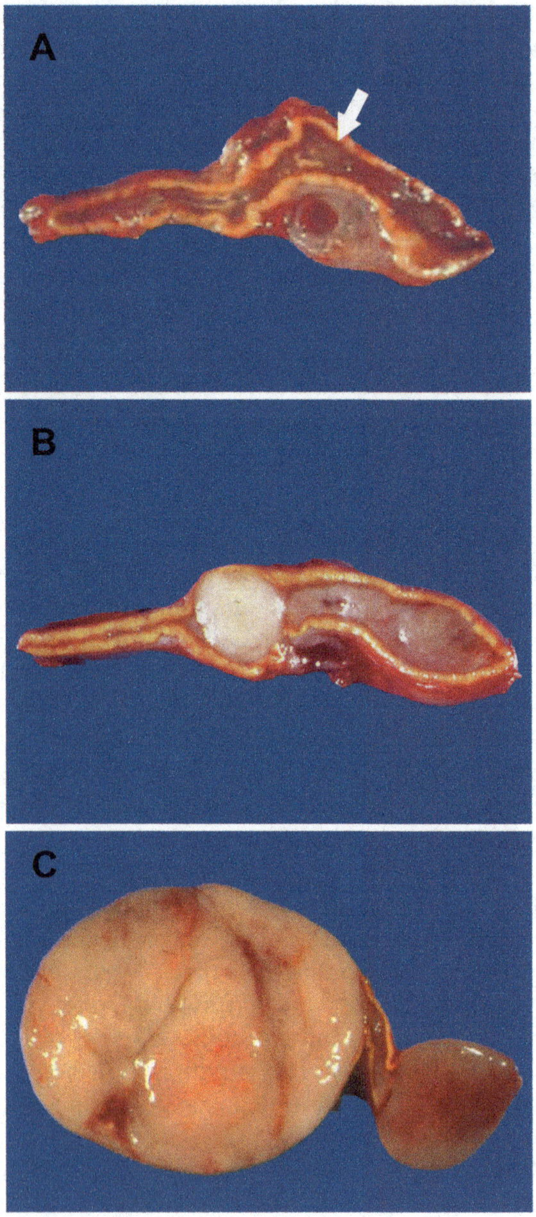

Fig. 1 (**A**) Transverse section of a normal adrenal gland. Medullary tissue (*arrow*) is *gray* and is normally localized to the head and body of the gland. It averages approximately 10% of the total adrenal volume but can account for slightly more or slightly less, as in this specimen. The more abundant brown tissue found throughout the gland is cortical zona reticularis. (**B**) Transverse section of an adrenal gland from a patient with MEN2A, showing diffusely expanded gray medullary tissue with ill-defined nodularity at right and a small pheochromocytoma at left. (**C**) Transverse section of an adrenal gland from a patient with MEN2A, showing two pheochromocytomas and a diffusely expanded medulla. Note that the color of pheochromocytomas can appear identical to medulla or somewhat different, but is distinct from yellow and brown cortex

cortical tumors [22]. Pigment (Fig. 2B,C)) can be present in sympathetic or parasympathetic PGL and is sometimes abundant [23–25]. Usually the pigment consists of neuromelanin or lipofuscin-like material, but true melanosomes are sometimes seen. Parasympathetic PGL often have more pronounced Zellballen (Fig. 4) and somewhat clearer cytoplasm than their sympathetic counterparts, but overlap exists between the two types of tumors.

Both PCC and PGL are highly vascular neoplasms. In addition to the small capillary vessels characteristic of tumor angiogenesis in most tissues, we have noticed that the tumors sometimes contain vessels suggestive of "arteriogenesis," a term applied to tumor-induced growth of large feeder vessels that are more typically upstream of the tumors themselves [26] (Fig. 2D). Large, malformed vascular channels reminiscent of arteriovenous malformations can also be present, most often in parasympathetic PGL (Fig. 4). Perivascular edema and/or hyalinization around large or small vessels can create striking histological patterns (Fig. 5). In some cases immunohistochemical staining for the proliferation marker Ki67 shows more labeling of the endothelial cells in large or small tumor blood vessels than of the tumor cells themselves.

Specific considerations in differential diagnosis and corresponding diagnostic strategies vary according to anatomic site. In the adrenal gland, the principal differential diagnosis is adrenal cortical adenoma or carcinoma. Elsewhere, possibilities include hepatic and hepatoid tumors, alveolar soft part sarcoma, melanoma, glomus tumors and other vascular neoplasms, and primary or metastatic carcinomas with endocrine or non-endocrine phenotype. Immunohistochemical staining can be used to distinguish between these various entities.

The single most specific and reliable generic neuroendocrine marker currently utilized in pathology practice is chromogranin A (CgA), a major constituent of the matrix of catecholamine-containing secretory granules [27]. Immunoreactivity for CgA will readily distinguish PCC and PGL from adrenal cortical tumors and non-endocrine tumors. Staining of PCC for CgA is usually extensive and the diagnosis should be made with caution for tumors that show little or no staining. Vice versa, the vast majority of adrenal cortical tumors will show reactivity for inhibin and/or Melan A, which are rare to absent in PCC and PGL. It must be noted that some adrenal cortical tumors contain cells with large numbers of mitochondria and/or large amounts of lipofuscin, which may lead to nonspecific interactions with antibodies. Consequently, oncocytic tumors of the adrenal cortex can show very convincing but nonspecific staining for a variety of antigens, or normal cortical cells can show spurious staining for neuroendocrine markers.

Distinction of PCC and PGL from other neuroendocrine tumors that also express CgA is a process of deduction that often requires panels of antibodies, for example, demonstration of immunoreactivity for the catecholamine

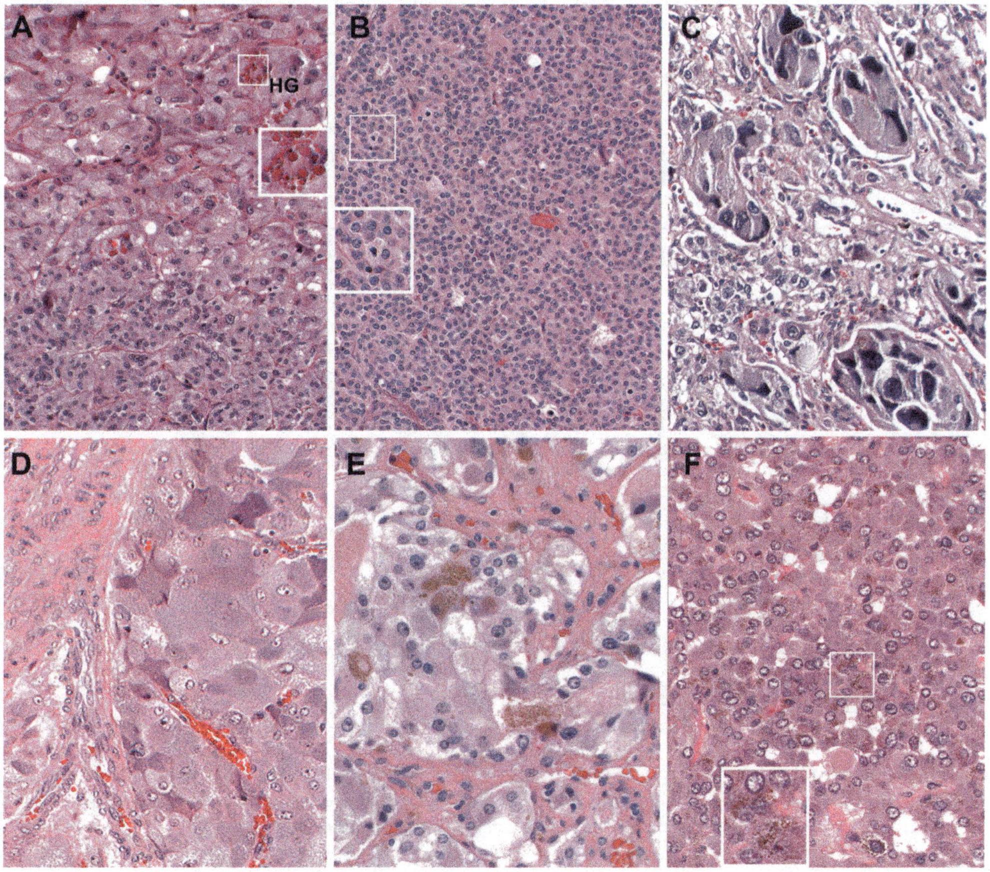

Fig. 2 Cytological and architectural pattern variations in pheochromocytomas. (**A**) (from a patient with MEN2A). Adjacent areas of large (*top*) and small (*bottom*) tumor cells, both growing in typical rounded packets (Zellballen). Large pheochromocytoma cells such as those shown are larger than normal chromaffin cells and often have vesicular nuclei with prominent nucleoli, resembling the nuclei of neurons. However, they contain numerous secretory granules, therefore stain intensely for CgA and usually lack other neuronal characteristics such as neurofilament protein expression or high level expression of RET. "HG" indicates a cluster of hyaline globules, which are frequently seen in PCC but also occasionally occur in cortical neoplasms. (**B**) (from a patient with neurofibromatosis).A monomorphous population of cells identical to those at bottom of panel A, growing in a diffuse pattern. Several mitotic figures are present. (**C**) Extreme cytological atypia and pleomorphism. (**D**) A mosaic pattern of basophilic and amphophilic cells most likely to be observed in well-fixed PCC. Tumor cell "embracing," in which cytoplasm of one tumor cell appears to envelop that of another, is often conspicuous in tumors with this pattern, as shown. The tumor cells are similar in size and nuclear morphology to those at the top of panel A. An artery-like blood vessel within the tumor (*top left*) gives rise to several small vessels. (**E**) and (**F**) Pigmented cells in PCCs. Cellular "monotony," a diffuse growth pattern, prominent mitoses, pleomorphism, and hyperchromasia are among the putative adverse parameters scored in the PASS system [38] but are often not as clear-cut as in panels (**B**) and (**C**). Original magnifications (**A–C**) 200x; (**D–F**) approximately 400×. Insets show the *small boxed areas* at higher magnification

biosynthetic enzyme tyrosine hydroxylase (TH) and exclusion of staining for keratins expressed in pulmonary and gastrointestinal neuroendocrine tumors. The distinction is particularly challenging if individual patients have both PGL and carcinoid tumors [10], as can occur in NF1 or VHL [28–30]. Although normal parasympathetic paraganglia express both TH and CgA, staining for either or both of those markers tends to be weaker and more variable in parasympathetic than in sympathoadrenal PGL, and may actually be absent in some parasympathetic tumors [31, 10, 32]. Some parasympathetic PGL preferentially express chromogranin B (CgB) instead of CgA [32] (Fig. 4).

Correlations of Pathology and Genotype

Small or large nodules often coexist with varying degrees of diffuse hyperplasia in the adrenals of patients with MEN2 (Fig. 1). Identification of these clues pointing to occult hereditary disease is an important service that a pathologist can provide to patients and their families, and they should be searched for carefully. They are usually not present in other hereditary PCC/PGL syndromes. Other correlations between genetics and morphology are at present mostly of academic interest. A distinctive histological pattern of small vessels interspersed between small tumor cells has been reported in PCC of patients

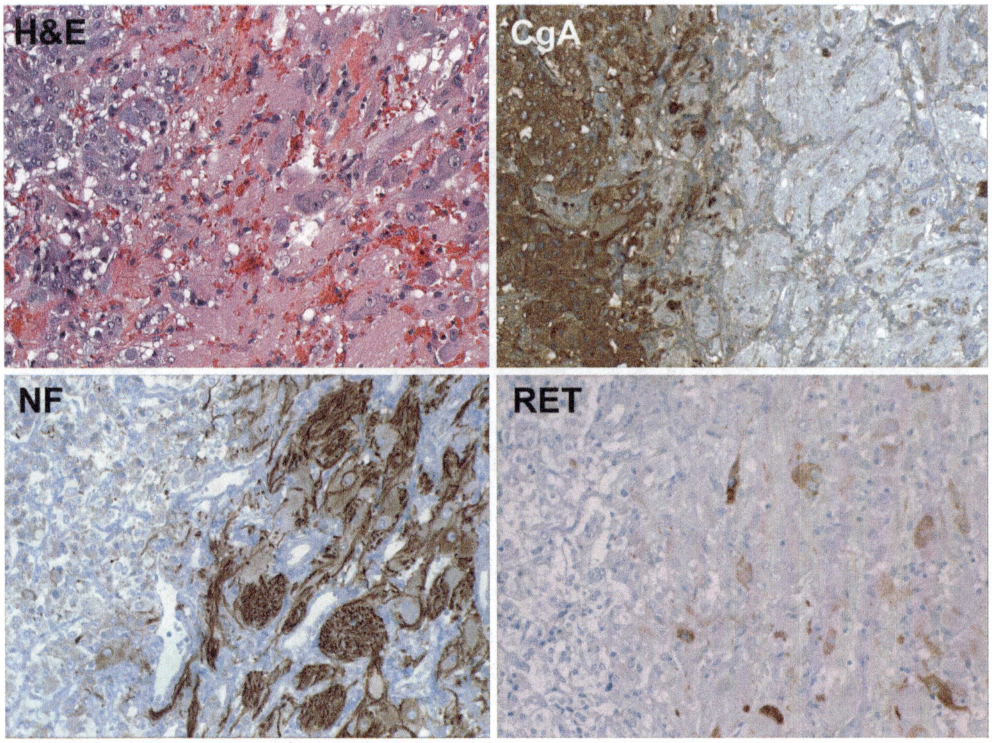

Fig. 3 Composite pheochromocytoma (*left*) with ganglioneuroma (*right*). These tumors recapitulate the functional cytology of normal chromaffin cells and sympathetic neurons. Chromaffin cells contain numerous cytoplasmic secretory granules and therefore stain strongly and diffusely for CgA. In contrast, the granules in neurons are relatively sparse and tend to migrate away from cell bodies into processes. In neuronal areas of the tumors immunoreactive CgA is therefore weak or absent in most of the neuronal cell bodies and is often seen as linear or punctuate staining in processes. This finding can help to identify areas of neuronal differentiation. The reverse pattern is seen with staining for neurofilament protein, which demonstrates axon-like processes. In addition, areas of neuronal differentiation sometimes stain strongly for receptor tyrosine kinase RET, which normally is expressed at high levels in sympathetic neurons but only weakly, if at all, in chromaffin cells

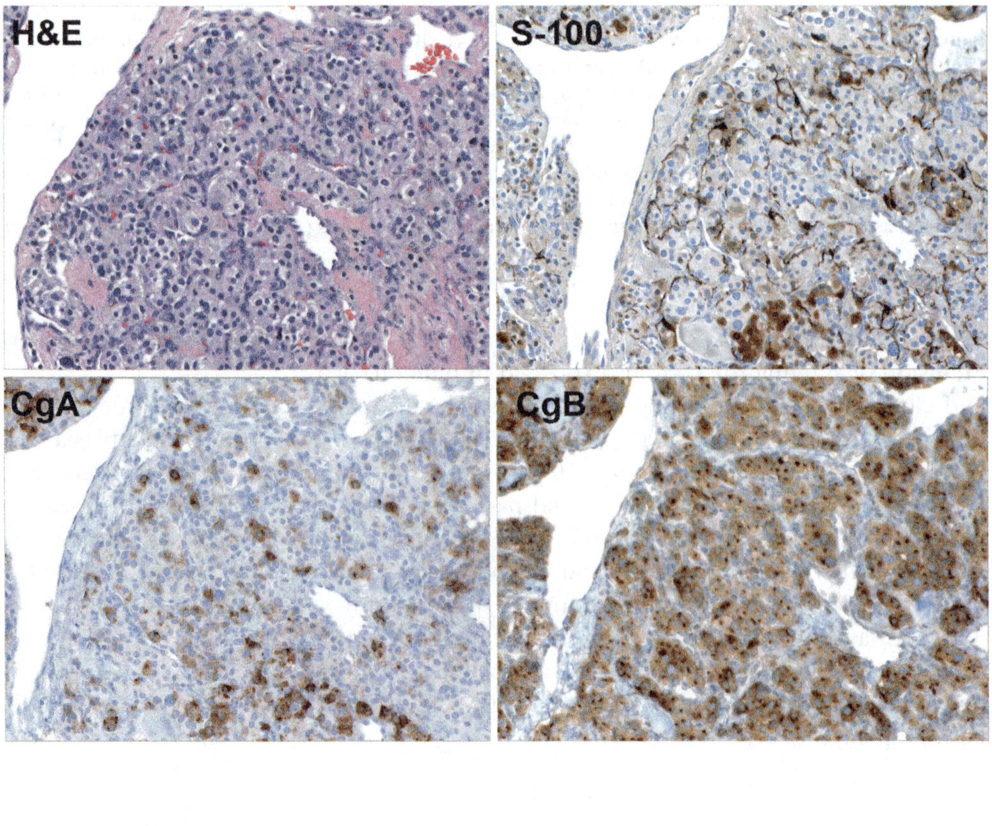

Fig. 4 Carotid PGL showing prominent Zellballen and large vascular channels. Immunohistochemical stain for S100 shows sustentacular cells at the periphery of Zellballen and a few positive chief cells. S100 staining should be nuclear in order to be interpreted as positive, but nuclear and cytoplasmic staining often occur together. In contrast to sympathetic PGL, carotid and other parasympathetic PGL sometimes show relatively little immunoreactivity for chromogranin A (CgA) while staining extensively for chromogranin B (CgB) as shown. In this tumor, CgB staining has a prominent dot-like Golgi distribution and weaker diffuse localization in the rest of the cytoplasm

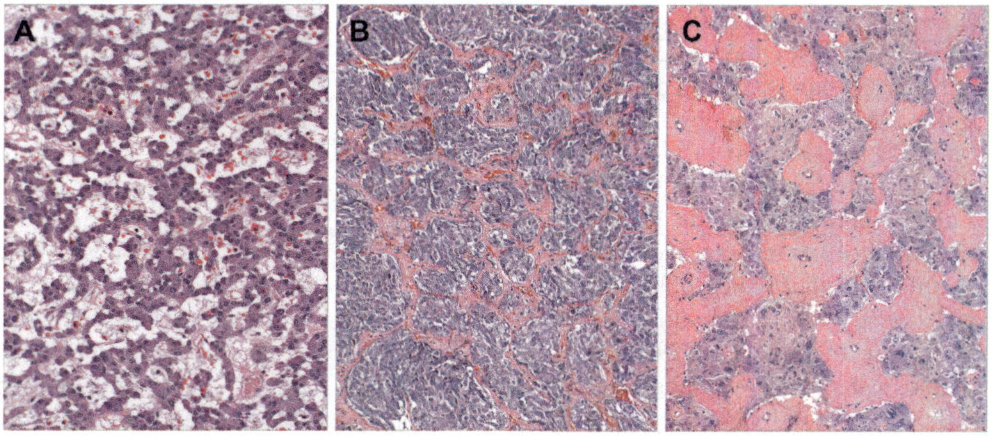

Fig. 5 Histological pattern changes caused by alterations of capillary vasculature in pheochromocytomas. (**A**) Pericapillary edema imparting a sinusoid-like appearance reminiscent of hepatocellular neoplasms. (**B**) Mild pericapillary fibrosis. (**C**) Marked pericapillary hyalinization. These three patterns as seen here in separate tumors may represent a biological continuum starting with leakage of proteinaceous exudate. Original magnifications 100×

with VHL [33]. The observation is intriguing in view of a known association of the most common VHL subtypes with hypoxic signaling pathways that influence vasculogenesis [34], but it is an inconsistent finding. In addition, it must be remembered that the pathogenicity of mutations leading to type 2 VHL subtypes, and especially those leading to type 2C, may not be due primarily to hypoxia-mimetic effects. The vascularity of parasympathetic PGL is also noteworthy in view of the tumors' frequent association with SDH mutations that affect hypoxic signaling and the important roles of at least the carotid body in physiological responses to hypoxia. Hyaline globules tend to be more common in PCC of patients with MEN2 than with VHL [33] and probably also more so than in other hereditary disorders, possibly contributing to the inverse correlation of globules with malignancy.

Malignancy

PCC and PGL may show local invasive growth into other organs, such as the liver, spleen, or kidney. However, according to the current WHO classification, malignancy is defined by the presence of metastases [6], not local invasion. Despite its potential lethality, local invasion alone is a poor predictor of metastases, and apparent absence of invasion does not preclude development of metastases. The two types of aggressive behavior may therefore have different biological underpinnings. Precise reporting of which behavior a tumor exhibits is critical for assessing criteria that in the future will better define risk from either metastases *or* local invasion.

The most stringent definition of malignancy stipulates that metastases must be to a site where paraganglionic tissue is not normally present, e.g., liver or bone, in order to avoid confusion with multiple primary tumors. This concern is particularly applicable to clinical imaging studies because lymph nodes and paraganglia are normally present in close proximity [1]. A retroperitoneal hot spot on a scan, for example, could therefore represent either a metastasis or a new tumor. From the perspective of histopathology, tumor clearly identifiable within a lymph node can be classified as malignant. However, paraganglionic cells in soft tissue are problematic because normal or hyperplastic paraganglia can be confused with foci of metastatic or infiltrating tumor. It is important to remember this potential of confusion not only with respect to PCC/PGL but also for common tumors such as those of prostate (Fig. 6), bladder, or other locations, where failure to recognize normal paraganglia can result in incorrect tumor staging [35–37].

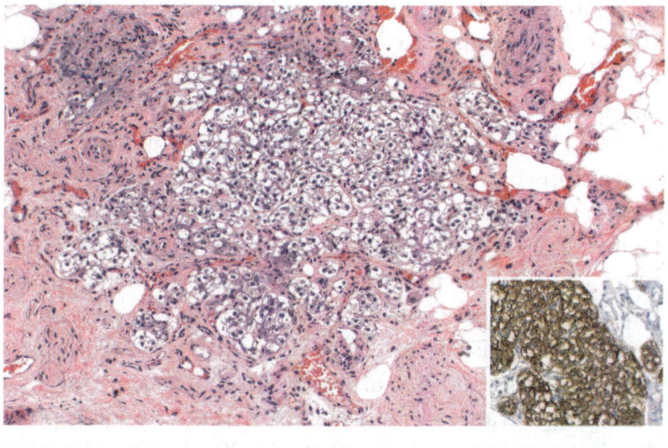

Fig. 6 Normal paraganglion in periprostatic soft tissue of a patient who underwent radical prostatectomy for adenocarcinoma. The structure is suggestive of Gleason 4 prostate cancer but its correct identity is confirmed by diffuse strong immunoreactivity for CgA (inset). Deposits of paraganglionic tissue in or near pelvic organs can have irregular contours as in this example and can be closely apposed to sympathetic nerve fibers, mimicking soft tissue and perineural infiltration. Clear cytoplasm is a common finding, although its cause is unknown

Determining metastatic potential of a PCC or PGL before metastases have occurred is more problematic and there is currently no consensus that it can reliably be done. An important obstacle to determining predictive criteria is the fact that PCC and PGL metastasize infrequently and often late. No individual histological feature is able to predict metastatic potential, including capsular or vascular invasion, extreme cytological atypia, or areas resembling pediatric neuroblastoma [21]. However, some evidence suggests that multifactorial scoring systems can be helpful. In a seminal 1990 study examining multiple histological and non-histological parameters of 120 sympathetic PGL and PCC, [8] Linnoila et al. developed a statistical model, according to which >70% of the tumors could be classified correctly on the basis of four factors: extra-adrenal location, coarse nodularity, confluent necrosis, and absence of hyaline globules. Most malignant tumors had two or three of those features, while 89% of benign tumors had one or none. Unfortunately, a number of subsequent papers assessing markers for malignancy blur the distinction between intra-adrenal and extra-adrenal tumors, thereby obscuring the independent predictive value of extra-adrenal location demonstrated as the most powerful predictor ($P<0.001$) in the Linnoila et al. study.

In 2002 Thompson proposed the PASS system (*p*heochromocytoma of the *a*drenal *s*caled *s*core), specific to the adrenal gland, that scores multiple microscopic findings, including dependent and independent variables identified by Linnoila et al. to arrive at a total score correlated with metastatic potential [38]. Parameters scored are necrosis (confluent or in the center of Zellballen); vascular, capsular, and soft tissue invasion; a high mitotic count (>3/10HPF), atypical mitotic figures, tumor cell spindling, and the more subjective features of diffuse growth or large Zellballen, high cellularity, cellular monotony, nuclear hyperchromasia, and profound nuclear pleomorphism (Fig. 2B,C). All tumors that metastasized had a score of >4, but 17/50 with score of >4 had not metastasized in a follow-up period of ~5 years, and one with a score of >15 had not metastasized in ~28 years. In his paper Thompson notes that the PASS score provides a threshold for risk but does not quantitate the risk above that threshold and he further notes that a score of = 3 does not guarantee that a patient will not at some point develop metastases. A recent study [39] showed considerable intra- and interobserver variation for the PASS, due to the subjective nature of several criteria. Calculation of a score or reporting each of its components is optional, but a high score should not be considered equivalent to a diagnosis of malignancy.

A 2005 scoring system proposed by Kimura for both PCC and extra-adrenal sympathetic PGL combines histological, immunohistochemical, and biochemical characteristics to arrive at a score reported to predict both the metastatic potential of tumors and the prognosis for patients with tumors that metastasize [40]. An interesting aspect of the system is scoring of whether a tumor is adrenergic or noradrenergic, thereby anticipating incorporation of this element into patient management algorithms later proposed by clinicians [9]. Anatomic site in this system is indirectly given additional weight because extra-adrenal PGL are almost invariably noradrenergic.

Use of immunohistochemistry as an ancillary technique to assess malignant potential has produced mixed results. The marker most consistently reported to correlate with malignancy is the proliferation marker Ki-67 [40–42]. However, even those results are disputed. Studies of MIB-1 labeling show a striking lack of methodological consistency and many papers do not provide sufficient methodological detail to permit replication. Although many pathologists now include an assessment of Ki-67 labeling in diagnostic reporting of PCC and PGL, there is currently no prospect of standardization and reporting of a labeling index remains optional. Numerous additional markers are reported to correlate with malignancy, but their usefulness is still limited to research purposes [41, 43]. Among those are VEGF expression and microvessel density. Although the utility of microvessel density as a predictor of metastasis has been challenged, tumor vessels are of interest as potential targets of therapy [44]. Malignant PCC tend to be larger than their benign counterparts, although this criterion cannot be used in the individual case, as there is a large overlap.

The Interplay of Pathology and Genetic Testing

The genotype–phenotype correlations in familial syndromes with PCC and/or PGL and the high prevalence of unsuspected hereditary disease have led to recommendations for genetic testing and subsequent patient management [9, 19, 45]. Tumor location, presence of multiple tumors, presence of metastases, and type of catecholamine produced are useful as guides in deciding which genes to test. However, specific algorithms differ somewhat according to institutional preference and test availability. The most stringent recommendations favor genetic testing of all patients with apparently sporadic tumors for *RET*, *VHL*, and *SDH* mutations in order to avoid being misled by individual differences in presentation and penetrance, low penetrance of some mutations, de novo mutations, and imprinting of *SDHD* [45]. Alternatively, PCC, especially bilateral ones, should be tested first for *RET* and *VHL* abnormalities, whereas PGL should be tested first for *SDHB* and *SDHD* gene mutations. The number of *SDHC* mutations is presently so low that routine testing is not advocated. Routine genetic testing is not currently available for *NF1* mutations because the gene is extremely large and, in contrast to the other susceptibility genes, does not have discrete mutation "hot spots" leading to development of these tumors [46].

Because extra-adrenal location correlates with *SDHB* mutation and *SDHB* mutation correlates with malignancy, it might be speculated that the pathology findings associated with malignancy point indirectly toward *SDHB* and that genetic testing for *SDHB* mutations [47] might outweigh the predictive value of current pathology criteria in many cases.

Concluding Remarks and Future Prospects

Several recent developments described in this chapter are important to practicing pathologists, as they have direct impact on the content of pathology reports:

- There are now three groups of tumors to be distinguished: PCC, which are adrenal tumors; sympathetic PGL, which are their extra-adrenal counterparts; and parasympathetic PGL, which occur in the head and neck.
- The mainstay of diagnosis of tumors in each of these three groups is histology, supplemented by immunohistochemistry if necessary. The required elements of pathology reports are essentially the basics required for all tumors, including size and weight and comments on the presence or absence of necrosis, vascular or capsular invasion, mitoses, resection margins, and unusual features [48, 49].
- Malignancy is defined by the presence of metastases in sites where chromaffin cells normally do not occur. Histopathological scoring systems await further validation. Risk of malignancy can be inferred partly from tumor location and specific gene mutations. Most notably, SDHB mutations are likely to occur in extra-adrenal sympathetic PGL and these tumors are frequently malignant.
- The "10% rule" is no longer valid and should be abandoned. Molecular genetic research has shown that 25–30% of PCC and PGL have a hereditary basis, which should be signaled by pathologists to the clinicians. Mutation analysis should be advised, especially in young patients or patients having more than one tumor or a positive family history.

It is to be expected that further research will yield a refinement of the above conclusions and new markers for the distinction of PCC with adverse clinical behavior. Ongoing studies may also yield new insights into pathogenesis and new treatment strategies for malignant PCC, which presently have a poor prognosis with less than 50% 5-year survival.

References

1. Tischler AS. Paraganglia. In: Mills SE, ed. Histology For Pathologists. Third ed. Philadelphia: Lippincott Williams and Wilkins; 2007:1211–33.
2. Kohn A. Die chromaffinen Zellen des sympathicus. Anat Anz 1898;15:399–400.
3. Kohn A. Die Paraganglien. Arch Mikr Anat 1903;52:262–365.
4. Cronin C. Charles Sugrue, M.D., of Cork (1775–1816) and the first description of a classical medical condition: phaeochromocytoma. Ir J Med Sci 2008;177(2):171–5.
5. Manger WM. An overview of pheochromocytoma: history, current concepts, vagaries, and diagnostic challenges. Ann N Y Acad Sci 2006;1073:1–20.
6. DeLellis RA, Lloyd RV, Heitz PU, Eng C, eds. Tumours of Endocrine Organs. Lyon: IARC Press; 2004.
7. Karsner HT. Tumors of the Adrenal. Atlas of Tumor Pathology, Section VIII-Fascicle 29. Washington, DC: Armed Forces Institute of Pathology; 1950.
8. Linnoila RI, Keiser HR, Steinberg SM, Lack EE. Histopathology of benign versus malignant sympathoadrenal paragangliomas: clinicopathologic study of 120 cases including unusual histologic features. Hum Pathol 1990;21(11):1168–80.
9. Pacak K, Eisenhofer G, Ahlman H, et al. Pheochromocytoma: recommendations for clinical practice from the First International Symposium. October 2005. Nat Clin Pract Endocrinol Metab 2007;3(2):92–102.
10. Tischler AS. Pheochromocytoma and Extra-Adrenal Paraganglioma: Updates. Arch Pathol Lab Med 2008;132(8):1272–84.
11. Neumann HP, Bausch B, McWhinney SR, et al. Germ-line mutations in nonsyndromic pheochromocytoma. N Engl J Med 2002;346(19):1459–66.
12. Gimenez-Roqueplo AP, Burnichon N, Amar L, Favier J, Jeunemaitre X, Plouin PF. Recent advances in the genetics of phaeochromocytoma and functional paraganglioma. Clin Exp Pharmacol Physiol 2008;35(4):376–9.
13. Baysal BE. Genomic imprinting and environment in hereditary paraganglioma. Am J Med Genet C Semin Med Genet 2004;129(1):85–90.
14. Baysal BE. Role of mitochondrial mutations in cancer. Endocr Pathol 2006;17(3):203–12.
15. Dahia PL, Hao K, Rogus J, et al. Novel pheochromocytoma susceptibility loci identified by integrative genomics. Cancer Res 2005;65(21):9651–8.
16. Dannenberg H, Komminoth P, Dinjens WN, Speel EJ, de Krijger RR. Molecular genetic alterations in adrenal and extra-adrenal pheochromocytomas and paragangliomas. Endocr Pathol 2003;14(4):329–50.
17. Astuti D, Morris M, Krona C, et al. Investigation of the role of SDHB inactivation in sporadic phaeochromocytoma and neuroblastoma. Br J Cancer 2004;91(10):1835–41.

18. Braun S, Riemann K, Kupka S, et al. Active succinate dehydrogenase (SDH) and lack of SDHD mutations in sporadic paragangliomas. Anticancer Res 2005;25(4):2809–14.
19. Korpershoek E, Petri BJ, van Nederveen FH, et al. Candidate gene mutation analysis in bilateral adrenal pheochromocytoma and sympathetic paraganglioma. Endocr Relat Cancer 2007;14(2):453–62.
20. Eisenhofer G, Bornstein SR, Brouwers FM, et al. Malignant pheochromocytoma: current status and initiatives for future progress. Endocr Relat Cancer 2004;11(3):423–36.
21. Lack EE. Tumors of the Adrenal Gland and Extraadrenal Paraganglia. Washington, DC: American Registry Of Pathology; 2007.
22. Al-Zaid T, Alroy J, Pfannl R, et al. Oncocytic Adrenal Cortical Tumor with Cytoplasmic Inclusions and Hyaline Globules. Virchows Arch 2008;453(3):301–6.
23. Bellezza G, Giansanti M, Cavaliere A, Sidoni A. Pigmented "black" pheochromocytoma of the adrenal gland: a case report and review of the literature. Arch Pathol Lab Med 2004;128(10):e125–8.
24. Lack EE, Kim H, Reed K. Pigmented ("black") extraadrenal paraganglioma. Am J Surg Pathol 1998;22(2):265–9.
25. Reddy CE, Panda NK, Vaiphei K, Powari M. Pigmented vagal paraganglioma. J Laryngol Otol 2003;117(7):584–7.
26. Yu JL, Rak JW. Host microenvironment in breast cancer development: inflammatory and immune cells in tumour angiogenesis and arteriogenesis. Breast Cancer Res 2003;5(2):83–8.
27. Feldman SA, Eiden LE. The chromogranins: their roles in secretion from neuroendocrine cells and as markers for neuroendocrine neoplasia. Endocr Pathol 2003;14(1):3–23.
28. Fuller CE, Williams GT. Gastrointestinal manifestations of type 1 neurofibromatosis (von Recklinghausen's disease). Histopathology 1991;19(1):1–11.
29. Sinkre PA, Murakata L, Rabin L, Hoang MP, Albores-Saavedra J. Clear cell carcinoid tumor of the gallbladder: another distinctive manifestation of von Hippel-Lindau disease. Am J Surg Pathol 2001;25(10):1334–9.
30. Griffiths DF, Williams GT, Williams ED. Duodenal carcinoid tumours, phaeochromocytoma and neurofibromatosis: islet cell tumour, phaeochromocytoma and the von Hippel-Lindau complex: two distinctive neuroendocrine syndromes. Q J Med 1987;64(245):769–82.
31. Lloyd RV, Sisson JC, Shapiro B, Verhofstad AA. Immunohistochemical localization of epinephrine, norepinephrine, catecholamine-synthesizing enzymes, and chromogranin in neuroendocrine cells and tumors. Am J Pathol 1986;125(1):45–54.
32. Schmid KW, Schroder S, Dockhorn-Dworniczak B, et al. Immunohistochemical demonstration of chromogranin A, chromogranin B, and secretogranin II in extra-adrenal paragangliomas. Mod Pathol 1994;7(3):347–53.
33. Koch CA, Mauro D, Walther MM, et al. Pheochromocytoma in von hippel-lindau disease: distinct histopathologic phenotype compared to pheochromocytoma in multiple endocrine neoplasia type 2. Endocr Pathol 2002;13(1):17–27.
34. Dahia PL, Ross KN, Wright ME, et al. A HIF1alpha Regulatory Loop Links Hypoxia and Mitochondrial Signals in Pheochromocytomas. PLoS Genet 2005;1(1):e8.
35. Ostrowski ML, Wheeler TM. Paraganglia of the prostate. Location, frequency, and differentiation from prostatic adenocarcinoma. Am J Surg Pathol 1994;18(4):412–20.
36. Rode J, Bentley A, Parkinson C. Paraganglial cells of urinary bladder and prostate: potential diagnostic problem. J Clin Pathol 1990;43(1):13–6.
37. Makinen J, Nickels J. Paraganglion cells mimicking metastatic clear cell carcinoma. Histopathology 1979;3(6):459–65.
38. Thompson LD. Pheochromocytoma of the Adrenal gland Scaled Score (PASS) to separate benign from malignant neoplasms: a clinicopathologic and immunophenotypic study of 100 cases. Am J Surg Pathol 2002;26(5):551–66.
39. Wu et al., Am J Surg Pathol 2009;33(4):599–608.
40. Kimura N, Watanabe T, Noshiro T, Shizawa S, Miura Y. Histological grading of adrenal and extra-adrenal pheochromocytomas and relationship to prognosis: a clinicopathological analysis of 116 adrenal pheochromocytomas and 30 extra-adrenal sympathetic paragangliomas including 38 malignant tumors. Endocr Pathol 2005;16(1):23–32.
41. August C, August K, Schroeder S, et al. CGH and CD 44/MIB-1 immunohistochemistry are helpful to distinguish metastasized from nonmetastasized sporadic pheochromocytomas. Mod Pathol 2004;17(9):1119–28.
42. Liu TH, Chen YJ, Wu SF, et al. [Distinction between benign and malignant pheochromocytomas]. Zhonghua Bing Li Xue Za Zhi 2004;33(3):198–202.
43. Portela-Gomes GM, Stridsberg M, Grimelius L, Falkmer UG, Falkmer S. Expression of chromogranins A, B, and C (secretogranin II) in human adrenal medulla and in benign and malignant pheochromocytomas An immunohistochemical study with region-specific antibodies. Apmis 2004;112(10):663–73.
44. Zielke A, Middeke M, Hoffmann S, et al. VEGF-mediated angiogenesis of human pheochromocytomas is associated to malignancy and inhibited by anti-VEGF antibodies in experimental tumors. Surgery 2002;132(6):1056–63; discussion 63.
45. Benn DE, Robinson BG. Pheochromocytoma-quo vadis? Nat Clin Pract Endocrinol Metab 2007;3(5):377.
46. Bausch B, Borozdin W, Mautner VF, et al. Germline NF1 mutational spectra and loss-of-heterozygosity analyses in patients with pheochromocytoma and neurofibromatosis type 1. J Clin Endocrinol Metab 2007;92(7):2784–92.
47. Amar L, Baudin E, Burnichon N, et al. Succinate dehydrogenase B gene mutations predict survival in patients with malignant pheochromocytomas or paragangliomas. J Clin Endocrinol Metab 2007;92(10):3822–8.
48. Lack EE, Lloyd RV, Carney JA, Woodruff JW. Recommendations for the reporting of extra-adrenal paragangliomas. The Association of Directors of Anatomic and Surgical Pathology. Hum Pathol 2003;34(2):112–3.
49. Lack EE. Recommendations for the reporting of tumors of the adrenal cortex and medulla. Association of Directors of Anatomic and Surgical Pathology. Virchows Arch 1999;435(2):87–91.

Endocrine Tumors of the Lung and Upper Airways

Armando E. Fraire, Ulrike M. Gruber-Mösenbacher, and Helmut H. Popper

Abstract Neuroendocrine tumors stand alone among other members of the larger family of tumors of the lung and upper airways. While relatively uncommon, they have, over the years, been the subject of considerable attention and study. A recent search of the literature yielded thousands of citations for small cell carcinoma, a single entity within the spectrum of neuroendocrine tumors. This chapter discusses the intriguing putative role of neuroendocrine cell hyperplasia as a possible precursor of these tumors. In addition, this chapter explores the similarities as well as differences between neuroendocrine and non-neuroendocrine tumors. Lastly, this chapter attempts to provide concise up-to-date information on both current, consensus –based morphologic criteria and the application of modern techniques, particularly immunohistochemical techniques that may facilitate histopathological diagnosis.

Keywords Lung • Upper airways • Larynx • Neurosecretory granules • Neuroendocrine cells • Neuroendocrine hyperplasia • Carcinoid tumorlets • Typical carcinoids • Atypical carcinoids • Large cell neuroendocrine carcinoma • Small cell carcinoma • Immunohistochemistry • Thyroid transcription factor-1 • Chromogranin • Synaptophysin • Calcitonin

The remarkable family of lung and upper airways tumors collectively known as neuroendocrine tumors differs considerably from their non-neuroendocrine counterparts on account of their distinct light microscopic architecture, ultrastructural features, unique immunohistochemical properties, and perhaps more importantly, on account of their clinical behavior. To emphasize their carcinoma – like nature and morphology, these tumors were first described as "carcinoid tumors" by Oberndorfer in the early 1900s [1]. These tumors have been traditionally compartmentalized by the World Health Organization Classification of Tumors and other classification schemes into several categories of tumors, which have evolved over time [2]. Currently, widely accepted categories include carcinoid tumors (both typical and atypical), large cell neuroendocrine carcinoma and small cell carcinoma, along with a subset of atypical carcinoids of the upper airways characterized by immunoreactivity to calcitonin and TTF-1 (thyroid transcription factor-1) and known to behave clinically as low-grade neuroendocrine carcinomas [3–5]. A special category recognized as possible precursors of neuroendocrine tumors are minute diffuse neuroendocrine proliferations of the lung known as diffuse idiopathic pulmonary neuroendocrine cell hyperplasia [6] and less diffuse, actually nodular aggregates of hyperplastic neuroendocrine cells known as tumorlets [7]. In this chapter, we consider these categories of neuroendocrine tumors of the lung but first we briefly discuss their cell of origin and the concept of a dispersed neuroendocrine system throughout the body [7–10].

Pulmonary neuroendocrine cells and the concept of a dispersed neuroendocrine system: Neuroendocrine cells are not unique to the lung. In fact they are found dispersedly in a great variety of organs and tissues. First proposed by Feyrter [8], the concept of a dispersed neuroendocrine system throughout the human body was later advanced by Gould and DeLellis in the early 1980s and further discussed by Hammar and others in more recent years [9–12]. According to this concept, a dispersed neuroendocrine system encompassing a variety of endocrine cells in the skin, thyroid, parathyroid, thymus, pancreas, lung, and other anatomical sites, would constitute the cellular basis for the development of neuroendocrine tumors in such sites. Notorious within this group of organs are the calcitonin producing C cells of the thyroid

A.E. Fraire (✉)
Professor of Pathology, Director, Pulmonary and Autopsy Pathology, University of Massachusetts Medical School, UMassMemorial Medical Center, Three Biotech, One Innovation Drive, Worcester, MA, USA
e-mail: frairea@ummhc.org

A. Khan (ed.), *Surgical Pathology of Endocrine and Neuroendocrine Tumors*, Current Clinical Pathology,
DOI 10.1007/978-1-60327-396-1_10,

and neuroendocrine cells of the skin known as Merkel cells [13]. In the lung, neuroendocrine cells (also known as Kultzchisky or Feyrter cells) [8] co-exist with four other major types of cells that can be found along the tracheobronchial tree. These include columnar ciliated cells, goblet (mucin-producing) cells, basal cells, and clara cells. Neuroendocrine cells in the airways of normal lungs can be seen microscopically as single cells (Fig. 1) or as small aggregates of cells near the basal membrane known as neuroepithelial bodies [14]. (Fig. 2) Within these bodies, individual cells appear as small eosinophilic cells extending from the basement membrane of the bronchial mucosa to the luminal surface of the bronchial epithelium. They occur singly or in clusters of 4–10 cells, each having oval nuclei and inconspicuous nucleoli. These cells are argyrophilic and contain electron dense, membrane-bound neurosecretory granules, by electron microscopy. The granules are said to be 70–170 nm in size and to be surrounded by a clear halo [14]. Immunohistochemically, these cells show positivity to a wide array of markers regarded as markers of neuroendocrine differentiation. These include chromogranins, neurofilaments, synaptophysin and neuron-specific enolase, as well as Leu-7 and others such as calcitonin, vasoactive polypeptide, and adrenocorticotrophic hormone [11, 15, 16]. In addition, these cells are immunoreactive for CD117 (c-kit) and the thyroid transcription factor (TTF-1). As we will see later, markers of neuroendocrine differentiation play a pivotal role in clinical medicine, facilitating the recognition and diagnosis of tumors derived from neuroendocrine cells.

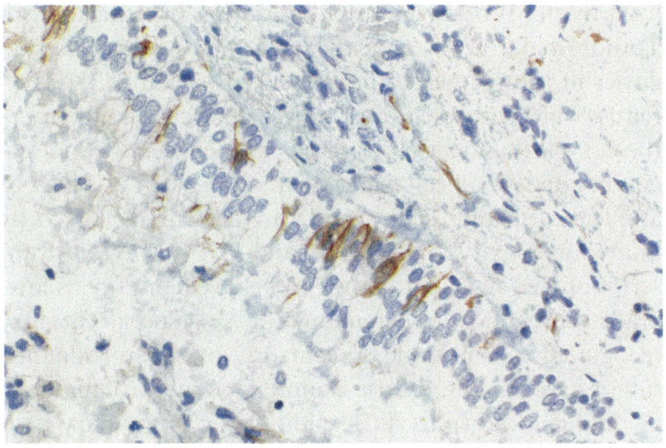

Fig. 1 Neuroendocrine cells within ciliated bronchial epithelium. In this illustration, the neuroendocrine nature of the cells is highlighted by their immunoreactivity to n-CAM (CD56). (CD56 immunostain)

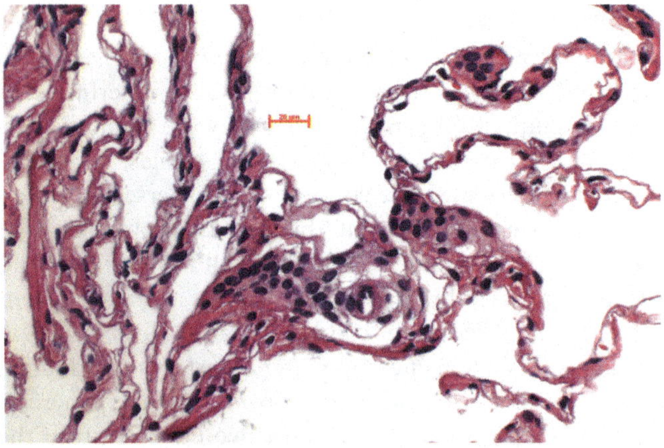

Fig. 2 Neuroepithelial body. Note three groups of small, highly uniform cells with neuroendocrine phenotype, 2.0 mm scale. Hematoxylin and eosin

Diffuse Idiopathic Pulmonary Neuroendocrine Hyperplasia

Long known to occur in association with high altitude and lung disorders of cigarette smokers, neuroendocrine cell hyperplasia, herein referred to as diffuse idiopathic pulmonary neuroendocrine hyperplasia (DIPNECH) is a disorder still awaiting formal classification both in terms of its pre-neoplastic potential and clinical significance. Early in the 1990s, Aguayo et al. called attention to DIPNECH occurring in six patients with small airway disease [6]. This small airway disease was characterized histopathologically by peribronchiolar fibrosis, hyperplasia/dysplasia of neuroendocrine cells, and multiple carcinoid tumorlets. None of the six patients were cigarette smokers but all had symptoms and radiographic and physiologic abnormalities. Later, Armas and collaborators called attention to a patient with DIPNECH who presented clinically with an interstitial lung process [17]. In this patient, an open lung biopsy showed a florid intraepithelial population of neuroendocrine cells involving distal small airways and alveoli with desquamation and filling of airspaces by nests of proliferating cells with neuroendocrine phenotype. While these nests of cells were only positive for the Grimelius reaction and neuron-specific enolase (while negative for serotonin, calcitonin and chromogranin) they showed ultrastructural evidence of neurosecretory dense-core granules. In their report, the authors favored a hyperplastic process showing no evidence of any associated tumorlets or carcinoid tumors. Subsequently, however, other reports have described the association of DIPNECH and tumorlets. We have also seen this association.

Typically, patients with DIPNECH are 40–60 years old, with some excess of females presenting with a slowly progressive disease characterized by dry cough and shortness of breath [6, 7, 17]. Some of these patients are initially misdiagnosed as having bronchial asthma, partly due to similar symptomatology and/or results of pulmonary function testing, showing evidence of mixed obstructive/restrictive patterns of disease with impaired gas transfer across the alveolocapillary membrane. Radiographically, DIPNECH is manifested essentially as bronchiolitis obliterans [18, 19]. On CT scans, Lee and Associates described mosaic pattern of air trapping as the predominant finding in five adult women with documented DIPNECH (Fig. 3). In four of the five women, the airway walls were thickened. Nodular lesions were noted in two of the five patients. The nodules ranged from six to eight in number and ranged in diameter of 0.2–1.5 mm [19]. Given their small size, lesions of DIPNECH are not readily visible on surgically resected specimens of lung and are found only incidentally upon microscopic examination. Microscopically, DIPNECH presents as small clusters of cells or small linear or nodular aggregates of cells that protrude into the bronchiolar lumina (Fig. 4). Peribronchiolar fibrosis may be present but the surrounding lung may be entirely normal. As noted earlier, in some cases there may be associated carcinoid tumorlets. Tumorlets are small nodular aggregates of hyperplastic neuroendocrine cells often no more than 2–3 mm, fundamentally differing from DIPNECH only on account of size and their nodular configuration. Rare cases of multiple tumorlets with associated bronchiolitis obliterans have been successfully treated by single lung transplantation [20].

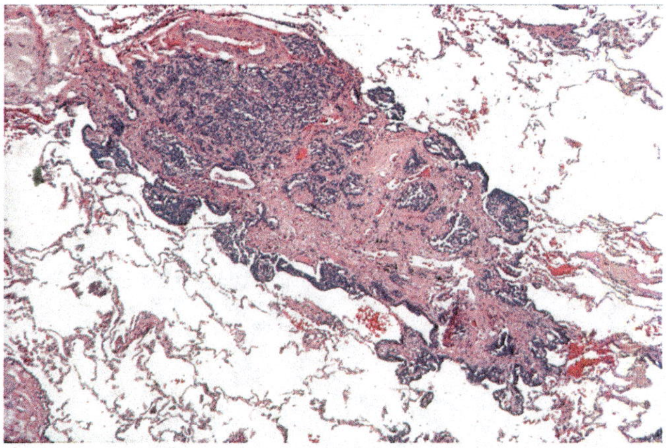

Fig. 4 DIPNECH lesion showing multiple clusters of small uniform looking cells with a fibrous background. Hematoxylin and eosin

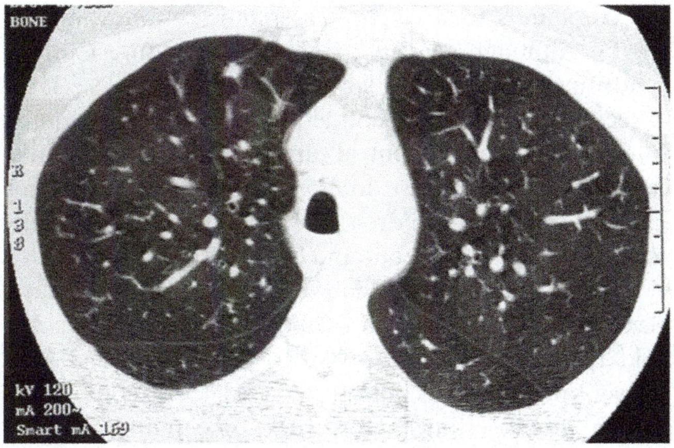

Fig. 3 DIPNECH Lesion. High resolution computed tomography of chest. A 48-year-old woman with shortness of breath for 8 years. Note mosaic pattern at the level of the aortic arch and a small nodule at the anterior segment of the left upper lobe. Histopathology documented a focus of DIPNECH. (Reproduced with permission, Courtesy of Dr. J.S. Lee) [19]

DIPNECH, current status: Diffuse idiopathic pulmonary neuroendocrine cell hyperplasia (DIPNECH) is a rare lesion. Along with two other conditions, atypical adenomatous hyperplasia of the alveolar epithelium and squamous dysplasia of the bronchial epithelium, DIPNECH is recognized in the World Health Organization classification of tumors as a pre-invasive (pre-neoplastic) disorder because some patients with DIPNECH may go on to develop tumorlets and/or single or multiple cell carcinoid tumors [7]. Gosney, however, has cautioned that carcinoid tumors that accompany DIPNECH and are presumed to develop from it appear to be invariably peripheral and always of low grade [21]. Gosney further notes that the emergence of central pulmonary neuroendocrine tumors from DIPNECH has not been documented as of yet [21]. Similarly, convincing evidence of DIPNECH as a forerunner of large cell neuroendocrine carcinoma or small cell carcinoma regardless of their central or peripheral location, has not been reported in the literature.

Carcinoid Tumorlets

Initially described by Whitwell in 1955 as carcinoid tumorlets, tumorlets are essentially small nodular aggregates of hyperplastic neuroendocrine cells [22–24]. (Fig. 5) By convention, tumorlets are small lesions, never more than 5 mm in maximum diameter. According to this definition, any lesion over 5 mm must be considered a carcinoid tumor. Most lesions are single but can be multiple in some patients [25]. Ultrastructurally, the cells of tumorlets show features common to neuroendocrine cells, namely dense core neurosecretory granules and prominent lysosomes. Most cases can be readily distinguished from other minute pulmonary lesions such as minute meningothelial-like bodies (formerly known as chemodectomas). In

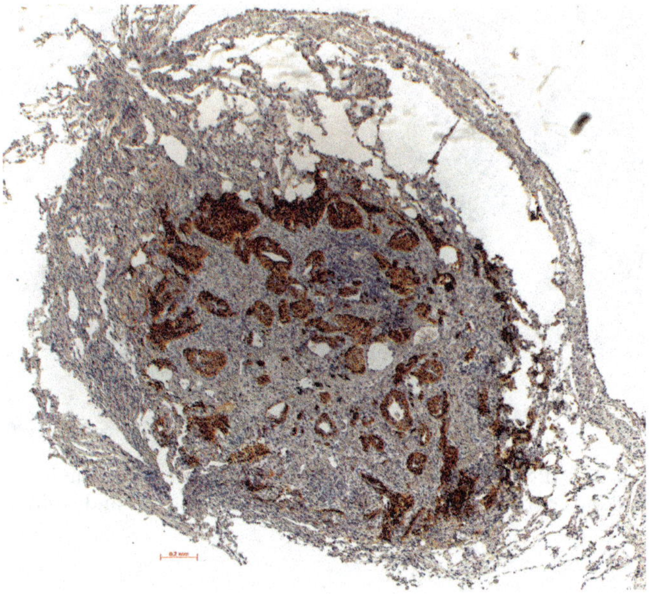

Fig. 5 Carcinoid tumorlet, note nodular configuration and high immunoreactivity of tumor cells to chromogranin. Scale at bottom left corner. Chromogranin immunostain

difficult cases, immunostains for pancytokeratin, smooth muscle actin (SMA), and progesterone receptor (PR) will be of help since meningothelial like bodies will usually be cytokeratin negative and SMA and PR positive.

As is the case with DIPNECH, some carcinoid tumorlets are associated with fibrotic obliteration of bronchioles [20]. Other associations include diffuse panbronchiolitis, intralobar sequestration, and congenital adenomatoid malformation of the lung [26]. Given their smallness, tumorlets are almost never symptomatic and are often found on incidental basis, at autopsy or in lung surgical specimens resected for a variety of reasons. The clinical behavior of tumorlets is benign with only isolated instances of metastases of regional lymph nodes having been described [27, 28]. Given that the diagnosis of DIPNECH and tumorlets is largely based on quantitative assessment, the distinction between DIPNECH and carcinoid tumorlets, at least for the time being, remains hazy, awaiting molecular genetics or other studies that may facilitate the distinction on better-defined basis. In this regard, a promising avenue of future investigation is the expression of neutral endopeptidase (NEP) in neuroendocrine cells. NEP has been reported in neuroendocrine cells of DIPNECH, possibly as a secondary effect, since pulmonary neuroendocrine cells are rich in bombesin-like proteins, the substrate of neutral endopeptidase [29]. Whether tumorlets are forerunners of carcinoid tumors is not known. What is known is that tumorlets and carcinoid tumors frequently co-exist, providing at least circumstantial evidence for some pre-neoplastic role of tumorlets.

Carcinoid Tumors

In the 2004 classification scheme of the World Health Organization (WHO), carcinoid tumors now occupy a separate and distinct niche among the various families of lung tumors [30]. Interestingly, in the WHO classification scheme carcinoids are not grouped within the family of neuroendocrine tumors of the lung. Two major variants of carcinoid tumors are recognized: typical and atypical [30]. Objective and non-objective histopathologic criteria have been formulated to distinguish these two variants. Yet, as we will discuss below this distinction is not always easy.

Typical Carcinoid Tumors: As currently defined by the 2004 WHO Classification of Tumors, typical carcinoid tumors of the lung are "tumors characterized by a variety of microscopic patterns of growth that suggest neuroendocrine differentiation." Further, the WHO classification of lung tumors states that "individual tumor cells have uniform cytologic features with moderate eosinophilic cytoplasm [30]. Carcinoid tumors are usually centrally located, i.e., in the major airways but an important minority develops in the peripheral (subpleural) areas of the lung parenchyma. As noted earlier these peripherally located carcinoids are the type of carcinoids, which are likely to emerge from DIPNECH lesions [21]. Some patients with typical carcinoids, particularly the centrally located ones, present with symptoms related to bronchial obstruction. In contrast, peripherally located carcinoid tumors tend to be clinically silent and to become apparent only as incidental radiographic findings. Of note, peripheral carcinoids tend to show a spindle cell morphology [31–33]. Although frequently cited in the literature, Cushing Syndrome and other similar endocrine syndromes related to secretion of ectopic peptide moieties are not common [30]. The incidence of central carcinoids is almost equal in the two sexes and most develop in adults although they can also occur in children [31–33]. Although generally accessible to the endoscope and hence endoscopic biopsies, biopsy procedures may result in copious post procedural bleeding. This has led to a legendary reputation of carcinoid tumors as tumors prone to profusely bleed after biopsy, an issue anecdotally referred to at conferences and in other settings. However, some pulmonologists dispute this assertion indicating that bleeding in these cases is not greater than bleeding related to biopsies of other tumors (personal observation). It is nonetheless true, as is the case with other neuroendocrine tumors, that carcinoids are richly vascularized tumors and therefore susceptible to some degree of bleeding following biopsy procedures.

At the microscopic level, the major feature of carcinoid tumors is their organoid pattern with formation of nests,

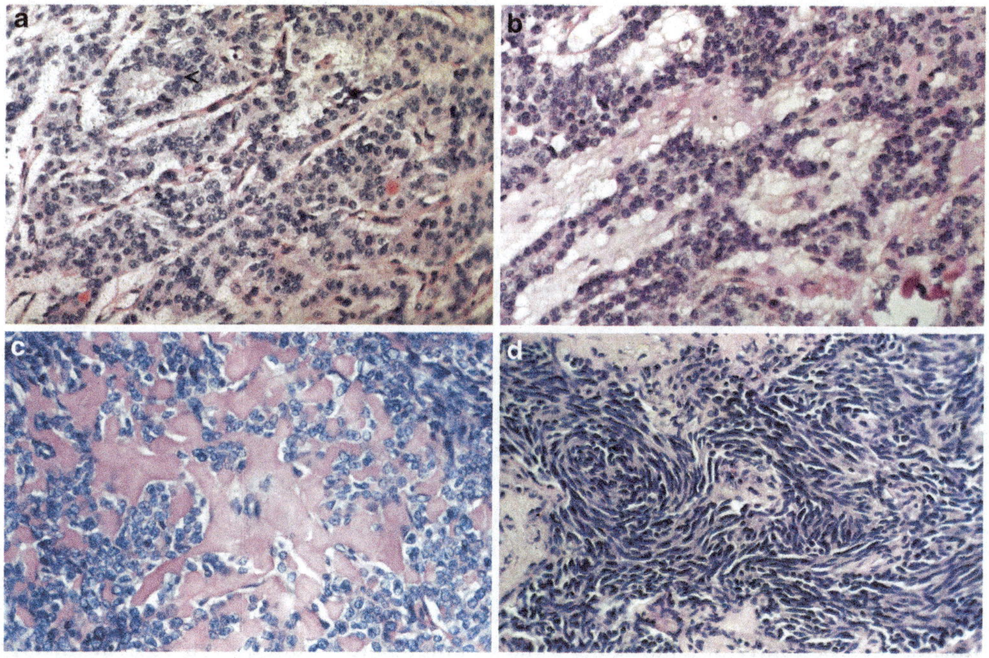

Fig. 6 Typical carcinoid. (**A–D**) The morphologic appearance of typical carcinoids is variable. (**A**) This panel displays rosette formation, (**B**) In this field, a ribbony pattern is evident, (**C**) This carcinoid shows masses of pink amorphous material corresponding to amyloid, (**D**) a spindle cell morphology is often seen in peripherally located carcinoids. Hematoxylin and eosin

cords, or trabeculae of cells, separated by thin fibrovascular septae. Other patterns of growth include ribbons, festoons, and microacinar rosette-like structures [34]. (Fig. 6) A number of variants have been recognized: clear, papillary, oncocytoid, spindle type, and others. Islands of bone, cartilage, and deposition of amyloid can also be seen within some tumors [35–39] (Fig. 6). Necrosis is not a common feature and if present, should raise the possibility of atypical carcinoid. At the individual cell level, the hallmark of the tumor cells is their well-known nuclear chromatin distribution pattern. This is a pattern variously described as granular, punctate, or "salt and pepper" pattern [34], which, however, can also be seen in higher-grade neuroendocrine tumors. Importantly, necrosis and increased mitotic activity are not features of typical carcinoid tumors. However, a low level of mitotic activity can be seen in some typical carcinoids [34, 40]. Individual cell atypia may be present, i.e., nucleomegaly but most authors regard this feature as not helpful in terms of diagnosis.

Typical carcinoid tumors also occur in the upper respiratory tract, but are not common. In fact, typical carcinoids are said to be the least common of neuroendocrine tumors arising from the larynx, with only 42 cases reported as of 2005 [3, 4]. These tumors show a 3:1 predilection for males presenting with a mean age of 34 and a range of 45–80 years at the time of diagnosis [3]. Most laryngeal carcinoids are microscopically quite similar if not identical to those occurring in the lung. While their clinical course is generally favorable, typical carcinoids of the larynx can metastasize in about 33% of the cases [3–5].

Atypical Carcinoid Tumors: These tumors share many of the histopathologic and clinico-demographic features of typical carcinoids but fundamentally differ from them in terms of clinical behavior. Microscopically, the 2004 WHO classification of tumors regards atypical carcinoids as tumors with increased mitotic activity (2–10 mitoses per 10 high power fields and/or foci of necrosis. (Fig. 7) To be meaningful, at least three sets of 10 high power fields should be counted and averaged [40]. While

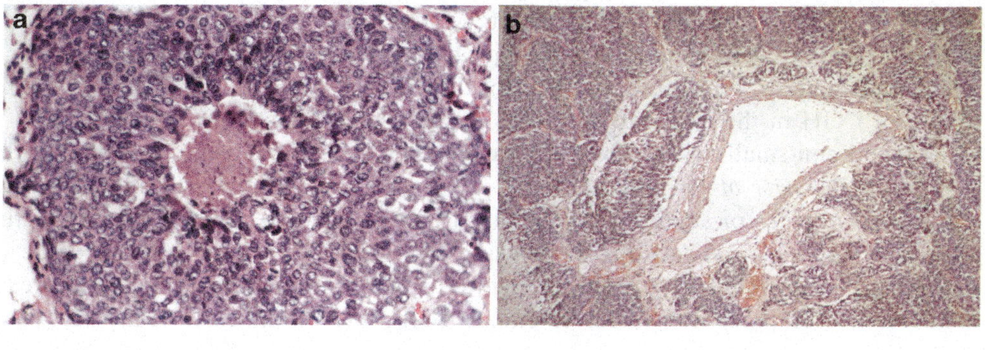

Fig. 7 Atypical carcinoid, (**A**) Atypical carcinoid showing an island of tumor cells with central necrosis. Mitosis not visible at this magnification and (**B**) Vascular invasion. Hematoxylin and eosin

considerable cellular atypia (nuclear irregularity, nucleomegaly) may be present, cellular atypia is a subjective criterion, difficult to estimate and is not generally regarded or accepted as a helpful diagnostic feature [30]. The diagnosis of atypical carcinoid tumor can be made on basis of bronchoscopic biopsies but the distinction of typical from atypical carcinoid is best made on basis of surgically resected specimens, unless mitosis and/or necrosis are evident on a (generous) bronchoscopic biopsy [30].

Nearly one-fifth of all carcinoids of the lung are said to be cytokeratin negative. However, in the experience of one of us (HHP) all carcinoids of lung have been positive for cytokeratin. Neuroendocrine markers such as CD56, CD57, chromogranin, synaptophysin, and neuron-specific enolase are generally positive. Thyroid Transcription Factor 1 is said to be positive in about one-third of all typical carcinoids and nearly all of the atypical carcinoids [30, 40, 41]. If positive, immunoreactivity for the S100 protein may indicate the presence of sustentacular cells raising the possibility of a paraganglioma of lung. Cytokeratin 20 is typically negative [40].

Immunoelectron microscopy contributes to the differential diagnosis between typical and atypical carcinoids of the lung. While neurosecretory electron-dense, membrane-based granules occur in both of these two tumors, there is some evidence that differences exist in terms of the quantity and quality of such granules [42]. Fukayama and associates examined these granules in the case of a 56-year-old female with an atypical endocrine tumor of the lung bearing morphologic resemblance to an atypical carcinoid. In their case, the authors identified secretory granules that were positive for gastrin-releasing peptide, human chorionic gonadotrophin, calcitonin, and serotonin, calling attention that in their patient the granules appeared to be more numerous and larger in size than conventional neurosecretory granules, presumably referring to granules in non-atypical endocrine tumors of the lung [42]. In difficult cases, comparative genomic hybridization (CGH) can be of considerable assistance in making the distinction between typical and atypical carcinoid tumors. Using CGH, Ulmann et al. analyzed 15 typical carcinoids and 20 atypical carcinoid tumors. The study showed loss of 11q in 58% of the atypical tumors but only 12% of the typical ones. Deletions of 3p were seen in 25% of the atypical carcinoids but none of the typical ones [43]. Using metaanalysis, the authors further documented the ability of CGH in the differentiation between carcinoid tumors and non-small cell carcinoma of the lung [43].

Clinical Behavior of Pulmonary Carcinoid Tumors: A substantial number of studies have examined this issue with most investigators agreeing in that atypical carcinoids behave in a clinically significant more aggressive behavior as compared to typical carcinoids [44]. One important caveat to remember is, however, that all carcinoid tumors are malignant tumors, albeit with a different level of malignancy. For example, in the study by Warren and Gould, of 27 patients with typical bronchial carcinoids, two patients had nodal metastases at the time of resection and distant metastases were identified at a later time in two additional patients, 5 and 10 years after diagnosis [45]. In a study of 35 patients with peripheral spindle cell carcinoids Ranchod et al. found nodal metastases in seven patients and distant bone metastases in one other patient [31]. Abdi and collaborators reported on eleven patients with peripheral carcinoid tumors, three of who also had regional lymph node metastases [32]. Slodkowska and associates reported their findings on 77 patients with carcinoid tumors, 62 with typical and 15 with atypical morphology. The typical tumors occurred in younger patients and were smaller than the atypical ones [46]. On follow up, regional lymph node metastases were identified not only in 33% of the atypical carcinoids but also in 10% of the typical variants [46].

Atypical Carcinoid Tumors of the Upper Airways: Atypical carcinoids of the upper airways are also known as neuroendocrine carcinomas [3]. Characteristically, they occur in the larynx forming submucosal masses sometimes in association with ulceration of the squamous mucosa [3]. The morphology and immunohistochemistry of these tumors is similar to those of the lung. Major features to look for are necrosis, mitosis, and cellular atypia. Features of atypia include larger cells, prominent eosinophilic cytoplasm, nuclear pleomorphism, and small or inconspicuous nucleoli. Mitotic activity may be prominent and focal areas of necrosis as well as vascular invasion may be seen [3].

While the morphology and immunohistochemical properties of atypical carcinoids in the upper airway, particularly the larynx, are generally similar to those seen in their pulmonary counterparts, there are differences in nomenclature and also in the immuno-expression of some markers such as p53, TTf-1, and calcitonin. For example, investigators have called attention to the difficult diagnostic problem that may arise in distinguishing atypical carcinoid from medullary carcinoma of the thyroid. This problem is due in part to morphologic overlap and/or in part to similarities of their immunoreactivity patterns. A number of studies have addressed the issue [47].

A case in point is the study of a cohort of eight patients with atypical carcinoids of the larynx and 10 patients with medullary carcinoma of the thyroid by Hirsch and collaborators looking to define the usefulness of p53, TTF-1, and calcitonin in the distinction between these two neoplasms [47]. As would be expected and based on previous data, positive immunoreactivity to calcitonin was found in all cases of atypical laryngeal carcinoid tumors and in all cases of thyroid medullary carcinoma [47]. Weak, focal immunoreactivity for TTF-1 was observed in one of eight (13%) laryngeal atypical carcinoids whereas nine of ten (90%) medullary carcinomas were positive for this marker. P53 was positive in three of six (50%) laryngeal atypical carcinoids and three of 10 (30%) of medullary carcinomas of the thyroid [47]. These workers concluded that immunoreactivity for TTF-1 but not calcitonin or p53 may be helpful in distinguishing laryngeal atypical carcinoids and thyroid medullary carcinoma. In their conclusion, the authors further noted diffuse and/or strong TTF-1 immunoreactivity favored a diagnosis of primary thyroid medullary carcinoma over atypical carcinoid tumor of the larynx [47].

Akin to their pulmonary counterparts, atypical carcinoids of the upper airways are aggressive tumors with reported 5- and 10-year survival rates of 48% and 30%, respectively [3]. Metastases to cervical nodes is said to occur in up to 43% of cases [3].

Large Cell Neuroendocrine Carcinoma

Large cell neuroendocrine carcinomas are not common. In a large study from Japan, Takei and collaborators reported an overall frequency of 3.1% of all patients undergoing surgical resection for primary lung cancers [48]. As we will see below, the 2004 World Health Organization classification of tumors has laid out detailed histopathologic criteria needed for the diagnosis of this high-grade neoplasm. Large cell neuroendocrine carcinomas are tumors of middle-aged or elderly cigarette smokers, and are said to behave clinically as small cell carcinomas [49]. Large cell neuroendocrine carcinomas must be differentiated from large cell carcinomas with neuroendocrine features [50–52]. Both of these neoplasms are highly malignant and carry an unfavorable prognosis. However, the distinction between the two neoplasms is an important one since large cell neuroendocrine carcinomas are more aggressive in their clinical behavior and more likely to be treated with therapeutic regimens similar to those of small cell carcinoma while large cell carcinomas with neuroendocrine features are more likely to be treated surgically and in advanced cases with therapeutic regimens that are more appropriate for non-small cell carcinomas.

Radiographically, these tumors present as peripherally located nodular masses with highly irregular contours. In a study of 36 (33 men, three women) patients using high resolution CT of the chest, Akata and associates found only one tumor that was centrally located [53]. Mediastinal lymphadenopathy was found in 12 of the 36 patients. Frequent findings in the series included notching, calcifications, and pleural indentations. Cavitation of tumors was said to be infrequent [53]. The morphologic criteria for the diagnosis of large cell neuroendocrine carcinoma by the WHO classification of lung tumors are simple and straightforward. Essentially, for a tumor to be diagnosed as large cell neuroendocrine carcinoma, a tumor must have light microscopic features of neuroendocrine morphology, i.e., organoid patterns such as nesting, palisading, trabeculation, and/or rosette-like structures, plus a high mitotic rate (with counts of 11 mitoses or more per 10 high power fields) and extensive necrosis. (Fig. 8) In addition, such tumors must have strong immunoreactivity for at least one neuroendocrine marker (other than

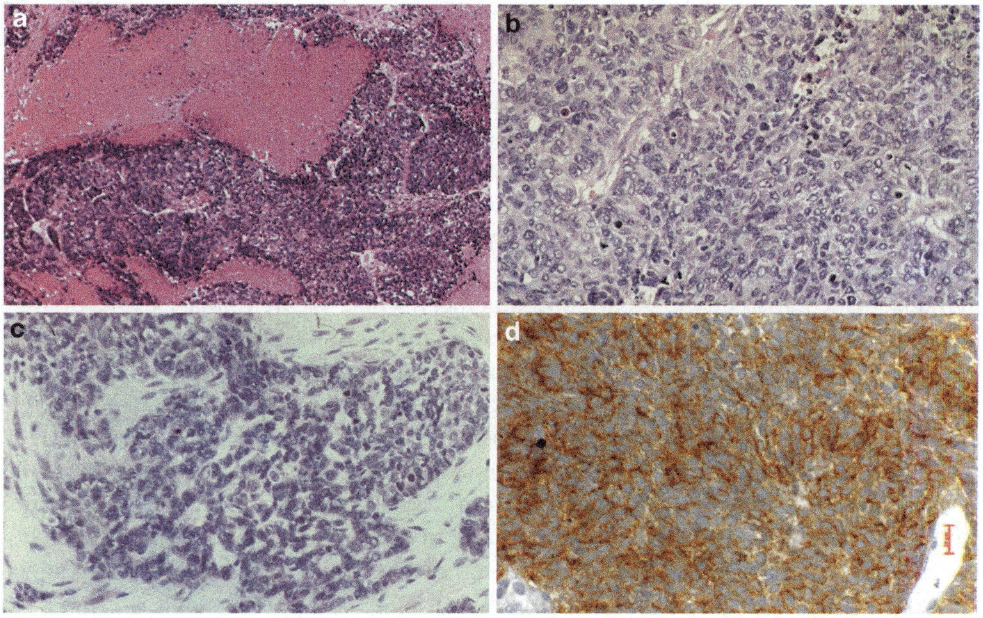

Fig. 8 Large cell neuroendocrine carcinoma, (**A–D**) (**A**) Low power view showing extensive tumor necrosis, (**B**) Note focal palisading of tumor cells in *left upper* quadrant, (**C**) An area showing resetting, (**D**) Strong immunoreactivity to N-CAM (CD56)

neuron-specific enolase). An immunohistochemical panel consisting of CD56, chromogranin, and synaptophysin used in our laboratory to characterize these tumors has been found useful in the majority of cases.

As noted, a tumor made up of large neoplastic cells and showing necrosis, high mitotic rate and immunoreactivity to neuroendocrine markers but not showing light microscopic evidence of organoid nesting, palisading, trabeculation, or rosette-like structures should be classified as a large cell carcinoma with neuroendocrine features and not as a large cell neuroendocrine carcinoma. Interestingly, the above histopathologic criteria for the diagnosis of large cell neuroendocrine carcinoma are also helpful in separating such tumors from atypical carcinoids and small cell carcinoma. At times, however, histopathology alone may not permit a definite diagnosis to be made. In these instances, ancillary testing may be of help. For instance, the distinction between typical and atypical carcinoids on one hand and between atypical carcinoids and higher-grade neuroendocrine carcinoma on the other can further be facilitated with the study of PAX-5 expression. In a study by Sica et al., PAX-5 expression was found in 78% of high-grade neuroendocrine carcinomas. In contrast, these investigators found that none of the 51 carcinoids in their series (both typical and atypical) expressed PAX-5 [54]. A well-studied marker in the diagnosis of gastrointestinal stromal tumors is C-kit. C-kit (CD117) has been found to be positive in large cell neuroendocrine carcinoma of lung, but only in 25% of the cases. Therefore, it appears to be of non-diagnostic value [55].

Large cell neuroendocrine carcinomas can occur in a "combined fashion" with classic small cell carcinoma. These combined tumors are known to have genetic alterations suggesting that divergent differentiation do not exclude a monoclonal origin from a common ancestor. In a study of 22 pulmonary endocrine tumors by D'Adda et al., six tumors were combined, eight were pure large cell carcinomas, and eight were pure small cell carcinomas [56]. In that study, the authors separately extracted DNA from each of the two cytologically different populations in the combined tumors. Allelic imbalance was investigated by PCR amplification of 30 highly polymorphic microsatellite markers located at 11 different chromosomal regions [56]. A common background of genetic alterations, similar in both components of the combined neoplasms was demonstrated at 17p123.1, 3p14.2–3p21.2, 4q24, 5q21, and 9p21 [56]. In fact, the authors noted two components in the combined tumors appeared to be more similar to each other than to their respective pure forms. In addition, the study showed allelic imbalances preferentially involving one of the two components [56]. These alterations often appeared to be specific for this histological variant, as compared with those observed in pure forms or in data obtained from the literature. These investigators concluded that the two phenotypic components of combined neuroendocrine had a significantly close genetic relationship to each other, supporting the notion of a tumor with a monoclonal origin from a common ancestor showing divergent differentiation [56].

Small Cell Carcinoma

Small cell carcinomas are defined by the 2004 World Health Organization Classification of Tumors as malignant epithelial tumors consisting of small cells with scant cytoplasm, poorly defined nuclear borders, finely granular nuclear chromatin, and absent or inconspicuous nucleoli [57]. Small cell carcinomas are known to represent about 25% of all major types of lung cancers and to account for a significant level of morbidity and mortality. Previous terms applied to these tumors such as oat cell carcinoma and small cell anaplastic carcinoma or small cell undifferentiated carcinoma are no longer recognized and their use is to be discouraged. Likewise, previous classification schemes dividing small cell carcinomas into various subtypes (such as intermediate, lymphocyte-like, and others) have failed to achieve prognostic significance and are no longer in use [58, 59]. Accordingly, at present time, only classic forms or combined forms with elements of either squamous carcinoma or adenocarcinoma or large cell carcinoma are recognized and in use today by most practicing pathologists. Hammar has indicated that in these combined tumors, the non-small cell component should comprise at least 10% of the entire tumor [11].

The published literature on small cell carcinoma of lung is massive. A recent search for PubMed access line yielded greater than 33,000 citations. This information overload has no doubt contributed to a greater understanding of the natural history, histopathology, cytogenetics, and management of this tumor. Yet, the overall morbility and mortality of small cell carcinoma remains exceedingly high, justifying the reputation of small cell carcinoma as one of the most lethal forms of cancers known to man. Small cell carcinoma is a disease of smoking older men and women who usually are in the sixth or seventh decade of life. Symptoms reflect the central location of these tumors [57]. Stridor and hemoptysis are comparatively rare while hoarseness and vocal cord paralysis are more common. In advanced cases, the symptoms are more apt to reflect disseminated disease such as bone marrow or liver metastases [57]. Paraneoplastic syndromes such as the Eaton–Lambert syndrome or the

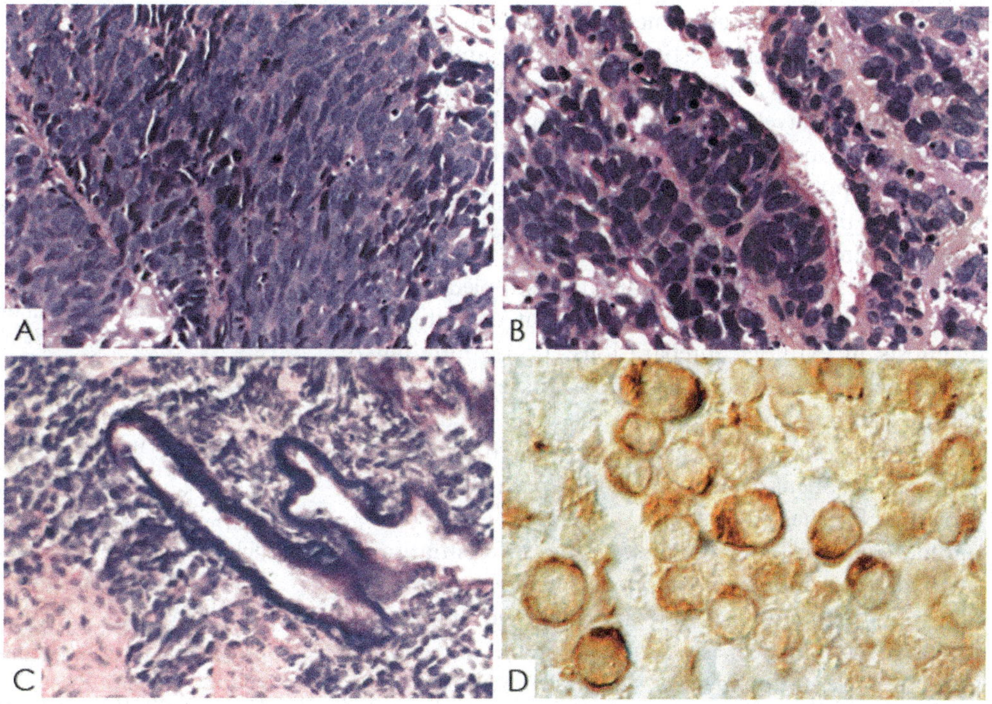

Fig. 9 Small cell carcinoma, (**A–D**) (**A**) Low power view. Note compact arrangement of somewhat spindly tumor cells, (**B**) Tumor cells invade ciliated respiratory epithelium, (**C**) DNA incrustation of small pulmonary venules, the "Azzopardi Effect," (**D**) Tumor cells showing immunoreactivity to pancytokeratin

Cushing syndrome are not commonly seen in patients with small cell carcinoma but in a small subset of patients, a paraneoplastic syndrome may actually precede the discovery of the lung tumor.

As is the case with squamous cell carcinomas, the majority of small cell carcinoma are centrally located but a small minority [60, 61] are peripherally located, mimicking spindle cell carcinoids. Centrally located small cell carcinomas tend to occlude the lumen of major airways and to grow to a large extent in the adjacent mediastinal structures. As a result, radiographic and CT studies of chest show relatively small lung tumors (at times inconspicuous) with relatively large mediastinal components. CT imaging is superior to conventional radiographs to detect mediastinal nodal involvement and involvement of the superior vena cava, a life threatening condition that may require immediate medical intervention [57].

Grossly, small cell carcinomas present as fleshy poorly outlined masses with specks of anthracotic pigment encircling airways and obliterating the underlying lung parenchyma. In their early stage, however, bronchial mucosal irregularities or loss of endobronchial longitudinal grooving may be the only gross manifestations. Despite the prevalence of necrosis (see below) and in contrast to squamous cell carcinomas, small cell carcinomas rarely undergo cavitation. This is an important and clinically relevant issue since it may assist the radiologist to fine tune the diagnosis of mass lesions in the lung.

Microscopically, individual cells of small cell carcinoma may have a variety of shapes and sizes including fusiform, polygonal, and even small round lymphocyte-like variants. Small cell carcinomas are high-grade neoplasms with mitotic rates exceeding those of atypical carcinoids, usually with greater than 11 mitoses per 10 high power fields [57]. Necrosis, crush artifact, and DNA smearing around small vessels (Azzopardi Effect) are characteristic but not pathognomonic of these tumors [62] (Fig. 9). This artifactual DNA smearing phenomenon is a reflection of increased cell fragility and can also be seen in lymphomas and other malignancies (see below). Crush DNA artifact is greater in biopsy samples as compared to samples from surgically resected cases. Areas affected by this DNA smearing are positive for the Feulgen reaction. Necrosis, when extensive may obscure the morphologic features of small cell carcinoma making the distinction from lymphomas and other small blue cell tumors difficult. In this regard, recent communications from investigators in the United Kingdom and other sites have called attention to the usefulness of CD56 and Ki-67 immunostaining [63, 64]. In most cases of biopsies with extensive DNA smearing this immunohistochemical marker in conjunction with lymphoid markers such as CD3, CD20, and CD45, and neuroendocrine markers such as chromogranin and synaptophysin (and low molecular cytokeratin) will facilitate the diagnosis.

The cytologic features of small cell carcinoma are unique. The tumor cells arrange themselves in clusters, often linear. Despite their name, the tumor cells are two to three times the size of a resting lymphocyte and typically have a very limited amount of cytoplasm. Morphometric studies in past have shown that considerable nuclear size overlap exists between "small cells" and "large cells" in high-grade pulmonary neuroendocrine carcinomas [65] suggesting that estimation of cell size is not always a useful adjunct in diagnosis. The nuclear chromatin is "salt and pepper" as a reflection of its stippled distribution, a useful feature that when present contributes to diagnosis in cytologic preparations. Loose molding of neighboring cells is another important cytopathologic feature that in combination with the other cited features may allow the cytopathologic diagnosis to be made in sputum specimens or cytological preparations such as bronchial brushes or washings.

One problem that may arise is the differentiation of small cell carcinoma from poorly differentiated squamous cell carcinoma. Aside morphologic similarities, extensive tumor necrosis, crush artifact, and limited tumor representation in tissue samples contribute to making this distinction a difficult one. Zhang et al. studied 28 cases of small cell carcinoma and an equal number of poorly differentiated squamous cell carcinoma with a panel of antibodies that included p63, TTF-1, and a high molecular weight cytokeratin [66]. In their study, the authors found that 93% of the small cell carcinomas showed TTF-1 immunoreactivity and no staining for p63 or high molecular weight cytokeratin. In contrast, 95% of the cases of poorly differentiated squamous cell carcinoma showed no TTF-1 positivity and strong positivity for p63 and high molecular weight cytokeratin [66]. The authors concluded that this panel of antibodies is highly effective in making the distinction between these two tumors [66]. Another consideration is the distinction between lymphoma and small carcinomas, particularly in the case of carcinomas with a lymphocyte-like morphology. In this instance, a basic panel of immunostain that includes CD45 and CD56 is generally helpful.

References

1. Oberndorfer S. (1907) Karzinoide Tumoren des diinndarms. Frankfurt Zeitschr Pathol 1:426–432.
2. World Health Organization Classification of Tumors. (2004) Pathology and Genetics of Tumours of the Lung, Pleura, Thymus and Heart. In: WD Travis, E Brambila, HK Müller-Hermelink and CC Harris, Eds. Pathology and Genetics, Head and Neck Tumours. IARC Press. Lyon.
3. L Barnes. (2005) Neuroendocrine Tumors. In: L Barnes, JW Eveson, P Reichart and D Sidransky, Eds. World Health Organization Classification of Tumours. Pathology and Genetics. Head and Neck Tumours. IARC Press. Lyon, pp. 135–139.
4. Soga J, Ferlito A, Rinaldo A. (2004) Endocrine carcinomas (Carcinoids and their variants of the larynx): A comparative consideration with those of other sites. Oral Oncol 40:668–672.
5. El-Naggar AK, Batsakis JG. (1991) Carcinoid tumor of the larynx: A critical review of the literature. ORL J Otorhinolaryngol Relat Spec 53:188–193.
6. Aguayo SM, Miller YE, Waldron JA et al. (1992) Brief report: Idiopathic diffuse hyperplasia of pulmonary neuroendocrine cells and airways disease. NEJM 18:1285–1288.
7. Kerr KM and Fraire AE 2008. Ch 34. Preinvasive Disease. In: JF Tomshefski, PT Cagle, C Farver and AE Fraire, Eds. Dail and Hammar Pulmonary Pathology, 3rd Ed. Springer. New York Berlin Heidelberg, pp. 158–215.
8. Feyrter F. (1938) Ueber diffuse endokrine epitheliate organe. Zentralbl Inn Med 59:545–561.
9. Gould VE, Dellelis RA. (1983) The neuroendocrine cell system: Its tumors, hyperplasia and dysplasia. In: SG Silverberg, Ed. Principles and Practice of Surgical Pathology. Wiley. New York, 1:488–1501.
10. Pearse AGE. (1969) The cytochemistry and ultrastructure of polypeptide hormone-producing cells of the APUD series and the embryologic, physiologic and pathologic implications of this concept. J Histochem Cytochem 17:303–313.
11. Boers JE, den Brok JLM, Koudtaal J et al. (1996) Number and proliferation of neuroendocrine cells in normal human airway epithelium. Am J Respir Crit Care Med 154:758–763.
12. Hammar SP. (1993) Ch 32 Common Neoplasms. In: DH Dail and SP Hammar, Eds. Pulmonary Pathology 2nd Ed. Springer-Verlag. Berlin New York Heidelberg, pp. 1123–1278.
13. Gould VE, Moll R, Moll I, Lee I, Franke WW. (1985) Neuroendocrine (Merkel) cells of the skin: hyperplasias, dysplasias and neoplasms. Lab Invest 52:334–353.
14. Hasleton PS, Curry A. (1996) Anatomy of the lung. In: P.S. Hasleton, Ed. Spencer's Pathology of the Lung. Fifth Ed. McGraw-Hill, New York, St. Louis, San Francisco, pp. 1–44.
15. Said JW, Vimadalal S, Nash G, et al. (1985) Immunoreactive neuron-specific enolase, bombesin, and chromogranin as markers for neuroendocrine lung tumors. Hum Pathol 16:236–240.
16. Connor DT, Deftos LJ. (1986) Secretion of chromogranin A by peptide-producing endocrine neoplasms. N Engl J Med 314:1145–1151.
17. Armas OA, White DA, Erlandson RA et al. (1995) Diffuse idiopathic pulmonary neuroendocrine cell proliferation presenting as interstitial lung disease. Amer J Surg Pathol 19:963–970.
18. Brown MJ, English J, Müller NL. (1997) Bronchiolitis obliterans due to neuroendocrine hyperplasia. CT-pathologic correlation. Am J Roentgenol 168:1561–1562.
19. Lee JS, Brown KK, Cool C, Lynch DA. (2002) Diffuse pulmonary cell hyperplasia: Radiologic and clinical features. J Comput Assist Tomogr 26:180–184.
20. Sheerin N, Harrison NK, Sheppard MN et al. (1995) Obliterative bronchiolitis caused by multiple tumourlets and microcarcinoids successfully treated by single lung transplantation. Thorax 50,207–209.
21. Gosney JR. (2004) Diffuse idiopathic pulmonary neuroendocrine cell hyperplasia as a precursor to pulmonary neuroendocrine tumors. Chest 125:108S.
22. Whitwell F. (1955) Tumourlets of the lung. J Pathol Bact 70:529–541.
23. Churg A, Warnock ML. (1976) Pulmonary tumorlet. A form of peripheral carcinoid. Cancer 37:1469–1477.
24. Gmelich JT, Bensch KG, Liebow AA. (1967) Cells of Kulchitsky type in bronchioles and their relation to the origin of peripheral carcinoid tumours. Lab Invest 17:88–98.
25. Pelosi IG, Zancanaro C, Sbubo L, Bresaola E, Martignoni G, Bontempini L. (1992) Development of innumerable neuroendocrine

tumorlets in pulmonary lobe scarred by intralobar sequestration: Immunohistochemical and ultrastructural study of an unusual case. Arch Pathol Lab Med 116:1167–1174.
26. Neuroendocrine neoplasms. (1999) Ch 32 In: RS Fraser, N Colman, NL Müller and PD Paré, Eds. Fraser and Paré's Diagnosis of Diseases of the Chest, 4th Ed. WB Saunders, Philadelphia, London, Toronto, pp. 1229–1261.
27. Hausman DH, Weimann RB. (1967) Pulmonary tumourlet with hilar lymph node metastases. Cancer 20:1515–1519.
28. D'Agati VD, Perzin KH. (1985) Carcinoid tumorlets of the lung with metastasis to a periobronchial lymph node. Report of a case and review of the literature. Cancer 55:2472–2476.
29. Cohen AJ, King TE, Gilman LB et al. (1998) High expression of neutral endopeptidase in idiopathic diffuse hyperplasia of pulmonary neuroendocrine cells. Am J Respir Crit Care Med 158:1593–1599.
30. Beasley M, Thunnissen FB, Hasleton PhS et al. (2004) Carcinoid tumour. In: WD, Brambilla AE, Müller-Hermelink HK and Harris CC, Eds. Pathology and genetics of tumours of the lung, pleura, thymus and heart. Travis. IARC Press, Lyon, pp. 59–62.
31. Ranchod M, Levine GD. (1980) Spindle cell carcinoid tumors of the lung: a clinicopathologic study of 35 cases. Am J Surg Pathol 4:315–331.
32. Abdi EA, Goel R, Bishop S et al. (1988) Peripheral carcinoid tumours of the lung. A clinicopathologic study. J Surg Oncol 39:190–196.
33. Klemen H, Smolle-Jüttner FM, Popper HH. 1994 Morphologic and immunohistochemical study of typical and atypical carcinoids of the lung, on the basis of 55 cases with clinical correlation of a new classification. Endocrine-Related Cancer 1:53–62.
34. Moran CA, Suster S. (2000) Neuroendocrine Carcinomas: In: CDM Fletcher, Ed. Diagnostic Histopathology of Tumors, 2nd Ed. Churchill Livingstone. London Edinburgh New York, pp. 176–179.
35. Mark EJ, Quay SC, Dickersin GR. (1981) Papillary carcinoid tumor of the lung. Cancer (Philadelphia) 48:316–324.
36. Ghadially FN, Block HJ. (1985) Oncocytic carcinoid of the lung. J Submicrosc Cytol 17:435–442.
37. Gaffey MJ, Mills SE, Frierson HF Jr, et al. (1998) Pulmonary clear cell carcinoid tumor; another entity in the differential diagnosis of pulmonary clear cell neoplasia. Am J Surg Pathol 22:1020–1025.
38. Bonikos DS, Bensch KG, Jamplis RW. (1976) Peripheral pulmonary carcinoid tumours. Cancer 37:1977–1998.
39. Okike N, Bernatz PE, Woolner LB. (1976) Carcinoid tumors of the lung. Ann Thorac Surg 22:270–275.
40. Beasley MB. (2008) Part 7, Atypical Carcinoids. In: PT Cagle Chief, Ed. Color Atlas and text of pulmonary pathology. The Wolters Kluwer Co. Philadelphia, Baltimore, New York, pp. 58–59.
41. Kaufmann O, Dietel M. (2000) Expression of thyroid transcription factor-1 in pulmonary and extrapulmonary small cell carcinomas and other neuroendocrine carcinomas of various primary sites. Histopathology 36:415–420.
42. Fukayama M, Furukawa E, Shiozawa Y et al. (1990) Atypical endocrine granules in atypical endocrine tumor (AET) of the lung. Acta Pathol Jpn 40:361–366.
43. Ullmann R, Petzmann S, Klemen H et al. (2002) The position of lung carcinoids within the spectrum of neuoendocrine tumors of the lung and other tissues. Genes Chromosomes Cancer 34:78–85.
44. Arrigoni MG, Woolner LB, Bernatz PE. (1972) Atypical carcinoid tumors of the lung. J Thorac Cardiovasc Surg 64:413–421.
45. Warren WH, Gould VE. (1990) Long term follow-up of clinical bronchial carcinoid tumors: Clinicopathologic Observations. Scand. J. Thorac Cardiovasc Surg 24:125–130.
46. Slodkowska J, Langfort R, Rudzinski P et al. (1998) Typical and atypical carcinoids – Pathologic and clinical analysis of 77 cases. Pneumol Alergol Pol 66:297–303.
47. Hirsch MS, Faquin WC, Krane JF (2004) Thyroid transcription factor – 1 but not p53 is helpful in distinguishing moderately differentiated neuroendocrine carcinoma of the larynx from medullary carcinoma of the thyroid. Modern Pathol 17:631–636.
48. Takei H, Asamura H, Maeshima A et al. (2002) Large cell neuroendocrine carcinoma of the lung: Clinicopathologic study of eighty seven cases. J Thorac Cardiovasc Surg 124:285–292.
49. Pathology of the Lungs. (2000) Corrin B, Editor in Chief. Churchill Livingstone, London Edinburgh, New York, pp. 479–480.
50. Visscher DW, Zarbo RJ, Trojanowski JW, Sakr W, Crissman JD. (1990) Neuroendocrine differentiation in poorly differentiated lung carcinomas. A light microscopic and immunohistologic study. Mod Pathol 3:508–512.
51. Wick M, Berg L, Hertz M. (1992) Large cell carcinoma of the lung with neuroendocrine differentiation. A comparison with large cell "undifferentiated" pulmonary tumors. Am J Clin Pathol 97:796–805.
52. Travis WD. (2004) The concept of pulmonary neuroendocrine tumours. In: WD Travis, E. Brambilla, HK Müller-Hermelink and CC Harris, Eds. World Health Organization Classification of Lung Tumours. Pathology and Genetics of Tumours of the Lung, Pleura, Thymus and Heart. IARC Press, Lyon, pp. 19–20.
53. Akata S, Okada S, Maeda J et al. (2007) Computed tomographic findings in large cell neuroendocrine carcinoma of the lung. Clin Imaging 31:379–384.
54. Sica G, Vasquez MF, Altorki N et al. (2008) PAX-5 expression in pulmonary neuroendocrine carcinomas: its usefulness in surgical and fine-needle aspiration biopsy specimens. Am J Clin Pathol 129:556–562.
55. Butnor KJ, Burchette JL, Sporn TA et al. (2004) The spectrum of c-kit (CD117) immunoreactivity in lung and pleural tumors: A study of 96 cases using a single source antibody with a review of the literature. Arch Pathol Lab Med 128:538–543.
56. D'Adda T, Pelosi G, Lagrasta C et al. (2008) Genetic alterations in combined neuroendocrine neoplasms of the lung. Mod Pathol 21:414–422.
57. Travis W, Nicholson S, Hirsch FR et al. (2004) Small Cell Carcinoma. In: WD Travis, E Brambilla, HK Müller-Hermelink and CC Harris, Eds. World Health Organization Classification of Tumours. Pathology and Genetics of Tumours of the Lung, Pleura, Thymus and Heart. IARC Press Lyon, pp. 31–34.
58. Hirsch FR, Matthews MJ, Aisner S, et al. (1988) Histopathologic classification of small cell lung cancer: changing concepts and terminology. Cancer 62:973–977.
59. Fraire AE, Johnson EH, Yesner R, Zhang XB, Spjut HJ, Greenberg SD. (1992) Prognostic significance of histopathologic subtype and stage in small cell lung cancer. Hum Pathol 23:520–528.
60. Mark EJ, Ramirez JF. (1985) Peripheral small-cell carcinoma of the lung resembling carcinoid tumor: A clinical and pathologic study of 14 cases. Arch Pathol Lab Med 109:263–269.
61. Kreisman H, Wolkove N, Quoix E. (1992) Small cell lung cancer presenting as a solitary pulmonary nodule. Chest 101:225–229.
62. Azzopardi JG (1959) Oat cell carcinoma of the bronchus. J Pathol Bacteriol 78:513–519.
63. Kontogiannis K, Nicholson AG, Butcher D et al. (2005) CD 56: A useful tool for the diagnosis of small cell lung carcinomas on biopsies with extensive crush artifact. J Clin Pathol 58:978–980.

64. Aslan DL, Gulbahce HE, Pambuccian SE et al. (2005) Ki-67 immunoreactivity in the differential diagnosis of pulmonary neuroendocrine neoplasms in specimens with extensive crush artifact. Am J Clin Pathol 123:874–878.
65. Marchevsky AM, Gal AA, Shah S, et al. (2001) Morphometry confirms the presence of considerable nuclear size overlap between "small cells" and "large cells" in high-grade pulmonary neuroendocrine neoplasms. Am J Clin Pathol 116:466–472.
66. Zhang H, Liu J, Cagle PT et al. (2005) Distinction of pulmonary small cell carcinoma from poorly differentiated squamous cell carcinoma: An immunohistochemical approach. Modern Pathol 18:111–118.

Neuroendocrine Tumors of the Pancreas

Runjan Chetty

Abstract This is an overview that incorporates the recommended nomenclature, classification, immunohistochemistry, precursor lesions, and pathologic types of pancreatic neuroendocrine tumors. In addition, both sporadic and inherited forms together with the relevant genetics are highlighted.

Keywords Pancreatic neuroendocrine tumor • Islet hyperplasia • Islet cell dysplasia • Nesidioblastosis • Multiple endocrine neoplasia (MEN)

Introduction

The term "karzinoid" (carcinoid) was introduced by Oberndorfer based on his observation of peculiar tumors ("little carcinomas") in the small intestine. Other names used for this entity include APUDoma and islet cell tumor/adenoma.

Use of the term carcinoid has become entrenched in the medical literature and has been applied to different entities by pathologists and clinicians. Some pathologists label all tumors with neuroendocrine features "carcinoid," while some clinicians restrict the use of the term carcinoid to the so-called carcinoid syndrome, due to a serotonin-producing tumor. It is also known that a carcinoid in one site is not equivalent to a similar tumor in another site within the gastrointestinal tract (GIT). Originally thought to be benign, it is now known that the full histopathological spectrum from very low-grade to high-grade malignancy can be encountered within this family of tumors.

R. Chetty (✉)
Professor of Pathology, Director of Surgical Pathology, University Health Network/Toronto Medical Laboratories, Department of Laboratory Medicine and Pathobiology, University of Toronto, Toronto, Canada
e-mail: runjan.chetty@uhn.on.ca

Should they be called endocrine or neuroendocrine cells/tumors? The cells of the dispersed endocrine system and their tumors that occur in the GIT share several antigens with nerve elements such as neuron-specific enolase (NSE), protein gene product 9.5 (PGP 9.5), chromogranin A, B, and C, and synaptophysin. It is for this reason that "neuroendocrine" is the preferred designation and the term "neuroendocrine tumor" (NET) will be used in this chapter.

There are at least 15 discrete neuroendocrine cell types distributed throughout the GIT and these cells are the progenitors of the characteristic tumors that form the rubric of neuroendocrine tumors of the gastroenteropancreatic (GEP) tract.

Pancreatic neuroendocrine tumors (PNET) have been associated with a certain mystique despite their somewhat obvious and easily recognizable clinical and pathologic manifestations. Perhaps it is the syndromic clinical scenario and its infrequency that has intensified fascination amongst pathologists and clinicians alike, and has ensured that PNETs have come under closer scrutiny of late, especially in terms of molecular pathogenesis.

Incidence

It has been estimated that the incidence of PNETs is 0.4–1 per 100,000 people [1–4]. Autopsy surveys have shown the incidence to range from 0% to 10% of autopsies depending on the thoroughness of sectioning and sampling of the pancreas [5, 6]. In a surgical series, PNETs were found to account for about 15% of pancreatic neoplasms [7, 8].

PNETs are encountered in adults and the vast majority occurs in patients over the age of 30 years [9]. Clinically, there are functioning and nonfunctioning PNETs depending on whether clinical symptoms due to hormone/peptide production are present or not. Immunohistochemically detected peptides within a tumor do not necessarily equate

A. Khan (ed.), *Surgical Pathology of Endocrine and Neuroendocrine Tumors*, Current Clinical Pathology,
DOI 10.1007/978-1-60327-396-1_11, © Humana Press, a part of Springer Science+Business Media, LLC 2009

to clinically functional tumors. Distinct functional states have been ascribed to PNETs depending on the dominant hormone that is produced and the associated clinical symptoms (Table 1). These may be due to excess of gastrin (Zollinger-Ellison syndrome), insulin, vasoactive intestinal peptide (VIP), glucagon, somatostatin, growth hormone releasing hormone (GHRH), adrenocorticotrophic hormone (ACTH), 5-hydroxy tryptamine or serotonin (carcinoid syndrome), parathyroid hormone-related peptide (PTHrP), and calcitonin. Of the functional tumors, some controversy exists as to whether insulin- or gastrin-producing tumors are commoner. Some studies suggest that the former account for the majority of PNETs (range: 46–85%) [9, 10], whilst others are of the opinion that the gastrin-producing tumors are most frequently encountered [11–15]. Overall, nonfunctioning tumors are commoner than the functional ones [4].

Table 1 Classification of Gastroenteropancreatic Endocrine Cells and Tumors

Hormone	Cell type	Clinical syndrome
Insulin	β	Hypoglycemia
Glucagon/GLP's	α	Diabetes Mellitus; Skin Rash
Somatostatin	δ	Somatostatinoma Syndrome
Gastrin	γ	Zollinger-Ellison Syndrome
Pancreatic Polypeptide	PP	
Vasoactive Intestinal Peptide (VIP)	?	Verner-Morrison Syndrome
Secretin	σ	WDHA ("Pancreatic Cholera")
Prostaglandins	?	? WDHA
Serotonin	EC	Carcinoid Syndrome
Cholecystokinin (CCK)	?	
ACTH/MSH;CRH	?	Cushing's Syndrome
Vasopressin	?	Diabetes Insipidus
Growth hormone-releasing hormone (GRH); growth hormone (GH)	?	Acromegaly
Parathyroid hormone-related peptide	?	Hypercalcemia

Histogenesis/Origin

The concept of a totipotential stem cell within ductules as a progenitor of both exocrine and endocrine cells is now well established and generally accepted. In addition, it is thought that both exocrine and endocrine pancreatic tissue can be derived from preexisting, differentiated exocrine and endocrine cells. This observation is based on experimental models that demonstrate regeneration of both exocrine and endocrine pancreas from existing cells and regenerating ductules [16]. A slightly opposing view has been proposed based on studies in transgenic mice that develop PNETs [17]; in these models it appears that endocrine tumors develop from mature endocrine cells located within preexisting islets of Langerhans. It is therefore likely that there is more than one source of origin for PNETs: arising from totipotential stem cells and differentiated, mature endocrine cells, that it is a multi-step process of genetic alterations with tumor cell proliferation mediated by growth factors including insulin-like growth factor-1 (IGF-1) [18].

Pathology

The gross and microscopic appearances of PNETs are well characterized and detailed descriptions are available, especially in some of the recently written textbooks [1, 2]. However, there are a few associated entities that are worth highlighting.

Islet Hyperplasia

In islet hyperplasia the size and shape of normal islets of Langerhans varies (Fig. 1). Whilst the most recognizable islet is spherical or round, more elongated or "arching" islets are also described [1]. The size of islets varies from 50 to 150 μm in newborns and from 50 to 250 μm in adults. Thus, islets larger than 250 μm but less than 0.5 mm are regarded as hyperplastic islets. Lesions 0.5–5 mm in diameter are considered microadenomas.

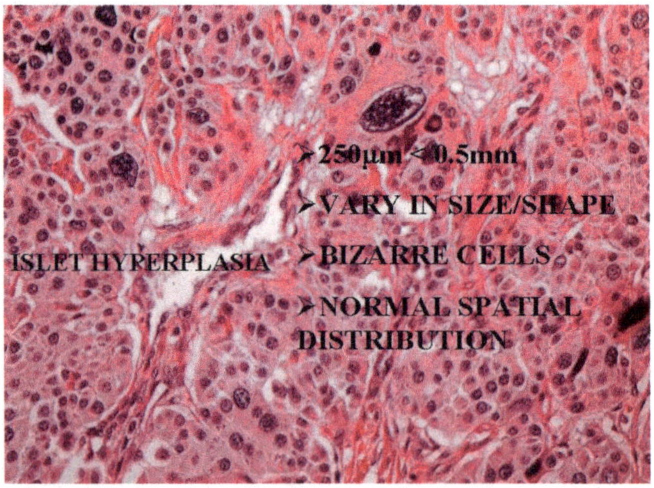

Fig. 1 Islet hyperplasia is typified morphologically by variation in size and shape of the islets together with the presence of occasional large bizarre cell. (H&E× 400)

Islet hyperplasia is considered to be an increase in volume density of the endocrine component that is accomplished by increase in both islet size and islet number. This condition has been encountered in a diverse range of conditions and has even been documented in asymptomatic patients with normal pancreatic function. Some of the discrepancies may be explained by failure to recognize the important differences in islet mass in the various parts of the pancreas; islet mass in the tail is greater than that in the body and head of the organ, and there are regional differences in cell distribution, with more PP cells in the islets of the uncinate process. Conditions that have been associated with islet hyperplasia include: α-1 anti-trypsin deficiency, hyperinsulinism, Zollinger-Ellison syndrome, Verner-Morrison syndrome, maternal diabetes, erythroblastosis fetalis, acquired immunodeficiency syndrome (AIDS), Simpson-Golabi-Behmel syndrome, hereditary tyrosinemia of hepatorenal type, Zellweger's cerebrohepatorenal syndrome, leprechaunism, and Beckwith-Wiedemann syndrome [19].

Microscopy of islet hyperplasia reveals large islets that vary in size and shape and exhibit a degree of coalescence. Within the islets there is retention of the spatial arrangement and distribution of the four main endocrine cell types. Markedly enlarged, bizarre β cells are sometimes encountered, especially in cases of neonatal nesidioblastosis.

Islet Dysplasia

See Fig. 2. La Rosa and colleagues highlighted three characteristic features of islet dysplasia [19]:

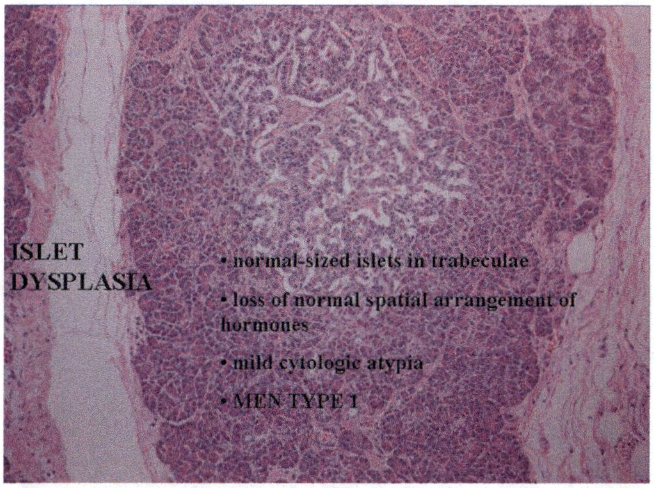

Fig. 2 Islet dysplasia, on the other hand, is composed of more uniform islets with a trabecular arrangement. However, there is loss of the normal spatial arrangement of the constituent hormones with one often dominating. (H&E× 200)

i) normal-sized or slightly enlarged islets with cells often arranged in trabeculae,
ii) loss of the normal spatial and quantitative arrangement of the four main cell types with altered dominance of one cell type, and
iii) mild cytologic atypia.

Once islet dysplasia attains a size of 0.5 mm, it is called microadenoma [1]. Islet dysplasia is most frequently associated with multiple endocrine neoplasia (MEN) type 1.

Nesidioblastosis

The definition of nesidioblastosis, in the broadest sense, is the occurrence of endocrine cells often in clusters, intimately associated with pancreatic ductules, and forming so-called ductulo-insular complexes. Often associated with this is so-called endocrine cell "mal-distribution" or islet hyperplasia with prominent, hypertrophic, bizarre, β-cells resulting in hyperinsulinemic hypoglycemia [20]. The term "nesidioblastosis" was coined in 1938 by Laidlaw to describe the phenomenon of islet cells originating from pancreatic duct epithelium [21]. The term has embryologic roots in that the same phenomenon or process occurs during embryonic or fetal life. After 10–11 weeks of gestation, endocrine cells can be seen budding off from pancreatic duct epithelium and then proliferating to form the islets of Langerhans [22]. Thus, nesidioblastosis is a reflection of this particular embryologic event, but the term has also been used to describe islet hyperplasia. The frequent coexistence of ductulo-insular complexes and islet hyperplasia and the overlap of conditions in which both have been described (alone or together such as MEN type 1, chronic pancreatitis), lends to the concept that they are part of the same spectrum of lesions. From a purist's point of view, nesidioblastosis is the presence of endocrine cells budding off from pancreatic ductule epithelium, a condition that is seen in many pancreatic conditions, including chronic pancreatitis with ductular proliferation.

Unusual Histopathological Appearances

The vast majority of PNETs confirm to the typical neuroendocrine pattern with the well-recognized "zellballen" or packeted arrangement evident (Fig. 3). Equally commonly seen is a trabecular pattern. (Pseudo)-glandular or acinar (Fig. 4) and mixed patterns of the aforementioned types are also frequently seen. The cells have readily

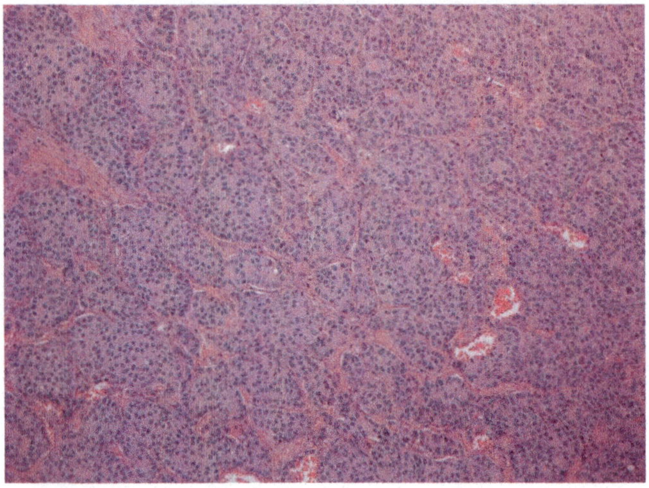

Fig. 3 The classic pattern of a neuroendocrine tumor with nests of uniform cells surrounded by a fibrovascular stroma. (H&E× 100)

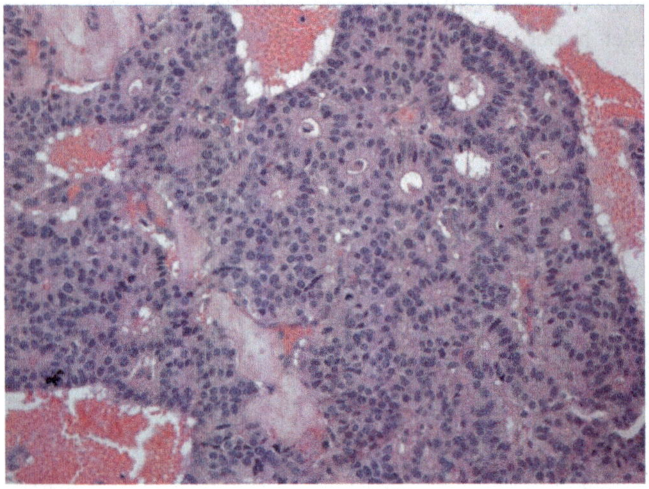

Fig. 4 A micro-acinar/pseudo-glandular pattern that often causes confusion with an acinar cell carcinoma. (H&E× 200)

recognizable cytological features: round-to-ovoid cells with eosinophilic, slightly granular cytoplasm and nuclei with a dispersed chromatin pattern ("salt and pepper") and not infrequently, discernible nucleoli. Ancillary findings such as intracytoplasmic hyaline globules, nuclear pseudo-inclusions, and associated amyloidosis are also seen. Variations in both cell morphology and pattern have been well described.

Less commonly, cystic, papillary, and so-called angiomatoid/angiomatous patterns may also be seen. The presence of calcification is sometimes noted (Fig. 5) and when psammomatous in nature in duodenal NET, it is diagnostic of a duodenal somatostatin-producing NET.

The constituent cells may have abundant granular eosinophilic cytoplasm due to accumulation of mitochondria

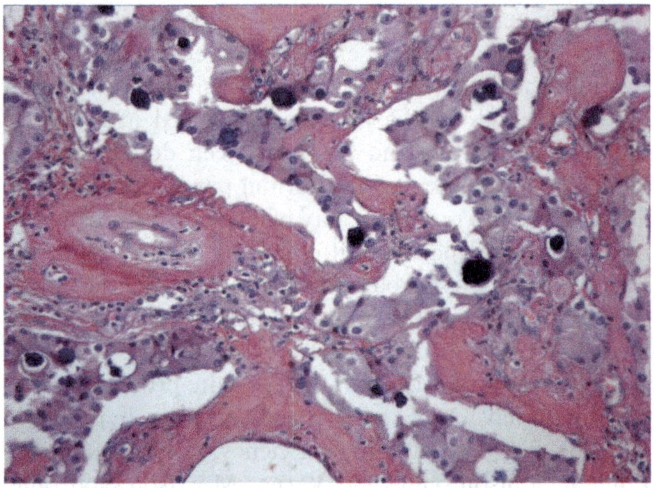

Fig. 5 Somatostatin-producing pancreatic neuroendocrine tumor containing psammoma bodies. Usually they are less frequently seen in pancreatic tumors as compared to periampullary tumors. (H&E× 400)

resulting in an oncocytic/oxyphilic appearance (Fig. 6) or the tumor cells may be spindle shaped, have a clear or finely vacuolated cytoplasm, be large and pleomorphic, sometimes with multiple nuclei or so-called rhabdoid (Fig. 7). The latter cell has a characteristic appearance that is due to collapse of the cytoskeleton (misfolded proteins) with formation of aggresomes, which are perinuclear in location, often displace the nucleus peripherally and appear as deeply eosinophilic globules in the cytoplasm. Another morphological variant is a PNET with ductules. This is not a mixed neuroendocrine-epithelial tumor but a NET with ductules that are either entrapped as the tumour

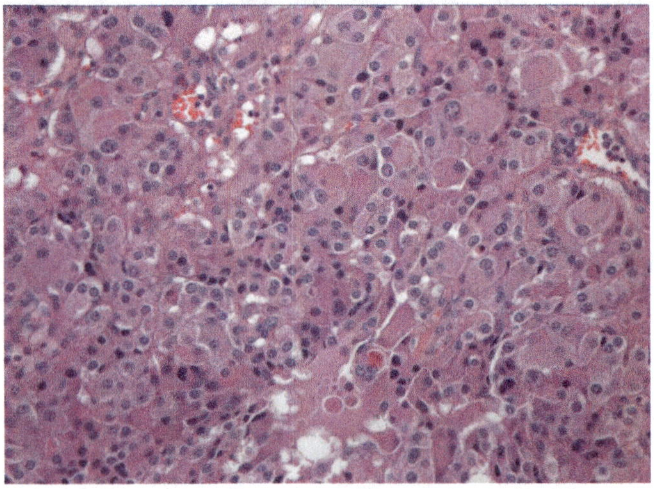

Fig. 6 An oncocytic neuroendocrine tumor composed of eosinophilic cells that also harbor hyaline globules within the cytoplasm. (H&E× 400)

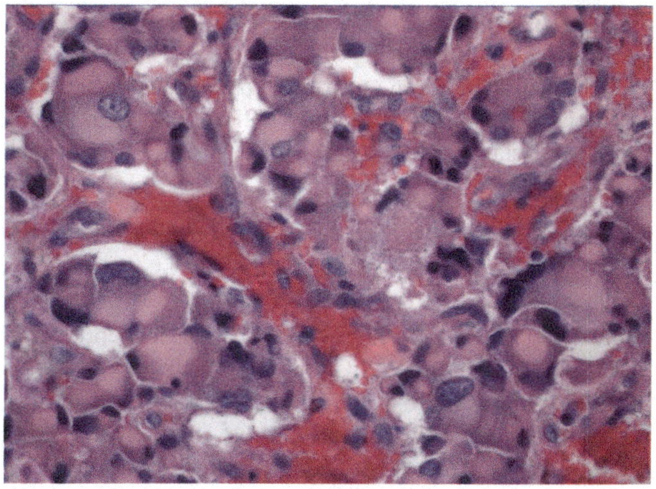

Fig. 7 Very characteristic "rhabdoid" cells have distinct cytoplasmic paranuclear aggregations of intermediate filaments. (H&E× 400)

grows into surrounding normal pancreatic tissue or as a result of secondary ductular proliferation occurring as a reactive phenomenon.

Immunohistochemistry

These lesions are readily classified by the immunohistochemical localization of common markers of neuroendocrine differentiation. They almost uniformly stain for synaptophysin, a 38 kd molecular weight molecule that is associated with synaptic vesicles of neurons and neuroendocrine cells. It is a small vesicle-associated marker. Most PNET stain for chromogranin, a large secretory granule-associated marker. There are two families of chromogranins, A and B; to appropriately classify these lesions one needs to identify both chromogranins. Moreover, chromogranin immunoreactivity is directly related to the number of secretory granules that may be scarce in some tumors that are poorly differentiated or those that rapidly secrete their hormone product without storing it in significant amounts. Other markers of neuroendocrine differentiation include CD57 (Leu-7), neural cell adhesion molecule (NCAM; CD56), neuron-specific enolase (NSE), and protein gene product 9.5 (PGP 9.5) that stain variable subpopulations of endocrine lesions and some, such as NCAM and NSE stain some non-endocrine tumors as well.

The structure-function correlations of these lesions are best defined by their immunoreactivity for specific peptide hormones. Those associated with clinical symptoms and predictive of biological behavior are the most important to evaluate and are listed in Table 1. In most laboratories the panel of antisera available for characterization of hormone production is limited, however, at a minimum, these lesions should be examined for production of the eutopic hormones; insulin, glucagon, somatostatin, pancreatic polypeptide, as well as for the important common ectopic substances; gastrin and VIP.

Often times, the functional status and clinical symptoms of the patient will determine specific markers done in a particular case. Included in the baseline work-up of PNET is Ki-67, as the Ki-67 index separates benign, well-differentiated NET (<2%) from those of uncertain behavior (>2%).

Other markers that are available include

1. Neuroendocrine secretory protein-55 (NESP-55): this protein is a 241 amino acid polypeptide that belongs to the chromogranin family and is thus located within large dense core secretory granules. The value of NESP-55 lies in its ability to stain PNET (in addition to pheochromocytomas), whilst GIT NET are negative.
2. Somatostatin receptors: somatostatin analogs have been used in the treatment of clinically apparent GEP NET. Five somatostatin receptors have been identified. Several NET express somatostatin receptors, but up to 90% of serotonin- and gastrin-producing NET of the distal jejunum and ileum, and about 60% of insulin-producing PNET are positive for receptors 2 and 5.
3. CDX-2: is a homeobox gene that is essential for intestinal development and differentiation. Approximately 80% of GIT NET are CDX-2 positive, especially those occurring in the ileum and appendix. NET occurring in the stomach tend to be CDX-2 negative.
4. Histidine decarboxylase: expression occurs in most NE cells but PNET are most frequently positive for this marker.

Hereditary Forms of PNET

Multiple Endocrine Neoplasia (MEN) Syndrome, Type 1

This is an autosomal dominant condition and affected individuals show 94% penetrance with manifestation of associated pathology by the age of 50 years [25]. There are germline mutations of the *MEN-1* tumor suppressor gene located on chromosome 11q13 and consequent loss of a 610 amino acid nuclear protein, menin, which suppresses cell proliferation [26]. Hereditary PNETs occur in more than 60% of patients with MEN-1 [27, 28]. Patients usually manifest primary hyperparathyroidism before pancreatic lesions [29]. MEN-1 involvement of the pancreas is in the form of multiple, small, nonfunctioning benign PNETs, often microadenomas, associated with foci of nesidioblastosis. If a functional tumor occurs, 50% will be gastrin-producing and 20% insulin-producing tumors. It is worth remembering that in MEN-1, duodenal gastrin-producing tumors are more common than those arising in the pancreas. In contrast to sporadic PNETs, those associated with MEN-1 tend to present at an earlier age, have a higher rate of post-operative recurrence and are a common cause of death in these patients [28].

Von Hippel-Lindau Disease

Von Hippel-Lindau (VHL) disease is an autosomal dominant condition due to deletions or mutations in a tumor suppressor gene located on chromosome 3p25.5 [29]. The disease profile is typified by retinal and central nervous system hemangioblastomas, cysts in the kidney, epididymis (papillary cystadenoma) and liver, hemangiomas of the adrenal, liver and lung, renal cell carcinoma, pheochromocytoma, and endolymphatic sac tumors. Pancreatic pathology in VHL is usually in the form of benign cysts and serous microcystic adenomas, which occur in 35–70% of VHL patients [30–33]. The frequency of pancreatic endocrine tumors, on the other hand, is less common and encountered in only 2–12% of patients [32–35].

Neuroendocrine tumors of the pancreas in VHL are uncommon, also occur in young patients, occur anywhere in the pancreas, are said to be functionally inactive (immunohistochemistry does demonstrate focal positivity for pancreatic polypeptide, somatostatin, glucagon, and/or insulin in 30–40% of cases), multiple (up to five), and not associated with either microadenomas (endocrine cell foci less than 0.5 cm in diameter) or nesidioblastosis [32]. However, we have observed a case of VHL in which these latter findings were present [36]. VHL-associated PNETs tend to be arranged in trabeculae, glandular configurations, and solid foci. Characteristically, up to 60% of the tumors contain clear cells or multi-vacuolated lipid-rich cells in varying proportions.

Neurofibromatosis, Type 1

Rare cases of somatostatin-producing PNETs have been encountered in neurofibromatosis. These tumors are far commoner in the duodenum or periampullary region in patients with neurofibromatosis. The *VHL* gene has been found to contain inactivating somatic mutations in neurofibromatosis-associated PNETs [10].

Tuberous Sclerosis

Rare PNETs have been reported in patients with tuberous sclerosis [37, 38]; it is not clear if there is a causal or a casual association.

Nomenclature

Functional PNETs have been named after the peptide that is released by the tumor. Insulinomas, gastrinomas, glucagonomas, and somatostatinomas have all become popular appellations for PNETs elaborating the corresponding peptide or hormone. However, as pointed out by Wick and Graeme-Cook [7], this occurrence is not specific and several neuroendocrine tumors such as paragangliomas and neuroblastomas are also capable of producing some of the aforementioned hormones. It is recommended that the morphologic and functional status should be recorded and a more appropriate diagnosis is: "primary pancreatic neuroendocrine tumor/neoplasm producing somatostatin," or "somatostatin-producing pancreatic neuroendocrine tumor/neoplasm." It is worth reiterating that immunohistochemically detected peptides do not imply that the patient has clinical symptoms, nor does this finding imply that the tumor is functional. If clinically nonfunctional, these tumors may be designated thus: "nonfunctioning pancreatic neuroendocrine tumor/neoplasm composed mainly of somatostatin-producing cells." However, it must be recognized that absence of recognized clinical features may not necessarily reflect true lack of clinical function and subtle clinical manifestations may be missed. Most patients are not evaluated biochemically for the full spectrum of peptide products of PNETs. Should no dominant hormone be detected immunohistochemically, the tumor is simply a: "primary pancreatic neuroendocrine tumor/neoplasm, with insulin, glucagon, VIP, and somatostatin-producing cells present." The above nomenclature is allied to the classification of PNETs, which will also convey the biologic behavior of the tumor in question.

Classification

Several classification systems have been suggested, both morphological and functional. The World Health Organization (WHO) classification factors in both histopathological and functional parameters [23] (see Table 2). Wick has proposed an all-embracing classification of neuroendocrine tumors, irrespective of site [24]. Whatever classification system is applied, it is clear that tumor size,

Table 2 WHO Classification of Pancreatic Neuroendocrine Tumors

I. Well-differentiated neuroendocrine neoplasm/tumor
***Benign behavior*:**
confined to pancreas, no angioinvasion, < 2 cm in size, </= 2 mitoses per 10HPF,
</= 2% Ki-67 proliferation/10 HPF,
nonfunctioning tumors,
insulin-producing tumors.
***Uncertain behavior*:**
confined to pancreas, >/= 2 cm in size, >2 mitoses per 10 HPF,
> 2% Ki-67 proliferation/10HPF, or angioinvasive,
functioning tumors (gastrin, insulin, VIP, glucagon, somatostatin or ectopic ACTH, GH or PTHrP), nonfunctioning tumors.
II. Well-differentiated neuroendocrine neoplasm/tumor
***Low-grade malignant*:**
Gross local invasion and/or metastases, angioinvasion and/or perineural invasion, 2–9
mitoses per 10 HPF, Ki-67 proliferative index of 2–10%,
functioning tumors (gastrin, insulin, VIP, glucagon, somatostatin or ectopic ACTH, GH or PTHrP), nonfunctioning tumors.
III. Poorly-differentiated neuroendocrine carcinoma
High-grade malignant tumors with markedly atypical cells, small or intermediate sized cells,
or undifferentiated carcinoma, >/= 10 mitoses per 10HPF, Ki-67 proliferation index >10%,
prominent angioinvasion.

lymphovascular invasion, nuclear atypia, mitotic rate, extension through the tumor capsule, lymph node spread, and distant metastases are features that impact on tumor behavior. It has also been demonstrated that hormone production, detected by immunohistochemistry and not necessarily clinically functional, also influences behavior. Hormone production may be subdivided into production of hormones that are intrinsic to the pancreas (insulin, pancreatic polypeptide, somatostatin, and glucagon), and hormones that are identified as enteric in origin (vasoactive intestinal peptide and gastrin) [4]. Tumors producing the former behave better than those that produce the latter. Insulin-producing tumors have a low risk of behaving aggressively, while those producing pancreatic polypeptide, somatostatin, and glucagon, have a worse prognosis. In addition, tumors producing inappropriate hormones such as ACTH, calcitonin, or GHRH are also associated with aggressive behavior.

Types of Pancreatic Neuroendocrine Tumor

Insulin-Producing PNET

This is the commonest of the functioning PNET. Whilst the vast majority occurs sporadically, about 8% occur in the setting of MEN 1. Insulin-producing PNET synthesize and secrete insulin autonomously in the presence of low blood glucose. Hypoglycemia-induced catecholamine surge results in symptoms such as: tremor, irritability, weakness, tachycardia, and hunger. Neuroglycopenic symptoms on the other hand include: bizarre behavior, seizures, speech disturbances, and coma. Those occurring in MEN 1 and producing hypoglycemia are usually larger than 1 cm. They can occur anywhere in the pancreas but 65% occur in the body and tail and 35% in the head. They usually are single tumors when sporadic. Insulin-producing PNET have a propensity for amyloid, association with ductules, and dystrophic calcification (even psammoma bodies) may be encountered. These PNET usually have a good prognosis.

Gastrin-Producing PNET

This is the second commonest PNET accounting for 20% of all cases and 30% of functioning PNET. It is typically associated with ZE syndrome. The hypersecretion of gastrin results in upper GI peptic ulceration accompanied by abdominal pain and weight loss. Compared to those occurring in the duodenum, pancreatic gastrin-producing NET are larger (1–3 cm). Histologically, osseous metaplasia, intracytoplasmic hyaline globules, and signet-ring type cells are most frequently encountered in this variant. Although slow growing, these PNETs have a worse prognosis than insulin-producing PNET.

Glucagon-Producing PNET

It accounts for 8% of all functioning PNET and is uncommonly associated with MEN 1. Most occur in the pancreatic tail, then body and head, are solitary and large (7 cm). This PNET results in the glucagonoma syndrome: diabetes mellitus, necrolytic migratory erythema, anemia, malnutrition, glossitis, loss of weight, venous thrombosis, and neuropsychiatric manifestations. About 80% are malignant and 75% show evidence of metastasis to the liver at the time of presentation.

Somatostatin-Producing PNET

This is slightly more common in women and seen in the fourth–sixth decades. Usually seen in the head and then tail of the pancreas. This NET is commoner in the duodenum than the pancreas. Patients present with a wide variety of symptoms but the somatostatinoma syndrome symptoms are commoner with pancreatic somatostatin-producing NET: diabetes mellitus, steatorrhea, cholelithiasis together with abdominal pain, nausea, vomiting, loss of weight, and anemia. Pancreatic somatostatin-producing NET, unlike their duodenal counterparts, are not associated with NF-1 or MEN 1, contain fewer psammoma bodies, and have poorer prognosis. These are usually large tumors (7 cm), solitary, and 5% are malignant.

Vasoactive Intestinal Peptide-Producing PNET

These are solitary, well–circumscribed, and most often seen in the tail and/or body of the pancreas; present with the Verner Morrison syndrome: watery diarrhea, hypokalemia, and achlorhydria (WDHA). Over 50% are malignant with liver spread at the time of diagnosis.

Molecular Pathogenesis of PNETs

Whilst much is known about the morphology and immunohistochemical aspects of PNETs, very little is known about the cellular and molecular mechanisms that are at play in the pathogenesis of these lesions. In the last few years several studies using a wide variety of techniques have been published. The results published thus vary according to the technique employed in a particular study. For the sake of simplicity, the molecular events in PNETs can be divided into hereditary (syndromic) and sporadic forms.

Syndromic PNETs

MEN-1 Syndrome

The majority of MEN-1 families have heterozygous germline mutations scattered throughout the MEN-1 protein-coding region [19]. Numerous unique mutations have been described but the majority (about 70%) are truncation mutations, resulting from frame shift deletions, insertions, deletion/insertion or splice site defects, and nonsense mutations [39, 40]. No correlation has, thus far, been shown between specific genetic aberrations in MEN-1 and clinical features in these patients. MEN-1-associated PNETs display a wide variety of molecular abnormalities including chromosomal loss, chromosomal loss with duplication, mitotic recombination, or a point mutation of the second wild-type allele [19]. The molecular aberrations in MEN-1 lead to loss of growth suppressive effects of the tumor suppressive protein, menin. Menin may play a role in DNA repair or synthesis and it may also interact with a host of transcription factors [19]. Hessman and colleagues undertook a genome-wide scan of PNETs arising in the clinical context of MEN-1 and showed multiple allelic deletions involving chromosomes 6, 8, 10, 11, 18, and 21 [41]. Interestingly, they also found inter- and intra-tumoral genetic heterogeneity or variation suggesting that there is chromosomal instability in these tumors [41].

Von Hippel-Lindau

As mentioned earlier PNETs are not commonly encountered in VHL. However, unlike MEN-1, a distinct genotype-phenotype correlation exists in VHL, especially with regard to the development of pheochromocytomas [29]. Missense mutations are found more frequently in patients with pheochromocytoma (so-called type 2), while those without (type 1) have large deletions or premature truncation mutations [29]. Lubensky et al. performed a histopathological and molecular genetic analysis of 30 PNETs from 14 VHL patients [31]. They showed loss of heterozygosity of one VHL allele in informative cases [31]. VHL protein has several functions including regulation of ubiquitination of the hypoxia-inducible factor HIF1α, resulting in upregulation of angiogenic substances, as well as a role in the cell cycle at the G0/G1 checkpoint [19]. It is thought that loss of these tumor suppressive effects of VHL protein is responsible for tumorigenesis.

Sporadic PNETs

In terms of molecular pathogenesis, it is the tumor suppressor pathway with genomic instability rather than a mutator phenotype that is operative in sporadic PNET. The common oncogenes and tumour suppressor genes such as *p53*, *p16*, *k-ras*, and *DPC-4* are not usually involved in sporadic PNET.

MEN-1 Gene

Somatic mutations of the *MEN-1* gene have been found in approximately 30% of sporadic or nonfamilial PNETs, while 46% show LOH [45–47]. In terms of the different types of PNET, there is variation in the frequency of mutations of *MEN-1*. *MEN-1* mutations are found in 55% of gastrin-producing and 50% of VIP-producing PNETs, but in only 7% of tumors that produce insulin

[4, 46–50]. Primary sporadic gastrin-producing PNETs more frequently exhibit mutations in exon 2 of the *MEN-1* gene than seen in similar tumors occurring in the duodenum [19]. In addition, PNETs less than 1 cm in size are less likely to harbor exon 2 mutations of *MEN-1* [19]. These mutations, associated with the frequent loss of 11q as detailed above, explain biallelic inactivation of the tumor suppressive effects of menin.

VHL Gene

A study to ascertain the frequency of allelic loss in the 3p region encompassing the *VHL* gene was undertaken in 43 sporadic PNETs [51]. Allelic loss was identified in 33% of cases but the smallest common region of allelic loss was not at the *VHL* locus but more centromeric, at 3p25 [51]. Furthermore, those PNETs harboring 3p allelic loss were associated with metastatic disease, while those with an intact 3p region were more likely to be benign. These authors concluded that the *VHL* gene is not involved in the development of sporadic PNETs, rather some other novel gene close by [52]. Moore and colleagues who found only 1 of 39 sporadic PNETs to show a somatic mutation of the *VHL* gene confirmed this conclusion [42]. As mentioned earlier, some neurofibromatosis-associated PNETs contain inactivating mutations of the *VHL* gene.

K-Ras

Most studies on K-*ras* in sporadic NPETs indicate that mutations in this gene are infrequent [52–56]. K-*ras* mutations, if present, are most commonly seen in insulin-producing PNETs [53–55].

p16

Somewhat disparate results have been shown with regard to *p16* (located on chromosome 9p21) abnormalities in sporadic PNETs. Muscarella et al. reported that inactivating alterations of *p16* were present in 91.7% of the cases that they analyzed [57]. However, others found only 1 case in 41 to have a *p16* aberration [58], and in another study only 17% of insulin-producing PNETs contained a *p16* alteration [59]. The general consensus is that *p16* plays an insignificant role in sporadic PNET tumorigenesis [4].

PTEN

This tumor suppressor gene located on chromosome 10q23 was regarded as a possible candidate in PET tumorigenesis because of the frequent chromosomal loss of 10q [4]. With this in mind Perren and colleagues analyzed 33 sporadic PNETs [60]. Loss of heterozygosity for *PTEN* was found in 53% of malignant PNETs but not in any of the benign tumors [60]. On further investigation, only one tumor was found to contain a mutated *PTEN* gene. These authors postulated that mutations of the gene are uncommon but impaired cellular localization of the protein may contribute to tumorigenesis [60].

Chromosomal Imbalances

A wide range of chromosomal alterations has been observed in PNETs. The most consistent and recurring chromosomal abnormality is allelic loss of chromosome 11q, which includes the *MEN-1* locus [42]. This particular abnormality occurs frequently in conjunction with loss of chromosome 6 in neurofibromatosis-associated PETs [43, 44]. Genome-wide studies, using several techniques including comparative genomic hybridization and genome-wide allelotyping, have yielded the following genetic aberrations: Losses on chromosomes 3p, 3q, 6q, 6p, 10q, 11q, 11p, 16p, 20q, 21q, 22q, Xq, and Y, ranging from 25% to 50% of PETs. Gains on chromosomes 5q, 7q, 7p, 9q, 12q, 17p, and 20q, ranging from 25 to 35% of PETs [4, 43, 44].

Noteworthy is the observation that PNETs harboring losses of 3p, 6pq, and 10pq , and gains of 5q, 14q, and Xq, are associated with advanced tumor stage, suggesting these chromosomal abnormalities are important in tumor progression [4, 43, 44].

Chromosomal deletions occur most frequently on chromosomes 3, 6, and 11 [43, 44].

PNETs from females show frequent loss of chromosome X, and males show loss of chromosome Y and rarely of X [4]. In addition, loss of a sex chromosome was associated with metastasis, local invasion, and poor survival [4].

References

1. Lack EE. Pathology of the pancreas, gallbladder, extrahepatic biliary tract, and ampullary region. Pancreatic endocrine neoplasms. New York, Oxford University Press, 2003;323–73.
2. Lubensky I. Endocrine Pancreas. In: LiVolsi VA, Asa SL, eds. *Endocrine Pathology*. Philadelphia, Churchill Livingstone, 2002;205–236.
3. Kloppel G, IntVeld PA, Komminoth P, et al. The endocrine pancreas. In: Kovacs K, Asa SL, eds. *Functional Endocrine Pathology*, 2nd edition. Cambridge, Blackwell Scientific Publications, 1998;415–87.
4. Gumbs AA, Moore PS, Falconi M, et al. Review of the clinical, histological, and molecular aspects of pancreatic endocrine neoplasms. *J Surg Oncol* 2002;81:45–53.

5. Grimelius L, Hultquist GT, Stenkvist B. Cytological differentiation of asymptomatic pancreatic islet cell tumors in autopsy material. *Virchows Arch* 1975;365:275–88.
6. Kimura W, Kuroda A, Morioka Y. Clinical pathology of endocrine tumors of the pancreas. *Dig Dis Sci* 1991;36:933–42.
7. Wick MR, Graeme-Cook FM. Pancreatic neuroendocrine neoplasms. A current summary of diagnostic, prognostic, and differential diagnostic information. *Am J Clin Pathol* 2001;115: S28–S45.
8. Lam KY, Lo CY. Pancreatic endocrine tumour: a 22-year clinico-pathological experience with morphological, immunohistochemical observation and a review of the literature. *Eur J Surg Oncol* 1997;23:36–42.
9. Owen DA, Kelly JK. *Pathology of the gallbladder, biliary tract and pancreas. Major problems in Pathology, vol 39*. Philadelphia, WB Saunders Co, 2001.
10. Mullan MH, Gauger PG, Thompson NW. Endocrine tumours of the pancreas: review and recent advances. *ANZ J Surg* 2001;71:475–82.
11. Legaspi A, Brennan M. Management of islet cell carcinoma. *Surgery* 1988;104:1018–23.
12. Lo CY, van Heerden JA, Thompson GB, et al. islet cell carcinoma of the pancreas. *World J Surg* 1996;20:878–83.
13. Dial P, Braasch J, Rossi R, et al. Management of non functioning islet cell tumors of the pancreas. *Surg Clin North Am* 1985;65:291–9.
14. Falconi M, Bonora A, Bassi C, et al. Non-functioning pancreatic tumours. In: Dervenis C, Bassi C, eds. *Pancreatic tumours, Achievements and Prospective*. Stuttgart, Georg Thieme Verlag, 2000;345–52.
15. Cheslyn-Curtis S, Sitaram V, Williamson RCN. Management of non-functioning neuroendocrine tumours of the pancreas. *Br J Surg* 1993;80:625–7.
16. Bonner-Weir S, Baxter LA, Schuppin GT, et al. A second pathway for regeneration of adult exocrine and endocrine pancreas. *Diabetes* 1993;42:1715–20.
17. Rindi G. Transgenic models of endocrine tumours. In: Polak JM, ed. *Diagnostic histopathology of neuroendocrine tumours*. Edinburgh, Churchill-Livingstone, 1993;67–89.
18. Smith FE, Rosen KM, Villa-Komaroff L, et al. Enhanced insulin-like growth factor I gene expression in regenerating rat pancreas. *Proc Natl Acad Sci USA* 1991;61:6152–6.
19. La Rosa S, Furlan D, Sessa F, et al. The endocrine pancreas. In: Lloyd RV, ed. *Endocrine Pathology. Differential diagnosis and Molecular advances*. New Jersey, Humana Press, 2004; 291–328.
20. Chetty R. Pot pourri of pancreatic and periampullary pathology. *Curr Diagn Pathol* 2000;6:165–70.
21. Laidlaw GF. Nesidioblastoma, the islet cell tumor of the pancreas. *Am J Pathol* 1938;14:125–34.
22. Liu MH, Potter EL. Development of the human pancreas. *Arch Pathol* 1962;74:439–52.
23. Solcia E, Kloppel G, Sobin LH, et al. *Histological typing of endocrine tumours. WHO International histological classification of tumours, 2nd ed.* Berlin, Springer, 2000.
24. Wick MR. Neuroendocrine neoplasia: current concepts. *Am J Clin Pathol* 2000;113:331–5.
25. Trump D, Farren B, Wooding C, et al. Clinical studies of multiple endocrine neoplasia type 1 (MEN I). *Q J Med* 1996;89:653–69.
26. Chandrasekharappa SC, Guru SC, Manickam P, et al. Positional cloning of the gene for multiple endocrine neoplasia-type 1. *Science* 1997;276:404–7.
27. Burgess JR, Greenaway TM, Shepherd JJ. Expression of the MEN-1 gene in a large kindred with multiple endocrine neoplasia type 1. *J Intern Med* 1999;243:465–70.
28. Jensen RT. Pancreatic endocrine tumors: recent advances. *Ann Oncol* 1999;10:S170–S176.
29. Friedrich CA. Von Hippel-Lindau syndrome. A pleomorphic condition. *Cancer* 1999;86:2478–2482.
30. Hough MT, Stephens DH, Johnson CD, et al. Pancreatic lesions in von Hippel-Lindau disease: prevalence clinical significance, and CT findings. *Am J Roentgenol* 1994;162:1091–1094.
31. Lubensky IA, Pack S, Ault D, et al. Multiple neuroendocrine tumors of the pancreas in von Hippel-Lindau disease. *Am J Pathol* 1998;153:223–231.
32. Neumann HPH, Dinkel E, Brambs H, et al. Pancreatic lesions in the von Hippel-Lindau syndrome. *Gastroenterology* 1991;101:465–471.
33. Binkovitz LA, Johnson CD, Stephens DH. Islet cell tumors in von Hippel-Lindau disease: increased prevalence and relationship to the multiple endocrine neoplasias. *Am J Roentgenol* 1990;155:501–505.
34. Hammel PR, Vilgrain V, Terris B, et al. Pancreatic involvement in von Hippel-Lindau disease. *Gastroenterology* 2000;119:1087–1095.
35. Libutti SK, Choyke PL, Bartlett DL, et al. Pancreatic neuroendocrine tumors associated with von Hippel-Lindau disease: diagnostic and management recommendations. *Surgery* 1998; 124:1153–1159.
36. Chetty R, Kennedy M, Ezzat S, Asa SL. Pancreatic neuroendocrine pathology in a patient with Von Hippel-Lindau disease: An expanding spectrum of lesions. *Endocr Pathol* 2004;15:141–8.
37. Verhoef S, van Diemen-Steenvoorde R, Akkersdijk WL, et al. Malignant pancreatic tumor within the spectrum of tuberous sclerosis complex in childhood. *Eur J Pediatr* 1999;158:284–7.
38. Francalanci P, Diomedi-Camassei F, Purifacto C, et al. Malignant pancreatic endocrine tumor in a child with tuberous sclerosis. *Am J Surg Pathol* 2003;27:1386–9.
39. Guo SS, Sawaicli MP. Molecular and genetic mechanisms of tumorigenesis in multiple endocrine neoplasia type 1. *Mol Endocrinol* 2001;15:1653–64.
40. Calender A, Vercherat C, Gaudray P, et al. Deregulation of genetic pathways in neuroendocrine tumors. *Ann Oncol* 2001; 12:S3–S11.
41. Hessman O, Skogseid B, Westin G, et al. Multiple allelic deletions and intratumoral genetic heterogeneity in MEN 1 pancreatic tumors. *J Clin Endocrinol Metab* 2001;86:1355–61.
42. Moore PS, Missiaglia E, Antonello D, et al. Role of disease-causing genes in sporadic pancreatic endocrine tumors: MEN 1 and VHL. Genes Chromosome Cancer 2001;32:177–81.
43. Rigaud G, Missiaglia E, Moore PS, et al. High resolution allelotype of nonfunctional pancreatic endocrine tumors: Identification of two molecular subgroups with clinical implications. *Cancer Res* 2001;61:285–92.
44. Speel EJ, Richter J, Moch H, et al. Genetic differences in endocrine pancreatic tumor subtypes detected by comparative genomic hybridization. *Am J Pathol* 1999;155:1787–94.
45. Hessman O, Lindberg D, Skogseid B, et al. Mutation of the multiple endocrine neoplasia type 1 gene in nonfamilial, malignant tumors of the endocrine pancreas. *Cancer Res* 1998; 58:377–9.
46. Shan L, Nakamura M, Yokoi T, et al. Somatic mutations of multiple endocrine neoplasia type 1 gene in the sporadic endocrine tumors. *Lab Invest* 1998;78:471–5.
47. Zhuang Z, Vortmeyer AO, Pack S, et al. Somatic mutations of the MEN1 tumor suppressor gene in sporadic gastrinomas and insulinomas. *Cancer Res* 1997;57:4682–6.
48. Debelenko LV, Zhuang Z, Emmert-Buck MR, et al. Allelic deletions on chromosome 11q13 in multiple endocrine neoplasia type1-associated and sporadic gastrinomas and pancreatic endocrine tumors. *Cancer Res* 1997;57:2238–43.

49. Cupisti K, Hoppner W, Dotzenrath C, et al. Lack of MEN1 gene mutations in 27 sporadic insulinomas. *Eur J Clin Invest* 2000;30:325–9.
50. Gortz B, Roth J, Krahenmann A, et al. Mutations and allelic deletions of the MEN1 gene are associated with a subset of sporadic endocrine pancreatic and neuroendocrine tumors and not restricted to foregut neoplasms. *Am J Pathol* 1999;154:429–36.
51. Chung DC, Smith AP, Louis DN, et al. A novel pancreatic endocrine tumor suppressor gene locus on chromosome 3p with clinical prognostic implications. *J Clin Invest* 1997;100:404–10.
52. Pavelic K, Hrascan R, Kapitanovic S, et al. Molecular genetics of malignant insulinoma. *Anticancer Res* 1996;16:1707–17.
53. Pavelic K, Hrascan R, Kapitanovic S, et al. Multiple genetic alterations in malignant metastatic insulinomas. *J Pathol* 1995;177:395–400.
54. Yoshimoto K, Iwahana H, Fukuda A, et al. Ras mutations in endocrine tumors: mutation detection by polymerase chain reaction-single strand conformation polymorphism. *Jpn J Cancer Res* 1992;83:1057–62.
55. Beghelli S, Pelosi G, Zamboni G, et al. Pancreatic endocrine tumours: evidence for a tumour suppressor pathogenesis and for a tumour suppressor gene on chromosome 17p. *J Pathol* 1998;186:41–50.
56. Yashiro T, Fulton N, Hara H, et al. Comparisons of mutations of ras oncogene in human pancreatic exocrine and endocrine tumors. *Surgery* 1993;114:758–64.
57. Muscarella P, Melvin WS, Fisher WE, et al. Genetic alterations in gastrinomas and nonfunctioning pancreatic neuroendocrine tumors: an analysis of p16/MTS1 tumor suppressor gene inactivation. *Cancer Res* 1998;58:237–40.
58. Moore PS, Rigaud G, Zamboni G, et al. Pancreatic tumors: molecular pathways implicated in ductal cancer are involved in ampullary but not in exocrine nonductal or endocrine tumorigenesis. *Br J Cancer* 2001;84:253–62.
59. Bartsch DK, Kersting M, Wild A, et al. Low frequency of p16 (INK4a) alterations in insulinomas. *Digestion* 2000; 62:171–7.
60. Perren A, Komminoth P, Saremaslani P, et al. Mutation and expression analyses reveal different subcellular compartmentalization of PTEN in endocrine pancreatic tumors compared to normal islet cells. *Am J Pathol* 2000;157:1097–103.

Neuroendocrine Tumors of the Gastrointestinal Tract

Runjan Chetty

Abstract Endocrine tumors in gastrointestinal tract are uncommon yet distinctive lesions. They vary in different locations and are associated with distinct clinical settings. This chapter outlines endocrine tumors from the stomach through to the rectum, including the appendix, and relevant precursor lesions and clinical associations. After each site there is a table provided that will enable the pathologist to provide a framework on which a comment on possible behavior can be gauged.

Keywords Gastric neuroendocrine cell hyperplasia • Gastric neuroendocrine cell dysplasia • Gastric neuroendocrine tumor • Duodenal neuroendocrine tumor • Gangliocytic paraganglioma • Ileal neuroendocrine tumor • Appendiceal neuroendocrine tumor • Colon and rectal neuroendocrine tumor

Introduction

Neuroendocrine tumors of the GIT, whilst morphologically similar, do vary in terms of associations and perhaps even behavior according to the site at which they are encountered.

The gastroenteropancreatic tract contains as many as 15 endocrine cell types, all of which may be a potential source for the development of endocrine tumors [1]. These cells, together with endocrine cells scattered in other endodermal derivatives such as the biliary tree, lung, thyroid, and urethra, constitute the diffuse or dispersed neuroendocrine system.

R. Chetty (✉)
Professor of Pathology, Director of Surgical Pathology, Health Network/Toronto Medical Laboratories, Department of Laboratory Medicine and Pathobiology, University of Toronto, Toronto, Canada
e-mail: runjan.chetty@uhn.on.ca

Classification and Terminology

Recently, there has been an acute awareness that the so-called "carcinoid tumor" spans a wide range of morphologic appearances and these tumors have varied biologic behavior, which is often site-specific. The WHO classification has attempted to introduce a uniform approach to the diagnosis of neuroendocrine tumors within the gastroenteropancreatic tract and for the purposes of this overview it will be used [2]. An important, and somewhat overdue, development is the appearance of a TNM staging consensus proposal from the European Neuroendocrine Tumor Society (ENETS). A group of 62 experts in gastrointestinal neuroendocrine tumors from 20 countries proposed TNM classifications for foregut and mid- and hind-gut neuroendocrine tumors [3, 4]. This represents a potentially reproducible and meaningful classification on which treatment options can be based. Thus, the term "carcinoid tumor" on its own should be avoided. It would be more prudent and indeed helpful to the clinician to use the WHO classification and indicate the extent of disease [5].

Immunohistochemistry

A core panel of markers is advocated with all cases and includes chromogranin, synaptophysin, serotonin, gastrin, and Ki-67. This may be supplemented by histamine, other markers such as somatostatin and vesicular monoamine transporter type 2 (VMAT-2), which is thought to be a marker of ECL cell tumors, and others depending on the site of the tumor and its functional status. CDX-2 stains a proportion of midgut neuroendocrine tumors.

Gastric Neuroendocrine Tumors

In the human gastric mucosa at least six different endocrine cell types have been identified and characterized [6].

A. Khan (ed.), *Surgical Pathology of Endocrine and Neuroendocrine Tumors*, Current Clinical Pathology,
DOI 10.1007/978-1-60327-396-1_12, © Humana Press, a part of Springer Science+Business Media, LLC 2009

In the antrum, G cells are most numerous, while the enterochromaffin-like (ECL) cells, which produce histamine, are the largest endocrine population in the gastric acidopeptic mucosa. Somatostatin-producing D cells are present throughout the gastric mucosa in smaller numbers. Serotonin-producing enterochromaffin (EC) cells are also present in smaller numbers. The EC, ECL, and G cells form tumors, and most are well-differentiated, nonfunctioning ECL tumors in the body or fundus of the stomach [1]. The well-known exceptions are occasional gastrin, histamine, and 5HT-producing endocrine tumors that result in symptoms of hormone production [7, 8]. A morphologic spectrum of lesions may be encountered from hyperplasia through to tumor. See Table 1.

Table 1 Spectrum of Gastric endocrine lesions

A. Precursor lesions
• Neuroendocrine cell hyperplasia/dysplasia
B. Well differentiated neuroendocrine tumor
• ECL-like neuroendocrine tumor: types I, II, and 25% of cases of type III
• EC cell neuroendocrine tumor (serotonin-producing): rare
• G cell neuroendocrine tumor (gastrin-producing); rare
C. Poorly differentiated neuroendocrine carcinoma
• ECL-like neuroendocrine carcinoma: type III (75% of cases)
• ACTH-producing neuroendocrine carcinoma
D. Small cell carcinoma

Gastric Neuroendocrine Cell Hyperplasia

Hyperplastic change of ECL cells of the oxyntic mucosa is a frequent finding in gastric atrophy and represents a proliferation due to long-standing, severe hypergastrinemia. Both *H. pylori* infection and inflammation promote the ECL cell growth.

Solcia categorized hyperplasia into several types [9]:

1. Simple or diffuse hyperplasia: This is defined as an increased density of ECL cells of more than twice the standard deviation compared to age and sex matched controls. Argyrophilic, often hypertrophic, ECL cells are scattered or clustered in less than five cell aggregates. This is frequently seen in patients with Zollinger-Ellison syndrome with duodenal ulcers with moderate hypergastrinemia.
2. Linear hyperplasia: Here, there are linear sequences of five or more ECL cells along the basement membrane of the gastric glands (Fig. 1). It is seen in severe hypergastrinemia associated with Zollinger-Ellison syndrome or pernicious anemia. At least two lines per linear millimeter of gastric mucosa are seen.

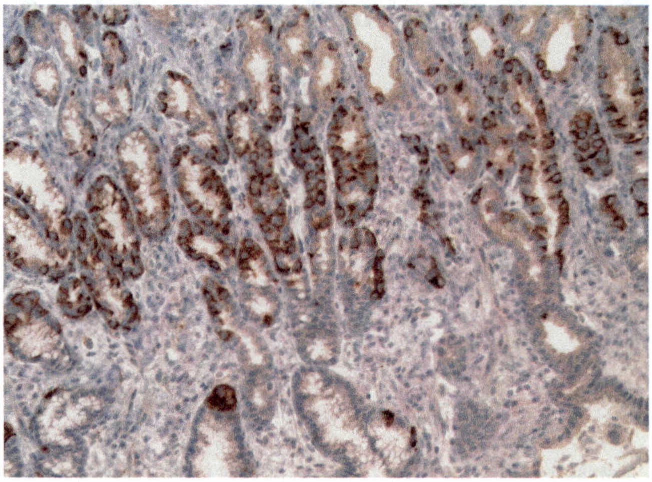

Fig. 1 Gastric mucosa showing a linear array of five or more endocrine cells highlighted by the chromogranin stain. This represents linear endocrine cell hyperplasia (chromogranin × 400)

3. Micronodular hyperplasia: Clusters of five or more endocrine cells between 50 and 150 μm in size, with at least one cluster per linear millimeter of mucosa are seen. Micronodular hyperplasia and linear hyperplasia in combination are often seen in severe hypergastrinemia with diffuse autoimmune type chronic atrophic gastritis of the body and fundus of the stomach, with or without pernicious anemia. ECL cell clustering or "micronodular pseudohyperplasia" may result from gland atrophy in normogastrinemic or mildly hypergastrinemic *H. pylori* gastritis. These clusters are not associated with the diffuse or linear hyperplasia, are small (usually less than 50 μ in diameter), and are composed of small cells with pyknotic nuclei and scanty cytoplasm.
4. Adenomatoid hyperplasia: This is a collection of five or more micronodules adherent to each other with interposition of basement membranes and thin strands of lamina propria. This is associated with micronodular hyperplasia in atrophic gastritis or the Zollinger-Ellison syndrome.

Gastric Neuroendocrine Cell Dysplasia/Micronodules

Dysplastic or pre-carcinoid endocrine cell growths are lesions between 150 and 500 μm in diameter, composed of slightly atypical endocrine cells with enlarged nuclei. These foci are scattered deeply in the mucosa and although they are precursors of full-fledged tumors, the dysplastic growths are always intramucosal and do not infiltrate beyond the muscularis mucosae. These lesions escape endoscopic detection and are diagnosed by microscopy. Their detection should encourage extensive biopsy sampling in pursuit of a possible tumor. These micronodular foci are sentinel lesions for the Zollinger-Ellison syndrome and chronic atrophic gastritis associated multiple endocrine tumors. Solcia described five patterns to the micronodules [9]:

1. Enlarged micronodules: The growths are more than 150 μm in size.
2. Adenomatous micronodules: One or more collections of at least five of micronodules that are closely adherent with interposition of basement membrane only. This arrangement mimics the back-to-back gland pattern seen in some cancers.
3. Fused micronodules: This is characterized by disappearance of basement membrane between adjacent micronodules.
4. Micro-infiltrative micronodules: There is micro-infiltration of the lamina propria by endocrine cells that fill the space between the normal gastric glands.
5. Nodules with stroma formation: The neuroendocrine cells have a trabecular or micro- and lobular pattern.

Gastric Neuroendocrine Tumors

Gastric neuroendocrine tumors are extremely uncommon with only one to two cases occurring per 1 million people every year and they account for about 9% of all GIT neuroendocrine tumors [10].

Three basic types (I–III) of gastric neuroendocrine tumor related to ECL-like cells have been described in three well-defined clinicopathologic settings (see Table 2). Non-ECL-like tumors are rare and may arise from G cells in the antrum leading to the Zollinger-Ellison syndrome or they may be EC cell tumors which produce serotonin, or tumors causing Cushing's syndrome due to excess ACTH (usually poorly differentiated neuroendocrine carcinomas).

Table 2 Comparison of the three types of ECL-like gastric neuroendocrine tumors

	Type I	Type II	Type III
Incidence	70–80%	5%	15–25%
Gender	Females	Males	Males
Age	>50	<50	>50
Number	Multiple	Multiple	Single
Size	<1–2 cm	<1–2 cm	>2 cm
Hyperplasia/dysplasia	Occasionally	Frequent	Uncommon
Association	Atrophic gastritis	ZES and/or MEN 1	None
Gastrin level	Elevated	Elevated	Normal
Gastric pH	Elevated	Decreased	Normal
Metastasis risk	5%	10%	50–100%

Type I

Here the neuroendocrine tumor exists in a background of chronic atrophic (autoimmune) gastritis involving mainly the body/fundus with associated achlorhydria. It is the commonest of the three types and accounts for 70–80% of gastric neuroendocrine tumors. These lesions are commonly encountered in females, are small (usually less than 1–2 cm in maximal diameter), well-differentiated, single or multiple, and are located within the mucosa where they may produce flat lesions or a polypoid excrescence. As a result of the atrophic gastritis with loss of specialized cells, there is an increase in gastrin levels and an elevation of the gastric pH because of achlorhydria. These tumors have an extremely small risk of metastases and thus tumor-related death. Approximately 5% of cases may have lymph node spread.

With regard to surveillance of these patients, it should be borne in mind that multiple biopsies of the body and fundus are required, as the lesions may not be visible endoscopically. Although indolent and slow growing both surgical and non-surgical modes of treatment have been recommended. Endoscopic resection, partial and even total gastrectomy have all been suggested. The somatostatin analog, octreotide has been reported to be efficacious in achieving tumor regression, controlling hypergastrinemia, and ECL proliferation [11]. In general, endoscopic surveillance and biopsy is sufficient management, unless the tumor assumes a high-grade appearance, a scenario which is very rare.

Type II

These lesions occur in the characteristic setting of either Zollinger-Ellison (ZE) and/or type 1 multiple endocrine neoplasia (MEN) syndromes. It is interesting to note that with ZE/MEN1 overlap syndrome have up to a 35% risk of developing a type II endocrine tumor of the stomach. This contrasts sharply with patients with ZES without concomitant MEN1 who have about a 1% chance of developing a tumor [12]. As mentioned above, these tumors are associated with a range of endocrine cell abnormalities from hyperplasia through to micronodules with the spectrum of lesions often observed within the same case. Located mainly in the body/fundus, occasional cases have been described in the antrum too. They account for about 5% of gastric endocrine lesions and are invariably multiple, 1–2 cm in diameter, well differentiated and also associated with elevated gastrin levels. In contrast to type I endocrine tumors, the gastric pH is acidic (low). The risk of spread to lymph nodes is up to 30%, to liver is up to 10% of cases; and the overall tumor-related death risk is about 5–10%. Similar therapeutic options to type I tumors have been considered for type II tumors, although the multiplicity of tumors makes endoscopic resection difficult.

Type III

This type represents the so-called 'sporadic" variety and constitutes 15–25% of endocrine tumors in the stomach. They tend to occur more commonly in males over the age of 50, are single tumors, large (greater than 2 cm in maximal diameter), ulcerated polypoid masses, which display a range of differentiation from well (25%) to poorly differentiated (75%). The patients are normogastrinemic and the gastric pH is normal as well. The usual clinical presentation is due to a tumor mass (pain, hemorrhage, obstruction) and not due to endocrine manifestations. With the poorly differentiated examples there is a very high risk of metastasis and hence tumor-related deaths. These cases have been associated with adenocarcinomas (sometimes labeled as type IV tumors), the mixed endocrine-exocrine carcinomas. Type III tumors should be treated aggressively with essentially the same approach as to a gastric adenocarcinoma.

Morphology

The type I and II tumors are characterized by small micronodular, trabecular aggregates of uniform cells that are devoid of mitotic activity, necrosis, and angioinvasion (Fig. 2). They tend to remain within the mucosa and occasionally breach the muscularis mucosae. The higher grade tumors encountered in type III manifest a more solid, sheet-like growth pattern with attendant cytologic atypia: pleomorphism, mitoses, necrosis. Small carcinoma histologic features are the same as a similar tumor encountered in other sites. Invariably, these tumors extend deeply into the gastric wall at the time of presentation.

Prognostic Features

See Table 3. Gastric neuroendocrine tumors displaying the following features are associated with a good outcome: limited to the mucosa or submucosa, <1 cm in diameter, types I (especially) and II tumors, and nonfunctioning tumors. Those showing deeper extension into the gastric wall with associated cytologic atypia have a worse prognosis.

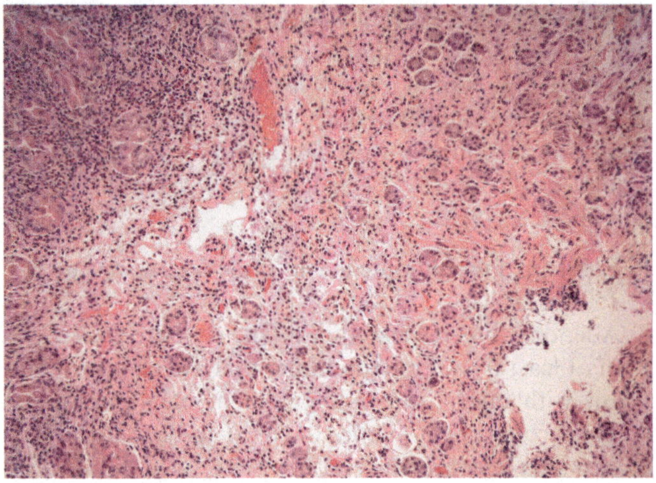

Fig. 2 A type I gastric neuroendocrine tumor composed of nest and aggregates of bland endocrine cells within the lamina propria and focally extending through muscularis mucosae. (H&E × 200)

Table 3 Behavior guidelines for gastric neuroendocrine tumors

Well-differentiated, benign behavior:
- nonfunctioning
- < or = to 1 cm in diameter
- confined to mucosa/submucosa
- no angioinvasion

Well-differentiated, uncertain behavior:
- nonfunctioning, 1–2 cm in diameter, confined to mucosa/submucosa, no angioinvasion

Well-differentiated, low-grade malignant behavior:
- nonfunctioning, >2cm diameter, with or without angioinvasion
- nonfunctioning, extending beyond submucosa, usually >2 cm diameter, with or without angioinvasion
- functioning, well differentiated histology, any size, any depth of invasion

Poorly-differentiated, high-grade malignant behavior:
- functioning/nonfunctioning, poorly differentiated neuroendocrine carcinoma with >10 mitoses per 10 HPF, necrosis, angioinvasion
- small cell carcinoma

Duodenal and Jejunal Neuroendocrine Tumors

Neuroendocrine tumors that occur in the duodenum and proximal jejunum are similar and for the purposes of this discussion can be regarded as a single site.

Incidence

The duodenum is by far the commoner site for a neuroendocrine tumor than the proximal jejunum and accounts for about 20% of these tumors in the GIT, while only 1% occur in the proximal jejunum [13]. There is, however, some discrepancy with this incidence of 20%, and Modlin and Kidd quote an incidence of around 5% [10].

Neuroendocrine Tumor Types

Four main neuroendocrine tumor types occur in the duodenum/proximal jejunum:

1. G cell neuroendocrine tumors: functioning or nonfunctioning
2. Somatostatin (δ) cell neuroendocrine tumors: rarely associated with the somatostatinoma syndrome
3. Gangliocytic paraganglioma
4. Enterochromaffin (EC) cell (serotonin-producing) neuroendocrine tumors

Rare cases of L cell, pancreatic polypeptide-producing tumors, and primary small cell carcinoma of the duodenum have also been encountered.

Location

Most are located in the first and second parts of the duodenum. Gastrin-producing tumors associated with the ZE syndrome can occur in the first, second, or third parts of the duodenum or proximal jejunum. On the other hand, nonfunctioning G cell tumors tend to arise in the duodenal bulb. Somatostatin cell tumors and gangliocytic paraganglioma have a predilection for the duodenal papilla at the ampulla of Vater.

G-Cell Neuroendocrine Tumor

This is the commonest of the duodenal neuroendocrine tumors, accounting for 66% of cases. Approximately one-third of tumors are associated with ZE syndrome that may also be part of MEN1. However, in patients with MEN1 and ZES, the incidence of a duodenal gastrin-producing neuroendocrine tumor is of the magnitude of 90%. About 15–40% of ZE syndrome cases not associated with MEN1 (so-called sporadic ZES) have a duodenal G-cell tumor. From a histologic point of view the syndrome-associated gastrinomas tend to be multicentric but are otherwise typical of other neuroendocrine tumors (Fig. 3). Presenting symptoms are usually related to the presence of a duodenal mass: obstructive jaundice, cholangitis, pancreatitis, hemorrhage, and bowel obstruction, or sometimes related to hormone production.

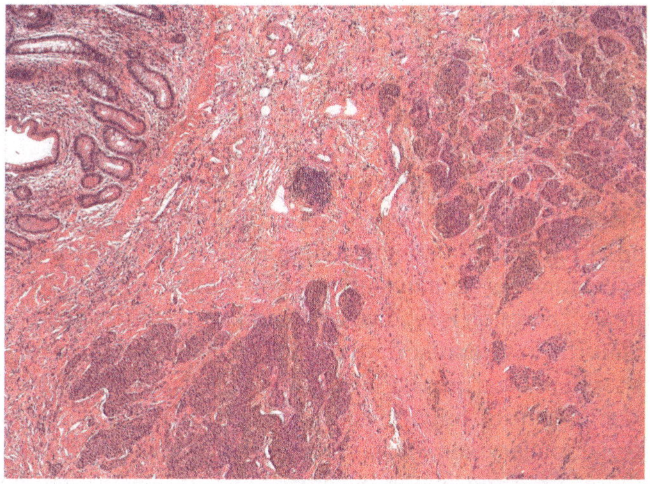

Fig. 3 An ileal gastrin-producing neuroendocrine tumour within the submucosa. The tumor has a typical packeted arrangement with peripheral palisading. The cytoplasm also displays the characteristic eosinophilic granularity. (H&E × 100)

Functioning tumors irrespective of any syndromic association behave as low-grade malignant tumors while nonfunctioning tumors are accompanied by a benign course. Those associated with ZES and/or MEN1 are associated with a poorer prognosis. Although they tend to be small (average <1 cm in diameter), 10% of functioning tumors metastasize to regional lymph nodes at the time of presentation. In fact, the lymph node metastases may be larger than the primary tumor. Liver spread is rare and if present occurs late in the disease.

Somatostatin Cell Neuroendocrine Tumor

This is the second commonest neuroendocrine tumor in the duodenum and make up 15–20% of cases.

Somatostatin-producing neuroendocrine tumors of the duodenum are particularly associated with type I neurofibromatosis [14, 15]. Indeed, a somatostatinoma of the periampullary region should alert one to the possibility of coexistent type I neurofibromatosis. Their periampullary location, glandular morphology, and psammomatous calcification characterize these somatostatinomas. Whether associated with neurofibromatosis or not, somatostatinomas usually produce local symptoms. Clinical symptoms are related to the local effects of the periampullary mass: obstructive jaundice, cholangitis, pancreatitis, hemorrhage, and obstruction. Some cases may be asymptomatic. Despite the strong immunostaining for somatostatin, most patients with duodenal somatostatinomas do not usually manifest the somatostatin syndrome of diarrhea, diabetes mellitus, dyspepsia, and cholelithiasis. However, pancreatic somatostatinomas often present with somatostatin syndrome [16]. These tumors are less frequent in the pancreas and represent less than 1% of all functional pancreatic endocrine tumors and are rarely, if ever, associated with MEN type I (see Table 4 for differences between duodenal and pancreatic somatostatinomas). The microscopic appearance of somatostatinomas is similar in both locations. The lesion is typified by glandular structures lined by uniform, eosinophilic granular cells. Solid, nested foci may be seen in focal areas. Psammomatous calcification, which is of diagnostic importance and is characteristic, is seen in periampullary somatostatinomas but is less common in those occurring in the pancreas (Fig. 4). There may be occasional mitoses and mild cytologic atypia is frequently present. The tumor has a characteristic infiltrative growth pattern and can be seen extending between the muscle bundles of the muscularis propria. It is important to distinguish this from an adenocarcinoma and awareness of the entity will go a long way towards making this distinction. They often (66% of cases) behave as low-grade malignant tumors and 25% of cases metastasize to regional lymph nodes, especially those tumors more than 2 cm in diameter. Liver metastases are uncommon [16].

Table 4 Differences between periampullary and pancreatic somatostatinomas

Periampullary	Pancreatic
More common	Less common
Often associated with NF-1	Not associated with NF-1
May be associated with MEN 1	Not associated with MEN 1
Rarely cause somatostatin syndrome	Often cause somatostatin syndrome
Psammoma bodies frequent	Psammoma bodies infrequent
Good prognosis	Poor prognosis

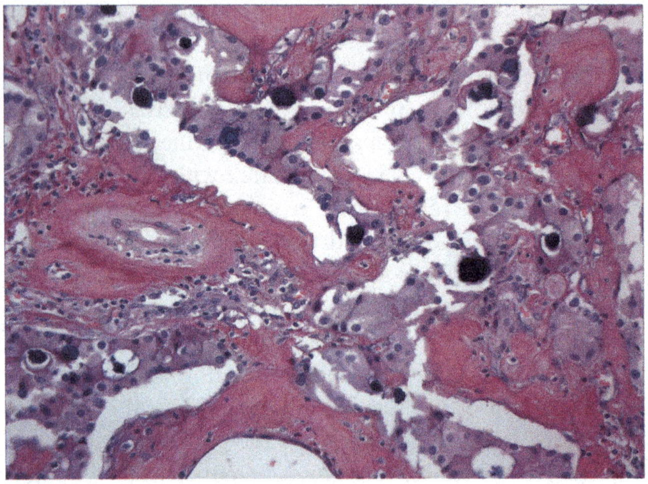

Fig. 4 Somatostatin-producing neuroendocrine tumors are typified by psammomatous calcification that is almost pathognomonic for this tumor. (H&E × 400)

Table 5 Behavior guidelines for duodenal/proximal jejunal neuroendocrine tumors

Well-differentiated, benign behavior:
- Nonfunctioning, 1 cm or less in diameter, mucosa/submucosa, no angioinvasion
- Gangliocytic paraganglioma, irrespective of size/depth of invasion/lymph node status

Well-differentiated, uncertain behavior:
- Nonfunctioning, 1–2 cm diameter, mucosa/submucosa, no angioinvasion

Well-differentiated, low-grade malignant behavior:
- Nonfunctioning, > 2 cm, with or without angioinvasion
- Nonfunctioning, extending beyond submucosa, usually >2 cm diameter, with or without angioinvasion
- Functioning, well differentiated histology, any size, any depth of invasion

Poorly-differentiated, high-grade malignant behavior:
- Functioning/nonfunctioning, poorly differentiated neuroendocrine carcinoma with >10 mitoses per 10 HPF, necrosis, angioinvasion
- Small cell carcinoma

Gangliocytic Paraganglioma

Histopathological Definition

This is a characteristic tumor composed of three elements: endocrine cells, ganglion and ganglion-like cells, and spindle cells. Classically, it is located in the second part of the duodenum (ampullary/periampullary) but rare cases have also been encountered in the jejunum, pylorus of the stomach, appendix, lung, and nasopharynx. Some cases have been described in neurofibromatosis type I.

Morphologic Description

This is a triphasic tumor in which the proportion of the different elements varies within and between cases. The elements are haphazardly distributed and anyone can predominate. It is a hybrid tumor of a neuroendocrine, paraganglioma, and ganglioneuroma. The endocrine cells are epithelioid or columnar, round to polygonal in appearance arranged in nests demarcated by thin-walled vascular channels that impart the nested or zellballen pattern. These cells may also be arranged in trabeculae or gland-like structures. The endocrine cells are cytologically bland but they may exhibit focal mild atypia. The ganglion cells are reminiscent of their normal counterparts and may be uni- or multi-nucleated. They are distributed within the endocrine and spindle cell components. The spindle cell proliferation forms the substratum or background matrix and surrounds the nests of endocrine cells. They resemble Schwann and sustentacular cells. Rarely, psammoma bodies and stromal amyloid can be encountered.

They are often large (>2 cm in diameter) and often extend into the muscularis propria. This is a relatively well-circumscribed tumor but can have an infiltrative growth margin (not uncommonly seen) and even lymph node metastasis that are not indicative of aggressive behavior or malignancy.

Depending on which element dominates, the differential diagnoses varies. These include a neuroendocrine tumor, paraganglioma, ganglioneuroma, Schwannoma, and even carcinoma, if the ganglion-like cells dominate.

The endocrine cells are positive for: CAM 5.2, synaptophysin, protein gene product (PGP) 9.5, chromogranin A (not all cases), Leu-7, pancreatic polypeptide, somatostatin, leuenkephalin, serotonin, glucagon, vasoactive intestinal peptide (VIP), pancreatic polypeptide, insulin, and gastrin.

Ganglion cells are immunoreactive with neurofilament, chromogranin A (sometimes), GFAP, synaptophysin, pancreatic polypeptide, somatostatin, PGP 9.5, and leuenkephalin.

The spindle cells are positive with neurofilament, S100 protein, neuron-specific enolase, and PGP 9.5.

The pale cells corresponding to endocrine cells contain membrane-bound neurosecretory granules and intracytoplasmic intermediate filaments often in whorls, and dark cells representing spindle cells contain microfilaments. Rare elongated processes are seen and the sustentacular cells investing the endocrine cells can be visualized. The ganglion cells show evidence of neuronal differentiation with prominent stacks of cisternae of rough endoplasmic reticulum (corresponding to Nissl substance) and numerous intermediate filaments. Between ganglion-like cells, axon-like extensions containing filaments are seen. Interestingly, hybrid cells containing neurosecretory granules, neurofilaments, and features of ganglion cells are seen as well.

This is an indolent, benign tumor with a low growth fraction.

Enterochromaffin (EC) Cell (Serotonin-Producing) Neuroendocrine Tumors

Unlike the ileum, a serotonin-producing tumor is rare in the duodenum and proximal jejunum. If they do occur, then they are morphologically identical to those that occur in the ileum. Exceptional cases with liver metastasis from a duodenal primary and resultant "carcinoid syndrome" have been described.

The behavior of duodenal and proximal jejunal neuroendocrine tumors is outlined in Table 5.

Distal Jejunal/Ileal/Right Colonic Neuroendocrine Tumors

These three midgut sites have similar neuroendocrine tumors are thus linked embryologically. In contrast to the stomach and proximal small intestine, enterochromaffin (EC) cell tumors (serotonin-producing) are most frequently encountered in the midgut and account for 95% of cases. Rare L cell, glucagon-like peptide, and pancreatic polypeptide-producing tumors are also described in the ileum. After the appendix, the ileum is the next commonest site for neuroendocrine tumors, accounting for about 20–30% of all neuroendocrine tumors occurring in the GIT. The pre-eminent site of involvement is the terminal ileum, but involvement of the ileocaecal region is not infrequent.

They occur in patients in the sixth or seventh decades of life and have no gender predilection. Patients usually present with abdominal pain, intestinal obstruction, or nondescript symptomatology related to the GIT. Only about 5% of patients present with the prototype "carcinoid syndrome": flushing, diarrhea, and right heart fibrosis.

The lesions are typically yellow macroscopically and are usually small ranging between 1 and 2 cm in diameter and in 30–40% of cases, there may be multiple tumors [17]. Histologically, the tumors are typified by a well-developed zellballen pattern with solid nests or islands of cells, often with prominent peripheral palisading (Fig. 3). Pseudoglandular structures with PAS-positive luminal material may also be present within the nests. A common finding in midgut neuroendocrine tumors is a hyalinized, paucicellular stroma. When infiltrating, the tumor is characteristically aligned in cords and linear runs of cells. In addition to the usual immunohistochemical markers, some cases are CDX-2 and carcino-embryonic antigen (CEA) positive. Interestingly, approximately one-third of cases show patchy positivity with prostatic acid phosphatase.

The overall mortality rate for ileal neuroendocrine tumors is about 20%. With liver metastases, the 10-year survival is only 10–15%. Overall, 20% of patients with ileal neuroendocrine tumors have lymph node and liver metastases [18]. Tumors which are 1 cm or less in diameter have an excellent prognosis with less than 5% risk of lymph node spread. However, this risk rises precipitously to 80–85% in tumors larger than 2 cm [19]. See Table 6.

Colon and Rectal Neuroendocrine Tumors

Distal to the caecum, neuroendocrine tumors are relatively rare and the commonest site is the rectum. If tumors are present in the colon, they tend to be poorly differentiated

Table 6 Behavior guidelines for distal jejunal/ileal/colon neuroendocrine tumors

Well-differentiated, benign behavior:
- Nonfunctioning, 1 cm or less, mucosa/submucosa, no angioinvasion

Well-differentiated, uncertain behavior:
- Nonfunctioning, 1 cm or less, mucosa/submucosa, with angioinvasion

Well-differentiated, low-grade malignant behavior:
- Nonfunctioning, >2 cm, with or without angioinvasion
- Nonfunctioning, invasion of muscularis propria and/or beyond

Poorly-differentiated, high-grade malignant behavior:
- Functioning/nonfunctioning, poorly differentiated neuroendocrine carcinoma with >10 mitoses per 10 HPF, necrosis, angioinvasion
- Small cell carcinoma

neuroendocrine carcinomas. Rectal neuroendocrine tumors are well differentiated, small (less than 1 cm), and generally confined to the mucosa or submucosa. An association with inflammatory bowel disease (both ulcerative colitis and Crohn's disease) has been suggested. Histologically, rectal tumors have a trabecular pattern rather than the solid islands of tumor as seen in the ileum. Rectal neuroendocrine tumors tend to be negative for chromogranin A but are positive for synaptophysin, glucagon, glicentin, and pancreatic polypeptide. In addition, the well-differentiated rectal tumors also show immunoreactivity to prostatic acid phosphatase.

In general, tumors 1 cm or less in diameter and located in the mucosa/submucosa have a very low risk of metastasis. Tumors that are 1–2 cm in diameter have a 5% risk of regional lymph node spread. The poorly differentiated neuroendocrine carcinomas have invariably spread to regional lymph nodes at the time of presentation. See Table 7. Occasional cases of composite neuroendocrine carcinoma and conventional adenocarcinoma have been described.

Table 7 Behavior guidelines for distal colon and rectum neuroendocrine tumors

Well-differentiated, benign behavior:
- Nonfunctioning, 2 cm or less, mucosa/submucosa, no angioinvasion

Well-differentiated, uncertain behavior:
- Nonfunctioning, 2 cm or less, mucosa/submucosa, with angioinvasion

Well-differentiated, low-grade malignant behavior:
- Nonfunctioning, >2 cm, with or without angioinvasion
- Nonfunctioning, invasion of muscularis propria and/or beyond

Poorly-differentiated, high-grade malignant behavior:
- Functioning/nonfunctioning, poorly differentiated neuroendocrine carcinoma with >10 mitoses per 10 HPF, necrosis, angioinvasion
- Small cell carcinoma

Composite tumors (neuroendocrine and conventional adenocarcinoma)

Appendiceal Neuroendocrine Tumors

The appendix is the commonest site in the GIT for neuroendocrine tumors. Unlike the appendix, the vast majority of classical neuroendocrine tumors are indolent and hence, associated with an excellent prognosis. In addition to neuroendocrine tumors of the usual type, the so-called "goblet cell carcinoid" tumor is also encountered in the appendix. Historically and nomenclaturally, this lesion has been regarded as a variant of neuroendocrine tumor or carcinoid. However, recent immunohistochemical evidence points towards overlap with adenocarcinoma [19, 20]. In addition, the behavior of this lesion is more aggressive and warrants it being separated from the usual neuroendocrine tumors that occur in the appendix. It should be borne in mind that goblet cell carcinoid does share some molecular similarity with neuroendocrine tumors. Some have suggested that they be regarded as crypt cell or amphicrine carcinomas; others have opined that mucin-producing neuroendocrine tumors is a more appropriate term. Whatever terminology is applied, it must be remembered that these are aggressive lesions.

Neuroendocrine tumors tend to occur in patients in their fourth and fifth decades of life, and there is a slight female predilection. Tubular neuroendocrine tumors occur in younger patients: usually in their twenties. Since spread to the liver is extremely rare, appendiceal neuroendocrine tumors that are serotonin positive rarely result in carcinoid syndrome.

The typical neuroendocrine tumor of the appendix is located in the tip of the appendix and is frequently found "incidentally" in appendectomy specimens for appendicitis. They may also be causally related to appendicitis.

They frequently permeate into the muscularis propria and serosal fat of the mesoappendix; two features that belie its indolent nature. Unless the tumor is large and in excess of 2–3 cm, then only is lymph node involvement seen. These tumors resemble their ileal counterparts, both morphologically (solid, nested growth pattern) and immunohistochemically (most being serotonin positive). A rare variant from L cells has also been described and resembles the tumor that occurs in the rectum.

The tubular variant resembles a carcinoma, in being composed of tubular structures containing inspissated luminal mucin. They are frequently arranged in a trabecular growth pattern. To aid in the distinction from carcinoma the following features are useful: origin from the crypt base, absence of overt cytologic atypia, especially mitoses, and a non-destructive infiltrative growth pattern. In addition, these tumors are chromogranin positive.

Goblet cell carcinoid is an uncommon, yet distinctive neoplasm that is characterized by dual endocrine and glandular differentiation in the same cell, a feature that led to confusion regarding histogenesis, nomenclature, and clinical management of this neoplasm (Fig. 5). A variety of names have been applied to this lesion: mucinous carcinoid, adenocarcinoid, amphicrine carcinoma, crypt cell carcinoma, and mucin-producing neuroendocrine tumor. These tumors tend to permeate the appendix wall in a diffuse, often times, concentric fashion, and as such do not produce a mass. Hence, size criteria cannot easily be applied to this variant in determining behavior. The biological behavior and outcome of GCC are a little controversial. Early reports considered GCC a more aggressive variant of classical appendiceal "carcinoid" with potential for distant metastases and recurrence. Standard appendectomy was deemed adequate treatment. However, worrisome morphological features and evidence for more aggressive clinical behavior with frequent angiolymphatic permeation, perineural/intraneural invasion, extensive mesoappendiceal extension, lymph node spread, and peritoneal and liver metastases, have all been documented [21]. Accordingly, GCC is now considered a distinct neoplasm with morphological and clinical features intermediate between classical appendiceal well-differentiated neuroendocrine tumor and adenocarcinoma. Although some still consider simple appendectomy sufficient treatment for localized GCC, a right hemicolectomy is currently recommended and viewed as the standard mode of surgical treatment [22].

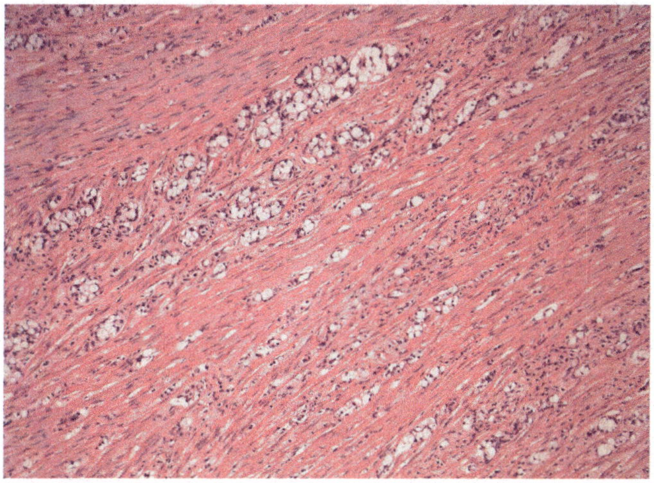

Fig. 5 The so-called goblet cell carcinoid composed of vacuolated cells that permeate the muscle layer in a diffuse fashion. (H&E × 100)

Table 8 Behavior guidelines for appendiceal neuroendocrine tumors

Well-differentiated, benign behavior:
• Nonfunctioning, 2 cm or less, confined to appendix wall, no angioinvasion
Well-differentiated, uncertain behavior:
• Nonfunctioning, greater than 2 cm, extending into mesoappendix, no angioinvasion
Well-differentiated, low-grade malignant behavior:
• Nonfunctioning or functioning, greater than 2 cm, extending into mesoappendix, with angioinvasion
• Nonfunctioning or functioning, any size, with lymph node or liver metastases
• "Goblet cell carcinoid"
Poorly-differentiated, high-grade behavior:
• Functioning/nonfunctioning, poorly differentiated neuroendocrine carcinoma with >10 mitoses per 10 HPF, necrosis, angioinvasion
• Small cell carcinoma

See Table 8 for the behavioral features of neuroendocrine tumors of the appendix. The overall 5-year survival for well-differentiated neuroendocrine tumors localized to the appendix is around 95% and this drops to about 85% with regional lymph node involvement. The tubular variant is essentially innocuous. Goblet cell carcinoids are considerably more aggressive as mentioned above.

References

1. Rindi G, Capella C, Solcia E. Cell biology, clinicopathological profile, and classification of gastro-enteropancreatic endocrine tumors. J Mol Med 1998;76:413–20.
2. Solcia E, Kloppel G, Sobin LH, et al. Histologic typing of Endocrine Tumours. In: WHO International Classification of Tumours. Heidelberg: Springer-Verlag, 2000.
3. Rindi G, Kloppel G, Ahlman H, et al. TNM staging of foregut (neuro)endocrine tumors: a consensus proposal including a grading system. Virchows Arch 2006;449:395–401.
4. Rindi G, Kloppel G, Couvelard A, et al. TNM staging of midgut and hindgut (neuro) endocrine tumors: a consensus proposal including a grading system. Virchows Arch 2007;451:757–62.
5. Chetty R. Requiem for the term "carcinoid tumour" in the gastrointestinal tract? Can J Gastroenterol 2008;22:357–8.
6. Simonsson M, Eriksson S, Hakanson R, et al. Endocrine cells in the human oxyntic mucosa. A histochemical study. Scand J Gastroenterol 1988;23:1089–99.
7. Rindi G, Luinetti O, Cornaggia M, et al. Three subtypes of gastric argyrophil carcinoid and the gastric neuroendocrine carcinoma: a clinicopathologic study. Gastroenterol 1993:104:994–1006.
8. Rindi G, Bordi C, Rappel S, eta al. Gastric carcinoids and neuroendocrine carcinomas: pathogenesis, pathology and behavior. World J Surg 1996;20:168–72.
9. Solcia E, Rindi G, Larosa S, et al. Morphological, molecular, and prognostic aspects of gastric endocrine tumors. Microsc Res Tech 2000;48:339–48.

10. Modlin IM, Lye KD, Kidd M. A 5-decade analysis of 13,715 carcinoid tumors. Cancer 2003;97:934–59.
11. Ferraro G, Annibale B, Marignani M, et al. Effectiveness of octreotide in controlling fasting hypergastrinemia and related enterochromaffin-like cell growth. J Clin Endocrinol Metab 1996;81:677–83.
12. Delle Fave G, Capurso G, Annibale B, et al. Gastric neuroendocrine tumors. Neuroendocrinol 2004;80:16–9. (Supplement).
13. Capella C, Solcia, E, Sobin LH, et al. Endocrine tumours of the small intestine. In: Pathology and Genetics of tumours of the digestive system. WHO classification of Tumours. Eds: Hamilton SR, Aaltonen LA. IARC press, Lyon 2000; 77–82.
14. Dayal Y, Tallberg KA, Nunnemacher G, et al. Duodenal carcinoids in patients with and without neurofibromatosis. Am J Surg Pathol 1986;10:348–57.
15. Burke AP, Federspiel BH, Sobin LH, et al. Carcinoids of the duodenum. A histologic and immunohistochemical study of 65 tumors. Am J Surg Pathol 1989;13:828–37.
16. Chetty R. Pot Pourri of pancreatic and periampullary pathology. Curr Diagn Pathol 200;6:165–70.
17. Burke AP, Thomas RM, Elsayed AM, et al. An immunohistochemical and clinicopathologic study of 167 cases. Cancer 1997;79:1086–93.
18. Stinner B, Kisker O, Zielke A, et al. Surgical management for carcinoid tumors of small bowel, appendix, colon, and rectum. World J Surg 1996;20:183–8.
19. Alsaad KO, Serra S, Schmitt A, Perren A, Chetty R. Cytokeratins 7 and 20 immunoexpression profile in goblet cell and classical carcinoids of appendix. Endocr Pathol 2007;18:16–22.
20. Alsaad KO, Serra S, Perren A, Hsieh E, Chetty R. CK19 and CD99 immunoexpression profile in goblet cell (mucin-producing neuroendocrine tumors) and classical carcinoids of the vermiform appendix. Int J Surg Pathol 2007;15:252–257.
21. Pahlavan PS, Kanthan R. Goblet cell carcinoid of the appendix. World J Surg Oncol 2005;20:3:36.
22. Pham TH, Wolff B, Abraham SC, et al. Surgical and chemotherapy treatment outcomes of goblet cell carcinoid: A tertiary cancer center experience. Ann Surg Oncol 2006;13:370–6.

Neuroendocrine Tumours of the Breast

Andrew M. Hanby and Rebecca A. Brannan

Abstract There is debate about the existence of neuroendocrine cells in the normal breast, however, tumours with varying degrees of neuroendocrine differentiation occur. The latest WHO classification identifies solid neuroendocrine carcinoma, small and large cell carcinoma. In addition mucinous carcinoma contributes to a large number of tumours with neuroendocrine differentiation. The biology and molecular pathology of solid neuroendocrine and mucinous carcinomas do not appear independent of grade and these are generally low-grade lesions with an oestrogen receptor positive or negative, chromogranin A positive, TTF1 negative, molecular profile. Small and large cell carcinomas are aggressive tumours with often (but not always) an oestrogen receptor negative and chromogranin A positive, TTF1 positive profile. Metastasis of tumours with neuroendocrine attributes from elsewhere should always be considered when encountered in breast biopsy material.

Keywords Solid neuroendocrine tumour • Small cell carcinoma • Large cell • Neuroendocrine carcinoma • Merkel cell carcinoma

Introduction

As with breast tumours in general, neuroendocrine carcinoma of the breast and breast tumours with lesser degrees of neuroendocrine differentiation encompass a diverse range of tumours differing from each other in morphology, molecular pathology, and clinical course. Tumours with neuroendocrine attributes were first described by Feyrter in 1962 [1], and have been described in male as well as female breasts [2].

A.M. Hanby (✉)
Leeds Institute of Molecular Medicine, Yorkshire Cancer Research and Liz Dawn Pathology and Translational Sciences Centre Section of Pathology and Tumour Biology Wellcome Trust Brenner Building, Level 4, Room 4.13 St James's University Hospital, Beckett Street Leeds, LS9 7TF, United Kingdom
e-mail: a.m.hanby@leeds.ac.uk

The Origin of Neuroendocrine Carcinomas Arising in the Breast

The origin of these tumours is debated in the literature. A number of studies have detailed the immunohistochemical profile of the benign breast using a variety of antibodies said to be associated with endocrine differentiation. Chromogranin A-positive argyrophilic cells were demonstrated between the basal myoepithelial and the luminal epithelial cells in normal mammary tissue by Bussolati et al. [3]. These cells were variously globoid, cylindrical, or stellate with rounded oval nuclei and granular cytoplasm [3]. Other studies, however, failed to identify such a population [4, 5]. Two main theories, therefore, emerge for the provenance of breast tumours with neuroendocrine attributes; either that these tumours derive from neuroendocrine cells normally present in the breast or alternatively that the endocrine differentiation or features of endocrine differentiation within some breast carcinomas reflect an altered gene profile consequent upon the oncogenic process [6–8]. The existence of small numbers of pre-existing neuroendocrine cells as tumour precursors and the differentiation of malignant breast epithelium along neuroendocrine lines are not, in our opinion, mutually exclusive.

Incidence

Because of the variation of classification employed in the literature, which blurs the difference between neuroendocrine carcinoma and neuroendocrine differentiation in tumours arguably categorized otherwise, there is a great breadth of incidence figures reported. Van Krimpen reports 40 cases showing neuroendocrine differentiation in a series of 317 breast carcinomas [9], but many of these cases may not have fulfilled the stricter criteria for neuroendocrine carcinoma detailed below [10].

A. Khan (ed.), *Surgical Pathology of Endocrine and Neuroendocrine Tumors*, Current Clinical Pathology,
DOI 10.1007/978-1-60327-396-1_13,

Clinical Profile

The age of patients with neuroendocrine tumours in the breast range from 40 to 89 [11, 12] in the published literature, with the range for the small cell subset 46–71 [13, 14]. Whilst, historically, the term carcinoid tumour has often been used to describe neuroendocrine tumours arising in the breast, [1, 15], a search of the literature reveals only one description of the systemic carcinoid symptoms related to the breast, a carcinoid crisis induced by mammographic compression [16] of a mammary metastasis from an ileal primary. No compelling evidence of this in the context of a primary mammary neuroendocrine carcinoma can be found in the literature to date. Equally, no distinguishing presentation or prognostic profile of these neoplasms from the generality of breast neoplasms has been reported. A variety of presentations have been documented in the literature – commonly as a mass with sizes ranging from 1 to 18 mm [13, 17, 18] or radiologically detected by virtue of radioopacity or microcalcifications [13, 18]. These lesions are occasionally multicentric [13].

More details regarding the natural history of these lesions is discussed in the sub-sections below. There is no evidence that focal neuroendocrine differentiation has a special prognostic significance [9].

Classification

Immunohistochemical and histochemical studies of series of breast tumours will reveal a range of positivity with "endocrine/neuroendocrine" markers and to an extent, therefore, the definition of "endocrine/neuroendocrine" can be subjective. The World Health Organization (WHO) suggestion that these lesions should have a similar histological appearance to those seen in the gastrointestinal tract and lung and that these tumours should express neuroendocrine markers in more that 50% of the tumour cells [19] is most helpful.

As implied above, considerable diversity occurs in mammary tumours exhibiting neuroendocrine features. This diversity is both temporal, in other words neuroendocrine differentiation can be identified within in situ lesions, so called E-DCIS [20, 21] as well as invasive, and also qualitative, in other words there are different species of breast tumours, which manifest neuroendocrine features. This spectrum ranges from mucinous carcinomas of the breast, which may show varying degrees of endocrine differentiation through to tumours identical in morphology to small cell carcinomas arising in the lung.

Multiple different classifications have been proposed for neuroendocrine carcinomas arising within the breast, for example, Papotti proposed seven types [22], and Sapino five [23]. Perhaps the most pragmatic is the WHO classification which defines three principle tumours; solid neuroendocrine tumour, small/oat cell carcinoma, and large cell neuroendocrine carcinoma [19]. It should be appreciated that not all tumours in the breast exhibiting neuroendocrine features fit snugly into the WHO classification categories and, for the purposes of this chapter, we also discuss type B pattern mucinous carcinomas and Merkel cell/Merkel-like tumours.

In practice multiple patterns can occur precluding easy 'pigeonholing,' and the associated DCIS pattern may appear to differ from the invasive component [6].

Solid Neuroendocrine Carcinoma

This pattern of neuroendocrine carcinoma of the breast has been recognized under a number of other names including 'solid variant' of papillary carcinoma proposed by Maluf [24] in recognition of the ramifying fibrovascular cores throughout the lesion [Fig. 1a,b]. These tumours often grow in an insular fashion so much so that it can be quite difficult to distinguish between an in situ and invasive lesion. Pseudorosettes or palisades are seen in many tumours. The tumour cells are typically medium sized, commonly polygonal or plasmacytoid, and are loosely cohesive; eosinophilic granular cytoplasm is commonly seen. The component cells are typically relatively monotonous and small with equally small mildly atypical, round-to-ovoid nuclei with small or inconspicuous nucleoli, and finely dispersed chromatin [20, 18]; however, in our experience, on high power examination the nuclear pleomorphism can be greater than at first suspected. In general, the nuclear morphology in the invasive component is matched by those within associated DCIS [20]. Little mitotic activity is typical [18]. Spindle cells can be variably present and are often prominent, so much so that where they dominate, a spindle cell variant has been proposed [25].

As both epithelioid and spindle cell morphologies can co-exist this can lead the misinterpretation of such tumours as usual type ductal hyperplasia (UDH) [18, 20]. Unlike UDH the epithelioid and spindle cells are not intermingled so intimately, and the spindle cells may be arranged in fascicles of cells rather than a mixed pattern, see Fig. 1c. Also the presence of fibrovascular cores throughout the lesion supports the diagnosis of a neuroendocrine carcinoma.

Typical solid neuroendocrine carcinomas and mucinous carcinomas are ER [26–28], PR [26, 27, 29], chromogranin A [11–13, 26, 30–33], NSE [31, 13, 17, 27, 33], and

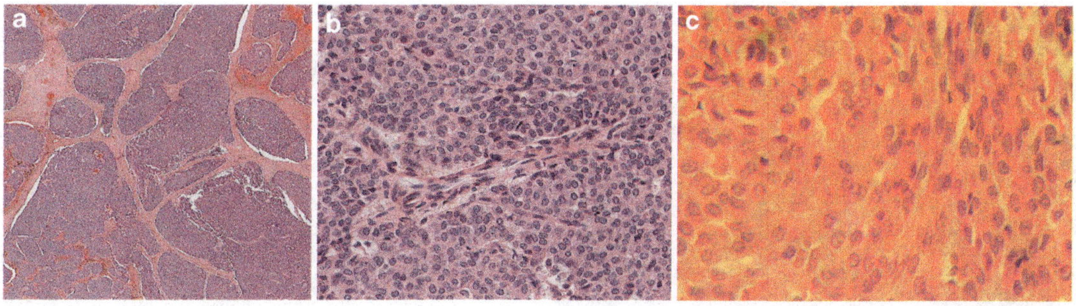

Fig. 1 Solid neuroendocrine tumour. (**a**) Shows the overall structure of a typical example with ramifying fibrovascular cores throughout the lesion and islands of invasive tumour resembling in situ disease. (**b**) From the same tumour demonstrates the presence of smaller calibre arborizing blood vessels punctuating the cellular tumour islands. This feature is also seen in the associated in situ disease but is not seen in a usual type ductal hyperplasia (UDH) – a benign lesion, which it may mimic. (**c**) From a different example where the component cells show a mix of spindle and epithelioid morphologies. Unlike UDH, fascicles of spindles cells may be seen (*right* side of the image)

synaptophysin [11, 13, 17, 26, 27, 30–33] positive with some variation between series. It is worth noting that PR is often positive in extramammary neuroendocrine tumours, though ER expression is rare, for example, in one series of pancreatic endocrine tumours 58% were PR positive, though none were ER positive [34]. Other markers that can be expressed include GCDFP15 [31, 35], CEA [12]. Grimelius silver stain [26], neurotensin [26, 21], CD56 [11, 36], bcl-2 [17], CAM 5.2 [17], cytokeratin AE1/3 [17], and α-hCG [26]. A great range of markers have been reported as being negative in these lesions but idiosyncratic variation between cases is likely and it is hard to generalize. However, it is worth noting that ER and PR can be negative in these tumours [30] and those studies which have looked for overexpressed Her-2/neu [30, 26, 37] have not found it, though a distinctive fine granular cytoplasmic staining pattern with the HercepTest™ has been reported in a single case of breast carcinoma with neuroendocrine differentiation [37].

A distinctive molecular pathology and clinical profile is yet to be firmly established for these tumours and as yet no specific targeted therapy has been identified related to their endocrine characteristics. There are also no large studies defining a specific molecular signature in these tumours and the treatment described in the literature, for example, see [12, 13, 18], do not differ from the practice of managing breast cancer as a whole. Many of these tumours, particularly occurring in elderly patients, are relatively indolent [18, 23].

Small Cell/Oat Cell Carcinoma (SLNC)

Less than 30 of small cell carcinoma of the breast cases have been reported in the literature [14]. In this form of mammary carcinoma the tumour is morphologically identical to lesions arising within the bronchus and may possess a similarly identical immunophenotype; consequently consideration of a metastasis from the bronchus should always be considered when such a tumour is encountered in a breast biopsy (see below) [38, 39]. These tumours grow as highly cellular sheets. The component cells are mitotically active, densely packed, and have minimal cytoplasm with hyperchromatic millet seed-like nuclei. Striking chromatin smearing is often seen [Fig. 2]. In situ disease is a common accompaniment and may have either small cell or ductal features [28, 39] see Fig. 3. Apart

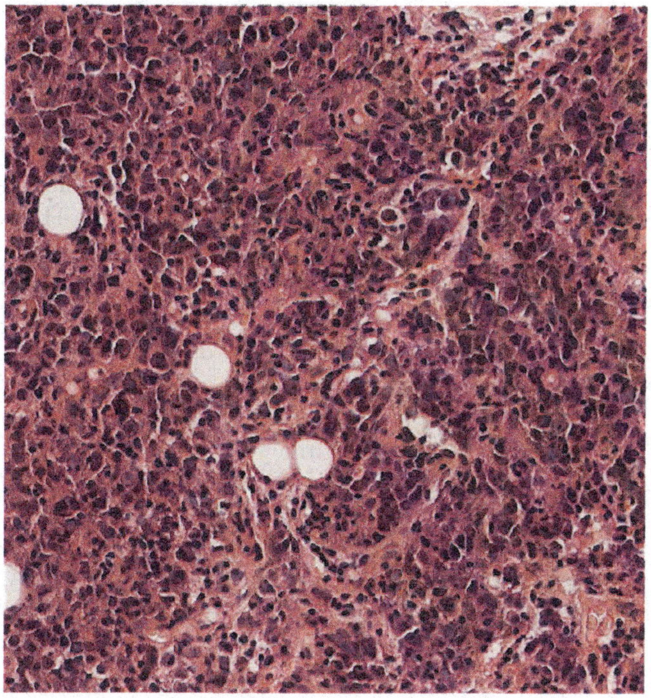

Fig. 2 Small cell carcinoma of the breast. These tumours are morphologically similar to such lesions arising in the bronchus. This is a typical field showing high cellularity, nuclear hyperchromasia, and some of the nuclear smearing typical of these lesions

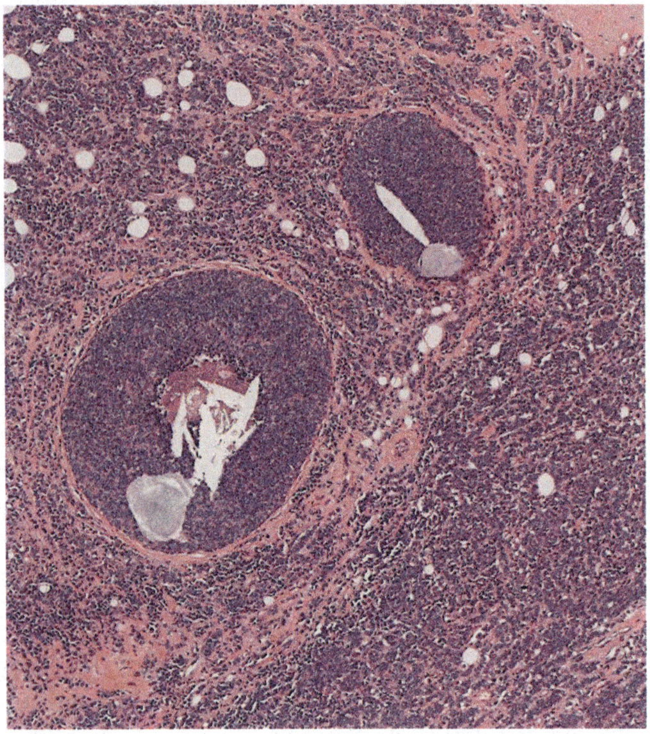

Fig. 3 Small cell carcinoma of the breast. These lesions need to be distinguished from tumours metastatic to the breast from the bronchus. The presence of in situ disease (the *rounded* configurations towards the centre of the image) supports the diagnosis of this lesion as a primary mammary tumour

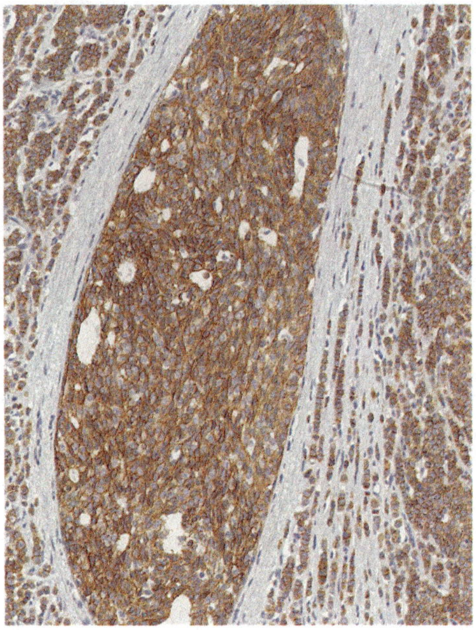

Fig. 4 Small cell carcinoma of the breast; same case as 13.3; Immunohistochemical stain for E-cadherin. Small cell carcinoma can resemble lobular carcinoma – in this example lines of tumour cells identical to the 'Indian files,' more commonly associated with lobular carcinoma, can be seen. Unlike typical lobular carcinoma membrane localized E-cadherin is present both in the invasive and in situ component

from a metastasis, these lesions need to be distinguished from lymphoma and lobular carcinoma. The latter should not be a problem in good quality samples but poor fixation may make this distinction more challenging. If there is any doubt, positive membrane staining with E-cadherin should exclude the diagnosis of lobular carcinoma [Fig. 4]. However, the picture is often complicated a by mixed pattern of disease, for example, in one of the largest series four of nine cases showed mixed pathology with lobular and ductal represented in different cases [39]. The distinction between atypical carcinoid tumour and small cell carcinoma has been stated to be difficult; an organized trabecular pattern of tumour cells favours the former [6], however, in writing this chapter, we were unable to find a bona fide description of an atypical carcinoid tumour occurring in the breast.

Small cell neuroendocrine carcinomas typically express synaptophysin [13, 17], NSE [13, 17], and chromogranin A [13]. They can also express markers typical of these lesions occurring outside the breast, most notably TTF1 [36, 38] (Fig. 5), but also including NCAM [13], Leu-7 [13], and CD56 [36]. They are usually ER and PR negative, but in the largest series 5/9 were positive; none have been documented as overexpressing HER2 [13, 17, 39].

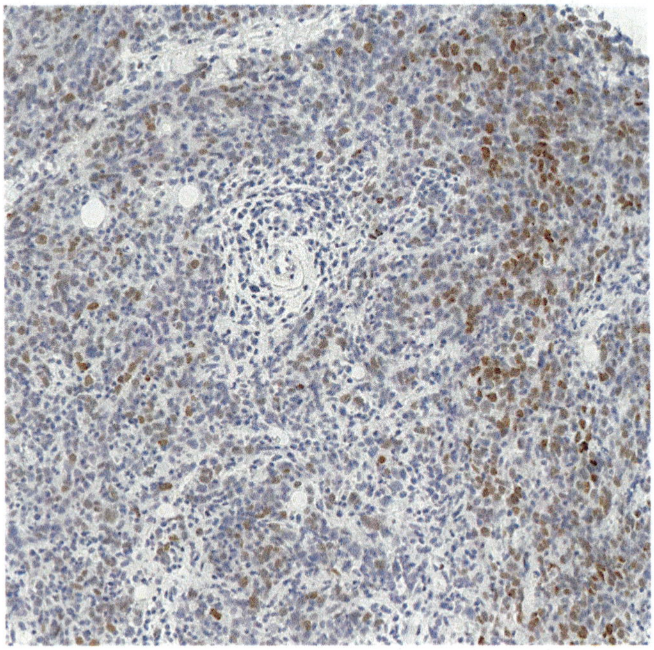

Fig. 5 Small cell carcinoma of the breast, immunohistochemical stain demonstrating nuclear localization for TTF1

These tumours are aggressive; most of the reported pure SCNC cases show an appreciably worse prognosis [14]. Given the resemblance of these carcinomas to those arising in the bronchus, treatment most appropriate for tumours primary to the bronchus may need to be considered.

Large Cell Neuroendocrine Carcinoma

This category probably includes the tumours described by Sapino et al. as poorly differentiated and comprised 8 out of a series of 50 tumours with evidence of neuroendocrine differentiation [35]. Other than this, the literature is sparsely populated by case studies rather than series [27]. These tumours are comprised of much larger cells than seen in small cell carcinoma and internal nuclear detail such as nucleoli may be more readily appreciated. Sometimes more cytoplasm may also be evident. Mitoses may be plentiful, up to 65 per 10 high power fields (HPF) [35]. They may be Chromogranin A, Synaptophysin, NSE, estrogen, and progesterone receptor positive [27].

Mucinous Carcinoma of the Breast

Whilst these lesions are not formally within the WHO heading of neuroendocrine tumours, they are probably the commonest lesions with neuroendocrine differentiation occurring within the breast [40] and can show areas identical to solid neuroendocrine carcinoma.

These tumours have been divided into type A and type B, on the basis of the studies of Capella et al. [41], with a type 'C' also being suggested, but not generally adopted [42]. It is the 'B' type that shows neuroendocrine differentiation. In this pattern, cellular islands are present within pools of mucin. Incidentally identical tumours can be seen in the skin and these can be morphologically and immunohistochemically identical [43]. Interestingly one study showed that mucinous carcinomas with neuroendocrine differentiation showed relatively higher PR positivity [29]. It has been suggested in a small series of mucinous carcinomas that neuroendocrine differentiation (type B) confers a better prognosis [29]. Mixed pattern tumours with both mucinous features and areas resembling solid neuroendocrine carcinoma may be seen, and endocrine DCIS is a common accompaniment [20], see Fig. 6.

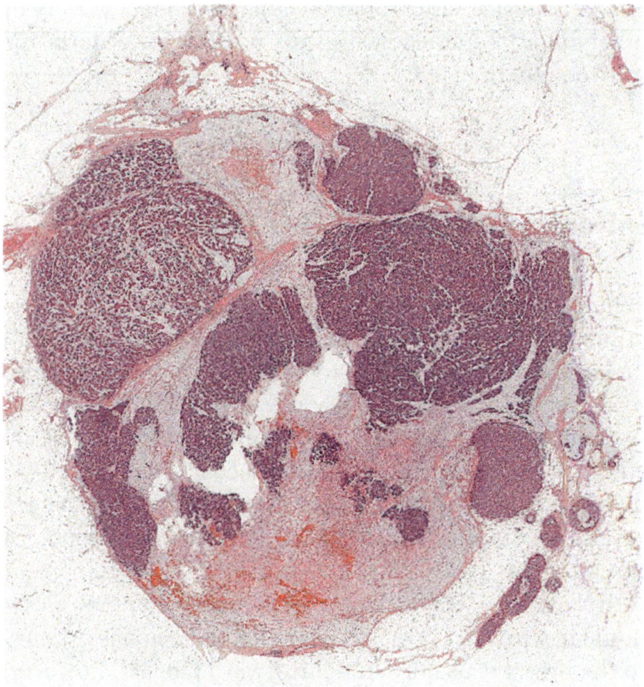

Fig. 6 Type B mucinous carcinoma. Neuroendocrine differentiation is a hallmark of these lesions which, as in this example, (for example from the 12–4 o' clock positions), can include areas identical to solid pattern neuroendocrine carcinoma. Elsewhere copious mucin production characterizes these lesions (for example 4–7 o' clock positions)

Merkel Cell/Merkel Cell Like

Tumours with these features are rare and have been variously described as Merkel cell or Merkel cell like. At least one such tumour has been reported in the male breast [44]. These tumours are 'small round blue cell tumours.' They are cellular, mitotically active with either epitheloid or spindle cells, having scant cytoplasm. Necrosis is common [18, 44–46]. At least two cases in the literature demonstrated the characteristic dot-like positivity with Cytokeratin 20 demonstrable in true Merkel cell tumours, a feature which distinguishes them from small cell carcinomas [44, 46]. The data is too limited to form a firm view on outcome; an 82-year-old patient with a CK20 positive tumour died 15 months after diagnosis [46], whilst a 38-year-old described as having a 'Merkel cell-like' tumour was well 6 years after diagnosis [45].

Neuroendocrine Differentiation Occurring in Other Mammary Carcinomas

Carcinomas may exhibit hybrid features with neuroendocrine differentiation – notably, for example, having apocrine characteristics [35, 47]. Indeed it has been suggested that androgen receptor activation may switch on neuroendocrine differentiation in elderly patients and is associated with low-grade tumours [35]. Lesser degrees of neuroendocrine differentiation can be seen in a variety of other breast tumours, which do not fill the criteria for 'neuroendocrine' [48].

Differential Diagnosis

Where the diagnosis of primary neuroendocrine carcinoma of the breast is considered, particularly if small or large cell, it is prudent to consider the possibility of a metastasis from a primary site outside of the breast. A number of easily more recognizable endocrine carcinomas from other sites have been documented as metastasizing to the breast, for example, medullary carcinoma of the thyroid and islet cell carcinoma of the pancreas [48].

In general, where there is appropriate ductal carcinoma in situ (DCIS) the decision that the lesion is primary to the breast is usually straightforward [26, 28], however, there is one report of secondary colonization of sclerosing adenosis, mimicking DCIS, by a metastatic islet cell tumour of the pancreas [48].

If DCIS cannot be identified then this can be more problematic. Under these circumstances, in the practical diagnostic setting it is prudent to suggest total body imaging and a search for a primary tumour of extra-mammary sites be undertaken. As indicated below the immunohistochemical profile of these tumours may be identical to similar tumours occurring outside the breast and therefore much reliance on the overall clinical picture has to be made.

Up to 90% of tumours said to be of neuroendocrine type stain positively with the Grimelius' silver stain. The overall immunohistochemical profile documented for these lesions over multiple publications is varied and encompasses diverse tumours. As a group, most stain for chromagranin A and synaptophysin. A range of other products have been documented including neurotensin, however, many of these specific products are idiosyncratic to particular tumours and in many cases no specific product can be identified at all in such lesions.

It is important to note that markers in isolation cannot be relied on to identify a neuroendocrine tumour to be of breast origin or not. For example, the marker TTF1 can be expressed by primary breast small cell neuroendocrine carcinomas [11], and progesterone receptor can be expressed in a number of non-mammary neuroendocrine tumours. Other important differential diagnoses to consider include lymphoma and melanoma for which negative CD45 [14, 17] and HMB45 [14, 17] labelling provides useful information.

Cytopathology

The cytology of neuroendocrine tumours in the breast and mammary tumours with neuroendocrine differentiation does not differ from similar tumours seen elsewhere [49]. Like lobular carcinoma, loss of cell cohesion may be a prominent feature [50]. The FNA may be cellular with single or loose clusters of cells. The amount of cytoplasm may be scant or arranged eccentrically in a plasmacytoid fashion [6, 30, 33]. Some peripherally located cytoplasmic granularity may be observed. The nuclear-cytoplasmic ratio is typically high and the nuclei are hyperchromatic with inconspicuous nucleoli [30]. Architectural configurations such as rosette-like formations or papillary fronds may be present [6, 33, 51]. PAS-positive mucin containing vacuoles can be sometimes demonstrated [52]. The eosinophilic cytoplasm, also noticeable on H&E stained histological sections can be observed in Giemsa or Diff-Quick stained preparations, but is not so obvious in Papanicolaou preparations [52].

Ultrastructure

There is very little work examining in detail the ultrastructure of endocrine tumours of the breast and therefore, what is documented is relatively anecdotal, given the diversity of such tumours occurring in the breast. In general, where this ultrastructural examination has been done the findings resemble those for neuroendocrine tumours occurring outside the breast [6, 20, 21, 26].

Serum Neoplastic Markers

The data in the literature regarding secreted markers are limited. One case study reported that CEA, CA 15.3, CA 125, and CA 19.9 were not elevated in the serum whereas the neuroendocrine markers NSE and chromogranin were raised [40]. The value of serum chromogranin A as a feature specific to neuroendocrine tumours is weakened by the observation that in a series of non-endocrine malignancies, 34 out of a total of 72 showed elevated chromogranin A levels [53].

Summary

Endocrine neoplasms of the breast are represented by a diverse group of neuroendocrine tumours. Most are relatively low grade but high-grade tumours with an immunophenotype similar to small cell carcinoma of the bronchus also occur. Neuroendocrine differentiation in a mammary neoplasm does not add any additional information regarding tumour biology to that supplied by the established prognostic indicators of tumour size, grade, and nodal status [54].

References

1. Feyrter F, Hartmann G. [On The Carcinoid Growth Form Of The Carcinoma Mammae, Especially The Carcinoma Solidum (Gelatinosum) Mammae.]. Frankf Z Pathol 1963;73:24–39.
2. Alm P, Alumets J, Bak-Jensen E, Olsson H. Neuroendocrine differentiation in male breast carcinomas. Apmis 1992; 100(8):720–6.
3. Bussolati G, Gugliotta P, Sapino A, Eusebi V, Lloyd RV. Chromogranin-reactive endocrine cells in argyrophilic carcinomas ("carcinoids") and normal tissue of the breast. Am J Pathol 1985;120(2):186–92.
4. Nesland JM, Lunde S, Holm R, Johannessen JV. Electron microscopy and immunostaining of the normal breast and its benign lesions. A search for neuroendocrine cells. Histol Histopathol 1987;2(1):73–7.
5. Fetissof F, Dubois MP, Arbeille-Brassart B, Lansac J, Jobard P. Argyrophilic cells in mammary carcinoma. Hum Pathol 1983;14(2):127–34.
6. Kurisu Y, Tsuji M, Akashi K, et al. Composite type of breast carcinoma with endocrine differentiation: A cytological and immunohistochemical study. Pathol Int 2004;54(2):105–10.
7. Fukunaga M. Neuroendocrine carcinoma of the breast: a case report of pure type. Apmis 1998;106(11):1095–100.
8. Maluf HM, Koerner FC. Carcinomas of the breast with endocrine differentiation: a review. Virchows Arch 1994; 425(5):449–57.
9. van Krimpen C, Elferink A, Broodman CA, Hop WC, Pronk A, Menke M. The prognostic influence of neuroendocrine differentiation in breast cancer: results of a long-term follow-up study. Breast 2004;13(4):329–33.
10. Sapino A, Bussolati G. Is detection of endocrine cells in breast adenocarcinoma of diagnostic and clinical significance? Histopathology 2002;40(3):211–4.
11. Fujimoto Y, Yagyu R, Murase K, et al. A case of solid neuroendocrine carcinoma of the breast in a 40-year-old woman. Breast Cancer 2007;14(2):250–3.
12. Tanaka N, Katayama K, Negishi T, Kano H, Uchida N, Kuwano H. Case of breast cancer with endocrine differentiation. Int Surg 2007;92(4):214–7.
13. Jochems L, Tjalma WA. Primary small cell neuroendocrine tumour of the breast. Eur J Obstet Gynecol Reprod Biol 2004; 115(2):231–3.
14. Adegbola T, Connolly CE, Mortimer G. Small cell neuroendocrine carcinoma of the breast: a report of three cases and review of the literature. J Clin Pathol 2005;58(7):775–8.
15. Van Laarhoven HA, Gratama S, Wereldsma JC. Neuroendocrine carcinoid tumours of the breast: a variant of carcinoma with neuroendocrine differentiation. J Surg Oncol 1991; 46(2):125–32.
16. Ozgen A, Demirkazik FB, Arat A, Arat AR. Carcinoid crisis provoked by mammographic compression of metastatic carcinoid tumour of the breast. Clin Radiol 2001;56(3):250–1.
17. Bigotti G, Coli A, Butti A, del Vecchio M, Tartaglione R, Massi G. Primary small cell neuroendocrine carcinoma of the breast. J Exp Clin Cancer Res 2004;23(4):691–6.
18. Zekioglu O, Erhan Y, Ciris M, Bayramoglu H. Neuroendocrine differentiated carcinomas of the breast: a distinct entity. Breast 2003;12(4):251–7.
19. Tavasssoli FA, Devilee P, eds. Tumours of the breast and female genital organs. 1 ed. Lyon: IARC press; 2003.
20. Tsang WY, Chan JK. Endocrine ductal carcinoma in situ (E-DCIS) of the breast: a form of low-grade DCIS with distinctive clinicopathologic and biologic characteristics. Am J Surg Pathol 1996;20(8):921–43.
21. Cross AS, Azzopardi JG, Krausz T, van Noorden S, Polak JM. A morphological and immunocytochemical study of a distinctive variant of ductal carcinoma in-situ of the breast. Histopathology 1985;9(1):21–37.
22. Papotti M, Macri L, Finzi G, Capella C, Eusebi V, Bussolati G. Neuroendocrine differentiation in carcinomas of the breast: a study of 51 cases. Semin Diagn Pathol 1989;6(2):174–88.
23. Sapino A, Righi L, Cassoni P, Papotti M, Pietribiasi F, Bussolati G. Expression of the neuroendocrine phenotype in carcinomas of the breast. Semin Diagn Pathol 2000;17(2):127–37.
24. Maluf HM, Koerner FC. Solid papillary carcinoma of the breast. A form of intraductal carcinoma with endocrine differentiation frequently associated with mucinous carcinoma. Am J Surg Pathol 1995;19(11):1237–44.
25. Paties C, Zangrandi A, Taccagni GL, Kindl S, Vassallo G. Spindle cell non-argyrophil carcinoma of the breast with neuroendocrine differentiation. Histopathology 1996; 29(5):471–3.
26. La Rosa S, Usellini L, Riva C, Capella C. Well-differentiated neurotensin-producing neuroendocrine carcinoma of the breast. Report of a case. Histopathology 2007;51(6):846–7.
27. Tsai WC, Yu JC, Lin CK, Hsieh CT. Primary alveolar-type large cell neuroendocrine carcinoma of the breast. Breast J 2005;11(6):487.
28. Papotti M, Gherardi G, Eusebi V, Pagani A, Bussolati G. Primary oat cell (neuroendocrine) carcinoma of the breast. Report of four cases. Virchows Arch A Pathol Anat Histopathol 1992;420(1):103–8.
29. Tse GM, Ma TK, Chu WC, Lam WW, Poon CS, Chan WC. Neuroendocrine differentiation in pure type mammary mucinous carcinoma is associated with favorable histologic and immunohistochemical parameters. Mod Pathol 2004; 17(5):568–72.
30. McIntire M, Siziopikou K, Patil J, Gattuso P. Synchronous metastases to the liver and pancreas from a primary neuroendocrine carcinoma of the breast diagnosed by fine-needle aspiration. Diagn Cytopathol 2008;36(1):54–7.
31. Yaren A, Kelten C, Akbulut M, Teke Z, Duzcan E, Erdem E. Primary neuroendocrine carcinoma of the breast: a case report. Tumori 2007;93(5):496–8.
32. Vidulich KA, Donley SE, Duvic M. Multinodular cutaneous spread in neuroendocrine tumor of the breast: an unusual presentation. Am J Clin Dermatol 2007;8(6):379–83.
33. Mardi K, Sharma J. Fine needle aspiration cytology of breast carcinoma with neuroendocrine features–a case report with histopathological and immunohistochemical correlation. Indian J Pathol Microbiol 2007;50(1):65–8.
34. Viale G, Doglioni C, Gambacorta M, Zamboni G, Coggi G, Bordi C. Progesterone receptor immunoreactivity in pancreatic endocrine tumors. An immunocytochemical study of 156 neuroendocrine tumors of the pancreas, gastrointestinal and respiratory tracts, and skin. Cancer 1992;70(9):2268–77.
35. Sapino A, Righi L, Cassoni P, Papotti M, Gugliotta P, Bussolati G. Expression of apocrine differentiation markers in

neuroendocrine breast carcinomas of aged women. Mod Pathol 2001;14(8):768–76.
36. Salman WD, Harrison JA, Howat AJ. Small-cell neuroendocrine carcinoma of the breast. J Clin Pathol 2006;59 (8):888.
37. Mieda J, Ohaki Y, Oguro T, et al. Breast cancer with neuroendocrine differentiation detected by unique staining pattern of neoplastic cells in hercep test. J Nippon Med Sch 2004;71(3):203–8.
38. Shin SJ, DeLellis RA, Rosen PP. Small cell carcinoma of the breast–additional immunohistochemical studies. Am J Surg Pathol 2001;25(6):831–2.
39. Shin SJ, DeLellis RA, Ying L, Rosen PP. Small cell carcinoma of the breast: a clinicopathologic and immunohistochemical study of nine patients. Am J Surg Pathol 2000;24 (9):1231–8.
40. Panareo S, Carcoforo P, Lanzara S, et al. Radiolabelled somatostatin analogs for diagnosis and radio-guided surgery of neuroendocrine breast cancer undetectable with conventional imaging procedures. Breast 2008;17(1):111–114.
41. Capella C, Eusebi V, Mann B, Azzopardi JG. Endocrine differentiation in mucoid carcinoma of the breast. Histopathology 1980;4(6):613–30.
42. Coady AT, Shousha S, Dawson PM, Moss M, James KR, Bull TB. Mucinous carcinoma of the breast: further characterization of its three subtypes. Histopathology 1989;15 (6):617–26.
43. Hanby AM, McKee P, Jeffery M, et al. Primary mucinous carcinomas of the skin express TFF1, TFF3, estrogen receptor, and progesterone receptors. Am J Surg Pathol 1998; 22(9): 1125–31.
44. Alzaraa A, Thomas GD, Vodovnik A, Modgill VK. Merkel cell carcinoma in a male breast: a case report. Breast J 2007; 13(5):517–9.
45. Fukunaga M. Neuroendocrine carcinoma of the breast with Merkel cell carcinoma-like features. Pathol Int 1998;48(7): 557–61.
46. Asioli S, Dorji T, Lorenzini P, Eusebi V. Primary neuroendocrine (Merkel cell) carcinoma of the nipple. Virchows Arch 2002;440(4):443–4.
47. Berruti A, Saini A, Leonardo E, Cappia S, Borasio P, Dogliotti L. Management of neuroendocrine differentiated breast carcinoma. Breast 2004;13(6):527–9.
48. Judson K, Argani P. Intraductal spread by metastatic islet cell tumor (well-differentiated pancreatic endocrine neoplasm) involving the breast of a child, mimicking a primary mammary carcinoma. Am J Surg Pathol 2006;30(7):912–8.
49. Loo CK, Burchett IJ. Fine needle aspiration biopsy of neuroendocrine breast carcinoma metastatic to the thyroid. A case report. Acta Cytol 2003;47(1):83–7.
50. Tang W, Taniguchi E, Wang X, et al. Loss of cell cohesion in breast cytology as a characteristic of neuroendocrine carcinoma. Acta Cytol 2002;46(5):835–40.
51. Veilleux C, Trophilme D, Le Charpentier M, Dutrillaux B, Klijanienko J, Vielh P. Fine-needle sampling of a case of carcinoma of the breast with neuroendocrine differentiation. Diagn Cytopathol 1996;14(3):233–7.
52. Hussein KA, Sanders DS, Preece PE, Hunter SM, Nicoll SM. Argyrophil carcinoma of the breast: a cytologic, histochemical, and ultrastructural study of a case. Diagn Cytopathol 1989;5 (2):217–20.
53. Tropea F, Baldari S, Restifo G, Fiorillo MT, Surace P, Herberg A. Evaluation of chromogranin A expression in patients with non-neuroendocrine tumours. Clin Drug Investig 2006; 26(12): 715–22.
54. Miremadi A, Pinder SE, Lee AH, et al. Neuroendocrine differentiation and prognosis in breast adenocarcinoma. Histopathology 2002;40(3):215–22.

Neuroendocrine Tumors of Female Genital Tract

Khush Mittal and Fan Chen

Abstract Neuroendocrine tumors are relatively rare in the female genital tract, and therefore may present a diagnostic challenge. It is important to recognize these tumors as their management and prognosis may differ from the more common tumors with which these may be confused.

Keywords Carcinoid • Small cell carcinoma • Small cell carcinoma • hypercalcemic type • Small cell carcinoma • pulmonary type • Large cell neuroendocrine carcinoma

Neuroendocrine tumors of the female genital tract are rare but well recognized. A classification of these tumors is presented in Table 1. They can involve the ovary, fallopian tube, uterine cervix and corpus, and vagina and vulva.

Table 1 Neuroendocrine Tumors of the Female Genital Tract

Neuroendocrine tumors of the ovary
- Small cell carcinoma, hypercalcemic type
- Small cell carcinoma, pulmonary type
- Large cell neuroendocrine carcinoma
- Carcinoid

Neuroendocrine tumors of the Fallopian tube
- Carcinoid
- Small cell carcinoma

Neuroendocrine tumors of the uterine cervix

Carcinoid tumor of the uterine corpus
- Small cell carcinoma of the endometrium

Neuroendocrine tumors of the vagina
- Carcinoid
- Small cell carcinoma

Small cell carcinoma of the vulva

K. Mittal (✉)
Associate Professor of Pathology, NYU School of Medicine and Hospitals, Director, Surgical and Ob-Gyn pathology, Bellevue Hospital – Building H, Room 4west, NY 10016, USA
e-mail: khush.mittal@med.nyu.edu

Small Cell Carcinoma, Hypercalcemic Type, of the Ovary

Small cell carcinoma of the ovary, hypercalcemic type (SCC-HT), is rare. It generally occurs in young women (mean age 24 years), although it has been reported in an 8-year-old girl [1–5]. It is almost always unilateral, but bilateral and rare familial cases have been reported [1, 6]. Patients usually present with abdominal pain and swelling, two-thirds of the cases are associated with hypercalcemia and 50% of the patients show extra-ovarian involvement at the time of diagnosis [1–7].

Gross examination usually shows a large mass, between 6 and 26 cm (average 15 cm) [1–6]. The tumor is typically solid, lobulated, and pale white to gray. Areas of hemorrhage, necrosis, and cystic degeneration may be present (Fig. 1). Microscopic examination shows tumor cells growing in a diffuse pattern (most common) or as small islands/nests, trabeculae, and cords. Follicle-like

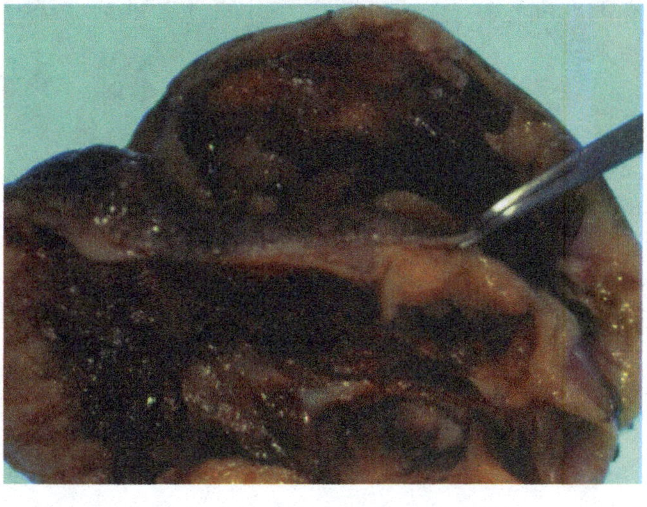

Fig. 1 Gross appearance of small cell carcinoma of the ovary, hypercalcemic type. The cut sections show areas of hemorrhage and necrosis

A. Khan (ed.), *Surgical Pathology of Endocrine and Neuroendocrine Tumors*, Current Clinical Pathology,
DOI 10.1007/978-1-60327-396-1_14, © Humana Press, a part of Springer Science+Business Media, LLC 2009

spaces containing eosinophilic fluid are present in 80% of the cases (Figs. 2 and 3) [1]. The tumor cells are uniformly small and round to spindled with scant cytoplasm, hyperchromatic nuclei, and small nucleoli. Characteristically, there is brisk mitotic activity and there are foci of necrosis (Fig. 4). The stroma is usually scant and fibrotic, but occasionally can be edematous and even myxoid. Fifty percent of the tumors have a large cell component, which may show epithelioid or rhabdoid features with eosinophilic cytoplasm, intracytoplasmic eosinophilic hyaline globules, large eccentrically located vesicular nuclei, and prominent nucleoli [8–9]. Ten to twelve percent of the tumors are associated with benign or malignant mucinous epithelium [1].

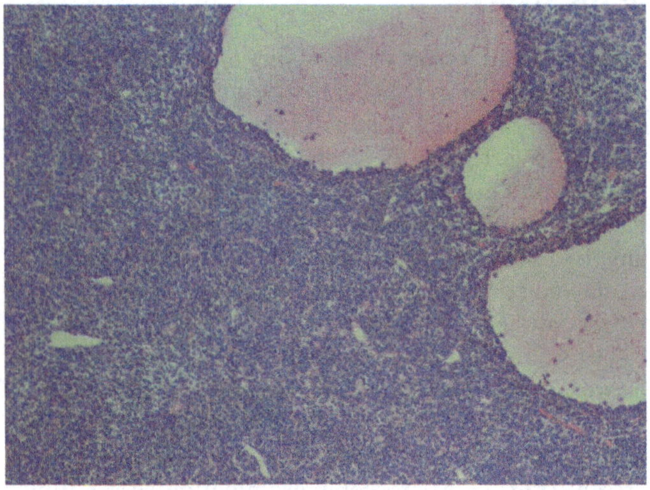

Fig. 2 Small cell carcinoma of the ovary, hypercalcemic type, showing closely packed tumor cells with diffuse growth pattern and follicle-like spaces (H&E × 40)

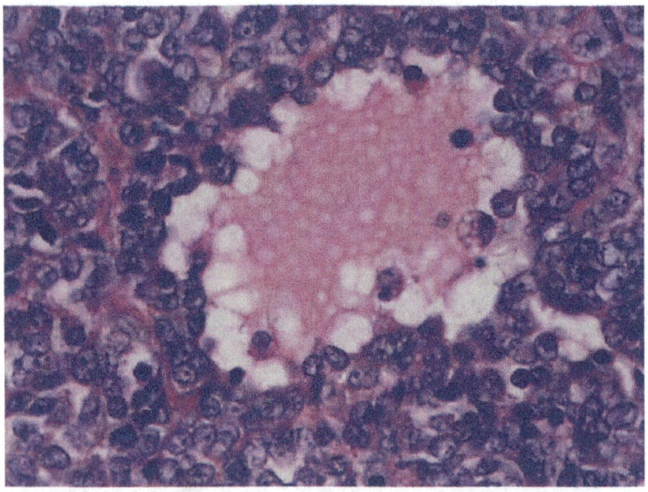

Fig. 3 Small cell carcinoma of the ovary, hypercalcemic type, showing tumor cells with follicular arrangement, small round to oval hyperchromatic nuclei, scant cytoplasm, and small nucleoli (H&E × 200)

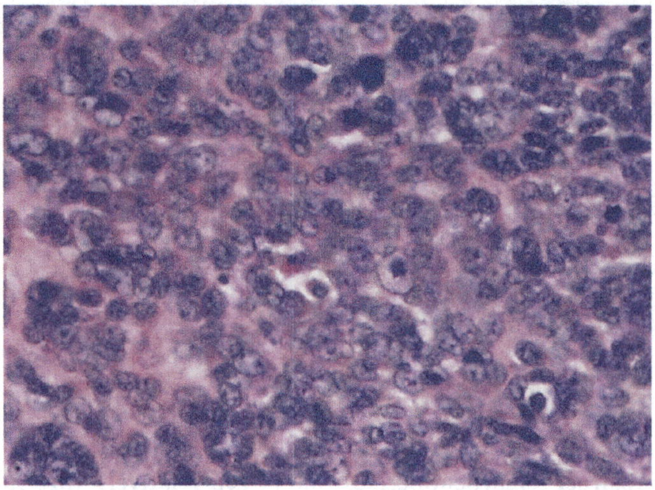

Fig. 4 Small cell carcinoma of the ovary, hypercalcemic type, showing small tumor cells with brisk mitotic activity (H&E × 200)

Immunohistochemical studies typically show immunoreactivity for one or more epithelial markers such as pan-cytokeratin, epithelial membrane antigen, or CAM 5.2 (Fig. 5). Variable immunoreactivity for vimentin, neuron-specific enolase, parathyroid hormone-related protein, chromogranin, or synaptophysin has been observed (Fig. 6). α-Inhibin, S100, B72.3, and desmin are generally immunonegative [1, 2, 4, 10, 11].

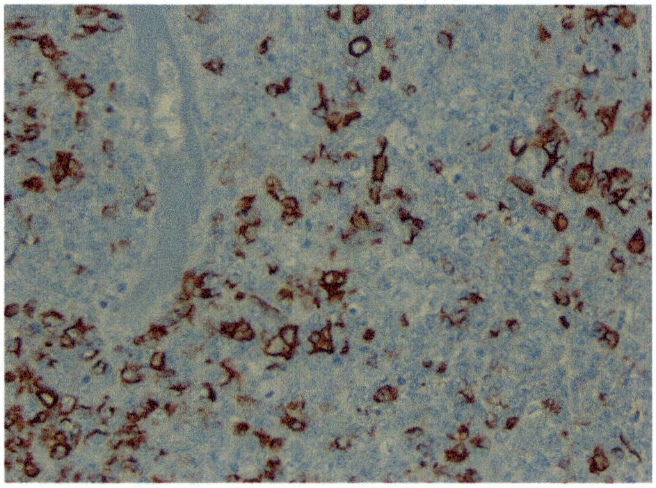

Fig. 5 Small cell carcinoma of the ovary, hypercalcemic type, showing tumor cells with patchy staining for cytokeratin Cam5.2

The differential diagnosis is broad and includes adult and juvenile granulosa cell tumor, primitive germ cell tumor, lymphoma, primitive neuroectodermal tumor, neuroblastoma, desmoplastic small round cell tumor, small cell carcinoma (pulmonary type), and metastatic

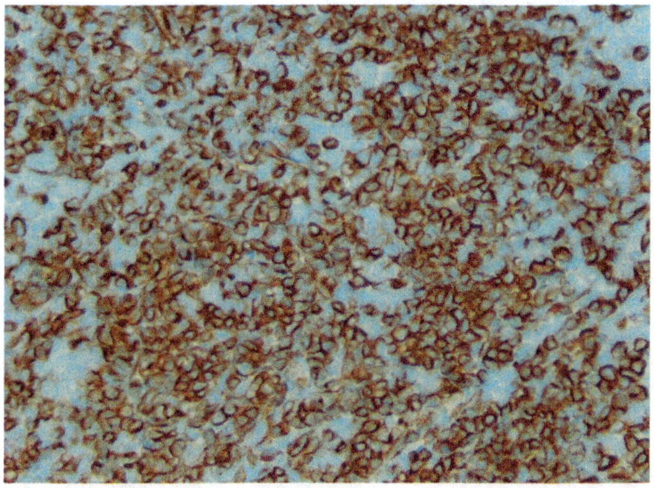

Fig. 6 Small cell carcinoma of the ovary, hypercalcemic type, showing tumor cells strongly positive for vimentin

small cell carcinoma. Large cell variant must be differentiated from undifferentiated large cell carcinoma and malignant melanoma. Thorough sampling of the tumor with attention to the characteristic clinical, microscopic, and immunohistochemical features of these other tumors should allow distinction from SCC-HT. In adult granulosa cell tumor, the tumor cells with grooved nuclei growing in a microfollicular pattern and Call-Exner bodies are characteristic, and tumor cells are immunoreactive for α-inhibin [1, 11].

The prognosis for SCC-HT is generally poor. Most tumors have spread beyond the ovary at the time of diagnosis. Surgery is the mainstay of therapy. Adjuvant chemotherapy and radiation are often used as well [1, 2, 4]. In the review by Young et al., only 33% of the patients with stage IA disease were alive and free of tumor for an average of 5.7 years postoperatively. In contrast, only 10% of patients with stage IC disease and 6.5% of patients with stages II, III, and IV disease were alive without recurrence at the last follow-up. In their study, favorable prognostic factors for stage IA tumor included age older than 30 years, normal preoperative calcium level, tumor less than 10 cm in diameter, and the absence of a large cell component [1].

Small Cell Carcinoma, Pulmonary Type, of the Ovary

Small cell carcinoma of the ovary, pulmonary type (SCC-PT), is extremely rare. It generally occurs in perimenopausal and postmenopausal women with a wide age range between 28 and 85 years (mean age 59 years). Fifty percent of the tumors are bilateral. Patients usually present with pelvic or abdominal mass. Most patients present with high-stage disease. Occasionally patients also present with carcinoid syndrome, such as, Cushing's syndrome and SIADH [2, 4, 12–15].

Gross examination usually shows a large mass, between 4.5 and 26 cm (average 13–14 cm) [12–15]. The tumor is typically solid with a cystic component. Areas of hemorrhage and necrosis may be present. Microscopic examination shows small to medium sized cells with scant cytoplasm, hyperchromatic nuclei with finely stippled chromatin, nuclear molding, and inconspicuous nucleoli. Typically, numerous mitotic figures and abundant necrosis are present. Many SCC-PTs are associated with surface epithelial-stromal tumor, especially endometrioid adenocarcinoma with or without squamous or mucinous differentiation. The association with Brenner tumor, mucinous tumor with atypical cells, and mature cystic teratoma has been reported [2, 4, 12–15].

Immunohistochemical studies typically show immunoreactivity for cytokeratin, EMA, and neuron-specific enolase. Chromogranin and Leu-7 can be immunopositive [4, 12, 14].

The differential diagnosis includes metastatic small cell carcinoma especially from the lung, carcinoid, Merkel cell carcinoma, malignant melanoma, and other small round blue cell tumors, discussed earlier [2, 12–15].

Patients with SCC-PT are typically treated with surgery followed by chemotherapy. The survival is dismal [2, 4, 12–15].

Large Cell Neuroendocrine Carcinoma of the Ovary

Large cell neuroendocrine carcinoma of the ovary (LCNEC) generally occurs in women during or beyond reproductive age, between 22 and 77 years of age (mean age 48.5 years). It is usually unilateral. Patients usually present with abdominal pain/distension, pelvic mass/pain, and about half of the patients present with advanced stage disease [14, 16–18].

Gross examination shows a large partially solid and partially cystic mass, between 9 and 30 cm (average 16.6 cm) [14, 16–18]. Microscopic examination shows tumor cells growing in sheets, islands, cords, and trabeculae. The tumor cells are medium to large with abundant cytoplasm, vesicular nuclei, and prominent nucleoli. Necrosis is extensive and mitotic figures are abundant. Most cases are associated with surface epithelial-stromal tumor, which can be endometrioid or mucinous.

Mucinous neoplasm of low malignant potential (borderline tumor) can be also present [14, 16–18].

Immunohistochemical studies typically show the tumor cells are immunoreactive for cytokeratin, neuron-specific enolase, chromogranin, synaptophysin, and peptide hormones, including serotonin and vasoactive intestinal peptide [14, 16–18].

The differential diagnosis includes undifferentiated carcinoma, anaplastic carcinoma, dysgerminoma, sertoli cell tumor, and adult granulosa cell tumor [16–18].

The prognosis for LCNEC is poor. Surgery followed by chemotherapy is the mainstay of the treatment. Most patients die of disease despite the extensive treatment [14, 16–18].

Carcinoid Tumor of the Ovary

Carcinoid tumor of the ovary generally occurs in women from early reproductive age to postmenopausal age, between 16 and 83 years of age (mean age 50.8 years). [14, 19–25, 32]. There are three main categories, including a component of mature cystic teratoma, primary ovarian carcinoid, and metastatic carcinoid [21]. Up to 75% of carcinoids are associated with mature cystic teratoma [14, 19, 20, 22–25]. Primary carcinoid is usually unilateral. About 5–15% of carcinoids show contralateral ovary with mature cystic teratoma, and sometimes mucinous or Brenner tumor [14, 20, 22, 23, 25]. Patients usually present with pelvic mass, abdominal pain and enlargement. Irregular menstruation and abnormal vaginal bleeding have also been reported [14, 19–25]. Approximately one-fourth to one-third of these patients have associated carcinoid syndrome [14, 19, 20]. Androgenic or estrogenic manifestation, chronic constipation, hyperinsulinemic hypoglycemia, hyperthyroidism, and carcinoid heart disease have been reported [14, 20, 26–28, 32].

Gross examination usually shows a large mass, between 2 and 28 cm (average 10 cm) [19, 20, 22–25]. The external surface is smooth, bosselated, and fibrous adhesion can be present. The carcinoid tumor is typically solid, firm, tan-yellow, and homogenous. Carcinoid associated with mature cystic teratoma or other tumor appears to arise from the wall of a cystic mass, protruding into the lumen.

Microscopic examination of primary ovarian carcinoid tumor shows four different patterns: insular, trabecular, mucinous, and strumal.

The insular pattern resembles carcinoid of midgut. The tumor cells grow in nests, some forming glands, separated by fibromatous stroma. Eosinophilic secretion, sometimes with calcification is present in the lumen. The tumor cells are columnar cells with abundant cytoplasm, cytoplasmic granularity, and round and uniform nuclei with coarse chromatin. Characteristically, mitotic activity is rare (Figs. 7–8).

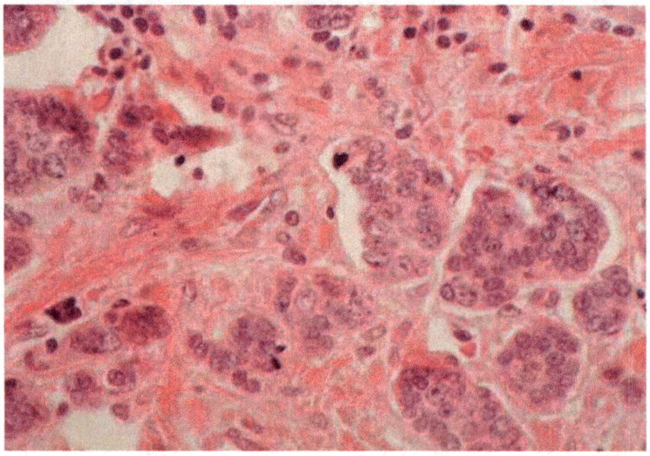

Fig. 7 Primary ovarian carcinoid with insular growth pattern (H&E × 40)

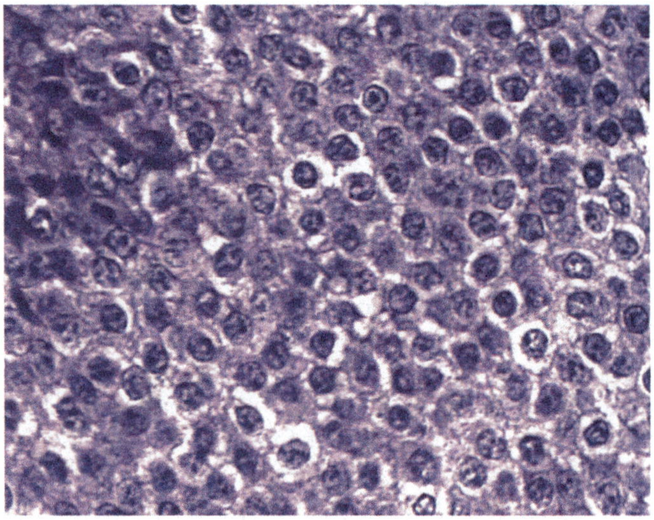

Fig. 8 Primary ovarian carcinoid with insular growth pattern (H&E × 200)

The trabecular pattern resembles carcinoid of foregut and hindgut. The tumor cells grow in long wavy parallel ribbons, cords, or trabeculae, separated by fibrous stroma. The tumor cells are tall columnar cells with abundant granular cytoplasm, oblongated nuclei with coarse chromatin, perpendicular to the long axis of the ribbons or cords. Typically, few mitotic figures are present (Figs. 9–10).

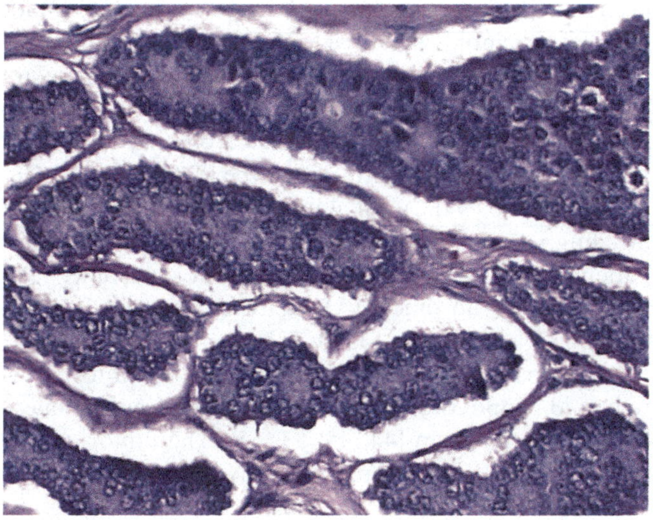

Fig. 9 Primary ovarian carcinoid with trabecular growth pattern (H&E × 40)

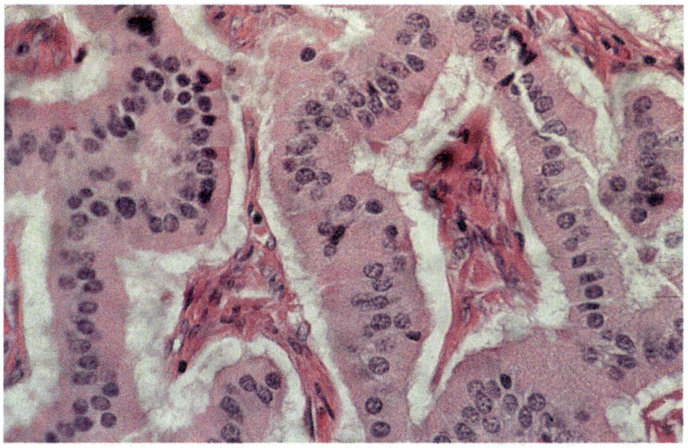

Fig. 10 Primary ovarian carcinoid with trabecular growth pattern (H&E × 200)

The mucinous pattern (*aka* goblet cell carcinoid) resembles carcinoid of appendix. The tumor is subdivided into three groups: well differentiated, atypical, and adenocarcinoid. In the well-differentiated group, the tumor cells either infiltrate into stroma or float in the pool of mucin. The tumor cells are goblet, cuboidal, or columnar cells with small uniform round-to-oval nuclei. Atypical mucinous carcinoid shows glandular crowding with cribriform or microcyst architecture and moderate nuclear atypia. The tumor cells are similar to those in the well-differentiated group. Adenocarcinoid is a carcinoid with a carcinomatous component. The tumor cells grow in island or large nodules of packed glands or single cells, which are mainly signet ring cells. Non-signet ring tumor cells grow in large islands, some forming glands. The tumor cells contain variable amount of eosinophilic and granular cytoplasm, large nuclei, and prominent nucleoli. Necrosis is present and mitotic figures are abundant.

The strumal carcinoid consists of both strumal and carcinoid component. The strumal component can be normal thyroid tissue or follicular adenoma, and may contain calcium oxalate crystals. The carcinoid component is mainly trabecular carcinoid, although some are insular or mucinous carcinoid (Figs. 11–12).

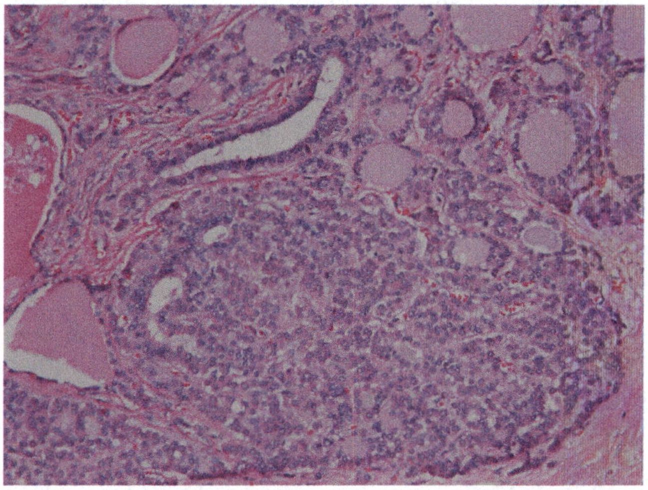

Fig. 11 Primary ovarian strumal carcinoid, showing carcinoid trabeculae admixed with thyroid follicles (H&E × 40)

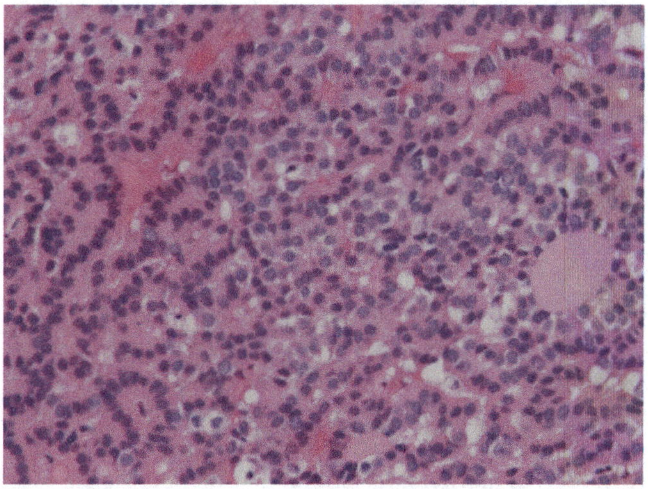

Fig. 12 Primary ovarian strumal carcinoid, showing carcinoid trabeculae admixed with thyroid follicles (H&E × 200)

Immunohistochemical studies typically show immunoreactivity for neuron-specific enolase, chromogranin, synaptophysin, and serotonin. Variable immunoreactivity for peptide hormones has been observed [14, 19, 26–29].

The differential diagnosis is broad and includes metastatic carcinoid (almost always from gastrointestinal tract), granulosa cell tumor, Sertoli-Leydig cell tumor and Brenner tumor. Features suggestive of metastatic carcinoid include bilateral ovarian involvement, multifocality, and extraovarian involvement [14, 21, 22, 25].

The prognosis is generally good. Surgery is the mainstay of the treatment for primary ovarian carcinoid that is confined to the ovary. Patients with primary ovarian carcinoid with extraovarian involvement at the time of diagnosis should be treated with surgery followed by radiotherapy or chemotherapy. Primary mucinous carcinoid is more aggressive, especially when a carcinomatous component is involved. Approximately 5% of patients die of disease. Most of these are patients with tumors showing extra-ovarian spread at the time of diagnosis [14, 20, 22–25, 30–32].

Carcinoid Tumor of the Fallopian Tube

So far, only a few carcinoid tumors have been reported, all arising in teratoma of the fallopian tube. Gross examination of the tumor in one case showed a large solid, lobulated tan-yellow mass with a smooth surface (>10 cm). Microscopic examination shows tumor cells growing in an acinar or trabecular pattern. The tumor cells contain eosinophilic cytoplasm with mild cytologic atypia. Carcinoid was associated with teratoma of the fallopian tube in all three cases. Immunohistochemical studies typically show the tumor cells are immunoreactive for chromogranin. The main differential diagnosis is metastatic carcinoid from GI tract or elsewhere [14, 33].

Small Cell Carcinoma of the Fallopian Tube

Only two cases of undifferentiated small cell carcinoma of the Fallopian tube have been reported. Microscopic examination shows tumor cells that resemble the small cell carcinoma of the lung. Immunohistochemical studies show that the tumor cells are immunonegative for neuroendocrine markers, including, neuron-specific enolase, synaptophysin, and Leu-7 [34].

Neuroendocrine Tumors of the Cervix

Neuroendocrine tumors of the uterine cervix are uncommon, which generally occur in women with a wide age range between 21 and 94 years of age (mean age, fifth decade) [14, 37, 40, 44, 48, 49, 53, 55]. These have recently been classified as those in the lung as typical carcinoid, atypical carcinoid, small cell carcinoma, and large cell neuroendocrine carcinoma [35, 54]. These tumors mostly occur in a pure form, however, they may coexist with squamous cell carcinoma or adenocarcinoma of the cervix and are associated with HPV, type 16 or 18 [14, 35, 36, 38, 39, 45, 55, 57]. Most patients present with vaginal bleeding, discharge, or post-coital spotting. However, patients can also present with carcinoid syndrome, such as Cushing's syndrome, SIADH, hypercalcemia, or hypoglycemia [7, 14, 37, 40–43, 48, 53].

Gross examination usually shows either a white-yellow polypoid/exophytic, or an infiltrative or ulcerated mass, between 1 and 6 cm [44, 45, 53, 55]. The tumor can be either well demarcated or infiltrative into the adjacent structures.

Microscopic examination of neuroendocrine tumors in the cervix shows four different categories: carcinoid, atypical carcinoid, small cell carcinoma, and large cell neuroendocrine carcinoma.

In a typical carcinoid, the tumor cells grow in an organoid, trabecular, nested, cord-like, or micro-acinar growth pattern. The tumor cells show modest amount of amphophilic to eosinophilic granular cytoplasm, small to medium sized round-to-oval nuclei with finely granular chromatin. Characteristically, there are few mitotic figures, usually less than 5/10 HPF and there is no necrosis.

In an atypical carcinoid, the tumor cells grow in a similar growth pattern to those of carcinoid. The tumor cells show coarsely distributed chromatin and mild-to-moderate cytologic atypia. Characteristically, there are 5–10 mitotic figures/10 HPF and foci of necrosis can be present.

In a small cell carcinoma, the tumor cells grow in sheet, irregular aggregate, or nest pattern. The tumor cells are small uniform cells and loosely cohesive, with scant amount of cytoplasm, hyperchromatic nuclei, and nuclear molding. Characteristically, mitotic figures can be more than 10/10 HPF. Geographic necrosis and lymphovascular invasion can be present.

In a large cell neuroendocrine carcinoma, the tumor cells lose the organoid growth pattern, but can grow in pseudotrabecular, insular, nest, or solid pattern. The tumor cells are large, polygonal with moderate to abundant amount of eosinophilic cytoplasm, large nuclei with coarse, vesicular chromatin, and prominent nucleoli. Characteristically, more than 10 mitotic figures/10 HPF, areas of geographic necrosis, and vascular invasion are present. Immunohistochemical studies typically show immunoreactivity for neuron-specific enolase, chromogranin, synaptophysin, cytokeratin, and CEA. Variable immunoreactivity for peptide hormones like serotonin, intestinal polypeptide, or somatostatin has been observed. Surprisingly, TTF-1 immunopositivity has been reported in rare small and large cell neuroendocrine carcinomas of the cervix [14, 42–45, 48, 50–53, 55, 58].

The differential diagnosis of well-to-moderately differentiated neuroendocrine tumor includes primary or metastatic adenocarcinoma with micro-acinar architectures. The differential diagnosis of poorly differentiated neuroendocrine tumor includes small cell non-keratinizing squamous cell carcinoma, undifferentiated carcinoma, solid adenocarcinoma, PNET, lymphoma, granulocytic sarcoma, malignant melanoma, and undifferentiated sarcoma [40, 53, 55].

The prognosis for neuroendocrine tumor in the uteri cervix is generally poor and is related to the degree of differentiation. Surgery followed by chemotherapy and radiation is the mainstay of therapy. The tumor may metastasize to the liver, lung, and brain. Unfavorable prognostic factors are high mitotic figures, necrosis, high clinical stage, and small cell component [13, 32, 37, 40, 43–49, 51–53, 55–57].

Carcinoid Tumor of the Uterine Corpus

Only one primary carcinoid tumor of the uterine corpus has been reported thus far [59]. It occurred in an 82-year-old woman, causing uterine enlargement. Microscopic examination showed tumor cells growing in nests and islands. The tumor cells were uniform with little pleomorphism, granular cytoplasm, and finely dispersed chromatin. Immunohistochemical studies showed the tumor cells were immunoreactive for cytokeratin, chromogranin, and S100. Interestingly, the tumor cells were immunonegative for synaptophysin [59].

Small Cell Carcinoma of the Endometrium

Small cell carcinoma of endometrium is uncommon. It generally occurs in women between 23 and 78 years of age (mean age 60 years) [13–14, 60–62, 64]. It may coexist with adenocarcinoma, adenosquamous cell carcinoma, malignant mixed Müllerian tumor, or endometrial stromal sarcoma [13, 14, 60–62]. Most patients present with abnormal vaginal bleeding, however, abdominal/pelvic mass can also be observed. Most patients present with advanced stage disease. Two cases associated with ocular paraneoplastic syndrome have been reported [13, 14, 60–63].

Microscopic examination shows tumor cells growing in sheets. The tumor cells are small- to medium-sized cells with scant amount of cytoplasm, hyperchromatic round nuclei, and inconspicuous nucleoli.

Immunohistochemical studies typically show immunoreactivity for one of the neuroendocrine markers, such as neuron-specific enolase, synaptophysin, or chromogranin. Variable immunoreactivity for vimentin has been observed [14, 60–64].

The differential diagnosis includes metastatic small cell carcinoma from elsewhere, PNET, malignant mixed Müllerian tumor, or endometrial stromal sarcoma [13, 61, 62].

The prognosis for small cell carcinoma of endometrium is generally poor. Surgery followed by radiation and/or chemotherapy is the mainstay of treatment. However, majority of patients die of disease despite the treatment [13, 60–62, 64].

Carcinoid Tumors of the Vagina

Only one primary carcinoid tumor of the vagina has been reported [65]. It occurred in a 32-year-old woman and was noted during routine examination. Microscopic examination showed tumor cells growing in cords, nests with acinar formation. The patient was treated surgically followed by chemotherapy. The patient died of disease [65].

Small Cell Carcinoma of the Vagina

Small cell carcinoma of the vagina is extremely rare. It generally occurs in women between 32 and 78 years of age (mean age 59 years) [13, 14, 68, 69]. Patients usually present with vaginal bleeding. Patients with this tumor may have Cushing syndrome [14, 67].

Gross examination usually shows friable mass, ranging in size from 0.5 to 10 cm, in greatest dimension [69]. The tumor can be exophytic, fungating, and yellow in color. Areas of hemorrhage may be present. Microscopic examination shows tumor growing in solid sheets of tightly packed small, round, oval-to-spindle cells with scant amount of cytoplasm, small nuclei with finely granular chromatin, nuclear molding, and inconspicuous nucleoli.

Immunohistochemical studies typically show immunoreactivity for cytokeratin and EMA. Variable immunoreactivity for neuron-specific enolase, chromogranin, and synaptophysin has been observed. Interestingly, one case has been reported where the tumor cells are immunoreactive for thyroid transcription factor-1 (TTF-1) [66, 69].

The differential diagnosis is broad and includes metastatic small cell carcinoma from elsewhere, especially from lung and cervix, other small round blue cell tumors, including lymphoma, PNET, embryonal rhabdomyosarcoma, small cell non-keratinizing squamous cell carcinoma, and basaloid squamous cell carcinoma [13, 69].

The prognosis for small cell carcinoma of the vagina is generally poor. There is no optimal treatment consensus so far since the disease is so rare. Radiation, chemotherapy, or combination of the two is usually used and treatment failure is very common [13, 14, 66, 6–69].

Small Cell Carcinoma of the Vulva

It is not known how many small cell carcinomas of the vulva actually occur, since the early literature also included Merkel cell carcinoma into this category. Rare cases have been reported. Microscopic examination shows tightly packed tumor cells growing in sheets. The tumor cells are small, with scant amount of cytoplasm, hyperchromatic nuclei with finely granular chromatin, nuclear molding, and inconspicuous nucleoli. Characteristically, there is brisk mitotic activity [13].

References

1. Young RH, Oliva E, Scully RE. Small cell carcinoma of the ovary, hypercalcemic type. A clinicopathological analysis of 150 cases. Am J Surg Pathol. 1994 Nov;18(11):1102–16.
2. McCluggage WG. Ovarian neoplasms composed of small round cells: a review. Adv Anat Pathol. 2004 Nov;11(6): 288–96. Review.
3. Dickersin GR, Kline IW, Scully RE. Small cell carcinoma of the ovary with hypercalcemia: a report of eleven cases. Cancer. 1982 Jan 1;49(1):188–97.
4. Clement PB. Selected miscellaneous ovarian lesions: small cell carcinomas, mesothelial lesions, mesenchymal and mixed neoplasms, and non-neoplastic lesions. Mod Pathol. 2005 Feb;18 Suppl 2:S113–29. Review.
5. Schleef J, Wagner A, Kleta R, Schaarschmidt K, Dockhorn-Dworniczak B, Willital G, Jürgens H. Small-cell carcinoma of the ovary of the hypercalcemic type in an 8-year-old girl. Pediatr Surg Int. 1999 Jul;15(5–6):431–4.
6. Lamovec J, Bracko M, Cerar O. Familial occurrence of small-cell carcinoma of the ovary. Arch Pathol Lab Med. 1995 Jun;119(6):523–7.
7. Clement PB, Young RH, Scully RE. Clinical syndromes associated with tumors of the female genital tract. Semin Diagn Pathol. 1991 Nov;8(4):204–33. Review.
8. Popiolek DA, Kumar AR, Mittal K. Large cell variant of small cell carcinoma, hypercalcemic type, of primary peritoneal origin. Gynecol Oncol. 2005 Jan;96(1):249–53.
9. Di Vagno G, Melilli GA, Cormio G, Piscitelli D, Ciampolillo A, Resta L, Selvaggi L. Large-cell variant of small cell carcinoma of the ovary with hypercalcaemia. Arch Gynecol Obstet. 2000 Nov;264(3):157–8.
10. Aguirre P, Thor AD, Scully RE. Ovarian small cell carcinoma. Histogenetic considerations based on immunohistochemical and other findings. Am J Clin Pathol. 1989 Aug;92(2):140–9.
11. Choi YL, Kim HS, Ahn G. Immunoexpression of inhibin alpha subunit, inhibin/activin betaA subunit and CD99 in ovarian tumors. Arch Pathol Lab Med. 2000 Apr;124(4):563–9.
12. Eichhorn JH, Young RH, Scully RE. Primary ovarian small cell carcinoma of pulmonary type. A clinicopathologic, immunohistologic, and flow cytometric analysis of 11 cases. Am J Surg Pathol. 1992 Oct;16(10):926–38.
13. Crowder S, Tuller E. Small cell carcinoma of the female genital tract. Semin Oncol. 2007 Feb;34(1):57–63. Review.
14. Eichhorn JH, Young RH. Neuroendocrine tumors of the genital tract. Am J Clin Pathol. 2001 Jun;115 Suppl:S94–112. Review.
15. Mebis J, De Raeve H, Baekelandt M, Tjalma WA, Vermorken JB. Primary ovarian small cell carcinoma of the pulmonary type: a case report and review of the literature. Eur J Gynaecol Oncol. 2004;25(2):239–41. Review.
16. Eichhorn JH, Lawrence WD, Young RH, Scully RE. Ovarian neuroendocrine carcinomas of non-small-cell type associated with surface epithelial adenocarcinomas. A study of five cases and review of the literature. Int J Gynecol Pathol. 1996 Oct;15(4):303–14. Review.
17. Lindboe CF. Large cell neuroendocrine carcinoma of the ovary. APMIS. 2007 Feb;115(2):169–76.
18. Veras E, Deavers MT, Silva EG, Malpica A. Ovarian nonsmall cell neuroendocrine carcinoma: a clinicopathologic and immunohistochemical study of 11 cases. Am J Surg Pathol. 2007 May;31(5):774–82.
19. Soga J, Osaka M, Yakuwa Y. Carcinoids of the ovary: an analysis of 329 reported cases. J Exp Clin Cancer Res. 2000 Sep;19(3):271–80.
20. Davis KP, Hartmann LK, Keeney GL, Shapiro H. Primary ovarian carcinoid tumors. Gynecol Oncol. 1996 May;61(2): 259–65. Review.
21. Robboy SJ, Scully RE, Norris HJ. Carcinoid metastatic to the ovary. A clinocopathologic analysis of 35 cases. Cancer. 1974 Mar;33(3):798–811.
22. Robboy SJ, Norris HJ, Scully RE. Insular carcinoid primary in the ovary. A clinicopathologic analysis of 48 cases. Cancer. 1975 Aug;36(2):404–18.
23. Robboy SJ, Scully RE, Norris HJ. Primary trabecular carcinoid of the ovary. Obstet Gynecol. 1977 Feb;49(2):202–7.
24. Alenghat E, Okagaki T, Talerman A. Primary mucinous carcinoid tumor of the ovary. Cancer. 1986 Aug 1;58(3):777–83.
25. Robboy SJ, Scully RE. Strumal carcinoid of the ovary: an analysis of 50 cases of a distinctive tumor composed of thyroid tissue and carcinoid. Cancer. 1980 Nov 1;46(9):2019–34.
26. Motoyama T, Katayama Y, Watanabe H, Okazaki E, Shibuya H. Functioning ovarian carcinoids induce severe constipation. Cancer. 1992 Jul 15;70(2):513–8.
27. Yaegashi N, Tsuiki A, Shimizu T, Kobayashi N, Sato S, Namiki T, Motoyama T, Katayama Y, Yajima A. Ovarian carcinoid with severe constipation due to peptide YY production. Gynecol Oncol. 1995 Feb;56(2):302–6.
28. Sporrong B, Falkmer S, Robboy SJ, Alumets J, Håkanson R, Ljungberg O, Sundler F. Neurohormonal peptides in ovarian carcinoids: an immunohistochemical study of 81 primary carcinoids and of intraovarian metastases from six mid-gut carcinoids. Cancer. 1982 Jan 1;49(1):68–74.
29. Sidhu J, Sánchez RL. Prostatic acid phosphatase in strumal carcinoids of the ovary. An immunohistochemical study. Cancer. 1993 Sep 1;72(5):1673–8.

30. Basham KL, Hajdu SI, Teichberg S, Menzin A. Adenocarcinoid tumor of the ovary diagnosed during pregnancy. A case report. J Reprod Med. 2000 Sep;45(9):758–61.
31. Baker PM, Oliva E, Young RH, Talerman A, Scully RE. Ovarian mucinous carcinoids including some with a carcinomatous component: a report of 17 cases. Am J Surg Pathol. 2001 May;25(5):557–68.
32. Modlin IM, Shapiro MD, Kidd M. An analysis of rare carcinoid tumors: clarifying these clinical conundrums. World J Surg. 2005 Jan;29(1):92–101. Review.
33. Astall EC, Brewster JA, Lonsdale R. Malignant carcinoid tumour arising in a mature teratoma of the fallopian tube. Histopathology. 2000 Mar;36(3):282–3.
34. Alvarado-Cabrero I, Young RH, Vamvakas EC, Scully RE. Carcinoma of the fallopian tube: a clinicopathological study of 105 cases with observations on staging and prognostic factors. Gynecol Oncol. 1999 Mar;72(3):367–79.
35. Albores-Saavedra J, Gersell D, Gilks CB, Henson DE, Lindberg G, Santiago H, Scully RE, Silva E, Sobin LH, Tavassoli FJ, Travis WD, Woodruff JM. Terminology of endocrine tumors of the uterine cervix: results of a workshop sponsored by the College of American Pathologists and the National Cancer Institute. Arch Pathol Lab Med. 1997 Jan;121(1):34–9. Review.
36. Ueda G, Yamasaki M. Neuroendocrine carcinoma of the uterus. Curr Top Pathol. 1992;85:309–35. Review.
37. Collinet P, Lanvin D, Declerck D, Chevalier-Place A, Leblanc E, Querleu D. Neuroendocrine tumors of the uterine cervix. Clinicopathologic study of five patients. Eur J Obstet Gynecol Reprod Biol. 2000 Jul;91(1):51–7.
38. Stoler MH, Mills SE, Gersell DJ, Walker AN. Small-cell neuroendocrine carcinoma of the cervix. A human papillomavirus type 18-associated cancer. Am J Surg Pathol. 1991 Jan;15(1):28–32.
39. Ambros RA, Park JS, Shah KV, Kurman RJ. Evaluation of histologic, morphometric, and immunohistochemical criteria in the differential diagnosis of small cell carcinomas of the cervix with particular reference to human papillomavirus types 16 and 18. Mod Pathol. 1991 Sep;4(5):586–93. Erratum in: Mod Pathol 1992 Jan;5(1):40.
40. Albores-Saavedra J, Rodríguez-Martínez HA, Larraza-Hernández O. Carcinoid tumors of the cervix. Pathol Annu. 1979;14 Pt 1:273–91. Review.
41. Stockdale AD, Leader M, Phillips RH, Henry K. The carcinoid syndrome and multiple hormone secretion associated with a carcinoid tumour of the uterine cervix. Case report. Br J Obstet Gynaecol. 1986 Apr;93(4):397–401.
42. Koch CA, Azumi N, Furlong MA, Jha RC, Kehoe TE, Trowbridge CH, O'Dorisio TM, Chrousos GP, Clement SC. Carcinoid syndrome caused by an atypical carcinoid of the uterine cervix. J Clin Endocrinol Metab. 1999 Nov;84(11):4209–13.
43. van Nagell JR Jr, Powell DE, Gallion HH, Elliott DG, Donaldson ES, Carpenter AE, Higgins RV, Kryscio R, Pavlik EJ. Small cell carcinoma of the uterine cervix. Cancer. 1988 Oct 15;62(8):1586–93.
44. Gersell DJ, Mazoujian G, Mutch DG, Rudloff MA. Small-cell undifferentiated carcinoma of the cervix. A clinicopathologic, ultrastructural, and immunocytochemical study of 15 cases. Am J Surg Pathol. 1988 Sep;12(9):684–98.
45. Abeler VM, Holm R, Nesland JM, Kjørstad KE. Small cell carcinoma of the cervix. A clinicopathologic study of 26 patients. Cancer. 1994 Feb 1;73(3):672–7.
46. Sykes AJ, Shanks JH, Davidson SE. Small cell carcinoma of the uterine cervix: a clinicopathological review. Int J Oncol. 1999 Feb;14(2):381–6.
47. Delaloge S, Pautier P, Kerbrat P, Castaigne D, Haie-Meder C, Duvillard P, Guivarch C, Goupil A, Borel C, Lhommé C. Neuroendocrine small cell carcinoma of the uterine cervix: what disease? What treatment? Report of ten cases and a review of the literature. Clin Oncol (R Coll Radiol). 2000;12(6):357–62. Review.
48. Conner MG, Richter H, Moran CA, Hameed A, Albores-Saavedra J. Small cell carcinoma of the cervix: a clinicopathologic and immunohistochemical study of 23 cases. Ann Diagn Pathol. 2002 Dec;6(6):345–8.
49. Weed JC Jr, Graff AT, Shoup B, Tawfik O. Small cell undifferentiated (neuroendocrine) carcinoma of the uterine cervix. J Am Coll Surg. 2003 Jul;197(1):44–51.
50. Ishida GM, Kato N, Hayasaka T, Saito M, Kobayashi H, Katayama Y, Sasou S, Yaegashi N, Kurachi H, Motoyama T. Small cell neuroendocrine carcinomas of the uterine cervix: a histological, immunohistochemical, and molecular genetic study. Int J Gynecol Pathol. 2004 Oct;23(4):366–72.
51. Viswanathan AN, Deavers MT, Jhingran A, Ramirez PT, Levenback C, Eifel PJ. Small cell neuroendocrine carcinoma of the cervix: outcome and patterns of recurrence. Gynecol Oncol. 2004 Apr;93(1):27–33.
52. Tsunoda S, Jobo T, Arai M, Imai M, Kanai T, Tamura T, Watanabe J, Obokata A, Kuramoto H. Small-cell carcinoma of the uterine cervix: a clinicopathologic study of 11 cases. Int J Gynecol Cancer. 2005 Mar–Apr;15(2):295–300.
53. Gilks CB, Young RH, Gersell DJ, Clement PB. Large cell neuroendocrine [corrected] carcinoma of the uterine cervix: a clinicopathologic study of 12 cases. Am J Surg Pathol. 1997 Aug;21(8):905–14. Erratum in: 1997 Oct;21(10):1260.
54. Krivak TC, McBroom JW, Sundborg MJ, Crothers B, Parker MF. Large cell neuroendocrine cervical carcinoma: a report of two cases and review of the literature. Gynecol Oncol. 2001 Jul;82(1):187–91. Review.
55. Sato Y, Shimamoto T, Amada S, Asada Y, Hayashi T. Large cell neuroendocrine carcinoma of the uterine cervix: a clinicopathological study of six cases. Int J Gynecol Pathol. 2003 Jul;22(3):226–30.
56. Dikmen Y, Kazandi M, Zekioglu O, Ozsaran A, Terek MC, Erhan Y. Large cell neuroendocrine carcinoma of the uterine cervix: a report of a case and review of the literature. Arch Gynecol Obstet. 2004 Nov;270(3):185–8. Epub 2003 Apr 25. Review.
57. Cetiner H, Kir G, Akoz I, Gurbuz A, Karateke A. Large-cell neuroendocrine carcinoma of the cervix associated with cervical-type invasive adenocarcinoma: a report of case and discussion of histogenesis. Int J Gynecol Cancer. 2006 Jan–Feb;16(1):438–42. Review.
58. McCluggage WG, Sargent A, Bailey A, Wilson GE. Large cell neuroendocrine carcinoma of the uterine cervix exhibiting TTF1 immunoreactivity. Histopathology. 2007 Sep;51(3): 405–7.
59. Chetty R, Clark SP, Bhathal PS. Carcinoid tumour of the uterine corpus. Virchows Arch A Pathol Anat Histopathol. 1993;422(1):93–5.
60. Campo E, Brunier MN, Merino MJ. Small cell carcinoma of the endometrium with associated ocular paraneoplastic syndrome. Cancer. 1992 May 1;69(9):2283–8. Review.
61. Huntsman DG, Clement PB, Gilks CB, Scully RE. Small-cell carcinoma of the endometrium. A clinicopathological study of sixteen cases. Am J Surg Pathol. 1994 Apr;18(4):364–75. Review.
62. van Hoeven KH, Hudock JA, Woodruff JM, Suhrland MJ. Small cell neuroendocrine carcinoma of the endometrium. Int J Gynecol Pathol. 1995 Jan;14(1):21–9. Review.

63. Varras M, Akrivis Ch, Demou A, Hadjopoulos G, Stefanaki S, Antoniou N. Primary small-cell carcinoma of the endometrium: clinicopathological study of a case and review of the literature. Eur J Gynaecol Oncol. 2002;23(6):577–81. Review.
64. Katahira A, Akahira J, Niikura H, Ito K, Moriya T, Matsuzawa S, Makinoda S, Oda T, Fujiwara K, Yaegashi N. Small cell carcinoma of the endometrium: report of three cases and literature review. Int J Gynecol Cancer. 2004 Sep–Oct;14 (5):1018–23.
65. Sulak P, Barnhill D, Heller P, Weiser E, Hoskins W, Park R, Woodward J. Nonsquamous cancer of the vagina. Gynecol Oncol. 1988 Mar;29(3):309–20.
66. Rusthoven JJ, Daya D. Small-cell carcinoma of the vagina. A clinicopathologic study. Arch Pathol Lab Med. 1990 Jul;114 (7):728–31.
67. Colleran KM, Burge MR, Crooks LA, Dorin RI. Small cell carcinoma of the vagina causing Cushing's syndrome by ectopic production and secretion of ACTH: a case report. Gynecol Oncol. 1997 Jun;65(3):526–9.
68. Kaminski JM, Anderson PR, Han AC, Mitra RK, Rosenblum NG, Edelson MI. Primary small cell carcinoma of the vagina. Gynecol Oncol. 2003 Mar;88(3):451–5. Review.
69. Bing Z, Levine L, Lucci JA, Hatch SS, Eltorky MA. Primary small cell neuroendocrine carcinoma of the vagina: a clinicopathologic study. Arch Pathol Lab Med. 2004 Aug;128(8):857–62. Review.

Neuroendocrine Tumors of Prostate, Urinary Bladder and Kidney

Zhong Jiang

Abstract Overall, neuroendocrine tumors in genitourinary system are rare. However, it is crucial to recognize these tumors because patients with neuroendocrine tumors have significant differences in clinical treatment and prognosis from patients with other tumors in the genitourinary system. In this chapter, important neuroendocrine tumors in the prostate, urinary bladder, and kidney are discussed. Highlights also mark imperative elements of each tumor including tumor epidemiology, diagnosis, prognosis, and treatment.

Keywords Focal neuroendocrine differentiation in prostatic adenocarcinoma • Prostatic carcinoid tumor • Small cell carcinoma of the prostate • Large neuroendocrine carcinoma of the prostate • Paraganglioma of the urinary bladder • Small cell carcinoma of the urinary bladder • Neuroendocrine tumors of the kidney

Neuroendocrine Tumors of the Prostate

Normal Neuroendocrine Cells of Prostate

Normal prostatic gland contains secretory luminal cells and basal cells. In addition, there is also a small population of isolated, randomly scattered neuroendocrine cells that represent a third type of epithelial cells in prostate glands [1]. Most of neuroendocrine cells are located in transition zone and peripheral zone of the prostate [2]. Neuroendocrine cells of the prostate arise from endodermal-devised prostate stem cells [3] and rest on the basal cell layer and have an apical cytoplasmic process that extends to the lumen and has long specialized surface microvilli [4]. They also show lateral dendritic processes [4].

These neuroendocrine cells are not reliably recognized by routine H&E staining but they can be identified by immunohistochemical staining with antibodies for neuroendocrine markers including chromogranin, synaptophysin, and neuron-specific enolase (NSE) [2]. Subpopulations of these cells also contain a variety of peptide hormones such as serotonin, somatostatin, calcitonin, and gastrin releasing peptide [4, 5].

The functions of these neuroendocrine cells in the prostate are not known. They may have paracrine function, perhaps in response to neural stimulation [4]. Consistently, lack of Ki67 (a cell proliferation marker) expression in neuroendocrine cells of the prostate indicates that they do not participate in the cell cycle during normal and hyperplastic growth [6].

Neuroendocrine Tumors of the Prostate

Classification:

1) **Focal Neuroendocrine Differentiation in Prostatic Adenocarcinoma**
2) **Carcinoid Tumor**
3) **Small Cell Carcinoma**
4) **Large Neuroendocrine Carcinoma**

Focal Neuroendocrine Differentiation in Prostatic Adenocarcinoma

Highlights:

- **Diagnostic criteria for focal neuroendocrine differentiation in prostatic adenocarcinoma: single and/or cluster**

Z. Jiang (✉)
Professor of Pathology, Director, Genitourinary Pathology, University of Massachusetts Medical School, Three Biotech, One Innovation Drive, Worcester, MA, USA
e-mail: jiangz@ummhc.org

A. Khan (ed.), *Surgical Pathology of Endocrine and Neuroendocrine Tumors*, Current Clinical Pathology,
DOI 10.1007/978-1-60327-396-1_15, © Humana Press, a part of Springer Science+Business Media, LLC 2009

of neuroendocrine cells are present in conventional prostatic adenocarcinoma.

- **Neuroendocrine cells are often present in primary and metastatic adenocarcinoma of the prostate (10–100% of primary conventional prostatic adenocarcinoma with focal neuroendocrine differentiation).**
- **Neuroendocrine cells co-express prostate specific antigen (PSA).**
- **Ectopic peptides made by neuroendocrine cells in prostate cancer are associated with paraneoplastic syndromes.**
- **The prognostic significance of focal neuroendocrine differentiation in conventional prostatic adenocarcinoma is not conclusive.**

Neuroendocrine differentiation appears to be more common in prostatic adenocarcinoma than in carcinomas arising in other organs of the genitourinary tract [1, 7]. Single or cluster of neuroendocrine cells can be detected in 10–100% of conventional prostatic adenocarcinoma [1, 3, 7–9]. Neuroendocrine cells are also present in approximately 55% of metastatic prostatic adenocarcinomas with a similar pattern of distribution of primary counterparts [8].

Immunohistochemical stains with neuroendocrine markers including chromogranin, synaptophysin, NSE, serotonin, and somatostatin are important for identifying the neuroendocrine differentiation in conventional prostate cancer [1, 7]. These neuroendocrine cells also co-express PSA, suggesting a common precursor cell of origin, prostate stem cells [8]. Some studies suggested that the neuroendocrine differentiation in prostatic adenocarcinomas has developed from the hormonal therapy for these cancers [10, 11].

Ectopic peptides such as adrenocorticotrophic hormone (ACTH), leuenkephalin, and endorphin have been found in some neuroendocrine cells of prostatic adenocarcinoma [1]. The abnormal secretion of these ectopic substances is believed to account for the paraneoplastic syndromes, which are occasionally found in association with prostate cancer [1].

Evidence of the prognostic significance of focal neuroendocrine differentiation in conventional prostatic adenocarcinoma is not conclusive. Earlier studies suggested correlation to exist between neuroendocrine differentiation and prognosis [1, 10, 12, 13]. However, more recent publications could not demonstrate that neuroendocrine differentiation in prostatic adenocarcinoma is a prognostic marker for predicting poor clinical outcome [8, 13–15]. The expression of neuroendocrine cells does not appear to be suppressed with androgen ablation and does not correlate with pathologic stage [8].

Carcinoid Tumor of the Prostate

Highlights:

- **Primary carcinoid tumor of the prostate is extremely rare.**
- **Unlike tumor with neuroendocrine differentiation, primary carcinoid tumor should be an individual tumor that is separated from conventional prostatic adenocarcinoma.**
- **Histological criteria for prostatic carcinoid tumor: (1) typical neuroendocrine nuclei; (2) positivity of neuroendocrine markers; (3) no significant cytological atypia, mitosis, and necrosis.**
- **Co-expression of PSA can be seen in prostatic carcinoid tumor.**
- **The prognosis is unknown.**

Primary prostatic carcinoid tumor is very rare. Since Wasserstein first described a prostate carcinoid tumor in 1979 [16] there were only several individual case reports about primary prostate carcinoid [16–20].

Common features of primary prostate carcinoid tumor include: (1) primary carcinoid tumor of the prostate needs all features of carcinoid tumor in other organs including neuroendocrine nuclear appearance, low mitotic activity, lack of significant cytological atypia, and necrosis; (2) unlike neuroendocrine differentiation in prostate adenocarcinoma, primary carcinoid tumor of the prostate should be an independent tumor that is separated from prostatic adenocarcinoma, although they may be associated with conventional prostatic adenocarcinoma. The so-called carcinoid-like growth pattern that mixed with conventional prostatic adenocarcinoma should not be classified as primary prostatic carcinoid tumor. (3) The tumor cells usually co-express PSA [16–20].

A single case of primary prostatic carcinoid in conjunction with multiple endocrine neoplasia 2B in a child has also been documented [20]. Although there has been a report about metastasis of primary prostatic carcinoid [16], its prognosis is still uncertain, as currently there have been only rare reported cases.

Small Cell Carcinoma of the Prostate

Highlights:

- **Primary small cell carcinoma of the prostate accounts for 0.5–2% of all prostatic carcinomas.**
- **Diagnostic criteria for prostatic small cell carcinoma are same as those for small cell carcinoma in other organs.**
- **A Gleason score should not be assigned to prostatic small cell carcinoma.**

- **About 90% of prostatic small cell carcinomas are positive for at least one neuroendocrine marker.**
- **PSA, P501S, thyroid transcription factor-1 (TTF-1) can be positive in prostatic small cell carcinoma.**
- **Serum PSA levels are often not elevated in prostatic small cell carcinoma.**
- **Its therapy is different from conventional prostatic adenocarcinoma.**
- **The prognosis of prostatic small cell carcinoma is very poor.**

Primary small cell carcinoma of the prostate is rare and accounts for 0.5–2% of all prostatic carcinomas [13]. Diagnostic criteria for prostatic small cell carcinoma are same as those for small cell carcinoma in other organs [21]. The tumor cells are small, round, or oval shaped with scant cytoplasm (Fig. 1A,B). The nuclei are hyperchromatic without prominent nucleoli. Nuclear molding, mitosis, and necrosis are often seen (Fig. 1A,B).

Approximately 45% of prostatic small cell carcinomas are mixed with conventional prostatic adenocarcinoma [21]. Interestingly, the incidence of prostatic small cell carcinoma increased after long-term androgen deprivation therapy [22–24] while many of patients with prostatic small cell carcinoma often showed normal serum PSA [21]. Approximately 90% of prostatic small cell carcinomas are positive for at least one neuroendocrine marker [21]. CD56 is the most sensitive marker for prostatic small cell carcinoma [21]. Immunohistochemical staining for the neuroendocrine markers is a useful tool to identify prostatic small cell carcinoma. When the diagnosis is confirmed, a Gleason score should not be assigned to prostatic small cell carcinoma.

Clinically, it is important to distinguish between prostatic small cell carcinoma and poorly differentiated adenocarcinoma because treatments of these two entities are different. Prostatic small cell carcinoma is treated with chemotherapy, whereas prostatic adenocarcinoma is treated with hormonal therapy.

Approximately 20%, 30%, and 25% of prostatic small cell carcinoma were positive for PSA, P501S, and prostate-specific membrane antigen (PSMA), respectively [21]. These prostatic markers (if they are positive in small cell carcinoma) may help to identify prostatic origin of metastatic small cell carcinoma, whereas more than 50% prostatic small cell carcinoma are also positive for thyroid transcription factor-1 (TTF-1); TTF-1 cannot be used as marker to distinguish between lung and prostate origin of small cell carcinoma [21]. The prognosis of prostatic small cell carcinoma is very poor with a mean survival time of only 7 months [13, 25, 26].

Large Neuroendocrine Carcinoma of the Prostate

Highlights:

- **Large cell neuroendocrine carcinoma of the prostate is extremely rare.**
- **Diagnostic criteria for large cell neuroendocrine carcinoma of the prostate are same as those for large cell neuroendocrine carcinoma in other organs.**
- **Gleason score should not be assigned to large cell neuroendocrine carcinoma of the prostate.**
- **Most of large cell neuroendocrine carcinomas are positive for at least one neuroendocrine marker.**
- **PSA, P504S/alpha methylacyl CoA racemase (AMACR), and prostate acid phosphatase (PSAP) can be positive in large cell neuroendocrine carcinoma of the prostate.**
- **Most of the patients with large cell neuroendocrine carcinomas had a history of prostatic adenocarcinoma treated with hormone therapy.**
- **The prognosis of large cell neuroendocrine carcinoma of the prostate is very poor.**

Primary large cell neuroendocrine carcinoma of the prostate is very rare and so far there are only several case

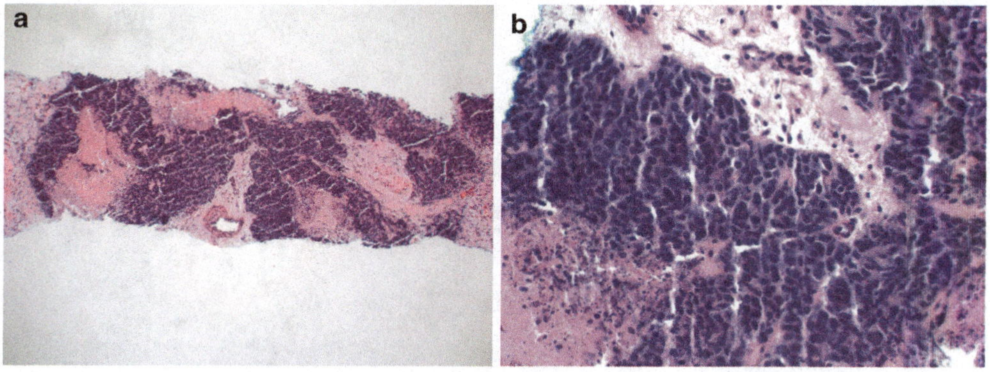

Fig. 1 Small cell carcinoma of the prostate. (**A**) Prostatic needle biopsy showing small cell carcinoma with extensive necrosis. (**B**) Typical cytological appearance of small cell carcinoma with small, round, or oval nuclei and scant cytoplasm

reports [7, 27–29] and one large series with seven cases [30]. Diagnostic criteria for prostatic large cell neuroendocrine carcinoma are same as those for small cell carcinoma in other organs [30]. The tumor cells are large and polygonal shaped with low nuclear to cytoplasmic ratio. The nuclei show coarse chromatin and frequent nucleoli. Mitosis and necrosis are often seen. Most of large cell neuroendocrine carcinomas are positive for at least one neuroendocrine marker and CD56 is a most sensitive marker [30]. Although the tumors show foci of admixed prostatic adenocarcinomas that have long-term hormonal therapy, a Gleason score should not be assigned to the large cell neuroendocrine carcinoma of the prostate [30]. All of prostatic large cell neuroendocrine carcinomas have shown to be positive for P504S/AMACR. They are also positive for either PSA or PSAP [30].

The prognosis of prostatic large cell neuroendocrine carcinoma is very poor. A recent study reported that all of patients died with metastatic disease at mean of 7 months after platinum-based chemotherapy [30].

Neuroendocrine Tumors of the Urinary Bladder and the Kidney

Paraganglioma of the Urinary Bladder

Highlights:

- **Primary paraganglioma of the urinary bladder is rare.**
- **Diagnostic criteria for paraganglioma of the bladder are same as those for paraganglioma in other organs.**
- **The tumor cells are negative for epithelial markers and positive for neuroendocrine markers. Sustentacular cells are positive for S100.**
- **The main differential diagnosis is urothelial carcinoma.**
- **The tumor is treated by complete surgical resection.**
- **The prognosis depends on the depth of tumor invasion. Histological findings of nuclear pleomorphism, mitotic figures, and necrosis are not reliable predictors of the clinical outcome.**

Paraganglioma of the urinary bladder is an extra-adrenal pheochromocytoma derived from paraganglion cells in the bladder wall. Primary paraganglioma of the urinary bladder is rare and accounts for <0.1% of bladder tumors [31–35]. Diagnostic criteria for paraganglioma of the bladder are same as these for paraganglioma in other organs [31–35]. Tumor cells with abundant granular cytoplasm form nest, so call "Zellballen" pattern (Fig. 2A,B). Bizarre nuclei can be seen but they should not be considered as evidence of malignancy. Tumor cells are often negative for epithelial markers and positive for neuroendocrine markers including chromogranin, synaptophysin, NSE, et al. [31, 33, 34, 36, 37]. Around nests of tumor cells, there are vascularized fibrous septa, and sustentacular cells can be identified by S100 immunostaining [31, 33, 34, 36, 37].

It is important to distinguish between paraganglioma of the bladder and nested variant of urothelial carcinoma [31]. S100 immunoreactivity in sustentacular cells and diffuse positivity of neuroendocrine markers in tumor cells can be very useful to confirm the diagnosis of paraganglioma. The criteria for malignant paraganglioma are metastasis. Histological findings of nuclear pleomorphism, mitotic figures, and necrosis are not reliable predictors of the clinical outcomes of patients with paraganglioma of the urinary bladder [31, 36, 37].

Bladder paraganglioma is treated by surgical resection [38]. As there is a significant risk of local recurrence if the tumor is not completely resected, partial cystectomy is usually recommended [38]. However, with small tumors, transurethral resection may be adequate [38].

Metastases occur in approximately 15% of cases [36]. The depth of tumor invasion through the bladder wall is a very important prognostic factor to predict recurrence and metastasis of bladder paraganglioma [31]. Patients with tumor of advanced classification (>=T3) are at risk of recurrence, metastasis, and dying of the disease,

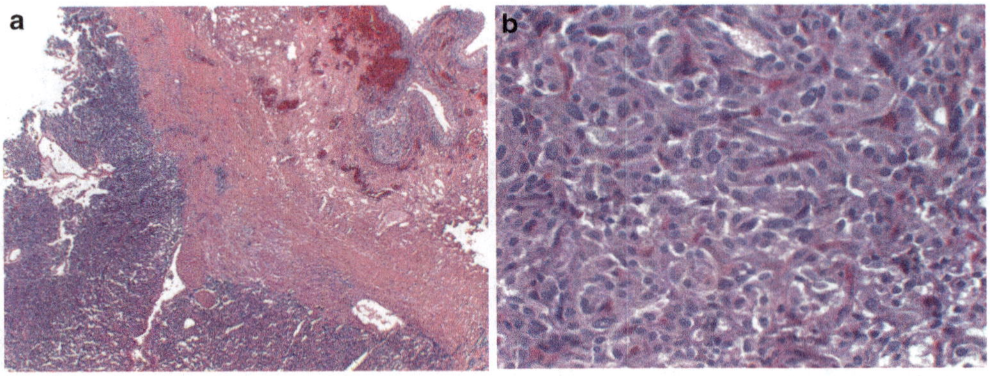

Fig. 15.2 Paraganglioma of the urinary bladder. (**A**) Urothelial mucosa with paraganglioma in the muscularis propria (**B**) Tumor cells with nest, the so-called "Zellballen" pattern

whereas patients with T1 or T2 disease had favorable outcome after complete tumor resection [31].

Small Cell Carcinoma of the Urinary Bladder

Highlights:

- **Primary small cell carcinoma of the urinary bladder accounts for 0.35–0.7% of all bladder tumors.**
- **Diagnostic criteria for small cell carcinoma of the bladder are same as those for small cell carcinoma in other organs.**
- **Some small cell carcinomas coexist with other carcinoma components including urothelial carcinoma and adenocarcinoma.**
- **Localized small cell carcinoma of the bladder should undergo radical cystectomy. Chemotherapy should also be considered.**
- **The prognosis of small cell carcinoma of the urinary bladder is poor and also depends on tumor stage.**

Primary small cell carcinoma of the urinary bladder is rare and accounts for 0.35–0.7% of all bladder tumors [39, 40]. It may arise from stem cells present in the urinary bladder or from urothelial metaplastic changes. Diagnostic criteria for bladder small cell carcinoma are same as those for small cell carcinoma in other organs [32, 38, 41]. The tumor cells are small, round, or oval, with scant cytoplasm. The nuclei are hyperchromatic without prominent nucleoli. Nuclear molding, mitosis, and necrosis are often seen. Immunohistochemical staining for the neuroendocrine markers is a useful tool to identify small cell carcinoma. Approximately 68% of small cell carcinomas are mixed with urothelial carcinoma or adenocarcinoma of the bladder [42], whereas these non-small cell components comprised <10% of the total tumor areas [42]. It is important to recognize bladder small cell carcinoma because of its distinctive treatment and prognosis.

Patients with localized small cell carcinoma of the bladder should undergo radical cystectomy while treatment for metastatic disease is a platinum-based chemotherapy [41, 43, 44]. Adjuvant treatment is not indicated for patients with stage II disease after radical cystectomy but should be considered for patients with stage III and IV disease [43, 44].

The prognosis of bladder small cell carcinoma is poor. Most of patients with bladder small cell carcinoma presented at least localized advanced disease [42]. The overall median survival was 1.7 years [44]. The 5-year survival rates for patients with stage II, III, and IV disease were 64%, 15%, and 11%, respectively [44].

Neuroendocrine Tumors of the Kidney

Highlights:

- **Renal neuroendocrine tumors including carcinoid tumor and small cell carcinoma are extremely rare.**
- **Diagnostic criteria for renal neuroendocrine tumors are same as those for the neuroendocrine tumors in other organs.**
- **TTF-1 can be used to rule out a lung metastasis, as a lung carcinoid tumor is positive for TTF-1 while primary renal carcinoid is negative for TTF-1.**
- **WT-1 is also negative in renal carcinoid. Therefore, it is useful to distinguish between adult Wilms' tumor in the kidney and primary carcinoid tumor.**

Renal neuroendocrine tumors including carcinoid tumor and small cell carcinoma are extremely rare [32, 38]. Diagnostic criteria of renal neuroendocrine tumors are same as those of the neuroendocrine tumors in other organs [32, 38].

Renal carcinoid tumors with average size of 6.4 cm [45] often are well circumscribed [32, 46–48] and show tan and red color [38]. The tumor consists of cords or nests of cells with fine nuclear chromatin, low mitotic activity, and lack of necrosis. The tumor cells are positive for neuroendocrine markers [45]. Differential diagnoses of primary renal carcinoid include metastatic carcinoid tumor from the lung and adult Wilms' tumor. TTF-1 can be used to rule out a lung metastasis, as a lung carcinoid tumor is positive for TTF-1 while primary renal carcinoid is negative for TTF-1 [45]. WT-1 is also negative in renal carcinoid. Therefore, it is useful to distinguish between adult Wilms' tumor in the kidney and primary carcinoid tumor [45]. Patients with renal carcinoid tumors often present with lymph node metastasis and may progress to distant metastasis, but usually have a prolonged clinical course in spite of wide metastasis [45].

Renal small cell carcinomas form whitish and necrotic mass located close to the renal pelvis [32]. The tumor cells are small, round, or oval with scant cytoplasm. The nuclei are hyperchromatic without prominent nucleoli. Nuclear molding, mitosis, and necrosis are often seen. It is important to differentiate renal small cell carcinoma from other small blue cell tumors including lymphoma and primitive neuroectodermal tumor (PNET) in the kidney. Immunohistochemical stains will be very useful in the differential diagnosis. The tumor cells of renal small cell carcinoma are positive for pan-cytokeratin and neuroendocrine markers, whereas lymphoma cells are negative for pan-cytokeratin and neuroendocrine markers but are positive for vimentin, CD45, and other lymphoma markers [32]. The tumor cells in PNET are positive for vimentin, CD99, and CD117 that are negative in renal small cell carcinoma [32].

The prognosis of renal small cell carcinoma is poor. Nephrectomy combined with chemotherapy is common treatment for renal small cell carcinoma [49]. One study showed that a significant improvement in overall survival was seen with the use of platinum-based chemotherapy (20 months vs. 8 months, P = 0.02).

References

1. Abrahamsson PA. Neuroendocrine differentiation in prostatic carcinoma. Prostate 1999;39:135–48.
2. Santamaria L, Martin R, Martin JJ, Alonso L. Stereologic estimation of the number of neuroendocrine cells in normal human prostate detected by immunohistochemistry. Appl Immunohistochem Mol Morphol 2002;10:275–81.
3. Bonkhoff H. Neuroendocrine differentiation in human prostate cancer. Morphogenesis, proliferation and androgen receptor status. Ann Oncol 2001;12 Suppl 2:S141–4.
4. Sternberg S. Histology for Pathologists. 2nd ed. Philadelphia: Lippincott-Raven; 1997.
5. Abrahamsson PA, Dizeyi N, Alm P, di Sant'Agnese PA, Deftos LJ, Aumuller G. Calcitonin and calcitonin gene-related peptide in the human prostate gland. Prostate 2000;44:181–6.
6. Bonkhoff H, Stein U, Remberger K. Endocrine-paracrine cell types in the prostate and prostatic adenocarcinoma are postmitotic cells. Hum Pathol 1995;26:167–70.
7. di Sant'Agnese PA. Neuroendocrine differentiation in carcinoma of the prostate. Diagnostic, prognostic, and therapeutic implications. Cancer 1992;70:254–68.
8. Aprikian AG, Cordon-Cardo C, Fair WR, Reuter VE. Characterization of neuroendocrine differentiation in human benign prostate and prostatic adenocarcinoma. Cancer 1993;71:3952–65.
9. di Sant'Agnese PA. Neuroendocrine differentiation in prostatic carcinoma: an update. Prostate Suppl 1998;8:74–9.
10. Abrahamsson PA, Falkmer S, Falt K, Grimelius L. The course of neuroendocrine differentiation in prostatic carcinomas. An immunohistochemical study testing chromogranin A as an "endocrine marker". Pathol Res Pract 1989;185:373–80.
11. Stratton M, Evans DJ, Lampert IA. Prostatic adenocarcinoma evolving into carcinoid: selective effect of hormonal treatment? J Clin Pathol 1986;39:750–6.
12. Cohen RJ, Glezerson G, Haffejee Z, Afrika D. Prostatic carcinoma: histological and immunohistological factors affecting prognosis. Br J Urol 1990;66:405–10.
13. Helpap B, Kollermann J, Oehler U. Neuroendocrine differentiation in prostatic carcinomas: histogenesis, biology, clinical relevance, and future therapeutical perspectives. Urol Int 1999;62:133–8.
14. Abrahamsson PA, Cockett AT, di Sant'Agnese PA. Prognostic significance of neuroendocrine differentiation in clinically localized prostatic carcinoma. Prostate Suppl 1998;8:37–42.
15. de Matteis A. Tissue markers in the diagnosis and prognosis of prostatic carcinoma. Eur Urol 1992;21 Suppl 1:66–70.
16. Wasserstein PW, Goldman RL. Primary carcinoid of prostate. Urology 1979;13:318–20.
17. Ghannoum JE, DeLellis RA, Shin SJ. Primary carcinoid tumor of the prostate with concurrent adenocarcinoma: a case report. Int J Surg Pathol 2004;12:167–70.
18. Reyes A, Moran CA. Low-grade neuroendocrine carcinoma (carcinoid tumor) of the prostate. Arch Pathol Lab Med 2004;128:e166–8.
19. Tash JA, Reuter V, Russo P. Metastatic carcinoid tumor of the prostate. J Urol 2002;167:2526–7.
20. Whelan T, Gatfield CT, Robertson S, Carpenter B, Schillinger JF. Primary carcinoid of the prostate in conjunction with multiple endocrine neoplasia IIb in a child. J Urol 1995;153:1080–2.
21. Wang W, Epstein JI. Small cell carcinoma of the prostate. A morphologic and immunohistochemical study of 95 cases. Am J Surg Pathol 2008;32:65–71.
22. Miyoshi Y, Uemura H, Kitami K, Satomi Y, Kubota Y, Hosaka M. Neuroendocrine differentiated small cell carcinoma presenting as recurrent prostate cancer after androgen deprivation therapy. BJU Int 2001;88:982–3.
23. Turbat-Herrera EA, Herrera GA, Gore I, Lott RL, Grizzle WE, Bonnin JM. Neuroendocrine differentiation in prostatic carcinomas. A retrospective autopsy study. Arch Pathol Lab Med 1988;112:1100–5.
24. Shah RB, Mehra R, Chinnaiyan AM, et al. Androgen-independent prostate cancer is a heterogeneous group of diseases: lessons from a rapid autopsy program. Cancer Res 2004;64:9209–16.
25. Helpap B, Kollermann J. Undifferentiated carcinoma of the prostate with small cell features: immunohistochemical subtyping and reflections on histogenesis. Virchows Arch 1999;434:385–91.
26. Ro JY, Tetu B, Ayala AG, Ordonez NG. Small cell carcinoma of the prostate. II. Immunohistochemical and electron microscopic studies of 18 cases. Cancer 1987;59:977–82.
27. Fernandes RC, Matsushita MM, Mauad T, Nascimento Saldiva PH. Prostate carcinoma with neuroendocrine differentiation: case report and literature review. Rev Hosp Clin Fac Med Sao Paulo 2001;56:153–8.
28. Patel S, Rosenthal JT. Hypercalcemia in carcinoma of prostate. Its cure by orchiectomy. Urology 1985;25:627–9.
29. Wynn SS, Nagabundi S, Koo J, Chin NW. Recurrent prostate carcinoma presenting as omental large cell carcinoma with neuroendocrine differentiation and resulting in bowel obstruction. Arch Pathol Lab Med 2000;124:1074–6.
30. Evans AJ, Humphrey PA, Belani J, van der Kwast TH, Srigley JR. Large cell neuroendocrine carcinoma of prostate: a clinicopathologic summary of 7 cases of a rare manifestation of advanced prostate cancer. Am J Surg Pathol 2006;30:684–93.
31. Cheng L, Leibovich BC, Cheville JC, et al. Paraganglioma of the urinary bladder: can biologic potential be predicted? Cancer 2000;88:844–52.
32. Eble J, Sauter G, Epstein J, Sesterhenn I. WHO Tumors of the Urinary System and Male Genital Organs: WHO, IARC Press; 2004.
33. Leestma JE, Price EB, Jr. Paraganglioma of the urinary bladder. Cancer 1971;28:1063–73.
34. Linnoila RI, Keiser HR, Steinberg SM, Lack EE. Histopathology of benign versus malignant sympathoadrenal paragangliomas: clinicopathologic study of 120 cases including unusual histologic features. Hum Pathol 1990;21:1168–80.
35. Murphy W, Beckwith J, Farrow G. Atlas of Tumor Pathology. Tumors of the Kidney, Bladder, and Related Urinary Structures. 3rd ed. Washington, D.C: AFIP; 1994.
36. Davaris P, Petraki K, Arvanitis D, Papacharalammpous N, Morakis A, Zorzos S. Urinary bladder paraganglioma (U.B.P.). Pathol Res Pract 1986;181:101–6.
37. Grignon DJ, Ro JY, Mackay B, et al. Paraganglioma of the urinary bladder: immunohistochemical, ultrastructural, and DNA flow cytometric studies. Hum Pathol 1991;22:1162–9.
38. Bostwick DG, Eble J. Urologic Surgical Pathology. St. Louis: Mosby; 1997.

39. Holmang S, Borghede G, Johansson SL. Primary small cell carcinoma of the bladder: a report of 25 cases. J Urol 1995;153:1820–2.
40. Lohrisch C, Murray N, Pickles T, Sullivan L. Small cell carcinoma of the bladder: long term outcome with integrated chemoradiation. Cancer 1999;86:2346–52.
41. Grignon DJ, Ro JY, Ayala AG, et al. Small cell carcinoma of the urinary bladder. A clinicopathologic analysis of 22 cases. Cancer 1992;69:527–36.
42. Cheng L, Pan CX, Yang XJ, et al. Small cell carcinoma of the urinary bladder: a clinicopathologic analysis of 64 patients. Cancer 2004;101:957–62.
43. Oesterling JE, Brendler CB, Burgers JK, Marshall FF, Epstein JI. Advanced small cell carcinoma of the bladder. Successful treatment with combined radical cystoprostatectomy and adjuvant methotrexate, vinblastine, doxorubicin, and cisplatin chemotherapy. Cancer 1990;65:1928–36.
44. Choong NW, Quevedo JF, Kaur JS. Small cell carcinoma of the urinary bladder. The Mayo Clinic experience. Cancer 2005;103:1172–8.
45. Hansel DE, Epstein JI, Berbescu E, Fine SW, Young RH, Cheville JC. Renal carcinoid tumor: a clinicopathologic study of 21 cases. Am J Surg Pathol 2007;31:1539–44.
46. Acconcia A, Miracco C, Mattei FM, deSanti MM, Del Vecchio MT, Luzi P. Primary carcinoid tumor of kidney. Light and electron microscopy, and immunohistochemical study. Urology 1988;31:517–20.
47. Ghazi MR, Brown JS, Warner RS. Carcinoid tumor of kidney. Urology 1979;14:610–2.
48. Zak FG, Jindrak K, Capozzi F. Carcinoidal tumor of the kidney. Ultrastruct Pathol 1983;4:51–9.
49. Majhail NS, Elson P, Bukowski RM. Therapy and outcome of small cell carcinoma of the kidney: report of two cases and a systematic review of the literature. Cancer 2003;97:1436–41.

Neuroendocrine Tumors of Other Miscellaneous Sites: Thymus and Skin

Francoise Truong and Ashraf Khan

Abstract Neuroendocrine tumors usually arise in endocrine organs but have also been described in unusual sites like the thymus and the skin. Neuroendocrine neoplasia in these sites is rare but does exist. The following chapter will discuss neuroendocrine carcinoma arising in the thymus and skin, the latter referred to as Merkel cell carcinoma of the skin.

Keywords Merkel cell carcinoma • Neuroendocrine carcinoma of the thymus • Neuroendocrine carcinoma of the skin • Skin • Thymus

Thymic Neuroendocrine Carcinomas

Thymus Normal Anatomy and Histology

Embryologically, the thymus is predominantly derived from the third pouch. At birth, it weighs between 10 and 35 g (mean weight of 20 g), progressively enlarges until puberty when it achieves a maximum weight of approximately 20–50 g. From puberty, the thymus involutes and persists in an atrophic state [1].

The fully mature thymus is an encapsulated pyramid-shaped organ situated in the anterosuperior mediastinum. It is composed of two fused lobes further divided into lobules by fibrous extensions of the capsule. The lobules are composed of the cortex and medulla. The two predominant cells in the thymus are the epithelial cells and bone marrow-derived lymphocytes but other cells, like neuroendocrine cells, are also present in a lesser number.

F. Truong (✉)
Pathologist, William Osler Health Center,
101 Humber College Blvd, Etobicoke, ON,
Canada, M9V 1R8
e-mail: francoise_truong@oslerhc.org

Neuroendocrine cells are a minor but constant component of the normal thymus [2]. Peptide- and amine-producing neuroendocrine cells have been identified in the thymus glands of reptiles and birds and, to a lesser degree, in mammalian thymus. Some of these cells may be analogous to C cells of the thyroid gland. The exact physiologic role of the neuroendocrine cells in the thymus is not clearly understood. But we know that these cells give rise to neuroendocrine neoplasms in the thymus.

Neuroendocrine Tumors

Definition

Rosai and Higa were the first to propose the existence of primary neuroendocrine neoplasms in the thymus. These thymic tumors had identical morphological features to neuroendocrine tumors arising at other location [3]. Tumors of the thymus that are exclusively or predominantly composed of neuroendocrine cells are termed and classified as neuroendocrine carcinomas of the thymus (NCT). Since these tumors have a malignant nature (they can metastasize and recur), many authors favor the use of the term "carcinoma" instead of "carcinoid."

The neoplastic cells show neuroendocrine differentiation. Morphologically, the nuclei have a fine chromatin with the typical "salt and pepper" appearance. The cytoplasm can be abundant and is usually eosinophilic. Their neuroendocrine nature can be demonstrated by immunohistochemistry studies with antibodies directed against chromogranin, synaptophysin, CD56, and neuron-specific enolase. Also, the presence of neurosecretory granules seen by electron microscopy is another helpful tool to confirm neuroendocrine differentiation [4–8].

A. Khan (ed.), *Surgical Pathology of Endocrine and Neuroendocrine Tumors*, Current Clinical Pathology,
DOI 10.1007/978-1-60327-396-1_16, © Humana Press, a part of Springer Science+Business Media, LLC 2009

Incidence and Epidemiology

Overall, primary neuroendocrine carcinomas (NEC) of the thymus are very rare. Only about 250 cases have been described in the literature. They constitute 2–5% of all thymic epithelial tumors and less than 5% of all anterior mediastinal neoplasms. The well-differentiated neuroendocrine carcinomas comprise the typical and atypical carcinoid. The majority of well-differentiated cases are atypical and occur in men in their fifties. The poorly differentiated neuroendocrine carcinomas are further divided into small cell carcinoma and large cell carcinomas.

Classification

The classification of thymic neuroendocrine carcinomas is similar to other neuroendocrine carcinoma classifications in other sites of the human body and is the one proposed by the WHO, see Table 1. Others have also used a three-tiered classification according to histopathologic features: low, intermediate, and high grade [6]. This latter classification is based on a combination of cytologic features, architectural characteristics, and mitotic activity. In this chapter, the preferred classification is the one used by the WHO. This classification is based upon the one used in other sites, like the lung and the gastrointestinal tract. It provides a morphological basis for clinical studies. Table 2 compares the WHO classification and the three-tiered classification.

Table 1 Histologic classification of thymic neuroendocrine carcinoma

Well differentiated
- Typical carcinoid
  - Less than 2 mitoses per 2 mm^2 or 10 high power field
- Atypical carcinoid
  - 2–10 mitoses per 2 mm^2 or 10 high power field
  - Foci of necrosis

Poorly differentiated
- Large cell carcinoma
  - More than 2 mitoses per 2 mm^2or 10 high power field
- Small cell carcinoma
  - Small cell features
  - Numerous mitoses, more than 10 per high power field

Macroscopy

Well-differentiated and poorly differentiated thymic neuroendocrine carcinomas look very much alike macroscopically. They can appear as a solid nodular or invasive mass. They can range from 2–20 cm with a tan-brown color [7]. Their cut surface is homogeneous and can show areas of hemorrhage, necrosis, or both (Fig. 1).

Table 2 Comparison between the WHO and three-tiered histologic classification

Three-tiered classification	WHO classification
Well-differentiated NEC Mild atypia Less than 3 mitoses per HPF Small foci of necrosis (less than 5 mm^2)	Well-differentiated NEC
Moderately-differentiated NEC Moderate atypia 4–9 mitoses per HPF Areas of necrosis (1–2 cm)	Well-differentiated NEC
Poorly differentiated NEC Marked atypia More than 10 mitoses per HPF Extensive areas of necrosis	Poorly differentiated NEC

HPF: high power field
NEC: neuroendocrine carcinoma
Reference [5].

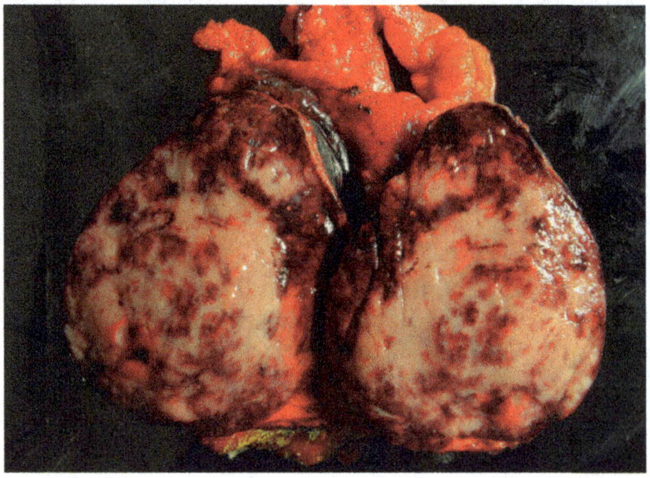

Fig. 1 Atypical thymic neuroendocrine carcinoma

Clinical Presentation

Local Symptoms

Patients have a radiographic mediastinal mass and may present with local symptoms: chest pain, dyspnea, and superior vena cava syndrome [7]. The poorly differentiated neuroendocrine carcinomas are more prone to cause local symptoms.

Systemic Symptoms

Neuroendocrine carcinoma of the thymus may cause Cushing syndrome (central obesity, moon facies, hirsutism, hypertension, osteoporosis, etc.). A little less than 30 cases of neuroendocrine carcinoma with Cushing syndrome have been reported in the literature. Some articles show that 10% of all cases of ectopic ACTH syndrome are due to thymic carcinoids. Carcinoid syndrome is almost never encountered.

Multiple Neuroendocrine Neoplasia

Thymic neuroendocrine carcinoma can occur in the setting of multiple endocrine neoplasia type 1 (MEN 1). Approximately 25% of NEC of the thymus are associated with MEN 1. This is an autosomal-dominant syndrome arising from mutations of a tumor suppressor gene, MEN 1, located on chromosome 11q13. It is usually characterized by multifocal endocrine tumors affecting principally the parathyroids, pancreas, anterior pituitary gland, and adrenal glands. Affected patients are almost all males and the majority do not show signs and symptoms of endocrine disorders like carcinoid or Cushing syndrome. In the setting of MEN 1, NEC of the thymus are aggressive and often show local invasion, distant metastases at diagnosis, and recurrence. Previous hyperparathyroidism seems to play a role in the pathogenesis and in the development of NEC of the thymus in MEN 1 [9–13].

Well-Differentiated Neuroendocrine Carcinomas

Typical Carcinoids

According to the WHO classification, typical carcinoids have less than 2 mitoses per 2 mm^2 (10 high power field) and no necrosis. Typical carcinoids are very rare since most carcinoid tumor of thymus possess small foci of necrosis, therefore epidemiological data is missing.

Morphologically, they are composed of a uniform population of polygonal cells. They have scant to moderate amount of eosinophilic cytoplasm and the nuclei have a finely granular chromatin with inconspicuous nucleoli. The cells can be arranged in ribbons, festoons, and rosettes. Solid nests can also be seen. The accompanying stroma is highly vascularized and can be hyalinized.

Atypical Carcinoids

As previously mentioned, the great majority of well-differentiated neuroendocrine carcinoma of the thymus is considered atypical. It is a tumor of adults, it occurs in their fifties and has a slight male predominance. According to the WHO classification, necrosis and/or 2–10 mitoses per 2 mm^2needs to be present.

Morphologically, they have the same histological features as the typical carcinoids but they show areas of necrosis and have a proliferation rate of 2–10 mitoses per 10 HPF (2 mm^2). See Figs. 1–4.

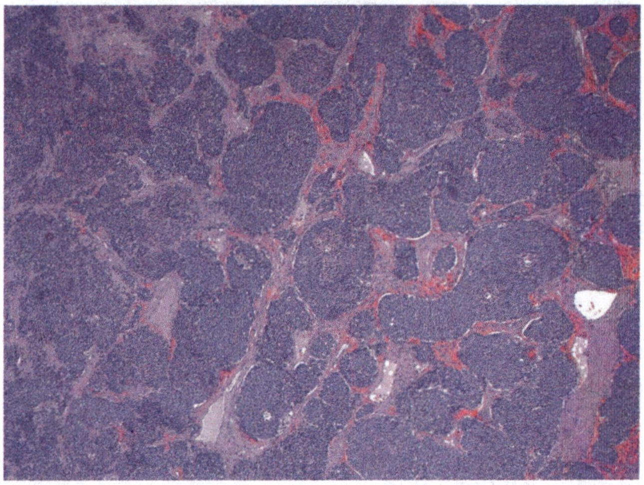

Fig. 2 Atypical thymic neuroendocrine carcinoma, solid nests of tumor with hyalinized stroma

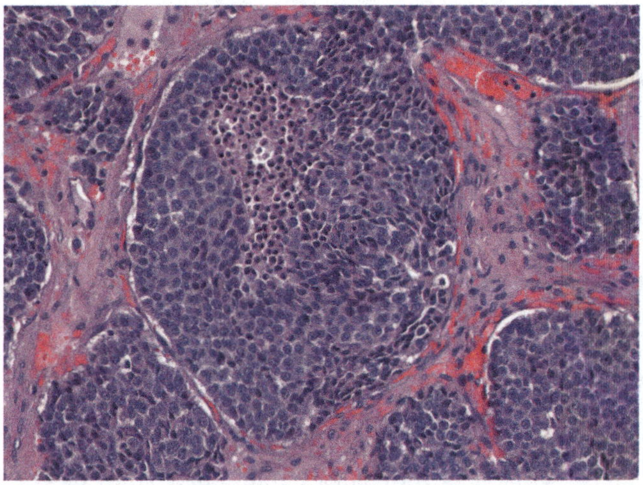

Fig. 3 Atypical thymic neuroendocrine carcinoma, foci of necrosis

Morphological Variants

Large series studying the morphologic features of primary neuroendocrine carcinoma of the thymus indicate that they have a broad range of cytologic features. Indeed,

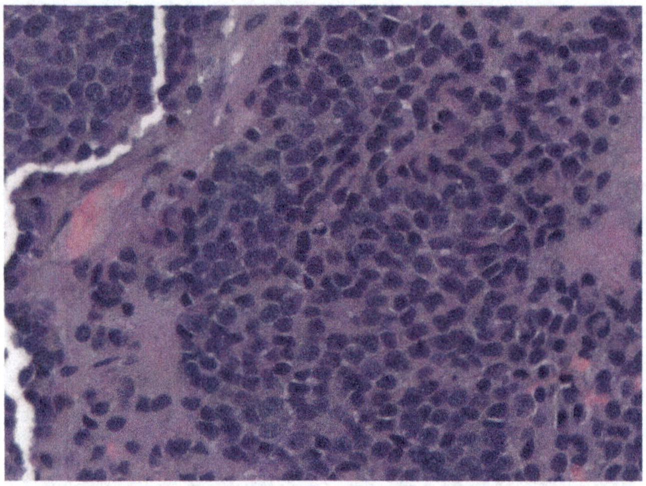

Fig. 4 Atypical thymic neuroendocrine carcinoma, tumor cells with salt and pepper chromatin

many morphologic variants of well-differentiated NEC of the thymus have been described despite the rarity of this tumor.

Spindle Cell Carcinoid

They are composed of a dense proliferation of spindle cells arranged in fascicles. They can focally have an organoid pattern [14].

Pigmented Carcinoid

They show a monotonous proliferation of tumor cells arranged in a nesting or trabecular pattern. Areas of intra- and extracellular dark pigment deposition are seen. The pigment is positive for Fontana-Masson stain confirming that the pigment is melanin [15].

Oncocytic Carcinoid

The tumor cells have an oxyphilic cytoplasm. Like other tumors with oncocytic changes, this is due to the excessive accumulation of mitochondria in the cytoplasm [16].

Mucinous

In this variant of the tumor, there is abundant stromal mucin in which the neuroendocrine tumor cells are embedded. This mucinous matrix is positive for Alcian blue at pH 2.5 [17, 18].

Angiomatoid

The tumor shows numerous dilated, cavernous spaces filled with blood. These cystic spaces are lined by tumor cells with neuroendocrine differentiation [19].

Sarcomatoid

The tumor is accompanied by sarcomatous stroma with areas of chondroid and osseous differentiation [20].

Poorly Differentiated Neuroendocrine Thymic Carcinoma

Large Cell Neuroendocrine Carcinoma

They are composed of large atypical cells with moderate to abundant cytoplasm. Their nuclei often have prominent nucleoli. Architectural features of neuroendocrine differentiation are usually seen, such as organoid nesting, trabeculae, or rosettes. The mitotic rate is high with more than 10 mitoses per 10 high power field and necrosis is frequent and extensive. The tumor lacks any characteristics of small cell carcinoma (see below). This type of neuroendocrine carcinoma of the thymus is extremely rare.

Small Cell Carcinoma

These tumors are composed of small cells (less than the size of three resting lymphocytes) with scant cytoplasm. The cell borders are ill defined and nuclear molding is often seen. The nuclei can be round, oval, and even spindly with a fine granular cytoplasm. Usually, nucleoli are absent or inconspicuous. There are numerous mitotic figures and apoptotic bodies. A sheet-like growth is more often encountered than the typical neuroendocrine architecture, such as nesting, trabeculae, and rosettes.

A variant of small cell carcinoma exists and encompasses all the small cell neuroendocrine carcinoma that are seen combined with the non-neuroendocrine carcinoma (squamous cell carcinoma and adenocarcinoma of the thymus).

Combined Thymic Tumors

Combined Thymic Epithelial Tumors

This corresponds to thymic neoplasms composed of at least two distinct types of thymic cancer: thymoma and thymic carcinoma. Combined "non-neuroendocrine thymic carcinoma with thymic neuroendocrine carcinoma" and "thymoma with thymic neuroendocrine carcinoma" are seen but are extremely rare. In these cases, the prognosis is based upon the most aggressive tumor.

Combined Thymic Neuroendocrine Carcinoma

Many cases of thymic neuroendocrine carcinoma reported in the literature show combined features of well-differentiated to poorly differentiated NEC with a spectrum of differentiation [21].

Immunophenotype and Ultrastructure

Because of their neuroendocrine differentiation, the tumor cells will react with the usual neuroendocrine markers such as chromogranin, synaptophysin, neuron-specific enolase, and CD56. Similar to other neuroendocrine tumors, broad spectrum cytokeratin like cytokeratin AE 1/3 and CAM5.2 will also be positive. A special stain for Grimelius will also be positive.

Hormones like ACTH, HCG, calcitonin, somatostatin, and cholecystokinin can be detected in a few cases. There is no correlation between the clinical symptoms and the detection of these hormones. Tumors are negative for TTF-1 and cytokeratin 20.

Like other tumors with neuroendocrine differentiation, dense-core neurosecretory granules in the cytoplasm will be detected by electron microscopy.

Differential Diagnosis

Thymic neuroendocrine carcinomas are rare and must be differentiated from more common type of cancer that can mimic morphologically neuroendocrine tumors and metastatic neuroendocrine carcinomas from other sites.

Metastatic Neuroendocrine Carcinomas

Of utmost importance, a thorough clinical history and thoracic imaging with help in assessing the origin of the tumor. A positive immunostaining of the tumor for TTF-1 is more in favor of a lung origin.

Mediastinal Paraganglioma

Paraganglioma do not show mitotic activity or necrosis. Both tumors will be positive for neuroendocrine markers but paraganglioma are negative for cytokeratins.

Parathyroid Tumors

Ectopic parathyroid adenoma and carcinoma can mimic thymic neuroendocrine carcinoma. Parathyroid lesions usually have glycogen in their cytoplasm and can be highlighted with a periodic acid-Schiff stain; this will be negative in thymic neuroendocrine carcinoma. Also, an immunohistochemical stain for parathyroid hormones will be positive in parathyroid tumors.

Thymoma Type A

A thymoma with spindle cells (type A) can mimic a thymic neuroendocrine carcinoma with spindle cell features. This type of thymoma lacks neuroendocrine markers.

Synovial Sarcoma

These tumors can be cytokeratin positive but will lack the neuroendocrine markers of thymic NEC.

Medullary Thyroid Carcinoma

These tumors usually are positive for calcitonin, carcinoembryonic antigen, and TTF-1.

Genetics

Few comparative genomic hybridization data are available in the literature. Varied chromosomal abnormalities have been noted. Interestingly, one study shows genetic alterations similar to those seen in type B3 and C thymomas such as losses on chromosomal arms 6p, 6q, 13q, and 3p. This may be suggestive of a genetic relationship between thymomas and thymic NEC [22]. Also, one study including one case of thymic NEC in a patient with MEN 1 and 10 sporadic cases failed to show chromosomal alterations of 11q (allelic losses on 11q is frequently found in sporadic and MEN 1-associated neuroendocrine tumors of the lung and the digestive system). Therefore, the authors consider that a distinctive cytogenetic mechanism is involved in the development of thymic NEC. This could explain the different clinical behavior between thymic NEC and neuroendocrine tumors of the lung and gut (thymic NEC behaving more aggressively than the non-thymic carcinoid tumors) [23].

Prognosis and Treatment

Prognosis

Compared with lung carcinoid, atypical carcinoids of the thymus are more aggressive with a high rate of local invasion and metastases. Prognosis is closely related to histology and stage. Poorly differentiated tumors do worse than the well-differentiated ones.

Amongst well-differentiated carcinomas, the more the mitoses (more than 3 per high power field) and foci of necrosis, the worse the prognosis. The more advanced the tumor is (capsular invasion, lymph node involvement, and distant metastases), the worse the prognosis [4].

In studies using a three-tiered histological classification, well-differentiated tumors, moderately differentiated, and poorly differentiated had a 5-year survival of 50%, 25%, and 0%, respectively [7]. Unresectable tumors and advanced clinical stage are associated with higher mortality [5].

Treatment

Patients with MEN 1 should have a cervical thymectomy followed by radiographic surveillance. Because of the aggressive nature of this tumor and a high rate of recurrence despite prophylactic thymectomy, some suggest perioperative use of radiotherapy [11, 12].

For sporadic cases, complete surgical resection excision is the treatment of choice with adjuvant radiotherapy and chemotherapy [4, 24, 25].

Primary Neuroendocrine Carcinoma of the Skin

Merkel Cells

Merkel cells were first described by F.S. Merkel in 1875. These cells are scattered in the basal cell layer of the epidermis. They can group in clusters but are not seen in routine histologic sections. These are present in higher concentration in the digits, lips, oral cavity, and the outer root sheath of hair follicles. They play a role in tactile sensation. By electron microscopy, these cells have neurosecretory granules in their cytoplasm and they stain for chromogranin, synaptophysin, neuron-specific enolase, and neural cell adhesion molecule antigens. They have paranuclear aggregates of cytokeratins that will stain for cytokeratin 20.

Primary Neuroendocrine Cell Carcinoma of the Skin

Primary neuroendocrine cell carcinoma of the skin (Merkel cell carcinoma) has been first described by Toker in 1972. It was thought to be of eccrine or of sudoriferous origin. Subsequently, cytoplasmic neurosecretory granules were detected in the cells of this tumor and this linked the neoplasm and Merkel cells of the skin, hence the name Merkel cell carcinoma. Although the tumor cells in Merkel cell carcinoma and Merkel cells of the epidermis share immunohistochemical and ultrastructural features, a direct histogenetic relationship is yet to be proven [26, 27].

Epidemiology

The incidence of Merkel cell carcinoma has been increasing in the past years. The number of new cases is estimated at 1500 per year in the United States [28]. It affects predominantly Caucasian males in their sixties.

Risk Factors

Exposure to sun (and ultraviolet B) is a major risk factor for the development of Merkel cell carcinoma. Immunosuppression, solid organ transplant, and chronic arsenic exposure are also considered risk factors.

Clinical Presentation

These tumors arise most often on sun-exposed areas like the head and neck and extremities. It usually presents as a solitary, painless, and rapidly growing nodule. The dome shaped nodule is pink, violaceous, and can sometimes be ulcerated.

Histology

Microscopically, Merkel cell carcinoma is a poorly defined proliferation of small blue cells (Figs. 4–8). The tumor is located in the dermis and can infiltrate subcutaneous fat, fascia, and even muscle. The overlying epidermis is usually uninvolved but pagetoid involvement of the epidermis can be seen. Various growth patterns are encountered, but a sheet-like growth is most commonly seen. Other architectural patterns include nests and trabeculae. Characteristically, the periphery of the tumor shows a trabecular pattern of infiltration (Fig. 5). The small tumor cells are monotonous and uniform in size, round to oval and are about two to three times the size of a mature resting lymphocyte (Fig. 6). The cytoplasm is scant and amphophilic. The nucleoli are round and have a fine granular chromatin with multiple nucleoli that are not prominent. Mitotic figures are numerous and areas of necrosis are common, especially in large tumors. The stroma shows many vessels with plump endothelial cells. Merkel cell carcinoma can be seen in association with squamous cell carcinoma (in about 30% of the cases) [27].

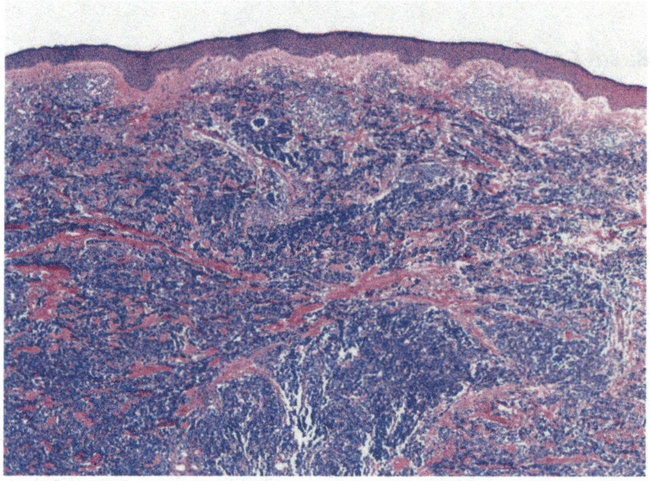

Fig. 5 Merkel cell carcinoma involving the dermis

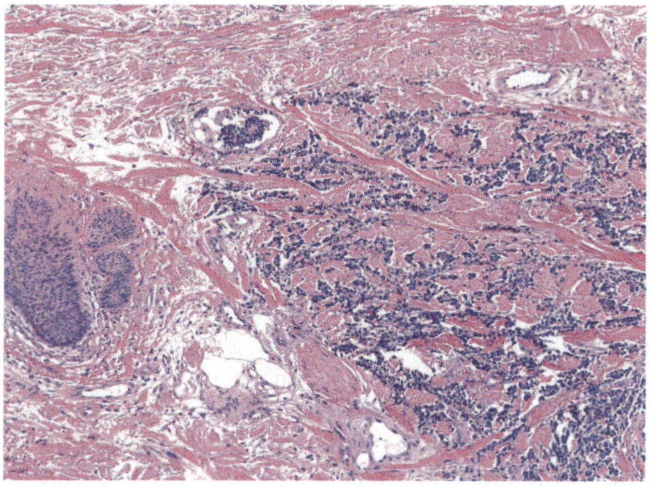

Fig. 6 Periphery of the Merkel cell carcinoma showing a trabecular pattern of infiltration

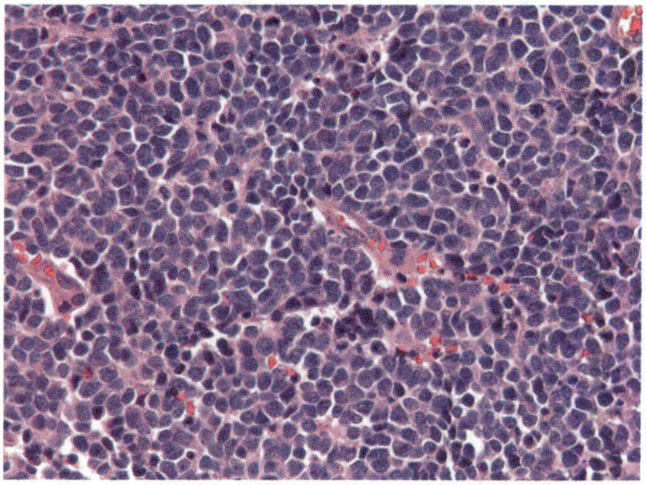

Fig. 7 Merkel cell carcinoma, the tumor cells have a fine chromatin, scant amphophilic cytoplasm

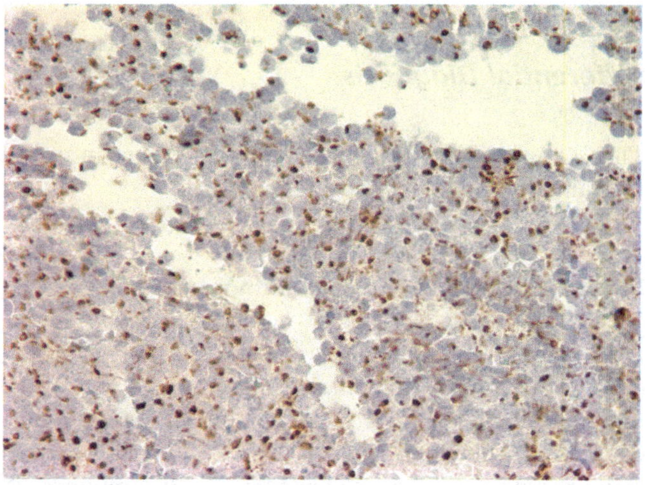

Fig. 8 Merkel cell carcinoma, immunostaining with Cytokeratin 20 show a characteristic paranuclear dot-like staining

Immunohistochemistry and Electron Microscopy

Merkel cell carcinoma shows neuroendocrine and epithelial differentiation. The neuroendocrine differentiation is highlighted by a positive staining for antigens such as chromogranin, synaptophysin, neuron-specific enolase, somatostatin, and calcitonin. The epithelial differentiation is confirmed with stains for low molecular weight keratin, epithelial membrane antigen, and BER-EP4. A characteristic feature for Merkel cell carcinoma is a paranuclear dot-like staining with cytokeratin 20 (see Fig. 8). In addition to these markers, a positive staining can be seen with CD117 and CD99 in some cases [29].

Ultrastructurally, the tumor cells contains dense-core neurosecretory granules, often just beneath the cell membrane. Tightly packed perinuclear intermediate filaments in the cytoplasm are also present and account for the positive immunostaining with cytokeratin 20.

Differential Diagnosis

The various tumors described below may mimic morphologically Merkel cell carcinoma.

Metastatic Neuroendocrine Carcinoma

A major differential diagnosis is with metastatic neuroendocrine carcinoma from other primary sources such as the lung and medullary thyroid carcinoma. It can be differentiated by the clinical history and the dot-like pattern staining with cytokeratin 20 in Merkel cell carcinoma. A positive staining for TTF-1 is in favor of lung origin. Medullary thyroid carcinoma will be positive for TTF-1 and CEA.

Melanoma

Merkel cell carcinoma can resemble a variant of melanoma, the small cell melanoma. The latter will have epidermal involvement and the tumor cells will be negative for cytokeratin 20 and positive for protein S100 and Melan A.

Lymphoma

Various lymphomas, especially lymphoblastic lymphoma, can have features of Merkel cell carcinoma. Cytokeratin and leucocyte common antigen (CD45) can help separate the two entities.

PNET/Ewing Sarcoma

These tumors are more often positive for CD99 and Fli-1 than Merkel cell carcinoma (though they can sometimes be positive in Merkel cell carcinoma) [29]. A negative staining for cytokeratin 20 will rule out Merkel cell carcinoma.

Metastatic Neuroblastoma

Similar to PNET/Ewing sarcoma tumors, metastatic neuroblastoma will not stain for cytokeratin 20.

Basal Cell Carcinoma

The nuclear features of basal cell carcinoma are different from those of Merkel cell carcinoma. The nuclei in basal cell carcinoma lack the fine granular chromatin and they also lack the cytokeratin 20 staining of Merkel cell carcinoma [30].

Prognosis and Treatment

No established staging system for MCC is recognized. A 4-tiered and 3-tiered system exists [31, 32]. Most clinicians use a 3-tiered system (stage I: tumor dimension is less than 2 cm, stage II: tumor dimension is more than 2 cm, stage III: regional or distant metastasis are present). Merkel cell carcinoma is an aggressive tumor with high recurrence rate (55–79% within the first 6–12 months after initial diagnosis). Favorable clinical prognostic factors include age (less than 55 years old), a location to the head and neck, female sex, and stage (tumors less than 2 cm in size and no lymph node involvement) [33–35]. Histologically, a poor prognosis is associated with a high level of mitoses and angiolymphatic invasion [36]. A positive p63 staining is an independent prognostic marker of aggressiveness [37]. Recently, a positive staining with survivin (a inhibitor of apoptosis) was shown to be associated with a poor prognosis [38].

Currently, there is no consensus for the treatment of MCC. Local disease is usually treated with surgical resections with the Mohs technique. The role of adjuvant therapy like radiotherapy and chemotherapy is yet to be established [32, 39].

Genetics

Numerous chromosomal abnormalities are seen in Merkel cell carcinoma [40]. The most frequent chromosomal rearrangement involves the short arm of chromosome 1 and is observed in 40% of patients. Also, UV-B-specific mutations in the p53 and Ha-ras genes are commonly seen [41]. As of now, no candidate gene has been identified in Merkel cell carcinoma.

References

1. Vinay K, Nelso F, Abul A. Robbins & Cotran Pathologic Basis of Disease, Seventh Edition. Elsevier Science, 2004, p.706
2. Stacey EM. Histology For Pathologists, Third Edition. Lippincott Williams & Wilkins, p. 511
3. Rosai J, Higa E. Mediastinal endocrine neoplasm, of probable thymic origin, related to carcinoid tumor. Clinicopathologic study of 8 cases. Cancer 1972;29(4):1061–74.
4. Chaer R, Massad MG, Evans A, Snow NJ, Geha AS. Primary neuroendocrine tumors of the thymus. The Annals of Thoracic Surgery 2002;74(5):1733–40.
5. Gal AA, Kornstein MJ, Cohen C, Duarte IG, Miller JI, Mansour KA. Neuroendocrine tumors of the thymus: a clinicopathological and prognostic study. The Annals of Thoracic Surgery 2001;72(4):1179–82.
6. Moran CA. Primary neuroendocrine carcinomas of the mediastinum: review of current criteria for histopathologic diagnosis and classification. Seminars in Diagnostic Pathology 2005;22 (3):223–9.
7. Moran CA, Suster S. Neuroendocrine carcinomas (carcinoid tumor) of the thymus. A clinicopathologic analysis of 80 cases. American Journal of Clinical Pathology 2000;114(1): 100–10.
8. Tiffet O, Nicholson AG, Ladas G, Sheppard MN, Goldstraw P. A clinicopathologic study of 12 neuroendocrine tumors arising in the thymus. Chest 2003;124(1):141–6.
9. Vidal A, Lorenzo MJ, Isidro ML, Cordido F. Atypical thymic carcinoid in multiple endocrine neoplasia type 1 syndrome. Journal of Endocrinological Investigation 2007;30 (7):601–2.
10. Takagi J, Otake K, Morishita M, et al. Multiple endocrine neoplasia type I and Cushing's syndrome due to an aggressive ACTH producing thymic carcinoid. Internal Medicine (Tokyo, Japan) 2006;45(2):81–6.
11. Lim LC, Tan MH, Eng C, Teh BT, Rajasoorya RC. Thymic carcinoid in multiple endocrine neoplasia 1: genotype-phenotype correlation and prevention. Journal of Internal Medicine 2006;259(4):428–32.
12. Gibril F, Chen YJ, Schrump DS, et al. Prospective study of thymic carcinoids in patients with multiple endocrine neoplasia type 1. The Journal of Clinical Endocrinology and Metabolism 2003;88(3):1066–81.
13. Ferolla P, Falchetti A, Filosso P, et al. Thymic neuroendocrine carcinoma (carcinoid) in multiple endocrine neoplasia type 1 syndrome: the Italian series. The Journal of Clinical Endocrinology and Metabolism 2005;90(5):2603–9.
14. Moran CA, Suster S. Spindle-cell neuroendocrine carcinomas of the thymus (spindle-cell thymic carcinoid): a clinicopathologic and immunohistochemical study of seven cases. Modern Pathology 1999;12(6):587–91.
15. Klemm KM, Moran CA, Suster S. Pigmented thymic carcinoids: a clinicopathological and immunohistochemical study of two cases. Modern Pathology 1999;12(10):946–8.
16. Moran CA, Suster S. Primary neuroendocrine carcinoma (thymic carcinoid) of the thymus with prominent oncocytic features: a clinicopathologic study of 22 cases. Modern Pathology 2000; 13(5):489–94.
17. Suster S, Moran CA. Thymic carcinoid with prominent mucinous stroma. Report of a distinctive morphologic variant of thymic neuroendocrine neoplasm. The American Journal of Surgical Pathology 1995;19(11):1277–85.
18. Gao Z, Kahn L, Bhuiya T. Thymic carcinoid with mucinous stroma: a rare variant of carcinoid with an aggressive clinical course. Annals of Diagnostic Pathology 2006;10 (2):114–6.
19. Moran CA, Suster S. Angiomatoid neuroendocrine carcinoma of the thymus: report of a distinctive morphological variant of neuroendocrine tumor of the thymus resembling a vascular neoplasm. Human Pathology 1999;30(6):635–9.
20. Kuo TT. Carcinoid tumor of the thymus with divergent sarcomatoid differentiation: report of a case with histogenetic consideration. Human Pathology 1994;25(3):319–23.
21. Moran CA, Suster S. Thymic neuroendocrine carcinomas with combined features ranging from well-differentiated (carcinoid) to small cell carcinoma. A clinicopathologic and immunohistochemical study of 11 cases. American Journal of Clinical Pathology 2000;113(3):345–50.
22. Rieker RJ, Aulmann S, Penzel R, et al. Chromosomal imbalances in sporadic neuroendocrine tumours of the thymus. Cancer Letters 2005;223(1):169–74.
23. Pan CC, Jong YJ, Chen YJ. Comparative genomic hybridization analysis of thymic neuroendocrine tumors. Modern Pathology 2005;18(3):358–64.
24. Filosso PL, Actis Dato GM, Ruffini E, Bretti S, Ozzello F, Mancuso M. Multidisciplinary treatment of advanced thymic neuroendocrine carcinoma (carcinoid): report of a successful case and review of the literature. The Journal of Thoracic and Cardiovascular Surgery 2004;127(4):1215–9.
25. Dosios T, Nikou GC, Toubanakis C, Filippides T, Papachristou D. Multimodality treatment of neuroendocrine tumors of the thymus. The Thoracic and Cardiovascular Surgeon 2005;53(5):305–9.
26. Dinh V, Feun L, Elgart G, Savaraj N. Merkel cell carcinomas. Hematology/Oncology Clinics of North America 2007;21 (3):527–44; ix.
27. Walsh NM. Primary neuroendocrine (Merkel cell) carcinoma of the skin: morphologic diversity and implications thereof. Human Pathology 2001;32(7):680–9.
28. Lemos B, Nghiem P. Merkel cell carcinoma: more deaths but still no pathway to blame. The Journal of Investigative Dermatology 2007;127(9):2100–3.
29. Llombart B, Monteagudo C, Lopez-Guerrero JA, et al. Clinicopathological and immunohistochemical analysis of 20 cases of Merkel cell carcinoma in search of prognostic markers. Histopathology 2005;46(6):622–34.
30. Ball NJ, Tanhuanco-Kho G. Merkel cell carcinoma frequently shows histologic features of basal cell carcinoma: a study of 30 cases. Journal of Cutaneous Pathology 2007;34(8):612–9.
31. Allen PJ, Bowne WB, Jaques DP, Brennan MF, Busam K, Coit DG. Merkel cell carcinoma: prognosis and treatment of patients from a single institution. Journal Of Clinical Oncology 2005;23(10):2300–9.
32. Tai P. Merkel cell cancer: update on biology and treatment. Current Opinion in Oncology 2008;20(2):196–200.

33. Coit DG. Merkel cell carcinoma. Annals of Surgical Oncology 2001;8(9 Suppl):99S–102S.
34. Goessling W, McKee PH, Mayer RJ. Merkel cell carcinoma. Journal Of Clinical Oncology 2002;20(2):588–98.
35. Smith PD, Patterson JW. Merkel cell carcinoma (neuroendocrine carcinoma of the skin). American Journal of Clinical Pathology 2001;115 Suppl:S68–78.
36. Skelton HG, Smith KJ, Hitchcock CL, McCarthy WF, Lupton GP, Graham JH. Merkel cell carcinoma: analysis of clinical, histologic, and immunohistologic features of 132 cases with relation to survival. Journal of the American Academy of Dermatology 1997;37(5 Pt 1):734–9.
37. Asioli S, Righi A, Volante M, Eusebi V, Bussolati G. p63 expression as a new prognostic marker in Merkel cell carcinoma. Cancer 2007;110(3):640–7.
38. Kim J, McNiff JM. Nuclear expression of survivin portends a poor prognosis in Merkel cell carcinoma. Modern Pathology 2008;21(6):764–9.
39. Eng TY, Boersma MG, Fuller CD, et al. A comprehensive review of the treatment of Merkel cell carcinoma. American Journal of Clinical Oncology 2007;30(6):624–36.
40. Van Gele M, Leonard JH, Van Roy N, et al. Combined karyotyping, CGH and M-FISH analysis allows detailed characterization of unidentified chromosomal rearrangements in Merkel cell carcinoma. International Journal of Cancer 2002;101(2):137–45.
41. Bichakjian CK, Lowe L, Lao CD, et al. Merkel cell carcinoma: critical review with guidelines for multidisciplinary management. Cancer 2007;110(1):1–12.

Endocrine Tumors and Tumor-Like Lesions of Infancy, Childhood, and Adolescents and Inherited Tumor Syndromes

Vânia Nosé

Abstract The endocrine system is an embryological diverse system composed of a variety of glands, such as pituitary, pineal, thyroid, parathyroid, adrenal, endocrine pancreas, and the diffuse neuroendocrine system. Neoplasms of all of these organs seen in adults are also found in infancy, childhood, and adolescents, both sporadic and as part of an inherited tumor syndrome. Besides these neoplastic diseases, young children and adolescents may present with a mass-like lesion that may be developmental or an embryological defect in nature and may mimic neoplasms. These diseases may include enlargement and hyperplasia, a single mass, or atrophy accompanied by hypofunction. We will discuss some of the different types of pathology that occur in adults and may also be present in infancy, childhood, and adolescents, as well as, tumors and tumor-like conditions that occur almost exclusively in these groups. We will cover also sporadic tumors and tumors occurring in a familial setting.

Keywords Endocrine tumors • Pediatric endocrine pathology • Pituitary • Thyroid • Parathyroid • Adrenal • Inherited tumor syndrome • Multiple endocrine neoplasia • PTEN hamartoma tumor syndrome • Familial diseases

Introduction

The signs and symptoms of endocrine lesions come from hormonal hyperfunction, hormonal hypofunction, or mass effect symptoms.

Most endocrine tumors that are seen in adults [1–4] may also be seen in infancy or childhood, either as a sporadic event or as part of an inherited tumor syndrome. The tumors and tumor-like lesions in children and adolescents can be developmental, acquired, or neoplastic in origin. This chapter focuses on tumor-like lesions and neoplastic disorders involving the pituitary, thyroid, parathyroid, and adrenal glands in the pediatric and adolescent populations. We will start each discussion with a brief summary of the embryology of that particular organ, as most tumor-like lesions at this age group may be related to embryonal development. We will discuss the tumors and tumor-like lesions occurring specifically in this age group and briefly discuss the tumors that are similar to the adults. We will also discuss tumors and tumor-like lesions that are related to hereditary and developmental disorders, that are sporadic, and as part of a multiple endocrine tumor syndromes. Refer to other organ-specific chapters for details of tumors occurring in adults.

V. Nosé (✉)
Associate Director of Surgical Pathology, Chief, Endocrine Pathology Service, Associate Professor of Pathology, Department of Pathology, Harvard Medical School, Brigham and Women's Hospital, Boston, MA 02115, USA
e-mail: vnose@partners.org

Pituitary

The pituitary gland of the neonate is prominent and undergoes involution in the postnatal period, followed by increased growth through the age of 3. The pituitary can be recognized by the third month of fetal development and the hormone producing cells of the anterior gland can be recognized as early as 5 weeks of gestation (corticotroph). Somatotroph are identified by 8 weeks and lactotroph by 12 weeks of gestation. The adenohypophysis and the neurohypophysis form the human pituitary gland and arise developmentally from two anlages. The adenohypophysis develops from an evagination of the primitive oral region, Rathke's pouch. The posterior wall of Rathke's pouch gives rise to the pars tuberalis. The neurohypophysis originates from the infundibular process of the diencephalon.

The signs and symptoms of pituitary lesions come from hormonal hyperfunction, hormonal hypofunction, or compression of surrounding structures such as the optic chiasm.

A. Khan (ed.), *Surgical Pathology of Endocrine and Neuroendocrine Tumors*, Current Clinical Pathology,
DOI 10.1007/978-1-60327-396-1_17, © Humana Press, a part of Springer Science+Business Media, LLC 2009

A. Hyperfunction is due to excess secretion of trophic hormones. The most common cause of hyperfunction in childhood and adolescents is a functional adenoma, less frequently hyperplasia. Non-pituitary tumors and hypothalamic diseases are rare causes of hyperpituitarism. Ectopic nests of adenohypophyseal cells trapped in the pharyngeal mucosa may give rise to ectopic adenoma.
B. Hypofunction is caused by deficiency of trophic hormones due to lesions within the sella turcica with destruction of the hormone-producing cells. The most common cause in infancy is agenesis, a developmental disorder due to failure of Rathke's pouch to fuse with infundibular process. Pituitary adenoma and less commonly inflammatory diseases leading to hypopituitarism rarely occur in this age group. Patients may also show signs of isolated anterior pituitary hormone deficiency such as hypothyroidism or hypogonadism.
C. Local mass effects: Due to its location adjacent to a variety of normal structures, the mass effects of a tumor-like lesion or an adenoma can manifest as sellar expansion, bone erosion, disruption of the diaphragma sellae, and compression of the optic chiasm with bitemporal hemianopsia, elevated intracranial pressure, headaches, seizures, obstructive hydrocephalus, and cranial nerve palsies.

The most common findings in the pituitary gland present in infancy, childhood, and adolescents are (Table 1):

Table 1 Pituitary pathology in children

Neoplastic	Non- neoplastic
Pituitary Adenoma	Hyperplasia
Craniopharyngioma	Inflammatory conditions
Gangliocytoma/ganglioglioma	Rathke's cleft pouch remnants
Hamartoma or choristoma	Rathke's cleft cysts
	Arachnoid cysts
	Dermoid cysts
	Epidermoid cysts
	Meningoencephalocele
	Hamartoma
	Pituitary aplasia or hypoplasia
	Empty sella syndrome

Hereditary and Developmental Disorders

Persistence of Rathke's pouch remnants: These are small nests of squamous cells in the posterior lobe adjacent to the cleft. They can be found in up to 30% of normal human pituitaries at autopsy. If large lesion, children may present with growth retardation or pituitary dwarfism.

Persistence of cleft of Rathke's pouch: This developmental abnormality is frequent. It is a colloid-filled space, between the anterior and posterior pituitary, which can give rise to Rathke's cleft cysts. These cysts are usually small, but when large, they can be symptomatic either from pressure or hypopituitarism including diabetes insipidus. When suprasellar extension is present, headaches and visual fields defects can occur. The cyst contains watery-to-mucinous fluid, is lined by columnar epithelium (Fig. 1) or ciliated cuboidal epithelium with occasional goblet cells.

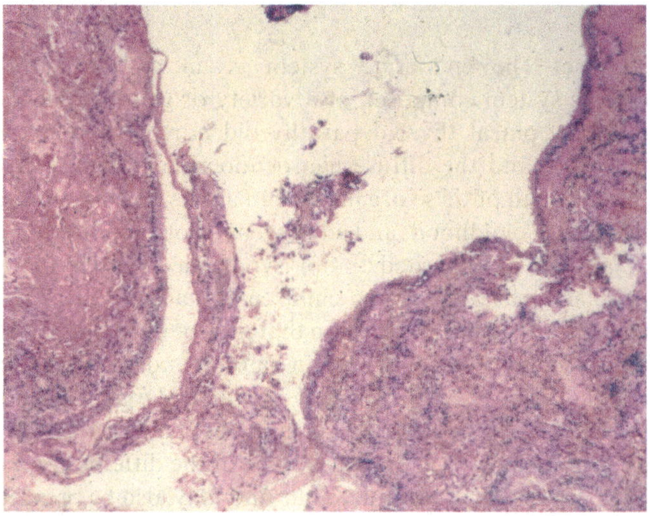

Fig. 1 Microscopic view of a Rathke's cleft cyst, lined by cuboidal epithelium

Arachnoid Cysts: These cysts may be congenital or acquired and originate in the arachnoid of the sella or parasellar regions. As with Rathke's cleft cysts, arachnoid cysts may present with mass effect from suprasellar extension or hypopituitarism due to pituitary compression. The cyst is filled with clear fluid and the cyst wall is lined by a simple epithelial layer covering arachnoid laminar connective tissue.

Dermoid cysts: Dermoid cysts are rare intracranially and in the pituitary region. They can be intrasellar, suprasellar, or both. They originate from ectopic or implanted epithelial cells. They usually occur in the midline. As with the other previously described cysts, the symptoms are of mass effect or hypopituitarism. And as with dermoid cysts elsewhere, the pituitary region dermoid cysts are lined by squamous epithelium with sweat glands and hair follicles.

Epidermoid cysts: These rare pituitary/sellar cysts, also known as epidermal inclusion cysts, are more commonly seen than dermoid cysts. They are generally in the midline. Epithelial rests in the pituitary may be involved in the genesis of these cysts. They have similar imaging and clinical findings to other cysts in this region. They are lined by keratinizing squamous epithelium. They usually occur in the fifth decade of life.

Pituitary aplasia and hypoplasia: Congenital absence of the pituitary is rare. Congenital hypopituitarism is usually associated with hypoplasia of the adrenals, thyroid, and gonads. Even if the anterior pituitary is not formed, the posterior pituitary may be present. It may be associated with anencephaly, where the number of cells may be normal, but the ACTH-producing cells are decreased and have poorly developed organelles.

Empty sella syndrome: Empty sella syndrome is an anatomical description of the appearance of the sella turcica. Empty sella syndrome can be primary or secondary. The primary empty sella syndrome is a developmental disorder due to incomplete development of the diaphragma sella with flattening of the pituitary gland. This has been reported as a cause for hypogonadotrophic hypogonadism in boys and short stature in females. The secondary empty sella syndrome occurs after resection, irradiation, necrosis, or infarction, leading to almost complete absence of pituitary.

Acquired Disorders of the Pituitary Gland

The differential diagnosis of mass-like lesions in the pituitary of children include inflammatory disorders as congenital syphilis, lymphocytic and granulomatous hypophysitis, sarcoidosis, Langerhans cell histiocytosis, pituitary adenomas, and craniopharyngiomas. The great majority of the lesions arising in anterior pituitary in children are adenomas and constitute 2% of all intracranial tumors in children and up to 9% of the pituitary adenomas in adolescents.

Pituitary Adenomas: In the pediatric population, these tumors are primarily seen in adolescents, are sporadic or be a component of multiple neoplasia syndrome. Functional pituitary adenomas are the most common cause of hyperpituitarism. We have recently reviewed 22 pituitary adenomas occurring in childhood, and the clinical and morphological findings parallel those of the adult tumors.

Ectopic Adenomas: Ectopic adenomas are extremely rare. They are derived from pituitary cells in the pharynx and can occur in the sphenoid sinus, mouth, nasal cavity, or in the suprasellar region.

Pituitary Diseases in Familial Syndromes

Pituitary adenomas are integral components of the type 1 multiple endocrine neoplasia syndrome (MEN1). The pituitary adenomas in the MEN1 syndrome are usually hormonally active. They may produce all types of hormones, but there is a preponderance of prolactin and/or growth hormone production. Null cell adenomas in MEN1 are less frequent than in sporadic pituitary adenomas [1]. GH-producing adenomas are present in about 10% of patients with Carney complex (Table 2).

Table 2 Inherited neoplasia syndromes associated with pituitary tumors

Syndrome	Gene/ chromosomal location	Pituitary pathology
MEN1	*MEN1*/11q13	Growth hormone or prolactin-producing adenoma or non-functional adenoma
Carney complex	*PRKAR1A*/ 2p16	Growth hormone-producing adenoma

Tumors of the Hypothalamus, Neurohypophysis, and Sellar Region

The region of the sella has a variety of tissues and cell types, including central and peripheral nervous system, endocrine, germinal, epithelial, meningeal, mesenchymal, and hematopoietic cells. Besides the great variety of neoplasms that can occur in this region, the neoplasms can mimic each other, clinically and morphologically. Immunohistochemistry is most of the time necessary for the differential diagnosis of the lesions in this region.

Craniopharyngiomas

Craniopharyngiomas are an uncommon neoplasm but are the second most common neoplasm of the sellar region, up to 9% of the intracranial neoplasms, following pituitary adenomas and the most common suprasellar neoplasm in children. The vast majority of craniopharyngiomas are in the suprasellar region. The usual symptoms are headache and visual changes, such as diplopia. Craniopharyngiomas are usually cystic, irregular nodular masses of firm tissue with yellow-brown viscid contents (Fig. 2). The fluid contains large numbers of cholesterol crystals. Pseudostratified columnar cells palisade around stellate cells forming the adamantinomatous pattern (Fig. 2). The basaloid epithelium keratinizes without maturing, giving rise to nests of keratin in the tumor. The tumors frequently contain calcific debris, cholesterol clefts, and foreign body giant cells. Papillary craniopharyngioma is a distinct neoplasm that differs from the

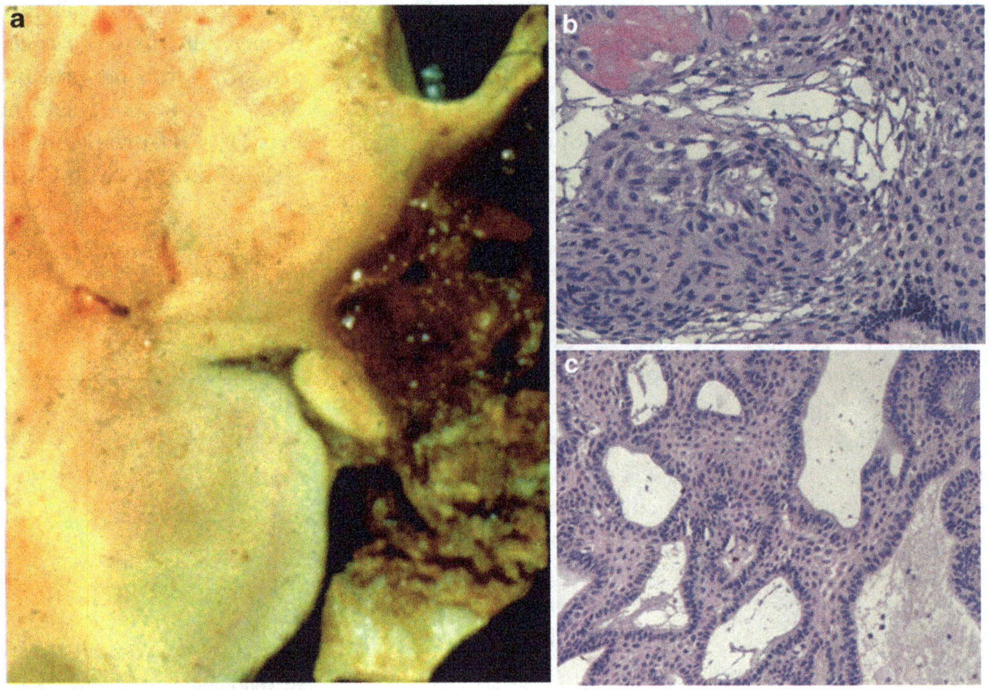

Fig. 2 Craniopharyngioma: (**A**) Gross appearance of a craniopharyngioma; (**B**) Microscopic appearance of the epithelial squamous differentiation; and (**C**) Microscopic appearance of adamantinous pattern

classical form by the absence of the histological features of the classical type and by an older age incidence. Radical excision is rarely curative and may lead to hypothalamic dysfunction and psychological abnormalities, as well as hypopituitarism, and recurrence is common.

Hamartoma or Choristoma

Hamartomas or choristomas are rare and usually located in the hypothalamus. Hamartomas are lesions attached to the tuber cinereum or the mammillary bodies, located usually behind the pituitary stalk. They present with visual field defects or endocrinologic disturbances, such as precocious puberty. The association of neuronal hamartomas and growth hormone producing pituitary adenomas has suggested that the growth hormone releasing factor has a paracrine effect. Hamartomas and choristomas are firm, round masses formed by mature neurons in clusters separated by unmyelinated axons.

Parathyroid

The four parathyroid glands originate from the endodermal third and forth pharyngeal pouches during the fifth gestational week and tend to be solid without fat in children; adipocyte infiltration is first seen at puberty. In children younger than 10 years, the mean weight of the combined four parathyroid glands is less than 60 mg, and from 11 to 20 years of age the combined weight is between 10 and 80 mg, and less than 100 mg.

The parathyroid diseases have been classified according to their metabolic and hormonal status as hypoparathyroidism and hyperparathyroidism. Hyperparathyroidism refers to a status of increased production of parathyroid hormone with normal or abnormal serum calcium. It is classified as primary or secondary. Primary hyperparathyroidism is a common endocrinopathy, familial or not in origin, due to hyperplasia, adenoma, or carcinoma. Most cases of non-familial hyperparathyroidism in children are due to a single adenoma. Multiglandular parathyroid hyperplasia is less frequent and mostly seen in infants. The usual histology in the hyperparathyroidism is primary chief cell hyperplasia.

Hereditary and Developmental Disorders

Over 15% of the population may have supernumerary parathyroid gland or abnormally located within the thyroid, thymus, or as small nests in the neck and mediastinum.

Agenesis and Hypoplasia

Agenesis is due to a defect in the pharyngeal pouch development and is responsible for congenital hypoparathyroidism and is usually associated with other syndromes as DiGeorge Syndrome.

Parathyroid Cysts

Parathyroid cysts are rare in children. A parathyroid cyst may present as a neck mass or be discovered as an incidental finding. It can also present due to cystic degeneration of a parathyroid adenoma. Parathyroid cysts can be divided into three groups according to the mechanism of cyst formation: developmental (arising from vestigial remnants of the third and fourth branchial clefts) (Fig. 3); coalescence of microcysts into macrocysts; or degeneration of an adenoma (forming a pseudocyst) [2].

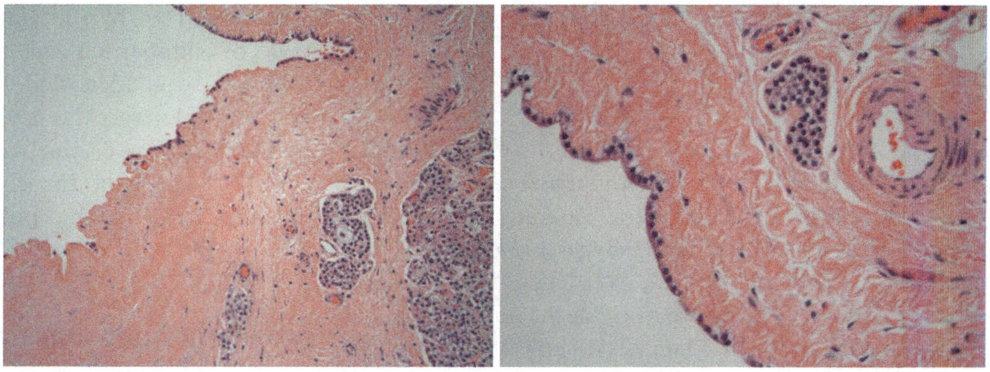

Fig. 3 Microscopic view of a parathyroid cyst, focally lined by chief cells, with a dense fibrous wall with scattered parathyroid tissue

Parathyroid Disease in the Setting of Inherited Tumor Syndromes

The familial form of hyperparathyroidism (Table 3) is found in many autosomal dominant disorders including MEN1 and MEN2A (Table 4), hereditary hyperparathyroidism-jaw tumor syndrome, and familial isolated hyperparathyroidism, neonatal severe hyperparathyroidism, familial hypocalciuric hypercalcemia, autosomal dominant mild hyperparathyroidism, and familial hypercalcemia and hypercalciuria [1, 3].

Familial hyperparathyroidism is usually part of multiple endocrine lesions. Hyperparathyroidism also occurs in families without evidence of other endocrine disease. The diagnosis of chief cell hyperplasia should be followed by the study of any other organ involvement in the patient or in the family.

Neonatal Severe Hyperparathyroidism: Neonatal severe hyperparathyroidism is a rare disorder characterized by extreme hypercalcemia due to diffuse chief cell hyperplasia and bony changes as demineralization and pathologic fractures [3]. Total parathyroidectomy in the neonatal period is necessary for survival of the patient. Neonatal hyperparathyroidism is an aggressive expression of hyperparathyroidism and it is caused by loss-of-function mutations in the calcium-sensing gene (*CaSR*). Neonatal hyperparathyroidism and hypocalciuric hypercalcemia are apparently different manifestations of one mutation of the *CaSR* gene.

Familial Hypocalciuric Hypercalcemia (FHH): Hypercalcemia and hypercalciuria and familial benign hypocalciuric hypercalcemia (FHH) characterize familial hyperparathyroidism. This is the most common cause of hereditary hypercalcemia. FHH is inherited as an autosomal dominant trait with mild-to-moderate hypercalcemia, accompanied by few symptoms. The condition does not require treatment and responds poorly to parathyroidectomy. Familial hypocalciuric hypercalcemia prevails in about half the cases of hypercalcemia during the first two decades of life [3]. Loss-of-function mutations in the *CaSR* gene are responsible for this disease.

Table 3 Inherited causes of primary hyperparathyroidism

Syndrome	Gene/chromosomal location	Parathyroid pathology
MEN1 (Table 4)	*MEN1*/11q13	Multiglandular hyperplasia and/or adenoma
MEN2A (Table 4)	*RET*/10q11.2	Multiglandular hyperplasia
Familial hypocalciuric hypercalcemia (FHH)	*CaSR*/3q13.3-21	Primary hyperplasia due to insensitivity to calcium levels
Neonatal severe primary hyperparathyroidism	*CaSR*/3q13.3-21	Primary hyperplasia due to insensitivity to calcium levels
Hyperparathyroidism–jaw tumor syndrome (HPT-JT)	*HRPT2*/1q25-q32	Adenomas and carcinomas
Familial isolated hyperparathyroidism (FIHPT)	Multiple associations	Multiglandular hyperplasia

Table 4 Multiple endocrine neoplasia syndromes

Multiple endocrine neoplasia syndromes
Multiple endocrine neoplasia 1:
• Primary hyperparathyroidism (90%)
• Enteropancreatic tumors (60–70%)
• Pituitary tumors (10–20%)
• Thymic or bronchial endocrine tumors
• Adrenal cortical tumors
Multiple endocrine neoplasia 2A:
• Medullary thyroid carcinoma (90–100%)
• Pheochromocytoma (40–60%)
• Parathyroid hyperplasia (10–30%)
Multiple endocrine neoplasia 2B:
• Medullary thyroid carcinoma (100%)
• Pheochromocytoma (40–60%)
• Mucosal neuromas
• Ganglioneuromatosis of the intestine
• Marfanoid habitus

Familial Isolated Hyperparathyroidism (FIH): Familial isolated hyperparathyroidism without association of other tumors has been described as a separate entity. These patients present with profound hypercalcemia more frequently as compared with MEN1. There is a tendency towards malignant transformation in the glands. In parathyroid tumors from FIH families, there is repeated allelic losses of the *HRPT2* region in 1q25-31. Screening for other tumors associated with MEN1 and HPT-JT should be performed for the diagnosis of FIH.

Hereditary Hyperparathyroidism – Jaw Tumor (HPT-JT): The maxillary and mandibular tumors can be differentiated from the brown tumors of hyperparathyroidism (ossifying fibroma of the jaw). Parathyroid enlargement is primarily due to an adenoma with occurrence of cysts. Other diseases have been described in this syndrome, such as renal hamartomas, Wilms tumor, polycystic kidney disease, and cysts. There is evidence that parathyroid carcinoma and Wilms tumor are part of the HPT-JT syndrome. The HPT-JT syndrome is an autosomal dominant familial disorder, linked to the chromosomal region of 1q25-q32 (*HRPT2* locus). In cystic sporadic parathyroid adenomas of HPT-JT, LOH was found on 1q, 1p, and 11q13.

Thyroid

The thyroid gland develops from the larger median anlage and the two lateral anlagen. The medial anlage, which forms the major portion of the thyroid, is derived from the floor of the foregut and the two lateral anlagen are derived from the endoderm of the fourth and fifth branchial pouches as the ultimobranchial bodies. The medial anlage appears by day 24 as median endodermal diverticulum from the base of the tongue in the region of the foramen cecum. The diverticulum descends down from the foramen cecum into the neck along the midline attached to the thyroglossal duct. It reaches its final position anterior to the trachea by about 7 weeks; it then grows laterally and becomes bilobed. Early during the fifth week, the thyroglossal duct loses its lumen and shortly afterwards breaks into fragments. However, the caudal end of the thyroglossal duct may persist in some embryos and this constitutes the pyramidal process. The lateral thyroid anlage becomes attached to the posterior surface of the thyroid during the fifth week and is thought to give rise to the calcitonin producing C cells and solid cell nests. The thyroid gland initially consists of a solid mass of endodermal cells, but small groups of epithelial cells are soon identified. The first follicles form from epithelial plates at the beginning of the eighth week and by the twelfth week the plates are entirely converted into follicles. At birth, the thyroid weighs 1–2 g, and it increases to 10–15 g at puberty.

Hereditary and Developmental Disorders

Thyroid agenesis and hypoplasia: Agenesis and hypoplasia are the main causes of nongoitrous cretinism at birth.

Ectopic thyroid tissue: Ectopic thyroid tissue may be present along the path of the thyroglossal duct cyst and can be seen as a mass-forming lesion such as lingual, sublingual, suprahyoid, and in the mediastinum [2]. It may be also found within striated muscle and fibroadipose tissue in the neck.

Thyroglossal duct cyst: Thyroglossal duct cyst arises from a cystic dilatation of a persistent thyroglossal duct and is most commonly found in children as a tumor-like mass in the midline. Thyroid tissue in the wall of the cyst is not present in all cases [2]. These cysts have to be differentiated from intrathyroidal branchial cleft cysts, occasionally found as a cystic thyroid mass in children (Fig. 4).

Thyroid teratoma: Most head and neck teratomas arise in neonates and infants, and thyroid teratomas are typically congenital and diagnosed in the prenatal or neonatal period. Thyroid teratomas are very rare and account for less than 3% of thyroid masses in childhood. We recently reviewed 11 cases (seven boys, four girls) of thyroid teratomas from 28 cervical teratomas; all tumors were present before or at birth [5]. The tumors ranged in size from 3.5 cm to 13.5 cm (Fig. 5A,B). The tumors were cystic and solid and immature neuroepithelium and immature glial tissue predominated (Fig. 5C). An admixture of thyroid and other tissues was present in eight of these cases. The follow up on these patients was up to 45 years. None of

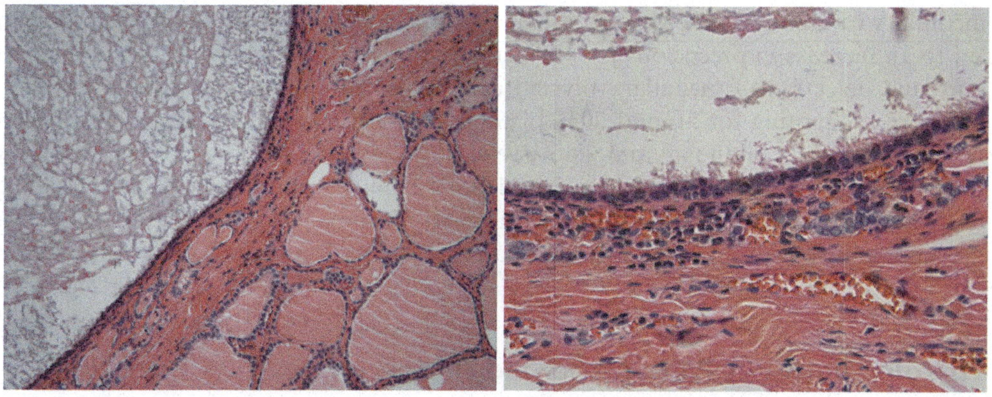

Fig. 4 Microscopic view of an intrathyroidal branchial cleft cyst, lined by a ciliated epithelium

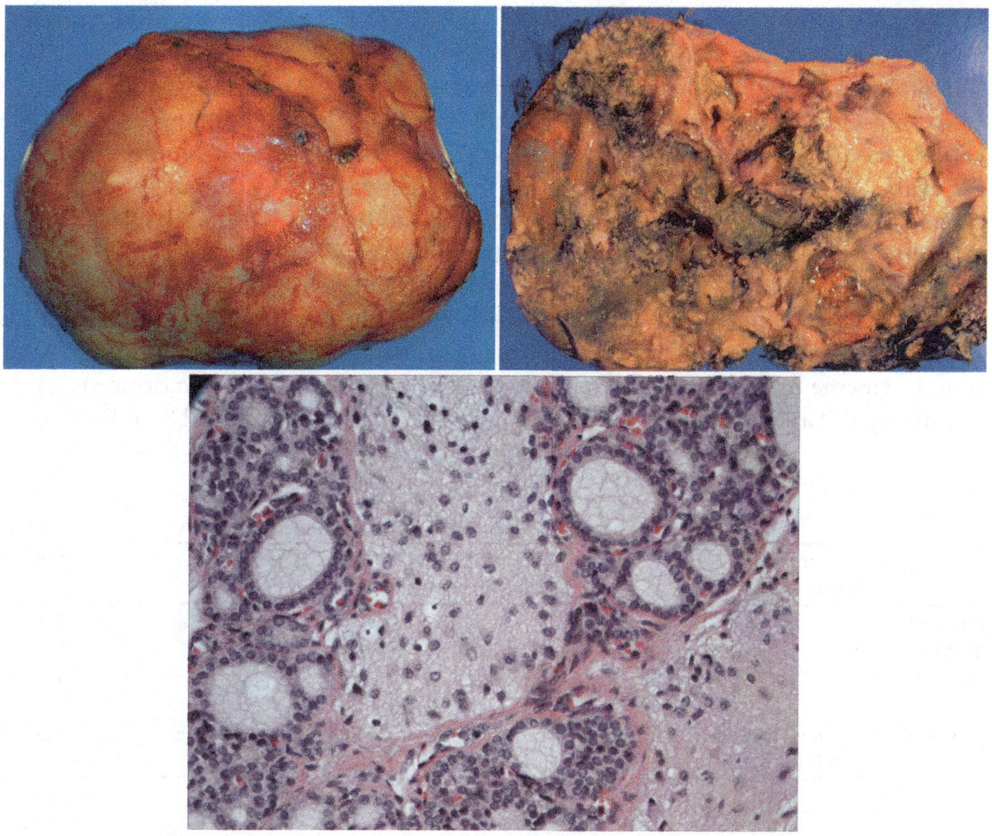

Fig. 5 Thyroid teratoma in neonates and infants. Gross appearance of intact tumor and cut surface showing a *solid* and *cystic* appearance. Microscopic view of the tumor with thyroid follicles intermixed with glial tissue

these patients had tumor recurrence and there was no difference in outcome among patients with mature or immature teratomas [5].

Thyroid nodules in children and adolescents: The majority of thyroid nodules in children are benign including nodular hyperplasia, adenomatous hyperplasia, and adenomatous nodules. Thyroid carcinoma in children account for approximately 40% of the thyroid nodules, about 2–3% of all malignancies in the pediatric age group; however, thyroid carcinoma is the most common site of malignancy in childhood and adolescents with a peak of incidence between 13 and 16 years of age. Thyroid carcinomas have been found in children following radiation administered for various conditions and has been reported as soon as 3 years after treatment up to 14 years after radiation. The children exposed to irradiation after the Chernobyl incident had increased incidence of *RET-PTC* rearrangement papillary thyroid carcinoma. As in adults, papillary thyroid carcinoma is the most common thyroid neoplasm in children accounting for about 25% of the pediatric thyroid lesions and represent over 80% of pediatric thyroid tumors. As in any other organ site, follicular tumors can be either benign or malignant [24–26]. Children and adolescents may have the classical tumors seen in adults such as follicular adenomas and carcinomas, papillary thyroid carcinomas, and medullary carcinomas. The genetic tests in children have led to an increase in precocious prophylactic thyroidectomy and detection of medullary thyroid carcinomas in children, accounting for around 20% of thyroid lesions removed during childhood and adolescence [10]. No benign counterpart of the C cell tumor is identified; however, various degrees of C cell hyperplasia represent the precancerous stage of medullary carcinoma.

Thyroid Tumors as Part of Inherited Tumor Syndromes

Familial thyroid cancer can arise from follicular cells (familial non-medullary thyroid carcinoma) or from the calcitonin-producing C cell (familial medullary thyroid carcinoma). This is usually a component of MEN 2A or 2B (Table 4) or a pure familial medullary thyroid carcinoma syndrome (Table 5). The genetic events in the familial C-cell derived tumors are known and genotype–phenotype correlations are well established [7–10]. In contrast, the case for a familial predisposition of non-medullary thyroid carcinoma (NMTC) is only now beginning to emerge as familial forms have been described in recent years (Table 6).

Although the majority of papillary (PTC) and follicular thyroid carcinomas (FTC) are sporadic, familial tumors account for over 10% of cases [6, 14–23]. Familial syndromes are classified as familial medullary thyroid carcinoma (FMTC) and familial non-medullary thyroid carcinoma (FNMTC). These are sub-classified into two subgroups: familial syndromes characterized by a predominance of non-thyroidal tumors and familial tumor syndromes characterized by a predominance of non-medullary thyroid carcinoma [11].

Familial Syndromes Characterized by a Predominance of Non-thyroidal Tumors

The first group of non-medullary thyroid carcinoma includes familial syndromes characterized by a predominance of non-thyroidal tumors, such as *PTEN* hamartoma tumor syndrome (PHTS), familial adenomatous polyposis (*FAP*), Carney complex type 1, and Werner syndrome (Table 7) [11].

PTEN Hamartoma Tumor Syndrome (PHTS): PHTS is a complex disorder caused by germline inactivating mutations of the *PTEN* tumor suppressor gene, including Cowden syndrome (CS), Bannayan-Riley-Ruvalcaba syndrome (BRRS), Proteus syndrome (PS), and Proteus-like syndrome. Affected individuals develop both benign and malignant tumors in a variety of tissues, including thyroid tumors in two-thirds of PHTS patients. Breast carcinoma and thyroid carcinoma are the two most common malignancies present in individuals with CS. Thyroid pathologic findings in this syndrome typically affecting the follicular cells include multinodular goiter, multiple adenomatous nodules, follicular adenoma, follicular carcinoma, and less frequently papillary carcinoma. Follicular carcinoma is an important feature in CS and BRRS. These tumors are more frequently multicentric and are believed to progress from a pre-existing follicular adenoma. According to the diagnostic criteria for Cowden syndrome follicular carcinoma with a frequency of 5–10% is a major criterion and multinodular goiter,

Table 5 Sporadic and familial medullary thyroid carcinoma

	Age at tumor diagnosis	Associated diseases	Multiple thyroid tumors	Bilateral thyroid tumors
Sporadic	50	None	No	No
FMTC	50	None	Yes	Yes
MEN2A	30	Pheochromocytoma and hyperparathyroidism	Yes	Yes
MEN2B	Infancy or early childhood	Pheochromocytoma, mucosal ganglioneuromas, marfanoid habitus	Yes	Yes

Table 6 Classification of familial non-medullary thyroid carcinoma

1. Syndromic or familial tumor syndrome with a preponderance of non-thyroidal tumors:

- *PTEN*-hamartoma tumor syndrome (PHTS)
- Familial adenomatous polyposis syndrome (FAP)
- Carney complex
- Werner syndrome

2. Non-syndromic or familial tumor syndrome with a preponderance of NMTC:

- Familial papillary thyroid carcinoma (FPTC)
- Familial PTC associated with renal papillary neoplasia
- Familial non-medullary thyroid carcinoma type 1 (fNMTC1)
- Familial multinodular goiter (FMNG)

Table 7 Non-medullary thyroid carcinoma as a component of a familial tumor syndrome

Disorder	Gene/ chromosomal location	Inheritance	Thyroid pathology
Familial adenomatous polyposis (FAP)	*APC*/5q21	AD	PT CMv
***PTEN*-hamartoma tumor syndrome (PHTS)**	*PTEN*/10q22-23	AD	MAN FA FC PTC LT
Carney complex	*PRKAR1a*/ 17q24	AD	MAN, FC FA, PTC
Werner syndrome	*WRN*/8p11-21	AR	PTC ATC

PTC: Papillary thyroid carcinoma
CMv: Cribriform-morular variant
MAN: Multiple adenomatous nodules
FA: Follicular adenoma
FC: Follicular carcinoma
LT: Lymphocytic thyroiditis
ATC: Anaplastic thyroid carcinoma

adenomatous nodules, and follicular adenomas are minor criteria, with a frequency of 50–67% [11–15].

Multiple adenomatous nodules (MAN) are a characteristic finding in these syndromes and grossly present as multiple firm yellow-tan well-circumscribed nodules diffusely involving the thyroid gland; secondary cystic and hemorrhagic areas are usually absent (Fig. 6A). These nodules are multicentric, bilateral, well-circumscribed, unencapsulated, solid cellular nodules sharing features similar to follicular adenomas (Fig. 6B). Follicles are not dilated and some nodules may have a discontinuous rim of fibrous tissue. In our experience [11], we believe the morphologic findings of multiple adenomatous nodules should be considered as a possible major criterion in CS and BRRS.

Follicular carcinoma is an important feature in CS and BRRS. It has been described that these tumors are more frequently multicentric. We [11] have also found that the majority of carcinomas arise in a background of MAN (Fig. 7A,B). The mean age of diagnosis of follicular carcinoma in our series of BRRS was 14 years (7–24 years). While cancer risk in BRRS was expected to be similar to the general population, we found four cases of follicular thyroid carcinoma (67%), showing that this type of carcinoma was more frequent in the pediatric population; we believe that these patients should follow the same management guidelines as CS.

Medullary thyroid carcinoma is not considered a part of the spectrum of PHTS, however, previous studies including two studies by our group [11, 14, 15] have identified C-cell hyperplasia in individuals affected with this syndrome. Most studies have failed to demonstrate a consistent genotype-phenotype relationship in PHTS. Careful phenotyping gives further support for the suggestion that BRRS and CS are actually one condition, presenting at different stages. In summary the presence of numerous adenomatous nodules in a background of lymphocytic thyroiditis in younger patients should raise the suspicion for the diagnosis of PHTS. Multicentric thyroid pathology characterized by the presence of numerous adenomatous nodules, follicular adenomas, and the presence of follicular thyroid carcinoma is a common thyroid pathology finding of PHTS [11, 14].

Familial adenomatous polyposis (FAP): FAP is an inherited autosomal dominant syndrome caused by germline mutations in the adenomatous polyposis coli (*APC*) gene on chromosome 5q21, characterized by hundreds to thousands of adenomatous colonic polyps that develop during early adulthood. Extracolonic manifestations in FAP include osteomas, epidermal cysts, desmoid tumors, upper gastrointestinal tract polyps-hamartomas, congenital hypertrophy of the retinal pigment epithelium (CHRPE), hepatoblastomas, and thyroid tumors. Papillary thyroid carcinoma occurs in 2% of patients. Adolescents and young women with FAP are at particular risk of developing thyroid cancer and their chance of being affected is approximately 160 times higher than that of normal individuals (PTC occurs with a frequency of about 10 times that expected for sporadic PTC) [17]. We have recently reviewed nine cases of papillary carcinoma in the setting of FAP [11], all were females and the youngest patient with cribriform morular variant of papillary thyroid carcinoma was 17 years old at the time of the thyroid diagnosis. This patient had total colectomy with multiple, over 100, adenomatous colonic polyps, a year prior to total thyroidectomy. The thyroid was multinodular with multiple nodules on both thyroid lobes and isthmus. There were seven foci of papillary thyroid carcinoma (PTC), six of a cribriform morular variant (CMv) (Fig. 8), and one classical variant, measuring from 0.1 cm to 1.6 cm, with lymphovascular invasion present. This patient had a positive lymph node. The immunostaining for β-catenin was positive in the nucleus and in the cytoplasm in all foci of cribriform morular variant of papillary thyroid carcinoma. β-Catenin was negative in the classical variant of PTC and it is only expressed in cell membrane of the non-tumoral follicular cells. The adenomatous polyposis coli (*APC*) gene is ubiquitously expressed in normal tissue and it is a negative regulator of Wnt pathway [18]. Inactivation of the *APC* tumor suppressor gene initiates colorectal neoplasia and is also involved in FAP-related thyroid tumors. Mutations of the *APC* gene lead to a truncated protein that lacks the β-catenin binding site and therefore cannot degrade β-catenin. One of the

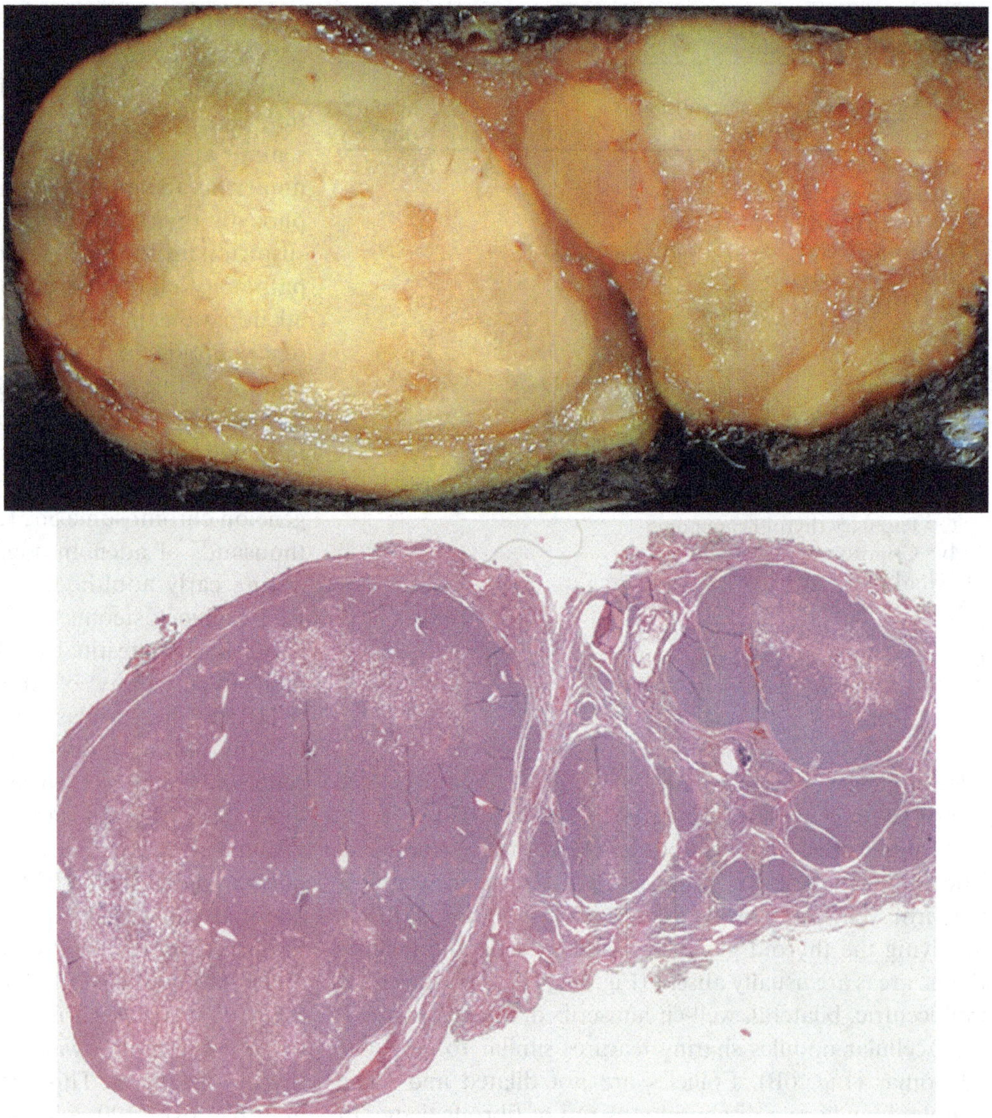

Fig. 6 Thyroid pathology on PTEN-Hamartoma Tumor Syndrome: multiple adenomatous nodules

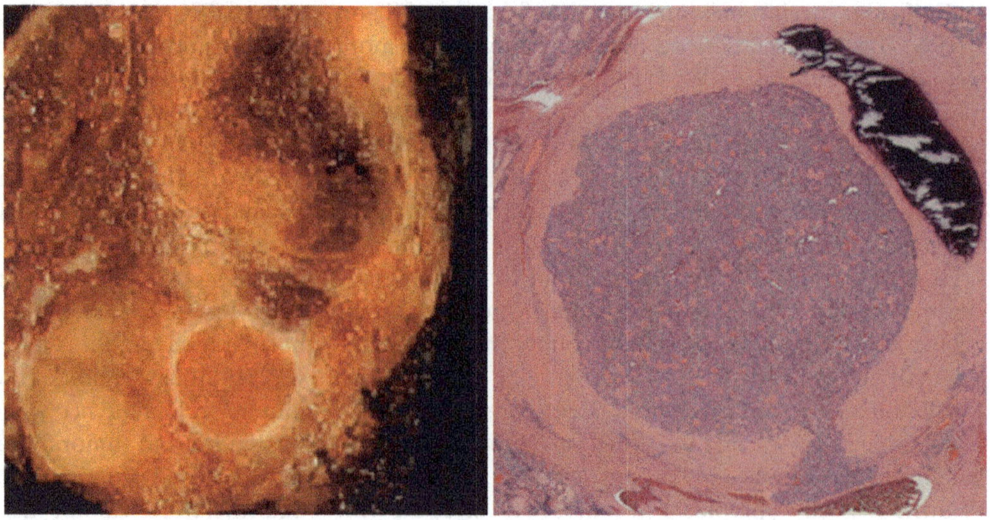

Fig. 7 Thyroid pathology on PTEN-Hamartoma Tumor Syndrome: follicular carcinoma and multiple adenomatous nodules

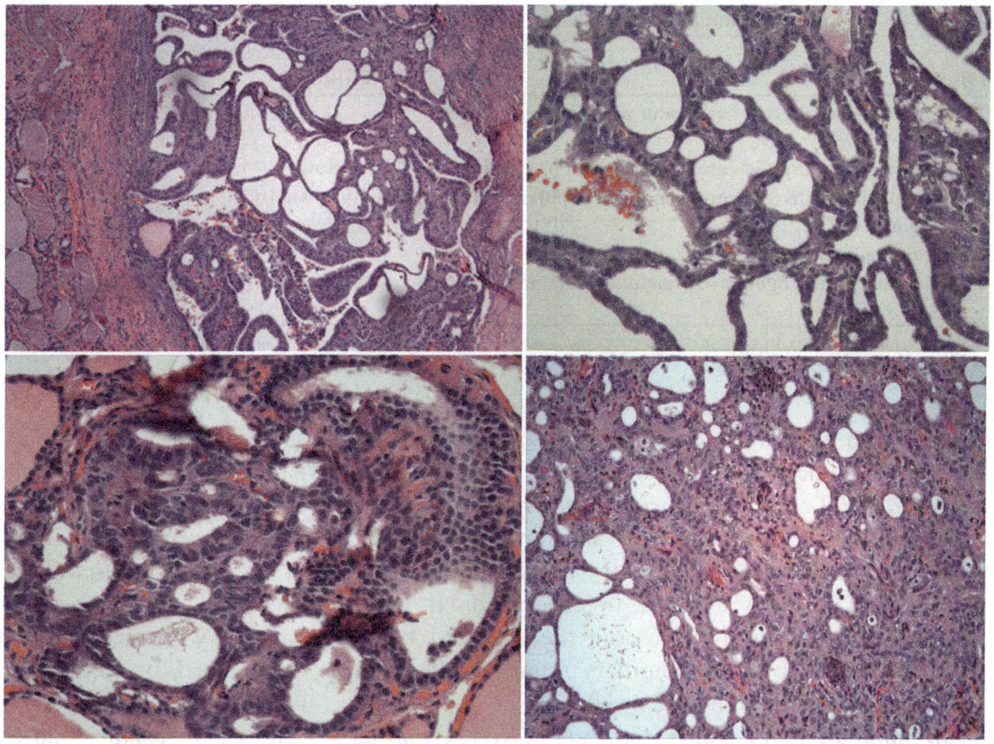

Fig. 8 Microscopic appearances of the FAP-associated papillary thyroid carcinoma: cribriform-morular variant

biochemical activities associated with the APC protein is down-regulation of transcriptional activation mediated by β-catenin.

The distinct CMv-PTC seen in FAP-related thyroid carcinomas is very unusual in sporadic PTC and its identification should raise the possibility of this familial tumor syndrome, and any patient presenting with this rare carcinoma should be evaluated for FAP.

Carney complex: Carney complex is an autosomal dominant disease characterized by skin and mucosal pigmentation, diverse pigmented skin lesions, non-endocrine and a variety of endocrine neoplasias (pituitary adenoma, pigmented nodular adrenal disease, Sertoli and Leydig cell tumors, and thyroid tumors). Patients with Carney complex may share similar components with other familial multiple endocrine neoplasia. The thyroid is usually multinodular with multiple adenomatous nodules, follicular adenomas, and both PTC and FTC are present in about 15% of patients with Carney complex [19].

Familial Tumor Syndromes Characterized by a Predominance of Non-medullary Thyroid Carcinoma

The second group of non-medullary thyroid carcinoma includes familial syndromes characterized by a predominance of NMTC, such as pure familial (f) PTC with or without oxyphilia, fPTC with papillary renal cell carcinoma, and fPTC with multinodular goiter (Table 8). Familial non-medullary thyroid carcinoma syndrome (FNMTC) is diagnosed when three or more family members have non-medullary thyroid cancer in the absence of other known associated syndromes. Statistical estimates suggest that a grouping of two family members with NMTC could represent the concurrence of sporadic tumors but thyroid tumors in three or more members in kindred, or the diagnosis of PTC in men and children is more suggestive of a familial predisposition. Familial non-medullary thyroid carcinoma is now recognized as a distinct clinical entity and accounts for up to 10.5% of all follicular cell origin thyroid carcinomas [21–23]. Familial non-medullary thyroid carcinoma has a high incidence of multifocality and association with multiple benign nodules. FNMTC patients have shorter disease-free survival than do sporadic disease patients because of frequent locoregional recurrence. The genetic inheritance of FNMTC remains unknown, but it is believed to be an autosomal dominant mode.

Familial Papillary Thyroid Carcinoma (fPTC) is characterized by multicentric tumors and multiple adenomatous nodules with or without oxyphilia. Familial PTC enriched in thyroid carcinoma with oxyphilia (*TCO*) has been mapped to chromosomal region 19p13 and FNMTC without oxyphilia has also been mapped to 19p13.31. Tumor-specific loss of heterozygosity is found in sporadic FTC with and without oxyphilia at both 19p13 and 2q21.32.

The familial nonmedullary thyroid carcinoma type 1 (fNMTC1) syndrome (chromosomal region 2q21) is characterized by PTC without any distinguishing pathologic

Table 8 Familial tumor syndromes characterized by a predominance of non-medullary thyroid carcinoma

Disorder	Gene/chromosomal location	Inheritance	Thyroid pathology
Familial papillary thyroid carcinoma with oxyphilia	*(TCO)* Unknown/19p13.2	AD	PTC with or without oxyphilia, multicentric
Familial papillary thyroid carcinoma without oxyphilia	Unknown/19p13.2	AD	Classical PTC
Familial papillary thyroid carcinoma with papillary renal cell neoplasia (fPTC/PRN)	Unknown/1q21	Unknown	Classical PTC
Familial papillary thyroid carcinoma (f/PMTC1)	Unknown/2q21	Unknown	Classical PTC
Familial multinodular goiter with papillary thyroid carcinoma	Unknown/14q	AD	PTC in a background multinodular cyst formation

PTC: Papillary thyroid carcinoma
AD: Autosomal dominant

features and without an obvious increase in frequency of non-thyroidal neoplasms in kindred members.

Familial PTC associated with renal papillary neoplasia presents with the usual classical variant of PTC and with no special features. The papillary renal neoplasia syndrome (fPTC/PRN) mapped to chromosomal region 1q21 includes not only PTC and the expected benign thyroid nodules but also papillary renal neoplasia and possibly other malignancies as well.

In familial multinodular goiter (FMNG) syndrome, which is mapped to 14q, some patients may develop an associated PTC.

C Cell Hyperplasia and Medullary Thyroid Carcinoma

Medullary thyroid carcinoma (MTC) refers to those neoplasms arising from the calcitonin-producing C thyroid cells derived from neural crest and represents approximately 5% of all thyroid tumors and about 15% of all thyroid cancer-related deaths. Medullary thyroid carcinomas occur in sporadic or hereditary (25% of cases) forms, as part of MEN 2 syndromes or as the MTC-only syndrome (Table 5). MEN 2A is associated with pheochromocytoma and parathyroid hyperplasia, while MEN 2B is associated with marfanoid habitus, mucosal neuromas, ganglioneuromatosis, pheochromocytoma, and rarely with parathyroid disease. Medullary Thyroid Carcinoma can occur in these four different settings, summarized in Table 5.

Both sporadic and familial MTC arise at the junction of the upper and middle thirds of the lateral lobes, corresponding to the areas where C cells are present. All patients with medullary thyroid carcinoma should then be screened for familial disease [7]. The hereditary tumor is usually preceded by C-cell hyperplasia (CCH) and these tumors are usually bilateral and multicentric. The presence of C-cell hyperplasia is considered a paradigm of a genetically determined condition. The tumors are sharply circumscribed but not encapsulated. A germline point mutation in the *RET* gene on chromosome 10q11.2 is responsible for the hereditary MTC and about 98% of all mutations responsible for familial MTC are known. The aggressiveness of MTC is usually related to the clinical presentation, if present as a hereditary or sporadic form, and the type of *RET* mutation present [8]. In familial syndromes, there is a known relationship between specific *RET* protooncogene mutations, disease phenotype, and prognosis. The youngest patient submitted to a prophylactic thyroidectomy in a setting of known MEN2B we have seen with bilateral medullary thyroid carcinoma was 4 years old (Fig. 9A,B).

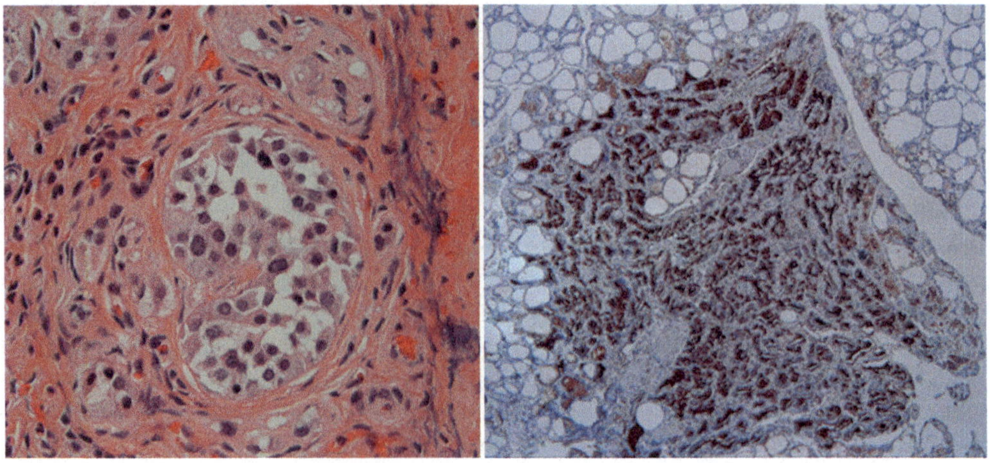

Fig. 9 MEN2B: A 4-year-old patient submitted to prophylactic thyroidectomy with bilateral medullary thyroid carcinoma

Adrenal

The adrenal glands are composite endocrine tissues that form two distinct regions, the cortex and medulla, each with diverse embryology, physiology, and morphology. The pathological processes of the cortex and medulla also differ. The classification of adrenal cortical lesions is primarily based on their functional status, such as decreasing or increasing steroids, or whether or not they affect endocrine function. The adrenal medulla, which originates from the neural crest, is the site of disorders that produce hyperfunction through overproduction of catecholamines.

The adrenal cortex originates from peritoneal cells at the base of the dorsal mesentery at 5 weeks.

The fetal cortex or provisional zone is an outer layer composed of large cells with eosinophilic cytoplasm that primarily secretes dehydroepiandrosterone sulfate. By the tenth week of gestation the adult cortex appears in the subcapsular area. It is formed of smaller cells with clear cytoplasm. Histologically, the zonation shows the outer region, the glomerulosa, is about 15% of the cortex and produces mineralocorticoids. The thicker middle zone, 70–80% of the cortex, is the fasciculata and produces glucocorticoids and sex steroids. The inner cortical layer, the reticularis, occupies 5–15% of the cortical width. It is formed by eosinophilic cytoplasm and compact cells that also produce glucocorticoids and sex steroids.

Hereditary and Developmental Disorders

Adrenal Cortical Nodules and Tumor-like Lesions

Nodular Adrenal Cortical Hyperplasia

The correlation of morphologic and functional classifications provides valuable diagnostic information and better classification of these lesions.

The manifestations associated with nodular adrenal cortical hyperplasia range from no-clinical or endocrinological/laboratorial evidence of excess of corticosteroids to a full Cushing's syndrome secondary to an excess of ACTH.

The endocrine status of the patient leads to a functional classification of the lesions, as seen below:

1. Adrenal cortical nodule with eucorticalism
2. Hypercorticolism
   - Pituitary-dependent with diffuse and/or nodular hyperplasia
   - Ectopic ACTH secretion with predominantly diffuse hyperplasia
   - Primary pigmented nodular adrenocortical disease
   - Ectopic secretion of corticotropin releasing factor with diffuse and/or nodular hyperplasia.
3. Hyperaldosteronism with diffuse and/or nodular hyperplasia without an adrenal neoplasm.
4. Virilization with predominantly diffuse hyperplasia – congenital adrenal hyperplasia. The histological findings of nodular hyperplasia are similar to those of the adrenal cortical neoplasms. In most cases, the nodular adrenal cortical hyperplasia is bilateral and the size of the nodules is variable. The presence of a dominant macronodule makes the differential diagnosis between the nodular hyperplasia and adrenal cortical adenoma difficult. The classification of these lesions can be based on gross morphology as bilateral or unilateral; diffuse or nodular; micro (<1 cm) or macro-nodular (> or = 1 cm).

Heterotopic and Accessory Adrenal Cortical Nodules

These heterotopic adrenal tissues are non-neoplastic adrenal cortical tissues located along the "path" of the gonadal descent, from periadrenal connective tissue, near fallopian tubes and ovaries, vas deferens, and hilum of the testis. They are common incidental findings in herniorrhaphy contents. These heterotopic solitary nodules are composed of cortical cells, almost always with no medulla, and can become hyperplastic with an ACTH stimulus. These are mostly hyperplastic and rarely become a true adrenal cortical neoplasm. The commonly found cortical extrusions also can become hyperplastic.

Primary Pigmented Nodular Adrenocortical Disease

This rare pituitary-independent form of Cushing syndrome is characterized by the presence of multiple pigmented nodules of cortical cells intermixed with atrophic cortical tissue. The adrenal glands can be smaller than normal, normal in size, or enlarged. The individual nodules are small, usually from 1 to 3 mm in diameter, and are pale to black in color. The cells of this lesion are large, with granular eosinophilic cytoplasm, and filled with lipochrome pigment. The nuclei are hyperchromatic and enlarged, with prominent nucleoli. This disorder can occur in a familial autosomal dominant form associated with Carney's complex or as a sporadic, non-familial form. Carney complex consists of spotty pigmentation, such as lentigines, blue nevi, cutaneous and cardiac myxomas, and endocrine overactivity. Almost half of patients with Carney complex have primary pigmented nodular adrenocortical disease (Fig. 10).

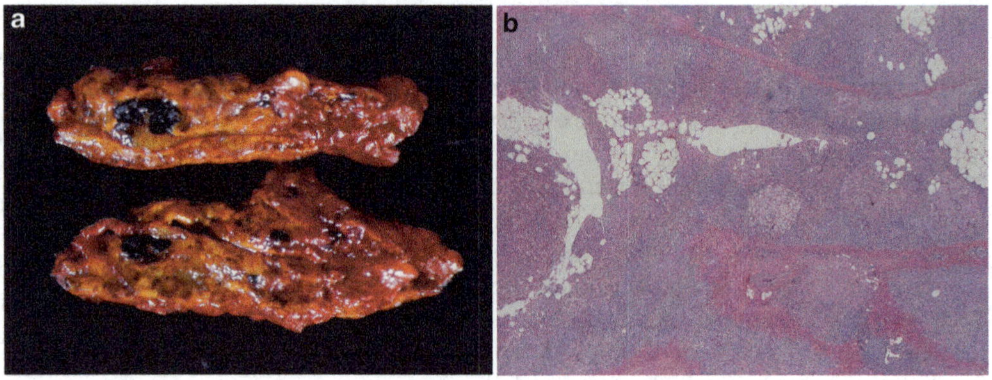

Fig. 10 Gross (**A**) and microscopic (**B**) pictures of a Carney complex related pigmented nodular adrenal cortical disease (PPNAD)

Macronodular Hyperplasia with Marked Adrenal Enlargement

This is a rare cause of ACTH-independent Cushing syndrome in which both adrenal glands are typically enlarged due to nodular hyperplasia. Usually both adrenals may be large enough to simulate a neoplasm, with a combined weight of over 80 g. The histological findings are similar to nodular hyperplasia with an extraordinary degree of nodular cortical hyperplasia. There may also be myelolipomatous foci.

Adrenal Cytomegaly

Adrenal cortical cytomegaly can be an incidental finding in the adrenal fetal cortex at autopsy or can be associated with Beckwith-Wiedemann syndrome (Fig. 10). Adrenal cortical cytomegaly involving both glands is a common finding in this syndrome. Cytomegaly is defined as nuclear enlargement with hyperchromasia and pleomorphism and presence of pseudoinclusion.

Myelolipoma

Myelolipomas of the adrenal gland are tumor-like masses composed of hematopoietic precursor cells and mature adipose tissue in varying proportions, not associated with glucocorticoid production. It occurs primarily in one gland and the mass is usually yellow to red-brown. Histological findings include mature adipose tissue and trilinear hematopoietic cells. Myelolipomatous metaplasia can occur in adrenal glands of patients with Carney complex, ACTH-dependent and ACTH-independent Cushing's syndrome, associated with glucocorticoid activity.

Adrenal Cysts

Adrenal cysts are uncommon in childhood. These cystic lesions of the adrenal cortex are usually unilateral, occurring predominantly in women. The most common type of adrenal cyst is the endothelial cyst, which is composed of lymphatic and vascular channels. The adrenal pseudocyst, mostly of unclear origin, is the most common clinically recognized type. Some pseudocysts may have a vascular or mesothelial origin. True epithelial cysts are rare and most adrenal cysts are not associated with endocrine symptoms. These cysts vary in size from 0.1 cm to larger pseudocysts of 10 cm or larger. Pseudocysts lack any epithelial or endothelial cell lining and have a thick fibrous capsule with focal calcification. The content of the cysts is usually dark hemorrhagic fluid. Differential diagnosis with a cystic neoplasm is difficult.

Acquired Disorders of the Adrenal Glands

Adrenal Cortical Tumors (Adenoma and Carcinoma)

Adrenal cortical neoplasms of the adrenal gland in infancy, childhood, and adolescents are rare. Girls are more frequently affected than boys; the majority (about 75%) of these tumors are malignant and hormonally functional with clinical evidence of different syndromes, according to the hormone production. These patients usually present with signs and symptoms of endocrine abnormality such as virilization and Cushing syndrome; more frequently as mixed syndrome or as pure Cushing syndrome, feminization syndrome, and very rarely as hyperaldosteronism syndrome.

The pediatric adrenal cortical tumors may have similar morphology to the adult counterpart but may behave in a different fashion. The established criteria distinguishing benign from malignant adrenal cortical neoplasms in the adult are not applicable to the pediatric cases, as it cannot predict the biological behavior. The pediatric adrenal cortical tumors have also distinct pathological criteria for malignancy from the adult counterpart (Table 9).

Table 9 Comparison of adult and childhood criteria for malignancy of adrenocortical tumors

Criteria for malignancy of adult tumors (Weiss System):

- High nuclear grade
- Mitotic figures >5/50 HPF
- Atypical mitosis
- Eosinophilic cytoplasm >75% tumor cells
- Confluent necrosis
- Diffuse architecture
- Venous invasion
- Sinusoidal invasion
- Capsular invasion

Criteria for malignancy in pediatric patients (Wieneke, Thompson, Heffess, 2003):

- Tumor weight of >400 g
- Tumor size >10.5 cm
- Extension into periadrenal soft tissue
- Extension into adjacent organs
- Invasion into vena cava
- Venous invasion
- Capsular invasion
- Presence of tumor necrosis
- Mitosis >15/20HPF
- Presence of atypical mitosis

In the USA, only about 25 new cases occur each year, representing only 0.2% of all children malignancies. In Brazil, approximately 10 times that many cases are diagnosed each year; the distribution of these tumors following a regional, rather than a familial pattern, raising a possibility of an environmental factor. There is a biphasic age distribution, the infantile group with a peak of incidence of 1 year and with a survival of 53%, and the adolescent group with a peak of incidence of 9–16 years and with a survival of 17%.

Adenomas have variable histological features, so there are no reliable criteria in distinguishing benign from malignant lesions. The same criteria used in adult-type adrenal cortical tumors can be used in pediatric adrenal cortical neoplasms; however, this will classify some pediatric lesions as carcinoma histologically even though they behave less aggressively than those in adults and will not ultimately metastasize. The likelihood of a malignant behavior increases as the tumor size increases and tumors over 400 g are predictive of a malignant behavior; however, the size alone cannot predict behavior. In pediatric patients, another important factor to predict malignant behavior is the extension into periadrenal soft tissues, invasion to adjacent organs and inferior vena cava. Nuclear pleomorphism with hyperchromatism can be seen in adenomas or carcinomas, but mitoses are rarely seen in the benign neoplasms. Sometimes, the histological features can mimic adrenal medullary neoplasia. Adrenal cortical and adrenal medullary tumors may have common features such as nesting pattern, compact eosinophilic cytoplasm, nuclear irregularities, intracytoplasmic hyaline globules, and synaptophysin immunostaining. Discerning malignancy in adrenal cortical neoplasms is one of the most difficult and controversial areas in surgical pathology. No single histological criterion is reliable to accurately and independently distinguish between benign and malignant tumors and predict patient outcome. Evaluation of multiple histological criteria is necessary. A recent (2003) study [27] of 83 adrenal cortical neoplasms in the pediatric population proposed a criteria to predict an aggressive behavior (Table 9). As no single finding is able to separate benign from malignant tumors these authors proposed a three part separation: two or less than two criteria present in a tumor (benign outcome); three criteria (uncertain malignant potential); four or more criteria (poor clinical outcome). According to these authors, these breakpoints accurately classify 78% of all cases that will behave in a clinically malignant fashion. Adrenal cortical tumors in the pediatric age group, which proved to be clinically malignant, showed extensive tumor necrosis, increased number of mitoses, and vascular invasion.

Adrenal Tumors as Part of Inherited Tumor Syndromes

Both adrenal cortical tumors and adrenal medullary tumors can be components of inherited neoplasia syndromes [1, 4]. The mechanisms or etiology of adrenocortical tumorigenesis are unknown, but there is specific susceptibility to inherit adrenocortical carcinoma in some familial syndromes. The study of genetic syndromes associated with adrenocortical tumors such as Beckwith-Wiedemann, Li-Fraumeni, McCune-Albright, Carney, and MEN 1 (Table 10), has shed light on the molecular basis of tumorigenesis. Beckwith-Wiedemann Syndrome and adrenal cytomegaly are usually associated with

Table 10 Inherited neoplasia syndromes associated with adrenocortical tumors

Syndrome	Gene/ chromosomal location	Adrenal pathology
Beckwith-Wiedemann	*CDKN1C*/	*NSD1*/11p15.5
Carcinoma		
Carney complex	*PRKAR1A*/2p16	Nodular hyperplasia
Li-Fraumeni syndrome	p53/17p13	Carcinoma
McCune-Albright syndrome	*GNAS1*/20q13.2	Nodular hyperplasia
Multiple endocrine neoplasia 1	*MEN1*/11q13	Adenoma/carcinoma
Congenital adrenal hyperplasia	*CYP21*/6p21.3	Nodular/hyperplasia adenoma/carcinoma

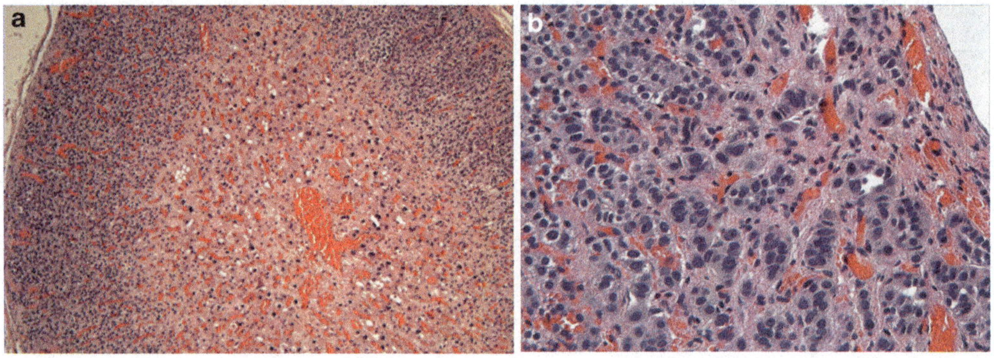

Fig. 11 Beckwith-Wiedemann Syndrome with focal adrenal cytomegaly (**A**) and an adrenal cortical tumor in this setting (**B**)

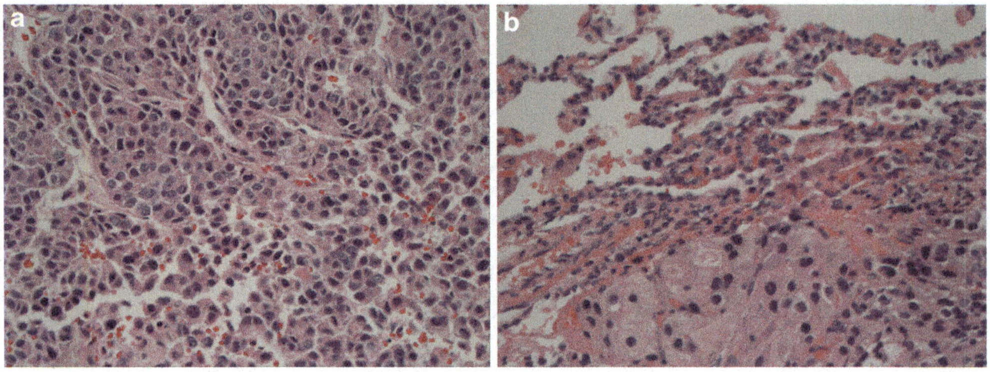

Fig. 12 Adrenal cortical carcinoma (**A**) in a 6-month-old baby with metastases to the lung (**B**) 5 months after diagnosis

adrenal cortical carcinoma (Figs. 11 and 12), nephroblastoma, and hepatoblastoma. While Carney complex, Peutz-Jeghers syndrome, and Cowden disease share clinical features such as mucocutaneous lentigines and multiple tumors such as thyroid, breast, ovarian, and testicular neoplasms, and autosomal dominant inheritance, the genetic locus differs:Carney complex on chromosome 2p16; the gene for Peutz-Jeghers syndrome is on chromosome 19q13, gene *STK11/LKB1*, and Cowden disease on 10q23, *PTEN* 12.

Pheochromocytomas and Paragangliomas

Pheochromocytomas are rare in the pediatric population and accounts for up to 15% of pheochromocytomas. These tumors present in the first two decades of life and have a greater likelihood of being in a familial tumor syndrome. Their behavior is difficult to predict based on histology alone. There are a few proposed criteria in predicting an aggressive behavior in adult population, but there remains no comprehensive clinicopathologic study of pediatric tumors. In addition, several studies report histologic differences between tumors occurring in different genetic settings (i.e., von Hippel-Lindau, multiple endocrine neoplasia, neurofibromatosis, familial paraganglioma syndrome, sporadic) (Table 11). Pheochromocytomas and paragangliomas are sporadic in about 70% of cases or be part of syndromes [1, 4] as MEN2A, MEN2B, NF1, VHL, and the familial paraganglioma-pheochromocytoma syndromes caused by SDHB, SDHC, and SDHD mutations (Table 11).

Table 11 Inherited neoplasia syndromes associated with paragangliomas and pheochromocytomas

Syndrome	Gene/ chromosomal location	Adrenal pathology
MEN2A and MEN2B	*RET*/10q11.2	Adrenal pheochromocytoma
Neurofibromatosis, type1	*NF1*/17q11	Adrenal pheo/H&N paraganglioma
Von Hippel-Lindau disease	*VHL*/ 3p25-26	Adrenal pheo/ABD paraganglioma
PGL1	*SDHD*/11q23	Adrenal pheo/H&N, and ABD paraganglioma
PGL3	*SDHC*/ 1q21-23	H&N paraganglioma
PGL4	*SDHB*/1p36	Adrenal pheo/H&N, THOR and ABD paraganglioma

MEN: Multiple endocrine neoplasia
PGL: Pheochromocytoma-paraganglioma syndrome
H&N: head and neck
ABD: abdominal
THOR: thoracic
Pheo: pheochromocytomas

We recently studied 37 paragangliomas (21 pheochromocytomas, 16 extra-adrenal paragangliomas) in 34 pediatric patients and correlated clinical, multiple histologic, and genetic parameters. Thirty-four histologic criteria were evaluated by two pathologists. Genetic screening for VHL, SDHB, SDHD, and RET mutations was performed on frozen tissue by direct sequencing in 11 tumors. The patients ranged in age from 4 to 20 years (mean 12.9 years); there was a male predominance (22 males, 12 females). Four patients had bilateral pheochromocytomas and two had multiple paragangliomas. Several syndromes with genetic predisposition are represented, including neurofibromatosis-1 (n = 1), Carney's syndrome (n = 1), von Hippel-Lindau syndrome (n = 10), familial paraganglioma syndrome type 3/SDHB (n = 1), and other uncharacterized familial pheochromocytomas (n = 4). Follow-up was available for 23 patients, ranging from 4 months to 23 years (mean 5.7 years). Four patients had local recurrence (three paragangliomas recurred at 4, 9, and 23 years; one familial pheochromocytoma recurred at 3 years). Two patients (5%), including one paraganglioma and one pheochromocytoma developed metastases. In contrast to adult tumors, pediatric tumors are well encapsulated and only rarely do tumor cells encroach upon the adjacent adrenal cortex. Large amphophilic cells and hyaline globules are much less common (Fig. 13). Twelve pheochromocytomas (57%) had histologic features suggestive of increased malignant potential based on a scaled score of ≥4; one recurred and one metastasized. The VHL and SDHB-related tumors showed a thick tumor capsule, small to medium-sized clear-to-pale eosinophilic cells, absence of hyaline globules, and variable desmoid-type fibrosis. Some sporadic tumors had mixed VHL and non-VHL features. In conclusion, the histopathologic findings in pediatric paraganglioma/pheochromocytoma differ from adult tumors and the proposed criteria for malignant potential may overestimate aggressiveness. In addition, tumors associated with particular genetic profiles appear histologically distinct from sporadic counterparts.

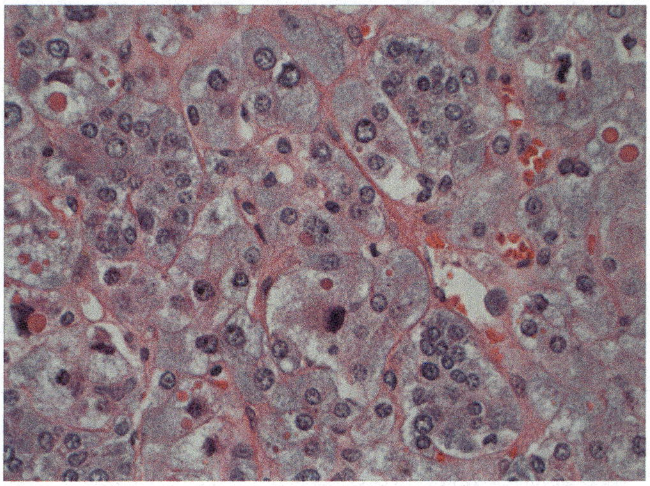

Fig. 13 Pediatric pheochromocytoma in a young patient with neurofibromatosis type 1

Neuroblastomas and Ganglioneuroblastoma

Neuroblastoma is the most common solid tumor in childhood outside the central nervous system and is the fourth most common malignancy after leukemia, brain tumors, and lymphoma. Over 88% of all cases occur in the first 5 years of life; it is rare in adults. Most neuroblastomas are sporadic but familial occurrence has been reported.

Neuroblastoma is a primitive neoplasm of neuroectodermal origin and arises primarily in the sympathoadrenal neuroendocrine system arising from neuroblasts. Over half occur in the abdomen and 15% in the thorax. Other less common sites include neck, head, orbit, and kidney. Approximately one-third of tumors are adrenal in origin. In 10% of cases the primary site is unknown.

A variety of clinical manifestations and associated disorders have been reported with neuroblastic tumors including Horner's syndrome, heterochromia iridis, and opsoclonus/myoclonus, as well as watery diarrhea syndrome, due to production of vasoactive intestinal peptide (VIP).

The adrenal tumors are usually unilateral, solitary, and unicentric. Bilateral tumors are rare. The macroscopic findings are variable ranging from small and well circumscribed to large and irregular masses. The cut surface ranges from maroon to tan, is often variegated, and hemorrhage, necrosis, and calcification may be present. In young infants there may be variable cystification.

The International Neuroblastoma Pathology Classification in 1999 [28, 29] provided a uniform nomenclature for neuroblastic tumors depending upon the degree of neuroblastic and Schwannian differentiation (Table 12).

Table 12 International neuroblastoma Shimada classification

Prognosis	Histopathological features/age
Favorable	Stroma rich, all ages, no nodular pattern
	Stroma poor, age 1.5–5 years, differentiated, MKI <100
	Stroma poor, age <1.5 years, MKI <200
Unfavorable	Stroma rich, all ages, nodular pattern
	Stroma poor, age >5 years
	Stroma poor, age 1.5–5 years, undifferentiated
	Stroma poor, age 1.5–5 years, differentiated, MKI >100
	Stroma poor, age <1.5 years, MKI >200

MKI: mitosis-karyorrhexis index (# mitoses and karyorrhexis per 5000 cells)

They were thereby classified into four categories: neuroblastoma; ganglioneuroblastoma, intermixed; ganglioneuroblastoma, nodular; and ganglioneuroma, maturing and mature subtypes. Neuroblastoma was further stratified into three subtypes. Undifferentiated neuroblastomas are composed of small undifferentiated cells and ancillary studies are necessary to identify them as neuroblastoma. Poorly differentiated neuroblastomas (Fig. 14) have at least some neuropil and differentiating neuroblastomas often have abundant neuropil and at least 5% of cells showing differentiation toward ganglion cells. Ganglioneuroblastoma, intermixed, requires at least 50% Schwannian stroma. Ganglioneuroblastoma, nodular, is a ganglioneuroma or ganglioneuroblastoma with one or more macroscopic nodules of neuroblastoma. Ganglioneuroma of the maturing subtype has a minor component of scattered differentiating neuroblasts and/or maturing ganglion cells that do not form distinct microscopic nests. Ganglioneuroma of the mature subtype is composed of mature Schwannian stroma and mature ganglion cells.

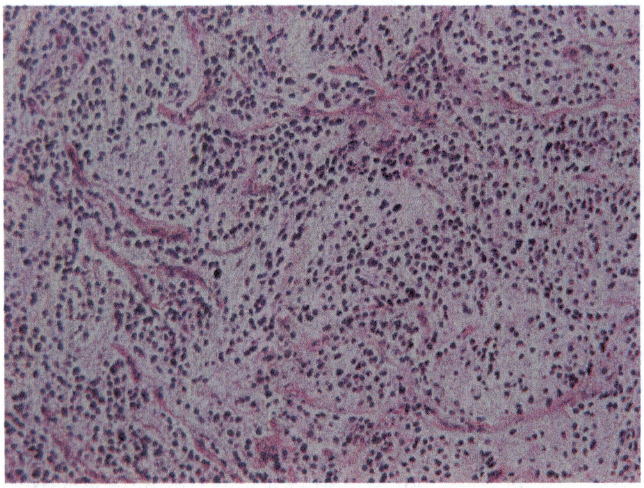

Fig. 14 Poorly differentiated neuroblastoma

This system also separates neuroblastic tumors into favorable and unfavorable prognostic groups depending upon the degree of differentiation of the tumor and its mitosis karyorrhexis index, both of which are linked to the age of the patient.

Unfavorable group:

- neuroblastoma, undifferentiated or high MKI, in ages < 1.5 years
- neuroblastoma, undifferentiated or poorly differentiated, or intermediate or high MKI, in ages 1.5–5 years
- neuroblastoma, all tumors, in ages >5 years
- ganglioneuroblastoma, nodular subtype

Favorable group:

- neuroblastoma, poorly differentiated or differentiated, MKI < 200, in age < 1.5 years
- neuroblastoma, differentiated, MKI <100, in ages 1.5–5 years
- ganglioneuroblastoma, intermixed
- ganglioneuroma, maturing and mature subtypes

The mitosis karyorrhexis index (MKI) is the number of mitoses and karyorrhectic figures per 5,000 cells.

N-Myc amplification is the best characterized genetic abnormality, is present in one-third of neuroblastomas, correlates with poor prognosis and rapid tumor progression and is a prognostic variable independent of stage and age [30].

Primary Benign or Malignant Mesenchymal Tumors

Mesenchymal tumors of the adrenal in children are extremely rare. Hemangiomas, leiomyomas, lipomas, and solitary fibrous tumors are rarely described. Other rare tumors are the adenomatoid tumor, sex-cord stromal tumors, and other tumor-like lesions.

References

1. DeLellis RA, Lloyd RV, Heitz PU, et al., 2004. World Health Organization Classification of Tumours. Pathology and Genetics of Tumour of Endocrine Organs. Lyon: IARC Press.
2. Lloyd RV, Douglas BR, Young WF. 2002. Endocrine Diseases. Atlas of Non-Tumor Pathology. American Registry of Pathology. Armed Forces Institute of Pathology. Washington DC. First Series, Fascicle 1.
3. Lloyd RV. 2004. Endocrine Pathology: Differential Diagnosis and Molecular Advances. Totowa: Humana Press.
4. Lack EE. 2007. Tumors of the adrenal Glans and Extraadrenal Paraganglia. Atlas of Tumor Pathology. American Registry of Pathology. Armed Forces Institute of Pathology. Washington DC, Volume 8, Series 4.
5. Riedlinger WF, Lack EE, Robson CD, Rahbar R, Nosé V. 2005. Primary thyroid teratomas in children: a report of 11 cases with a proposal of criteria for their diagnosis. Am J Surg Pathol. 29(5):700–6.
6. Nosé V. 2008. Familial Non-medullary thyroid carcinoma: An update Endocr Pathol 19(4):226–240.
7. Wolfe HJ, DeLellis RA. 1981. Familial medullary thyroid carcinoma and C cell hyperplasia. Clin Endocrinol Metab 10(2):351–365.
8. Eng C, Clayton D, Schuffenecker I, et al. 1996. The relationship between specific RET proto-oncogene mutations and disease phenotype in multiple endocrine neoplasia type 2. International RET mutation consortium analysis. JAMA 276:1575–1579.
9. Carney JA. 2005. Familial multiple endocrine neoplasia: the first 100 years. Am J Surg Pathol 29(2):254–74.
10. Machens A, Niccoli-Sire P, Hoegel J, et al. Early malignant progression of hereditary medullary thyroid cancer. N Engl J Med 2003; 349:1517–1525.
11. Dotto J, Nosé V. Familial thyroid carcinoma: a diagnostic algorithm. Adv Anat Pathol 2008;15:332–349.

12. Zbuk KM, Eng C. 2007. Cancer phenomics: RET and PTEN as illustrative models. Nat Rev Cancer 7(1):35–45.
13. Eng C. 2003. PTEN: one gene, many syndromes. Hum Mutat 22(3):183–198.
14. Harach HR, Soubeyran I, Brown A, et al. 1999. Thyroid pathologic findings in patients with Cowden disease. Ann Diagnost Pathol 3:331–340.
15. Zambrano E, Holm I, Glickman J, et al. 2004. Abnormal distribution and hyperplasia of thyroid C-cells in PTEN-associated diseases. Endoc Pathol 15:1;55–64.
16. Harach HR, Williams GT, Williams ED. 1994. Familial adenomatous polyposis associated thyroid carcinoma: a distinct type of follicular cell neoplasm. Histopathology 25:549–561.
17. Herraiz M, Barbesino G, Faquin W, et al. 2007. Prevalence of thyroid cancer in familial adenomatous polyposis syndrome and the role of screening ultrasound examinations. Clin Gastroenterol Hepatol 5(3):367–373.
18. Uchino S, Noguchi S, Yamashita H, et al. 2006. Mutational analysis of the APC gene in cribriform-morula variant of papillary thyroid carcinoma. World J Surg 30:775–779.
19. Stratakis CA, Courcoutsakis NA, Abati A, et al. 1997. Thyroid gland abnormalities in patients with the syndrome of spotty skin pigmentation, myxomas, endocrine overactivity, and schwannomas (Carney Complex). J Clinical Endocrine Metabolism 82: 2037–2043.
20. Ishikawa Y, Sugano H, Matsumoto T, et al. 1999. Unusual features of thyroid carcinomas in Japanese patients with Werner syndrome and possible genotype-phenotype relations to cell type and race. Cancer 85:1345–1352.
21. Bakhsh A, Kirov G, Gregory GW, et al. 2006. A new form of familial multi-nodular goiter with progression to differentiated thyroid cancer. Endocrine-Related Cancer 13: 475–483.
22. Charkes ND. 2006. On the prevalence of familial nonmedullary thyroid cancer in multiple affected kindreds. Thyroid 16:181–186.
23. Uchino S, Noguchi S, Kawamoto H, et al. 2002. Familial nonmedullary thyroid carcinoma characterized by multifocality and a high recurrence rate in a large study population. World J Surg 26:897–902.
24. McGregor LM, Rosoff PM. 2001. Follicle-derived thyroid cancer in young people: the Duke experience. tr Hematol Oncol 18(2):89–100.
25. Millman B, Pellitteri PK. 1995. Thyroid carcinoma in children and adolescents. Arch Otolaryngol Head Neck Surg 121 (11):1261–4.
26. Josefson J, Zimmerman D. Thyroid nodules and cancers in children. Pediatr Endocrinol Rev 2008; 6(1):14–23.
27. Weineke JA, Thompson LDR, Heffess CS. 2003 Adrenal cortical neoplasms in the pediatric population: a clinicopathologic and immunophenotypic analysis of 83 patients. Am J Surg Pathol 27(7):867–81.
28. Qualman SJ, Bowen J, Fitzgibbons PL, Cohn SL, Shimada H; Cancer Committee, College of American Pathologists. 2005. Protocol for the examination of specimens from patients with neuroblastoma and related neuroblastic tumors. Arch Pathol Lab Med 129(7):874–83.
29. Shimada H, Umehara S, Monobe Y, Hachitanda Y, Nakagawa A, Goto S, Gerbing RB, Stram DO, Lukens JN, Matthay KK. 2001. International neuroblastoma pathology classification for prognostic evaluation of patients with peripheral neuroblastic tumors: a report from the Children's Cancer Group. Cancer 92(9):2451–61.
30. Goto S, Umehara S, Gerbing RB, Stram DO, Brodeur GM, Seeger RC, Lukens JN, Matthay KK, Shimada H. 2001 Histopathology (International Neuroblastoma Pathology Classification) and MYCN status in patients with peripheral neuroblastic tumors: a report from the Children's Cancer Group. Cancer 92(10):2699–708.

Application of Molecular Diagnosis Techniques in the Diagnosis and Management of Endocrine Tumors

Jennifer L. Hunt

Abstract Molecular alterations in endocrine tumors can be related to genetic syndromes or can be somatic mutations that are restricted to tumor tissues. Tumors associated with genetic syndromes have been described for all endocrine organs and include medullary thyroid carcinoma, parathyroid tumors, pituitary adenomas, adrenal cortical tumors, and pheochromocytomas. The endocrine syndromes are discussed in detail, with particular attention to mutational analysis. In terms of somatic mutations, the most advanced understanding is for thyroid and parathyroid lesions, where established markers are making their way slowly into clinical practice. Somatic mutations for endocrine tumors are also discussed, with an emphasis on testing that has clinical diagnostic and therapeutic implications.

Keywords Papillary carcinoma • Follicular carcinoma • Medullary carcinoma • Multiple endocrine neoplasia syndrome • BRAF mutation • RAS mutation • RET/PTC translocation • RET mutation • Parathyroid adenoma • Parathyroid carcinoma • Hyperparathyroidism-jaw tumor syndrome • HRPT2 gene • Pituitary adenoma • Carney complex • McCune-Albright syndrome • Adrenal cortical adenoma • Adrenal cortical carcinoma • Beckwith-Wiedemann syndrome • Li-Fraumeni syndrome • Pheochromocytoma • Von Hippel-Lindau syndrome • Neurofibromatosis • Familial paragangliomatosis syndrome

J.L. Hunt (✉)
Associate Chief of Pathology, Director of Quality and Safety, James Homer Wright Pathology Laboratories, WRN225, Massachusetts General Hospital, 55 Fruit Street, Boston, MA 02114, USA
e-mail: huntj2@ccf.org

Thyroid Tumors

Papillary Carcinoma

Papillary thyroid carcinoma (PTC) is the most common tumor of the thyroid gland and is also one of the best-studied tumors from the perspective of molecular alterations. A number of molecular mutations have been described in these tumors, including alterations in both oncogenes and tumor suppressor genes. Not only do these mutational events serve as potential diagnostic and prognostic markers, but they are also likely to be important for novel targeted therapies of the future.

The first mutations in PTCs were identified in the *RAS* genes (*KRAS, HRAS*, and *NRAS*), which are involved in the very important RAS-RAF-MEK-MAPK/ERK pathway [1]. In PTC, *RAS* mutations are relatively uncommon, described in less than 20% of PTCs, with the most common mutations being in *KRAS* codons 12 and 13 [2–4]. *RAS* mutations are much more commonly implicated in the follicular tumor pathway.

One of the first mutations that was found to be relatively specific to papillary carcinoma was the *RET/PTC* translocation. Since the first reports of this translocation, multiple different partner genes have been identified for *RET* fusions, and translocations between other genes have also been identified [5, 6] (Table 1). The most common two partners in the *RET/PTC* translocations are *PTC1*, which is the *H4* gene, and *PTC3*, which is the *ELE1* gene [6]. Together, these two mutations represent over 90% of all translocations in PTC, with the other variants being rare. *H4* and *ELE1* are both located on chromosome 10 (as is the RET gene) and therefore the fusions are better classified as intrachromosomal rearrangements.

RET/PTC translocations are found in a subset of PTCs and are particularly prominent in radiation induced tumors [7–9]. This includes tumors secondary to nuclear fallout, such as those seen after the Chernobyl disaster, and tumors related to therapeutic radiation. In most

A. Khan (ed.), *Surgical Pathology of Endocrine and Neuroendocrine Tumors*, Current Clinical Pathology,
DOI 10.1007/978-1-60327-396-1_18,

Table 1 RET-PTC translocations

Translocation	Partner gene	Partner gene location
RET/PTC1	*H4*	10q21
RET/PTC2	*RIα*	17q23
RET/PTC3	*ele1*	10q11.2
RET/PTC4 (OR 3R2)	*ele1*	10q11.2 alternate breakpoint
RET/PTC5	*RFG5*	14q22.1
RET/PTC6	*HTIF1*	7q32-34
RET/PTC7	*RFG7*	1p13.1
RET/PTC8	*KTN1*	18q21-22
RET/PTC9	*RFG9*	14q22.1
RET/ELKS	*ELKS*	12p13.3
RET/PCM1	*PCM-1*	8p21-22
RET-RFP	*RFP*	6p22
TRK/T1	*TPR*	1q25
TRK/T2	*TPR*	1q25
TRK/TPM3	*TPM3*	1q22-23
TRK/T3	*TFG*	3q11-12
HF/PTEN	PTEN	10q23

This table details the translocation partners for the *RET* gene and other genes that harbor translocations in papillary thyroid carcinoma. Aut dom = Autosomal dominant; aut rec = Autosomal recessive; TSG = tumor suppressor gene.

studies, the overall incidence of the *RET/PTC* translocation in PTCs is approximately 20%, though there are geographic differences [4, 10]. There is unlikely to be prognostic significance for the *RET/PTC* translocation [10].

RET/PTC can be detected using either reverse-transcription polymerase chain reaction (RT-PCR) or by using fluorescence in situ hybridization (FISH). RT-PCR is usually most successful when it is performed on RNA extracted from fresh tissue, since DNA and RNA are significantly degraded in paraffin embedded samples. RT-PCR assays can be designed for paraffin samples, but they require smaller products and robust controls. FISH, on the other hand, can be performed on most anatomic pathology specimens.

The *BRAF* gene mutation is another very common gene to harbor somatic alterations in PTC. The *BRAF* gene is also involved in the RAS-RAF-MEK-MAPK/ERK pathway. The mutation associated with PTC was originally designated as V599E, but upon discovery of a counting error in the codons, the designation was changed to V600E (or T1799A). The mutation replaces an A with a T at nucleotide 1799 in exon 15 of the BRAF gene [11, 12] (Fig. 1)

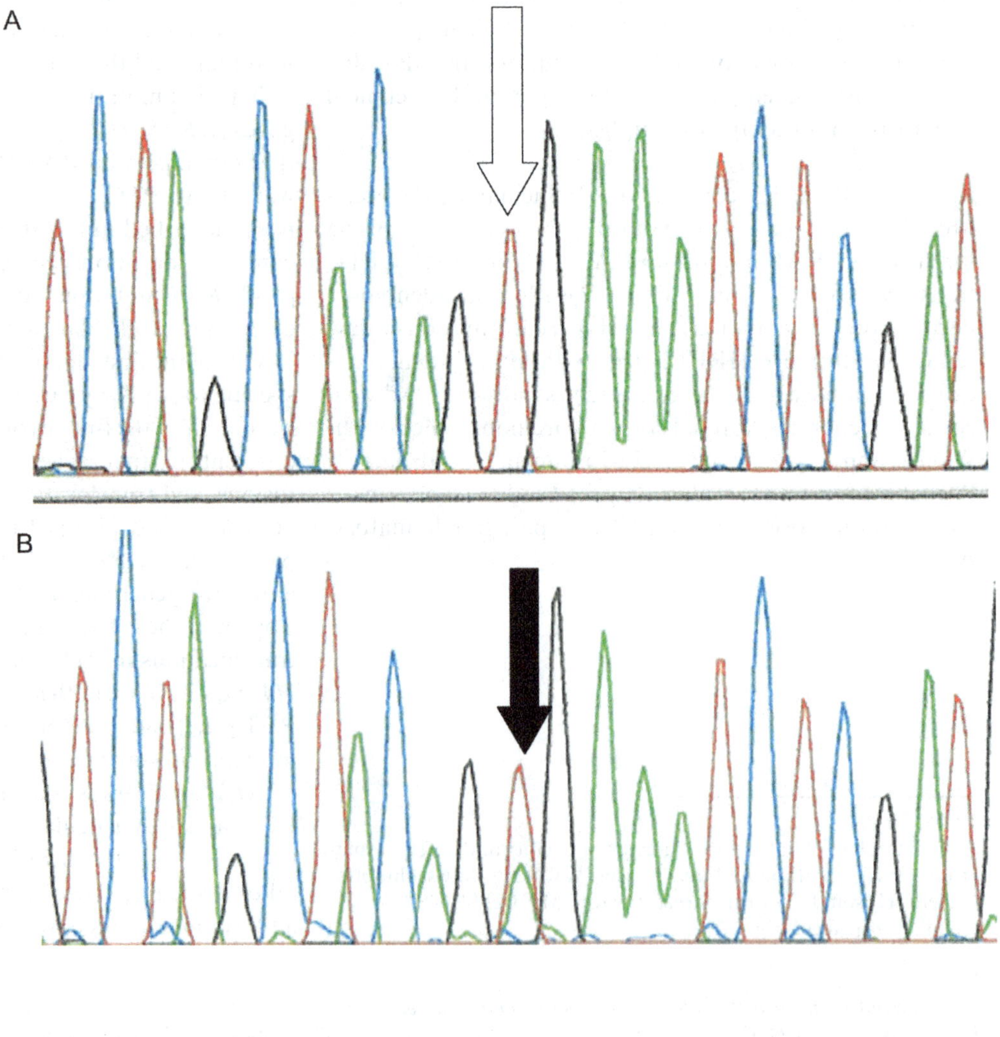

Fig. 1 ***BRAF* gene sequencing in papillary thyroid carcinoma.** (**A**) demonstrates the normal sequence for the *BRAF* gene at codon 600 (nucleotide 1799, *white arrow*). (**B**) shows the mutant sequence, with the T (*red peak*) being replaced with an A (*green peak*) (*black arrow*)

BRAF mutations are primarily seen in sporadic, non-radiation induced PTCs [13, 14]. Most studies have found between 30% and 50% of PTCs harbor the *BRAF* mutation. A recent metaanalysis found an overall incidence of *BRAF* mutations of 49% [15]. Some studies have suggested that *BRAF* mutations in PTC may have prognostic significance [1, 15, 16], but others have found that it is not an independent prognostic indicator [17, 18]. It is found in higher frequencies in tall cell variant of PTC, and is associated with higher risk factors, such as extrathyroidal extension and lymph node metastases [14, 19]. Follicular variants of papillary carcinoma have a lower incidence of *BRAF* mutations [20, 21].

The use of diagnostic molecular assays in PTCs is not widespread in practice today. However, given the potential for diagnostic, prognostic, and therapeutic information from the molecular mutational panel, it is likely that these assays will become more readily available to the practicing pathologist. Some studies have already been published reporting good diagnostic utility of mutational screening on cytology fine-needle aspiration specimens [22, 23].

Importantly, *BRAF* and *RET/PTC* mutations have been found to be almost entirely mutually exclusive, though rare cases can harbor more than one mutation [5]. These mutational pathways have implications for therapeutic approaches [1, 24]. In fact, new therapies are currently in clinical trials for malignant melanomas, which also harbor the *BRAF* V600E mutation, targeting activated *BRAF* or other downstream effectors in the RAS-RAF-MEK-MAPK/ERK pathway.

The *BRAF* mutation can be detected by a variety of techniques. The gold standard assay is a gene-sequencing assay using genomic DNA from tumor tissue. However, other types of assays can also be used, including pyrosequencing assays and allele specific polymerase chain reaction (PCR). These assays have the advantage of being more sensitive than traditional gene sequencing. In fact, gene sequencing can usually identify mutations only when the mutant population represents more than 20–25% of the sample. All types of samples can be used to do the molecular testing, including paraffin embedded tissues and fine-needle aspirations [22, 23, 25].

Follicular Carcinoma

Follicular neoplasms, including both adenomas and carcinomas, have long been known to harbor mutations in the *RAS* genes (*KRAS, HRAS*, and *NRAS*). The most common mutations in follicular carcinomas are in the *HRAS* and *NRAS* genes, particularly in codon 61 [3], though mutations in the common hotspots in the KRAS gene are also seen (Fig. 2). The clinical utility of detecting *RAS* mutations in clinical samples has been limited, since they can be found in both benign and malignant neoplasms [26, 27]. However, there has been some suggestion that tumors with *RAS* mutations may have a worse prognosis, and therefore there may be a role for *RAS* testing in the future [28].

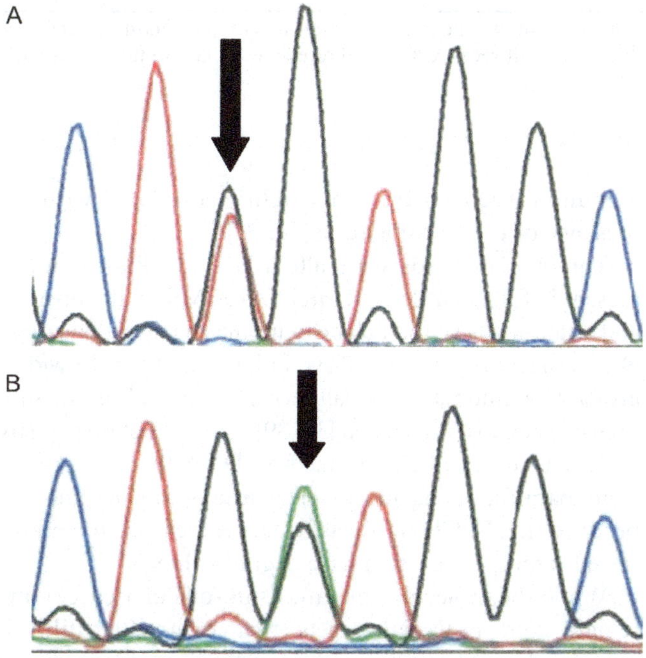

Fig. 2 ***KRAS* gene sequencing in thyroid follicular carcinoma. (A, B)** demonstrate two different mutations in the *KRAS* gene. (**A**) shows the mutation in the first nucleotide of codon 12 (*black arrow* GGT → TGT) and (**B**) shows the mutation in the second nucleotide (black arrow GGT → GAT)

A translocation has also been described in follicular carcinomas, between the *PPARγ* gene and the *PAX8* gene (*PPARγ/PAX8*) [29]. This translocation is seen in between 30 and 50% of follicular carcinomas [30]. The translocation has also been identified in a small number of follicular adenomas and possibly in a subset of follicular variant of papillary carcinomas [30–34]. Hürthle cell tumors or oncocytic variants of follicular carcinomas do not appear to harbor the translocation. Several studies have demonstrated that follicular tumors with and without the *PPARγ/PAX8* translocation are different in terms of behavior, prognosis, and expression profile by microarray analysis [35, 36].

The *PPARγ/PAX8* translocation can be detected either by RT-PCR or by FISH, using similar techniques as are used for detecting the *RET/PTC* translocation in papillary carcinomas. An antibody for PPARγ is commercially available. Unfortunately, the presence of expression by

Table 2 MEN syndromes with medullary thyroid carcinoma and specific mutations that are seen

Syndrome Name	Pattern	Gene	Locus	Type	Clinical Features
MEN Type 2A (MEN2A)	Aut Dom	RET (codons 609, 611, 618, 620, 634)	10q21	Oncogene	• Medullary carcinoma • Multiglandular PT disease (20–30%) • Pheochromocytoma (50%)
MEN Type 2B (MEN2B)	Aut Dom	RET (codon 918)	10q21	Oncogene	• Medullary Carcinoma • Pheochromocytoma (50%) • Ganglioneuroma
Familial Medullary thyroid carcinoma	Aut Dom	RET (codons 609, 611, 618, 620, 634)	10q21	Oncogene	• Medullary carcinoma

This table shows the most common hereditary conditions that are associated with medullary thyroid carcinoma. Aut dom = Autosomal dominant; aut rec = Autosomal recessive; TSG = tumor suppressor gene.

immunohistochemistry is not tightly correlated with the presence of the translocation [31, 37].

Tumor suppressor gene alterations are known to be present in follicular derived carcinomas. Minimally invasive and angio-invasive follicular carcinomas have far fewer loss of heterozygosity events (allelic imbalance) than do widely invasive carcinomas, especially when a panel of tumor suppressor gene loci is assessed [38, 39]. Loss of heterozygosity (LOH) assays can be performed on DNA that is extracted from paraffin tissue blocks. The assays are designed to produce small PCR products, which is ideal for these processed samples that often have degraded DNA.

While the molecular mutations in follicular carcinoma remain good potential targets, their diagnostic utility is currently limited because of the overlap in profiles between benign and malignant tumors. Novel targeted therapies hold some promise in the treatment of follicular tumors, particularly in the setting of tumors that are refractory to radioactive iodine. For example, there are drugs targeting PPARγ, as well as those targeting the downstream effectors of *RAS* activating mutations [40–42]. Currently, however, there are no large-scale clinical trials that are studying the effects of these drugs in follicular thyroid tumors.

Medullary Carcinoma

Medullary thyroid carcinoma (MTC) is associated with the characteristic *RET* oncogene mutations, particularly in the setting of syndromic cases in families with multiple endocrine neoplasia syndromes (MEN 2A and MEN2B) and familial medullary thyroid carcinoma syndrome. The *RET* proto-oncogene is located on chromosome 10q21, and the protein product is a receptor tyrosine kinase. The mutations in the *RET* oncogene that are associated with MEN syndromes occur predominantly in codons 609, 611, 618, 620, 634 (for MEN2A), and 918 (for MEN2B) (Table 2). Patients with the MEN syndromes have a constellation of additional tumor findings, but the highest risk comes from a very high incidence of medullary carcinoma. Because the C-cell derived tumors can occur early in life, current management recommendations are for total thyroidectomy in early childhood for patients who carry the germline mutations [43].

Interestingly, sporadic medullary carcinomas have been shown to harbor somatic *RET* mutations in around 50% of cases [44, 45]. These mutations affect the same codons as in hereditary disease, but in a different distribution. In a small subset of tumors, multiple different *RET* mutations are found within the same lesion [44]. There may be some prognostic significance for somatic *RET* mutations in sporadic medullary carcinomas, particularly when the mutation is in codon 918 [45, 46].

Detecting germline *RET* oncogene mutations from genomic DNA from the patient's blood is performed using a gene sequencing approach, concentrating on the most common mutations in the front-line assay. Testing recommendations have changed in recent years, to include potentially testing of all patients with MTC, since MEN syndromes can present later in life [47, 48]. Testing of tumors for somatic mutations is currently not performed clinically. Unfortunately, early studies using drugs that target tyrosine kinases, including RET, have not had promising results [49]; it is likely that experimentation with other targeted therapies will continue, however, since traditional chemotherapy and radiation therapy are not generally affective for MTC.

Poorly Differentiated Thyroid Carcinoma

Poorly differentiated thyroid carcinoma (PDTC) is a poorly understood entity that has suffered from lack of consensus about the diagnostic criteria. Some PDTCs arise from pre-existing well-differentiated tumors, including both papillary and follicular carcinomas. The literature on PDTC is also complicated by the inclusion of some variants of papillary carcinoma (i.e., tall cell variant, diffuse sclerosis variant, and solid variant) in some of the series [50]. In order to understand the molecular mutational profile of PDTC, it is essential that the definition is better established [50].

Partly because of the lack of consensus in diagnostic features and partly because these tumors are relatively rare, there is very little known about the molecular events in poorly differentiated thyroid carcinoma [51]. Several studies have addressed the molecular mutations associated with well-differentiated precursor lesions [52]. For example, *RET/PTC* translocations and *BRAF* mutations are found in PDTC, but mainly in cases that are derived from more obvious PTC precursor lesions [52–55]. Similarly, *RAS* mutations have been found in approximately 20% of PDTC [56].

A few series of tumors diagnosed as insular carcinoma have suggested that the tumor suppressor gene *p53* is involved in pathogenesis; p53 has been reported to be over-expressed by immunohistochemistry in insular carcinomas, but in a variable number of cases (16–50%) [57]. At the DNA level, *p53* mutations can also be seen in PDTC [58–60]. *BRAF* mutations do not appear to be present in insular carcinomas, unless the pattern is seen as a part of a well-differentiated PTC [16, 61].

Anaplastic Thyroid Carcinoma

Anaplastic thyroid carcinoma (ATC) is a highly malignant tumor of thyroid origin. ATC may arise from well-differentiated precursor lesions. As such, the molecular profile of ATC includes many of the same genetic alterations as are seen in the well-differentiated tumors [62]. In contrast to well-differentiated tumors, however, the mutational profile of ATC is much more complex and multiple alterations in tumor suppressor genes are also found. Several studies examining the progression from well-differentiated tumors to ATC have shown transformation at the molecular level as well [52, 63–69].

Across the literature, approximately 22% of ATCs harbor mutations in the *BRAF* gene, though the range is broad (6–50%) [16, 17, 64–66]. This is not surprising, since up to 50% of ATCs are associated with a histologically identifiable papillary carcinoma. Additionally, the average incidence of *RAS* gene mutations in ATC is 25%, again signifying that some ATCs probably derive from follicular lesions (Fig. 3) [64–66, 70]. As with many high-grade epithelial malignancies, alterations in the *p53* gene

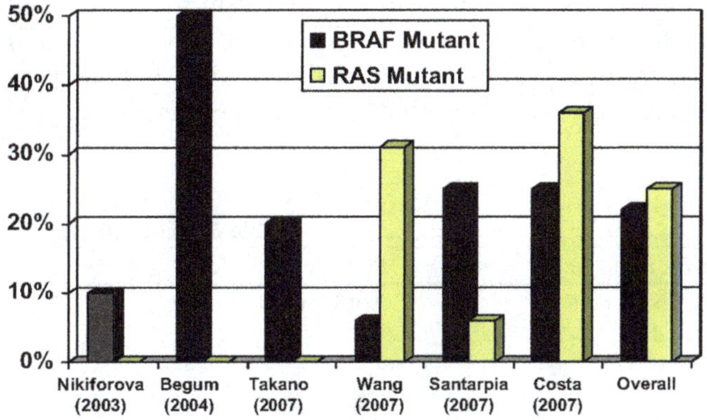

Fig. 3 ***KRAS* and *BRAF* in anaplastic thyroid carcinoma.** This graph shows the percentage of cases of anaplastic thyroid carcinoma that were positive for *BRAF* and *RAS* gene mutations across several studies. The final bar is the combination of the cases in all of the studies

are also quite common in ATC. Mutations, loss of heterozygosity, and protein over-expression have all been described [51, 71, 72].

There are diagnostic implications for mutational testing in ATC, particularly in cases where a differential diagnosis is being entertained. For example, the finding of a *BRAF* gene mutation in a high-grade spindle cell neoplasm in the thyroid will be strongly supportive of a diagnosis of ATC. But, there are also potential therapeutic implications for molecular testing. ATC is notoriously refractory to all conventional therapies for carcinoma. In fact the 1-year survival for ATC is less than 10% [73, 74]. Targeted therapies, particularly when combined with conventional chemotherapy, hold some promise for future treatment protocols for ATC, but data regarding efficacy in humans is still lacking [75–77].

Parathyroid Tumors

There have been some studies of the molecular mutational findings in parathyroid neoplasia. One feature that is consistently noted is that parathyroid adenomas and carcinomas have a high rate of loss of the short arm of chromosome 1 (1p) [78–82]. Other genes have also been implicated in parathyroid adenomas and carcinomas, including retinoblastoma (*RB*, 13q14.3), the *MEN* gene (11q13), and the *BRCA2* gene (13q12.3) [83–85]. Loss of RB protein expression is seen in the majority of parathyroid carcinomas [86] and at the DNA level, alterations and loss of heterozygosity of the *RB* gene are seen in the majority of parathyroid carcinomas [82, 83, 85].

Some forms of hyperparathyroidism are associated with genetic syndromes. The different types of familial hyperparathyroidism are listed in Table 3. One very interesting syndrome that involves the parathyroids is hyperparathyroidism-jaw tumor syndrome [78]. Molecular studies of this entity have provided insight into the pathogenesis of sporadic parathyroid neoplasia. The responsible gene in this syndrome is a tumor suppressor gene mapping to 1q25-31, designated as *HRPT2*. This gene harbors germline mutations in hereditary cases of this syndrome. But, loss of heterozygosity and somatic point mutations have also been detected in sporadic parathyroid carcinomas [79, 87]. The burden of loss of heterozygosity across s a series of tumor suppressor genes has also been shown to correlate with malignancy [88].

Loss of heterozygosity and mutation of the *HRPT2* gene correlates with loss of expression of the protein product, parafibromin [89, 90]. With studies of both benign and malignant parathyroid neoplasia, studies have consistently shown loss of expression in carcinomas [91–93]. Diagnostic tests at the DNA level are not clinically available, but immunohistochemical analysis of parafibromin does present a possible diagnostic test for parathyroid carcinomas.

Table 3 Different types of familial hyperparathyroidism

Syndrome Name	Pattern	Gene	Locus	Type	Clinical Features
MEN Type 1 (MEN1)	Aut Dom	MEN1	11q13	TSG	• Multiglandular PT disease (>90%) • Gastroenteropancre-atic tumors (25–75%) • Pituitary adenomas (40%) • Adrenal cortical tumors (55%)
MEN Type 2A (MEN2A)	Aut Dom	RET (codons 609, 611, 618, 620, 634)	10q21	Onco-gene	• Medullary carcinoma • Multiglandular PT disease (20–30%) • Pheochromocytoma (50%)
Hyperparathyroidism-jaw tumor syndrome (HPT-JT)	Aut Dom	HRPT2	1q21-32	TSG	• Primary hyperparathyroidism with cystic parathyroids • Parathyroid carcinoma (10–15%) • Fibro-osseous lesions of jaws • Kidney lesions
Familial isolated hyperparathyroidism (FIHP)	Aut Dom	MEN1 CaSR	11q13 19p13.3	TSG	• Benign multiglandular PT disease • Carcinomas of breast, colon, endometrium, and others
Familial hypocalciuric hypercalcemic (FHH)	Aut Dom	CaSR	3q21.1 19p13.3 (type 2) 19q13 (type 3)		• Normal or increased calcium • Moderate hyperphosphatemia • Inappropriately low urine calcium • Increased or normal PTH levels
Neonatal severe hyperparathyroidism (NSHPT)	Aut Rec	CaSR	3q21.1		• Homozygous form of FHH
Autosomal dominant mild hyperparathyroidism (ADMH)	Aut Dom	CaSR	3q21.1		

This table shows the most common hereditary conditions that are associated with parathyroid neoplasia. Aut dom = Autosomal dominant; aut rec = Autosomal recessive; TSG = tumor suppressor gene; CaSR = calcium sensing receptor gene.

Pituitary Tumors

Pituitary tumors are classified by the hormone that is produced, with the most common being prolactin secreting adenomas and growth hormone secreting adenomas. Pituitary adenomas have been shown to be monoclonal by X-inactivation (HUMARA) assays [94, 95]. Other genetic alterations in sporadic tumors, however, are poorly understood. In fact, much of our understanding of the molecular alterations in pituitary neoplasia is through the study of hereditary or genetically derived disease [96, 97]. Pituitary neoplasia is seen in association with several well-known syndromes. Pituitary adenomas are seen in 40% of patients with multiple endocrine neoplasia type I (MEN1), in less than 25% of patients with Carney complex, and in patients with familial isolated pituitary adenomas (FIPA) (Table 4). Growth hormone or prolactin cell hyperplasia, and rarely pituitary adenomas are also seen in patients with McCune–Albright Disease.

Patients with MEN1 syndrome have a constellation of findings, including pituitary neoplasia, hyperparathyroidism, and pancreatic tumors [98]. The autosomal dominant MEN1 syndrome is caused by a mutation in the *MEN1* gene, which is located on 11q13 [99]. The *MEN1* gene is a classic tumor suppressor gene. The germline mutations in the *MEN1* gene are not clustered, but rather are scattered along the entire coding region of the 49 kb genomic sequence of the gene. Most families will have unique mutations, but up to 20% of the cases with clinical features of MEN1 will not have an identifiable mutation in the gene [91]. Sporadic pituitary adenomas have also been shown to have alterations in the *MEN1* gene [98].

Pituitary lesions can be seen in patients with Carney complex [91, 100]. These patients often present with acromegaly, but this finding is only associated with a pituitary adenoma in less than 20% [100, 101]. Approximately 60% of patients with Carney complex will have a germline inactivating mutation in the protein kinase A (PKA) type 1 regulatory (R1α) subunit (*PRKAR1A*) [100]. This gene, which is located on chromosome 17q22-24, also functions as a tumor suppressor gene. Germline mutations in *PRKAR1A* are found in approximately 60% of well-characterized patients who meet the diagnostic criteria for Carney complex. *PRKAR1A* mutations are spread across the coding region for the gene, approximately 21 kb [102].

A final group of familial cases of pituitary adenoma is in familial isolated pituitary isolation (FIPA). In "homogenous" FIPA, the affected family members have adenomas with identical hormone profiles, while "heterogeneous" FIPA family members have adenomas that have different hormone profiles [103]. Recent studies have identified germline mutations in the gene that encodes for aryl hydrocarbon receptor-interacting protein (*AIP*, chromosome 11q13.3) in 15–35% of families with FIPA [104, 105]. Germline mutations in *AIP* have also been identified in some patients with apparently sporadic GH-secreting tumors, suggesting under-recognition of familial cases with low penetrance [106].

Table 4 Syndromes associated with pituitary neoplasia

Syndrome name	Pattern	Gene	Locus	Type	Clinical features
MEN Type 1 (MEN1)	Aut Dom	MEN1	11q13	TSG	• Multiglandular PT disease (>90%) • Gastroenteropancreatic tumors (25-75%) • Pituitary adenomas (40%) • Adrenal cortical tumors (55%)
Carney complex	Aut Dom	PRKAR1A	17q22-24	Possibly TSG	• Acromegaly (pituitary adenoma <20%) • Cardiac myxomas • Breast myxomatosis • Spotty skin pigmentation • Large cell calcifying Sertoli cell tumors • Adrenocortical lesions (primary pigmented nodular adrenocortical disease) • Leydig-cell tumors • Psammomatous melanotic schwannoma • Epithelioid blue nevus • Ductal breast adenomas • Thyroid follicular neoplasms
Familial Isolated Pituitary Adenoma	Aut dom	*AIP*	11q13.3	Probable TSG	Pituitary adenomas
McCune-Albright Syndrome	Sporadic (>85%)	*GNAS1*(mosaicism)	20q13	Guanine nucleotide binding protein	• Polyostotic fibrous dysplasia • Pigmented skin lesions • Endocrine abnormalities (GH excess in 20%)

This table shows the most common hereditary conditions that are associated with pituitary neoplasia. Aut dom = Autosomal dominant; aut rec = Autosomal recessive; TSG = tumor suppressor gene.

McCune-Albright Syndrome (MAS) is not an inherited disease, but rather is caused by mosaicism for mutations in the *GNAS1* gene (20q13.3) [99]. These patients present with polyostotic fibrous dysplasia, pigmented skin lesions, and endocrine related abnormalities. Among the endocrine problems, GH excess is one of the common findings; this hormone excess is most commonly caused by GH-cell hyperplasia, and only rare cases of pituitary adenoma occur. Prolactin-cell hyperplasia can also occur. The *GNAS1* gene is located on chromosome 20q13 and encodes for the Gsα subunit of the G protein. Interestingly, mutations in the *GNAS1* gene are also found in sporadic GH-producing tumors [99, 107]. Between 30% and 50% of sporadic GH-secreting adenomas have been shown to have *GNAS1* mutations, but there are some geographic differences noted [64, 91, 100].

Other molecular alterations in pituitary tumors have also been described, including alterations in the retinoblastoma gene (*RB1*), which is again a classic tumor suppressor gene [108]. For example, loss of heterozygosity of 13q14.2, where the *RB1* gene is located, has been associated with more aggressive pituitary tumor behavior [99, 109, 110]. Lack of expression of the retinoblastoma protein has also been seen in pituitary adenomas, and recent evidence has suggested that *RB1* promoter methylation may be another route for inactivation of the *RB1* gene [111, 112].

Gastroenteropancreatic Neuroendocrine Tumors (GEP-NET)

Neuroendocrine tumors of the gastrointestinal tract are relatively rare lesions that are derived from the diffuse endocrine system. As is seen with other endocrine tumors, these tumors occur in both sporadic and hereditary settings. Hereditary tumors, however, only represent about 20% of tumors that arise in the gastrointestinal tract and pancreas [113]. The incidence of hereditary disease is much higher in nonfunctional tumors.

The syndromes that can harbor GEP-NETs include MEN1 syndrome, von Hippel Lindau syndrome, neurofibromatosis type 1, and tuberous sclerosis (Table 5). Most of these have been discussed in detail elsewhere within this chapter. The somatic mutational profiles of GEP-NETs are quite complex and depend upon the location of the tumors, among other things [114]. There are many different genes that have been implicated in the pathogenesis, including somatic mutations and loss of heterozygosity of the *MEN1*, *VHL*, and *NF1* genes [113]. Other tumor suppressor genes that have been studied show variable rates of loss of heterozygosity and somewhat lower rates of somatic point mutations [115]. These include *p16/MTS1* in some gastrinomas and *p53* in some higher-grade tumors [115].

There are more interesting data stemming from the expression of growth factors and growth factor receptors

Table 5 Syndromes associated with gastroenteropancreatic neuroendocrine tumors

Syndrome Name	Pattern	Gene	Locus	Type	Clinical Features
MEN Type 1 (MEN1)	Aut Dom	*MEN1*	11q13	TSG	• Multiglandular PT disease (>90%) • Gastroenteropancreatic tumors (25–75%) • Pituitary adenomas (40%) • Adrenal cortical tumors (55%)
Von Hippel-Lindau	Aut Dom	*VHL*	3p25-26	TSG	• Hemangioblastoma • Renal tumors • Pancreatic tumors • Endolymphatic sac tumors • Pheochromocytoma (10–20%) • Gastroenteropancreatic neuroendocrine tumors (12%)
Neurofibromatosis	Aut Dom	*NF1*	17q11.2	TSG	• Neurofibromas • Lisch nodules • Schwannomas • Gliomas • Meningiomas • Pheochromocytoma (<5%) • Gastroenteropancreatic neuroendocrine tumors (1–2%)
Tuberous Sclerosis	Aut Dom	Hamartin Tuberin	9q34 16p13.3	TSG	• Hamartomas • Astrocytomas • Well differentiated tumors (kidney, brain, heart, skin, lung, pancreas)

This table shows the most common hereditary conditions that are associated with gastroenteropancreatic neuroendocrine neoplasia. Aut dom = Autosomal dominant; aut rec = Autosomal recessive; TSG = tumor suppressor gene.

in these tumors, including VEGF, TGF-α, PDGF, and EGFR. Although the pathways are not completely well understood, the expression profiles for these lesions have begun to be exploited in early clinical trials that are targeting these molecules. The early results are promising for some (bevacizumab and everolimus) and have had disappointing results for others (imatinib and gefitinib) [116]. Finally, there are drugs that are coupled to somatostatin that target tumors that express somatostatin, and these have proven to be safe and potentially effective treatments [117].

Adrenal Cortical Tumors

Adrenal cortical lesions are classified as hyperplasia, adenoma (ACA), and carcinoma (ACC). A variety of syndromes are associated with adrenal cortical lesions, including Li-Fraumeni Syndrome, Beckwith-Wiedemann Syndrome, Carney complex, MEN1, and congenital adrenal hyperplasia (Table 6) [118, 119]. The genetics of Carney complex and MEN1 were discussed above in the section on pituitary lesions.

Li-Fraumeni syndrome (LFS) is characterized by kindreds with multiple tumors at an early age of onset [120,

Table 6 Syndromes associated with adrenal cortical neoplasia

Syndrome Name	Pattern	Gene	Locus	Type	Clinical Features
MEN Type 1 (MEN1)	Aut Dom	*MEN1*	11q13	TSG	• Multiglandular PT disease (>90%) • Gastroenteropancreatic tumors (25–75%) • Pituitary adenomas (40%) • Adrenal cortical tumors (55%)
Carney complex	Aut Dom	*PRKAR1A*	17q22-24	Possibly TSG	• Acromegaly (pituitary adenoma <20%) • Cardiac myxomas • Breast myxomatosis • Spotty skin pigmentation • Large cell calcifying Sertoli cell tumors • Adrenocortical lesions (primary pigmented nodular adrenocortical disease in 90%) • Leydig-cell tumors • Psammomatous melanotic schwannoma • Epithelioid blue nevus • Ductal breast adenomas • Thyroid follicular neoplasms
Beckwith-Wiedemann Syndrome	Sporadic	*IGF2* H19 CDKN1C	11p15	Imprinting	• Exomphalos • Macroglossia • Gigantism • Nephroblastoma • Hepatoblastoma • Rhabdomyosarcoma • Adrenal cortical carcinoma (5%)
McCune-Albright Syndrome	Sporadic	*GNAS*	20q13	Mosaicism	• Polyostotic fibrous dysplasia • Pigmented skin lesions • Endocrine abnormalities (GH excess in 20%)
Li-Fraumeni Syndrome	Aut Dom	*TP53* hCHK3	17q13.1	TSG	• Soft tissue sarcomas • Osteosarcomas • Breast cancers • Brain tumors • Leukemia • Adrenal cortical carcinomas (3–4%)
Congenital adrenal hyperplasia	Aut Rec	*CYP21B*	6p21.3	Inactivation from recombination with pseudogene	• Adrenal cortical hyperplasia (in 100% of patient) • Adrenal tumors (in 82% of patients and 45% of carriers) • Adrenal cortical carcinomas (rare)

This table shows the most common hereditary conditions that are associated with adrenal cortical neoplasia. Aut dom = Autosomal dominant; aut rec = Autosomal recessive; TSG = tumor suppressor gene.

121]. The tumors include soft tissue and bone sarcomas, breast carcinoma, brain tumors, and leukemia. Adrenal cortical carcinomas occur in 3–4% of patients with LFS [118, 119]. The syndrome is caused by germline mutations in the *p53* gene, located on chromosome 17q13.1. *p53* is a tumor suppressor gene and therefore the tumors have a second inactivating mutation, often a deletion mutation. These deletion mutations are detected by loss of heterozygosity analysis [119, 121, 122].

Beckwith-Wiedemann Syndrome (BWS) is usually sporadic, with only 15% representing familial disease [123]. BWS is also referred to as a congenital overgrowth syndrome since the patients present as neonates with macroglossia, gigantism, and exomphalos. The patients are at high risk for childhood tumors, as well, including nephroblastoma, hepatoblastoma, and rhabdomyosarcoma [124]. Approximately 5% will develop adrenal cortical carcinoma [118]. Genes mapping to chromosome 11p15, including insulin-like growth factor-2 (*IGF2*), *H19*, and cyclin-dependent kinase inhibitor 1C (*CDKN1C*, also known as $p57^{kip2}$) have been implicated in BWS [118]. This chromosomal region is involved in parental imprinting. Paternal uniparental isodisomy, which is loss of the maternal allele and duplication of the paternal allele, germline mutations in p57kip2, and methylation of H19, have all been described as mechanisms of the genetic alterations in BWS [119].

Sporadic adrenal cortical tumors have also been studied for molecular alterations. Many studies are driven by the search for markers that can distinguish between benign and malignant tumors [125]. The most common molecular alterations identified in sporadic tumors are also those involved in the syndromic causes of adrenal cortical tumors: *p53*, *CDKN1c*, *IGF2*, *H19*, and *MEN1*. Unfortunately, no markers have been identified that correlate well with malignancy in adrenal cortical tumors [118, 126]. *p53* mutations are considered to be later events in malignant transformation of adrenal cortical tumors [125]. Mutations are found in approximately 20% of adrenal cortical carcinomas [119], and most of these occur in the hotspots of this gene, which are in exons 5–8. Finally, there have been some efforts to separate adrenal cortical adenomas from carcinomas using other molecular techniques, including comparative genomic hybridization and molecular profiling. Some of the early work has shown potential for discriminating between aggressive and indolent disease, based on both techniques [127, 128].

Adrenal – Pheochromocytoma

Like adrenal cortical tumors, pheochromocytomas are associated with specific syndromes (Table 7), and also occur as sporadic tumors. Von Hippel-Lindau syndrome, neurofibromatosis, and the familial paraganglioma syndromes are caused by germline mutations in tumor suppressor genes (*VHL*, *NF1*, *SDHB*, and *SDHD*). These syndromes have typical constellations of clinical findings and pheochromocytoma is one of the possible manifestations of these diseases. In contrast to the other endocrine tumors with a potential hereditary etiology, there is growing evidence that up to 25–30% of patients with apparently sporadic pheochromocytomas will have a germline mutation when they are properly tested [129]. In fact,

Table 7 Syndromes associated with pheochromocytoma

Syndrome name	Pattern	Gene	Locus	Type	Clinical features
MEN2	Aut dom	*RET*	10q11.2	Oncogene	• Medullary thyroid carcinoma • Ganglioneuromas • Hyperparathyroidism • Pheochromocytoma (40–50%)
Von Hippel-Lindau	Aut dom	*VHL*	3p25-26	TSG	• Hemangioblastoma • Renal tumors • Pancreatic tumors • Endolymphatic sac tumors • Pheochromocytoma (10–20%)
Neurofibromatosis	Aut dom	*NF1*	17q11.2	TSG	• Neurofibromas • Lisch nodules • Schwannomas • Gliomas • Meningiomas • Pheochromocytoma (<5%) • Gastroenteropancreatic neuroendocrine tumors (1–2%)
Familial paraganglioma syndromes	Aut dom	*SDHB* *SDHD*	1p36.13 11q23	TSG	• Paragangliomas • Pheochromocytoma

This table shows the most common hereditary conditions that are associated with pheochromocytomas. Aut dom = Autosomal dominant; aut rec = Autosomal recessive; TSG = tumor suppressor gene.

recent guidelines have suggested that all patients who are diagnosed with a pheochromocytoma should be tested for possible hereditary disease [130].

In sporadic pheochromocytomas, much of the molecular work has also been directed at trying to discover markers associated with malignancy or prognosis. Unfortunately, specific markers have not been identified, and predicting prognosis at both the histologic and the molecular genetic level remains a challenge. There is some evidence that expression profile analysis by microarray can potentially separate tumors based on prognosis [131]. Currently, there are no diagnostic or prognostic tests available clinically for sporadic pheochromocytomas.

References

1. Xing M. BRAF Mutation in Papillary Thyroid Cancer: Pathogenic Role, Molecular Bases, and Clinical Implications. *Endocr Rev* 2007;28:742–62.
2. Capella G, Matias-Guiu X, Ampudia X, et al. Ras oncogene mutations in thyroid tumors: polymerase chain reaction-restriction-fragment-length polymorphism analysis from paraffin-embedded tissues. *Diagnostic Molecular Pathology* 1996;5:45–52.
3. Vasko V, Ferrand M, Di Cristofaro J, et al. Specific pattern of RAS oncogene mutations in follicular thyroid tumors. *J Clin Endocrinol Metab* 2003;88:2745–52.
4. Adeniran AJ, Zhu Z, Gandhi M, et al. Correlation between genetic alterations and microscopic features, clinical manifestations, and prognostic characteristics of thyroid papillary carcinomas. *Am J Surg Pathol* 2006;30:216–22.
5. Wang YL, Wang JC, Wu Y, et al. Incidentally simultaneous occurrence of RET/PTC, H4-PTEN and BRAF mutation in papillary thyroid carcinoma. *Cancer Lett* 2008;263:44–52.
6. Nikiforov YE. RET/PTC rearrangement in thyroid tumors. *Endocrine Pathology* 2002;13:3–16.
7. Nikiforov YE, Rowland JM, Bove KE, Monforte-Munoz H, Fagin JA. Distinct pattern of ret oncogene rearrangements in morphological variants of radiation-induced and sporadic thyroid papillary carcinomas in children. *Cancer Research* 1997;57:1690–4.
8. Thomas GA, Bunnell H, Cook HA, et al. High prevalence of RET/PTC rearrangements in Ukrainian and Belarussian post-Chernobyl thyroid papillary carcinomas: a strong correlation between RET/PTC3 and the solid-follicular variant. *J Clin Endocrinol Metab* 1999;84:4232–8.
9. Santoro M, Thomas GA, Vecchio G, et al. Gene rearrangement and Chernobyl related thyroid cancers. *Br J Cancer* 2000;82:315–22.
10. Nikiforova MN, Nikiforov YE. Molecular genetics of thyroid cancer: implications for diagnosis, treatment and prognosis. *Expert Rev Mol Diagn* 2008;8:83–95.
11. Cohen Y, Xing M, Mambo E, et al. BRAF mutation in papillary thyroid carcinoma. *J Natl Cancer Inst* 2003;95:625–7.
12. Kimura ET, Nikiforova MN, Zhu Z, et al. High prevalence of BRAF mutations in thyroid cancer: genetic evidence for constitutive activation of the RET/PTC-RAS-BRAF signaling pathway in papillary thyroid carcinoma. *Cancer Res* 2003;63:1454–7.
13. Lima J, Trovisco V, Soares P, et al. BRAF mutations are not a major event in post-Chernobyl childhood thyroid carcinomas. *J Clin Endocrinol Metab* 2004;89:4267–71.
14. Lupi C, Giannini R, Ugolini C, et al. Association of BRAF V600E mutation with poor clinicopathological outcomes in 500 consecutive cases of papillary thyroid carcinoma. *J Clin Endocrinol Metab* 2007;92:4085–90.
15. Lee JH, Lee ES, Kim YS. Clinicopathologic significance of BRAF V600E mutation in papillary carcinomas of the thyroid: a meta-analysis. *Cancer* 2007;110:38–46.
16. Nikiforova MN, Kimura ET, Gandhi M, et al. BRAF mutations in thyroid tumors are restricted to papillary carcinomas and anaplastic or poorly differentiated carcinomas arising from papillary carcinomas. *J Clin Endocrinol Metab* 2003;88:5399–404.
17. Costa AM, Herrero A, Fresno MF, et al. BRAF mutation associated with other genetic events identifies a subset of aggressive papillary thyroid carcinoma. *Clin Endocrinol (Oxf)* 2007;
18. Kim TY, Kim WB, Song JY, et al. The BRAF mutation is not associated with poor prognostic factors in Korean patients with conventional papillary thyroid microcarcinoma. *Clin Endocrinol (Oxf)* 2005;63:588–93.
19. Kebebew E, Weng J, Bauer J, et al. The prevalence and prognostic value of BRAF mutation in thyroid cancer. *Ann Surg* 2007;246:466–70; discussion 70–1.
20. Costa AM, Herrero A, Fresno MF, et al. BRAF mutation associated with other genetic events identifies a subset of aggressive papillary thyroid carcinoma. *Clin Endocrinol (Oxf)* 2008;68:618–34.
21. Trovisco V, Soares P, Preto A, et al. Type and prevalence of BRAF mutations are closely associated with papillary thyroid carcinoma histotype and patients' age but not with tumour aggressiveness. *Virchows Archiv* 2005;446:589–95.
22. Xing M, Tufano RP, Tufaro AP, et al. Detection of BRAF mutation on fine needle aspiration biopsy specimens: a new diagnostic tool for papillary thyroid cancer. *J Clin Endocrinol Metab* 2004;89:2867–72.
23. Cohen Y, Rosenbaum E, Clark DP, et al. Mutational analysis of BRAF in fine needle aspiration biopsies of the thyroid: a potential application for the preoperative assessment of thyroid nodules. *Clin Cancer Res* 2004;10:2761–5.
24. Fagin JA. How thyroid tumors start and why it matters: kinase mutants as targets for solid cancer pharmacotherapy. *J Endocrinol* 2004;183:249–56.
25. Shibru D, Chung KW, Kebebew E. Recent developments in the clinical application of thyroid cancer biomarkers. *Curr Opin Oncol* 2008;20:13–8.
26. Namba H, Gutman RA, Matsuo K, Alvarez A, Fagin JA. H-ras protooncogene mutations in human thyroid neoplasms. *J Clin Endocrinol Metab* 1990;71:223–9.
27. Namba H, Rubin SA, Fagin JA. Point mutations of ras oncogenes are an early event in thyroid tumorigenesis. *Mol Endocrinol*1990;4:1474–9.
28. Garcia-Rostan G, Zhao H, Camp RL, et al. ras mutations are associated with aggressive tumor phenotypes and poor prognosis in thyroid cancer. *J Clin Oncol* 2003;21:3226–35.
29. Kroll TG, Sarraf P, Pecciarini L, et al. PAX8-PPARgamma1 fusion oncogene in human thyroid carcinoma. *Science* 2000;289:1357–60.
30. Nikiforova MN, Biddinger PW, Caudill CM, Kroll TG, Nikiforov YE. PAX8-PPARgamma rearrangement in thyroid tumors: RT-PCR and immunohistochemical analyses. *Am J Surg Pathol* 2002;26:1016–23.
31. Marques AR, Espadinha C, Catarino AL, et al. Expression of PAX8-PPAR gamma 1 rearrangements in both follicular thyroid carcinomas and adenomas. *J Clin Endocrinol Metab* 2002;87:3947–52.
32. Cheung L, Messina M, Gill A, et al. Detection of the PAX8-PPAR gamma fusion oncogene in both follicular thyroid carcinomas and adenomas. *J Clin Endocrinol Metab* 2003;88:354–7.

33. Castro P, Roque L, Magalhaes J, Sobrinho-Simoes M. A subset of the follicular variant of papillary thyroid carcinoma harbors the PAX8-PPARgamma translocation. *Int J Surg Pathol* 2005;13:235–8.
34. Castro P, Rebocho AP, Soares RJ, et al. PAX8-PPARgamma rearrangement is frequently detected in the follicular variant of papillary thyroid carcinoma. *J Clin Endocrinol Metab* 2006;91:213–20.
35. Nikiforova MN, Lynch RA, Biddinger PW, et al. RAS point mutations and PAX8-PPAR gamma rearrangement in thyroid tumors: evidence for distinct molecular pathways in thyroid follicular carcinoma. *J Clin Endocrinol Metab* 2003;88:2318–26.
36. Giordano TJ, Au AY, Kuick R, et al. Delineation, functional validation, and bioinformatic evaluation of gene expression in thyroid follicular carcinomas with PAX8-PPARG translocation. *Clin Cancer Res* 2006;1:1983.
37. Marques AR, Espadinha C, Frias MJ, et al. Underexpression of peroxisome proliferator-activated receptor (PPAR)gamma in PAX8/PPARgamma-negative thyroid tumours. *Br J Cancer* 2004;91:732–8.
38. Hunt JL, Yim JH, Carty SE. Fractional allelic loss of tumor suppressor genes identifies malignancy and predicts clinical outcome in follicular thyroid tumors. *Thyroid* 2006;16:643–9.
39. Hunt JL, Livolsi VA, Baloch ZW, et al. A novel microdissection and genotyping of follicular-derived thyroid tumors to predict aggressiveness. *Human Pathol* 2003;34:375–80.
40. Feldman PL, Lambert MH, Henke BR. PPAR modulators and PPAR pan agonists for metabolic diseases: the next generation of drugs targeting peroxisome proliferator-activated receptors? *Curr Top Med Chem* 2008;8:728–49.
41. Haluska P, Dy GK, Adjei AA. Farnesyl transferase inhibitors as anticancer agents. *Eur J Cancer* 2002;38:1685–700.
42. Khuri FR, Cohen V. Molecularly targeted approaches to the chemoprevention of lung cancer. *Clin Cancer Res* 2004;10:15.
43. Ukkat J, Lorenz K, Hinze R, Thomusch O, Dralle H. Importance of early screening and prophylactic thyroidectomy in asymptomatic nonindex RET germline carriers. *World J Surg* 2001;25:713–7.
44. Dvorakova S, Vaclavikova E, Sykorova V, et al. Somatic mutations in the RET proto-oncogene in sporadic medullary thyroid carcinomas. *Mol Cell Endocrinol* 2008;284:21–7.
45. Elisei R, Cosci B, Romei C, et al. Prognostic significance of somatic RET oncogene mutations in sporadic medullary thyroid cancer: a 10-year follow-up study. *J Clin Endocrinol Metab* 2008;93:682–7.
46. Schilling T, Burck J, Sinn HP, et al. Prognostic value of codon 918 (ATG->ACG) RET proto-oncogene mutations in sporadic medullary thyroid carcinoma. *Int J Cancer* 2001;95:62–6.
47. Szinnai G, Sarnacki S, Polak M. Hereditary medullary thyroid carcinoma: how molecular genetics made multiple endocrine neoplasia type 2 a paediatric disease. *Endocr Dev* 2007;10:173–87.
48. Raue F, Frank-Raue K. Multiple endocrine neoplasia type 2: 2007 update. *Horm Res* 2007;68 Suppl 5:101–4.
49. Frank-Raue K, Fabel M, Delorme S, Haberkorn U, Raue F. Efficacy of imatinib mesylate in advanced medullary thyroid carcinoma. *Eur J Endocrinol* 2007;157:215–20.
50. Volante M, Collini P, Nikiforov YE, et al. Poorly differentiated thyroid carcinoma: the Turin proposal for the use of uniform diagnostic criteria and an algorithmic diagnostic approach. *Am J Surg Pathol* 2007;31:1256–64.
51. Farid NR. P53 mutations in thyroid carcinoma: tidings from an old foe. *J Endocrinol Invest* 2001;24:536–45.
52. Nikiforov YE. Genetic alterations involved in the transition from well-differentiated to poorly differentiated and anaplastic thyroid carcinomas. *Endocr Pathol* 2004;15:319–27.
53. Fugazzola L, Mannavola D, Cirello V, et al. BRAF mutations in an Italian cohort of thyroid cancers. *Clinical Endocrinol* 2004;61:239–43.
54. Tallini G, Santoro M, Helie M, et al. RET/PTC oncogene activation defines a subset of papillary thyroid carcinomas lacking evidence of progression to poorly differentiated or undifferentiated tumor phenotypes. *Clinical Cancer Res* 1998;4:287–94.
55. Santoro M, Papotti M, Chiappetta G, et al. RET activation and clinicopathologic features in poorly differentiated thyroid tumors. *J Clin Endocrinol Metab* 2002;87:370–9.
56. Basolo F, Pisaturo F, Pollina LE, et al. N-ras mutation in poorly differentiated thyroid carcinomas: correlation with bone metastases and inverse correlation to thyroglobulin expression. *Thyroid* 2000;10:19–23.
57. Soares P, Cameselle-Teijeiro J, Sobrinho-Simoes M. Immunohistochemical detection of p53 in differentiated, poorly differentiated and undifferentiated carcinomas of the thyroid. *Histopathology* 1994;24:205–10.
58. Fagin JA, Matsuo K, Karmakar A, et al. High prevalence of mutations of the p53 gene in poorly differentiated human thyroid carcinomas. *J Clin Invest* 1993;91:179–84.
59. Ho YS, Tseng SC, Chin TY, Hsieh LL, Lin JD. p53 gene mutation in thyroid carcinoma. *Cancer Lett* 1996;103:57–63.
60. Dobashi Y, Sugimura H, Sakamoto A, et al. Stepwise participation of p53 gene mutation during dedifferentiation of human thyroid carcinomas. *Diagn Mol Pathol* 1994;3:9–14.
61. Soares P, Trovisco V, Rocha AS, et al. BRAF mutations typical of papillary thyroid carcinoma are more frequently detected in undifferentiated than in insular and insular-like poorly differentiated carcinomas. *Virchows Archiv* 2004;444:572–6.
62. Quiros RM, Ding HG, Gattuso P, Prinz RA, Xu X. Evidence that one subset of anaplastic thyroid carcinomas are derived from papillary carcinomas due to BRAF and p53 mutations. *Cancer* 2005;103:2261–8.
63. Wiseman SM, Griffith OL, Deen S, et al. Identification of molecular markers altered during transformation of differentiated into anaplastic thyroid carcinoma. *Arch Surg* 2007;142:717–27; discussion 27–9.
64. Freda PU, Chung WK, Matsuoka N, et al. Analysis of GNAS mutations in 60 growth hormone secreting pituitary tumors: correlation with clinical and pathological characteristics and surgical outcome based on highly sensitive GH and IGF-I criteria for remission. *Pituitary* 2007;10:275–82.
65. Takano T, Ito Y, Hirokawa M, Yoshida H, Miyauchi A. BRAF V600E mutation in anaplastic thyroid carcinomas and their accompanying differentiated carcinomas. *Br J Cancer* 2007;96:1549–53.
66. Santarpia L, El-Naggar AK, Cote GJ, Myers JN, Sherman SI. PI3K/Akt and Ras/Raf-MAPK pathway mutations in anaplastic thyroid cancer. *J Clin Endocrinol Metab* 2007;
67. Santos L, Loo C, Chandraratnam E, Gune S. Anaplastic carcinoma dedifferentiation of solid variant of papillary thyroid carcinoma. *Pathology* 2004;36:196–211.
68. Nikiforova MN, Kimura ET, Gandhi M, et al. BRAF mutations in thyroid tumors are restricted to papillary carcinomas and anaplastic or poorly differentiated carcinomas arising from papillary carcinomas. *J Clin Endocrinol Metab* 2003;88:5399–404.
69. Hunt JL, Tometsko M, LiVolsi VA, et al. Molecular evidence of anaplastic transformation in coexisting well-differentiated and anaplastic carcinomas of the thyroid. *American J Surg Pathol* 2003;27:1559–64.
70. Wang HM, Huang YW, Huang JS, et al. Anaplastic carcinoma of the thyroid arising more often from follicular carcinoma than papillary carcinoma. *Ann Surg Oncol* 2007;14:3011–8.

71. La Perle KM, Jhiang SM, Capen CC. Loss of p53 promotes anaplasia and local invasion in ret/PTC1-induced thyroid carcinomas. *Am J Pathol* 2000;157:671–7.
72. Matias-Guiu X, Villanueva A, Cuatrecasas M, et al. p53 in a thyroid follicular carcinoma with foci of poorly differentiated and anaplastic carcinoma. *Pathol Res Pract* 1996;192:1242–9; discussion 50–1.
73. Patel KN, Shaha AR. Poorly differentiated and anaplastic thyroid cancer. *Cancer Control* 2006;13:119–28.
74. Jiang JY, Tseng FY. Prognostic factors of anaplastic thyroid carcinoma. *J Endocrinol Invest* 2006;29:11–7.
75. Miccoli P, Materazzi G, Antonelli A, et al. New trends in the treatment of undifferentiated carcinomas of the thyroid. *Langenbecks Arch Surg* 2007;392:397–404.
76. Cornett WR, Sharma AK, Day TA, et al. Anaplastic thyroid carcinoma: an overview. *Curr Oncol Rep* 2007;9:152–8.
77. Kim S, Schiff BA, Yigitbasi OG, et al. Targeted molecular therapy of anaplastic thyroid carcinoma with AEE788. *Mol Cancer Ther* 2005;4:632–40.
78. Carpten JD, Robbins CM, Villablanca A, et al. HRPT2, encoding parafibromin, is mutated in hyperparathyroidism-jaw tumor syndrome. *Nat Genet* 2002;32:676–80.
79. Shattuck TM, Valimaki S, Obara T, et al. Somatic and germline mutations of the HRPT2 gene in sporadic parathyroid carcinoma. *N Engl J Med* 2003;349:1722–9.
80. Rubio MP, Correa KM, Ueki K, et al. The putative glioma tumor suppressor gene on chromosome 19q maps between APOC2 and HRC. *Cancer Res* 1994;54:4760–3.
81. McPherson JD, Marra M, Hillier L, et al. A physical map of the human genome. *Nature* 2001;409:934–41.
82. Cryns VL, Thor A, Xu HJ, et al. Loss of the retinoblastoma tumor-suppressor gene in parathyroid carcinoma. *N Engl J Med* 1994;330:757–61.
83. Cetani F, Pardi E, Viacava P, et al. A reappraisal of the Rb1 gene abnormalities in the diagnosis of parathyroid cancer. *Clin Endocrinol (Oxf)* 2004;60:99–106.
84. Cetani F, Pardi E, Giovannetti A, et al. Genetic analysis of the MEN1 gene and HPRT2 locus in two Italian kindreds with familial isolated hyperparathyroidism. *Clinical Endocrinol* 2002;56:457–64.
85. Vaidya B, Imrie H, Perros P, et al. Evidence for a new Graves disease susceptibility locus at chromosome 18q21. *Am J Human Genetics* 2000;66:1710–4.
86. Szijan I, Orlow I, Dalamon V, et al. Alterations in the retinoblastoma pathway of cell cycle control in parathyroid tumors. *Oncol Rep* 2000;7:421–5.
87. Awwad RA, Sergina N, Yang H, et al. The role of transforming growth factor alpha in determining growth factor independence. *Cancer Res* 2003;63:4731–8.
88. Ranganathan S, Lynshue K, Hunt JL, Kane T, Jaffe R. Unusual adrenal cortical tumor of unknown biologic potential: a nodule in a nodule in a nodule. *Pediatr Dev Pathol* 2005;8:483–8.
89. Juhlin C, Larsson C, Yakoleva T, et al. Loss of parafibromin expression in a subset of parathyroid adenomas. *Endocr Relat Cancer* 2006;13:509–23.
90. Cetani F, Ambrogini E, Viacava P, et al. Should parafibromin staining replace HRTP2 gene analysis as an additional tool for histologic diagnosis of parathyroid carcinoma? *Eur J Endocrinol* 2007;156:547–54.
91. Gill AJ, Clarkson A, Gimm O, et al. Loss of nuclear expression of parafibromin distinguishes parathyroid carcinomas and hyperparathyroidism-jaw tumor (HPT-JT) syndrome-related adenomas from sporadic parathyroid adenomas and hyperplasias. *Am J Surg Pathol* 2006;30:1140–9.
92. Cetani F, Pardi E, Ambrogini E, et al. Different somatic alterations of the HRPT2 gene in a patient with recurrent sporadic primary hyperparathyroidism carrying an HRPT2 germline mutation. *Endocr Relat Cancer* 2007;14:493–9.
93. Juhlin CC, Villablanca A, Sandelin K, et al. Parafibromin immunoreactivity: its use as an additional diagnostic marker for parathyroid tumor classification. *Endocr Relat Cancer* 2007;14:501–12.
94. Asa SL, Ezzat S. Genetics and proteomics of pituitary tumors. *Endocrine* 2005;28:43–7.
95. Asa SL, Ezzat S. Molecular basis of pituitary development and cytogenesis. *Front Horm Res* 2004;32:1–19.
96. Hemminki K, Eng C, Chen B. Familial risks for nonmedullary thyroid cancer. *J Clin Endocrinol Metab* 2005;90:5747–53.
97. Ezzat S, Asa SL. Mechanisms of disease: The pathogenesis of pituitary tumors. *Nat Clin Pract Endocrinol Metab* 2006;2:220–30.
98. Trouillas J, Labat-Moleur F, Sturm N, et al. Pituitary tumors and hyperplasia in multiple endocrine neoplasia type 1 syndrome (MEN1): a case-control study of 77 patients versus 2509 non-MEN1 patients. *Am J Surg Pathol* 2008;32:534–43.
99. Horvath A, Stratakis CA. Clinical and molecular genetics of acromegaly: MEN1, Carney complex, McCune-Albright syndrome, familial acromegaly and genetic defects in sporadic tumors. *Rev Endocr Metab Disord* 2008;9:1–11.
100. Boikos SA, Stratakis CA. Molecular mechanisms of medullary thyroid carcinoma: current approaches in diagnosis and treatment. *Histol Histopathol* 2008;23:109–16.
101. Stergiopoulos SG, Abu-Asab MS, Tsokos M, Stratakis CA. Pituitary pathology in Carney complex patients. *Pituitary* 2004;7:73–82.
102. Kirschner LS, Sandrini F, Monbo J, et al. Genetic heterogeneity and spectrum of mutations of the PRKAR1A gene in patients with Carney complex. *Hum Mol Genet* 2000;9:3037–46.
103. Georgitsi M, Raitila A, Karhu A, et al. Molecular diagnosis of pituitary adenoma predisposition caused by aryl hydrocarbon receptor-interacting protein gene mutations. *Proc Natl Acad Sci U S A* 2007;104:4101–5.
104. Leontiou CA, Gueorguiev M, van der Spuy J, et al. The role of the aryl hydrocarbon receptor-interacting protein gene in familial and sporadic pituitary adenomas. *J Clin Endocrinol Metab* 2008;93:2390–401.
105. Toledo RA, Lourenco DM, Jr., Liberman B, et al. Germline mutation in the aryl hydrocarbon receptor interacting protein gene in familial somatotropinoma. *J Clin Endocrinol Metab* 2007;92:1934–7.
106. Vierimaa O, Georgitsi M, Lehtonen R, et al. Pituitary adenoma predisposition caused by germline mutations in AIP gene. *Science* 2006;312:1228–30.
107. Valler L, Spada A, Giannattasio G. Altered Gs and adenlyate cyclase activity in human GH-secreting pituitary adenomas. . *Nature* 1987;330:566–8.
108. Villa C, Magri F, Morbini P, et al. Silent Familial Isolated Pituitary Adenomas: Histopathological and Clinical Case Report. *Endocr Pathol* 2008;
109. Donangelo I, Araujo PB, Antenuzi D, et al. Tumor deletion mapping of chromosomal region 13q14 in 43 growth hormone secreting pituitary adenomas. *Endocrine* 2005;28:131–6.
110. Ogino A, Yoshino A, Katayama Y, et al. The p15(INK4b)/p16(INK4a)/RB1 pathway is frequently deregulated in human pituitary adenomas. *J Neuropathol Exp Neurol* 2005;64:398–403.
111. Yoshino A, Katayama Y, Ogino A, et al. Promoter hypermethylation profile of cell cycle regulator genes in pituitary adenomas. *J Neurooncol* 2007;83:153–62.
112. Donangelo I, Marcos HP, Araujo PB, et al. Expression of retinoblastoma protein in human growth hormone-secreting pituitary adenomas. *Endocr Pathol* 2005;16:53–62.

113. Toumpanakis CG, Caplin ME. Molecular genetics of gastroenteropancreatic neuroendocrine tumors. *Am J Gastroenterol* 2008;103:729–32.
114. Duerr EM, Mizukami Y, Ng A, et al. Defining molecular classifications and targets in gastroenteropancreatic neuroendocrine tumors through DNA microarray analysis. *Endocr Relat Cancer* 2008;15:243–56.
115. Vortmeyer AO, Lubensky IA, Skarulis M, et al. Multiple endocrine neoplasia type 1: atypical presentation, clinical course, and genetic analysis of multiple tumors. *Modern Pathol* 1999;12:919–24.
116. Yao JC, Hoff PM. Molecular targeted therapy for neuroendocrine tumors. *Hematol Oncol Clin North Am* 2007;21:575–81; x.
117. Modlin IM, Oberg K, Chung DC, et al. Gastroenteropancreatic neuroendocrine tumours. *Lancet Oncol* 2008;9:61–72.
118. Subramaniam MM, Putti TC, Anuar D, et al. Clonal characterization of sporadic cribriform-morular variant of papillary thyroid carcinoma by laser microdissection-based APC mutation analysis. *Am J Clin Pathol* 2007;128:994–1001.
119. Barlaskar FM, Hammer GD. The molecular genetics of adrenocortical carcinoma. *Rev Endocr Metab Disord* 2007;8:343–8.
120. Bougeard G, Sesboue R, Baert-Desurmont S, et al. Molecular basis of the Li-Fraumeni syndrome: an update from the French LFS families. *J Med Genet* 2008;45(8):535–8.
121. Gonzalez K, Fong C, Buzin C, Sommer SS, Saldivar JS. p53 Testing for Li-Fraumeni and Li-Fraumeni-like syndromes. *Curr Protoc Hum Genet* 2008; Chapter 10:Unit 10
122. Zambetti GP. The p53 mutation "gradient effect" and its clinical implications. *J Cell Physiol* 2007;213:370–3.
123. Cohen MM, Jr. Beckwith-Wiedemann syndrome: historical, clinicopathological, and etiopathogenetic perspectives. *Pediatr Dev Pathol* 2005;8:287–304.
124. Kerr NJ, Fukuzawa R, Reeve AE, Sullivan MJ, Fukazawa R. Beckwith-Wiedemann syndrome, pancreatoblastoma, and the wnt signaling pathway. *Am J Pathol* 2002;160:1541–2.
125. Volante M, Rapa I, Papotti M. Poorly Differentiated Thyroid Carcinoma: Diagnostic Features and Controversial Issues. *Endocr Pathol* 2008;
126. McNicol AM. Assessment of malignancy in adrenal cortical tumors. *Endocr Pathol* 2006;17:131–6.
127. Giordano TJ. Molecular pathology of adrenal cortical tumors: separating adenomas from carcinomas. *Endocr Pathol* 2006;17:355–63.
128. Stephan EA, Chung TH, Grant CS, et al. Adrenocortical carcinoma survival rates correlated to genomic copy number variants. *Mol Cancer Ther* 2008;7:425–31.
129. Kuruba R, Gallagher SF. Current management of adrenal tumors. *Curr Opin Oncol* 2008;20:34–46.
130. Gimenez-Roqueplo AP, Burnichon N, Amar L, et al. Recent advances in the genetics of phaeochromocytoma and functional paraganglioma. *Clin Exp Pharmacol Physiol* 2008;35:376–9.
131. Thouennon E, Elkahloun AG, Guillemot J, et al. Identification of potential gene markers and insights into the pathophysiology of pheochromocytoma malignancy. *J Clin Endocrinol Metab* 2007;92:4865–72.

Index

R

S

Made in the USA
Monee, IL
13 September 2026

62976344R00142